A. A. Vasiliev

HISTORY OF THE

BYZANTINE EMPIRE

324-1453

Volume II

THE UNIVERSITY OF WISCONSIN PRESS

Published 1952
The University of Wisconsin Press
Box 1379, Madison, Wisconsin 53701
The University of Wisconsin Press, Ltd.
70 Great Russell Street, London

SECOND ENGLISH EDITION

In one volume, 1952
In two volumes, 1958
Volume II printings 1958, 1961, 1964, 1971, 1976

Printed in the United States of America

ISBN 0-299-80926-9; LC 58-9277

TABLE OF CONTENTS

LIST OF MAPS

iv

HISTORY OF THE
BYZANTINE EMPIRE
324-1453

CHAPTER VII: BYZANTIUM AND THE CRUSADES

THE revolution of 1081 elevated to the throne Alexius Comnenus, whose uncle Isaac had been emperor for a short time at the end of the sixth decade of the eleventh century (1057–59). The Greek name of the Comneni, mentioned in the sources for the first time under Basil II, came originally from a village not far from Hadrianople. Later the family became large landowners in Asia Minor.[1] Both Isaac and his nephew Alexius distinguished themselves by their military talents. Under Alexius the military party and provincial large landowners triumphed over the bureaucrats and civil regime of the capital, and at the same time the epoch of troubles came to its end. The first three Comneni succeeded in keeping the throne for a century and transferring it from father to son.

Owing to his energetic and skillful rule, Alexius I (1081–1118) secured the Empire from serious external dangers which sometimes threatened the very existence of the state. But the succession of the throne created difficulties. Long before his death, Alexius had nominated his son, John, heir to the imperial dignity and thereby greatly irritated his elder daughter, Anna, the famous authoress of the historical work, *Alexiad*. She devised a complicated plot in order to remove John and force the recognition as heir to the throne of her husband, Nicephorus Bryennius, who was also an historian. The aged Alexius remained, however, firm in his decision, and after his death John was proclaimed Emperor.

Upon ascending the throne, John II (1118–1143) had at once to undergo a painful experience. A plot against him was discovered, in which his sister Anna took the leading part; his mother was also entangled. The conspiracy failed, but John treated the conspirators very leniently, only punishing the majority by depriving them of their property. Because of his lofty moral qualities, John deserved general respect; he was called Calojohn (Caloyan),

---

[1] See F. Chalandon, *Essai sur le règne d'Alexis Ier Comnène*, 21. Recently a hypothesis was set forth on the Wallachian (Vlachian) origin of the Comneni. G. Murnu, "L'origine des Comnènes," *Bulletin de la section historique de l'Académie roumaine*, XI (1924), 212–16.

that is to say, John the Good (or the Handsome). Both Greek and Latin writers are unanimous in their high appreciation of John's character. Nicetas Choniates said, "he was the best type (κορωνίς) of all the Emperors, from the family of the Comneni, who had ever sat upon the Roman throne."[2] Gibbon, who was always severe in his judgment of Byzantine rulers, wrote of this "best and greatest of the Comnenian princes," that even "the philosophic Marcus (Aurelius) would not have disdained the artless virtues of his successor, derived from his heart, and not borrowed from the schools."[3]

Opposed to needless luxury and wasteful prodigality, John stamped his mark upon the court, which, under his rule, lived a strict and economical life; there were no more entertainments, no festivities, no enormous expenses. On the other hand, the reign of this merciful, calm, and most moral Emperor was little but a continuous military campaign.

His son and successor, Manuel I (1143–1180) formed a complete contrast to John. A convinced admirer of the West who had chosen as his ideal the western knight, the new Emperor changed at once the austere court setting of his late father. Cheerful entertainments, love, receptions, sumptuous festivities, hunting parties after the western pattern, tournaments—all these spread widely over Constantinople. The visits to the capital of foreign sovereigns such as the kings of Germany and France, the sultan of Iconium, and several Latin princes from the East, with the king of Jerusalem, Amaury I, at their head, required enormous amounts of money.

A very great number of western Europeans appeared at the Byzantine court, and the most lucrative and responsible offices of the Empire began to pass into their hands. Manuel was married twice, each time to a western princess. His first wife, Bertha of Sulzbach, whose name was changed in Byzantium to Irene, was a sister-in-law of the king of Germany, Conrad III; his second wife, Mary (Maria), was a French lady of rare beauty, a daughter of a prince of Antioch. The whole reign of Manuel was regulated by his western ideals, as well as by his illusive dream of restoring the unity of the former Roman Empire; for that purpose he hoped, with the aid of the pope, to deprive the king of Germany of his imperial crown, and he was even ready to effect a union with the western Catholic church. Latin oppression and neglect of indigenous interests, however, evoked general discontent among the population; and a vigorous desire to change the system arose. But Manuel died before he saw the collapse of his policy.

Alexius II (1180–1183), son and successor of Manuel, was twelve years old at his father's death. His mother, Mary of Antioch, was proclaimed regent.

---

[2] Nicetas Choniates, *Historia,* ed. I. Bekker, *Corpus Scriptorum Historiae Byzantinae,* 64–65; hereafter referred to as Bonn ed.

[3] E. Gibbon, *The History of the Decline and Fall of the Roman Empire,* ed. J. B. Bury, V, 229.

But practically all power passed into the hands of the regent's favorite, Alexius Comnenus, Manuel's nephew. The new government relied upon the support of the hated Latin element. Popular exasperation, therefore, kept increasing. Empress Mary, formerly so popular, was now considered as a "foreigner." The French historian Diehl compared the condition of Mary to that of Marie Antoinette, who in the time of the French revolution was similarly called by the populace "the Austrian."[4]

A strong party formed against the all-powerful favorite Alexius Comnenus; at the head of that party stood Andronicus Comnenus, one of the most singular figures in the annals of Byzantine history, and an interesting type for both historian and novelist. Andronicus, a nephew of John II and cousin of Manuel I, belonged to the younger line of the Comneni, which had been removed from the throne and had distinguished itself by extraordinary energy, sometimes wrongly directed. Later, in the third generation, this line provided the sovereigns of the Empire of Trebizond who are known in history as the dynasty of the Grand Comneni. "Prince-exile" of the twelfth century, "the future Richard III of Byzantine history," in whose soul there was "something similar to that of Caesar Borgia," "Alcibiades of the Middle-Byzantine Empire," Andronicus represented "a perfect type of a Byzantian of the twelfth century with all his virtues and vices."[5] Handsome, elegant, and witty, an athlete and a warrior, well educated and charming, especially to the women who adored him, frivolous and passionate, skeptic and, in case of need, hypocrite and perjurer, ambitious conspirator and intriguer, terrible in his later days for his ferocity, Andronicus, as Diehl said, being a genius by nature, might have become the savior and regenerator of the exhausted Byzantine Empire; but for that purpose he lacked "perhaps, a little moral sense."[6]

An historian contemporary with Andronicus, Nicetas Choniates, wrote about him: "Who has been born of such strong rock or with a heart forged on such an anvil as not to be softened by the streams of Andronicus' tears nor to be charmed by the wiliness of his words which he poured out as from a dark spring." The same historian compared Andronicus to the "multiform Proteus."[7]

In spite of a semblance of friendship with Manuel, Andronicus was suspected by the latter and found no opportunities of presenting himself in his true light in Byzantium. He spent most of Manuel's reign in wandering over

[4] Charles Diehl, *Figures byzantines* (4th ed., 1909), II, 112.

[5] V. Vasilievsky, "The Alliance of the Two Empires," *Slavyansky Sbornik,* II (1877), 255–57; in *Works of V. G. Vasilievsky,* IV, 68–70. Diehl, *Figures byzantines,* II, 90, 93. R. von Scala, "Das Griechentum seit Alexander dem Grossen," in H. F. Helmolt, *Weltgeschichte,* V, 95.

[6] *Figures byzantines,* II, 93. L. Bréhier, "Andronic (Comnène)," *Dictionnaire d'histoire et de géographie ecclésiastiques,* II, 1782.

[7] Nicetas Choniates, *Historia,* Bonn ed., 317, 319.

the different countries of Europe and Asia. Having been sent by the Emperor first to Cilicia and then to the borders of Hungary, Andronicus was accused of political treason and plotting against Manuel's life; he was confined in a Constantinopolitan prison, where he spent several years; after many extraordinary adventures, he succeeded in escaping from his confinement through a neglected drain pipe; then he was caught again and imprisoned for several years more. But he escaped again to the north and took refuge in southwest Russia with the Prince of Galich, Yaroslav. Under the year 1165 a Russian chronicler said: "The Emperor's cousin Kyr (Sir) Andronicus took refuge from Tsargrad with Yaroslav of Galich; and Yaroslav received him with great love and gave him several cities in consolation."[8] As Byzantine sources report, Andronicus was kindly received by Yaroslav, had his residence in Yaroslav's house, ate and hunted with him, and even took part in his councils with the boyars (Russian nobility).[9] But the stay of Andronicus at the court of the Prince of Galich seemed dangerous to Manuel, whose restless relative was already entering into negotiations with Hungary, with which Byzantium had begun a war. Manuel accordingly determined to pardon Andronicus, who was dismissed by Yaroslav from Galich to Constantinople, "with great honor," as a Russian chronicler says.[10]

Appointed Duke of Cilicia, in Asia Minor, he did not stay there for long. He arrived in Palestine via Antioch; there he fell in love with Theodora, the Emperor's relative and widow of the King of Jerusalem, who yielded to his solicitations. The infuriated Emperor commanded Andronicus to be blinded, but warned in time of his danger, he fled abroad with Theodora and led a wandering life for several years in Syria, Mesopotamia, and Armenia, spending some time even in far-off Iberia (Georgia or Gruzia, in the Caucasus).

At last, Manuel's envoys succeeded in seizing the passionately beloved Theodora and the children she had borne to Andronicus; incapable of enduring that loss, he resolved to make his submission to Manuel. Pardon was granted, and Andronicus apparently repented the follies of his stormy life. His appointment as governor of Pontus, in Asia Minor on the shores of the Black Sea, was a sort of honorable exile of a dangerous relative. At that time, 1180, Manuel died, and his son, Alexius II, a child of twelve, became Emperor. Andronicus was then sixty years old.

Such was the biography of the man in whom the population of the capital, exasperated by the latinophile policy of the Empress-regent, Mary of Antioch,

---

[8] *Ipatyevskaya Lietopis* (Chronicle) under the year 6673, p. 359 = *Voskresenskaya Lietopis*, under the same year, in the *Complete Collection of Russian Chronicles*, VII, 78.

[9] Ioannis Cinnami *Historia*, Bonn ed., 232. Nicetas Choniates, *Historia*, Bonn ed., 172.

[10] *Ipatyevskaya Lietopis* = *Voskresenskaya Lietopis*.

and her favorite, Alexius Comnenus, reposed all their trust. Very skillfully pretending to protect the violated rights of the minor Alexius II, who was in the power of the wicked rulers, and to be "a friend of the Romans" (φιλορώμαιος), Andronicus succeeded in winning the hearts of the exhausted population, who deified him. A contemporary, Eustathius of Thessalonica, said Andronicus "to the majority of people, was dearer than God himself," or, at least, "immediately followed him."[11]

After having created the proper feeling in the capital, Andronicus set out for Constantinople. At the news of his march, the populace of the capital gave vent to their hatred for the Latins. A raging mob attacked the Latin quarter and began to massacre the Latins, without distinction of sex or age; the infuriated populace plundered not only private houses, but also Latin churches and charitable institutions; in a hospital the patients lying in bed were murdered; the papal legate was insulted and beheaded; many Latins were sold into slavery in the Turkish markets. By that massacre of the Latins in 1182, as Th. Uspensky said, "the seed of the fanatic enmity between West and East, if not planted, was watered."[12] The all-powerful ruler, Alexius Comnenus, was imprisoned and blinded. Then Andronicus entered the capital in triumph. In order to give stability to his position, he began gradually to destroy Manuel's relatives and commanded the Empress-mother, Mary of Antioch, to be strangled. Then Andronicus became joint emperor with Alexius II. Several days later, in spite of his solemn promise to protect Alexius' life, he commanded him also to be strangled in secret. Thereupon, in 1183, Andronicus, at sixty-three years of age, became the sole all-powerful emperor.

Ascending the throne with designs which became evident later, Andronicus could maintain his power only by a system of terrorism and unspeakable cruelty. In external affairs, he showed neither energy nor initiative. The mood of the populace turned against him. In 1185 a revolution broke out which elevated to the throne Isaac Angelus. Andronicus' attempt to escape met with failure. Dethroned, he was exposed to hideous tortures and insults, which he bore with superhuman courage. In his atrocious sufferings he many times repeated: "Lord, have mercy upon me! Why do you break a bruised reed?"[13] The new emperor did not even allow the lacerated remains of Andronicus to be buried; and with this tragedy the last brilliant Byzantine dynasty came to its end.

[11] Eustathii *De Thessalonica a Latinis capta*, Bonn ed., 388.
[12] "Emperors Alexius II and Andronicus Comneni," *Journal of the Ministry of Public Instruction*, CCXIV (1881), 73. Uspensky, "The Last Comneni. Beginnings of Reaction," *Vizantiysky Vremennik*, XXV (1927–28), 14.
[13] Nicetas Choniates, *Historia*, Bonn ed., 458. The numerous sources on the death of Andronicus are discussed in N. Radojčić, *Dva posljednja Komnena na corigradskom prijestola*, 94, n. 1.

Alexius I and external relations before the First Crusade

Anna Comnena, the educated and gifted daughter of the new Emperor, Alexius, said that her father, at the beginning of his reign, viewed the Turkish danger from the east and the Norman from the west, and "saw that his Empire was in fatal agony."[14] The external situation of the Empire was very serious and gradually became still more troublesome and complicated.

The Norman War.—The Duke of Apulia, Robert Guiscard, after conquering the Byzantine possessions in southern Italy, formed much wider plans. Ambitious to deal a blow at the very heart of Byzantium, he transferred hostilities to the Adriatic coast of the Balkan peninsula. He left the government of Apulia to his younger son Roger and, with his elder brother Bohemond, well-known as a participator in the First Crusade, sailed against Alexius, with a considerable fleet. His chief immediate aim was to seize the maritime city of Dyrrachium (formerly Epidamnus; Slavonic Drach [Drač] now Durazzo) in Illyria. Dyrrachium, the chief city of the theme of Dyrrachium, which had been organized under Basil II Bulgaroctonus, was very well fortified and justly considered the key to the Empire in the west. The famous military road of Egnatius (*via Egnatia*), constructed as far back as Roman times, led from Dyrrachium to Thessalonica and then farther to the east toward Constantinople. Therefore it was perfectly natural that Robert's chief attention should be directed upon Dyrrachium. This expedition was "the prelude of the Crusades and preparation (Vorbereitung) for the Frankish dominion in Greece,"[15] "the pre-crusade of Robert Guiscard, his great war against Alexius Comnenus."[16]

Realizing that with his own forces he was incapable of overcoming the Norman danger, Alexius Comnenus called on the West for aid, and among other rulers he appealed to Henry IV of Germany. Henry at that time had some difficulties within his own empire and had not yet settled his struggle with Pope Gregory VII so that he was able to afford no aid to the Byzantine Emperor. But Venice, with a view to her own interests, replied favorably to the appeal of Alexius. In return for the help of her fleet, the Emperor promised the Republic of St. Mark enormous trade privileges. It suited the interests of Venice to support the eastern Emperor in his war against the Normans because in case of military success the Normans could immediately seize the trade routes to Byzantium and the East, in other words, could obtain possession of what the Venetians themselves hoped in the course of time

---

[14] Anna Comnena, *Alexias*, III, 9; ed. A. Reifferscheid, I, 117.

[15] C. Hopf, *Geschichte Griechenlands vom Beginne des Mittelalters bis auf die neuere Zeit*, I, 141.

[16] H. Grégoire and R. de Keyser, "La Chanson de Roland et Byzance ou de l'utilité du grec pour les romanistes," *Byzantion*, XIV (1939), 274.

to control. Besides, a real and immediate danger pressed upon Venice: Norman possession of the Ionian Islands, especially Corfù and Cephalonia, and the west coast of the Balkan peninsula, would have barred the Adriatic to the Venetian vessels plying in the Mediterranean.

After the capture of the island of Corfù, the Normans besieged Dyrrachium by land and sea. Although the Venetian vessels had relieved the besieged city on the seaward side, the land army under Alexius, composed of Macedonian Slavs, Turks, the imperial Varangian-English bodyguard, and some other nationalities, was heavily defeated. At the beginning of 1082, Dyrrachium opened its gates to Robert. But a revolt which had broken out in south Italy called Robert away. Bohemond, to whom the command of the expeditionary corps had been delegated by his brother, was finally vanquished.[17] A new expedition undertaken by Robert against Byzantium was successful, but an epidemic broke out among his troops and Robert himself fell a victim to the disease. He died in 1085 in the north of the island of Cephalonia. Even today a small bay and village in the island, Fiscardo (Guiscardo, Portus Wiscardi, in the Middle Ages, from the name of Robert Guiscard), recalls the name of the powerful Duke of Apulia. With Robert's death the Norman invasion of Byzantine territory ceased, and Dyrrachium passed again to the Greeks.[18]

It has been shown that the aggressive policy of Robert Guiscard in the Balkan peninsula failed. But under him the question of the south Italian possessions of Byzantium was definitely decided. Robert had founded the Italian state of the Normans, because he was the first to succeed in unifying the various countries founded by his compatriots and in forming the Duchy of Apulia, which under him lived through a period of brilliance. A certain decline of the Duchy which came on after Robert's death, lasted for about fifty years, at the end of which the foundation of the Sicilian Kingdom opened a new era in the history of the Italian Normans. Robert Guiscard, the French historian Chalandon declared, "opened a new way to the ambition of his descendants: after him the Italian Normans were to direct their gaze toward the east; in the east and at the expense of the Greek Empire, twelve years later, Bohemond was to create a princedom for himself."[19]

Venice, in return for the aid given by her fleet, received from the Emperor enormous trade privileges which established for the Republic of St. Mark quite an exceptional position in the Empire. Besides magnificent presents to the Venetian churches and honorable titles with a fixed salary to the doge and

[17] See R. B. Yewdale, *Bohemond I, Prince of Antioch*, 18–22.

[18] Chalandon, *Alexis Ier Comnène*, 64–92. F. Chalandon, "The Earlier Comneni," *Cambridge Medieval History*, IV, 329–30. The

place of the death of Guiscard is not definitely fixed. Chalandon, *Alexis Ier Comnène*, 93, n. 9. Yewdale (*Bohemond I*, 23) says that Guiscard died at Cassiope on Corfù.

[19] Chalandon, *Alexis Ier Comnène*, 94.

Venetian patriarch and their successors, the imperial charter of Alexius (or *chrysobull,* i.e. the charter confirmed with a gold imperial seal) of May 1082 granted the Venetian merchants the right of buying and selling all over the Empire and made them free of custom, port, and other dues connected with trade; the Byzantine customs officers had no right of inspecting their merchandise. In the capital itself the Venetians received a large quarter with many shops and stores as well as three landing places, which were called in the East *scales* (*maritimas tres scalas*), where the Venetian vessels could be freely loaded and unloaded. The charter of Alexius gives an interesting list of the places of the Empire which were commercially most important, on the seashore and in the interior, which were open to Venice in Asia Minor, the Balkan peninsula and Greece, and in the islands of the Aegean, ending with Constantinople, which is called in this document Megalopolis, i.e. Great City. In their turn, the Venetians promised to be the faithful subjects of the Empire.[20] By the privileges accorded to the Venetian merchants in the charter they were treated much more favorably than the Byzantine merchants themselves. By the charter of Alexius Comnenus a solid foundation was laid for the colonial power of Venice in the East; the conditions established to create her economic preponderance in Byzantium were such as would seem likely to make competition impossible for a long time. But the same exceptional economic privileges granted Venice served in the course of time, under changed circumstances, as one of the causes of the political conflicts between the Eastern Empire and the Republic of St. Mark.

Struggle of the Empire against the Turks and Patzinaks.—The Turkish danger from the east and north, from the Seljuqs and Patzinaks, which had already been very threatening under the predecessors of Alexius Comnenus, increased in intensity under that monarch. The victory over the Normans and Guiscard's death had permitted Alexius to restore the Byzantine territory in the west as far as the Adriatic coast, but on the other borders, the attacks of the Turks and Patzinaks were so successful that the Empire was considerably reduced in territory. Anna Comnena rhetorically declared that at that time "the neighboring Bosphorus was the frontier of the Roman Empire in the east, and Hadrianople in the west."[21]

It seemed that in Asia Minor, which had been almost wholly conquered by the Seljuqs, circumstances were shaping themselves favorably for the Empire, because among the Turkish rulers (emirs) a struggle for power was weakening the Turkish strength and bringing the country into a state of anarchy. But

[20] G. L. F. Tafel and G. M. Thomas, *Urkunden zur ältern Handels- und Staatsgeschichte der Republik Venedig,* I, 51–54. See F. Dölger, *Corpus der griechischen Urkunden des Mittelalters und der neuern Zeit,* I (1), 27–28; contains very good bibliography.

[21] *Alexias,* VI, 11; ed. Reifferscheid, I, 214–15.

Alexius was unable to take full advantage of the distractions of the Turks because of the attacks of the Patzinaks from the north.

In their conflict with Byzantium the Patzinaks found allies within the Empire in the Paulicians who dwelt in the Balkan peninsula.[22] The Paulicians represented an Eastern dualistic religious sect, one of the chief branches of Manichaeism, which had been founded in the third century A.D. by Paul of Samosata and reformed in the seventh century. Living in Asia Minor, on the eastern border of the Empire, and firmly adhering to their doctrine, they sometimes caused grave trouble to the Byzantine government by their warlike energy. One of the familiar methods of Byzantine internal policy was to transport various nationalities from one place to another; for example, the Slavs were moved to Asia Minor and Armenians to the Balkan peninsula. The Paulicians also had been transported in great numbers from the eastern border to Thrace in the eighth century by Constantine V Copronymus, as well as in the tenth century by John Tzimisces. The city of Philippopolis in the Balkan peninsula became the center of the Paulicians. Tzimisces, by settling the eastern colony in the vicinity of that city, succeeded first in removing the stubborn sectarians from their strongholds and castles on the eastern border, where it was very difficult to manage them, and also he hoped that in their new settlement the Paulicians would serve as a strong bulwark against the frequent invasions of the northern "Scythian" barbarians. In the tenth century the Paulician doctrine had been carried into Bulgaria by the reformer of that doctrine, Pope Bogomile, after whom the Byzantine writers named his followers Bogomiles. From Bulgaria the Bogomile doctrine later passed into Serbia and Bosnia, and then into western Europe, where the followers of the eastern dualistic doctrine bore different names: Patarins in Italy, Cathari in Germany and Italy, Poblicans (i.e. Paulicians) and Albigensians in France.

The Byzantine government was disappointed in its expectations from eastern sectarians settled in the Balkan peninsula. First of all, the unexpected spreading of the heresy was speedy and wide. Secondly, the followers of the Bogomile doctrine became the spokesmen for the national Slavonic political opposition against the severe Byzantine administration in both ecclesiastical and secular matters, especially within Bulgaria, which had been conquered by Basil II. Therefore, instead of defending the Byzantine territory from the northern barbarians, the Bogomiles called on the Patzinaks to fight against Byzantium. The Cumans (Polovtzi) joined the Patzinaks.

The struggle with the Patzinaks, in spite of some temporary successes, taxed all the strength of Byzantium. At the end of the ninth decade Alexius Comnenus suffered a terrific defeat at Dristra (Durostolus, Silistria), on the lower

[22] See p. 256.

Danube, and was nearly captured himself. Only the quarrel resulting from the division of the spoil, which had broken out between the Patzinaks and Cumans, prevented the former from taking full advantage of their victory.

After a short relief obtained from the Patzinaks by payment, Byzantium had to live through the terrible time of 1090–1091. The Patzinaks came, after a stubborn struggle, up to Constantinople itself. Anna Comnena related that, on the day of the commemoration of the martyr Theodore Tyron, the inhabitants of the capital, who usually went to visit in great numbers the church of the martyr in a suburb beyond the city wall, could not do so; it was impossible to open the city gates, because the Patzinaks were standing under the walls.[23]

The situation of the Empire became still more critical when a Turkish pirate, Tzachas, began to menace the capital from the south. He had spent his youth in Constantinople at the court of Nicephorus Botaniates, had received a high Byzantine title, and on the accession of Alexius Comnenus, had fled to Asia Minor. Having taken possession by means of his fleet of Smyrna and some other cities of the western coast of Asia Minor and some islands of the Aegean, Tzachas boldly set himself the goal of dealing a blow to Constantinople from the sea and thereby cutting off all means of supply from the capital. To assure the effectiveness of his plan, he entered into negotiations with the Patzinaks in the north and the Seljuqs of Asia Minor in the east. Secure of success, Tzachas already called himself emperor (*basileus*), put on the insignia of imperial rank, and dreamt of making Constantinople the center of his state. Both the Patzinaks and Seljuqs were Turks who, thanks to their military and political relations, came to realize their ethnographic kinship. The Russian scholar V. Vasilievsky declared "in the person of Tzachas there appeared a foe of Byzantium who combined with the enterprising boldness of a barbarian the refinement of a Byzantine education and an excellent knowledge of all the political relations of eastern Europe of that time; he planned to become the soul of the general Turkish movement and would and could give a reasonable and definite goal and general plan to the senseless wanderings and robberies of the Patzinaks."[24] It seemed that on the ruins of the Eastern Empire a new Turkish state of the Seljuqs and Patzinaks would now be founded. "The Byzantine Empire," as Vasilievsky continued, "was drowning in the Turkish invasion."[25] Another Russian historian, Th. Uspensky, wrote: "In the winter of 1090–91 the condition of Alexius Comnenus can be compared only with that of the last years of the Empire, when

[23] *Alexias,* VIII, 3; ed. Reifferscheid, II, 6–7.

[24] V. G. Vasilievsky, "Byzantium and the Patzinaks," *Works,* I, 76. There is a Turkish monograph on Tzachas, Akdes Nimet Kurat, Çaka.

[25] *Ibid.,* I, 77.

the Ottoman Turks surrounded Constantinople on all sides and cut it off from outward relations."[26]

Realizing the whole horror of the condition of the Empire, Alexius followed the usual Byzantine diplomatic tactics of rousing one barbarian against the others: he appealed to the Khans (princes) of the Cumans (Polovtzi), those "allies in despair," asking them to help him against the Patzinaks. The savage and ferocious Cuman Khans, Tugorkhan and Boniak, very well known in the Russian chronicles,[27] were invited to Constantinople, where they were received in the most flattering way and sumptuously entertained. The Byzantine Emperor humbly solicited the aid of the barbarians, who were very proud to be on an equal footing with the Emperor. The Cuman Khans gave Alexius their word and kept it. On the twenty-ninth of April, 1091, a bloody battle took place; in all probability, the Russians as well as the Cumans took part in it. The Patzinaks were crushed and mercilessly annihilated. Anna Comnena noted: "One could see an extraordinary spectacle: the whole people, reckoning not in ten thousands but surpassing any number, entirely perished on that day with wives and children." This battle left its trace in a contemporary Byzantine song, "The Scythians" (so Anna Comnena calls the Patzinaks), "because of one day did not see May."[28] By their interference in favor of Byzantium the Cumans did an enormous service to the Christian world. "Their chiefs, Boniak and Tugorkhan, must be justly reckoned among the saviors of the Byzantine Empire."[29]

Alexius returned to the capital in triumph. Only a small part of the captured Patzinaks were left alive. This remnant of the terrific horde settled in the Balkan peninsula, east of the Vardar river, and later on entered the Byzantine army, in which they formed a special contingent. The Patzinaks who had succeeded in escaping beyond the Balkans were so weakened that for thirty years they could undertake nothing against Byzantium.

Tzachas, who had terrified Byzantium but had not succeeded in supporting the Patzinaks with his fleet, lost a part of his conquests in the conflict with the Greek maritime forces. Then the Emperor stirred up against him the sultan of Nicaea, who invited Tzachas to a festival and killed him with his own hand. Thereupon the sultan came to a peaceful agreement with Alexius. Thus the critical situation of 1091 was successfully settled for the Empire, and the following year, 1092, proceeded under quite different conditions.

[26] *The History of the Crusades,* 8.

[27] Anna Comnena, *Alexias,* VIII, 4; ed. Reifferscheid, II, 9: ὁ Τογορτάκ, ὁ Μανιάκ. See thereupon Vasilievsky, "Byzantium and the Patzinaks," *Works,* I, 98, n. 2.

[28] *Alexias,* VIII, 5; ed. Reifferscheid, II, 15. The battle took place April 29, 1091, just one day before May. In her edition of the *Alexiad* Elizabeth Dawes translated this song: "Just by one day the Scythians missed seeing the month of May." *Alexias,* trans. Dawes, 205.

[29] Vasilievsky, "Byzantium and the Patzinaks," *Works,* I, 107.

In the desperate days of 1091 Alexius had sought allies not only among the Cuman barbarians, but, apparently, also among the western Latins. Anna Comnena wrote that Alexius "was anxious to dispatch messages calling on mercenaries from all sides."[30] That such messages were dispatched also to the West is shown from another passage of the same authoress who stated that, soon afterwards, Alexius "was expecting the mercenaries from Rome."[31]

In connection with these events, historians usually discuss the problem of a message of Alexius Comnenus to his old friend, Count Robert of Flanders, who some years before had passed through Constantinople on his way back from the Holy Land. In his letter the Emperor depicted the desperate situation "of the most Holy Empire of the Greek Christians which is oppressed by the Patzinaks and Turks," told of the insulting and murdering of the Christians, children, youths, women, and girls, as well as of the almost complete occupation of the Empire's territory by enemies; "there is left almost nothing but Constantinople, which our enemies threaten to take away from us in the very near future, unless speedy help from God and from the faithful Latin Christians reach us"; the Emperor "is running before the Turks and Patzinaks" from one city to another and prefers to deliver Constantinople into the hands of the Latins rather than those of the pagans. In order to stimulate the ardor of the Latins, the message gives a long list of relics of the capital and reminds the Count of the uncounted wealth and treasure accumulated there. "Therefore, hasten with all your people; strain all your forces, lest such treasures fall into the hands of the Turks and Patzinaks. . . . Endeavor, so long as you have time, that the Christian Empire and, which is still more important, the Holy Sepulcre be not lost to you and that you may have in heaven no doom, but reward. Amen!"[32]

V. Vasilievsky, who referred this message to the year 1091, wrote: "In 1091, from the shores of the Bosphorus, there broke upon western Europe a real wail of despair, a real cry of a drowning man who already was uncertain whether a friendly or unfriendly hand would be lent for his salvation. The Byzantine Emperor did not hesitate now to reveal before the eyes of the foreigners the whole depth of shame, dishonor, and humiliation, into which the Empire of the Greek Christians had been precipitated."[33]

This document, depicting in such vivid colors the critical situation of Byzantium about 1091, has been the cause of many discussions among scholars. It survives only in a Latin version. Opinions are divided: some, for example the Russian scholars V. Vasilievsky and Th. Uspensky, considered the letter

---

[30] *Alexias,* VIII, 3; ed. Reifferscheid, II, 7.

[31] *Ibid.,* VIII, 5; ed. Reifferscheid, II, 12.

[32] P. E. Riant, *Alexii I Comneni ad Robertum I Flandriae comitem epistola spuria,* 10–20. H. Hagenmeyer, *Die Kreuzzugsbriefe aus* den Jahren 1088–1100, 130–36. Dölger, *Corpus der griechischen Urkunden,* II, 39–40 (no. 1152).

[33] "Byzantium and the Patzinaks," *Works,* I, 90.

authentic; others, for example the French scholar Riant, regarded it as spurious. The more recent historians who have been interested in this problem incline to recognize, with some limitations, the authenticity of the message, i.e. they acknowledge the existence of an original text, which has not been preserved of the message which was addressed by Alexius Comnenus to Robert of Flanders. The French historian Chalandon admitted that the middle part of the message was composed on the basis of the original letter; but the Latin message was drawn up by somebody in the West to stimulate the crusaders a short time before the First Crusade (in the form of an *excitatorium*).[34] The more recent publisher of the letter and investigator of it, the German scholar, Hagenmeyer, agreed in substance, but with some restrictions, with the opinion of Vasilievsky concerning the authenticity of Alexius' message.[35] In 1924 B. Leib wrote that this letter was but an amplification made shortly after the Council of Clermont and was doubtless inspired by the authentic message that the Emperor had sent Robert to remind him of the promised reinforcements.[36] Finally, in 1928, Bréhier wrote: "It is possible, following Chalandon's hypothesis, that Robert, after his return to Flanders, forgot his promise; then Alexius sent him an embassy and letter, but, of course, entirely different from the text which has come down to us. As far as this apocryphal document is concerned, it might have been composed, perhaps with the aid of the authentic letter, at the moment of the siege of Antioch, in 1098, to demand reinforcements in the West. Alexius' letter, then, has nothing to do with the origins of the crusade."[37] In his history of the First Crusade, H. Sybel considered the letter of Alexius to Robert of Flanders an official documentary source with reference to the crusade.[38]

Some time is devoted to the question of the message of Alexius Comnenus to Robert of Flanders, because with it is partly connected the important problem whether the Emperor called upon the aid of the West or not. The state-

---

[34] Chalandon, *Alexis Ier Comnène*, appendix, 325-36; see esp. 331, 334, and 336. The history of the problem of the letter of Alexis to the Count of Flanders is also given.

[35] "Der Brief des Kaisers Alxios I Komnenos an den Grafen Robert I von Flandern," *Byzantinische Zeitschrift*, VI (1897), 26. Hagenmeyer, *Die Kreuzzugsbriefe*, 38-40. See also H. Pirenne, "A propos la lettre d'Alexis Comnène à Robert le Frison, comte de Flandre," *Revue de l'instruction publique en Belgique*, L (1907), 217-27. G. Caro, "Die Berichterstattung auf dem ersten Kreuzzuge," *Neue Jahrbücher für das klassische Altertum*, XXIX (1912), 50-62.

[36] *Rome, Kiev et Byzance à la fin du XIe siècle*, 122; a brief French version of the letter, 188-89.

[37] L. Bréhier, *L'Église et l'Orient du moyen âge; Les Croisades* (5th ed., 1928), 58. N. Iorga, *Essai de synthèse de l'histoire de l'humanité*, II, 276-77; Iorga rejects any significance of this letter. G. Buckler (*Anna Comnena. A Study*, 457, n. 1) declared the letter apocryphal, if not wholly at least in the greater part. See also C. Erdmann, *Die Entstehung des Kreuzzugsgedankens*, 365: it is of less interest whether a genuine piece of writing served as a foundation for the falsified text or not.

[38] *Geschichte des ersten Kreuzzuges* (3rd ed., 1881), 7-9.

ment of the contemporary Anna Comnena that Alexius was sending messages to the West, supports the fact that he must have sent a message to Robert of Flanders, and the probability that this message is the basis of the embellished Latin text which exists today. It is very probable that the original message was sent by Alexius in the critical year 1091.[39] It is also very probable that in 1188–89 an imperial message was sent to the Croatian King Zvonimir to urge him to take part in the struggle of Alexius Comnenus "against the Pagans and Infidels."[40]

The success of Alexius with external enemies was followed by similar success with internal enemies. Conspirators and pretenders, who wished to profit by the difficult situation of the Byzantine Empire, were discovered and punished.

Besides the peoples mentioned, the Serbs and Magyars (Hungarians) had begun to assume importance under Alexius Comnenus before the First Crusade. In the second half of the eleventh century Serbia became independent, and her independence was sealed by the adoption by the Serbian prince of the title of king (*kral*). His was the first kingdom of Serbia with the capital at Scodra (Skadar, Scutari). The Serbs had taken part in the army of Alexius during his war with the Normans and abandoned the Emperor at the critical moment. But after Dyrrachium had been reconquered by Byzantium from the Normans, hostilities between Alexius and Serbia began, and under the difficult circumstances of the Empire, their issue could not be very fortunate for the Emperor. Shortly before the crusade, however, a peace was made between the Serbs and the Empire.

Relations with Hungary (Ugria), which had previously taken an active part in the Bulgaro-Byzantine war of the tenth century under Simeon, became strained in the reign of Alexius Comnenus. At the end of the eleventh century continental Hungary, under the kings of the dynasty of Arpad, began to expand south toward the sea, toward the coast of Dalmatia. This was the cause of dissatisfaction both to Venice and to Byzantium. Thus the international policy of the Empire toward the time of the First Crusade had grown considerably more extended and complicated, and raised new problems.

But almost at the end of the eleventh century Alexius Comnenus, who had overcome the numerous dangers which threatened him and seemed to have created peaceful conditions for the Empire, could gradually prepare for the struggle with the eastern Seljuqs. With that struggle in view, the Emperor undertook a number of offensive measures. Then he heard of the approach of the first crusading troops to the borders of his empire. The First Crusade had

---

[39] Dölger, *Corpus der griechischen Urkunden*, II, 39 (no. 1152) mentioned the letter under the year 1088.

[40] See F. Šišic, *Geschichte der Kroaten*, I, 315–16.

begun; it changed Alexius' plans and led him and the Empire into new ways which were later to prove fatal to Byzantium.

The First Crusade and Byzantium

The epoch of the crusades is one of the most important in the history of the world, especially from the point of view of economic history and general culture. For a long time the religious problem pushed into the background the other sides of this complicated and manifold movement. The first country to realize the full importance of the crusades was France, where in 1806 the French Academy and then the National Institute offered a prize for the best work which had for its purpose: "To examine the influence of the Crusades upon the civil liberty of the peoples of Europe, their civilization, and the progress of knowledge, commerce, and industry." Of course, at the beginning of the nineteenth century it was premature to discuss thoroughly such a problem; it has not even yet been solved. But it is worth pointing out that the epoch of the crusades ceased to be discussed exclusively from the narrower standpoint of the religious movements of the Middle Ages. Two volumes were crowned in 1808 by the French Academy: one book by a German, A. Heeren, which was published at the same time in German and French under the title *An Essay on the Influence of the Crusades Upon Europe;* the other book, the work of the Frenchman M. Choiseul Daillecourt, *Upon the Influence of the Crusades on the State of the European Peoples.* Though both these studies are now out of date, they do not lack interest, especially the first.

Of course, the crusades are the most important epoch in the history of the struggle of the two world religions, Christianity and Islam—the struggle which has been carried on from the seventh century. But in this process not only religious idealistic motives were involved. Even in the First Crusade, which reflected most plainly the ideals of the crusade movement to deliver the Holy Land from the hands of the infidel, secular objects and earthly interests were already evident. "There were two parties among the crusaders, that of the religious-minded, and that of the politicians."[41] Citing these words of the German scholar Kugler, the French historian, Chalandon, added: "This statement of Kugler's is absolutely true."[42] But the more closely scholars examine internal conditions of the life of western Europe in the eleventh century, especially the economic development of the Italian cities at that time, the more they are convinced that economic phenomena also played a very significant part in the preparation and carrying out of the First Crusade. With every new crusade the secular side was felt more and more

---

[41] B. Kugler, "Kaiser Alexius und Albert von Aachen," *Forschungen zur deutschen Geschichte,* XXIII (1883), 486.

[42] *d'Alexis Ier Comnène,* 161. Chalandon, "Earlier Comneni," *Cambridge Medieval History,* IV, 334.

strongly; finally, during the Fourth Crusade, this secular standpoint gained a definite victory over the primitive idea of the movement, as the taking of Constantinople and the foundation of the Latin Empire by the crusaders in 1204 demonstrated.

Byzantium played such an important role in that epoch that the study of the Eastern Empire is necessary to a full and complete understanding of the origin and development of the crusades. Moreover, the majority of those who have studied the crusades have treated the problem from a too "occidental" point of view, with the tendency to make of the Greek Empire "the scapegoat charged with all the faults of the crusaders."[43]

Since their first appearance in the stage of world history in the fourth decade of the seventh century, the Arabs, with extraordinary rapidity, had conquered on the territory of the Eastern Empire, Syria, Palestine, Mesopotamia, the eastern regions of Asia Minor, Egypt, the northern seashore of Africa, and then Spain, the major part of which had belonged to the Visigoths. In the second half of the seventh and at the beginning of the eighth century, the Arabs had twice besieged Constantinople, which had been rescued, not without difficulty, by the energy and talent of the Emperors Constantine IV and Leo III Isaurian. In 732 the Arabs who had invaded Gaul from beyond the Pyrenees were stopped by Charles Martel near Poitiers. In the ninth century they conquered Crete, and toward the beginning of the tenth century Sicily and the major part of the southern Italian possessions of the Eastern Empire passed over into their hands.

These Arabian conquests were of the greatest importance for the political and economic situation of Europe. The astounding offensive of the Arabs, as H. Pirenne said, "changed the face of the world. Its sudden thrust had destroyed ancient Europe. It had put an end to the Mediterranean commonwealth in which it had gathered its strength. . . . The Mediterranean had been a Roman lake; now it became, for the most part, a Moslem lake."[44] This statement of the Belgian historian must be accepted with some reservations. Commercial relations between western Europe and the eastern countries were restricted by the Muslims but were not suspended. Merchants and pilgrims continued to travel back and forth, and exotic oriental products were available in Europe, for example, in Gaul.[45]

[43] F. Chalandon, *Histoire de la première croisade*, preface, 1. The German dissertation of A. Gruhn, *Die Byzantinische Politik zur Zeit der Kreuzzüge*, is of no importance; there is no reference to sources.

[44] "Mahomet et Charlemagne," *Revue belge de philologie et d'histoire*, I (1922), 85. "Without Islam the Frankish Empire would prob-ably never have existed and Charlemagne, without Mahomet, would be unconceivable" (p. 86). Pirenne, *Medieval Cities*, 24, 26; in French, 25, 28. See R. S. Lopez, "Mohammed and Charlemagne: A Revision," *Speculum*, XVIII (1943), 14-38.

[45] See L. Halphen, "La Conquête de la Méditerranée par les Europeens au XIe et au XIIe

Primitive Islam had distinguished itself by tolerance. Some separate cases of assaults on the churches and Christians occurred in the tenth century, but they had no religious motive so that such unfortunate incidents were only sporadic. In the conquered regions the Arabs had, for the most part, preserved churches and Christian service. They had not prohibited the practice of Christian charity. In the epoch of Charlemagne, at the beginning of the ninth century, there were inns and hospitals in Palestine for the pilgrims; new churches and monasteries were being restored and built and for that purpose Charlemagne sent copious "alms" to Palestine. Libraries were being organized in the monasteries. Pilgrims visited the Holy Land unmolested. These relations between the Frankish empire of Charlemagne and Palestine, in connection with the exchange of some embassies between the western monarch and the caliph Harun ar-Rashid, led to the conclusion supported by some scholars that a kind of Frankish protectorate had been established in Palestine under Charlemagne as far as the Christian interests in the Holy Land were concerned, the political power of the caliph in that country remaining untouched.[46] On the other hand, another group of historians, denying the importance of those relations, say that the "protectorate" was never established and that "it is a myth quite analogous to the legend of Charlemagne's crusade to the Holy Land."[47] The title of one of the recent articles on this subject is "The Legend of Charlemagne's Protectorate in the Holy Land."[48] The term "Frankish protectorate," like many other terms, is conventional and rather vague; but a discussion of it is important in order to show that already at the opening of the ninth century the Frankish Empire had very important interests in Palestine, a fact which is of considerable significance for the further development of the international relations preceding the crusades.

In the second half of the tenth century the brilliant victories of the Byzantine troops under Nicephorus Phocas and John Tzimisces over the eastern Arabs made Aleppo and Antioch in Syria vassal states of the Empire, and after that the Byzantine army probably entered Palestine.[49] These military

siècles," *Mélanges d'histoire offerts à H. Pirenne*, I, 175. J. Ebersolt, *Orient et Occident*, I, 56–57. N. Iorga, in *Revue historique du sud-est européen*, VI (1929), 77.

[46] See A. A. Vasiliev, "Charlemagne and Harun ar-Rashid," *Vizantiysky Vremennik*, XX (1913), 63–116. Bréhier, *Les Croisades* (5th ed., 1928), 22–34. Bréhier, "Charlemagne et la Palestine," *Revue historique*, CLVII (1928), 277–91; Bréhier gave the full bibliography of the problem.

[47] E. Joranson, "The Alleged Frankish Pro-

tectorate in Palestine," *American Historical Review*, XXXII (1927), 260. See also V. Barthold, "Charlemagne and Harun ar-Rashid," *Christiansky Vostok*, I (1912), 69–94.

[48] A. Kleinclausz, "La Légende du protectorat de Charlemagne sur la Terre Sainte," *Syria*, VII (1926), 211–33. S. Runciman, "Charlemagne and Palestine," *English Historical Review*, L (1935), 606–19; the theory of Charlemagne's protective rights in Palestine must be treated as a myth (p. 619).

[49] See pp. 308–10.

successes of Byzantium had a repercussion in Jerusalem, so that the French historian Bréhier judged it possible to speak of the Byzantine protectorate over the Holy Land which put an end to the Frankish protectorate there.[50]

When, in the second half of the tenth century (in 969), Palestine had passed over to the Egyptian dynasty of the Fatimids, the new position of the country seems not to have brought about, at least at the beginning, any substantial change in the life of the eastern Christians, and pilgrims continued to come to Palestine in safety. But in the eleventh century circumstances changed. The insane Fatimid caliph Hakim, the "Egyptian Nero,"[51] began a violent persecution of Christians and Jews all over his possessions. In 1009 he caused the Temple of the Resurrection and Golgotha in Jerusalem to be destroyed. In his rage for destroying churches he stopped only because he was afraid that a similar fate would befall mosques in Christian regions.[52]

When L. Bréhier wrote of the Byzantine protectorate over the Holy Land, he had in view a statement of an Arabian historian of the eleventh century, Yahya of Antioch. The latter says that in 1012 a Bedouin chief who had revolted against the caliph Hakim took possession of Syria, forced the Christians to restore the Church of the Resurrection in Jerusalem, and made a bishop the patriarch of Jerusalem; then the Bedouin "helped him to build up the Church of the Resurrection and restore many places in it as much as he could."[53] Interpreting this text the Russian scholar V. Rosen remarked that the Bedouin acted "probably in order to win the good will of the Greek Emperor."[54] Bréhier ascribed Rosen's hypothesis to Yahya's text. Since this important statement of the Bedouin's motive does not belong to Yahya, one may not affirm Bréhier's theory of the Byzantine protectorate over Palestine as positively as he does in his book.[55]

But in any event, that was only the beginning of the restoration of the Holy Land. After Hakim's death in 1021, a time of tolerance for the Christians ensued. A peace was made between Byzantium and the Fatimids, and the Byzantine emperors were able to take up the real restoration of the Temple of the Resurrection. The restoration of the Temple was completed in the middle of the eleventh century under Emperor Constantine Monomachus. The Christian quarter was surrounded by a strong wall. Pilgrims again could go to the Holy Land, and among the other pilgrims mentioned in the sources is

[50] Bréhier, "Charlemagne et la Palestine," *Revue historique,* CLVII (1928), 38–39.

[51] G. Schlumberger, *L'Épopée byzantine à la fin du dixième siècle,* II, 442.

[52] M. Canard, "Les Expéditions des arabes contre Constantinople dans l'histoire et dans la légende," *Journal Asiatique,* CCVIII (1926), 94.

[53] V. Rosen, *The Emperor Basil Bulgaroc-*tonus, 47; in Russian, 49. Yahia Ibn Saïd Antiochensis, *Annales,* ed. L. Cheikho, 201.

[54] *Basil Bulgaroctonus,* 356.

[55] Bréhier gave Yahya's statement from Schlumberger, *L'Épopée byzantine,* II, 448. Schlumberger using Yahya from Rosen gave the correct account as far as Rosen's hypothesis is concerned.

a most celebrated man, Robert the Devil, Duke of Normandy, who died at Nicaea in 1035, on his way back from Jerusalem.[56] Perhaps at the same time, in the fourth decade of the eleventh century, the famous Varangian of that epoch, Harald Haardraade, supported by a body of Scandinavians who arrived with him from the north, came to Jerusalem and fought against the Muslims in Syria and Asia Minor.[57] Vexations against the Christians soon recommenced. In 1056 the Holy Sepulchre was closed, and more than three hundred Christians were exiled from Jerusalem.[58]

The destroyed Temple of the Resurrection was evidently restored with magnificence. A Russian pilgrim, the abbot (*igumen*) Daniel, who visited Palestine in the first years of the twelfth century, soon after the foundation of the Kingdom of Jerusalem in 1099, enumerated the columns of the Temple, described its marble decorated floor and the six doors, and gave interesting information on the mosaics. He also described many churches, relics, and places of Palestine mentioned in the New Testament.[59] Daniel and an Anglo-Saxon pilgrim, Saewulf, his contemporary, told how "the pagan Saracens" (i.e. Arabs), hiding themselves in the mountains and caves, sometimes attacked the traveling pilgrims and robbed them. "The Saracens, always laying snares for the Christians, lie hidden in the hollow places of the mountains and the caves of the rocks, watching day and night, and always on the lookout for those whom they can attack."[60]

The Arabs' tolerance toward the Christians also manifested itself in the West. When, for instance, at the end of the eleventh century the Spaniards conquered the city of Toledo from the Arabs, they were surprised to find Christian churches in the city untouched and to learn that services had continued there undisturbed. Similarly, when at the end of the eleventh century the Normans took possession of Sicily, they found there, in spite of more than two hundred years of Arabian rule in the island, a very large number of Christians who were freely professing their faith. Thus the first incident of the eleventh century which struck the Christian west painfully was the destruction of the Temple of the Resurrection and Golgotha in 1009. Another

[56] See E. Freeman, *The History of the Norman Conquest of England,* I, 473; II, 187. Ebersolt, *Orient et Occident,* 79. Bréhier, "Charlemagne and Palestine," *Revue historique,* CLVII (1928), 45.

[57] See V. G. Vasilievsky, "The Varangian-Russian and Varangian-English Company (druzina) in Constantinople in the Eleventh and Twelfth Centuries," *Works,* I, 265–66. K. Gjerset, *History of the Norwegian People,* I, 278.

[58] *Miracula S. Wulframni,* ed. D. T. Mabil-

lon, 381–82. See Ebersolt, *Orient et Occident,* 74.

[59] "Life and Pilgrimage of Daniel, igumen of the Russian Land," *Pravoslavny Palestinsky Sbornik,* no. 3 (1887), 15–16; ed. B. de Khitrowo, I, 12 ff. See H. Vincent and N. Abel, *Jérusalem. Recherches de topographie, d'archéologie et d'histoire,* II, 258.

[60] "Life and Pilgrimage of Daniel," ed. de Khitrowo, I, 12 ff. *Pilgrimage of Saewulf to Jerusalem and the Holy Land,* 8.

event connected with the Holy Land took place in the second half of the eleventh century.

The Seljuq Turks, after they had crushed the Byzantine troops at Manzikert, in 1071, founded the Sultanate of Rum or Iconium in Asia Minor and proceeded to advance successfully in all directions. Their military successes had repercussion at Jerusalem: in 1070, a Turkish general, Atzig, marched upon Palestine and captured Jerusalem. Shortly after the city revolted, so that Atzig had to lay siege to it again. Jerusalem was retaken and terribly sacked. Then the Turks conquered Antioch in Syria, established themselves at Nicaea, Cyzicus, and Smyrna in Asia Minor, and occupied the islands Chios, Lesbos, Samos, and Rhodes. The condition of European pilgrims in Jerusalem and other places grew worse. Even if the persecution and insults of the Christians that many scholars ascribe to the Turks are exaggerated, it is very difficult to agree with the judgment of W. Ramsay on the mildness of the Turks toward the Christians: "The Seljuk sultans governed their Christian subjects in a most lenient and tolerant fashion, and even the prejudiced Byzantine historians drop a few hints at the Christians in many cases preferring the rule of the sultans to that of the emperors. . . . Christians under the Seljuk rule were happier than the heart of the Byzantine Empire, and most miserable of all were the Byzantine frontier lands exposed to continual raids. As to religious persecution there is not a trace of it in the Seljuk period."[61]

The destruction of the Temple of the Resurrection in 1009 and the conquest of Jerusalem by the Turks in the eighth decade of the eleventh century were facts that profoundly affected the religious-minded masses of western Europe and evoked a powerful emotion of religious enthusiasm. Moreover, many Europeans realized that if Byzantium fell under the pressure of the Turks the whole of the Christian West would be exposed to terrible danger. "After so many centuries of terror and devastations," said a French historian, "will the Mediterranean world succumb again to the assault of the barbarians? Such is the anguished question that is raised toward 1075. Western Europe, slowly reconstructed in the course of the eleventh century, will take charge of replying to it: to the mass attacks of the Turks it prepares to reply by a crusade."[62]

But the most threatening danger from the ever-growing power of the Turks

[61] *The Cities and Bishoprics of Phrygia*, I, 16, 27. He is followed by J. W. Thompson, *An Economic and Social History of the Middle Ages*, 391, where a wrong reference was given to W. Ramsay's article, "The War of Moslem and Christian for the Possession of Asia Minor," *Contemporary Review*, XC (1906), 1–15. On the Turks in Palestine at the close of the eleventh century, cf., e.g., P. E. Riant, "Inventaire critique des lettres historiques de croisades," *Archives de l'orient latin*, I (1881), 65.

[62] L. Halphen, *Les Barbares: des grandes invasions aux conquêtes turques du XIe siècle*, 387. See also Erdmann, *Die Entstehung des Kreuzzugsgedanken*, esp. 363–77.

was felt by the Byzantine emperors, who, after the defeat of Manzikert, seemed to be unable to resist the Turks successfully with their own forces. Their eyes were turned to the West, mainly to the Pope, who as the spiritual head of the western European world could, through his influence, induce the western European peoples to furnish Byzantium with adequate assistance. Sometimes, as the message of Alexius Comnenus to Robert of Flanders shows, the emperors also appealed to individual rulers of the West. But Alexius had in mind merely some auxiliary troops, not powerful and well-organized armies.

The popes replied very favorably to the appeals of the eastern emperors. Besides the purely idealistic side of the question—aid for Byzantium and thereby for all the Christian world, as well as the liberation of the Holy Land —the popes had also in view, of course, the interests of the Catholic church; in case of the success of the enterprise the popes could hope to increase their influence still more and restore the eastern church to the bosom of the Catholic church. They could not forget the rupture of 1054. The original idea of the Byzantine Emperor to get some mercenary auxiliaries from the West gradually developed, especially under the influence of papal appeals, into the idea of a crusade, that is to say, into the idea of a mass movement of the western European peoples, sometimes under the direction of their sovereigns and the most eminent military leaders.

As late as the second half of the nineteenth century scholars believed that the first idea of the crusades and the first call was expressed at the close of the tenth century by the famous Gerbert, later Pope Sylvester II. Among his letters is one "From the ruined Church of Jerusalem to the Church Universal"; in this letter the Church of Jerusalem appealed to the Church Universal, asking the latter to come to her aid. Today the best authorities on Gerbert's problem consider this letter an authentic work of Gerbert written before he became pope; but they see in it no project of a crusade, merely an ordinary message to the faithful asking them to send charity to support Christian institutions at Jerusalem.[63] At the close of the tenth century the position of the Christians in Palestine was not yet such as to call for any crusading movement.

Yet before the Comneni, under the pressure of the Seljuq and Patzinak danger, the Emperor Michael VII Ducas had sent a message to Pope Gregory VII begging him for help and promising the reunion of the churches. Also the pope had written many letters, in which he exhorted his correspondents to support the perishing Empire. In his letter to the Duke of Burgundy he wrote: "We hope . . . that, after the conquest of the Normans, we shall cross

---

[63] T. Havet, *Lettres de Gerbert* (983–97), 22 and n. 3. N. Bubnov, *The Collection of Gerbert's Letters as a Historical Source*, II, 230 and n. 137. See also H. Sybel, *Geschichte des ersten Kreuzzuges* (2nd ed., 1881), 458–59.

over to Constantinople to help the Christians, who, deeply depressed by frequent attacks of the Saracens, anxiously beg that we lend them a helping hand."[64] In another letter Gregory VII spoke "of the pitiful destiny of the great Empire."[65] In a letter to the German king, Henry IV, the pope wrote that "most of transmarine Christianity is being destroyed by the pagans in crushing defeat and, like cattle, they are every day being murdered, and the Christian race is being exterminated"; they humbly beseech help in order "that the Christian religion may not entirely perish in our day, which Heaven forbid"; following the papal exhortations the Italians and the other Europeans (*ultramontani*) are equipping an army, of more than 50,000, and planning, if possible, to establish the pope at the head of the expedition; they are willing to rise against the enemies of God and to reach the Holy Sepulchre. "I am induced to do so," the pope continued, "because the Constantinopolitan Church, which disagrees with us concerning the Holy Ghost, desires to come to an agreement with the Apostolic throne."[66]

In these letters the question was not only of a crusade for the liberation of the Holy Land. Gregory VII was planning an expedition to Constantinople in order to save Byzantium, the chief defender of Christianity in the East. The aid procured by the pope was to be followed by the reunion of the churches and by the return of the "schismatic" eastern church to the bosom of the "true" Catholic church. One is given the impression that in these letters it is a question rather of the protection of Constantinople than of the conquest of the Holy Land. Moreover, all these letters were written before the eighth decade of the eleventh century, when Jerusalem passed into the hands of the Turks and when the position of the Palestinian Christians grew worse. Thus, in Gregory's plans the Holy War against Islam seems to have taken second place; it seems that, in arming the western Christians for the struggle with the Muslim east, the pope had in view the "schismatic" east. The latter seemed to Gregory more horrid than Islam. In one of his briefs concerning the regions occupied by the Spanish Moors, the pope openly declared that he would prefer to leave these regions in the hands of the infidel, that is to say, of the Muhammedans, rather than see them fall into the hands of the disobedient sons of the church.[67] If the messages of Gregory VII embody the first plan of the crusades, they show the connection between this plan and the separation of the churches in 1054.

Like Michael VII, Alexius Comnenus, especially under the pressure of the horrors of 1091, made appeals to the West, asking that mercenary auxiliaries

---

[64] J. P. Migne, *Patrologia Latina*, CXLVIII, 326.

[65] *Ibid.*, 329.

[66] *Ibid.*, 386.

[67] *Ibid.*, 290. See C. Kohler, in *Revue historique*, LXXXIII (1903), 156–57. Erdmann, *Die Entstehung des Kreuzzugsgedankens*, 149.

be sent. But the interference of the Cumans and the violent death of the Turkish pirate Tzachas ended the danger, so that from the point of view of Alexius, western auxiliaries seemed useless to the Empire in the following year, 1092. Meanwhile, the movement, created by Gregory VII in the West, spread widely, thanks especially to the confident and active Pope Urban II. The modest auxiliaries asked for by Alexius Comnenus were forgotten. Now it was a question of a mass movement.

The first critical investigation of a German historian, H. Sybel, published for the first time in 1841, advanced these principal causes for the crusades, from the western point of view:[68] (1) The first is the general religious spirit of the Middle Ages which increased in the eleventh century owing to the Cluniac movement. In a society depressed by the consciousness of its sins there is a tendency to asceticism, to seclusion, to spiritual deeds, and to pilgrimage; the theology and philosophy of the time were also deeply affected by the same influence. This spirit was the first general cause which roused the masses of the population to the deed of freeing the Holy Sepulchre. (2) The second is the growth of the papacy in the eleventh century, especially under Gregory VII. Crusades seemed very desirable to the popes, because they opened wide horizons for the further development of the papal power and authority; if the popes succeeded in the enterprise whose initiators and spiritual guides they were to become, they would spread their authority over many new countries and restore "schismatic" Byzantium to the bosom of the Catholic church. Thus, their idealistic desire to aid the eastern Christians and to deliver the Holy Land intermingled with their wish to increase their power and authority. (3) Worldly and secular motives also played a considerable part with the different social classes. Sharing in the general religious emotion, the feudal nobility, barons, and knights, were filled with the spirit of adventure and with the love of war. An expedition against the East was an unequaled opportunity to satisfy their ambition and bellicosity, and to increase their means. As far as the lower classes were concerned, the peasants, ground down by the burden of feudal despotism and swept away by rudimentary religious feeling, saw in the crusade at least a temporary relief from feudal oppression, a postponement of payment of their debts, a certain security for their families and their modest chattels, and release from sins. Later, other phenomena were emphasized by scholars in connection with the origin of the First Crusade.

In the eleventh century western pilgrimages to the Holy Land were particularly numerous. Sometimes pilgrimages were made by very large groups; along with the individual pilgrimages there were real expeditions to the Holy Land. In 1026–27 seven hundred pilgrims, at whose head was a French abbot and among whom were many Norman knights, visited Palestine. In

[68] Sybel, *Geschichte des ersten Kreuzzuges* (2nd ed., 1881).

the same year William, count of Angoulême, followed by several abbots of the west of France and by a great number of nobles, made a voyage to Jerusalem. In 1033 there was such a congestion of pilgrims at the Holy Sepulchre as had never been seen before. But the most famous pilgrimage took place in 1064–65, when more than seven thousand persons (usually said to be more than twelve thousand) under the leadership of Günther, the bishop of Bamberg, in Germany, undertook a pilgrimage. They passed through Constantinople and Asia Minor, and, after many adventures and losses, reached Jerusalem. The sources on this great pilgrimage state that "out of seven thousand, not two thousand returned," and these came back "measurably attenuated in material resources." Günther himself, the leader of the pilgrimage, died prematurely, "one of the many lives lost in this adventure."[69]

In connection with these precrusading peaceful pilgrimages the question has been raised whether the eleventh century might be regarded, as it has rather often been, as a period of transition from peaceful pilgrimages to the military expeditions of the crusading epoch. Many scholars have tried to prove that, because of new conditions established in Palestine after the Turkish conquest, troops of pilgrims began to travel armed to be able to defend themselves against possible attacks. Now, owing to E. Joranson, the fact has been established that the greatest pilgrimage of the eleventh century was made up· exclusively of unarmed men; and in this connection inevitably rises the question "whether any pilgrimage in the pre-crusading period really was an expedition under arms."[70] Of course, some of the pilgriming knights were armed, but "though some of them wore coats of mail they were still peaceful pilgrims," and they were not crusaders.[71] They played a considerable part in the history of the origin of the crusades, however, by informing western Europeans of the situation in the Holy Land and awakening and maintaining interest in it.[72] All these pilgrimaging expeditions took place before the Turks conquered Palestine. One of the results of the more recent investigation of the pilgrimages of the eleventh century before the Turkish conquest is the discovery that pilgrims in Palestine were sometimes maltreated by the Arabs many years before the Seljuq occupation of that land,[73] so that the statement

[69] See E. Joranson, "The Great German Pilgrimage of 1064–65," *The Crusades and Other Historical Essays Presented to Dana C. Munro*, 39.

[70] *Ibid.*, 40.

[71] O. Dobiache-Rojdestvensky, *The Epoch of the Crusades; the West in the Crusading Movement*, 16.

[72] See on the pilgrimages of the 11th century Bréhier, *Les Croisades*, 42–50. Cf. Joranson, "The Great German Pilgrimage," *Crusades and Other Essays*, 4, n. to p. 3; 40, n. 141. In *The Legacy of the Middle Ages*, ed. C. Crump and E. Jacob, 63, there is the following misleading statement: "the age of pilgrimage deepened the interest and the Crusades followed."

[73] Joranson, "The Great German Pilgrimage," *Crusades and Other Essays*, 42.

that "as long as the Arabs held Jerusalem, the Christian pilgrims from Europe could pass unmolested"[74] must now be considered too positive.

There is no information on pilgrimages from Byzantium to the Holy Land in the eleventh century. A Byzantine monk, Epiphane, the author of the first Greek itinerary to the Holy Land, described Palestine in the precrusading period, but the period of his life cannot be fixed definitely, and scholars variously place it between the end of the eighth century and the eleventh.[75]

Before the First Crusade Europe had actually experienced three veritable crusades: the wars in Spain against the Moors, the Norman conquest of Apulia and Sicily, and the Norman conquest of England in 1066. Moreover, a political and economic movement occurred in Italy in the eleventh century, centered in Venice. The pacification of the Adriatic coast laid a solid foundation for the maritime power of Venice, and the famous charter of 1082 granted to Venice by Alexius Comnenus opened to the Republic of St. Mark the Byzantine markets. "On that day began the world commerce of Venice."[76] At that time Venice, like some other south Italian cities which still remained under the power of Byzantium, did not hesitate to traffic with Muhammedan ports. At the same time Genoa and Pisa, which in the tenth century and at the beginning of the eleventh had been raided several times by the African Muhammedan pirates, undertook in 1015–16 an expedition against Sardinia, which belonged to the Muhammedans. They succeeded in conquering Sardinia and Corsica. The ships of these two cities thronged the ports of the opposite African coast, and in 1087, encouraged by the pope, they successfully attacked Mehdia on the north African coast. All these expeditions against the infidels were due not only to religious enthusiasm or to the spirit of adventure, but also to economic reasons.

Another factor in the history of western Europe which is associated with the origin of the crusades is the increase in population in some countries, which began about 1100. It is definitely known that the population increased in Flanders and France. One aspect of the mass movement at the end of the eleventh century was the medieval colonial expansion from some western European countries, especially France. The eleventh century in France was a time of frequent famines and drought and of violent epidemics and severe winters. These hard conditions of living made the population think of far distant lands full of abundance and prosperity. Taking all these factors into consideration one may conclude that, towards the end of the eleventh century,

[74] H. Loewe, "The Seljūqs," *Cambridge Medieval History,* IV, 316.

[75] See, e.g., K. Krumbacher, *Geschichte der byzantinischen Litteratur,* 420. Vincent and Abel, *Jérusalem,* II, xxxvii.

[76] Charles Diehl, *Une république patricienne: Venise,* 33.

Europe was mentally and economically ready for a crusading enterprise on a large scale.

The general situation before the First Crusade was entirely different from the situation before the Second. These fifty-one years, 1096–1147, were one of the most important epochs in history. In the course of these years the economic, religious, and whole cultural aspect of Europe changed radically; a new world was opened to western Europe. The subsequent crusades did not add very much to the achievements of this period; they only continued the processes developed in these fifty-one years. And it is strange to recall that an Italian historian names the first crusades "sterile insanities" (*sterili insanie*).[77]

The First Crusade presents the first organized offensive of the Christian world against the infidels, and this offensive was not limited to central Europe, Italy, and Byzantium. It began in the southwestern corner of Europe, in Spain, and ended in the boundless steppes of Russia.

As to Spain, Pope Urban II, in his letter of 1089 to the Spanish counts, bishops, *vice comites* and other nobles and powerful men, authorized them to stay in their own land instead of going to Jerusalem and to tax their energy for the restoration of Christian churches destroyed by the Moors.[78] This was the right flank of the crusading movement against the infidels.

In the northeast, Russia desperately defended itself against the barbarian hordes of the Polovtzi (Cumans), who appeared in the southern steppes about the middle of the eleventh century, laid waste the country, and destroyed trade by occupying all the routes leading east and south from Russia. The Russian historian, Kluchevsky, wrote: "This struggle between the Russians and Polovtzi—a struggle lasting for well-nigh two centuries—was not without its place in European history at large; for while the West was engaged in crusades against the forces of Asia and the Orient, and a similar movement was in progress in the Iberian peninsula against the Moors, Rus [Russia] was holding the left flank of Europe. Yet this historical service cost her dear, since not only did it dislodge her from her old settlements on the Dnieper, but it caused the whole trend of her life to become altered."[79] In this

[77] F. Cerone, "La politica orientale di Alfonso d'Aragona," *Archivio storico per le provincie Napolitane*, XXVII (1902), 425.

[78] Bulla Urbani II, July 1, 1089, Romae, in J. D. Mansi, *Sacrorum conciliorum nova et amplissima collectio*, XX, 701. Migne, *Patrologia Latina*, CLI, 302–3. P. Jaffé, *Regesta Pontificum Romanorum*, I, 663 (no. 5401). See Riant, "Inventaire critique," *Archives de l'orient latin*, I (1881), 68–69; Riant was somewhat doubtful, but without any plausible rea-

son, about the authenticity of this bull. See Erdmann, *Entstehung des Kreuzzugsgedankens*, 295 and n. 38.

[79] V. O. Kluchevsky, *A History of Russia*, trans. C. J. Hogarth, I, 192; (2nd ed. in Russian, 1906), I, 344–45. See Leib, *Rome, Kiev, et Byzance*, 276 n. 1, 277. Though Russian chroniclers say nothing about the Crusade, the crusading movement ought to have been known in Russia in the eleventh century. N. Iorga, *Choses d'Orient et de Roumanie*, 39–

way Russia participated in the general western European crusading movement; defending herself, she at the same time defended Europe against the barbarous infidels. "Had the Russians thought of taking the cross," said Leib, "they should have been told that their first duty was to serve Christianity by defending their own land, as the Popes wrote to the Spaniards."[80]

The Scandinavian kingdoms also participated in the First Crusade, but they joined the main army in smaller bands. In 1097 a Danish noble, Svein, led a band of crusaders to Palestine. In the north nothing was heard of any great religious enthusiasm, and, as far as is known, most of the Scandinavian crusaders were actuated less by Christian zeal than by love of war and adventure, and the prospect of gain and renown.[81]

There were two Christian countries in the Caucasus, Armenia and Georgia; but after the defeat of the Byzantine army at Manzikert in 1071 Armenia had come under the power of the Turks, so that there could be no question of the participation of the Caucasian Armenians in the First Crusade. As to Georgia, the Seljuqs had taken possession of that land in the eleventh century, and only after the taking of Jerusalem by the crusaders in 1099 did the king of Georgia, David the Restorer, drive out the Turks. This occurred in about 1100, or, as a Georgian chronicle asserted, when "a Frankish army had set forth on a march and, with divine assistance, taken Jerusalem and Antioch, Georgia restored itself, and David became powerful."[82]

When in 1095, in connection with west European complications and projected reforms, the victorious Pope Urban II summoned a council to meet at Piacenza, an embassy from Alexius Comnenus was present to make an appeal for aid. This fact has been denied by some scholars; but the more recent investigators of this problem have come to the conclusion that an appeal for aid was really made by Alexius at Piacenza.[83] Of course, this was

40, rejected any relation of Russia to the crusades. D. A. Rasovsky, "Polovtzi, Military History of Polovtzi," *Annales de l'Institut Kondakov*, XI (1940), 98.

[80] *Rome, Kiev, et Byzance*, 276, n. 1.

[81] Gjerset, *Norwegian People*, I, 313–14. See P. E. Riant, *Expéditions et pèlerinages des Scandinaves en Terre Sainte*, 127–71.

[82] M. Brosset, *Histoire de la Géorgie*, I, 352–53. See also A. Dirr, "Géorgie," *Encyclopédie de l'Islam*, II, 139–40. W. E. D. Allen, *A History of the Georgian People*, 95–97.

[83] See D. C. Munro, "Did the Emperor Alexius I Ask for Aid at the Council of Piacenza, 1095?" *American Historical Review*, XXVII (1922), 731–33. J. Gay, *Les Papes du XIe siècle et la chrétienté*, 366. Leib, *Rome*,

Kiev, et Byzance, 180. Bréhier, "Charlemagne and Palestine," *Revue historique*, CLVII (1928), 61–62. Dölger, *Corpus der griechischen Urkunden*, II, 43 (no. 1176); good bibliography. Chalandon, *La première croisade*, I, 156, thought that Alexius' ambassadors came to Piacenza to resume the negotiations concerning the reunion of the churches; see also pp. 17–18. R. Grousset, *Histoire des Croisades et du royaume franc de Jerusalem*, I, 5. In the middle of the nineteenth century F. Palgrave imagined the fantastic theory that the Greek legates at Piacenza were really disguised agents of Bohemond of Tarent: *The History of Normandy and of England*, IV, 509–10. See Yewdale, *Bohemond I*, 34, n. 1.

not "the final impulse," which caused the First Crusade, as Sybel asserted.[84] As before, if Alexius appealed for aid at Piacenza, he did not dream of crusading armies; he wanted no crusade, but mercenaries against the Turks, who during the last three years had become a great menace in their successful advance in Asia Minor. About the year 1095, Qilij Arslan had been elected sultan in Nicaea. "He sent for the wives and children of the men then staying in Nicaea, and bade them live there, and made this city the dwelling-place, as one might say, of the Sultans."[85] In other words Qilij Arslan made Nicaea his capital. In connection with those Turkish successes Alexius might have appealed for aid at Piacenza; but his intention was not a crusade to the Holy Land, but assistance against the Turks. His request was favorably received at Piacenza. But unfortunately there is little information about this episode. A recent historian remarked, "From the council of Piacenza to the arrival of the crusaders in the Byzantine empire, the relations between the East and the West are veiled in tantalizing obscurity."[86]

In November 1095, at Clermont (in Auvergne, middle France) the famous council was held. At this meeting so many people had assembled that not enough room was found in town for the visitors, and the multitude was quartered in the open air. After the close of the council, at which some most important current matters, strictly ecclesiastical, were discussed, Urban II delivered a very effective oration, the original text of which has been lost. Some witnesses of the council who wrote down the oration later from memory, give texts which differ very much from one another.[87] Fervently relating the persecutions of the Christians in the Holy Land, the pope urged the multitude to take arms for the liberation of the Holy Sepulchre and of the eastern Christians. With cries of *"Deus lo volt"* ("God wills it" or "It is the will of God") the throngs rushed to the pope. At his proposal, a red cross worn on the right shoulder was adopted as the emblem of the future crusaders (hence the name "crusaders"). They were promised remission of sins, relief from debts, and protection for their property during their absence. There was no compulsion; but there must be no turning back, and the renegade was to be excommunicated and regarded as an outlaw. From France enthusiasm spread all over Italy, Germany, and England. A vast movement to the east was forming, and the real scale and importance of it could not be anticipated or realized at the Council of Clermont.

Therefore, the movement aroused at the Council of Clermont, which in the ensuing year shaped itself into the form of a crusade, was the personal

[84] *Geschichte des ersten Kreuzzuges*, 182.

[85] Anna Comnena, *Alexias*, VI, 12; ed. Reifferscheid, I, 220; ed. Dawes, 163.

[86] F. Duncalf, "The Pope's Plan for the First Crusade," *Crusades and Other Essays*, 48–49.

[87] See D. C. Munro, "Speech of Pope Urban II at Clermont, 1095," *American Historical Review*, XI (1906), 231–42.

work of Urban II; and for carrying this enterprise into effect he found favorable conditions in the life of the second half of the eleventh century, not only from a religious, but also from a political and economic point of view.

While the danger that loomed in Asia Minor became steadily more imminent, the First Crusade had practically been decided upon at Clermont. The news of this decision came to Alexius as a sudden and disconcerting surprise; disconcerting because he neither expected nor desired assistance in the form of a crusade. When Alexius called mercenaries from the west, he called them for the protection of Constantinople, that is to say, his own state; and the idea of the liberation of the Holy Land, which had not belonged to the Empire for more than four centuries, had for him a secondary significance.

For Byzantium, the problem of a crusade did not exist in the eleventh century. Neither on the part of the masses nor of the Emperor himself did there exist religious enthusiasm, nor were there any preachers of a crusade. For Byzantium the political problem of saving the Empire from its eastern and northern enemies had nothing to do with the far-off expedition to the Holy Land. The Eastern Empire had witnessed "crusades" of her own. There had been the brilliant and victorious expeditions of Heraclius against Persia in the seventh century, when the Holy Land and the Holy Cross were restored to the Empire. Then there had been the victorious campaigns under Nicephorus Phocas, John Tzimisces, and Basil II against the Arabs in Syria when the Emperors definitely planned to regain possession of Jerusalem. This plan had not been realized, and Byzantium, under the menacing pressure of the overwhelming Turkish successes in Asia Minor in the eleventh century, had given up all hope of recovering the Holy Land. For Byzantium the Palestine problem at that time was too abstract; it was not connected with the vital interests of the Empire. In 1090–91 the Empire was on the verge of ruin, and when Alexius asked for western auxiliary troops, and was answered by the coming of crusaders, his motive was to save the Empire. In Alexius' *Muses,* written in iambic meter and supposed to be a sort of political will to his son and heir, John, there are these interesting lines about the First Crusade:

Do you not remember what has happened to me? Do you fail to think of and take into account the movement of the West to this country, the result of which is to be that all-powerful time will disgrace and dishonor the high sublimity of New Rome, and the dignity of the throne! Therefore, my son, it is necessary to take thought for accumulating enough to fill the open mouths of the barbarians, who breathe out hatred upon us, in case there rises up the force of a numerous army hurling lightnings angrily against us, at the same time many of our enemies encircling our city rebell.[88]

[88] P. Maas, "Die Musen des Kaisers Alexios I," *Byzantinische Zeitschrift,* XXII (1913), 357–58, lines 328–29. If I am not mistaken, this passage has not yet been used in connection with the history of the First Crusade.

With this fragment from Alexius' *Muses* one may compare the following passage from Anna Comnena's *Alexiad,* also on the First Crusade:

And such an upheaval of both men and women took place then as had never occurred within human memory; the simpler-minded were urged on by the real desire of worshipping at our Lord's Sepulchre, and visiting the sacred places, but the more astute, especially men like Bohemond and those of like mind, had another secret reason, namely, the hope that while on their travels they might by some means be able to seize the capital itself, finding a pretext for this.[89]

These two statements on the part of the Emperor himself and his learned daughter give an excellent picture of the real attitude of Byzantium towards the crusaders and the crusade itself. In Alexius' mind, the crusaders were on an equal footing with the barbarians menacing the Empire, the Turks and Patzinaks. Anna Comnena made only a passing mention of the "simpler-minded" among the crusaders who really desired to visit the Holy Land. The idea of a crusade was absolutely alien to the spirit of Byzantium at the end of the eleventh century. Only one desire was overwhelmingly prevalent in the leading Byzantine circles—to gain relief from the pressing Turkish danger from the east and north. Therefore the First Crusade was an exclusively occidental enterprise, politically slightly connected with Byzantium. True, the Eastern Empire gave the crusaders some troops, but these Byzantine troops did not go beyond Asia Minor. In the conquest of Syria and Palestine Byzantium took no part.[90]

In the spring of 1096, owing to the preaching of Peter of Amiens, who is often called Peter the Hermit and to whom a historical legend, now rejected, ascribed the arousing of the crusading movement, there gathered in France a multitude mostly of poor people, small knights, and homeless vagrants, almost without arms, who went through Germany, Hungary, and Bulgaria towards Constantinople. These undisciplined bands under Peter of Amiens and another preacher, Walter the Penniless, hardly realized through what countries they were passing, and unaccustomed to obedience and order, went on their way pillaging and destroying the country. Alexius Comnenus learned with dissatisfaction of the approach of the crusaders, and this dissatisfaction became alarm when he was informed of the pillage and destruction effected by the crusaders on their march. Nearing Constantinople the crusaders, as usual, indulged in pillaging in the neighborhood of the capital. Alexius Comnenus hastened to transport them across the Bosphorus into

[89] Anna Comnena, *Alexias,* X, 5; ed. Reifferscheid, II, 76; ed. Dawes, 250. Dawes translated the last words of this passage: "looking upon this as a kind of corollary."

[90] See an interesting study by M. Canard, "La Guerre sainte dans le monde islamique et dans le mond crétien," *Revue africaine,* LXXIX (1936), 605–23. Canard also emphasized that the idea of a crusade as a holy war did not exist in Byzantium in the eleventh century.

Asia Minor, where, near Nicaea, they were almost all easily killed by the Turks. Peter the Hermit had returned to Constantinople before the catastrophe.

The episode of Peter the Hermit and his bands was a sort of introduction to the First Crusade. The unfavorable impression left by these bands in Byzantium reacted against the later crusaders. As for the Turks, having so easily done away with Peter's bands, they were sure they would be victorious also over other crusading troops.

In the summer of 1096 in western Europe, began the crusading movement of counts, dukes, and princes; in other words, a real army assembled. No one of the west European sovereigns took part in the Crusade. Henry IV of Germany was entirely occupied by his struggle with the popes for investiture. Philip I of France was under excommunication for his divorce from his legitimate wife and for his marriage with another woman. The English king, William II Rufus, was engaged in a continuous struggle with his vassals, the church, and the people, and held his power insecurely.

Among the leaders of the crusading army the following should be mentioned. The first is Godfrey of Bouillon, the duke of Lower Lorraine, to whom a later legend imparted such a pious character that it is difficult to discern his real features; in reality, he was a brave and capable soldier and a religious-minded man, who wished in this expedition to repair losses sustained in his European possessions. His two brothers took part in the expedition, and one of them, Baldwin, was to become later the king of Jerusalem. Under Godfrey the Army of Lorraine set forth on the march. Robert, the duke of Normandy, son of William the Conqueror and brother of the king of England, William Rufus, took part in the crusade, but not for religious motives or chivalrous inducements; he was discontented with his small power in his duchy, which, just before his starting, he had pledged to his brother for a certain sum of money. Hugh, count of Vermandois, brother of the king of France, full of ambition, aspired to glory and new possessions and was greatly esteemed by the crusaders. The rude and irascible Robert II, count of Flanders, son of Robert of Flanders, also took part in the expedition and for his crusading exploits was called the Jerusalemite.[91] At the head of the three armies stood the following men: Hugh of Vermandois, at the head of the middle French army; Robert of Normandy and Robert of Flanders, at the head of the two north French armies. At the head of the south French army stood Raymond, count of Toulouse, a very well-known fighter against the Arabs in Spain, a talented leader and a deeply religious man. Finally, Bohemond of Tarentum, son of Robert Guiscard, and his nephew Tancred,

[91] On Robert II of Flanders see an article of M. M. Knappen, "Robert II of Flanders in the First Crusade," *Crusades and Other Essays,* 79–100.

who commanded the southern Italian Norman army, had no interest in religion; not improbably they hoped at the first opportunity to even their accounts with Byzantium, whose stubborn enemies they were, and apparently Bohemond had already fixed his ambitions upon the possession of Antioch.[92] Thus, the Normans carried into the crusade a purely worldly and political element which was in contradiction with the original idea of the crusading movement. Bohemond's army was perhaps the best prepared of all the crusading bands for such an expedition, "for there were many men in it who had come into contact both with the Saracens in Sicily and the Greeks in southern Italy."[93] All the crusading armies pursued their own aims; there was neither general plan nor commander in chief. The chief role in the First Crusade, then, belonged to the French.

One part of the crusading armies went to Constantinople by land, another part by sea. Like Peter the Hermit's bands, the crusaders ravaged the places they traversed and performed all kinds of violence. A witness of this passage of the crusaders, Theophylact, the archbishop of Bulgaria, explained in one of his letters the cause of his long silence and thereby accuses the crusaders; he wrote: "My lips are compressed; first of all, the passage of the Franks, or their invasion, or I do not know how one may call it, has so affected and seized all of us, that we do not even feel ourselves. We have drunk enough the bitter cup of invasion. . . . As we have been accustomed to Frankish insults, we bear misfortunes more easily than before, because time is a good teacher of all."[94]

It is obvious that Alexius Comnenus had good reason to distrust such defenders of the crusading idea. The Emperor waited with irritation and alarm for the crusading armies which were approaching his capital on all sides and which in their number were quite unlike the modest bodies of auxiliaries for which he had appealed to the West. Some historians have accused Alexius and the Greeks of perfidy and disloyalty to the crusaders. Such charges must be rejected, particularly after attention is turned to the pillaging, plundering, and incendiarism of the crusaders on their march. Also one must now reject the severe and antihistoric characterization of Gibbon, who wrote: "In a style less grave than that of history I should compare the Emperor Alexius to the jackal, who is said to follow the steps, and to devour the leavings, of the

[92] See Yewdale, *Bohemond I*, 44; during his march through the Balkan peninsula towards Constantinople Bohemond endeavored to comply as much as possible with the wishes of Alexius and his representatives (p. 40). But Yewdale remarked: "What Bohemond's exact plans were and precisely what end he had in view when he took the cross, beyond the very general end of personal aggrandizement, we shall probably never know" (p. 44).

[93] *Ibid.*, 38.

[94] *Epistola*, XI; ed. Migne, *Patrologia Graeca*, CXXVI, 324–25.

lion."[95] Of course, Alexius was not a man humbly to pick up what the crusaders left to him. Alexius Comnenus showed himself a statesman, who understood what a threat to the existence of his Empire the crusaders presented; therefore, his first idea was, as soon as possible, to transport the restless and dangerous comers to Asia Minor, where they were to carry on the task for which they had come to the East, that is to say, fighting the infidels. An atmosphere of mutual distrust and malevolence was created between the Latins and the Greeks; in their persons stood face to face not only schismatics, but also political antagonists, who later on were to settle their controversy by the power of the sword. An educated Greek patriot and learned literary man of the nineteenth century (Bikélas) wrote:

To the Western eye the Crusades present themselves in all the noble proportions of a great movement based upon motives purely religious, when Europe . . . appears the self-sacrificing champion of Christianity and of civilization, in the vigour of her strong youth and the glory of her intellectual morning. It is natural that a certain honourable pride should still inspire any family of the Latin aristocracy which can trace its pedigree to those who fought under the banner of the Cross. But when the Easterners beheld swarms of illiterate barbarians looting and plundering the provinces of the Christian and Roman Empire, and the very men who called themselves the champions of the Faith murdering the Priests of Christ on the ground that they were schismatics, it was equally natural that they should forget that such a movement had originally been inspired by a religious aim and possessed a distinctively Christian character. . . . The appearance (of the crusaders) upon the stage of history is the first act in the final tragedy of the Empire.[96]

The special historian of Alexius Comnenus, Chalandon, was inclined to apply, at least in part, to all the crusaders the characteristics attributed by Gibbon to the followers of Peter the Hermit: "The robbers, who followed Peter the Hermit, were wild beasts, without reason and humanity."[97]

Thus in 1096 began the epoch of the Crusades, so abounding and rich in its various consequences, and of such great importance both for Byzantium and the East and for western Europe.

The first account of the impression made on the peoples in the East by the beginning of the crusading movement came from an Arabian historian of the twelfth century, Ibn al-Qalanisi: "In this year (A.H. 490 = 19 December 1096 to 8 December 1097) there began to arrive a succession of reports that the armies of the Franks had appeared from the direction of the sea of Constantinople with forces not to be reckoned for multitude. As these reports

[95] *Decline and Fall of the Roman Empire*, ed. Bury, chap. 59.

[96] D. Bikélas, *La Grèce byzantine et moderne*, 29. Bikélas, *Seven Essays on Christian Greece*, trans. John, Marquess of Bute, 35–36.

[97] *La première croisade*, 159–60.

followed one upon the other, and spread from mouth to mouth far and wide, the people grew anxious and disturbed in mind."[98]

After the crusaders had gradually assembled at Constantinople, Alexius Comnenus, considering their troops as mercenary auxiliaries, expressed a wish to be acknowledged the head of the expedition and insisted that an oath of vassalage be sworn to him by the crusaders. A formal treaty was concluded between Alexius and the crusading chiefs, who promised to restore to Alexius, as their suzerain, any towns they should take which had formerly made part of the Byzantine Empire. Unfortunately the terms of the oath of vassalage which the crusading leaders took have not been preserved in their original form. In all likelihood, Alexius' demands varied concerning different regions. He sought for direct acquisitions in the regions of Asia Minor, which, shortly before, had been lost by the Empire after the defeat of Manzikert (1071), and which were the necessary conditions of the power and secure existence of the Byzantine Empire and Greek nationality. To Syria and Palestine, which had been lost by Byzantium long ago, the Emperor did not lay claim, but confined himself to claiming to be their suzerain.[99]

After crossing to Asia Minor, the crusaders opened hostilities. After a siege, in June 1097, Nicaea surrendered to them, and by virtue of the treaty made with Alexius was delivered to him. The next victory of the crusaders at Dorylaeum (Eski-Shehr), forced the Turks to evacuate the western part of Asia Minor and to draw back into the interior of the country; after that Byzantium had an excellent opportunity to restore its power on the coast of Asia Minor. Despite natural difficulties, climatic conditions, and the resistance of the Muslims, the crusaders advanced far to the east and southeast. In upper Mesopotamia, Baldwin took the city of Edessa and he soon established there his princedom which became the first Latin dominion in the East and a bulwark of the Christians against the Turkish attacks from Asia. But the example of Baldwin had its dangerous reverse side: the other barons might follow his example and found princedoms of their own, which, of course, would inflict great harm on the very aim of the crusade. Later on, this danger was fulfilled.

After a long and exhausting siege, the chief city of Syria, Antioch, a very strong fortress, surrendered to the crusaders; the way to Jerusalem was open. But because of Antioch a violent strife had broken out between the chiefs ending when Bohemond of Tarentum, following Baldwin's example, became the ruling prince of Antioch.[100] Neither at Edessa nor at Antioch did the crusaders

[98] *The Damascus Chronicle of the Crusaders*, trans. H. A. R. Gibb, 41.

[99] Cf. Yewdale, *Bohemond I*, 44. G. de Jerphanion, "Les Inscriptions cappadociennes et l'histoire de l'Empire Grec de Nicée," *Orientalia Christiana Periodica*, I (1935), 244-45.

[100] On the details see Yewdale, *Bohemond I*, 52-84. Chalandon, *La première croisade*, 177-249.

take the vassal oath to Alexius Comnenus. As the greater part of the troops remained with the chiefs who had founded their princedoms, only a very few, 20,000 to 25,000 in number, reached Jerusalem, and they arrived exhausted and thoroughly weakened.

At that time, Jerusalem had passed from the Seljuqs into the hands of a powerful caliph of Egypt, of the Fatimid dynasty. After a violent siege, on the 15th of July 1099, the crusaders took the Holy City by storm and effected therein terrible slaughter. They thoroughly pillaged it, and carried away many treasures. The famous Mosque of Omar was robbed. The conquered country, occupying a narrow seashore strip in the region of Syria and Palestine, received the name of the Kingdom of Jerusalem. Godfrey of Bouillon, who consented to accept the title of the "Defender of the Holy Sepulchre," was elected king of Jerusalem. The new state was organized on the western feudal pattern.

The First Crusade, which had ended in the formation of the Kingdom of Jerusalem and of several independent Latin possessions in the east, created a complicated political situation. Byzantium, satisfied with the weakening of the Turks in Asia Minor and with the restoring of a considerable part of that country to the power of the Empire, was alarmed, however, by the appearance of the crusading princedoms at Antioch, Edessa, and Tripoli, which became new political foes of Byzantium. The Empire's distrust gradually increased to such an extent that, in the twelfth century, Byzantium, opening hostilities against its former allies, the crusaders, did not hesitate to make alliance with its former enemies, the Turks. In their turn, the crusaders settled in their new dominions and fearing the strengthening of the Empire in Asia Minor, also concluded alliances with the Turks against Byzantium. Here, in the twelfth century, it was already obvious that the very idea of crusading enterprise had completely degenerated.

One cannot speak of a complete rupture between Alexius Comnenus and the crusaders. Of course, the Emperor was deeply discontented with the formation of the Latin possessions in the East, which had taken no vassal oath to him; nevertheless he did not refuse adequate help to the crusaders, for example, in transporting them from the east to the west, on their way home. A rupture took place between the Emperor and Bohemond of Tarentum, who, from the point of view of Byzantine interests, had become excessively powerful at Antioch, at the expense of his neighbors, the weak Turkish emirs, and of Byzantine territory. Therefore Antioch became the chief center of Alexius' aims. Raymond of Toulouse, the head of the Provençal troops, dissatisfied with his position in the East and also regarding Bohemond as his chief rival, drew closer to Alexius. At that time, for Alexius the fate of Jerusalem had secondary interest.

A struggle between the Emperor and Bohemond was unavoidable. An opportunity apparently presented itself to Alexius when Bohemond was suddenly captured by the Turks, that is by the Emir Malik Ghazi of the Danishmand dynasty, who at the very end of the eleventh century had conquered Cappadocia and established there an independent possession, which, however, was to be destroyed by the Seljuqs in the second half of the twelfth century. Alexius negotiated with the emir for the delivery of Bohemond in return for a certain amount of money, but the negotiations came to nothing. Bohemond was redeemed by others and returned to Antioch. On the basis of the treaty made with the crusaders, Alexius demanded that Bohemond deliver Antioch to him; but Bohemond decisively refused to do so.

At that time, in 1104, the Muslims won a great victory over Bohemond and the other Latin princes at Harran, south of Edessa. This defeat of the crusaders nearly destroyed the Christian dominions in Syria and reinvigorated the hopes both of Alexius and of the Muslims; both gladly anticipated Bohemond's unavoidable weakening. The battle of Harran destroyed his plans to establish in the East a powerful Norman state; he realized that he did not have strength enough to go to war again against the Muslims and the Emperor, his sworn enemy. His further stay in the East seemed to him aimless. Bohemond therefore determined to strike a blow to the Empire in Constantinople itself, with new troops collected in Europe. Having entrusted his nephew Tancred with the regency of Antioch, he embarked and sailed to Apulia. Anna Comnena gave an interesting though fictitious account, written not without humor, of how, in order to be safer from the Greek ships, Bohemond simulated death, was put into a coffin, and thus accomplished his crossing to Italy.[101]

Bohemond's return to Italy was greeted with the greatest enthusiasm. People flocked to gaze at him, said a medieval author, "as if they were going to see Christ himself."[102] Having gathered troops, Bohemond opened hostilities against Byzantium. The pope favored Bohemond's plans. His expedition against Alexius, explained an American scholar, "ceased to be a mere political movement; it had now received the approval of the Church and assumed the dignity of a Crusade."[103]

Bohemond's troops were probably drawn, for the most part, from France

---

[101] Anna Comnena, *Alexias*, XI, 12; ed. Reifferscheid, II, 140–41. See Chalandon, *La première croisade*, I, 236, n. 6. Yewdale, *Bohemond I*, 102, n. 99. This legend became widespread in the west, where in the Middle Ages, accounts of the pretended death and pretended burials of some prominent persons are given in several sources. See Vasilievsky, *Works*, I, 234–35.

[102] "Historia belli sacri (Tudebodus imitatus et continuatus)," ed. D. Bouquet, *Recueil des historiens des croisades*, III, 228. See Yewdale, *Bohemond I*, 106.

[103] Yewdale, *ibid.*, 108, 115. This view is supported by A. C. Krey, "A Neglected Passage in the *Gesta* and Its Bearing on the Literature of the First Crusade," *Crusades and Other Essays*, 76–77.

and Italy, but there were also, in all likelihood, English, Germans, and Spaniards in his army. His plan was to carry out his father Robert Guiscard's campaign of 1081, to take possession of Dyrrachium (Durazzo) and then through Thessalonica to march upon Constantinople. But the campaign turned out to be unsuccessful for Bohemond. He suffered defeat at Dyrrachium and was forced to make peace with Alexius on humiliating terms. The chief terms of the agreement between Bohemond and Alexius Comnenus were: Bohemond promised to consider himself the vassal of Alexius and his son, John; to take up arms against the Emperor's enemies; and to hand over to Alexius all conquered lands formerly belonging to the Empire. Those lands which had never been a part of the Empire and which Bohemond gained in any manner, were to be held by him as if they had been granted to him by the Emperor. He promised to make war on his nephew Tancred if Tancred did not consent to submit to the Emperor. The patriarch of Antioch was to be appointed by the Emperor from persons belonging to the Greek Eastern church, so that there would be no Latin patriarch of Antioch. The cities and districts granted to Bohemond are enumerated in the agreement. The document closes with Bohemond's solemn oath on the cross, the crown of thorns, the nails, and the lance of Christ, that he will fulfill the provisions of the agreement.[104]

With the collapse of Bohemond's vast and aggressive plans, his stormy career perhaps fatal to the crusading movement, came to its end. For the three last years of his life he was of no particular importance. He died in Apulia in 1111.

Bohemond's death made Alexius' position more difficult, because Tancred of Antioch refused to carry into effect his uncle's agreement, and would not hand Antioch over to the Emperor. Alexius had to begin all over again. The plan of an expedition against Antioch was discussed but was never brought into effect. It was evident that at that time the Empire was unable to undertake the difficult project. Tancred's death, which occurred soon after Bohemond's death, made the plan of marching on Antioch no easier. The last years of Alexius' reign were particularly occupied by nearly annual wars with the Turks in Asia Minor, which often were successful for the Empire.

In the external life of the Empire, Alexius succeeded in a very hard task. Very often Alexius' activity has been considered and estimated from the point of view of his relations to the crusaders, but not from the point of view of the total of his external policy. Such a point of view is undoubtedly wrong.

[104] Bohemond's document composed of an original draft is found in Anna Comnena, *Alexias,* XIII, 12; ed. Reifferscheid, II, 209–21; ed. Dawes, 348–57. See Yewdale, *Bohemond* I, 127–29; Dölger, *Corpus der griechischen Urkunden,* II, 51–52 (no. 1243); good bibliography.

In one of his letters, Alexius' contemporary, the archbishop of Bulgaria, Theophylact, using the words of a Psalm (79:13) compares the Bulgarian province with a grape-vine, whose fruit "is plucked by all who pass by."[105] This comparison, as says the French historian Chalandon, may be applied to the Eastern Empire of the time of Alexius.[106] All his neighbors tried to take advantage of the weakness of the Empire and to seize some of its regions. The Normans, Patzinaks, Seljuqs, and the crusaders threatened Byzantium. Alexius, who had received the Empire in a state of weakness, succeeded in making adequate resistance to them all and thereby delayed for a considerable time the process of the dissolution of Byzantium. Under Alexius, the frontiers of the state, both in Europe and in Asia, were extended. The Empire's enemies were forced to recede everywhere, so that, on the territorial side, his rule signifies an incontestable progress. The charges particularly often brought against Alexius concerning his relations to the crusaders must be given up, if we consider Alexius as a sovereign defending the interests of his state, to which the westerners, full of desire to pillage and spoil, were a serious danger. Thus, in his external policy Alexius successfully overcame all difficulties, improved the international position of the Empire, extended its limits, and for a time stopped the progress of the numerous enemies who on all sides pressed against the Empire.

External relations under John II

Increasing contacts with the western states.—The son and successor of Alexius, John II, was of the emperor-soldier type and spent the major part of his reign among the troops in military enterprises. His external policy chiefly continued that of his father, who had already pointed out all the important problems, European as well as Asiatic, in which the Empire of that time was particularly interested. John set as his goal progress along the political paths entered upon by his father. The father had hindered his enemies from invading Byzantium; the son determined "to take away from his neighbors the lost Greek provinces and dreamt of restoring the Byzantine Empire to its former brilliancy."[107]

Though he clearly understood the European situation, John was little interested in European affairs. He had from time to time to wage war in Europe, but there his wars were of a strictly defensive character. Only towards the end of his reign, owing to the threatening rise of the Normans, which expressed itself in the union of south Italy with Sicily and the formation of the Kingdom of Sicily, did European affairs become very important to Byzantium. John's

[105] *Epistola*, XVI; ed. Migne, *Patrologia Graeca*, CXXVI, 529.
[106] *La première croisade*, I, 321-22.

[107] F. Chalandon, *Les Comnène. Études sur l'Empire byzantin au XIᵉ au XIIᵉ siècles*, II, 10.

main interest in his external policy was concentrated in Asia Minor. With regard to John's relations to the West, there were a steadily increasing number of western European states with which Byzantium had to come into contact.

The Norman danger had caused Alexius to draw closer to Venice, who had pledged herself to support Byzantium with her fleet; thereupon Alexius had granted the Republic of St. Mark quite exceptional trade privileges. The Venetians, who had gone in throngs to the Empire, especially to Constantinople, grew rich and soon formed in the capital a Venetian colony so numerous and wealthy that it began to be of predominant importance. Gradually, forgetting that they were neither in their native country nor in a conquered land, the Venetians began to behave so arrogantly and impertinently towards not only the lower classes of the Byzantine population, but also the high officials and nobility, that they aroused strong discontent in the Empire. The small commercial privileges granted Pisa by Alexius were not important enough to alarm Venice.

In Alexius' lifetime, relations between the Byzantines and Venetians were not yet particularly strained. But with his death, circumstances changed. Learning that Norman Apulia was having internal troubles and therefore considering the Norman danger to Byzantium already over, John decided to abrogate the commercial treaty that his father had made with Venice. At once, the irritated Venetians sent their fleet to raid the Byzantine islands of the Adriatic and Aegean. Judging an adequate resistance to the Venetian vessels impossible, John was forced, still in the first years of his reign, to enter into negotiations with Venice which led to the complete restoration of the commercial treaty of 1082. Under John, the other Italian maritime cities, like Pisa and Genoa, also enjoyed certain commercial privileges but these, of course, could not be compared with those of Venice.

In these same first years of John's reign, the Patzinak problem was definitely solved. The Patzinaks, who had been crushed under Alexius Comnenus by the Cumans (Polovtzi), thereafter did not harass the Empire for thirty years. But at the beginning of the reign of John, the Patzinaks, who had somewhat recovered from their defeat, crossed the Danube and invaded the Byzantine territory. The imperial troops inflicted a heavy and decisive defeat upon them. In memory of this victory, John even instituted a special "Patzinak festivity," which, as the Byzantine historian Nicetas Choniates said, "was still celebrated at the end of the twelfth century."[108] After this defeat the Patzinaks had no importance at all in the external history of Byzantium. However, Patzinaks who were captured and who settled within the Empire constituted a separate group in the Byzantine troops and afterwards fought on the side of Byzantium.

[108] Nicetas Choniates, *Historia*, Bonn ed., 23.

The tendency of Hungary (Ugria) to extend its possessions towards the Adriatic coast had already rendered Alexius Comnenus discontented and strained his relations with the Hungarians. It seemed that the marriage of John to a Hungarian princess should improve relations. "But that intercourse," said the Russian historian C. Grot, "could not destroy the feeling of mutual distrust and rivalry that, in the course of time, formed in both neighbor states."[109] Besides the establishment of the Hungarians (Magyars) on the Dalmatian coast, which was dangerous to Byzantium, the increasing rapprochement between Hungary and Serbia was a source of dissatisfaction to the Empire. The Serbs who, along with the Bulgars, had been forced to come to Byzantium at the beginning of the eleventh century under Basil II Bulgaroctonus, had already begun by the middle of this century to revolt. The end of the eleventh century and the beginning of the twelfth was the time of the first liberation of Serbia from Byzantine power. Under John may be noticed a particular rapprochement between Serbia and Hungary, which was ready to help Serbia in obtaining its independence. A Serbian princess was given in marriage to a Hungarian prince. Thus, towards the end of the reign of John, in the northwest a new cause for alarm to Byzantium was created in the close connection of Hungary and Serbia.

John's military operations against them were fairly successful but had no definite result. An anonymous panegyrist of John, however, praised his military activities in the Balkan peninsula in these bombastic words: "How glorious are your campaigns against the European peoples! He [John] defeated the Dalmatians, terrified the Scythians and Nomads, the whole people living in wagons and unorganized; he coloured the waters of the Danube with much gore and many strong-flowing rivers of blood."[110]

In the last ten years of the reign of John, the relations to southern Italy completely changed. There a period of troubles was followed by a new epoch of power and glory. Roger II united in his hands Sicily and southern Italy, and on Christmas Day, 1130, he was solemnly crowned in Palermo with the royal crown. Owing to the union of these two territories, Roger II became at once one of the most powerful sovereigns of Europe. It was a tremendous blow to Byzantium. The Emperor, theoretically still claiming some rights to the south Italian lands, considered the occupation of them by the Normans but temporary. The restoration of Italy was a favorite dream of the emperors of the twelfth century. The assumption of the royal title by Roger seemed an offense

---

[109] *From the History of Ugria (Hungary) and the Slavs in the Twelfth Century,* 26–27.

[110] *Fontes rerum byzantinarum,* ed. W. Regel, II, 334. Until now no one has used this source. Under the Scythians and Nomads the panegyrist included the Patzinaks and other northern tribes invading Byzantine territory.

to the imperial dignity; to recognize this title would have been to give up all rights to the Italian provinces.

The sudden rise of Roger was undesirable not only to Byzantium, but also to the German sovereign, who had important interests in Italy. In view of the common danger, John II formed an entente, first with Lothar of Germany and after the latter's death, with Conrad III Hohenstaufen; somewhat later this developed into a real alliance between the two Empires. The main object of this entente and later alliance was to destroy the Norman power in Italy. This alliance became very important under John's successor, Manuel. If John failed to strike a blow at the power of Roger, he succeeded, at least, in preventing him from invading Byzantium. The subsequent wars of Roger with Manuel showed clearly that such a plan of invasion had hovered before his eyes. The most important parts of John's external policy in the West, then, were his attitude regarding the formation of the Sicilian kingdom and the creation of the alliance of the two Empires.

Relations of John to the East.—In Asia Minor, John carried on almost yearly and usually successful expeditions, so that in the fourth decade of the twelfth century he succeeded in restoring to the Empire the territories which had been lost long ago. Thereupon, thinking that the Turkish power had been greatly broken down, John believed that without affecting state interests he would be able to interrupt hostilities against the Turks and undertake a new and more distant campaign to the southeast against Armenian Cilicia and the crusading princedom of Antioch.

Armenian Cilicia or Armenia Minor had been established at the end of the eleventh century by the refugees from Armenia proper, in the north, who had fled from their country before the advancing Turks. Among other noble Armenian families, a family named Rupen (Ruben) began to play an important part in the government of the new country. Armenia Minor, which had extended its territory at the expense of Byzantium, came into close relations with the Latin princes in the east, showing thereby its hostile attitude toward the Empire. Then John Comnenus set forth on his march; he planned to punish Armenia Minor, which was in a state of revolt, and at the same time to settle the case of the princedom of Antioch, which in the time of the First Crusade had taken no oaths to the Emperor and later on had refused to submit to John in spite of the treaty concluded between Alexius Comnenus and Bohemond.

John's expedition was exceedingly successful. Cilicia was conquered, and the Prince of Armenia, with his sons, was sent to Constantinople. The Byzantine territory, enlarged by the annexation of Armenia Minor, reached the borders of the princedom of Antioch. In his struggle with the latter, John also obtained definite success. Besieged, Antioch was forced to ask him for peace, which John granted on the condition that the Prince of Antioch should acknowledge the suzerainty of the Empire. The Prince consented to take the oath of fealty to the Emperor and, as a sign of his submission, to raise the imperial standard over the citadel of Antioch. A year later, on his return to Antioch, the Emperor, as suzerain, made a solemn entry into the city surrounded by his sons, courtiers, officials, and soldiers. The triumphal procession moved through the decorated streets of the city. By the Emperor's side, as if he were his armiger, rode the Prince of Antioch. At the city gates, the Emperor was welcomed by the patriarch with his clergy; then, through an enormous multitude of people singing hymns and psalms, to the sound of music, John went first to the cathedral and thence to the palace.[111]

John's panegyrist said: "[Antioch] receives thee as lover of Christ, as athlete of the Lord, as zealous fighter against the barbarians, as carrying the sword of Elijah; it wipes off thy sweat and softly embraces thee. The whole numerous population of the city poured out; every age and both sexes formed brilliant procession and accorded a great triumph. . . . Shout was mixed and many-tongued, here Italian, there Assyrian. . . . Here commanders, there officers, and amidst them thou shonest as a brightest star!"[112]

The Emperor's plans went farther. According to the sources, he dreamt of re-establishing the Byzantine power in the Euphrates valley and seems to have intended to interfere in the affairs of the kingdom of Jerusalem;[113] it may be that, in John's mind, the project of such an interference was based upon the possibility that the king of Jerusalem might recognize the imperial suzerainty as the Prince of Antioch had done. Of those projects, the panegyrist said: "Be of good cheer, o men who love Christ and those who are pilgrims and strangers [on the earth] because of Christ" (cf. Hebr., xi:13); "do not fear any more murderous hands; the Emperor who loves Christ has put them in chains and broken to pieces the unjust sword. Thou hast cleared for them the way to the earthly and visible Jerusalem and hast opened to thyself another more divine and broad way,—that to the heavenly and holy Jerusalem."[114]

Nevertheless, those plans failed. In 1143, on a march against the Turks, during a hunting party in the mountains of Cilicia, John accidentally wounded his arm with a poisoned arrow and died, far from the capital. On his deathbed, he named his younger son Manuel as his successor. The whole time of his reign John devoted to the wars against the Empire's enemies. He handed

---

[111] William of Tyre, *Historia rerum in partibus transmarinis gestarum*, XV, 3; in *Recueil des historiens des croisades*, I, 658–59; in English by E. A. Babcock and A. C. Krey, II, 97.

[112] Regel, *Fontes rerum byzantinarum*, II, 358–59.

[113] Ioannis Cinnamus, *Historia*, Bonn ed., 25. Nicetas Choniates, *Historia*, Bonn ed., 56. William of Tyre, *Historia*, XV, 21; in *Recueil des historiens*, I, 691; in English, II, 126.

[114] Regel, *Fontes rerum byzantinarum*, II, 338, 339.

over to his heir a state even stronger and more vast than that which he had received from his energetic and talented father. John's panegyrist, considering him superior to Alexander of Macedon and Hannibal, exclaimed, "Strong was the Celtic oak, and thou hast pulled out its roots; high was the Cilician cedar, and thou, before us, hast lifted it and dashed it down!"[115]

Policies of Manuel I and the Second Crusade

Relations with the Turks.—If John, in his external policy, had turned his chief attention to the East, his successor Manuel, particularly because of the Norman relations and his personal sympathies with the West, was involved chiefly in western policy, which had sad consequences to the Empire. The Seljuq danger, which met no adequate resistance, became again very threatening on the eastern border.

The Byzantine border territory of Asia Minor was almost continuously exposed to the ruinous incursions of the Muslims who were exterminating or expelling the Christian population. Manuel had to secure order and safety in the border regions, and for that purpose he erected and restored a number of fortified places intended to check the invaders, mainly in those places where the enemy carried on most of their invasions.

It cannot be said, however, that Manuel's hostilities against the Turks were successful. In the first years of his reign he made an alliance with the Muhammedan emirs of Cappadocia, the above-mentioned Danishmandites, and began a war against his enemy of Asia Minor, the sultan of Iconium or Rum. The imperial troops successfully reached the chief city of the sultanate, Iconium (Konia); but, probably because they were aware that the sultan had received some reinforcements, they only pillaged the city suburbs and then withdrew; on their way back they met with a severe defeat from the Seljuqs, which barely escaped ending in a real catastrophe to the retreating troops. But the news of the crusade, which was threatening both to the Emperor and sultan, compelled both adversaries to seek peace, and a peace was concluded.

Alliance of the two empires.—In the first years of the reign of Manuel his western policy, like that of his predecessor, was regulated by the idea of the alliance with Germany which had been achieved under the pressure of the common danger from the growing power of the Italian Normans. The negotiations with Conrad III of Germany interrupted by the death of John were renewed. The question of the marriage of Manuel to the sister-in-law of Conrad, Bertha of Sulzbach, which had been proposed under John, was also renewed. In his letter to Manuel, Conrad wrote that this marriage should be

[115] *Ibid.,* 336, 346, 347, 353. I think that by the Celtic oak the panegyrist means the French dukedom of Antioch.

a pledge "of a permanent alliance of constant friendship," that the German sovereign promised to be "a friend of the Emperor's friends and an enemy of his enemies,"[116] as well as, in case of danger to the Empire, to come to its aid not only with some auxiliary troops, but, if necessary, in person with all forces of the German state. Manuel's marriage to Bertha, who received in Byzantium the name of Irene, set a seal upon the alliance of the two empires. This alliance gave Manuel the hope of getting rid of the danger which threatened his state from Roger II. Of course, while Roger faced two such adversaries as the Byzantine and German sovereigns, he did not venture to begin war with Byzantium with his former hopes for success.[117]

But an unexpected event suddenly destroyed Manuel's dreams and political speculations. The Second Crusade entirely changed the situation, at least for a time; it deprived Byzantium of German support and exposed the Empire to twofold danger from the crusaders and from the Normans.

The Second Crusade.—After the First Crusade the Christian rulers in the east, that is to say, the Byzantine Emperor and the Latin rulers of Antioch, Edessa, and Tripoli, as well as the king of Jerusalem, instead of endeavoring to crush with united forces the strength of the Muslims, were occupied with their internal dissensions and looked with distrust on the political strengthening of their neighbors. Particularly disastrous to the general welfare were the hostile relations of Byzantium to Antioch and Edessa. These conditions enabled the Muslims, who had been weakened and driven back by the forces of the First Crusade, to recover themselves and again threaten from Mesopotamia the Christian possessions.

In 1144 Zangi, one of the Muhammedan rulers or Atabegs of Mosul, as the Seljuq governors who had become independent, were called, suddenly seized Edessa. An anonymous Syriac chronicle recently translated into French affords a detailed account of the siege and capture of Edessa by Zangi. The latter, as the chronicler said, "left Edessa four days after the capture of the city. . . . The inhabitants of Edessa went to redeem their captives, and the city was repopulated. The governor Zain-ed-Din, who was a good-natured man, treated them very well."[118] But after Zangi's death in 1146 the former count of Edessa, Joscelin, retook the city. Zangi's son Nur-ad-Din easily took possession of it, and then the Christians were massacred, the women and children were sold into slavery, and the city was almost entirely destroyed. It was a heavy blow to the Christian cause in the east, because the county of Edessa, because of its geographical position, was a buffer state of the crusaders which had

---

[116] Otto of Freising, *Gesta Friderici I. imperatoris*, I, 24 (25); ed. G. Waitz, 33.

[117] See E. Caspar, *Roger II (1101–1154) und die Gründung der normannisch-sicilischen*

[Monarchie], 365.

[118] J. Chabot, "Un Épisode de l'histoire des croisades," *Mélanges offerts à M. Gustave Schlumberger*, I, 179.

to receive the first attacks of Muslim assaults. Neither Jerusalem nor Antioch nor Tripoli could help the prince of Edessa. Meanwhile, after the fall of Edessa, the Latin possessions, Antioch in particular, began to be seriously threatened.

The fall of Edessa produced a deep impression upon the west and evoked renewed interest in the cause of the Holy Land. But the pope of that time, Eugenius III, could not initiate or promote a new crusading enterprise, because the democratic movement which had broken out in the fifth decade at Rome and in which the famous Arnold of Brescia had taken part rendered the pope's position in the "eternal City" unstable, and even forced him to leave Rome for a time. The king of France, Louis VII, seems to have been the real initiator of the crusade, and its preacher who carried the idea into effect was the monk Bernard of Clairvaux, who by his fiery appeals first won over France. Then he passed to Germany and persuaded Conrad III to take the cross and inspired the Germans to take part in the expedition.

But the western peoples, who had learned caution through the bitter experience of the First Crusade and had been greatly disappointed in its results, did not manifest their former enthusiasm, and at the meeting of Vezelay, in Burgundy, the French feudaries were against the crusade. Not without difficulty Bernard won them over by his passionate and persuasive eloquence. In Bernard's conception the original plan of Louis VII widened. Owing to Bernard, simultaneously with the crusade to the East there were organized two other expeditions: the first against the Muslims who at that time were in possession of Lisbon in the Pyrenean peninsula, the other against the pagan Slavs in the north, on the Elbe (Laba) river.

Historians strongly disapprove of Bernard's idea of adding Germany to the crusade. The German scholar Kugler, who was especially interested in the Second Crusade, considered it as "a most unhappy idea";[119] the Russian scholar Th. Uspensky called it "a fatal step and great error of St. Bernard" and attributed the sad results of the crusade to the participation of the Germans.[120] In truth, the antagonism between the French and Germans during the crusade was one of its peculiar traits and of course could not contribute to its success.

The news of the crusade alarmed Manuel, who saw in it a danger to his state and to his influence with the Latin princes of the east, particularly at Antioch, which with support from the west could ignore the Byzantine Emperor. Also the participation of Germany in the crusade deprived Byzantium of the guarantee upon which the alliance of the two empires was based. If the king of Germany left his country for the East for long, he could not take

[119] *Studien zur Geschichte des zweiten Kreuzzuges,* 96.

[120] *A History of the Crusades,* 55, 57.

care of the western interests of the Byzantine Empire, which was therefore open to the ambitious plans of Roger. Knowing how dangerous to the capital the first crusaders had been, Manuel commanded its walls and towers to be restored, having evidently no confidence in the ties of friendship and relationship which bound Conrad to him.

According to V. Vasilievsky, "undoubtedly Manuel hoped to stand at the head of the whole Christian army against the common enemies of Christianity."[121] Besides the fact that Byzantium was very greatly interested in the future destinies of Islam in the East, Manuel, in the epoch of the Second Crusade, had also some special reasons for such a hope: at that time the Christian world had but one emperor, namely Manuel, because Conrad III Hohenstaufen had not been crowned by the pope in Rome and therefore did not bear the title of emperor.

In 1147 the leaders of the crusade decided to go to Constantinople by land, the way by which the first crusaders had already gone. First Conrad set out via Hungary; a month later Louis went the same way. The march of the crusaders towards Constantinople was followed by the same violence and pillaging as in the First Crusade.

When the German troops had pitched their camp under the walls of the capital, Manuel exerted himself to the utmost to transport them to Asia before the arrival of the French army; finally, after some altercations with his relative and ally Conrad, he succeeded. In Asia Minor the Germans began at once to suffer from the want of food, and then they were assaulted by the Turks and destroyed; only a pitiful remnant of the German army returned to Nicaea. Some historians ascribe the failure of the German expedition to the intrigues of Manuel, alleging that he made an agreement with the Muslims, stirring them up to attack the crusaders. Some historians, for example Sybel and following him Th. Uspensky, even spoke of the conclusion of an alliance between Manuel and the Seljuqs.[122] But the more recent scholars are inclined to believe that such charges against Manuel have no serious grounds and that he should not be considered responsible for the failure of the Germans.[123]

The French who had approached the capital soon after the passage of the Germans to Asia Minor alarmed Manuel still more. Manuel was particularly dubious about Louis with whom, shortly before the crusade, Roger had opened negotiations inducing him to go to the East through his Italian possessions; in Louis, Manuel suspected he saw a secret ally of Roger, or "the un-

[121] "The Alliance of the Two Empires," *Slavyansky Sbornik*, II (1877), 214; *Works*, IV, 22–23.

[122] H. Sybel, *Ueber den zweiten Kreuzzug*, 441. Uspensky, *The Crusades*, 61. Uspensky, "The Eastern Policy of Manuel Comnenus,"

Accounts of the Russian Palestine Society, XXIX (1926), 114. Cf. Kugler, *Studien zur Geschichte des zweiten Kreuzzuges*, 166, n. 60.

[123] Chalandon, *Les Comnène*, 287.

official ally of Sicily,"[124] and the Emperor's conjectures had serious grounds.

Knowing that at that time Manuel was entirely absorbed by the crusade and his relations to the crusaders, Roger abandoned the general interests of Christianity and following only his own political aims suddenly seized the island of Corfù and devastated some other Byzantine islands. Then the Normans landed in Greece and captured Thebes and Corinth, which were at that time famous for their silk factories and silk stuffs. Not satisfied with seizing a large quantity of precious silk stuffs "the Normans, among numerous other captives, carried into Sicily the most skilful silk weavers, both men and women." It is not true, however, as is sometimes stated in historical works, that these weavers who were transported to Palermo were the creators of the silk production and silk industry in Sicily; in reality the production of silk and the development of the silkworm had been known there before. But the arrival of the captured Greek women gave a new impetus to the industry.[125] Athens also was not spared by the Normans.[126]

When the news of the successful invasion of the Normans into Greece reached the French, who were standing under the walls of Constantinople, the latter, already irritated by the rumors of an agreement between Manuel and the Turks, became agitated. Some of Louis' chiefs suggested to him that he seize Constantinople. In the face of this danger the Emperor turned his mind to transporting the French also into Asia Minor. A rumor circulated that the Germans were meeting with success in Asia Minor, and Louis consented to cross over the Bosphorus and even took the oath to Manuel. Only when Louis made his appearance in Asia Minor did he learn the truth about the disaster of the German army. The sovereigns met and marched on together. The Franco-German troops are known to have suffered a complete failure at Damascus. The disappointed Conrad left Palestine on a Greek vessel and sailed for Thessalonica, where Manuel, who was preparing to open hostilities against the Normans, had his residence at the time. Manuel and Conrad met there, examined the general situation, and concluded a definite alliance against Roger. Thereafter Conrad returned to Germany.

Meanwhile the crusade accomplished nothing. Louis, who remained in the East, realizing the complete impossibility of doing anything with his own resources, returned some months later to France via southern Italy where he met with Roger.

Thus the Second Crusade, which had started so brilliantly, ended in the most miserable way. The Muslims in the East were not weakened; on the con-

[124] E. Curtis, *Roger of Sicily and the Normans in Lower Italy 1016–1154*, 227.

[125] See on that subject F. Chalandon, *Histoire de la domination normande en Italie et en Sicile*, II, 135–37. See also Caspar, *Roger II*, 376–84.

[126] Only western sources mention the capture and pillaging of Athens. See Caspar, *Roger II*, 382, n. 5.

trary, they gained in courage and began even to hope to destroy the Christian possessions in the East. Besides that, the strife between the French and German troops as well as between the Palestinian and European Christians did not add to the prestige of the crusaders. Manuel himself was glad to see the crusade finished, because now, strengthened by the conclusion of a formal alliance with Germany, he was free to proceed in his western policy against Roger. Nevertheless it would be unjust to charge the whole failure of the crusade upon the Emperor; the failure of the enterprise must be rather attributed to the lack of organization and general discipline among the crusaders. Also by his attack upon the islands of the Adriatic and Greece, Roger had fatally affected the project of the crusade. Generally speaking, the religious basis of the crusading enterprises was receding and the worldly political motives showed themselves henceforth more and more clearly.

External policy of Manuel after the Second Crusade.—During the crusade Manuel had already taken serious measures for the war against Roger, upon whom he wished to take vengeance for the treacherous incursion upon the islands of the Adriatic and Greece and for his continued occupation of Corfù. Venice, which, as before, watched the growing power of the Normans with some apprehension, willingly consented to support the Byzantine enterprise with her fleet and received for that aid new commercial privileges in the Empire; besides the quarters and landing places (*scalas*) in Constantinople which had been allotted to the Venetians by the former trade treaties, some new places and one more landing place (*scala*) were assigned to them.[127] While those negotiations were going on, the Emperor was energetically preparing for the war against "the western dragon," "a new Amalek,"[128] "the dragon of the island (i.e. Sicily) who was about to eject the flame of his anger higher than the craters of Etna," as the contemporary sources characterized Roger.[129] Manuel's plans were not confined to driving the enemy out of Byzantine territory; the Emperor hoped later on to transfer hostilities into Italy and to attempt to restore the former Byzantine power there.

He was temporarily diverted from his enterprise when his preparations were almost complete by the Cumans (Polovtzi), who crossed the Danube and invaded the Byzantine territory; but he succeeded in rapidly routing them. Then supported by the Venetian vessels, Manuel took possession of Corfù.

Roger realized what danger might threaten him from the alliance of Byzantium with Germany, who had promised to send the Emperor a land army, and Venice, who had already sent her vessels. Roger resorted to skillful

---

[127] The text of the treaty in Tafel and Thomas, *Urkunden zur ältern Handels- und Staatsgeschichte*, I, 109-13. Zachariä von Lingenthal, *Jus graeco-romanum*, III, 525-29.

[128] Cf. Exodus 17:8-14.

[129] Zachariä von Lingenthal, *Jus graeco-romanum*, III, 443. Eustathii Thessalonicensis *Manuelis Comneni Laudatio funebris*, par. 17; Migne, *Patrologia Graeca*, CXXXV, 984.

diplomatic maneuvers in order to create all possible difficulties for Byzantium. Owing to the Sicilian fleet and intrigues, the Duke Welf, an old enemy of the Hohenstaufens, rose against Conrad in Germany, who was therefore prevented from marching into Italy to support Manuel; then the Serbs supported by the Hungarians (Ugrians) also opened hostilities against Manuel, whose attention was thereby diverted towards the north. Finally, Louis VII, afflicted by the failure of the crusade and irritated at the Greeks, came, on his return journey from the East, to a friendly understanding with Roger and was preparing a new crusade which threatened Byzantium with unavoidable danger. The abbot Suger, who had governed France during Louis' absence, was the initiator of a new crusading enterprise, and the famous Bernard of Clairvaux was even ready himself to stand at the head of the army. A French abbot wrote to the Sicilian King: "Our hearts, the hearts of almost all our Frenchmen are burning with devotion and love for peace with you; we are induced to feel thus by the base, unheard of and mean treachery of the Greeks and their detestable king (*regis*) to our pilgrims. . . . Rise to help the people of God . . . take vengeance for such affronts."[130] Roger also was strengthening his relations with the pope. In general the West regarded with disfavor the alliance between the "orthodox" sovereign of Germany and the "schismatic" Emperor of Byzantium. It was thought in Italy that Conrad had already become affected with Greek disobedience, and the Papal curia was therefore making attempts to restore him to the path of truth and obedient service to the Catholic church. Pope Eugenius III, the abbot Suger, and Bernard of Clairvaux were working to destroy the alliance between the two empires. Thus, in the middle of the twelfth century, V. Vasilievsky explained, "there was on the point of coming into existence a strong coalition against Manuel and Byzantium at the head of which stood King Roger, to which Hungary and Serbia already belonged, which France as well as the Pope was about to join, and to which it was endeavored to draw Germany and her king. If the coalition had been realized, the year 1204 would have seen Constantinople already threatened."[131]

Nevertheless, the danger to the Empire proved not to be great. The plan of the king of France was not carried into effect partly because the French chivalry responded to the idea coldly and partly because Suger died shortly after. Conrad remained loyal to the alliance with the Eastern Empire.

But at the very time when Manuel might have expected a particular advantage from his alliance with Germany, Conrad III died (1152). His death, which had occurred just when the Italian campaign had been decided upon,

---

[130] Peter the Venerable, *Epistolae*, VI, 16; ed. Migne, *Patrologia Latina*, CLXXXIX, 424.
[131] "The Alliance of the Two Empires," *Slavyansky Sbornik*, II (1877), 244; *Works*, IV, 55–56.

evoked in Germany rumors that the king had been poisoned by his court physicians. They had come to Germany from Italy, from the famous medical school of Salerno, which was at that time in the power of Roger. Conrad's successor Frederick I Barbarossa ascended the throne believing in unlimited imperial power granted him by God; he would not admit that his power in Italy should be divided with the eastern Emperor. In a treaty with the pope concluded shortly after Frederick's accession to the throne the king of Germany, calling Manuel *rex,* not *imperator,* as Conrad had addressed him, pledged himself to expel the eastern Emperor from Italy. But, shortly after, for some unexplained reasons, Frederick changed his plans and seems to have intended to return to the idea of the Byzantine alliance.

In 1154 the terrible foe of Byzantium, Roger II, died. The new Sicilian king, William I, set as his goal the destruction of the alliance of the two empires and of the alliance between Byzantium and Venice. The Republic of St. Mark, aware of Manuel's plans for establishing himself in Italy, could not approve of them; it would have been just as bad for Venice as if the Normans had established themselves on the opposite coast of the Adriatic, for in either case both coasts would have belonged to one power, which would have barred to the Venetian vessels the free use of the Adriatic and Mediterranean. Accordingly Venice broke off her alliance with Byzantium and having obtained important trade privileges in the kingdom of Sicily, made an alliance with William I.

After the Byzantine arms had had some success in southern Italy, i.e. after Bari and some other cities had been captured, William inflicted a severe defeat on Manuel's troops at Brindisi in 1156, which at once nullified all the results of the Byzantine expedition. In the same year the capital of Apulia, Bari, was by order of William razed. A contemporary wrote: "The powerful capital of Apulia, famous for its glory, strong in its wealth, proud of the noble and aristocratic origin of its citizens, an object of general admiration for the beauty of its buildings, lies now as a pile of stones."[132]

The unsuccessful campaign of Manuel in Italy clearly showed Frederick Barbarossa that the Byzantine Emperor had in view the conquest of that country. Therefore he definitely broke with the Byzantine alliance. An historian contemporary with Frederick, Otto of Freising, wrote: "Although [Frederick] hated William, he did not, however, wish that the strangers might take away the territory of his Empire, which had been unjustly seized by the violent tyranny of Roger."[133] Any hope for a reconciliation with Barbarossa disappeared, and therewith disappeared all Manuel's hopes for the

---

[132] Hugo Falcandus, *Historia sicula;* in L. A. Muratori, *Scriptores rerum italicarum,* VII, 269.

[133] Otto of Freising, *Gesta Friderci I.,* II, 49.

restoration of Italy. In 1158 a peace was made between Manuel and William of Sicily. This peace, the exact conditions of which are not known, meant the abandonment by Byzantium of her long cherished and brilliant plans as well as "the rupture of the friendship and alliance between the two Empires which had existed under Lothar of Saxony and John Comnenus and later had been strengthened by the personal relations between Conrad and Manuel." The Byzantine troops never saw Italy again.[134]

Under the new conditions the aims of the Byzantine policy changed. Now it had to oppose the tendency of the Hohenstaufens to annex Italy, which Frederick Barbarossa believed must acknowledge his power. Byzantine diplomats began to work actively in a new direction. Manuel, wishing to destroy the relations between Frederick and the pope, sought the support of the papal curia in his coming struggle with Frederick and seduced the pope by hints of a possible union between the eastern and western churches. By evoking a conflict between the pope and the king of Germany, Manuel hoped "to restore the Eastern Empire in the whole fulness of its rights and put an end to the anomaly which existed in the shape of the Western Empire."[135] Yet those negotiations failed, because the popes were not at all willing to fall into a state of dependence from one emperor to the other; on the contrary, the popes of the twelfth century, imbued with theocratic ideals, wished themselves to reach superiority over the Byzantine Emperor.

When the war between Frederick Barbarossa and the north Italian cities started, Manuel actively supported the latter with money subsidies. The walls of Milan, demolished by Frederick, were restored by the aid of the Byzantine Emperor. The battle of Legnano, on May 29, 1176, which ended in Frederick's complete defeat in northern Italy and resulted in the triumph of the north Italian communes and their supporter, the papacy, seemed rather to improve Manuel's position in Italy. His relations were also particularly favorable in regard to Genoa, Pisa, and Venice; under the pressure of German danger the latter passed over again to Byzantium. But Manuel, willing, perhaps because of his lack of means, to profit by the enormous wealth of the Venetian merchants on the territory of his Empire, suddenly ordered all the Venetians of Byzantium to be arrested and their property confiscated. Venice, naturally incensed, sent a fleet against Byzantium which, owing to an epidemic, was forced to return without great success. In all probability, friendly relations between Byzantium and Venice were not restored in Manuel's lifetime.

Wishing to reply to the Byzantine policy in Italy in a similar way, Frederick Barbarossa entered into negotiations with the most dangerous foe of Byzantium in the East, the sultan of Iconium, Qilij Arslan, and tried to induce

[134] V. G. Vasilievsky, "The South Italian War (1156–57)," *Slavyansky Sbornik*, III (1876), 400; *Works*, IV, 138.
[135] Chalandon, *Les Comnène*, II, 557.

the latter to invade the Greek Empire, hoping that the difficulties in Asia Minor would divert Manuel from European affairs.

Meanwhile the situation in Asia Minor was growing threatening. In Cilicia, which had been conquered by John Comnenus, a revolt broke out under the leadership of Thoros. Two of Manuel's armies sent against Thoros failed. The situation became more alarming when Thoros made an alliance with his former enemy the prince of Antioch, Reginald of Chatillon, and together they marched against the Greeks. At the same time Reginald made a successful naval attack on Cyprus. Manuel came to Cilicia in person. His arrival was so sudden that Thoros barely escaped capture and fled. In 1158, Manuel became again the master of Cilicia. Thoros submitted himself to the Emperor and was pardoned by him. Now it was the turn of Antioch.

Reginald of Chatillon, realizing that he would be unable to resist the Byzantine forces, decided to sue for Manuel's pardon. The Emperor was at Mopsuestia (Mamistra of the crusaders), in Cilicia; Reginald "appeared there as a suppliant before the Great Comnenus."[136] A most humiliating scene took place: barefooted, he prostrated himself before the Emperor, presenting to him the hilt of his sword and submitting himself to his mercy. "At the same time," as William of Tyre said, "he cried for mercy, and he cried so long that everyone had nausea of it and that many French have disdained and blamed him for that."[137] Ambassadors from most of the Oriental peoples, including the far distant Abasgians (Abkhaz) and Iberians, were present at that spectacle and were profoundly impressed.[138] "This scene has rendered the Latins despicable in the whole of Asia."[139] Reginald acknowledged himself the vassal of the Empire, so that later (1178–1179) a certain Robert was sent to the court of Henry II, king of England, as ambassador on behalf of the two countries, Byzantium and Antioch.[140] The king of Jerusalem, Baldwin III, arrived personally in Mopsuestia where, in Manuel's camp, he was courteously received by the Emperor. But Baldwin was forced to enter into a treaty with him and pledged himself to furnish troops to the Emperor. Eustathius of Thessalonica in his oration to Manuel mentioned the king, who

---

[136] G. Schlumberger, *Renaud de Chatillon*, 107.

[137] *Historia*, XVIII, 23; in *Recueil des historiens*, I, 860–61; ed. M. Paulin, II, 232. The Latin version says: "As soon as he had thus surrendered his sword, he threw himself on the ground at the emperor's feet, where he lay prostrate till all were disgusted, and the glory of the Latins was turned into shame." William of Tyre, *Historia*, trans. E. A. Babcock and A. C. Krey, II, 277; on the same

subject see a poem of Prodrome in the *Recueil des historiens*, II, 305–10.

[138] Ioannes Cinnamus, *Historia*, IV, 18; Bonn ed., 183.

[139] Schlumberger, *Renaud de Chatillon*, 110, 111. William of Tyre, *Historia*, XVIII, 23; in *Recueil des historiens*, I, 861: Latinitatis gloriam verteret in opprobrium.

[140] *The Great Roll of the Pipe for the Reign of King Henry the Second*, XXVIII, 125. Collection is referred to hereafter as *Pipe Rolls*.

"ran to us from Jerusalem astounded by the fame and the deeds of the Emperor and recognizing from afar his sublimity."[141]

Then in April 1159, Manuel made his solemn entry into Antioch. Escorted by Reginald of Chatillon and the other Latin princes on foot and unarmed, and followed by the king of Jerusalem on horseback but also unarmed, the Emperor passed through streets decorated with carpets, hangings, and flowers, to the sound of trumpets and drums and to the singing of hymns, and was brought to the cathedral by the patriarch of Antioch in his pontifical robes. For eight days the imperial banners flew from the city walls.[142]

The submission of Reginald of Chatillon and the entry of Manuel into Antioch in 1159 mark the triumph of the Byzantine policy towards the Latins. It was the result of more than sixty years of efforts and struggle. Despite many difficulties and wars, the Byzantine Emperor "never lost sight of the problem of Antioch—the problem raised during the First Crusade and since never solved."[143]

In the church of the Nativity, at Bethlehem, an inscription dated by the year 1169 has been preserved which stated "the present work was completed by the painter and mosaist Ephraim in the reign of the Emperor Manuel Porphyrogenitus Comnenus and in the days of the Great King of Jerusalem Amaury, and of the most holy Bishop of the holy Bethlehem Raoul in the year 6677, indiction 2" (= 1169).[144] The name of Manuel put together with that of Amaury may indicate that a sort of suzerainty of the Greek emperor was established over the king of Jerusalem.[145]

As to the relations of Manuel with the Muhammedan princes, he and Qilij Arslan had had for some years a friendly connection, and in 1161–62 the Sultan had even come to Constantinople where a solemn reception had been accorded to him by the Emperor. This reception is thoroughly described in Greek and Oriental sources. The Sultan spent eighty days in Constantinople. All the wealth and treasures of the capital were ostentatiously shown to the famous guest. Dazzled by the brilliancy of the palace reception, Qilij Arslan

[141] Regel, *Fontes rerum byzantinarum*, I, 39.

[142] Chalandon, *Les Comnène*, II, 451–52.

[143] *Ibid.*, 446.

[144] See M. de Vogüé, *Les Églises de la Terre Sainte*, 99. *Corpus inscriptorum graecarum*, IV, 339 (no. 8736). H. Vincent and F. N. Abel, *Bethléem: Le Sanctuaire de la Nativité*, 157–61.

[145] Chalandon, *Les Comnène*, II, 449. Bréhier, *Les croisades* (5th ed., 1928), 109; Bréhier gives the wrong date, 1172. The idea of Manuel's suzerainty is denied by Vincent and Abel (*Bethléem*, 160) but vigorously supported by G. de Jerphanion ("Les inscriptions cappadociennes," *Orientalia Christiana Periodica, I* [1935], 245–46) and rejected by J. L. LaMonte ("To What Extent Was the Byzantine Empire the Suzerain of the Latin Crusading States?" *Byzantion*, VII [1932], 253–64, esp. 263: this inscription evidence is nothing more than the gift of a generous and pious prince to a church which was one of the most celebrated shrines in Christendom).

did not even dare to sit down by the side of the Emperor. Tournaments, races, and even a naval festival with a demonstration of the famous "Greek fire" were given in honor of the sultan. Twice a day, food was brought to him in gold and silver vessels, and the latter were not taken back, but left at the disposal of the guest. One day, when the Emperor and sultan had dinner together, all vessels and decorations were offered to Qilij Arslan as a gift.[146]

In 1171 the king of Jerusalem, Amaury I, arrived in Constantinople and was magnificently received by Manuel. William of Tyre gave a detailed account of this visit.[147] It was the climax of the international glory and overwhelming power of Manuel in the Near East.

But the political results of the visit of Qilij Arslan to the capital were not very important; a sort of friendly treaty was made, but it was of short duration. Some years later the sultan announced to his friends and officials that the greater damage he did to the Empire, the more precious presents he got from the Emperor.

In such circumstances, the peace on the eastern border could not last long. On the strength of some local causes as well as perhaps because of the instigation of Frederick, hostilities broke out. Manuel himself rode at the head of his troops. The aim of the campaign was the capture of the capital of the sultanate, Iconium (Konia). In 1176 the Byzantine troops became entangled in the mountainous gorge of Phrygia, where the stronghold of Myriocephalon was situated not far from the border. There the Turks suddenly assaulted them on several sides and, on September 17th, 1176,[148] inflicted upon them a complete defeat. The Emperor barely saved his life and escaped capture. The Byzantine historian, Nicetas Choniates, wrote: "The spectacle was really worthy of tears, or, it is better to say, the disaster was so great that it could not be sufficiently bemourned: pits were filled to the top with corpses; in ravines there were heaps of slain; in bushes, mountains of dead. . . . No one passed by without tears or moan; but all sobbed and called their lost friends and relatives by their names."[149]

A contemporary historian who spent some time in Constantinople in 1179, depicts Manuel's mood after the defeat at Myriocephalon as follows:

[146] Ioannes Cinnamus, *Historia,* V, 3; Bonn ed., 204–8. Nicetas Choniates, *Historia,* III, 5–6; Bonn ed., 154–58. *Chronique de Michel le Syrien,* trans. Chabot, III, 319; from him, Gregorii Abulpharagii sive Bar-Hebraei, *Chronicon Syriacum,* ed. Bruns and Kirsch, 358–59. See Chalandon, *Les Comnène,* II, 463–66. Th. I. Uspensky, "The Eastern Policy of Manuel Comnenus," *Accounts of the Russian Palestine Society,* XXIX (1926), 115–17.

[147] William of Tyre, *Historia,* XX, 22–24; in *Recueil des historiens,* I, 981–87; trans. Babcock and Krey, II, 377–83. See G. Schlumberger, *Campagnes du roi Amaury Iᵉʳ de Jérusalem en Egypte, au XIIᵉ siècle,* 311–31. Chalandon, *Les Comnène,* II, 546–49.

[148] On this date see A. A. Vasiliev, "Das genaue Datum der Schlacht von Myriokephalon," *Byzantinische Zeitschrift,* XXVII (1927), 288–90.

[149] Nicetas Choniates, *Historia,* 247.

From that day the emperor is said to have borne, ever deeply impressed upon his heart, the memory of that fatal disaster. Never thereafter did he exhibit the gaiety of spirit which had been so characteristic of him or show himself joyful before his people, no matter how much they entreated him. Never, as long as he lived, did he enjoy the good health which before that time he had possessed in so remarkable a degree. In short, the ever-present memory of that defeat so oppressed him that never again did he enjoy peace of mind or his usual tranquillity of spirit.[150]

In a long letter to his western friend, King Henry II Plantagenet, of England, Manuel announced his recent disaster and evidently tried to soften it a little. A detailed narration of the battle was given by the Emperor in that letter; among other things, he gave interesting information concerning the participation in the battle of Englishmen who after 1066 served the Byzantine emperors, especially in the imperial guard.[151]

In spite of the crushing defeat at Myriocephalon, an anonymous panegyrist of Manuel turned the Emperor's very flight before the Turks into one of his brilliant deeds when he said: "After a clash with a mass of attacking Ismaelitians [i.e. Turks] he [Manuel] rushed into flight alone without fearing so many swords, arrows, and spears."[152] A nephew of Manuel adorned his new house with paintings, and among other pictures, "he ordered the deeds of the Sultan (of Iconium) to be painted, thus illustrating upon the walls of his house that which would have been more proper to keep in darkness."[153] In all likelihood, this unusual picture represented the fateful battle of Myriocephalon.

But for reasons still unknown, Qilij Arslan used his victory with moderation and opened negotiations with the Emperor which led to the conclusion of a tolerable peace. Some Byzantine fortifications in Asia Minor were destroyed.

The battle of Manzikert in 1071 had already been a deathblow to Byzantine domination in Asia Minor. But the contemporaries had not understood this, and still hoped to recover, and get rid of the Seljuq danger. The two first crusades had not decreased that danger. The battle of Myriocephalon in 1176 definitely destroyed Byzantium's last hope of expelling the Turks from Asia Minor. After that the Empire could not possibly carry on any efficient offensive policy in the East. She could barely protect the eastern border and repulse the Seljuq hordes which were continually penetrating into her territory. "The

---

[150] William of Tyre, *Historia*, XXI, 12; in *Recueil des historiens*, I, 1025; trans. Babcock and Krey, II, 415.

[151] This letter is inserted in Rogeri de Houedene (Roger van Hoveden), *Chronica*, ed. W. Stubbs, II, 102–4.

[152] S. Lampros, " Ὁ Μαρκιανὸς Κῶδιξ,"

Νέος Ἑλληνομνήμων, VIII (1911), 149. See also S. P. Shestakov, "Notes to the Poems of the Codex Marcianus gr. 524," *Vizantiyski Vremennik*, XXIV (1923–26), 46–47.

[153] Ioannes Cinnamus, *Historia*, Bonn ed., 267. See Charles Diehl, *Manuel d'art byzantin*, I, 405.

battle of Myriocephalon," declared Kugler, "decided forever the destiny of the whole East."[154]

Soon after this defeat, Manuel also sent a letter to Frederick Barbarossa in which he portrayed the Seljuq sultan's position as weak; but Frederick had already been informed of the truth—Manuel's crushing defeat.[155] In replying to Manuel, Frederick announced that the German emperors, who had received their power from the glorious Roman emperors, had to rule not only the Roman Empire but also "the Greek Kingdom" (*ut non solum Romanum imperium nostro disponatur moderamine, verum etiam regnum grecie ad nutum nostrum regi et sub nostro gubernari debeat imperio*); therefore he bade Manuel recognize the authority of the western emperor and yield to the authority of the pope, and ended with the statement that in the future he would regulate his conduct by that of Manuel, who in vain was sowing troubles among the vassals of the western empire.[156] It was thus the belief of the authoritative Hohenstaufen that the Byzantine emperor should submit to him in his position as western emperor. The idea of a single empire did not cease to exist in the twelfth century; at first Manuel remembered it, and later when circumstances became unfavorable to Byzantium, Frederick began to dream of the single empire.

In 1177, the Congress of Venice, which was attended by Frederick, the pope, and the representatives of the victorious Italian communes, confirmed the independence of the latter and reconciled the German sovereign to the pope. In other words, the treaty of Venice put an end to the hostility which had existed between Germany, the Lombard communities, and the papal curia, which Manuel had utilized for his diplomatic combinations. "The Congress of Venice was a blow to the Byzantine Empire, equivalent to the defeat inflicted on it by the Sultan of Iconium at Myriocephalon," said Th. Uspensky. "Having reconciled the elements in the West which were hostile to Byzantium, the Congress was a prognostic of the coalition which was to conquer Constantinople in 1204 and form the Latin states in the East."[157]

The Congress of 1177 had exceptional significance for Venice, where assembled a brilliant European society headed by the western emperor and the pope. Over ten thousand foreigners came to Venice, and all admired the beauty, wealth, and power of that city. A contemporary historian, addressing the Venetian people, wrote: "Oh, how happy you are because such a peace

[154] Kugler, *Studien zur Geschichte des zweiten Kreuzzuges*, 222.

[155] A fragment of this letter is preserved in the *Annales Stadenses*, ed. K. Pertz, *Monumenta Germaniae Historica, Scriptores*, XVI, 349. It is erroneously ascribed to 1179. See H. von Kap-Herr, *Die abendländische Politik Kaiser Manuels*, 104, n. 6.

[156] *Ibid.*, 156–57 for the text of this letter.

[157] "Alexius II and Andronicus," *Journal of the Ministry of Public Instruction*, CCXII (1880), 123–24.

could be made in your country. It will be a permanent glory to your name."[158]

A short time before his death, Manuel succeeded in obtaining his last diplomatic success, namely, marriage of his son and heir Alexius to an eight-year-old daughter of the king of France, Louis VII. The little princess Agnes received in Byzantium the name of Anne. Owing to this marriage, the somewhat strained relations which had been established between Byzantium and France after the Second Crusade seem to have improved. Eustathius of Thessalonica wrote a eulogistic oration on the occasion of the arrival at Megalopolis, i.e. Constantinople, of the imperial bride from France.[159]

Moreover, after the famous letter sent by Manuel to the king of England, Henry II, after the disaster of Myriocephalon, the relations between those two sovereigns became very friendly, and in the last years of Manuel's reign there is some evidence that the Byzantine envoys appeared at Westminster, and an Englishman, Geoffrey de Haie (Galfridus de Haia) was entrusted by Henry II with the entertainment of the Greek ambassadors; the same Geoffrey de Haie was sent in return to Constantinople.[160] Henry II, evidently well informed on Manuel's favorite sports of which hunting was not the least, even sent him a pack of hunting dogs on a vessel sailing from Bremen.[161]

To sum up, Manuel's policy differed very much from the cautious and thoughtful policy of his grandfather and father. Absorbed by his delusive dream of restoring the unity of the Empire as heir to Augustus, Constantine, and Justinian, and strongly inclined to western tastes, customs and manners, he exerted himself to the utmost in the struggle with Italy and Hungary as well as in his relations with the Western Empire, France, Venice, and other Italian communes. Leaving the East without adequate attention, he failed to prevent the further growth of the sultanate of Iconium and finally witnessed the collapse of all the hopes of the Empire in Asia Minor after the disaster of Myriocephalon.

The preference given by Manuel to the West, which was uncongenial to Byzantium and whose culture at that time was not equal to Byzantine culture, also brought about consequences disastrous to the Empire. By receiving foreigners with open arms and granting them the most responsible and lucrative places, he roused so strong a dissatisfaction among his subjects that bloody conflicts might be expected on the first occasion.

The special historian of Manuel's epoch estimated his policy in these com-

---

[158] *Historia ducum Veneticorum, s. a. 1177;* Pertz, *Monumenta Germaniae Historica,* XIV, 83. See H. Kretschmayr, *Geschichte von Venedig,* I, 268. W. C. Hazlitt, *The Venetian Republic: Its Rise, Its Growth, and Its Fall,* I, 231–32. Diehl, *Venise,* 45–46.

[159] Regel, *Fontes rerum byzantinarum,* I, 80–92; see also xiii–xiv.

[160] *Pipe Rolls,* XXVI, 166, 187, 192, 208; XXVIII, 125.

[161] *Ibid.,* XXVII, 19.

ments: "Manuel chanced to die rather too soon to see the sad consequences of his policy; they had been already perceived by the perspicacious minds of some of his contemporaries. It was hard to receive the heritage of the Emperor, and no one among his successors was to be able to restore the position of the Empire. In ensuing years the decline of the Empire was to go on rapidly: it is just to say that it began with the reign of Manuel."[162]

It might be more correct to say that the decline of the Empire had begun much earlier, in the epoch of the Macedonian dynasty, after the death of Basil II Bulgaroctonus in 1025. The first two Comneni, Alexius and John, succeeded in retarding the progress of the decline, but they failed to stop it. The erroneous policy of Manuel led the Empire again into the path of decline and this time into definite decadence. Hertzberg commented: "with Manuel, the ancient brilliance and ancient greatness of Byzantium sank into the grave forever."[163] This opinion of the historian of the nineteenth century agrees with the words of a well-known writer of the end of the twelfth century, contemporary with the Comneni and Angeli, Eustathius of Thessalonica: "According to divine purpose, with the death of the Emperor Manuel Comnenus there has perished all that still remained intact from the Romans, and darkness has enveloped all our country as if it were under an eclipse of the sun."[164]

Such a colorful figure as that of Manuel Comnenus could not fail to leave a deep impress far beyond the confines of the Byzantine Empire. His name and his exploits, the latter mostly legendary, were well known in the Russian heroic epics and in Russian songs, as well as in the Russian annals. Manuel sent to the princess of Polotzk, Euphrosinia, an icon of the Mother of God, of Ephesus.[165] It should not be forgotten that the famous legendary letter of Prester John was addressed to Manuel.

Foreign affairs under the last Comneni, Alexius II and Andronicus I

"The five-year period comprising the reign of the two last Comneni, Alexius and Andronicus," wrote the Russian historian, Th. Uspensky, "is interesting particularly as a period of reaction and state reforms which had an entirely rational basis and were evoked by the well realized defects of the former system of administration."[166] After Manuel's death his twelve-year-old son, Alexius II (1180–83), ascended the throne, and his mother Mary

---

[162] Chalandon, *Les Comnène*, II, 607–8. See also F. Cognasso, *Partiti politici e lotte dinastiche in Bizanzio alla morte di Manuele Comneno*, 216 (4).

[163] *Geschichte der Byzantiner*, 318.

[164] *De Thessalonica a Latinis capta*, Bonn ed., 380.

[165] See A. Sedelnikov, "The Epic Tradition Concerning Manuel Comnenus," *Slavia*, III (1924–25), 608–18.

[166] "Alexius II and Andronicus," *Journal of the Ministry of Public Instruction*, CCXII (1880), 100.

(Maria) of Antioch was proclaimed regent; her favorite Alexius Comnenus, Manuel's nephew, however, had the direction of all state affairs. The violent struggle of the court parties as well as the continuing Latin preponderance led to the summoning of the famous Andronicus into the capital. He had already for a long time been filled with ambitious plans of seizing the imperial throne; and he snatched at the opportunity to appear as a defender of the weak Emperor Alexius II, surrounded by wicked advisers, as well as a protector of Greek national interests. A short time before he entered the capital, the massacre of the Latins had taken place. Venetian sources pass over the massacre of 1182. Nevertheless the Venetian merchants no doubt also suffered considerably.

In the same year, 1182, Andronicus entered Constantinople and, in spite of his solemn promise, began to aim openly at sole dominion. By his order, the powerful Alexius Comnenus was arrested and blinded; then the Regent Mary of Antioch and, shortly after, the unfortunate Emperor Alexius II were strangled. In 1183, Andronicus, then sixty-three years old, became all-powerful sovereign of the Empire. In order to make his position more solid, he married the widow of Alexius II, Agnes (Anne) of France, who, at the death of her fourteen-year-old husband, was not quite twelve years of age.

The enthusiasm with which the populace received Andronicus is explained by their expectations from the new Emperor. The two chief problems of the internal life of the Empire confronted Andronicus: first, to establish a national government and deliver Byzantium from the Latin preponderance; second, to weaken the office-holding aristocracy and large landowning aristocracy, because the preponderance of large landowners was bringing about the ruin and destruction of the agricultural class of peasants. Such a program, however hard its execution might be, met great sympathy among the mass of the population.

The archbishop of Athens, Michael Acominatus (Choniates), one of the most precious sources for the internal situation of the Empire in the twelfth century, wrote in eulogistic terms: "And first of all I shall remember how, at the troublesome and painful time, the Roman Empire appealed to its former darling, the great Andronicus, to overthrow the oppressive Latin tyranny which, like a weed, had grafted itself on the young offshoot of the kingdom. And he brought with him no huge body of foot and horse, but armed only with justice marched lightly to the loving city. . . . The first thing he gave the capital in return for its pure love was deliverance from the tyrannous Latin insolence and the clearing of the Empire from barbarian admixture."[167]

[167] Μιχαὴλ ᾿Ακομινάτου τοῦ Χωνιάτου τὰ σωζόμενα, ed. S. Lampros, I, 157. See Th. I. Uspensky, "The Last Comneni. The Beginning of Reaction," *Vizantiysky Vremennik,* XXV (1927–28), 20.

"With Andronicus, a new party came to power."[168] "This last representative of the dynasty of the Comneni," said Th. Uspensky, "was or at least seemed to be a popular king, a king of peasants. People sang songs about him and composed poetical tales, the traces of which have been preserved in the annals and marginal notes of the unpublished manuscripts of the History of Nicetas Choniates."[169] Among other things, Nicetas wrote that Andronicus commanded his statue to be erected near the northern gate of the Church of the Forty Martyrs, and the Emperor was represented there not arrayed in the imperial robes, not wearing golden ornaments as sovereign, but as a worker, oppressed with labor, in a very modest dress, holding a scythe.[170]

Andronicus set strenuously to work at reforms. The salary of many officials was raised in order to make them less bribable; honest and incorruptible men were appointed judges; tax burdens were considerably lightened, and severe punishments were inflicted upon the tax collectors who were furthering their own interests. Strong measures were taken against large landowners, and many members of the Byzantine aristocracy were put to death. Michael Acominatus wrote: "Long ago we have been convinced that you are mild to the poor, terrific to the covetous, that you are the protector of the weak and the enemy of the violators, that you incline the balance of Themis neither to the right nor to the left, and that you have hands pure from bribes."[171]

The struggle of Andronicus with the Byzantine aristocracy, both of birth and of wealth, reminded the Italian historian, Cognasso, of the struggle of the tsar of Russia, John (Ivan) the Terrible, in the sixteenth century, with the Russian nobility. He wrote:

As Andronicus had intended to destroy the preponderance of Byzantine aristocracy, so John, the power of *boyars* [Russian nobility], and both of them, but the Russian Tzar to a greater extent, were forced to resort to coercive measures. But it was unfortunate that by weakening aristocracy they both weakened the state: John IV found himself as helpless before the Poles of Stephen Batory as Andronicus before the Normans of William II. John, sovereign of a young and strong people, succeeded by rapid measures in saving Russia; Andronicus had fallen before the Empire was reformed and strengthened. The old organism could no longer be supported, and a new organic body, of which Andronicus was dreaming, was too soon entrusted to inexperienced hands.[172]

Of course, Andronicus was incapable of carrying out a radical reform of a social system which had resulted from a long historical process. Representa-

[168] L. Bréhier, "Andronic (Comnène)," *Dictionnaire d'histoire et de géographie ecclésiastiques*, II, 1780.

[169] Uspensky, "Alexius II and Andronicus," *Journal of the Ministry of Public Instruction*, CCXII (1880), 18, 21.

[170] *Ibid.*, 15: Uspensky speaks not of a statue, but of a picture, probably a mosaic. Nicetas Choniates, *Historia*, Bonn ed., 432.

[171] Uspensky, *ibid.*, 19. Michael Acominatos, *Works*, ed. S. Lampros, 142.

[172] *Partiti politici e lotte dinastiche in Bizanzio*, 290 (78).

tives of the persecuted landowning aristocracy were only waiting for the first opportunity to get rid of their hated ruler and replace him by a person who would keep up the social policy of the first three Comneni. Suspecting everywhere treason and plots, Andronicus adopted a system of terrorism which, without any distinction, crushed guilty and guiltless, and not only among the higher classes; an atmosphere of irritation and hatred for the Emperor gradually grew among the population. The people who had recently received their darling with frantic acclamations, deserted him as a man who had not kept his promises, and they were already looking for a new claimant to the throne. Nicetas Choniates gave a striking picture of the changeable mood of the Constantinopolitan populace of that time: "In any other city the populace is thoughtless and very unyielding in its tumultuous motion; but the mob of Constantinople is particularly tumultuous, violent, and 'walking in crooked ways,' because it is composed of different peoples. . . . Indifference towards the emperors is an evil innate in them; him whom they raise today legally as their master, they disparage next year as a criminal."[173]

The complicated and threatening internal situation became still more aggravated by the failure of the external policy. Andronicus came to the conclusion that the political isolation of the Empire was impracticable from the point of view of its essential and vital interests; in order to save the situation he must resume relations with the western powers that he so ostentatiously abhorred.

And in truth the attitude of the West towards Byzantium was exceedingly menacing. After Manuel's death there were two enemies of Byzantium in western Europe: Germany, and the Kingdom of Sicily. The alliance of the two empires which for a time, during the reign of Manuel, had been the basis of the western European policy, came to an end; at the same time the aid rendered by Byzantium to the Lombard communes in their struggle against Frederick Barbarossa made that enemy of the Eastern Empire gradually inclined to draw closer and closer to the Kingdom of Sicily.

Then the Latins who had escaped the massacre organized in 1182 in Constantinople returned to the West to their own countries; relating the horrors of their experiences, they urged revenge for the insults and damages inflicted upon them. The Italian trade republics, which had suffered great financial losses, were particularly irritated. The members of some noble Byzantine families persecuted by Andronicus also fled to Italy, and there they tried to induce the Italian governments to open hostilities against Byzantium.

Meanwhile, the western danger to the Eastern Empire was growing more and more threatening. Frederick Barbarossa married his son and heir, Henry, to the heiress of the Kingdom of Sicily, Constance; the betrothal had been

[173] Nicetas Choniates, *Historia*, Bonn ed., 304–5.

announced in Germany in 1184, a year before Andronicus' death. It was a very important event, because after Frederick's death his successor could annex Naples and Sicily to the possessions of the king of Germany. From two separate enemies there would be created against Byzantium one single terrible enemy whose political interests could not be reconciled with those of the Eastern Empire. It is even very probable that this matrimonial alliance with the Norman royal house was made to establish a point of departure in the Sicilian kingdom for the plans of the western emperor against Byzantium, in order to conquer more easily, with the help of the Normans, "the Kingdom" of the Greeks. At least, a western medieval historian remarked: "The Emperor hostile to the Kingdom of the Greeks [regno Grecorum infestus] endeavors to unite the daughter of Roger with his son."[174]

The king of Sicily, William II, a contemporary of Andronicus, taking advantage of the internal troubles in Byzantium, organized a great expedition against the latter, the purpose of which was certainly not only the desire of taking revenge for the massacre of 1182 or of supporting a possible claimant to the Byzantine throne, but also an intention to take possession of the Byzantine throne for himself. Andronicus decided to enter into negotiations both with the West and with the East.

He made a treaty with Venice before the beginning of 1185.[175] In coming to terms with the Republic of St. Mark "in order to support the Empire" (*pro firmatione Imperii*) Andronicus is said to have released the Venetians still imprisoned in Constantinople after the massacre of 1182 and to have promised compensation for loss, in annual payments. He actually began to discharge these obligations, and the first installment was paid in 1185.[176] He also attempted to draw closer to the pope of Rome, from whom he evidently hoped to get support, by pledging himself to grant some privileges to the Catholic church. By the end of 1182 Pope Lucius III had sent a legate to Constantinople.[177] Furthermore, a western chronicle affords very interesting evidence that in 1185 Andronicus, against the will of the patriarch, constructed a church in Constantinople upon which he bestowed an ample revenue, where the Latin Catholic priests officiated according to their rite; "up to this day that church is called the Latin church."[178]

---

[174] *Annales Colonienses Maximi, s. a. 1185,* in Pertz, *Monumenta Germaniae Historica, Scriptores,* XVII, 791.

[175] Cognasso, *Partiti politici e lotte dinastiche in Bizanzio,* 294–95 (82–83). Bréhier, "Andronic (Comnène)," *Dictionnaire d'histoire,* II, 1781.

[176] Andrae Danduli *Chronicon,* ed. Muratori, *Rerum italicarum scriptores,* XII, 309 (s. a. 1182). See also H. F. Brown, "The Vene-

tians and the Venetian Quarter in Constantinople to the Close of the Twelfth Century," *Journal of Hellenic Studies,* XL (1920), 86.

[177] Cognasso, *Partiti politici e lotte dinastiche in Bizanzio,* 298–99 (86–87). Bréhier, "Andronic (Comnène)," *Dictionnaire d'histoire,* II, 1781.

[178] Benedicti Abbatis, *Gesta regis Henrici Secundi,* ed. W. Stubbs, I, 257: construxerat ecclesiam quandam nobilem in civitate Con-

Finally, a short time before he died, Andronicus made a formal alliance with the sultan of Egypt, Saladin. As a western chronicler reported, "urged by grief and distress (Andronicus) has recourse to the advice and succor of Saladin."[179] The conditions of that alliance sealed by oath run as follows: if Saladin succeeded, with the advice and aid of the Emperor, in occupying Jerusalem, Saladin himself should keep any other country they might take for himself, Jerusalem and the whole sea coast, except Ascalon, becoming free; but he should hold this territory under the suzerainty of Andronicus; the Emperor should take possession of all the conquered territories of the sultan of Iconium as far as Antioch and Armenia Minor, if the new allies were able to annex them. But "prevented by death, Andronicus could not carry that plan into effect."[180] Thus according to that treaty Andronicus was ready to cede Palestine to Saladin on condition that the latter should recognize the suzerainty of the Empire. But neither the treaty with Venice, nor the overtures to the pope, nor the alliance with the famous Saladin could save the situation or preserve the power in the hands of Andronicus.

In the eastern portion of the Mediterranean the governor of the island of Cyprus, Isaac Comnenus, seceded from the Empire and proclaimed the independence of the island under his rule. Having no good fleet, Andronicus failed to put down the revolt. Cyprus was lost. The loss of Cyprus was a very severe blow to the Empire, for Byzantium had had there an important strategic and commercial point which had brought large revenues to the treasury, especially because of the trade with the Latin states in the East.

But the chief and decisive blow was struck from the West, when the well-organized expedition of William II of Sicily sailed against the Empire. As usual, hostilities opened at Durazzo which at once passed into the hands of the Normans; then they followed the military Egnatian road (via Egnatia) and marched towards Thessalonica. The powerful Norman fleet also arrived there. In this war Venice seems to have been strictly neutral.

The well-known ten days' siege of Thessalonica by land and sea began. A narrative of this siege, rather rhetorical but nevertheless valuable, was written by an eyewitness, the archbishop of Thessalonica, Eustathius. In August, 1185, Thessalonica, which ranked next to Constantinople, was captured by

---

stantinopolis, et eam honore et redditibus multis ditaverat, et clericos Latinos in ea instituit secundum consuetudinem Latinorum, quae usque hodie dicitur Latina. See the same story also in Rogeri de Houedene, *Chronica*, ed. Stubbs, II, 205.

[179] *Chronicon Magni Presbiteri* (*Annales Reicherspergenses*), ed. Pertz, *Monumenta Germaniae Historica, Scriptores*, XVII, 511.

[180] *Ibid.*, XVII, 511. See R. Röhricht, *Geschichte des Königreichs Jerusalem* (*1100–1291*), 494 (ein förmliches Bündniss). N. Radojčić, *Dva posljednja Komnena na carigradskom prijestolju*, 85. Cognasso, *Partiti politici e lotte dinastiche in Bizanzio*, 297 (85). Dölger, *Corpus der griechischen Urkunden*, II, 91 (no. 1563). Bréhier, "Andronic (Comnène)," *Dictionnaire d'histoire*, II, 1781.

the Normans, who affected there an appalling destruction and massacre, the revenge of the Latins for the massacre of 1182. Said a Byzantine historian of that time, Nicetas Choniates: "Thus, between us and them [the Latins] a bottomless gulf of enmity has established itself; we cannot unite our souls and we entirely disagree with each other, although we keep up our external relations and often live in the same house."[181] After some days of pillage and murder the Norman troops advanced farther to the east, towards Constantinople.

When the news of the capture of Thessalonica and of the approach of the Norman troops to the capital had reached Constantinople, the population of the city broke out in revolt, accusing Andronicus of making no preparations for resisting the enemy. With unexpected rapidity Isaac Angelus was proclaimed emperor. Andronicus was dethroned and died after atrocious tortures. With the revolution of 1185 the epoch of the Byzantine Comneni ended.

The short reign of Andronicus I, who on his accession to the throne had set himself the goal of protecting the agricultural class, or peasants, against the arbitrary domination of the large landowners, and of freeing the state from the foreign Latin preponderance, differs strikingly in character from the rule of all other Comneni. For this reason alone the reign of Andronicus deserves intense and strictly scientific investigation. In some respects, particularly in the sphere of social problems and interests, the time of Andronicus, which has not yet been satisfactorily elucidated, presents a fascinating field for further researches.

FOREIGN POLICY OF THE ANGELI

Characteristics of the Emperors of the House of the Angeli

The dynasty of the Angeli, elevated to the throne by the revolution of 1185, sprang from a contemporary of Alexius Comnenus, Constantine Angelus, of the city of Philadelphia in Asia Minor, a man of low birth, who was married to a daughter of the Emperor Alexius; he was the grandfather of Isaac II Angelus, the first emperor from this house, who was therefore related by the female side to the Comneni.

One of the aims of the late Andronicus had been to establish a national government; obviously he had failed in this task and at the close of his reign he had begun to incline to the West. After his death, the need of a national government became thoroughly felt, so that, as a recent Italian historian of the rule of Isaac II Angelus, Cognasso, wrote: "The revolution of the twelfth of September (1185) became especially nationalistic and aristocratic in its

---

181 Nicetas Choniates, *Historia*, Bonn ed., 391–92.

plans; thus, from the advantages derived from the revolution all classes were excluded except the Byzantine aristocracy."[182]

Isaac II (1185-95) who represented, to quote Gelzer, "the embodied evil conscience which sat now upon the rotten throne of the Caesars,"[183] possessed no administrative talents at all. The excessive luxury and foolish lavishness of the court together with arbitrary and unendurable extortions and violence, lack of will power and of any definite plan in ruling the state in its external relations, especially in the Balkan peninsula where a new danger to the Empire appeared in the Second Bulgarian Kingdom, and in Asia Minor, where the Turks continued their successful advance unchecked by the fruitless Third Crusade,—all this created an atmosphere of discontent and agitation in the country. From time to time revolts broke out in favor of one or another claimant to the throne. But perhaps the chief cause of general discontent was "the fatigue of the population at enduring the two evils well recognized by Andronicus: the insatiability of the fiscal administration and the arrogance of the rich."[184] Finally, in 1195, a plot against Isaac was formed by his brother Alexius, who, with the help of a certain part of the nobility and troops, dethroned the Emperor. Isaac was blinded and imprisoned, and his brother Alexius became Emperor. He is known as Alexius III Angelus (1195–1203), or Angelus Comnenus, sometimes surnamed Bambacoratius (Βαμβακορά-βδης).[185]

In his qualities and capacities the new Emperor scarcely differed from his brother. The same foolish lavishness, the same lack of any political talent or interest in government, the same military incapacity brought the Empire by rapid steps far on the way towards disintegration and humiliation. Not without malicious irony Nicetas Choniates remarked concerning Alexius III: "Whatever paper might be presented to the Emperor for his signature, he signed it immediately; it did not matter that in this paper there was a senseless agglomeration of words, or that the supplicant demanded that one might sail by land or till the sea, or that mountains should be transferred into the middle of the seas or, as a tale says, that Athos should be put upon Olympus."[186] The Emperor's conduct found imitators among the nobility of the capital, who exerted themselves to the utmost to compete with each other in expense and luxury. Riots took place in both the capital and the provinces. The foreigners who resided in Constantinople, the Venetians and Pisans, often met

[182] "Un imperatore Bizantino della decadenza Isacco II Angelo," *Bessarione*, XXXI (1915), 44; separate ed., 18.

[183] *Abriss der byzantinischen Kaisergeschichte*, 1032.

[184] Cognasso, "Un imperatore Bizantino,"

Bessarione, XXXI (1915), 59; separate ed., 33.

[185] See N. A. Bees, "Bambacoratius, ein Beiname des Kaisers Alexios III. Angelos (1195–1203)," *Byzantinisch-neugriechische Jahrbücher*, III (1922), 285–86.

[186] *Historia*, Bonn ed., 599–600.

in bloody conflicts on the streets of the capital. External relations were also unsuccessful.

Meanwhile, the son of the deposed Isaac II, the young prince Alexius, had succeeded in escaping on a Pisan vessel from Byzantium to Italy; he went then to Germany, to the court of Philip of Swabia, king of Germany, who was married to his sister Irene, daughter of Isaac Angelus. It was the time of the beginning of the Fourth Crusade. The prince begged the pope and the king of Germany, his brother-in-law, to help him to restore the throne to his blind father Isaac. After many complications Alexius succeeded in inducing the crusaders in the Venetian vessels to sail to Constantinople instead of Egypt. In 1203 the crusaders seized the capital of Byzantium and, deposing Alexius III, re-established upon the throne the old and blind Isaac (1203–1204); then they seated his son Alexius by the side of his father, as his co-emperor (Alexius IV). The crusaders encamped close to Constantinople expecting the accomplishment of the terms for which they had stipulated.

But it was impossible for the Emperors to fulfill those terms, and their complete obedience to the crusaders roused a riot in the capital which resulted in the proclamation as Emperor of a certain Alexius V Ducas Mourtzouphlos (1204), related to the family of the Angeli and married to a daughter of Alexius III. Isaac II and Alexius IV perished during the revolt. The crusaders, seeing that they had lost their chief support in the capital in the persons of the two dead Emperors, and realizing that Mourtzouphlos, who had raised the banner of the anti-Latin movement, was their enemy, decided to take Constantinople for themselves. After a stubborn attack by the Latins and desperate resistance by the inhabitants of the capital, on April 13, 1204, Constantinople passed over into the hands of the western knights and was given up to terrific devastation. Emperor Mourtzouphlos had time to flee from the capital. The Byzantine Empire fell. In its place there were formed the feudal Latin Empire with Constantinople as its capital and a certain number of vassal states in various regions of the Eastern Empire.

The dynasty of the Angeli or Angeli-Comneni, Greek in its origin, gave the Empire not one talented emperor; it only accelerated the ruin of the Empire, already weakened without and disunited within.

Relations with the Normans and Turks and the formation of the Second Bulgarian kingdom

In the year of the revolution of 1185, which dethroned Andronicus I and elevated Isaac Angelus to the throne, the condition of the Empire was very dangerous. After the taking of Thessalonica, the Norman land army started to advance towards the capital, where the Norman fleet had already arrived. But, drunk with their successes, the Normans began to pillage the captured regions; overconfident and having too little respect for the Byzantine army, they were defeated and forced to evacuate Thessalonica and Dyrrachium. This failure of the Normans to land obliged their vessels to leave Constantinople. A treaty of peace concluded between Isaac Angelus and William II put an end to the Norman war. As for the Seljuq danger in Asia Minor, Isaac Angelus succeeded in reducing it temporarily by rich presents and an annual tribute to the Turkish sultan.

For Isaac Angelus even a temporary interruption of hostilities against the Normans was of very great advantage, for in the first years of his reign events of great importance to the Empire had taken place in the Balkan peninsula. Bulgaria, which had been conquered by Basil II Bulgaroctonus in 1018, after several unsuccessful attempts to regain her independence finally threw off the Byzantine yoke and in 1186 established the so-called Second Bulgarian Kingdom.

At the head of this movement stood two brothers, Peter or Kalopeter and Asen (Asan). The question of their origin and of the participation of the Wallachian element in the insurrection of 1186 has been several times discussed, and formerly historians believed that the brothers had grown up among the Wallachs and had adopted their tongue. "In the persons of the leaders," said V. Vasilievsky, "there was embodied exactly that fusion into one unit of the two nationalities, Bulgarian and Wallachian, that has been obvious in all narratives of the struggle for freedom and has been emphasized by modern historians."[187] More recently, Bulgarian historians have traced the origin of Peter and Asen to the Cuman-Bulgarian racial elements in northern Bulgaria, denied the strength of the Wallachian-Roumanian element in the insurrection of 1186, and considered the foundation of the Second Bulgarian Kingdom of Trnovo a national Bulgarian achievement.[188] Modern Roumanian historians, however, vigorously emphasize again the importance of the part played by the Wallachians in the formation of the Second Bulgarian Kingdom and say that the dynasty of the new kingdom was of Wallachian, i.e. Roumanian, origin.[189]

Some elements of Bulgarian and Roumanian nationalism have become involved in this question, so that it is necessary to reconsider it with all possible scholarly detachment and disinterestedness. On the basis of reliable evidence,

[187] V. G. Vasilievsky's review in *Journal of the Ministry of Public Instruction*, CCIV (1879), 181.

[188] See, e.g., P. Mutafchiev, *The Rulers of Prosec. Pages from the History of Bulgaria at the End of the Twelfth and the Beginning of the Thirteenth Century*, 6–7. V. Zlatarsky, *The Origin of Peter and Asen, the Leaders of*

the Insurrection in 1185, 427. P. Nikov, *The Second Bulgarian Empire 1186–1936*, 23.

[189] See G. Brătianu, "Vicina. I. Contribution à l'histoire de la domination byzantine et du commerce gênois en Dobrogea," *Bulletin de la section historique de l'Academie roumaine*, X (1923), 136. Brătianu, *Recherches sur Vicina et Cetatea Alba*, 93.

the conclusion is that the liberating movement of the second half of the twelfth century in the Balkans was originated and vigorously prosecuted by the Wallachians, ancestors of the Roumanians of today; it was joined by the Bulgarians, and to some extent by the Cumans from beyond the Danube. The Wallachian participation in this important event cannot be disregarded. The best contemporary Greek source, Nicetas Choniates, clearly stated that the insurrection was begun by the Vlachs (Blachi); that their leaders, Peter and Asen (Asan), belonged to the same race; that the second campaign of the Byzantine Empire during this period was waged against the Vlachs; and that after the death of Peter and Asen the Empire of the Vlachs passed to their younger brother John. Whenever Nicetas mentioned the Bulgarians, he gave their name jointly with that of the Vlachs: Bulgarians and Vlachs.[190] The western cleric Ansbert, who followed the Emperor Frederick Barbarossa in his crusade (1189–1190), narrated that in the Balkans the Emperor had to fight against Greeks and Vlachs, and calls Peter or Kalopeter "Emperor of the Vlachs and of the most part of the Bulgarians" (*Blacorum et maxime partis Bulgarorum dominus*), or "*imperator* of the Vlachs and Cumans," or simply "Emperor of the Vlachs who was called by them the Emperor of Greece" (*Kalopetrus Bachorum [Blachorum] dominus itemque a suis dictus imperator Grecie*).[191] Finally, Pope Innocent III in his letters to the Bulgarian King John (Calojoannes) in 1204 addressed him as "King of Bulgarians and Vlachs" (*Bulgarorum et Blacorum rex*); in answering the pope, John calls himself "*imperator omnium Bulgarorum et Blacorum*," but signs himself "*imperator Bulgariae Calojoannes*"; the archbishop of Trnovo calls himself "*totius Bulgariae et Blaciae Primas*."[192]

Although the Wallachians initiated the movement of liberation, the Bulgarians without doubt took an active part in it with them, and probably contributed largely to the internal organization of the new kingdom. The Cumans also shared in the movement. The new Bulgarian kingdom was ethnologically a Wallachian-Bulgarian-Cuman state, its dynasty, if the assertion of Nicetas Choniates is accepted, being Wallachian.[193]

[190] Nicetas Choniates, *Historia,* Bonn ed., 482, 485, 487–89, 516, 622.

[191] *Historia de expeditione Frederici Imperatoris,* Ansbertus, 26, 44, 48, 54.

[192] Innocent III, *Epistolae,* VII; ed. Migne, *Patrologia Latina,* CCXV, esp. col. 287; VI, 290; VIII, 292–93; IX, 294; XI, 295; XII, 295–96.

[193] On the formation of the Second Bulgarian Kingdom see the old but very fine monograph by K. R. von Höfler; if I am not mistaken this monograph was never mentioned before 1943 by scholars dealing with the question; *Abhandlungen aus dem Gebiete der slavischen Geschichte.* I. *Die Wallachen als Begründer des zweiten bulgarischen Reiches, der Asaniden, 1186–1257,* 229–45. N. Bănescu, *Un problème d'histoire médiévale: Création et caractère du Second Empire Bulgare,* 84–93. Ostrogorsky remarked recently that in the movement launched by Peter and Asen, Cumans and Wallachians took a considerable part. *Geschichte des byzantinischen Staates,* 287, and n. 3. R. L. Wolff, "The Second Bulgarian Empire. Its Origin and History to 1204," *Speculum* (1949), 167–206.

The cause of the revolt was the discontent with the Byzantine sway felt by both Wallachians and Bulgarians, and their desire for independence. The time seemed particularly auspicious to them, since the Empire, which was still enduring the consequences of the troubles of Andronicus' time and the revolution of 1185, was unable to take adequate measures to put down the revolt. Nicetas Choniates naïvely said that the revolt was caused by the driving away of the Wallachs' cattle for the festivities held on the occasion of the marriage of Isaac Angelus to a daughter of the king of Hungary.[194]

Peter, this "renegade and evil slave," as he was called by the metropolitan of Athens, Michael Acominatus,[195] and Asen at first received some defeats from the Byzantine troops; but they were able to enlist the aid of the Cumans, who lived beyond the Danube. The struggle grew more difficult for the Empire, and Peter and Asen succeeded in concluding a sort of treaty. Peter had already assumed the title of tsar at the outset of the revolt and had begun to wear the imperial robes. Now the new Bulgarian state was recognized as politically independent of Byzantium, with a capital at Trnovo and an independent national church.[196] The new kingdom was known as the Bulgarian Kingdom of Trnovo.[197]

Simultaneously with the Bulgarian insurrection a similar movement arose in Serbian territory, where the founder of the dynasty of Nemanya, the "Great Župan" (Great Ruler) Stephen Nemanja, who laid the foundation for the unification of Serbia, made an alliance with Peter of Bulgaria for the common fight against the Empire.[198]

In 1189, as a participant in the Third Crusade, Frederick Barbarossa of Germany was passing across the Balkan peninsula towards Constantinople on his way to the Holy Land. The Serbs and Bulgarians intended to use that favorable opportunity and to obtain their aim with Frederick's help. During his stay at Nish Frederick received Serbian envoys and the Great Župan Stephen Nemanya himself, and at the same time opened negotiations with the Bulgarians. The Serbs and Bulgarians proposed to Frederick an alliance against the Byzantine Emperor, but on condition that Frederick should allow Serbia to annex Dalmatia and retain the regions which had been taken away from Byzantium, as well as that he should leave the Asens in permanent possession of Bulgaria and secure the imperial title to Peter. Frederick gave them no decisive reply and continued his march.[199] In this connection a his-

[194] Nicetas Choniates, *Historia,* Bonn ed., 481.

[195] Μιχαὴλ ᾿Ακομινάτου τοῦ Χωνιάτου τὰ σωζόμενα, ed. S. Lampros, I, 246–47.

[196] P. Nikov, *Studies in the Historical Sources of Bulgaria and in the History of the Bulgarian Church,* 8–13. V. Zlatarsky, *History of the Bulgarian Empire,* II, 441–83.

[197] *Ibid.* Also see P. Nikov, *Bulgarian Diplomacy from the Beginning of the Thirteenth Century,* 76–77.

[198] See C. Jireček, *Geschichte der Serben,* I, 270.

[199] *Ibid.,* 271–72.

torian of the nineteenth century, V. Vasilievsky, remarked: "There was a moment when the solution of the Slavonic problem in the Balkan peninsula was in the hands of the western Emperor; there was a moment when Barbarossa was about to accept the help of the Serbian and Bulgarian leaders against Byzantium, which undoubtedly would have led to the ruin of the Greek Empire."[200]

Soon after the crossing of the crusaders into Asia Minor the Byzantine army was severely defeated by the Bulgarians. The Emperor himself narrowly escaped capture. A contemporary source reported, "The many slain filled the cities with weeping and made villages sing mournful songs."[201]

In 1195 a revolution occurred in Byzantium which deprived Isaac of the throne and of his sight and made his brother Alexius Emperor. First of all, Alexius had to confirm himself on the throne and therefore he opened peace negotiations with the Bulgarians. But they presented unacceptable terms. Some time later, in 1196, by means of Greek intrigues, both the brothers, Asen and later Peter, were murdered. Thereupon John, their younger brother, who had formerly lived for some time in Constantinople as hostage and had become very well acquainted with Byzantine customs, reigned in Bulgaria. He was the famous Tsar Kalojan, "from 1196 a threat to the Greeks and later to the Latins."[202] Byzantium could not cope alone with the new Bulgarian tsar who, entering into negotiations with Pope Innocent III, received a royal crown through his legate. The Bulgarians recognized the pope as their head, and the archbishop of Trnovo was raised to the rank of primate.

Thus, during the dynasty of the Angeli a powerful rival to Byzantium arose in the Balkan peninsula in the person of the Bulgarian king. The Second Bulgarian Kingdom, which had increased in power towards the end of the reign of the Angeli, became a real menace to the Latin Empire which was founded in the place of the Byzantine Empire.

The Third Crusade and Byzantium

After the fruitless Second Crusade the condition of the Christian dominions in the East continued to cause serious apprehensions: the internal dissensions among the princes, the court intrigues, the quarrels of the military orders, and the pursuit of private interests—all these weakened the Christians more and more and facilitated the advance of the Muslims. The most important centers of the Christian dominions, Antioch and Jerusalem, were not strong enough to protect themselves successfully. The energetic ruler of Syria, Nur-

---

[200] Vasilievsky, *Journal of the Ministry of Public Instruction*, CCIV (1879), 196–97.
[201] Nicetas Choniates, *Historia*, Bonn ed.,

565.
[202] Vasilievsky, *Journal of the Ministry of Public Instruction*, XXIV (1879), 203.

ad-Din Mahmud, who in the middle of the twelfth century had taken possession of Damascus, began to threaten Antioch. Moreover, a real danger came from Egypt, where the Kurd Saladin, a talented leader and clever politician with ambitious plans, had overthrown the ruler of the Fatimid dynasty, which was ruling there, had taken possession of Egypt at the end of the seventh decade of the twelfth century, and had founded the dynasty of the Ayyoubids. Profiting by Nur-ad-Din's death, Saladin conquered Syria and then most of Mesopotamia, and thereby surrounded the Kingdom of Jerusalem on the south, east, and north.

At that time there were serious troubles in Jerusalem, of which Saladin was aware. Learning that one of the Muslim caravans, in which his sister was traveling, had been pillaged by the Christians, Saladin entered the territory of the Kingdom of Jerusalem and in 1187, in the battle of Hittin (Hattin), close to the sea of Tiberias, defeated the Christian army. The king of Jerusalem and many other Christian princes fell into the hands of Saladin. Then he took a number of maritime places, such as Beirut, Sidon, Jaffa and so on, and thus cut off the Christians from the possibility of getting reinforcements by sea. After that Saladin marched upon Jerusalem and in the autumn of the same year (1187), without much difficulty, captured the Holy City. All the sacrifices offered by Europe and all her religious enthusiasm were of no avail. Jerusalem passed again into the hands of the infidel. A new crusade was necessary.

The pope was acting energetically in the west in favor of the new crusade. He succeeded in rousing three sovereigns: Philip II Augustus, king of France, Richard I the Lion-Hearted (Coeur-de-Lion), king of England, and Frederick I Barbarossa, king of Germany, joined the movement. But in that crusade which began so brilliantly there was no general guiding idea. The participants in the crusade endeavored, first of all, to secure for themselves friendly relations with the rulers of the countries through which they had to pass. Philip Augustus and Richard marched via Sicily, and therefore they had to be on good terms with the king of Sicily. Intending to go to the east through the Balkan peninsula, Frederick Barbarossa entered into negotiations with the king of Hungary, the Great Župan of Serbia, the Emperor Isaac Angelus, and even with the sultan of Iconium in Asia Minor, Saladin's enemy, a Muslim. Political combinations and concerns forbade the sovereign-crusader to regard his Muslim ally with pride or indifference. At the same time the Christians faced as their adversary no disunited Muslim forces, as they had before, but Saladin, victorious—especially after the taking of Jerusalem—talented and energetic, who had concentrated in his hands the forces of Egypt, Palestine, and Syria. On hearing of the projected crusade he appealed to the Muslims for an energetic and untiring struggle against the Christians, these "barking dogs" and "foolish men," as he designated them in a letter to his brother.[203] It was a kind of countercrusade against the Christians. A medieval legend relates that Saladin himself had, before this, made a tour of Europe in order to become acquainted with the position of different Christian countries.[204] A modern historian stated, "No crusade had ever had before so clearly the character of a duel between Christianity and Islam."[205]

Frederick Barbarossa passed safely through Hungary and, advancing through the Balkan peninsula, entered into negotiations with the Serbs and Bulgarians. For the success of his further advance, the question of what relations he could establish with Isaac Angelus was extremely important.

Since the massacre of the Latins in Constantinople in 1182 relations between the Christian East and West had been strained. The friendly understanding of Frederick Barbarossa with the Normans, which had taken the form of the marriage of his son to the heiress of the Kingdom of Sicily, forced Isaac to regard him with still greater suspicion. Despite the treaty made at Nürnberg by an envoy of the Byzantine Emperor with Frederick before his departure for the crusade, Isaac Angelus opened negotiations with Saladin, against whom the crusade was being directed. Saladin's envoys made their appearance at the court of Isaac. They made an alliance against the sultan of Iconium, by virtue of which Isaac, as far as he could, was to hinder Frederick from advancing to the East; at the same time Saladin promised to return the Holy Land to the Greeks. Isaac's attitude toward Frederick was growing very doubtful. Frederick's negotiations with the Serbs and Bulgarians, which had been clearly aimed against Byzantium, could not but alarm Isaac.

Meanwhile the crusading army of Frederick occupied Philippopolis. In his message to the western Emperor, Isaac named him "the king of Alemannia"[206] and himself "the emperor of the Romans";[207] he accused him of intending to conquer the eastern Empire, but promised to help him cross the Hellespont, if Frederick would give him noble German hostages and pledge himself to deliver him half of the land conquered by the Germans in Asia. The German ambassadors who were in Constantinople were imprisoned. Matters came to such a pass that Frederick had already determined to conquer Constantinople and had written to his son Henry to assemble the fleet in Italy and to obtain

---

[203] See Röhricht, *Geschichte des Konigreichs Jerusalem*, 491.

[204] See Fr. J. da Aquis, *Chonaca dell' imagine mondo*, in *Monumenta Historiae Patria Scriptorum*, III, 1561. See also G. Paris, "La Légende de Saladin," *Journal des Savants* (1893), 7–34. A. Thomas, "La Légende de Saladin en Poitou," *Journal des Savants*

(1908), 467–71.

[205] Bréhier, *Les Croisades*, 121; (5th ed., 1928), 121.

[206] Nicetas Acominatus also calls Frederick Φρεδέρικος ὁ τῶν Ἀλαμανῶν ῥήξ.

[207] *Historia de expeditione Frederici Imperatoris*, ed. Ansbertus, *Fontes rerum austriacarum, I, Scriptores*, V, 37.

from the pope the preaching of a crusade against the Greeks. Meanwhile, after the taking of Hadrianople, Frederick's troops occupied Thrace, almost as far as the very walls of Constantinople. A source said, "the whole city of Constantinople is shivering with fright thinking that its destruction and the extermination of its population are near."[208]

At that critical moment Isaac yielded. He made peace with Frederick at Hadrianople, and the chief conditions were: Isaac provided the vessels for transferring Frederick's troops across the Hellespont into Asia Minor, delivered him hostages, and promised to supply the crusaders with food. In the spring, 1190, the German army crossed the Hellespont.

Frederick's expedition is known to have ended in complete failure. After an exhausting march through Asia Minor the crusading army reached the limits of the state of Armenia Minor, in Cilicia. There, in 1190, the Emperor was, by mere accident, drowned in a river; thereupon his army was dispersed. In Frederick the most dangerous adversary of Saladin passed away.

The expedition of the two other west European sovereigns, Philip II Augustus and Richard I the Lion-Hearted, who had gone to Palestine from Sicily by sea, encroached upon the interests of Byzantium much less. However, with the name of Richard is closely connected the problem of Byzantium's definite loss of the island of Cyprus, which was an important strategic point in the eastern part of the Mediterranean.

During the tyranny of Andronicus I, Isaac Comnenus had seceded from the Empire, proclaimed himself independent ruler of Cyprus, and entered into an agreement with the king of Sicily. Isaac Angelus' attempt to regain the island had ended in failure. During his expedition to the East Richard the Lion-Hearted was irritated by the attitude of the ruler of Cyprus towards the vessels bearing Richard's sister and bride, which had been wrecked off the shores of the island. Then Richard landed at Cyprus and, after Isaac Comnenus' defeat and deposition, handed over the island to Guy de Lusignan, ex-king of Jerusalem. In 1192 the latter became ruler of Cyprus and founded there the dynasty of the Lusignans, giving up his illusive rights to the Kingdom of Jerusalem, which at that time did not belong to the Christians. It seemed that the new Latin state in Cyprus should play a very important role as a strategic basis of operation for the future Christian enterprises in the East.

The crusade accomplished nothing. Without having obtained any result both the sovereigns returned to Europe. Jerusalem remained in the power of the Muhammedans. The Christians preserved for themselves only a narrow shore strip, from Jaffa to Tyre. Saladin was master of the situation.

[208] *Historia peregrinorum*, in K. Zimmert, "Der deutsch-Byzantinische Konflikt vom Juli 1189 bis Februar 1190," *Byzantinische Zeitschrift*, XII (1903), 63, n. 2.

Henry VI and his eastern plans

If the danger had been great for Byzantium under Frederick Barbarossa,
it became still more threatening under his son and successor, Henry VI. The
latter, filled with the Hohenstaufen idea of unrestricted power granted him
by God, could not, for this reason alone, have a friendly attitude towards another emperor who claimed to possess the same absolute power, that is, the
Emperor of Byzantium. But besides that, he inherited, as the husband of the
Norman princess Constance, the Kingdom of the Two Sicilies; therewith he
inherited also the whole stubborn enmity of the Normans for Byzantium, and
their aggressive plans. It seemed left for Henry VI to carry out what his father
had not done, namely to annex Byzantium to the Western Empire. A sort
of ultimatum was sent to Constantinople. In it Henry reclaimed from Isaac
Angelus the cession of the territory in the Balkan peninsula between Dyrrachium and Thessalonica, which had been conquered by the Normans but
later restored to Byzantium; in the same document the question was raised
of compensation for the damages which Frederick Barbarossa had suffered
during the crusade and of help for Henry by the Byzantine fleet in his expedition to Palestine.[209] Isaac had scarcely sent Henry an embassy when in
1195, he was dethroned and blinded by his brother, Alexius III.

After this revolution the conduct of Henry VI became still more threatening. He arranged the marriage of his brother Philip of Swabia to Irene,
daughter of the deposed Emperor Isaac, and thereby created for his brother
some rights to Byzantium. In the person of Henry VI the new Byzantine
Emperor "was to fear not only the Western Emperor, the heir of the Norman
kings and crusader, but also, first of all, an avenger in behalf of the dethroned
Isaac and his family."[210] The objective of the crusade which was being fitted
out by Henry was as much Constantinople as Palestine. His plans embraced
the possession of all the Christian East, including Byzantium. Circumstances
seemed to be favorable to his aim: an embassy from the ruler of Cyprus came
to Henry begging the Emperor to confer upon him the royal title and expressing the desire to be "forever a man (i.e., vassal) of the Roman Empire"
(homo imperii esse Romani).[211] The ruler of Armenia Minor applied to
Henry with a similar request for the royal title. Had Henry succeeded in establishing himself in Syria, he would have been able entirely to surround the
Byzantine Empire.

At this critical moment the pope took the side of Byzantium. He understood
very well that, if the dream of the Hohenstaufens of a universal monarchy,

[209] Nicetas Choniates, *Historia*, Bonn ed.,
627–28.

[210] W. Norden, *Das Papsttum und Byzanz*,

128.

[211] *Annales Marbacenses*, ed. Pertz, *Monumenta Germaniae Historica*, XVII, 167.

including Byzantium, should be realized, the papacy would be doomed to permanent impotence. Therefore the pope exerted himself to the utmost to restrain Henry from his offensive plans against the Eastern Empire; the schismatic belief of the Byzantine Emperor seems not to have alarmed the successor of St. Peter. Perhaps for the first time in history, as Norden suggested, the Greek problem almost entirely lost for the papacy its religious character and presented itself as exclusively political. "What would a spiritual victory signify for the curia if it were to be bought at the price of the political liquidation of the Papacy!" To the papacy it seemed a secondary question whether Byzantium, as a buffer state against western imperialism, would be a Catholic or schismatic state, whether a legitimate Greek emperor or a usurper would sit on the Byzantine throne; to the papacy of the end of the twelfth century the principal thing was that the Byzantine state should preserve its independence intact.[212]

Meanwhile Henry sent a threatening message to Alexius III, similar to that which had been sent before to Isaac. Alexius could buy peace only by paying to Henry an enormous amount of money; for that purpose Alexius introduced in the whole state a special tax, which was called "Alamanian" ($\dot{a}\lambda a\mu a\nu\iota\kappa\acute{o}\nu$) and took off precious ornaments from the imperial tombs.[213] Only by such humiliation did he succeed in buying peace from his terrible adversary. At the end of the summer of 1197 Henry arrived at Messina in order to attend personally the setting out of the crusade. An enormous fleet had been assembled, which had perhaps as its aim not the Holy Land, but Constantinople. But just at that moment the young and vigorous Henry fell ill with fever and died in the autumn of the same year, 1197. With Henry's death his ambitious plans broke down; for the second time within a brief period the East escaped the Hohenstaufens. Byzantium met the news of Henry's death and the release from the "Alamanian tax" with great joy. The pope also breathed a sigh of relief.

Henry's activity, which showed the complete triumph of political ideas in crusading enterprises, had a very important significance for the future destinies of Byzantium. "Henry raised definitely the problem of the Byzantine Empire, the solution of which was soon to become a preliminary condition of the success of the crusades."[214]

That Henry VI dreamed of a world monarchy and of the conquest of Constantinople is now absolutely denied by some historians, who point out that such a statement is based only on the authority of a Byzantine historian of that epoch, Nicetas Choniates, and that the western sources afford no evidence

[212] Norden, *Das Papsttum und Byzanz*, 130, 132.

[213] Nicetas Choniates, *Historia*, Bonn ed., 631–32.

[214] Bréhier, *Les Croisades*, 143.

for it. These writers contend that the statement emphasized by Norden, whom Bréhier followed, is not authentic; they believe that in 1196 Henry had no serious thought of any attack on Byzantium; that Henry's crusade had nothing to do with the Byzantine policy, and that the foundation of a world monarchy by Henry is to be referred to the realm of fables.[215] But one cannot reject the evidence of the contemporary Nicetas Choniates, who made a clear statement of Henry's aggressive plans against Byzantium. Such a policy, moreover, was an immediate continuation and result of that of his father, Frederick Barbarossa; in the course of the Third Crusade Frederick had been on the point of seizing Constantinople.[216] Therefore the policy of Henry VI was not only the policy of a crusader, but also the policy of a man absorbed in the illusive idea of creating a world monarchy in which Byzantium was to become the most important part.

The Fourth Crusade and Byzantium

The Fourth Crusade is an extremely complicated historical phenomenon in which the most various interests and emotions are reflected; lofty religious emotion, hope of reward in the life to come, craving for spiritual action, and devotion to the obligations which had been undertaken in behalf of the crusade were mingled with the desire for adventure and gain, inclination for traveling, and the feudal custom of spending life in war. The domination of material interests and worldly feelings over spiritual and religious emotions, which had already been felt in previous crusades, was particularly evident in the Fourth Crusade; this was demonstrated in the taking of Constantinople by the crusaders in 1204 and the foundation of the Latin Empire.

At the end of the twelfth century, and especially in the epoch of Henry VI, the German influence was preponderant in Italy, and Henry's eastern plans threatened danger to the Eastern Empire. After his sudden death circumstances changed. The new pope elected in 1198, the famous Innocent III, turned his attention to restoring in full the papal authority, which had been undermined by the policy of the German sovereigns, and to putting himself at the head of the Christian movement against Islam. Italy stood on the side of the pope in his struggle with the German influence. Seeing the chief foe of the papacy and Italy in the Hohenstaufens, the pope began to support in Germany Otto of Brunswick, elected king by a portion of Germany against

---

[215] See E. Traub, *Der Kreuzzugsplan Kaiser Heinrichs VI im Zusammenhang mit der Politik der Jahre 1195–97*, 51–52, 60. W. Leonhardt, *Der Kreuzzugsplan Kaiser Heinrichs VI*, 63, 67, 89. Cf. Dölger, *Corpus der griechischen Urkunden*, II, 101 (no. 1619). Leonhardt's point of view is adopted by J.

Haller, "Kaiser Heinrich VI," *Historische Zeitschrift*, CXIII (1914), 488–89, and esp. 503.

[216] See, e.g., a letter of Frederick Barbarossa sent to his son and heir Henry from Philippopolis shortly before he died, 1189, in J. F. Böhmer, *Acta imperii selecta*, 152.

Philip Hohenstaufen of Swabia, brother of the late Henry VI. A very good opportunity seemed presented to the Byzantine Empire to carry out the plans of the Comneni to replace the German world state by a similar Byzantine world state. With this in mind, probably, the Emperor Alexius III wrote Innocent III in the year of the latter's election to the papal throne: "We are the only two world powers: the single Roman Church and the single Empire of the successors of Justinian; therefore we must unite and endeavor to prevent a new increase in the power of the western emperor, our rival."[217] In reality, the complicated situation of Byzantium, both external and internal, left no hope for the success of such ambitious plans.

But Innocent III did not want to see the eastern emperor a schismatic; he opened negotiations for union. These progressed slowly, for in one of his letters to Alexius the irritated pope threatened, in case of resistance, to support the right to the Byzantine throne of the family of the dethroned and blinded Isaac,[218] whose daughter had been married to the German king, Philip of Swabia; probably the pope did not mean to carry out his threat. Alexius III, however, did not consent to his proposal of union, and in one of his letters he even brought forward the statement that the imperial power was higher than the spiritual.[219] Thereupon relations between Byzantium and Rome became somewhat strained.

While carrying on negotiations with Constantinople and subtle diplomatic propaganda in Germany, Innocent III was exerting extraordinary activity in organizing a general crusade in which western and eastern Christianities should be fused together in order to reach the common aim—the liberation of the Holy Land from the hands of the infidel. Papal messages were sent to all the Christian sovereigns; the papal legates were traveling over Europe and promising the participants in the crusade the remission of their sins and many worldly practical advantages; eloquent preachers were encouraging the masses. In a letter Innocent III described the sad conditions of the Holy Land and expressed his anger against the sovereigns and princes of his epoch who were devoting their time to pleasures and petty quarrels; he described what the Muslims, whom the pope named in his letter pagans, think and say about the Christians. The pope wrote:

Our enemies insult us and say, "Where is your God who can free from our hands neither Himself nor you? We have polluted your sanctuaries, put forth our hands against the objects of your adoration, and violently attacked the Holy Land. In spite of you we keep in our hands your fathers' cradle of superstition. We have reduced and broken the spears of the French, the efforts of the English, the vigour

[217] Norden, *Das Papsttum und Byzanz*, 134; such a conclusion has been drawn by Norden from the letter of Innocent III to Alexius III. Innocent III, *Epistolae*, I, 353; ed. Migne, *Patrologia Latina*, CCXIV, 326–27.

[218] *Epistolae*, V, 122; ed. Migne, *Patrologia Latina*, CCXIV, 1123–24.

[219] Migne, *ibid.*, 1082–83.

of the Germans, the heroism of the Spaniards. What has all this valor which you sent against us accomplished? Where is your God? Let Him rise and help you! Let Him show how He protects you and Himself! . . . We have no more to do except, after the extermination of the defenders left by you for the protection of the country, to fall upon your own land in order to eradicate your name and the remembrance of you." What may we reply to such aggressions? How may we refute their insults? Indeed, that which they say is partly the very truth. . . . When the pagans display their anger with impunity in the whole country, the Christians do not dare any more to go out of their cities. They cannot even stay in them without shuddering. The sword [of the infidel] waits for them without; within they are torpid from fear.[220]

None of the principal west European sovereigns answered the call of Innocent III. Philip II Augustus of France had been excommunicated by the Church for his divorce from his wife; John Lackland of England who had just ascended the throne, had first of all to establish himself there and was absorbed in a stubborn strife with the barons; finally, in Germany a struggle for the throne burst out between Otto of Brunswick and Philip of Swabia, so that neither of them could leave the country. Alone among sovereigns the king of Hungary took the cross. But the choicest of the western knights, particularly of northern France, took part in the crusade. Thibault, count of Champagne, Baldwin of Flanders, Louis of Blois, and many others assumed the cross. The crusading army was composed of French, Flemish, English, Germans, and Sicilians.

But the central figure of the crusade was the doge of Venice, Enrico Dandolo, a typical Venetian in mind and character. Although on his accession to the throne he was already eighty years of age, if not more, he resembled a young man by his powerful energy, devoted patriotism, and clear understanding of the most important purposes of Venice, especially of her economic aims. When the majesty, welfare, and benefit of the Republic of St. Mark were involved, Dandolo had no scruples regarding the means. Possessing the art of dealing with men, as well as extraordinary will power and circumspection, he was a remarkable statesman, an ingenious diplomat, and, at the same time, an expert economist.[221]

At the beginning of the Fourth Crusade, the relations between Byzantium and Venice were not particularly friendly. A legend relates that, about thirty years before, Dandolo, during his stay in Constantinople as a hostage, had been treacherously blinded by the Greeks by means of a concave mirror which strongly reflected the rays of the sun; this circumstance was the cause of Dandolo's deep hatred of Byzantium. Of course, the mutual distrust and rivalry of Byzantium and Venice were founded upon deeper reasons. Dandolo realized perfectly well what an inexhaustible mine of rich resources was the

[220] *Epistolae,* I, 336; ed. Migne, *ibid.,* 309.   [221] See Diehl, *Venise,* 47–48.

East in general, Christian and Muhammedan, for the economic development of the Republic; he turned his attention first of all to his nearest rival, Byzantium. He demanded that all the commercial privileges which had been obtained by Venice in Byzantium and had been somewhat curtailed under the last Comneni, beginning with Manuel, should be restored in full measure. Dandolo had chiefly in view the arrest of the Venetian merchants and the seizure of their ships and confiscation of their property under Manuel, as well as the massacre of the Latins in 1182. The Doge could not at all approve, after many years of Venetian trade monopoly in the Eastern Empire, the according of trade privileges to other Italian cities, Pisa and Genoa, whereby the Venetian commercial prosperity was considerably undermined. Gradually, in the mind of the keenly discerning and clever Dandolo, a plan was ripening to conquer Byzantium in order to secure definitely the Oriental market for Venice. Like Innocent III, Dandolo menaced Alexius III with supporting the rights of the family of the deposed and blinded Isaac Angelus to the Byzantine throne.

Thus, in the preparations for the Fourth Crusade, two men were of first importance: Pope Innocent III, as a representative of the spiritual element in the crusade sincerely wished to take the Holy Land from the hands of the Muhammedans and was absorbed in the idea of union; and the Doge Enrico Dandolo, as a representative of the secular, earthly element, put first material, commercial purposes. Two other men exercised considerable influence upon the course of the crusade: the Byzantine prince Alexius, son of the dethroned Isaac Angelus, who had escaped from Constantinople to the West, and Philip of Swabia, of Germany, who had married a daughter of Isaac Angelus, the sister of the prince Alexius.

Thibaut, count of Champagne, was elected the head of the crusading army. Beloved and highly esteemed by all, he was an animating force in the enterprise. But unfortunately Thibaut suddenly died before the crusade started. The crusaders, deprived of their leader, elected a new head in the person of Boniface, marquis of Montferrat. The leading role in the crusade passed, therefore, from a Frenchman to an Italian prince.

At that time Palestine belonged to the Egyptian dynasty of the Ayyoubids, among whom, at the end of the twelfth century, after the death of the famous Saladin (March, 1193), troubles and strife broke out. These circumstances seemed to facilitate the crusaders' task. Toward the beginning of the Fourth Crusade, in Syria and Palestine there remained in the hands of the Christians two important industrial centers, Antioch and Tripoli, and a coast fortress, Acre (Acra, Saint-Jean-d'Acre).

The crusaders had to assemble at Venice which, for a certain sum, offered to transport them on its vessels to the East. The nearest objective of the crusade was Egypt, under whose power Palestine was at that time; it was intended to conquer Egypt at first, and then, with that advantage, to obtain from the Muslims the restoration of Palestine. Venice, however, did not wish to start transporting the crusaders until the sum agreed upon should be paid in full. The sum not being forthcoming, the crusaders were finally obliged to agree to the Doge's proposal that they should help him to reconquer the city of Zara (Zadr), situated on the Dalmatian shores of the Adriatic, which had recently seceded from Venice and passed over to the king of Hungary. He had taken the cross; nevertheless the crusaders consented to the Doge's proposal and sailed towards Zara, a city which was to participate in the crusade. Thus, the crusade fitted out against the infidel began with a siege by crusaders of a city where crusaders lived. In spite of the indignant protests of the pope and his threats to excommunicate the crusading army, the crusaders attacked Zara, took it by storm for Venice, and destroyed it. The crucifixes exposed by the inhabitants of the city upon the walls did not deter the assailants. A historian exclaimed, "A beautiful starting for a crusade!"[222] The Zara case dealt a heavy blow to the crusaders' prestige, but gave Dandolo the right to celebrate his first victory in the crusade.

When the pope learned of the taking of Zara and heard the complaints of the king of Hungary against the allies, that is to say, the crusaders and Venetians, he excommunicated them. Innocent wrote the crusaders: "Instead of reaching the Promised Land, you thirsted for the blood of your brethren. Satan, the universal tempter, has deceived you. . . . The inhabitants of Zara hang crucifixes upon the walls. In spite of the Crucified you have stormed the city and forced it to surrender. . . . Under fear of anathema, halt in this matter of destruction and restore to the envoys of the king of Hungary all which has been taken away from them. If you will not, know that you are falling under excommunication and will be deprived of the privileges granted all the crusaders."[223]

The threats of the pope and his excommunication produced no effect upon the Venetians. But the crusaders—the so-called "Francs"—exerted themselves to the utmost to have the papal excommunication raised. Finally, the pope, having pity upon them, raised the excommunication, but left the Venetians under the ban. He did not, however, definitely forbid the pardoned crusaders to associate with the excommunicated Venetians. They continued to act together.

During the siege and surrender of Zara a new personality makes his ap-

[222] Kretschmayr, *Geschichte von Venedig,* I, 290.

[223] Such is the general content of a letter of Innocent III. *Epistolae,* V, 161; ed. Migne,

Patrologia Latina, CCXIV, 1178–79. See A. Luchaire, *Innocent III: la question d'Orient,* 103–5.

pearance in the history of the Fourth Crusade—the Byzantine prince Alexius Angelus, son of the dethroned and blinded Isaac. Alexius had escaped from prison and fled to the West in order to obtain help for restoring the throne to his unfortunate father. After a fruitless meeting with the pope in Rome, the prince went to the north, to Germany, to his brother-in-law Philip of Swabia, who had married Irene, Alexius' sister and Isaac's daughter. Irene begged her husband to help her brother, who, "without shelter and fatherland, was traveling like the floating stars and had nothing with him but his own body."[224] Philip, who was at that time absorbed in his struggle with Otto of Brunswick, was unable to support Alexius effectively, but he sent an embassy to Zara begging Venice and the crusaders to help Isaac and his son by restoring them to the Byzantine throne. For that aid Alexius promised to subordinate Byzantium to Rome as far as religion was concerned, to pay a large amount of money, and, after restoring his father to the throne, to take a personal part in the crusade.

Thus was raised the question of the possibility of completely changing the crusade in direction and character. Doge Dandolo immediately realized all the advantages of Philip's proposal for Venice. The chief role in the expedition against Constantinople and in restoring the dethroned Isaac to the throne opened wide horizons to the Doge. For some time the crusaders did not consent to the proposed change and demanded that the crusade should not be averted from its original aim. But, finally, both sides came to an agreement.

Most of the crusaders determined to participate in the expedition upon Constantinople, but on condition that after a short stay there they go to Egypt, as had been formerly planned. Thus, a treaty of the conquest of Constantinople was concluded between Venice and the crusaders at Zara. The prince Alexius himself came into the camp at Zara. In May, 1203, the fleet with Dandolo, Boniface of Montferrat, and the Prince Alexius sailed from Zara and a month after made its appearance before Constantinople.

A Russian chronicle of Novgorod, in which is preserved a detailed account, not yet sufficiently studied, of the Fourth Crusade, the taking of Constantinople by the crusaders, and the foundation of the Latin Empire, remarks, "The Franks and all their chiefs have loved the gold and silver which the son of Isaac has promised them, and have forgotten the precepts of the Emperor and Pope."[225] Thus, the Russian point of view holds the crusaders blameworthy for their deviation from their original aim. The most recent investigator of the account of Novgorod, P. Bizilli, considered it very important and said that it gives a special theory explaining the crusade upon Byzantium which

[224] Nicetas Choniates, *Historia,* Bonn ed., 712.
[225] *The Chronicle of Novgorod;* in Russian, 181; in Latin in C. Hopf, *Chroniques gréco-romanes inédites ou peu connues,* 94.

no west European source mentions, namely that "that crusade was decided by the Pope and Philip of Swabia together."[226]

Many scholars have devoted much attention to the problem of the Fourth Crusade. Their chief attention has been turned to the causes of the change of direction of the crusade. One party of scholars explained the whole unusual course of the crusading enterprise by accidental circumstances and were the followers of the so-called "theory of accidents." An opposing group of scholars saw the cause of the change in the premeditated policy of Venice and Germany and became the partisans of the so-called "theory of premeditation."[227]

Until about 1860 no dispute on that problem had existed because all historians had depended mainly on the statements of the chief western source of the Fourth Crusade and a participant in it, the French historian Geoffrey de Villehardouin. In his exposition the events of the crusade progressed simply and accidentally: not having vessels, the crusaders hired them at Venice and therefore assembled there; after having hired the vessels they could not pay the Republic of St. Mark the full amount fixed and were forced to support the Venetians in their strife with Zara; then followed the coming of the prince Alexius, who inclined the crusaders against Byzantium. Thus, there was no question of any treason of Venice nor of any complicated political intrigue.

In 1861, for the first time, a French scholar, Mas-Latrie, author of the very well-known history of the island of Cyprus, accused Venice, which had important commercial interests in Egypt, of making a secret treaty with the sultan of Egypt and thereupon skillfully forcing the crusaders to abandon the original plan of the expedition upon Egypt and to sail against Byzantium.[228] Then the German historian, Karl Hopf, seemed definitely to prove the treason of the Venetians towards the Christian task, stating that the treaty between Venice and the sultan of Egypt was concluded on the 13th of May, 1202.[229] Although Hopf produced no text of the treaty and did not even indicate where this text was to be found, the authority of the German scholar was so great that many scholars adopted his standpoint without any doubt. But it was shown soon after that Hopf had no new document in his hands at all and that his date was quite arbitrary. A French scholar, Hanotaux, who a little later investigated this problem, refuted the theory of Venetian treason and, consequently, "the theory of premeditation." But he thought that if the Venetians

---

[226] Bazilli, "The Version of Novgorod of the Fourth Crusade," *Istoricheskiya Izvestiya,* fasc. 3–4, 55.

[227] On the history of that problem see P. Mitrofanov, "The Change of the Direction of the Fourth Crusade," *Vizantiysky Vremennik,* IV (1897), 461–523; and E. Gerland,

"Der vierte Kreuzzug und seine Probleme," *Neue Jahrbücher für das Klassische Altertum,* XIII (1904), 505–14. Kretschmayr, *Geschichte von Venedig,* I, 480–89.

[228] *Histoire de l'île de Chypre,* I, 162–63.

[229] *Geschichte Griechenlands,* I, 188.

were the chief instigators of the change of direction of the Fourth Crusade, they had obvious motives: the desire to subdue Zara, which had revolted; the wish to restore their candidate to the Byzantine throne, to revenge themselves on Byzantium for the sympathy Alexius III had given the Pisans, and, possibly, the hope to obtain some profit, if the Empire fell to pieces.[230] The theory of Hopf at the present time is considered refuted. If the Venetians can be really accused of treason, they became traitors not because of a secret treaty with the Muslims, but exclusively because they had in view their commercial interests in the Byzantine Empire.

But the followers of "the theory of premeditation" did not confine themselves to the attempt to prove the fact of the treason of Venice. In 1875 a new motive was brought forward by a French scholar, Count de Riant, who tried to prove that the chief instigator of the change of direction of the Fourth Crusade was not Dandolo, but the king of Germany, Philip of Swabia, son-in-law of the deposed Isaac Angelus. In Germany a skillful political intrigue had been woven which was to direct the crusaders upon Constantinople. Boniface of Montferrat fulfilled Philip's plans in the East. In the change of direction of the crusade Riant sees one of the episodes of the long struggle between the papacy and the Empire.[231] By his leading role in the crusade Philip humiliated the pope and falsified his conception of the crusade; welcoming the restored Byzantine Emperor as an ally, Philip might hope to be successful in his strife with the pope and with his rival in Germany, Otto of Brunswick.[232] But a blow was struck to Riant's theory by an investigation of Vasilievsky, who showed that the flight of the prince Alexius to the West took place not in the year 1201, as all the historians believed, but in 1202, so that for a complicated and long conceived political intrigue "Philip was left neither place nor time; thus the German intrigue may be proved as illusive as the Venetian."[233] The accurate investigation of a Frenchman, Tessier, on the basis of examination of contemporary sources, refuted the theory of the German sovereign's role and returned to the acknowledgment of the great significance of the narrative of Villehardouin, that is to say, to the prevailing standpoint before 1860, "the theory of accidents." Tessier said that the Fourth

---

[230] G. Hanotaux, "Les Vénitiens ont-ils trahi la chrétienté en 1202?" *Revue historique,* IV (1887), 74-102. See also L. Streit, *Venedig und die Wendung des vierten Kreuzzugs gegen Konstantinopel,* 33-34: Dandolo was "Auctor rerum," defender and then avenger of Venice.

[231] Innocent III is known to have supported Otto of Brunswick, rival of Philip of Swabia.

[232] See P. E. Riant, "Innocent III, Philippe de Souabe et Boniface de Montferrat," *Revue*

des questions historiques, XVII (1875), 321-74; XVIII (1875), 5-75. Riant, "Le Changement de direction de la quatrième croisade d'après quelques travaux recents," *Revue des questions historiques,* XXIII (1878), 71-114.

[233] *Journal of the Ministry of Public Instruction,* CCIV (1879), 340. Vasilievsky's view was adopted by western European scholars. See Kretschmayr, *Geschichte von Venedig,* I, 483.

Crusade was a French crusade, and the conquest of Constantinople was an achievement neither Germanic nor Venetian, but French.[234] Of Riant's premeditation theory there remains only the fact that Philip of Swabia took part in the change of direction of the crusade and, like Henry VI, claimed the Eastern Empire; but the sources do not justify affirming the existence of a leading and subtle plan on Philip's part on which could depend the destiny of the whole Fourth Crusade.

At the end of the nineteenth century a German historian, W. Norden, definitely refuting "the theory of premeditation" and agreeing essentially with "the theory of accidents," endeavored to investigate the latter more deeply, discussed the problem of the Fourth Crusade in the light of the political, economic, and religious relations between the West and East, and tried to elucidate the inner connection between the Fourth Crusade and the history of the previous hundred and fifty years.[235]

To sum up: in the complicated history of the Fourth Crusade there were in action various forces originating in the motives of the pope, Venice, and the German king in the West, as well as forces originating in the external and internal conditions of Byzantium in the East. The interplay of these forces created an exceedingly complex phenomenon which is not entirely clear, in some details, even at the present day. "This," said the French historian Luchaire, "will never be known, and science has something better to do than interminably to discuss an insoluble problem."[236] Grégoire has recently even gone so far as to proclaim that "there is really no problem of the Fourth Crusade."[237]

But among all the plans, hopes, and complications it remains clear that over all prevailed the firm will of Dandolo and his unyielding determination to develop the trade activity of Venice, to which the possession of the eastern markets promised limitless wealth and a brilliant future. Moreover, Dandolo was greatly alarmed by the growing economic power of Genoa, which at that time, in the Near East in general and in Constantinople in particular, began to gain a strong foothold. The economic competition between Venice and Genoa must also be taken into consideration when the problem of the Fourth Crusade is discussed.[238] Finally the unpaid debt of Byzantium to Venice for

---

[234] *Quatrième croisade. La diversion sur Zara et Constantinople*, esp. 183–84. In connection with Tessier's book see also a very interesting article by F. Cerone, "Il Papa ed i Veneziani nella quarta crociata," *Archivio Veneto*, XXXVI (1888), 57–70, 287–97.

[235] W. Norden, *Der vierte Kreuzzug im Rahmen der Beziehungen des Abendlandes zu Byzanz*, 105–8. Norden, *Das Papsttum und Byzanz*, 152–55.

[236] *Innocent III: la question d'Orient*, 97. See also Charles Diehl, "The Fourth Crusade and the Latin Empire," *Cambridge Medieval History*, IV, 417.

[237] "The Question of the Diversion of the Fourth Crusade," *Byzantion*, XV (1941), 166.

[238] See J. K. Fotheringham, "Genoa and the Fourth Crusade," *English Historical Review*, XXV (1910), 20–57. The same considerations are repeated by the author in his

the Venetian property seized by Manuel Comnenus may also have had something to do with the diversion of the Fourth Crusade.[239]

At the end of June, 1203, the crusading fleet appeared before Constantinople, which at that time, in the eyes of western Europe, said Nicetas Choniates, "looked perfectly like Sybaris, which was well known for its effeminacy."[240] A participant in the crusade, the French writer Villehardouin, described the deep impression produced upon the crusaders by the view of the Byzantine capital:

Now you may imagine that those who had never before seen Constantinople looked upon it very earnestly, for they never thought there could be in all the world so rich a city, when they saw the high walls and magnificent towers that enclosed it round about, the rich palaces and mighty churches, of which there were so many that no one would have believed it who had not seen it with his own eyes,—and the height and length of that city which above all others was sovereign. And be it known to you that no man there was of such sturdy courage but his flesh trembled; and it was no wonder, for never was so great an enterprise undertaken by anyone since the creation of the world.[241]

It seemed probable that the fortified capital could successfully resist the crusaders, who were not very numerous. But the latter, having landed on the European shore and taken the suburb of Galata, on the left bank of the Golden Horn, forced the iron chain which protected the entrance into it, penetrated the Golden Horn and burned a great number of the Byzantine vessels. At the same time the knights stormed the city itself. In spite of a desperate resistance, particularly by the mercenary Varangian troops, the crusaders, in July, took possession of the city. Alexius III, having neither energy nor will power, abandoned the capital and fled, taking with him the public treasure and jewels. Isaac II was released from prison and restored to his throne; his son, the prince Alexius, who had arrived with the crusaders, was proclaimed his co-regent (Alexius IV). This first siege and first taking of Constantinople by the crusaders was in order to restore Isaac II upon the throne.

Having placed Isaac on the throne, the crusaders, with Dandolo at their head, demanded from the Emperor's son the fulfillment of the promises

Marco Sanudo Conqueror of the Archipelago, 16–20.

[239] Brown, "Venetians and the Venetian Quarter," *Journal of Hellenic Studies,* XL (1920), 86; he refers to the book of E. Besta, *La cattura dei Veneziani in Oriente,* 19. I have not seen this book.

[240] Nicetas Choniates, *Historia,* Bonn ed., 717.

[241] *La Conquête de Constantinople,* par.

128; ed. N. de Wailly, 72–73; ed. E. Faral, I, 130–31. See a very thorough study by Faral whose object is to show the reliability and veracity of Villehardouin; "Geoffroy de Villehardouin. La Question de la sincérité," *Revue historique,* CLXXVII (1936), 530–82. Some criticisms by Grégoire, "The Question of the Diversion of the Fourth Crusade," *Byzantion,* XV (1941), 159–65.

which he had made, that is to say, that he should pay them a large sum of money and start with them to the crusade, for the western knights were already insisting that they should set off. Alexius IV urged the crusaders not to stay in Constantinople, but to pitch their camp outside, in its suburb, and, unable to pay the whole amount, besought them to grant him a respite. This led to strained relations between the Latins and Greeks. In the city itself, meanwhile, the population grew discontented with the policy of the Emperors, whom they accused of having betrayed the Empire to the crusaders. An insurrection burst out. The son-in-law of the Emperor Alexius III, the ambitious Alexius Ducas Mourtzouphlos, was proclaimed Emperor at the beginning of 1204; Isaac II and Alexius IV were deposed. Isaac died very soon in prison, and Alexius IV, by order of Mourtzouphlos, was strangled.

Mourtzouphlos, known as the Emperor Alexius V, was a nominee of the national party, which was hostile to the crusaders. The crusaders had no relations with him, and after the death of Isaac and Alexius they considered themselves completely free from any obligation towards Byzantium. Conflict between the Greeks and crusaders was unavoidable. The crusaders began to discuss the plan of taking Constantinople for themselves. In March of the same year, 1204, a treaty between Venice and the crusaders concerning the division of the Empire after the conquest was elaborated and concluded. The first words of the treaty were impressive: "Calling upon the name of Christ, we must conquer the city with the armed hand!"[242] The chief points of the treaty were as follows: in the captured city the Latin government was to be established; the allies were to share in the booty of Constantinople according to agreement; then a committee formed of six Venetians and six Frenchmen was to elect as emperor that man who, in their opinion, could best govern the country "to the glory of God and the Holy Roman Church and Empire"; to the Emperor was to be assigned a quarter of the conquered territory within the capital and without, as well as two palaces in the capital; the other three-quarters of the conquered territory were to be divided, half for Venice, the rest for the other crusaders; the possession of St. Sophia and the election of a patriarch were to be left to the side which did not provide the Emperor; all the crusaders who received possessions large or small were to take feudal oath to the Emperor; only the Doge Dandolo was to be exempted from this oath.[243] This was the basis upon which the future Latin Empire was to be established.

Having agreed upon these conditions for the partition of the Empire the crusaders devoted themselves to the task of taking Constantinople, storming it by land and sea. For some days the capital stubbornly defended itself.

[242] Tafel and Thomas, *Urkunden zur altern Handels- und Staatsgeschichte*, I, 446, 449.
[243] *Ibid.*, 446–52.

Finally arrived the fatal day, the 13th of April, 1204, when the crusaders succeeded in taking possession of Constantinople. The Emperor Alexius V Ducas Mourtzouphlos, fearing to be caught and "to fall into the teeth of the Latins as a tidbit or dessert,"[244] fled. Constantinople passed into the hands of the crusaders. The capital of the Byzantine Empire "fell when assailed by that criminal filibustering expedition, the Fourth Crusade."[245]

Taking up the narration of the events of this period, Nicetas Choniates wrote: "What a state of mind must, naturally, be his who will narrate the public disasters which have befallen this queen of cities [Constantinople] in the reign of the earthly angels [Angeli]!"[246]

After the taking of the city, for three days, the Latins treated the city with appalling cruelty and pillaged everything which had been collected in Constantinople for many centuries. Neither churches, nor relics, nor monuments of art, nor private possessions were spared or respected. The western knights and their soldiers, as well as the Latin monks and abbots, took part in the pillaging.

Nicetas Choniates, an eyewitness of the capture of Constantinople, gives a striking picture of appalling sacking, violation, sacrilege, and ruin effected by the crusaders in the capital of the Empire; even the Muhammedans had been more merciful towards the Christians after the capture of Jerusalem than these men who claimed to be soldiers of Christ.[247] Another stirring description of the sack of Constantinople by the crusaders, was given by another eyewitness, Nicholas Mesarites, metropolitan of Ephesus, in his funeral oration on the occasion of the death of his elder brother.[248]

In those three days when the crusaders were allowed to pillage Constantinople, a mass of precious monuments of art perished; many libraries were plundered; manuscripts were destroyed. St. Sophia was mercilessly robbed. The contemporary Villehardouin observed: "Since the world was created, never had so much booty been won in any city!"[249] A Russian chronicle of Novgorod describes in particular detail the scenes of pillage in churches and monasteries.[250] The disaster of 1204 is also mentioned in Russian "chronographies."[251]

The spoils were collected and divided among the Latins, both laymen and

[244] Nicetas Choniates, *Historia*, Bonn ed., 755.

[245] N. H. Baynes, "Byzantine Civilization," *History*, X (1926), 289.

[246] Nicetas Choniates, *Historia*, Bonn ed., 710.

[247] *Ibid.*, 757–63.

[248] A. Heisenberg, *Neue Quellen zur Geschichte des lateinischen Kaisertums und der Kirchenunion*, I, 41–48.

[249] *La Conquête de Constantinople;* ed. de Wailly, par. 250, p. 147.

[250] *The Chronicle of Novgorod*, under 1204, 186–87; ed. Hopf, *Chroniques gréco-romanes inédites*, 97.

[251] *The Russian Chronography* (in the version of 1512), 391–92.

ecclesiastics. After this crusade the whole of western Europe became enriched with the treasures exported from Constantinople; most of the western European churches received something from "the holy relics" of Constantinople.[252] The greater part of the relics, which were in the monasteries of France, perished during the French Revolution. The four bronze horses of antique work which had served as one of the best ornaments of the Constantinopolitan Hippodrome were carried away by Dandolo to Venice, where they ornament today the portal of the cathedral of St. Mark.

Nicetas Choniates, in an eloquent lament, described and mourned the ruin of the city, imitating the Biblical lamentation of the Hebrew prophet, Jeremiah, and the Psalms. The Byzantine lamentation begins: "Oh, city, city, eye of all cities, subject of narratives over all the world, spectacle above the world, supporter of churches, leader of faith, guide of orthodoxy, protector of education, abode of all good! Thou hast drunk to the dregs the cup of the anger of the Lord and hast been visited with fire fiercer than that which in days of yore descended upon the five cities (Pentapolis)."[253] Meanwhile, the difficult task of organizing the captured territory confronted the conquerors. They decided to establish an empire like that which had existed before. The question of the selection of the emperor arose. One man seemed destined to occupy the throne—the leader of the crusade, Marquis Boniface of Montferrat. But Dandolo seems to have opposed his candidacy; he judged Boniface too powerful and his possessions situated too near Venice. Accordingly Boniface was passed over. Dandolo himself as doge of the Republic of Venice did not pretend to the imperial crown. The electoral college assembled to elect the new emperor and fixed its choice, not without the influence of Dandolo, on Baldwin, count of Flanders, more distant from Venice and less powerful than Boniface. He was duly elected Emperor and was crowned in St. Sophia with great pomp.

At the time of Baldwin's ascension to the throne three Greek rulers were living: the two Emperors, Alexius III Angelus and Alexius V Ducas Mourtzouphlos, and Theodore Lascaris, who was then still the despot of Nicaea. Baldwin succeeded in conquering the partisans of the two Emperors; the relations of the Latin Empire to Theodore Lascaris, who founded an empire at Nicaea, belongs to a later chapter.

After the election of the Emperor the next problem was how to divide the conquered territory among the participants in the crusade. "The sharing of Romania" (*Partitio Romanie*), as the Latins and Greeks often called the Eastern Empire, was carried out, generally speaking, upon the basis of the

---

[252] C. Riant, *Exuviae sacrae constantinopolitanae*, I, xl–xlviii.

[253] Nicetas Choniates, *Historia*, Bonn ed., 763.

conditions established in March, 1204.[254] Constantinople was divided between Baldwin and Dandolo, so that the Emperor received five-eighths of the city, and the Doge the other three-eighths and St. Sophia. Besides five-eighths of the capital, Baldwin was awarded the territory of southern Thrace and a small part of northwestern Asia Minor adjoining the Bosphorus, the Sea of Marmora, and the Hellespont; some of the larger islands of the Aegean (Archipelago), for example, Lesbos, Chios, Samos, and some others, were also assigned to him. Thus, both shores of the Bosphorus and Hellespont came under the power of Baldwin.

Boniface of Montferrat as compensation for having missed the imperial crown was promised some possessions in Asia Minor, but he actually received Thessalonica with the surrounding territory in Macedonia and the north of Thessaly, forming the Kingdom of Thessalonica, which he held as Baldwin's vassal.

Venice secured the lion's share of the partition of Romania. The Republic of St. Mark received some points on the Adriatic shore, for example, Dyrrachium, the Ionian islands, the greater part of the islands of the Aegean, some places in the Peloponnesus, the island of Crete, some seaports in Thrace, with Gallipoli on the Hellespont, and some territory in the interior of Thrace. Dandolo assumed the Byzantine title of "Despot," was released from paying homage to the Emperor, and styled himself "lord of the fourth and a half of all the Empire of Romania," that is to say, of three-eighths (quartae partis et dimidiae totius imperii Romanie dominator); this title was used by the doges until the middle of the fourteenth century. According to the treaty, the Church of St. Sophia was delivered into the hands of the Venetian clergy, and a Venetian, Thomas Morosini, was raised to the patriarchate and became the head of the Catholic church in the new Empire. A Byzantine historian, Nicetas Choniates, a strong partisan of the Greek Orthodox church, gave in his history a very unfavorable portrait of Thomas Morosini.[255]

It is clear that, owing to the acquisitions made by Venice, the new Empire was very weak compared with the powerful Republic, whose position in the East became commanding. The best part of the Byzantine possessions passed into the hands of the Republic of St. Mark, the best harbors, the most important strategic points, and many fertile territories; the whole maritime way from Venice to Constantinople was in the power of the Republic. The Fourth Crusade, which had created "the Colonial Empire" of Venice in the East, gave the Republic innumerable commercial advantages and raised her to the pin-

---

[254] The treaty of the year 1204 in Tafel and Thomas, *Urkunden zur altern Handels- und Staatsgeschichte,* I, 464–88.

[255] Nicetas Choniates, *Historia,* Bonn ed., 824, 854–55.

nacle of her political and economic power. It was a complete victory for the able, thoughtfully pondered, and egoistically patriotic policy of Doge Dandolo.

The Latin Empire was founded on the feudal basis. The conquered territory was divided by the Emperor into a great number of larger or smaller fiefs, for the possession of which the western knights were obliged to take vassal oath to the Latin Emperor of Constantinople.

Boniface of Montferrat, king of Thessalonica, marched through Thessaly southward into Greece, and conquered Athens. In the Middle Ages, Athens was a half-forgotten provincial city where upon the Acropolis, in the ancient Parthenon, an Orthodox cathedral in honor of the Virgin Mary was located. At the time of the Latin conquest, at the beginning of the thirteenth century, the famous Michael Acominatus (Choniates) had been archbishop of Athens for about thirty years. Michael left a rich literary inheritance in speeches, poetry, and letters, which gives good information on the internal history of the Empire under the Comneni and Angeli, as well as on the conditions of Attica and Athens in the Middle Ages. Those provinces are represented in Michael's works in a very dark aspect, with barbarian population, perhaps partly Slavonic, with barbarian language round about Athens, with Attica desolate, and its population poor. "Having stayed a long time at Athens I have become barbarian," wrote Michael and compared the city of Pericles to Tartarus.[256] An assiduous protector of medieval Athens who had devoted much time and work to his poor flock, Michael, judging it impossible to resist the troops of Boniface, abandoned his seat and spent the rest of his life in solitude on one of the islands close to the shores of Attica. The Latins conquered Athens, which, with Thebes, was transmitted by Boniface to a Burgundian knight, Othon de la Roche, who assumed the title of the Duke of Athens and Thebes (dux Athenarum atque Thebarum). The cathedral upon the Acropolis passed into the hands of the Latin clergy.

While the Duchy of Athens and Thebes was founded in central Greece, in southern Greece, that is to say, in the ancient Peloponnesus, which was at that time often called Morea, a name whose etymological origin is not clear, was formed the Principality of Achaia, which was organized by the French.

Geoffrey de Villehardouin, nephew of the famous historian, was off the shore of Syria when he learned of the taking of Constantinople by the crusaders; he hastened thither, but he was driven by stress of weather upon the southern shores of the Peloponnesus. He landed there and conquered a part of the country. But feeling that he could not maintain himself with merely his own forces, he asked help from the king of Thessalonica, Boniface, who

[256] Michael Acominatus, ed. Lampros, II, 44, 127.

at that time was in Attica. The latter granted the right of conquering Morea to one of his knights, a Frenchman, William de Champlitte, from the family of the counts of Champagne. In the course of two years he and Villehardouin subdued the whole country. Thus, at the beginning of the thirteenth century, the Byzantine Peloponnesus was converted into the French Principality of Achaia, with Prince William at the head of its government; it was divided into twelve baronies and received the western European feudal organization. After William, the princely power passed over to the house of the Ville-hardouins. The court of the prince of Achaia was marked by its brilliancy and "seemed larger than the court of any great king."[257] "There French was spoken as well as in Paris."[258] About twenty years after the formation of the Latin feudal states and possessions on the Byzantine territory, Pope Honorius III, in his letter to Blanche, queen of France, spoke of the creation in the east "as a sort of new France" (ibique noviter quasi nova Francia est creata).[259]

The Peloponnesus feudaries built fortified castles with towers and walls, on the west European model; the best known among them was Mistra, on the slopes of Mount Taygetus, in ancient Laconia, close to ancient Sparta. This imposing medieval feudal construction became in the second half of the thirteenth century the capital of the Greco-Byzantine despots in the Peloponnesus, when the Palaeologi had reconquered Mistra from the Franks. Even today Mistra strikes scholars and tourists, with its imposing half-ruined buildings, as one of the rarest spectacles of Europe, and preserves intact in its churches the precious frescoes of the fourteenth and fifteenth centuries, which are extremely important for the history of later Byzantine art. In the western part of the peninsula was the strongly fortified castle of Clermont, which was preserved almost intact until the third decade of the nineteenth century, when it was destroyed by the Turks. A Greek chronicler wrote of that castle that, if the Franks had lost Morea, the possession of Clermont only would have sufficed to reconquer the whole peninsula.[260] The Franks also built some other strongholds.

In the Peloponnesus the Franks succeeded in establishing themselves firmly in two of the three southern peninsulas; but in the central one in spite of two fortified castles that they built, they never really overcame the stubborn resistance of the Slavs (the tribe of Melingi) who lived in the mountains. The Greeks of Morea, at least the majority of them, might have seen in the rule

[257] Marino Sanudo, *Istoria del regno di Romania,* in C. Hopf, *Chroniques gréco-romanes,* 102.

[258] *Chronique de Ramon Muntaner,* chap. 261; ed. J. A. Buchon, *Chroniques étrangères,* 502; ed. K. Lanz, 468–69; ed. Lady Good-enough, 627.

[259] *Epistolae Honorii III* (May 20, 1224), in *Recueil des historiens des Gaules et de la France,* XIX, 754.

[260] *The Chronicle of Morea,* ed. J. Schmitt, vss. 2712–13; ed. P. Kalonares, 114.

of the Franks a welcome relief from the financial oppression of the Byzantine government.[261]

In the south of the Peloponnesus Venice possessed two important seaports, Modon and Coron, which were excellent stations for the Venetian vessels on their way to the East and at the same time very good points for observing the maritime trade of the Levant. They were the two "principal eyes of the commune" (oculi capitales communis).[262]

Concerning the epoch of the Latin sway in the Peloponnesus, there is a great deal of interesting information in various sources, particularly in the so-called Chronicle of Morea (fourteenth century) which survives in different versions, Greek (in verse), French, Italian, and Spanish. If from the point of view of exact exposition of fact the Chronicle of Morea cannot occupy a chief place among the other sources, it nevertheless gives a rich mine of precious material about the internal conditions of living in the epoch of the Frankish rule in the Peloponnesus, with the institutions, the public and private life, and, finally, with the geography of Morea at that time. The Chronicle of Morea, as a source exceptionally rich and various in its information on the internal and cultural history of the epoch, when Greco-Byzantine and western feudal elements united together to create exceedingly interesting living conditions, deserves particular attention.

Some scholars suppose[263] that certainly the Frankish rule in Morea, and probably the Chronicle of Morea itself, influenced Goethe, who in the third act of the second part of his tragedy "Faust" lays the scene in Greece, at Sparta, where the love story between Faust and Helena takes place. Faust himself is represented there as a prince of the conquered Peloponnesus surrounded by the feudaries; the character of his rule reminds us somewhat of one of the Villehardouins, as the latter is represented in the Chronicle of Morea. In a conversation between Mephistopheles, in the form of Phorcias, and Helena, J. Schmitt thinks that Mistra, which had been built precisely at the time of the Latin sway in Morea, is without doubt described. Phorcias said:

> Thus stood, for many years, forlorn the sloping ridge
> That northward to the height rises in Sparta's rear,
> Behind Taygetus, whence, still a merry brook
> Downward Eurotas rolls, and then, along our vale
> Broad-flowing among reeds, gives nurture to your swans.
> There in the mountain-vale, behind, a stalwart race
> Themselves establish'd, pressing from Cimmerian night,

261 See W. Miller, *The Latins in the Levant,* 6.

262 See Hopf, *Geschichte Griechenlands,* II, 10.

263 See, e.g., *Chronicle of Morea,* ed. Schmitt, lviii–lxvi.

And have uprear'd a fastness, inaccessible,
Whence land and folk around they harry, as they list.

Later appears a description of this castle, which has pillars, pilasters, arches, archlets, balconies, galleries, scutcheons, and so forth, like a typical medieval castle. All this passage of the tragedy seems to have been written under the influence of the Chronicle of Morea, and therefore from the conquest of Morea by the Franks came some of the material for the poetic scenes of *Faust*.[264]

The taking of Constantinople by the crusaders and the establishment of the Latin Empire put the pope in a difficult position. Innocent III had opposed the diversion of the crusade and had excommunicated the crusaders and Venetians after the seizure of Zara; but after the fall of the capital of the Byzantine Empire, he stood face to face with the accomplished fact.

The Emperor Baldwin, who in his letter to the pope named himself "by the Grace of God the Emperor of Constantinople and always Augustus," as well as "the vassal of the Pope" (*miles suus*),[265] notified the latter of the taking of the Byzantine capital and of his own election. In his reply Innocent III entirely disregards his former attitude. He "rejoices in the Lord" (*gavisi sumus in Domino*) at the miracle effected "for the praise and glory of His name, for the honor and benefit of the Apostolic throne, and for the profit and exaltation of the Christian people."[266] The pope called upon all clergy, all sovereigns, and all peoples to support the cause of Baldwin and expressed the hope that since Constantinople was taken it would be easier to reconquer the Holy Land from the hands of the infidel; and at the close of the letter the pope admonished Baldwin to be a faithful and obedient son of the Catholic Church.[267] In another letter Innocent wrote: "Of course, although we are pleased to know that Constantinople has returned to obedience to its mother, the Holy Catholic Church, nevertheless we should be still more pleased, if Jerusalem had been restored to the power of the Christian people."[268]

---

[264] This theory is sometimes refuted. See, e.g., O. Pniower, *Deutsche Literaturzeitung*, XXV (1904), 2739–41. But most scholars, including myself, are convinced that Goethe had Mistra in mind when he wrote this particular passage. E. Gerland, "Die Quellen der Helenaepisode in Goethes Faust," *Neue Jahrbücher für das Klassische Altertum*, XXV (1910), 735–39. A. Struck, *Mistra, eine mittelalterliche Ruinenstadt*, 17–18. H. Grégoire, *Byzantion*, V (1930), 781. A new theory has lately been advanced: Goethe's source was not the *Chronicle of Morea* but the late Byzantine *Chronicle of Dorotheus* of Monembasia. J. Moravcsik, "Zur Quellenfrage der Helenaepisode in Goethes Faust," *Byzantinisch-neugriechische Jahrbücher*, VIII (1931), 41–56. H. Grégoire, "Une Source byzantine du second Faust," *Revue de l'Université de Bruxelles*, XXXVI (1930–31), 348–54. F. Dölger, "Die neuentdeckte Quelle zur Helenaszene in Goethes Faust. Die Prophyläen," *Beilage zur Münchner Zeitung*, XXVIII (1931), 289–90.

[265] Tafel and Thomas, *Urkunden zur altern Handels- und Staatsgeschichte*, I, 502.

[266] *Ibid.*, 516–17.

[267] Innocent III, *Epistolae*, VII, 153; ed. Migne, *Patrologia Latina*, CCXV, 455.

[268] *Ibid.*, IX, 139; ed. Migne, *ibid.*, 957–58.

But the state of mind of the pope changed when he had become acquainted in more detail with all the horrors of the sack of Constantinople and with the text of the treaty concerning the partition of the Empire. The treaty had a purely secular character with a clear tendency to eliminate the interference of the Church. Baldwin had not asked the pope to confirm his imperial title; and Baldwin and Dandolo had independently decided the question of St. Sophia, of the election of the patriarch, of ecclesiastical property, and other religious affairs. During the sack of Constantinople many churches and monasteries as well as a great number of highly honored sanctuaries had been defiled and polluted. All this evoked in the heart of the pope alarm and discontent with the crusaders. He wrote the Marquess of Montferrat: "Having neither right nor power over the Greeks you seem to have imprudently deviated from the purity of your vow, when you marched not against the Saracens, but against the Christians, meaning not to reconquer Jerusalem, but to take Constantinople, preferring earthly riches to heavenly riches. But it is much more important that some (of the crusaders) spared neither religion, nor age, nor sex . . ."[269]

Thus, the Latin Empire in the East, established on feudal grounds, possessed no strong political power; moreover, in church affairs, the Empire was unable for a time to establish relations with the Roman curia that were entirely satisfactory.

The aim of the western knights and merchants was not thoroughly attained, for not all Byzantine territories were in the power of the new Latin possessions in the East. After 1204 there were three independent Greek states. The Empire of Nicaea, under the dynasty of the Lascaris, in the western part of Asia Minor, situated between the Latin possessions in Asia Minor and the territories of the Sultanate of Iconium or Rum, and possessing a part of the seashore of the Aegean, was the biggest independent Greek center and the most dangerous rival of the Latin Empire. Then, in the western part of the Balkan peninsula, in Epirus, there was founded the Despotat of Epirus under the rule of the dynasty of the Comneni-Angeli. Finally, on the remote southeastern shore of the Black Sea, in 1204, was founded the Empire of Trebizond with the dynasty of the "Great Comneni."

If the Latins in the East had no political unity, they had no religious unity either, for these three Greek states remained faithful to the doctrine and practice of the Greek Eastern Church; from the point of view of the pope they were schismatic. Nicaea was particularly displeasing to the pope; there the Greek bishop, paying no attention to the residence of the Latin patriarch in Constantinople, was called the patriarch of Constantinople. In addition, the Greeks of the Latin Empire, despite their political subjugation by the

[269] *Ibid.,* VIII, 133; ed. Migne, *ibid.,* 712.

Latins, did not adopt Catholicism. The military occupation of the country did not signify ecclesiastical union.

The results of the Fourth Crusade were as fatal for the Byzantine Empire as for the future of the crusades. The Empire could never recover from the blow inflicted on it in 1204; it lost forever the significance of a political world power. Politically, the Eastern Empire, as a whole, ceased to exist; it yielded its place to a number of west European feudal states and never again, even after the restoration of the Empire under the Palaeologi, did it regain its former brilliancy and influence.

As regards the significance of the Fourth Crusade for the general problem of the crusading movement, it showed, first of all, in the clearest way that the idea of the movement had become entirely secular; secondly, it bifurcated the single motive which had formerly drawn the western peoples to the East. After 1204 they had to direct their forces not only against the Muslims in Palestine or Egypt, but, on a larger scale, to their own new possessions on the territory of the Eastern Empire in order to support their power there. The result of this, of course, was to delay the struggle against the Muslims in the Holy Land.

INTERNAL AFFAIRS UNDER THE COMNENI AND ANGELI

Ecclesiastical relations

The ecclesiastical life of Byzantium under the Comneni and Angeli is important mainly in two directions: first, in internal ecclesiastical relations which centered in the attempts to resolve certain religious problems and doubts which agitated Byzantine society and were of the most vital interest in that epoch; secondly, in the relations of the eastern church to the western, of the patriarchate of Constantinople to the papacy.

In their attitude to the Church the emperors of the dynasties of the Comneni and Angeli firmly adopted the caesaropapistic view which was so very characteristic of Byzantium. In one version of the *History* of Nicetas Choniates Isaac Angelus is quoted: "On earth there is no difference in power between God and emperor; kings are allowed to do everything, and they may use without any distinction that which belongs to God along with their own possessions, because they have received the imperial power from God, and between God and them is no difference."[270] The same writer, speaking of the ecclesiastical policy of Manuel Comnenus, gave the general belief of the Byzantine emperors, who consider themselves "the infallible judges of matters of God and man."[271] This opinion was supported in the second half of

[270] Nicetas Choniates, *Historia,* Bonn ed., 583.   [271] *Ibid.,* 274.

the twelfth century by the clergy. A celebrated Greek canonist and commentator of the so-called pseudo-Photian Nomocanon (a canonical collection of fourteen titles), the patriarch of Antioch, Theodore Balsamon, who lived under the last Comnenus and the first Angelus, wrote: "The emperors and patriarchs must be esteemed as church teachers because of their holy anointment. Therefore, orthodox emperors have the power to teach Christian people and, like priests, to burn incense as an act of worship to God." Their glory is that, like the sun, they, by the brilliance of their orthodoxy, enlighten the world from one end to another. "The power and activities of the emperors concern body and soul (of man) while the power and activity of the patriarch concern only soul."[272] The same author stated: "The Emperor is subject neither to the laws nor to the canons."[273]

Ecclesiastical life under the Comneni and Angeli enabled the Emperors to apply widely their caesaropapistic ideas: on the one hand, numerous "heresies" and "false doctrines" considerably agitated the minds of the population. On the other hand, the menace from the Turks and Patzinaks, and the new relations between the Empire and the West resulting from the crusades, began to threaten the very existence of Byzantium as an independent state, and forced the Emperors to consider deeply and ponder seriously the problem of union with the Catholic church, which in the person of the pope, could prevent the political danger threatening the East from the West.

As regards religion, the first two Comneni were in general the defenders of the Eastern Orthodox faith and church; nevertheless, under the pressure of political reasons, they made some concessions in favor of the Catholic church. Alexius Comnenus' daughter, Anna, struck by the activity of her father, in her "Alexiad" calls him, doubtless with exaggeration, "the thirteenth Apostle"; or, if this honor must belong to Constantine the Great, Alexius Comnenus must "be set either side by side with the Emperor Constantine or, if any one objects to that, next to Constantine."[274] The third Comnenus, Manuel, inflicted great harm upon the interests of the eastern church for the sake of his illusive western policy.

In the internal church life of the Empire the chief attention of the emperors was directed to the struggle with dogmatic errors and heretic movements of their time. One side of the ecclesiastical life alarmed the emperors, the excessive growth of ecclesiastic and monastic property, against which the government, from time to time, had taken adequate measures.

---

[272] Ῥάλλη καὶ Πότλη, Σύνταγμα τῶν θείων καὶ ἱερῶν κανόνων, IV, 544, 545.

[273] Theodori Balsamonis, *In canonem XVI Concilii Carthaginiensis*, ed. Migne, *Patrologia Graeca*, CXXXVIII, 93. See G. Vernadsky, "Die kirchlich-politische Lehre der Epana-goge und ihr Einfluss auf das russische Leben im XVII. Jahrhundert," *Byzantinisch-neugriechische Jahrbücher,* VI (1928), 120.

[274] Anna Comnena, *Alexias,* XIV, 8; ed. Reifferscheid, II, 259.

In order to provide funds for state defense and the compensation of his supporters, Alexius Comnenus confiscated some monastic estates and converted several sacred vessels into money. But to appease the discontent which this measure aroused, the Emperor returned to the churches an amount equal to the value of the vessels and condemned his own action by a special Novel, "On abstaining from using the sacred vessels for public needs."[275] Manuel by restoring the abrogated Novel of Nicephorus Phocas (964) again limited the increase of the church and monastic property; but later he was forced by means of other Novels, as far as possible, to modify the harsh consequences of this decree.

Disorders and moral decline among the clergy also alarmed Alexius Comnenus, who, in one of his novels, declared, "The Christian faith is exposed to danger, for the clergy with every day becomes worse";[276] he planned some measures for raising the moral standard of the clergy by ameliorating their life according to the canonic rules, by improving their education, by widely developing pastoral activity, and so on. But unfortunately because of the general conditions of that time he did not always succeed in carrying out his good beginnings.

Though they sometimes declared themselves against the excessive increase of church property, the Comneni, at the same time, were often the protectors and founders of monasteries. Under Alexius Mount Athos was declared by the Emperor exempt forever from taxes and other vexations; "the civil officials had nothing to do with the Holy Mountain."[277] As before, Athos was not dependent on any bishop; the *protos,* that is, the chairman of the council of the igumens (abbots, priors) of the monasteries of Athos, was ordained by the Emperor himself, so that Athos was directly dependent on him. Under Manuel the Russians who had formerly lived on Mount Athos and possessed there a small monastery received, by the order of the *protaton* (the council of the igumens), the convent of St. Panteleimon, which is widely known even today.

Alexius Comnenus also supported St. Christodulus in founding in the island of Patmos, where, according to tradition, the Apostle John wrote his Apocalypse, a monastery of that Saint, which still exists today. In the *chrysobull* published on that matter the Emperor granted this island to Christodulus as his permanent and inalienable property, exempted it from all taxes, and prohibited any officials from appearing in the island.[278] The strictest regime

[275] Zachariä von Lingenthal, *Jus graeco-romanum*, III, 355–58. See V. Grumel, "L'Affaire de Léon de Chalcédoine. Le chrysobulle d'Alexis Ier sur les objets sacrés," *Études byzantines*, II (1945), 126–33.

[276] *Ibid.*, III, 414.

[277] P. Uspensky, *The Christian Orient. Athos,* III (1), 226–27. P. Meyer, *Die Haupturkunden für die Geschichte der Athosklöster,* 172.

[278] Zachariä von Lingenthal, *Jus graecoromanum*, III, 370–71. F. Miklosich and J.

was introduced into the life of the monastery.[279] Chalandon says, "the island of Patmos became a small ecclesiastical and almost independent republic where only monks could live."[280] The attacks of the Seljuqs on the islands of the Archipelago forced Christodulus and the monks to leave Patmos and take refuge in Euboea, where Christodulus died at the end of the eleventh century. Christodulus' reforms did not survive him, and his attempt in Patmos completely failed.[281]

John Comnenus built in Constantinople the monastery of the Pantokrator (Almighty) and instituted there a very well-organized hospital for the poor with fifty beds. The internal arrangement of this hospital is described in much detail in the statute (typicon) issued by the Emperor in this connection[282] and is an example, "perhaps the most touching that history has preserved, concerning humanitarian ideas in Byzantine society."[283]

The intellectual life of the epoch of the Comneni was distinguished by intense activity. Some scholars even call this period the epoch of the Hellenic renaissance which was brought about by such eminent men of the Empire as, for example, Michael Psellus. This intellectual revival expressed itself under the Comneni in various ways, including the formation of different heretical doctrines and dogmatic errors, with which the Emperors, as protectors of the Orthodox faith, had to come into collision. This feature of the epoch of the Comneni influenced the so-called *Synodicon,* that is, the list of heretical names and antichurch doctrines which is still read every year in the Eastern Orthodox church during the first week of Lent, when an anathema is pronounced against heretics and antichurch doctrines in general; and a considerable number of the anathematized names and doctrines

Müller, *Acta et diplomata graeca medii aevi,* VI, 45.

[279] See *Regula pro monasterio S. Ioannis Theologi in insula Patmo,* in Miklosich and Müller, *Acta et diplomata,* VI, 59–80; also in K. Boïnes, Ἀκολουθία ἱερὰ τοῦ ὁσίου καὶ θεοφόρου πατρὸς ἡμῶν Χριστοδούλου.

[280] Chalandon, *Alexis Ier Comnène,* 289. See also P. Yakovenko, *On the History of the Immunity in Byzantium,* 10–11.

[281] See E. LeBarbier, *Saint Christodule et la réforme des convents grecs au XIe siècle* (2nd ed., 1863), 51–56; this old biography contains many errors. R. P. Dom P. Renaudin, "Christodoule, higoumène de Saint-Jean, à Patmos (1020–1101)," *Revue de l'orient chrétien,* V (1900), 215–46. Oeconomos, *La Vie religieuse dans l'empire byzantin au temps des Comnènes et des Anges,* 142–52.

[282] The Greek text of the statute (*typicon*)

was published by A. Dmitrievsky, *The Description of the Liturgical Manuscripts Preserved in the Libraries of the Orthodox East,* I (1), 682–87.

[283] Th. I. Uspensky, "The Tendency of Conservative Byzantium to Adopt Western Influences," *Vizantiysky Vremennik,* XXII (1916), 26. See also L. Oeconomos, *La Vie religieuse dans l'empire byzantin,* 193–210. E. Jeanselme and L. Oeconomos, *Les Oeuvres d'assistance et les hopitaux byzantins au siècle des Comnènes,* 11–18. Charles Diehl, "La Société byzantine à l'époque des Comnènes," *Revue historique du sud-est européen,* VI (1929), 242–49; separate ed., 52–57. Pan S. Codellas, "The Pantocrator, the Imperial Byzantine Medical Center of the Twelfth Century A.D. in Constantinople," *Bulletin of the History of Medicine,* XII, 2 (1942), 392–410.

in the *Synodicon* were originated in the time of Alexius and Manuel Comnenius.[284]

The chief energies of Alexius were directed against the Paulicians and Bogomiles who had been established for a long time in the Balkan peninsula, especially in the district of Philippopolis. But neither persecution of the heretics nor public disputes organized by the Emperor nor the burning of the head of the Bogomilian doctrine, the monk Basil, could eradicate their doctrines, which, without spreading very widely throughout the Empire, nevertheless continued to exist. Then the Emperor appealed to the monk Euthymius Zigabenus, a man skilled in grammatical knowledge and rhetoric, a commentator of the books of the New Testament and the Epistles of St. Paul, asking him to expose all existing heretical doctrines, especially the Bogomile doctrine, and to refute them on the basis of the Church Fathers. In accordance with the Emperor's desire Zigabenus drew up a treatise *The Dogmatic Panoply of the Orthodox Faith* which, containing all the scientific proofs fitted to refute the arguments of the heretics and to show their emptiness, was to serve as a manual for the struggle with heretical errors.[285] In spite of this, however, under Manuel occurred the famous case of the monk Niphon who preached the Bogomile doctrine.[286]

Among the other events in the intellectual life of Byzantium under Alexius Comnenus was the case of a learned philosopher, John Italus (coming from Italy), a pupil of Michael Psellus, who was accused of suggesting "to his hearers the perverted theories and heretical doctrines condemned by the Church and opposed to the Scriptures and tradition of the Fathers of the Church, of not honouring sacred images,"[287] and so on. The official report on the accusation of John Italus of heresy, published and interpreted by a Russian scholar, Th. Uspensky, opens an interesting page in the intellectual life of the epoch of the first Comnenus. At the council which examined the case of Italus there was on trial not only a heretic preaching a doctrine dangerous to the Church, but also a professor of the high school teaching people of mature age who was himself influenced by the ideas of Aristotle, Plato in part, and other philosophers. Some of his disciples were also summoned to court. After having examined Italus' opinions the council declared them misleading and heretical. The patriarch to whom Italus was delivered for instruction in truth became himself, to the great scandal of the church and population, an adherent to Italus' doctrine. By order of the Emperor a list of Italus' errors was then drawn

[284] On *Syndicon* see Th. I. Uspensky, *Essays on the History of Byzantine Civilization*, 89–145.

[285] Migne, *Patrologia graeca*, CXXX, 9–1362.

[286] Oeconomos, *La Vie religieuse dans l'empire byzantin*, 38–47.

[287] Th. I. Uspensky, "The Official Report on the Accusation of John Italus of Heresy," *Transactions of the Russian Archeological Institute in Constantinople*, II (1897), 3, 10.

up. Finally, anathema was pronounced against the eleven items of his doctrine and against the heretic himself.[288]

As not all the works of Italus are published, it is impossible to form a fixed opinion about him and his doctrine. There is, therefore, some disagreement among scholars on this problem. While, as Th. Uspensky said, "the freedom of philosophical thought was limited by the supreme authority of the Scriptures and the works of the Fathers of the Church,"[289] Italus, as some investigators, Bezobrazov and Bryanzev, for example, state, "judged it possible, in some problems, to give the preference to pagan philosophy over church doctrine";[290] he "separated the domain of theology from that of philosophy, and admitted the possibility of holding independent opinions in one or the other domain."[291] Finally, in connection with the case of Italus, N. Marr raised "the most important question of whether the initiators of the trial of Italus were on his level in intellectual development, demanding the separation of philosophy from theology, and whether, having condemned the thinker for intrusion upon theology, they granted him his freedom in purely philosophical speculation?"[292] Of course, the answer is no: at that time such freedom was impossible. But Italus is not to be considered only as a theologian. "He was a philosopher who was condemned because his philosophical system did not conform to the doctrine of the Church";[293] and the most recent investigator of the religious life of the epoch of the Comneni said that all the information clearly shows that Italus belonged to the Neoplatonic school.[294] All the discrepancy and difference in opinion show how interesting is the problem of John Italus from the point of view of the cultural history of Byzantium at the end of the eleventh and the beginning of the twelfth century.

But this is not all. Attention has been paid to the doctrines which appeared in western European philosophy in the lifetime of John Italus and resembled the doctrines of the latter; for example, such a resemblance is to be found in the doctrine of Abelard, a famous French scholar and professor of the first half of the twelfth century, whose autobiography, *Historia calamitatum,* is still read with intense interest. In view of the complicated and insufficiently investigated problem of mutual cultural influences between the East and West in this epoch, it may be too sweeping a statement to say that the western European

---

[288] The eleven items were published by Th. I. Uspensky, *Synodikon for the First Sunday of Lent,* 14–18; in French in Oeconomos, *La Vie religieuse dans l'empire byzantin,* 25–28.

[289] *Essays on Byzantine Civilization,* 171.

[290] P. Bezobrazov, *Vizantiysky Vremennik,* III (1896), 128.

[291] D. Bryanzev, "John Italus," *Vera i Razum,* II, 1 (1904), 328.

[292] "John Petritzi, Iberian (Gruzinian) Neoplatonist of the Eleventh and Twelfth Centuries," *Zapiski Vostochnago otdeleniya russkago Archeologicheskago Obchestwa,* XIX (1909), 107.

[293] Chalandon, *Alexis Ier Comnène,* 316. Oeconomos, *La Vie religieuse dans l'empire byzantin,* 29.

[294] Oeconomos, *ibid.* The French author followed in his book the work of Uspensky.

scholasticism depended on that of Byzantium; but it may be affirmed that "the circle of ideas in which the European mind was working from the eleventh to the thirteenth century was the same that we find in Byzantium."[295]

In external ecclesiastical affairs the time of the first three Comneni was an epoch of active relations with the popes and the western church. The chief cause of those relations, as the appeal of the Emperor Michael VII Parapinakes to Pope Gregory VII showed, was the danger threatening Byzantium from her external enemies, the Turks and Patzinaks. This danger compelled the emperors to seek for aid in the West, even at the price of the union of the churches. Therefore, the tendency of the Comneni to conclude a union with the Roman Church is explained by purely external political reasons.

In the most terrible years, that is, at the end of the eighties and the beginning of the nineties of the eleventh century, Alexius Comnenus held out the hand of reconciliation and agreement to Pope Urban II, promising to summon a Council in Constantinople in order to discuss the question of the azyms and other subjects which separated the two churches. In 1089 a synod of the Greek bishops, with Alexius I presiding, took place in Constantinople. At this synod was discussed the motion of Urban II to put his name again into the diptychs and to mention him in divine services, and under the pressure of the Emperor this delicate problem was decided in the affirmative.[296] Probably to this time is to be referred a treatise of Theophylact of Bulgaria, *On the Errors of the Latins,* in which V. Vasilievsky saw a sign of the times.[297] The main theme of the treatise is very remarkable. The author did not adopt the common view of the definite separation of the churches; neither did he acknowledge the errors of the Latins to be so numerous as to make separation unavoidable; he expresses himself against the spirit of theological intolerance and haughtiness which was predominant among his learned contemporaries. In a word, Theophylact in many points was ready to grant reasonable concessions. But in the symbol of the Creed no ambiguity could be admitted, no addition; in other words, it was impossible to adopt *filioque* in the eastern symbol.

But the critical situation of the Empire and some difficulties which befell Pope Urban II in Rome, where an antipope had been elected, prevented the summoning of the council. The First Crusade, which took place some years later, and the hostilities and mutual distrust which arose between the Greeks and crusaders were unfavorable to an understanding between the two churches. Under John Comnenus negotiations were carried on concerning the

[295] Uspensky, *Essays on Byzantine Civilization,* 178, 181, 183.

[296] See a very interesting article by W. Holtzmann, "Die Unionsverhandlungen zwischen Alexios I. und Papst Urban II. im Jahre 1089," *Byzantinische Zeitschrift,* XXVIII (1928), 40; the author gives three unpublished Greek texts; the text relating to the synod of 1089, 60–62.

[297] Vasilievsky, "Byzantium and the Patzinaks," *Works,* I, 83–85. The treaty in Migne, *Patrologia Graeca,* CXXVI, 226–50.

union between the Emperor and Popes Calixtus II and Honorius II; two letters exist addressed by John to these popes. Papal envoys arrived in Constantinople with full powers to treat the question.[298] But they failed to arrive at any tangible result. On the other hand, some learned Latins from the West took part in theological disputations at Constantinople. A German, Anselm of Havelberg, who wrote about 1150, left a very interesting account of a disputation held before John Comnenus in 1136, at which "there were present not a few Latins, among them three wise men skilled in the two languages and most learned in letters, namely James, a Venetian, Burgundio, a Pisan, and the third, most famous among Greeks and Latins above all others for his knowledge of both literatures, Moses by name, an Italian from the city of Bergamo, and he was chosen by all to be a faithful interpreter for both sides."[299]

Relations became more active under John's latinophile successor, Manuel I. The latter, hopeful of the restoration of the single Roman Empire, and convinced that he could receive the imperial crown only from Rome, offered the pope the prospect of union. It is obvious, accordingly, that the cause of the negotiations for union was purely political. The German historian Norden rightly remarked, "The Comneni were hoping with the help of the papacy to rise to dominion over the west and thereupon over the papacy itself; the Popes were dreaming with the support of the Comneni of becoming the masters of the Byzantine church and thereupon of the Byzantine Empire."[300]

After the Second Crusade Manuel corresponded with several popes. The popes themselves also were sometimes ready to lend a friendly hand to the Emperor, especially Pope Hadrian IV, who was engaged in a quarrel with the king of Sicily and was angry with the Emperor Frederick Barbarossa, who had been recently crowned. In his message to the archbishop of Thessalonica, Basil, Hadrian IV expressed his desire "to help in bringing all the brethren into one church" and compared the eastern church with lost *drachma,* wandering sheep, and the dead Lazarus.[301]

Shortly after, Manuel through his envoy officially promised Pope Alexander III the union of the churches, provided the pope would return to him the crown of the Roman Empire which was then, against all rights, in the hands of the German king, Frederick; if, for that purpose, the pope needed money or military forces, Manuel would supply him with troops in abundance. But

[298] Kap-Herr, *Die abendländische Politik Kaiser Manuels,* 9. Norden, *Das Papsttum und Byzanz,* 91. Chalandon, *Alexis Ier Comnène,* II, x–xi, 162–63. Dölger, *Corpus der griechischen Urkunden,* II, 59 (nos. 1302, 1303).

[299] Anselmi Havelbergensis, *Dialogi,* II,

chap. 1; ed. Migne, *Patrologia Latina,* CLXXXVIII, 1163. See C. H. Haskins, *Studies in the History of Mediaeval Science,* 144, 197. Haskins, *The Renaissance of the Twelfth Century,* 294.

[300] *Das Papsttum und Byzanz,* 101.

[301] Migne, *Patrologia Graeca,* CXIX, 928–29.

Alexander III, whose situation in Italy had somewhat improved, refused this offer.

A council was summoned by the Emperor in the capital to put an end to the various causes of discontent existing between the Latins and Greeks, and to find some means for joining the churches. Manuel exerted himself to the utmost to incline the patriarch to concessions. "A Conversation" at the council between Manuel and the patriarch, is a very interesting document for the light it throws on the views of the two chief participants in the council. In this "Conversation" the patriarch says that the pope is "reeking with impiety," and prefers the yoke of the "Agarens" [i.e. Muhammedans] to that of the Latins. This statement of the patriarch, apparently reflecting the ecclesiastical and public feeling of the epoch, was to be many times repeated in the future, for example, in the fifteenth century, at the time of the fall of Byzantium. Manuel was forced to yield and declared that he would withdraw from the Latins "as from the serpent's poison."[302] Thus all the discussions at the council failed to produce any agreement. It was even decided to break off entirely with the pope and his partisans.

Thus Manuel, both in his secular external policy and in his ecclesiastical policy, was wholly unsuccessful. The cause of this failure may be explained by the fact that the Emperor's policy in both fields was only his own personal policy and had no solid and real basis in public opinion. The restoration of the one Empire had already for a long time been impossible and the unitarian tendencies of Manuel met with no sympathy in the masses of the Empire's population.

In the last five years of the rule of the Comneni (1180–85), especially under Andronicus I, the ecclesiastical causes were absorbed in the complicated external and internal conditions. Andronicus, an enemy of the Latin sympathies of his predecessor at the beginning of his reign, could not be a partisan of the union with the western church. In internal ecclesiastical affairs, he dealt harshly with the patriarch of Constantinople and allowed no disputes on faith.[303] "A Dialogue against the Jews," which is often ascribed to him, belongs to a later time.

The time of the Angeli, politically full of troubles, was equally disturbed in ecclesiastical life. The emperors of this house felt themselves to be masters of the situation. The first Angelus, Isaac, deposed at his leisure the patriarchs of Constantinople, one after another.

Under the Angeli the vigorous theological dispute of the Eucharist arose in

---

[302] C. Loparev, "Concerning the Unitarian Tendencies of Manuel Comnenus," *Vizantiysky Vremennik*, XIV (1907), 339, 341, 342–43, 350, 353, 355.

[303] On the relation of Andronicus to the patriarch and the church in general see Oeconomos, *La Vie religieuse dans l'empire byzantin*, 113–18.

Byzantinum; the Emperor himself took part in it. A historian of that epoch, Nicetas Choniates, said the question was "whether the body of Christ, of which we partake, is as incorruptible (ἄφθαρτον) as it became after His passion and resurrection, or corruptible (φθαρτόν), as it was before his passion."[304] In other words, in this dispute the question was "whether the eucharist of which we partake, is subject to the common physiological processes to which any food that man takes is subject, or not subject to those physiological processes."[305] Alexius Angelus stood as the protector of "the insolently defiled" truth and supported the doctrine of the "incorruptibility" of the Eucharist. A similar dispute in Byzantium at the end of the twelfth century can be explained by western influence, which was very strong in the Christian East in the epoch of the crusades. As is known, such disputes had begun in the West a long time before; even in the ninth century there had been men who taught that the Eucharist is subject to the same processes as ordinary food.

As far as the relations of the Angeli to the pope are concerned, the pope was guided by political expediency, desiring, of course, to induce the eastern church to adopt union. The pope's plan failed. The complicated international situation, especially just before the Fourth Crusade, brought forward the king of Germany, who seemed to take an important part in the solution of the Byzantine problem. As the king of Germany was the most dangerous foe of the papacy, the pope, in order to prevent the western Emperor from getting possession of the Eastern Empire, endeavored by all means to support the "schismatic" eastern Emperor, even a usurper such as Alexius III who had dethroned his brother Isaac. Innocent III was in a rather embarrassing position during the Fourth Crusade, when the head of the Catholic church, at first acting very energetically against the diversion of the crusade, was gradually forced to change his mind and to declare the compliance of God with the sack of Constantinople by the crusaders, almost unexampled in barbarity as it was.

In summary, religious life under the Comneni and Angeli, a period of one hundred and twenty-three years (1081–1204), was marked by extraordinary intensity and animation in external relations and especially by conflicting and contradictory internal movements. Without doubt, from the point of view of religious problems this epoch is of great importance and of vivid interest.[306]

Internal administration

Financial and social conditions.—As a general thesis one may say that the internal situation of the Byzantine Empire and the administrative system

[304] Nicetas Choniates, *Historia,* Bonn ed., 682.

[305] A. Lebedev, *The Situation of the Byzantine Eastern Church from the End of the* *Eleventh Century to the Middle of the Fifteenth Century* (2nd ed., 1902), 153.

[306] See Oeconomos, *La Vie religieuse dans l'empire byzantin,* 222.

changed little in the course of the twelfth century. Whereas the history of the Byzantine church under the Comneni and Angeli has been more or less fully investigated, conditions are quite different for internal social and economic life. And if the internal history of Byzantium has been inadequately investigated, there is a particular lack of thorough research in the period beginning with the epoch of the Comneni. Even today histories usually offer on this subject short chapters, based sometimes only on general speculations, some occasional remarks or excursus, or at the very best, small articles on one problem or another, so that, at least for the present, there is no adequate conception of the internal history of this epoch. The most recent investigator of this period, the French scholar Chalandon, died before he could publish the promised continuation of his book in which the problem of the internal life of Byzantium in the twelfth century was to have been fully discussed.[307]

A representative of the large landowning nobility of Asia Minor, Alexius Comnenus, became Emperor of a state in which the financial system was entirely disorganized both by numerous military enterprises and by internal troubles of an earlier period. In spite of the crippled financial condition, Alexius, especially in the beginning years of his rule, had to remunerate his partisans, who had supported him in gaining the throne, and to present the members of his family with rich gifts. Fierce wars with the Turks, Patzinaks, and Normans, and the events connected with the First Crusade also required enormous expenditures. The estates of large landowners and of monasteries served as a means for replenishing the treasury.

As far as one can judge from the fragmentary information of the sources, Alexius had no scruples in confiscating the property of large landowners; even in the case of political plots capital punishment was often replaced by confiscation of land. The lands of the monasteries, which were given as grants (in Greek *kharistikia*) for life to recipients who were thence called *kharistikarioi,* were exposed to similar confiscation.

The system of *kharistikia* was not invented by the Comneni, but because of their financial difficulties, they perhaps resorted to it more frequently than anyone else. The system is connected with the secularization of the monastic estates under the iconoclastic emperors and probably with some phenomena of the social life of a still earlier time. In the tenth and eleventh centuries the system of *kharistikia* was already in frequent use. Monasteries were granted both to ecclesiastics and laymen, even to women, and it happened sometimes that monasteries for men were granted to women, and those for women to men. The *kharistikarios* was expected to defend the interests of the monastery

---

[307] Chalandon, *Alexis Ier Comnène,* II, 316. See some data on Alexis' internal policy, financial and economic, supplied by the diplomatic sources, especially from the documents of Mount Athos, in Germaine Rouillard, "A propos d'un ouvrage récent sur l'histoire d'état byzantin," *Revue de philologie* (October, 1942), 175–80.

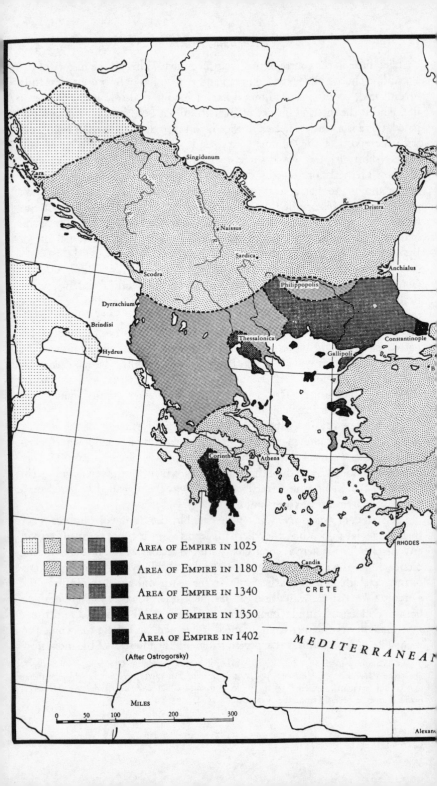

AREA OF EMPIRE IN 1025

AREA OF EMPIRE IN 1180

AREA OF EMPIRE IN 1340

AREA OF EMPIRE IN 1350

AREA OF EMPIRE IN 1402

(After Ostrogorsky)

MILES

0   50   100   200   300

MEDITERRANEAN

Singidunum

R. Dristra

Naissus

Sardica

Anchialus

Scodra

Philippopolis

Dyrrachium

Thessalonica

Brindisi

Gallipoli

Hydrus

Constantinople

Corinth

Athens

RHODES

Candia

CRETE

Zara

Alexan

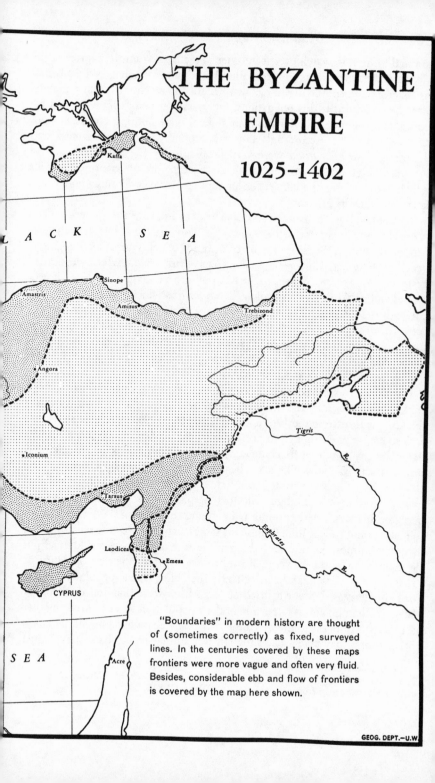

THE BYZANTINE EMPIRE

1025–1402

B L A C K   S E A

Kaffa

Amastris
Sinope
Amisus
Trebizond

Angora

Tigris

Iconium

Tarsus

Euphrates

Laodicea
Emesa

CYPRUS

S E A

Acre

"Boundaries" in modern history are thought
of (sometimes correctly) as fixed, surveyed
lines. In the centuries covered by these maps
frontiers were more vague and often very fluid.
Besides, considerable ebb and flow of frontiers
is covered by the map here shown.

GEOG. DEPT.—U.W.

granted to him, to watch over it in order to secure it from the caprice of the governor or tax gatherers and from illegal taxes, and to manage skillfully monastic economy, converting to his own benefit the revenues which remained after he had fulfilled his obligations. Of course, in reality he neglected his duties, and the monastic donations in general were nothing but a source of revenue and profit. Accordingly monastic economy was growing weak and declining. The *kharistikia* were very profitable for the receivers, and the Byzantine high officials sought for them eagerly. The ordinance of Alexius which provided for the conversion of some sacred vessels into money was later abrogated by him.

But confiscations of land were insufficient to improve the finances. Then Alexius Comnenus resorted to perhaps his worst financial measure, the corruption of money, the issue of debased coin, for which sources blame Alexius heavily. Along with the former golden coins of full weight, which were called *nomisma, hyperpyrus,* or *solidus,* he had put into circulation a certain alloy of copper and gold or silver and gold called *nomisma* which was circulated on a par with the full coin. The new *nomisma* as compared to the former, which consisted of twelve silver coins or *miliarisia,* was equal in value only to four silver coins, one-third as much.[308] But Alexius insisted that taxes be paid in money of full weight. Such measures brought still greater confusion into the finances of the Empire and irritated the population.

The difficult external situation and almost complete financial bankruptcy of the country, despite the measures taken, forced the government to collect the taxes with extreme severity; and as many large estates, secular as well as ecclesiastic, were exempt from taxes, the whole burden of taxation fell upon the lower classes who were completely exhausted under the unbearable pressure of fiscal exactions. The tax-collectors, who are called by a writer of the eleventh and the early twelfth century, the archbishop of Bulgaria, Theophylact, "rather robbers than collectors, despising both divine laws and imperial ordinances," were running wild among the people.[309]

The cautious rule of John Comnenus somewhat improved the state finances, in spite of almost continuous wars. But the rule of his successor Manuel put the country again on the verge of bankruptcy. At this time the population of the Empire decreased, and consequently the ability of the population to pay taxes also decreased. Some districts of Asia Minor were abandoned because of Muhammedan invasions; a portion of their population was captured, another part escaped in flight to the maritime cities. The abandoned territories could not, of course, pay taxes. The situation was similar in the Balkan peninsula

---

[308] The approximate value of a *nomisma* (*hyperpyrus* or *solidus*) was about two dollars, and of a *miliarision* from about fifteen to eighteen cents.

[309] *Epistola 24;* ed. Migne, *Patrologia Graeca,* CXXVI, 405.

owing to the aggressions of the Hungarians, Serbs, and the peoples beyond the Danube.

Meanwhile expenses were increasing. Besides the expenses of military enterprises, Manuel squandered enormous amounts of money on a mass of foreigners who had come to Byzantium because of the Emperor's Latin sympathies; at the same time he required money for buildings, for sustaining the absurd luxury at his court, and for supporting his favorites, both men and women.

The historian Nicetas Choniates drew a striking picture of universal discontent with the financial policy of Manuel.[310] The Greeks of the islands of the Ionian sea, unable to endure the burden of taxation, passed over to the Normans. Like Alexius Comnenus, Manuel tried to improve his finances by means of confiscation of the secular and ecclesiastic estates, and restored the famous Novel of Nicephorus Phocas, of 964, concerning church and monastic landownership.

Only in the reign of the last Comnenus, Andronicus I, whose short rule was marked by a reaction against Manuel's policy, did the situation of the taxable classes improve. Andronicus is known to have come out as protector of the national interests and the lower classes against Manuel's latinophile policy and support of the large landowners. Large landowners and tax collectors were brought sharply to account; provincial governors began to receive high salaries from the treasury; the sale of public offices ceased. A historian contemporary with Andronicus, Nicetas Choniates painted this idyllic picture:

Everyone, to quote a Prophet, lay quietly in the shade of his trees and having gathered grapes and the fruits of the earth ate them joyfully and slept comfortably, without fearing the tax collector's menace, without thinking of the rapacious or insatiable exactor of duties, without looking askance at the gleaner in his vineyard or being suspicious of the gatherer of cornstalks; but he who rendered unto Caesar those things which are Caesar's, of him no more was required; he was not deprived, as he used to be, of his last garment, and he was not reduced to the point of death, as formerly was often the case.[311]

The Byzantine sources give a sad picture of the internal life of the country under Manuel, and conditions could not, of course, improve greatly in the short and stormy reign of Andronicus. But the Jewish traveler, Benjamin, from the Spanish city of Tudela, who visited Byzantium in the eighth decade of the twelfth century, i.e. under Manuel, gave in the description of his journey some glowing praise of Constantinople as a result of his personal observation and oral communications. Benjamin wrote concerning Constantinople:

From every part of the Empire of Greece tribute is brought here every year, and strongholds are filled with garments of silk, purple, and gold. Like unto these storehouses and this wealth, there is nothing in the whole world to be found. It is said

[310] Nicetas Choniates, *Historia,* Bonn ed., 265–68.　　[311] *Ibid.,* 421–22.

that the tribute of the city amounts every year to 20,000 gold pieces, derived both from the rents of shops and markets, and from the tribute of merchants who enter by sea or land. The Greek inhabitants are very rich in gold and precious stones, and they go clothed in garments of silk with gold embroidery, and they ride horses, and look like princes. Indeed, the land is very rich in all cloth stuffs, and in bread, meat, and wine. Wealth like that of Constantinople is not to be found in the whole world. Here also are men learned in all the books of the Greeks, and they eat and drink every man under his vine and his fig tree.[312]

In another place the same traveler says: "All sorts of merchants come here from the land of Babylon, from the land of Shinar (Mesopotamia), from Persia, Media, and all the sovereignty of the land of Egypt, from the land of Canaan, and the empire of Russia, from Hungaria, Patzinakia, Khazaria, and the land of Lombardy and Sepharad (Spain). It is a busy city, and merchants come to it from every country by sea and land, and there is none like it in the world except Bagdad, the great city of Islam."[313] Under Manuel also, an Arabian traveler, al-Harawy (or el-Herewy) visited Constantinople, where he was well received by the Emperor; in his book he gave a description of the most important monuments of the capital and remarked: "Constantinople is a city larger than its renown proclaims. May God, in His grace and generosity, deign to make of it the capital of Islam!"[314] Perhaps one should compare the description of Benjamin of Tudela, with some verses of John Tzetzes, a poet of the epoch of the Comneni, relating also to Constantinople. Parodying two Homeric verses of the Iliad (IV, 437–38) "For they (the Trojans) had not all like speech nor one language, but their tongues were mingled, and they were brought from many lands," John Tzetzes said, not without bitterness and irritation: "The men are very thievish who dwell in the capital of Constantine; they belong neither to one language nor to one people; there are minglings of strange tongues and there are very thievish men, Cretans and Turks, Alans, Rhodians and Chians (of the island of Chios), . . . all of them being very thievish and corrupt are considered as saints in Constantinople."[315] The brilliant and bustling life of Constantinople under Manuel reminded A. Andreades of the life of certain capitals such as Paris in the last years of the Empire, on the eve of the catastrophe.[316]

It is difficult to say exactly what was the population of the capital at that

[312] Benjamin of Tudela, *Oriental Travels,* trans. M. N. Adler, 13; ed. L. Grünhut and M. N. Adler, 17–18; ed. M. Komroff, in *Contemporaries of Marco Polo,* 265–66.

[313] *Ibid.,* ed. Adler, 12; ed. Grünhut and Adler, 16. On Bagdad, *ibid.,* ed. Adler, 35–42; ed. Grünhut and Adler, 48–57; ed. Komroff, 264. Cf. G. Le Strange, *Bagdad During the Abbasid Caliphate,* 332.

[314] *Indications sur les lieux de pèlerinage,*

trans. C. Schefer, in *Archives de l'orient latin,* I, 589. A. A. Vasiliev, "Quelques Remarques sur les voyageurs du moyen âge à Constantinople," *Mélanges Charles Diehl,* I, 294–96.

[315] *Historiarum variarum Chiliades,* ed. T. Kiessling, Chilias XIII, vss. 360–68, p. 496. John Tzetzes is discussed later.

[316] A. Andreadès, "De la population de Constantinople sous les empereurs byzantins," *Metron,* I, 2 (1920), 97.

time. But perhaps, as a mere conjecture, the population of Constantinople towards the end of the twelfth century may be computed at between 800,000 and 1,000,000.[317]

In connection with the increase of large estates under the Comneni and Angeli, the landowners were steadily gaining in strength and power and becoming less dependent on the central government; feudal processes were sweepingly developing in the Empire. Referring to the epoch of the two last Comneni and Isaac II Angelus, Cognasso, wrote: "Feudalism covers thenceforth the whole Empire, and the Emperor must contend with grand provincial landlords who do not always consent to provide soldiers with the generosity shown, for example, for the struggle against the Normans. . . . As the equilibrium between the elements which formed the social and political platform of the Empire was broken, the aristocracy obtained the upper hand, and finally the Empire came under its power. The monarchy is deprived of its power and wealth in favor of the aristocracy." The Empire was hastening to its ruin.[318]

To the time of Manuel belongs a very interesting *chrysobull* which prohibited the transference to any but officials of senatorial or military rank of the immovable property granted by the Emperor; if, none the less, a transference had taken place contrary to this regulation, the immovable property was to go to the treasury.[319] This prohibition of Manuel, depriving the lower classes of the chance of possessing imperial land grants, made the aristocracy master of immense territories.[320] This *chrysobull* was abrogated in December, 1182, by Alexius II Comnenus. The abrogation was signed by the latter; but, without doubt, it was drawn up under the pressure of the all-powerful regent, Andronicus. From 1182 on the imperial grants in immovable properties might be transmitted to anyone regardless of his social rank.[321]

The *chrysobull* of 1182 must be interpreted in connection with the new policy of Andronicus towards the Byzantine aristocracy and large landowners, against whom he had to open a stubborn struggle. Alexius II Comnenus, who signed the law, was the mere mouthpiece of Andronicus' will. Therefore doubt is cast upon the opinion of some scholars who think that as Manuel's prohibition had clearly been aimed at the Franks and should have hindered the land purchases of those foreign traders, so the abrogation of the prohibi-

[317] *Ibid.*, 101.

[318] "Un Imperatore bizantino della decadenza Isacco II Angelo," *Bessarione*, XXI (1915), 52–53, 59–60, 269–89; separate ed., 26–27, 33–34, 56–76.

[319] Zachariä von Lingenthal, *Jus graeco-romanum*, III, 457; some years later this *chrysobull* was repeated (*ibid.*, 498). The date of

this *chrysobull* is debatable; see *ibid.*, 457, 498. F. Dölger, *Corpus der griechischen Urkunden*, II, 62–63 (no. 1333) and 70 (no. 1398).

[320] Cognasso, *Partiti politici e lotte dinastiche in Bizanzio*, 284 (72).

[321] Zachariä von Lingenthal, *Jus graeco-romanum*, III, 507.

tion was an act friendly to the Franks and entirely corresponded with the policy of Alexius II Comnenus.[322] True, the government of Alexius II, who was a child, and of his mother, had sought for the support of the hated Latin elements, but after Andronicus had entered Constantinople and been proclaimed regent, circumstances changed; the government fell into his hands, and towards the end of 1182 his policy was already openly hostile to the Latins.

Defense and commerce.—Because of almost permanent hostilities in the epoch of the Comneni, the army cost the state enormous sums of money, and the Comneni took care of the restoration and strengthening of their army. The army consisted of a great number of mercenaries of the most various nationalities besides the local elements supplied by the themes. Under the Comneni there was a new national element in the army—the Anglo-Saxon.

The cause of the appearance of the Anglo-Saxons in Byzantium was the conquest of England by the Normans under William the Conqueror in 1066, when the catastrophe which had burst upon England after the battle of Senlac, a few miles north of Hastings, delivered the country into the hands of the severe conqueror. Attempts at insurrection on the part of the Anglo-Saxons against the new ruler were severely quelled by executions and extinguished in streams of blood. Many Anglo-Saxons, in despair, abandoned their fatherland. In the eighties of the eleventh century, at the beginning of the rule of Alexius Comnenus, as the English historian Freeman emphasized in his very well-known work on the conquest of England by the Normans, some convincing indications of the Anglo-Saxon emigration into the Greek Empire were already evident.[323] A western chronicler of the first half of the twelfth century wrote: "After having lost their liberty the Anglians were deeply afflicted. . . . Some of them shining with the blossom of beautiful youth went to distant countries and boldly offered themselves for the military service of the Constantinopolitan Emperor Alexius."[324] This was the beginning of the "Varangian-English bodyguard" which, in the history of Byzantium of the twelfth century, played an important part, such as the "Varangian-Russian Druzhina" (Company) had played in the tenth and eleventh centuries. Apparently, there never was such a great number of mercenary foreign troops in Byzantium as during the latinophile rule of Manuel.

As far as the navy was concerned, the maritime forces which had been well organized by Alexius seem gradually to have been losing their fighting power, so that under Manuel they were in a state of decline. Nicetas Choniates, in his

---

[322] See Dölger, *Corpus der griechischen Urkunden,* II, 89 (no. 1553). Cf. Bréhier, "Andronic (Comnène)," *Dictionnaire d'histoire,* II, 1780.

[323] *Norman Conquest,* IV, 628. A. A. Vasiliev, "The Opening Stages of the Anglo-Saxon Immigration to Byzantium in the Eleventh Century," *Annales de l'Institut Kondakov,* IX (1937), 39-70.

[324] Orderici Vitalis *Historia ecclesiastica;* ed. Migne, *Patrologia Latina,* CLXXXVIII, 309.

history, sharply condemned Manuel for the destruction of the maritime power of the Empire.[325] Under the Comneni, the Venetian vessels which had made an alliance with the Empire helped Byzantium a great deal, but, of course, at the expense of Byzantine economic independence.

Manuel restored and fortified some places which were in a state of decay. He fortified a very important city and stronghold, Attalia (Satalia), on the southern shore of Asia Minor.[326] He also erected fortifications and constructed a bridge at Abydos, at the entrance into the Hellespont,[327] where one of the most important Byzantine customhouses was located and where, from the time of the Comneni, the Venetians and their rivals, Genoese and Pisans, had their residences.

Provincial administration under the Comneni has not yet been satisfactorily investigated. It is known that in the eleventh century the number of themes reached thirty-eight.[328] The reduction of the territory of the Empire in the eleventh and twelfth centuries made it impossible for the boundaries of the provinces and their number to remain the same. Information on this problem can be drawn from the Novel of Alexius III Angelus, of Nov. 1198.[329] where the trade privileges granted Venice by the Emperor are discussed and where are enumerated "by names all the provinces that were under the power of Romania and where (the Venetians) could conduct their trade business."[330] The list given in this Novel, a source which has not yet been adequately studied, gives an approximate idea of the changes which took place in the provincial division of the Empire in the course of the twelfth century.

Most of the former themes had been governed by military governors or *strategi*. Later, especially after the battle of Manzikert in 1071, and then in the course of the twelfth century in connection with the growing Turkish danger in Asia Minor and with the secession of Bulgaria in 1186, the territory of the Empire was considerably reduced. Owing to the reduction of territory, the very important title of *strategus* given to the governor general of the themes towards the end of the eleventh century fell into disuse. Under the Comneni the title of *strategus* entirely disappeared, because it became inappropriate to

[325] Nicetas Choniates, *Historia,* Bonn ed., 75.

[326] Benedicti Abbatis *Gesta regis Henrici Secundi,* ed. Stubbs, II, 195. The same information in Rogeri de Houedene, *Chronica magistri,* ed. Stubbs, II, 157.

[327] See two short poems of Theodore Prodromus in *Recueil des historiens,* II, 541–42.

[328] See Skabalanovich, *Byzantine State and Church in the Eleventh Century,* 186, 193–230.

[329] Zachariä von Lingenthal, *Jus graeco-romanum,* III, 560–61 (under the year 1199). Tafel and Thomas, *Urkunden zur ältern Handels- und Staatsgeschichte,* I, 258–72 (also under the year 1199). The correct date is November, 1198; this document is exactly dated. See Zachariä von Lingenthal, *Jus graeco-romanum,* III, 565. Tafel and Thomas, *ibid.,* 258.

[330] Zachariä von Lingenthal, *Jus graeco-romanum,* III, 560. Tafel and Thomas, *Urkunden zur ältern Handels- und Staatsgeschichte,* I, 258.

the smaller size of the provinces, and it was gradually replaced by *dux,* a title which had been already borne, in the ninth century and earlier, by the governors of some small provinces.[331]

In the commercial situation of the Empire under the Comneni and Angeli an exceedingly important change took place as a result of the crusades: the West and East began to engage in direct commercial relations with each other and Byzantium lost the role of intermediate commercial agent between them.[332] It was a severe blow to the international economic power of the Eastern Empire. Then in the capital itself, as in some other places, Venice had already gained a strong footing at the beginning of the reign of Alexius Comnenus. Under the same emperor the Pisans obtained very important commercial privileges at Constantinople; they received there a landing place (scala) and a special quarter with stores for their merchandise and private houses; reserved seats were guaranteed to the Pisans at St. Sophia during divine service and in the Hippodrome for public spectacles.[333] Towards the end of the reign of John Comnenus the Genoese opened negotiations for the first time with Byzantium, and it is certain that the main cause of these negotiations related to commercial questions. Manuel's policy was always closely connected with the commercial interests of Venice, Pisa, and Genoa, who, undermining the economic power of the Empire, were, in their turn, in a state of permanent commercial competition. In 1169 Genoa received exceptionally advantageous trade privileges all over the Empire, except in two places on the northern shores of the Black and Azov Sea.[334]

After the terrible massacre of the Latins in 1182 their position became again more favorable under the Angeli; and finally in November 1198 a *chrysobull* was reluctantly granted by Alexius III Angelus to Venice, reciting and confirming the previous bull of Isaac Angelus regarding the defensive alliance

[331] See E. Stein, "Untersuchungen zur spätbyzantinischen Verfassungs- und Wirtschaftsgeschichte," *Mitteilungen zur Osmanischen Geschichte,* II (1924), 21 (pagination of reprint); see also Stein's note on the *chrysobull* of November, 1198 (p. 20, n. 11).

[332] The best information on the commercial relations between Byzantium and the Italian republics under the Comneni and Angeli is to be found in W. Heyd, *Histoire du commerce du Levant au moyen âge,* I, 190–264. See also Chalandon, *Alexis Ier Comnène,* II, 625–27. Thompson, *Economic and Social History of the Middle Ages,* 380–439.

[333] The text in Miklosich and Müller, *Acta et diplomata graeca,* III, 9–13; also in J. Müller, *Documenti sulle relazioni della città Tos-*

cane coll 'Oriente cristiano e coi Turchi, 43–45, 52–54. See Heyd, *Histoire du commerce,* I, 193–94. Dölger, *Corpus der griechischen Urkunden,* II, 53–54 (no. 1255). See also A. Schaube, *Handelsgeschichte der Romanischen Völker des Mittelmeergebiets bis zum Ende der Kreuzzüge,* 247–74.

[334] "Nuova serie di documenti sulle relazioni di Genova coll 'Imperio Bizantino," ed. A. Sanguineti and G. Bertolotto, *Atti della Società ligure di storia patria,* XXVIII (1896–98), 351, 355, 360. Miklosich and Müller, *Acta et diplomata graeca,* III, 35. See Dölger, *Corpus der griechischen Urkunden,* II, 82 (no. 1488). G. Bratianu, *Recherches sur le commerce génois dans la mer Noire au XIIIe siècle,* 65–66.

with Venice, renewing the trading privileges and adding a number of new provisions. The boundaries of the Venetian quarter remained unchanged.[335] According to one writer, some clauses of this treaty exerted very great influence upon the institution of consular jurisdiction in the Ottoman Empire.[336]

Not only in the capital, but also in many provincial cities and islands of the Empire, the Venetians, Pisans, and Genoese took full advantage of their trading privileges and held quarters of their own. Thessalonica (Salonica) was, after Constantinople, the most important economic center of the Empire. There, as a source of the twelfth century testified, every year at the end of October, on the occasion of the feast of St. Demetrius, the patron of the city, a famous fair was held; and at that time Greeks and Slavs, Italians, Spaniards (Iberians) and Portuguese (Lusitanians), "Celts from beyond the Alps" (French), and men who came from the distant shores of the Atlantic, swarmed to Thessalonica and carried on their business transactions.[337] Thebes, Corinth, and Patras in Greece were famous for their silks. Hadrianople and Philippopolis, in the Balkan peninsula, were also very important commercial centers. The islands of the Aegean also took part in the industry and commerce of that time.

As the fatal year 1204 approached, the commercial importance of Byzantium was thoroughly undermined by the commercial efficiency and initiative of the Italian republics, Venice, Genoa, and Pisa. Venice occupied the first place. The monarchy lost, as the Italian historian, Cognasso, said, "its power and wealth in favor of the aristocracy, just as it is forced to lose its numerous other rights in favor of the commercial cosmopolitan class of the great cities of the Empire."[338]

EDUCATION, LEARNING, LITERATURE, AND ART

The time of the Macedonian dynasty was marked by intense cultural activity in the field of learning, literature, education, and art. The activity of such men as Photius in the ninth century, Constantine Porphyrogenitus in the tenth, and Michael Psellus in the eleventh, with their cultural environment, as well as the revival of the High School of Constantinople, which was reformed in the eleventh century, created favorable conditions for the cultural renaissance

---

[335] Concerning this *chrysobull*, see above. See also Brown, "Venetians and the Venetian Quarter," *Journal of Hellenic Studies,* XL (1920), 88.

[336] Mustafa Hamid, "Das Fremdenrecht in der Türkei," *Die Welt der Islam,* VII (1919), 26–27.

[337] *Timario* sive *De passionibus ejus.* Dialogus Satyricus, ed. M. Hase, *Notices et extraits des manuscrits de la Bibliothèque Nationale,* IX (1813), part 2, 171–74; ed. A. Ellissen, *Analecten der mittel- und neugriechischen Literatur,* IV (1), 46–53, 98 ff.

[338] "Un imperatore bizantino della decadenza Isacco II Angelo," *Bessarione,* XXXI (1915), 60; separate ed., 34.

of the epoch of the Comneni and Angeli. Enthusiasm for ancient literature was a distinctive feature of the time. Hesiod, Homer, Plato, the historians Thucydides and Polybius, the orators Isocrates and Demosthenes, the Greek tragedians and Aristophanes and other eminent representatives of various sections of ancient literature were studied and imitated by the writers of the twelfth century and the beginning of the thirteenth. This imitation was particularly evident in the language, which, in its excessive tendency towards the purity of the ancient Attic dialect, became artificial, grandiloquent, sometimes hard to read and difficult to understand, entirely different from the living spoken tongue. It was the literature of men who, as the English scholar Bury said, "were the slaves of tradition; it was a bondage to noble masters, but still it was a bondage."[339] But some writers expert in the beauty of the classic tongue nevertheless did not neglect the popular spoken language of their time and left very interesting specimens of the living tongue of the twelfth century. Writers of the epoch of the Comneni and Angeli understood the superiority of Byzantine culture over that of the western peoples, whom a source called "those dark and wandering tribes the greater part of which, if they did not receive birth from Constantinople, were at least raised and nourished by her, and among whom neither grace nor muse takes shelter," to whom pleasant singing seems "the cry of vultures or croak of crow."[340]

In the field of literature this epoch has a great number of interesting and eminent writers in both ecclesiastic and secular circles. The cultural movement also affected the family of the Comneni themselves, among whom many members, yielding to the influence of their environment, devoted a part of their time to learning and literature.[341] The highly educated and clever mother of Alexius I Comnenus, Anna Dalassena, whom her learned granddaughter Anna Comnena calls "this greatest pride not only of women but also of men, and ornament of human nature," often came to a dinner party with a book in her hands and there discussed dogmatic problems of the Church Fathers and spoke of the philosopher and martyr Maxim in particular.[342] The Emperor Alexius Comnenus himself wrote some theological treatises against heretics; Alexius' *Muses,* written a short time before his death, were published in 1913. They were written in iambic meter in the form of an "exhortation" and dedicated to his son and heir John.[343] These *Muses* were a kind of politi-

[339] Bury, *Romances of Chivalry,* 3.

[340] Nicetas Choniates, *Historia,* Bonn ed., 391, 764, 791.

[341] On this subject see the extremely interesting and instructive popular sketch by Charles Diehl, "La Société byzantine à l'époque des Comnènes," *Revue historique du sud-est européen,* VI (1929), 198–280.

[342] Anna Comnena, *Alexias,* III, 8; V, 9; ed. Reifferscheid, I, 113, 181–82.

[343] Maas, "Die Musen des Kaisers Alexios I," *Byzantinische Zeitschrift,* XXII (1913), 348–67.

cal will, concerned not only with abstract problems of morality, but also with many contemporary historical events, such as the First Crusade.

Alexius' daughter Anna and her husband Nicephorus Bryennius occupy an honorable place in Byzantine historiography. Nicephorus Bryennius, who survived Alexius and played an important role in state affairs under him and his son John, intended to write a history of Alexius Comnenus. Death prevented Nicephorus from carrying out his plan, but he succeeded in composing a sort of family chronicle or memoir the purpose of which was to show the causes of the elevation of the house of the Comneni and which was brought almost down to the accession of Alexius to the throne. The detailed narrative of Bryennius discusses the events from 1070 to 1079, that is to say, to the beginning of the rule of Nicephorus III Botaniates; since he discussed the activities of the members of the house of the Comneni, his work is marked by some partiality. The style of Bryennius is rather simple and has none of the artificial perfection that is, for example, peculiar to the style of his learned wife. The influence of Xenophon is clearly evident in his work. Bryennius' work is of great importance both for internal court history and for external policy, and throws special light on the increase of Turkish danger to Byzantium.

The gifted and highly educated wife of Bryennius, the eldest daughter of Emperor Alexius, Anna Comnena, is the authoress of the *Alexiad,* an epic poem in prose.[344] This first important achievement of the literary renaissance of the epoch of the Comneni is devoted to describing the glorious rule of Anna's father, "the Great Alexius, the luminary of the universe, the sun of Anna."[345] One of Anna's biographers remarked: "Almost as far down as the nineteenth century a woman as an historian was indeed a *rara avis.* When therefore a princess arose in one of the most momentous movements in human history she surely deserves the respectful attention of posterity."[346] In the fifteen books of her great work Anna described the time from 1069 to 1118; she drew a picture of the gradual elevation of the house of the Comneni in the period before the accession of Alexius to the throne and brought the narrative down to his death, thus making an addition to and a continuation of the work of her husband, Nicephorus Bryennius. The tendency to panegyrize her father is evident throughout the whole *Alexiad,* which endeavors to show to the reader the superiority of Alexius, this "thirteenth Apostle,"[347] over the other members of the Comneni family. Anna had received an excellent education and had read many of the most eminent writers of antiquity, Homer,

[344] Hesseling, *Byzantium,* 336; in French, 321; complete English translation by E. Dawes (1028).

[345] Anna Comnena, *Alexias,* XV, 11; ed. Reifferscheid, II, 315, 316.

[346] F. J. Foakes-Jackson, "Anna Comnena," *Hibbert Journal,* XXXIII (1934–35), 430.

[347] Anna Comnena, *Alexias,* XIV, 8; ed. Reifferscheid, II, 259.

the lyric writers, the tragedians, Aristophanes, the historians Thucydides and Polybius, the orators Isocrates and Demosthenes, the philosophers Aristotle and Plato. All this reading affected the style of the *Alexiad,* in which Anna adopted the external form of the ancient Hellenic tongue and used, as Krumbacher said, an artificial, "almost entirely mummiform school language which is diametrically opposed to the popular spoken language which was used in the literature of that time."[348] Anna even apologized to her readers when she chanced to give the barbarian names of the western or Russian (Scythian) leaders, which "deform the loftiness and subject of history."[349] Despite her unhistorical partiality for her father, Anna produced a work which is extremely important from the historical point of view, a work based not only upon her personal observation and oral reports, but also upon the documents of the state archives, diplomatic correspondence, and imperial decrees. The *Alexiad* is one of the most important sources for the First Crusade. Modern scholars acknowledge that "in spite of all defects, those memoirs of the daughter about her father remain one of the most eminent works of medieval Greek historiography,"[350] and "will always remain the noblest document" of the Greek state regenerated by Alexius Comnenus.[351]

It is not known whether Alexius' son and successor, John, who spent almost all his life in military expeditions, was in accord with the literary taste of his environment or not. But his younger brother *sebastokrator* Isaak was not only an educated man who was fond of literature but was even the author of two small works on the history of the transformation of the Homeric epic in the Middle Ages, as well as of the introduction to the so-called Constantinopolitan Code of the Octateuch in the Library of Seraglio. Some investigations suppose that the writings of the *sebastokrator* Isaac Comnenus were much more various than might be judged from two or three published short texts, and that in him there is a new writer, who arouses interest from various points of view.[352]

The Emperor Manuel, who was fond of astrology, wrote a defense "of astronomic science," that is to say, of astrology, against the attacks made upon it by

[348] Krumbacher, *Geschichte der byzantinischen Litteratur,* 277.

[349] Anna Comnena, *Alexias,* X, 8; VI, 14; ed. Reifferscheid, I, 122; II, 81.

[350] Krumbacher, *Geschichte der byzantinischen Litteratur,* 276.

[351] C. Neumann, *Geschichte Geschichtschreiber und Geschichtsquellen im zwölften Jahrhundert,* 28. For long Anna Comnena has been known chiefly by the appearance of her name in Sir Walter Scott's *Count Robert of Paris,* but she has been so transformed "by

the touch of the Wizard of the North" as to be quite unrecognizable. In one of the scenes of the novel (in chap. IV) Anna reads an extract from her history, the story of the retreat of Laodicea, which does not appear in the *Alexiad.* Foakes-Jackson, "Anna Comnena," *Hibbert Journal,* XXXIII (1934–35), 441.

[352] Th. I. Uspensky, "The Constantinopolitan Code of Seraglio," *Transactions of the Russian Archeological Institute at Constantinople,* XII (1907), 30–31.

the clergy, and in addition he was the author of various theological writings and of public imperial speeches.[353] Because of Manuel's theological studies, his panegyrist, Eustathius of Thessalonica, calls his rule an "imperial priesthood" or "a kingdom of priests" (Exodus, 19:6).[354] Manuel was not only himself interested in literature and theology but he endeavored to interest others. He sent Ptolemy's famous work, the *Almagest,* as a present to the king of Sicily and some other manuscripts were brought to Sicily from Manuel's library at Constantinople. The first Latin version of the *Almagest* was made from the manuscript at about 1160.[355] Manuel's sister-in-law Irene distinguished herself by her love for learning and by her literary talent. Her special poet and, probably, teacher, Theodore Prodromus, dedicated to her many verses, and Constantine Manasses composed his chronicle in verse in her honor, calling her in the prologue "a real friend of literature," (φιλολογωτάτη).[356] *A Dialogue Against the Jews,* which is sometimes ascribed to the period of Andronicus I, belongs to a later time.

This brief sketch shows how powerfully the imperial family of the Comneni was imbued with literary interests. But, of course, this phenomenon reflected the general rise of culture which found expression especially in the development of literature and was one of the distinctive features of the epoch of the Comneni. From the time of the Comneni and Angeli, historians and poets, theological writers as well as the writers in various fields of antiquity, and, finally, chroniclers, left works which give evidence of the literary interests of the epoch.

A historian, John Cinnamus, a contemporary of the Comneni, wrote a history of the rule of John and Manuel (1118–76) which was a continuation of Anna Comnena's work. This history followed the examples of Herodotus and Xenophon, and was also influenced by Procopius. The central figure of the evidently unfinished history is Manuel; it is therefore somewhat eulogistic. Cinnamus was an earnest defender of the rights of the eastern Roman imperial power and a convinced antagonist of the papal claims and of the imperial power of the German kings. He chose as his hero Manuel, who had treated him with favor; nevertheless he gave a trustworthy account based upon the study of reliable sources and written in very good Greek, "in the style of

[353] Cinnamus, *Historia,* Bonn ed., 290. Nicetas Choniates, *De Manuele,* VII, 5; Bonn ed., 274–75. Manuel's defense of astrology is written in the form of a letter to a monk who had "disparaged astronomic science and called its study impiety," and is published in the *Catalogus codicum astrologorum,* V (1), 108–25.

[354] *Fontes rerum byzantinarum,* I (1), 6; see also vii.

[355] See C. H. Haskins, "The Spread of Ideas in the Middle Ages," *Speculum,* I (1926), 24. Haskins, *Studies in Medieval Science,* 143, 161. Haskins, *The Renaissance of the Twelfth Century,* 292.

[356] *Compendium chronicum,* Bonn ed., 3, v. 3.

an honest soldier, full of natural and frank enthusiasm for the Emperor."[357]

Michael and Nicetas Acominati, two brothers from the Phrygian city of Chonae (in Asia Minor), were prominent figures in the literature of the twelfth and the early thirteenth centuries. They are sometimes also surnamed Choniatae after their native city. The elder brother, Michael, who had received an excellent classical education in Constantinople with Eustathius, bishop of Thessalonica, chose a religious career and for more than thirty years was archbishop of Athens.[358] An enthusiastic admirer of Hellenic antiquity, he had his residence in the episcopal building on the Acropolis where in the Middle Ages the cathedral of the Holy Virgin was located within the ancient Parthenon. Michael felt particularly fortunate to be situated on the Acropolis, where he seemed to reach the "peak of heaven." His cathedral was to him a constant source of delight and enthusiasm. He looked upon the city and its population as if he were a contemporary of Plato, and he was therefore thoroughly amazed to see the enormous chasm that separated the contemporary population of Athens from the ancient Hellenes. Michael was an idealist and at first was not able to appreciate properly the completed process of ethnographic change in Greece. His idealism clashed with dull reality. He could say: "I live in Athens, but I see Athens nowhere."

His brilliant inaugural oration delivered before the Athenians assembled in the Parthenon was, he himself asserted, a specimen of simplicity of style. In this speech he reminded the audience of the bygone greatness of the city, the mother of eloquence and wisdom, expressed his firm conviction in the continuous genealogy of the Athenians from ancient times to his day, urged the Athenians to keep to the noble customs and manners of their ancestors, and cited the examples of Aristides, Ajax, Diogenes, Pericles, Themistocles and others.[359] But this oration, in reality constructed in an elevated style, filled with antique and biblical quotations, embellished with metaphors and tropes, remained incomprehensible and dark to the hearers of the new metropolitan; it was beyond the understanding of the Athenians of the twelfth century, and Michael felt it. In one of his later sermons he exclaimed with deep sorrow: "Oh, city of Athens! Mother of wisdom! To what ignorance thou hast sunk! . . . When I addressed you with my inaugural oration, which was very simple and natural, it seemed that I spoke of something inconceivable, in a foreign

[357] Neumann, *Geschichte Geschichtschreiber und Geschichtsquellen*, 99; Krumbacher, *Geschichte der byzantinischen Litteratur*, 280.

[358] The most important monograph by Georg Stadtmüller, "Michael Choniates Metropolit von Athen (ca. 1138–ca. 1222)," *Orientalia Christiana*, XXXIII, 2 (1934), 125–325. Ida Carleton Thallon, *A Medieval Humanist:*

Michael Akominatos, 273–314. Very good study based on Michael's correspondence. Another valuable study by Kenneth M. Setton, "Athens in the Later Twelfth Century," *Speculum*, XIX (1944), 179–207.

[359] Michael Acominatus, ed. Lampros, I, 93–106.

language, Persian or Scythian."[360] The learned Michael Acominatus soon ceased to see in the contemporary Athenians the immediate descendants of the ancient Hellenes. He wrote: "There has been preserved the very charm of the country, the Hymettos rich in honey; the still Peiraeus, the once mysterious Eleusis, the Marathonian plain, the Acropolis,—but the generation which loved science has disappeared, and their place has been taken by a generation ignorant and poor in mind and body."[361] Surrounded by barbarians, Michael feared he himself would grow uncultivated and barbarous; he deplored the corruption of the Greek language, which had become a sort of barbarian dialect and which he was able to understand only after a residence of three years in Athens.[362] It is probable that his jeremiads were not without exaggeration; but he was not far from the truth when he wrote that Athens had been a glorious city but was no longer alive. The very name of Athens would have perished from the memory of men had not its continued existence been secured by the valiant deeds of the past and by famous landmarks, the Acropolis, the Areopagus, Hymettus, and Piraeus, which like some unalterable work of nature were beyond the envy and destruction of time.[363] Michael remained at Athens until the beginning of the thirteenth century. After the conquest of the city by the Franks in 1204 he was forced to give up his seat to a Latin bishop, and he spent the rest of his life in the small island of Ceos, off the shores of Attica, where he died and was buried about 1220 or 1222.

Michael Acominatus left a rich literary inheritance in the form of sermons and speeches on various subjects, as well as a great number of letters and some poetry, which give very valuable information on the political, social, and literary conditions of his time. Among his poems the first place belongs to an iambic elegy in honor of the city of Athens, "the first and also the only lamentation of the ruin of the ancient glorious city that has come down to us."[364] Gregorovius called Michael Acominatus a ray of sunlight which flashed in the darkness of medieval Athens, "the last great citizen and the last glory of that city of the sage."[365] Another writer said: "Alien by birth, he so identified himself with his adopted home that we may call him the last of the great Athenians worthy to stand beside those noble figures whose example he so glowingly presented to the people of his flock."[366]

In the barbarism which surrounded Athens and of which Michael wrote, as well as in the corruption of the Greek language, one may see some traces of Slavonic influence. Moreover, some scholars, for example Th. Uspensky, judge it possible, on the basis of Michael's works, to affirm the existence in the twelfth

[360] *Ibid.*, 124.
[361] *Ibid.*, II, 12.
[362] *Ibid.*, 44.
[363] *Ibid.*, I, 316. See Setton, "Athens in the Later Twelfth Century," *Speculum*, XIX

(1944), 207.
[364] Gregorovius, *Geschichte der Stadt Athen im Mittelalter*, I, 243.
[365] *Ibid.*, I, 204.
[366] Thallon, *A Medieval Humanist*, 314.

century around Athens of the important phenomenon of Slavonic community and free peasant landownership.[367] I cannot agree with this statement.

The younger brother of Michael, Nicetas Acominatus or Choniates, holds the most important place among the historians of the twelfth and the beginning of the thirteenth century. Born about the middle of the twelfth century in the Phrygian city of Chonae, Nicetas, like his brother, had been sent in his childhood to Constantinople, where he studied under the guidance of his elder brother Michael. While the latter devoted himself to a spiritual career, Nicetas chose the secular career of an official; beginning, apparently, with the last years of the rule of Manuel, and rising to especial importance under the Angeli, he was attached to the court, and reached the highest degrees. Forced to flee from the capital after its sack by the crusaders in 1204, he sought refuge at the court of the Nicean emperor, Theodore Lascaris, who treated him with consideration, restored to him all his lost honors and distinctions, and enabled him to devote the last years of his life to his favorite literary work and to bring to an end his great history. Nicetas died at Nicaea soon after 1210. Michael outlived Nicetas and wrote at his death an emotional funeral oration which is very important from the point of view of Nicetas' biography.

His chief literary achievement is the great historical work in twenty books comprising the events from the time of John Comnenus' accession to the throne to the first years of the Latin Empire (1118–1206). Nicetas' work is a priceless source for the time of Manuel, the interesting rule of Andronicus, the epoch of the Angeli, the Fourth Crusade, and the taking of Constantinople by the crusaders in 1204. The beginning of his history, which treats of the time of John Comnenus, is very brief. The work breaks off with a minor event and accordingly fails to represent a complete whole; perhaps, as Th. Uspensky supposed, it has not yet been published in its complete form.[368] For his history Nicetas acknowledged only two sources: narratives of eyewitnesses and personal observation. The opinions of scholars vary as to whether Nicetas used John Cinnamus as his source.[369] The history of Nicetas is written in an inflated, eloquent, and picturesque style; revealing profound knowledge both of ancient literature and of theology. However, the author himself held quite a different opinion of his style; in the introduction he wrote: "I did not care for a bombastic narrative, stuffed with ununderstandable words and elevated expressions, although many esteem it highly. . . . As I have already said, artificial and ununderstandable style is most repugnant to history, which, on the contrary, greatly prefers a simple, natural, and plain narrative."[370]

---

[367] "On the History of the Peasant Landownership in Byzantium," *Journal of the Ministry of Public Instruction*, CCXXV (1883), 85–86.

[368] *A Byzantine Writer Nicetas Acominatus of Chonae*, 128.

[369] *Ibid.*, 153–60. Krumbacher, *Geschichte der byzantinischen Litteratur*, 283.

[370] Nicetas Choniates, *Historia*, Bonn ed., 6.

In spite of some partiality in the exposition of the events of one reign or the other, Nicetas, who was firmly convinced of the full cultural superiority of "the Roman" over the western "barbarian," deserves as a historian great trust and deep attention. In his special monograph on Nicetas Choniates, Th. Uspensky wrote: "Nicetas is worthy of study if only for the reason that, in his history, he treats of the most important epoch of the Middle Ages, when the hostile relations between west and east reached their highest point of strain and burst out in the Crusades and in the founding of the Latin Empire in Tsargrad (Constantinople). His opinions of the western crusaders and the mutual relations between west and east are distinguished by a deep truth and ingenuous historical sense that we do not find in the best works of western medieval literature."[371]

Besides the *History,* to Nicetas Choniates belong perhaps a small treatise upon the statutes destroyed by the Latins in Constantinople in 1204; some rhetorical writings, formal eulogies in honor of various emperors; and a theological treatise which has not yet been published in full, *The Treasure of Orthodoxy* (Θησαυρὸς ὀρθοδοξίας); this work, a continuation of the *Panoply* of Euthymius Zigabenus, was written after study of numerous writers and has as its object the refutation of a great number of heretical errors.

Among the celebrated figures of the twelfth century in the field of general culture belongs also the talented teacher and friend of Michael Acominatus, the archbishop of Thessalonica, Eustathius, "the most brilliant luminary of the Byzantine world of learning since Michael Psellus."[372] He received his education in Constantinople, became deacon of the church of St. Sophia, and was a teacher of rhetoric. He wrote most of his works there, but his historical writings and various occasional compositions he wrote later at Thessalonica. Eustathius' house in Constantinople was a sort of school for young students; it became a center around which the best minds of the capital and youths anxious to learn collected.[373] As religious head of Thessalonica, the city next in importance to the capital, Eustathius devoted much of his energy to raising the spiritual and moral standard of contemporary monastic conditions, which sometimes created enemies against him among the monks.[374] From a cultural point of view his repeated appeals to the monks not to squander the treasures of the libraries are very interesting; he wrote: "Woe to me! Why will you, O dunces, liken a monastic library to your souls? As you do not possess any knowledge, you are willing to deprive the library also of its scientific means?

[371] *A Byzantine Writer,* v.

[372] Gregorovius, *Geschichte der Stadt Athen,* I, 205, 207.

[373] See the excellent article on Eustathius by Cohn in *Real-Encyclopädie der Classischen Altertumswissenschaft,* ed. A. F. Pauly, G.

Wissowa and others, VI, 1454.

[374] See Oeconomos, *La Vie religieuse dans l'empire byzantin,* 153–65 (on the basis of Eustathius' work, *De emendanda vita monachica,* ed. Migne, *Patrologia Graeca,* CXXXV, 729–910).

Let it preserve its treasures. After you there will come either a man of learning or an admirer of science, and the first, by spending a certain time in the libraries, will grow more clever than he was before; the other, ashamed of his complete ignorance, will, by reading books, find that which he desires."[375] Eustathius died between 1192 and 1194. His pupil and friend, the metropolitan of Athens, Michael Acominatus, honored his memory with a moving funeral oration.

A thoughtful observer of the political life of his epoch, an educated theologian who boldly acknowledged the corruption of monastic life, as well as a profound scholar whose knowledge in ancient literature secured him an honorable place not only in the history of Byzantine civilization but also in the history of classical philology, Eustathius is undoubtedly a prominent personality in the cultural life of Byzantium in the twelfth century. His literary legacy may be divided into two groups: in the first group are his vast and accurate commentaries on the Iliad and Odyssey, on Pindarus, and some others; to the second group belong the works written at Thessalonica: a history of the conquest of Thessalonica by the Normans in 1185; his very important correspondence; the famous treatise on the reforms of monastic life; an oration on the occasion of the death of the Emperor Manuel, and other writings. Eustathius' works have not yet been adequately used for the study of the political and cultural history of Byzantium.[376]

At the close of the eleventh century and at the beginning of the twelfth there lived a very prominent theologian, Theophylact, archbishop of Achrida (Ochrida) in Bulgaria. He was born on the island of Euboea and for some time officiated as a deacon in St. Sophia in Constantinople. He received a very good education under the famous Michael Psellus. Then, probably under Alexius I Comnenus, he was appointed to the archbishopric of Achrida in Bulgaria, which at that time was under Byzantine power. Under the severe and barbarous living conditions in this country he was unable to forget his former life in Constantinople, and with all the force of his soul he wished to return to the capital. This wish was not fulfilled. He died in Bulgaria at the beginning of the twelfth century (about 1108, though the exact date is unknown). He was the author of some theological works, and his commentaries on the books of the Old and New Testament are particularly well known. But from the modern point of view his most important literary legacies are his letters and his book *On the Errors of the Latins.* Almost all his letters were written between 1091 and 1108,[377] and they draw an exceedingly interesting

---

[375] Migne, *Patrologia Graeca,* CXXXV, 836.

[376] See Krumbacher, *Geschichte der byzantinischen Litteratur,* 536–41. Regel, *Fontes rerum byzantinarum,* I (1), xi–xvii. On Eustathius' literary activity see an interesting ar-

ticle in modern Greek, P. Koukoulès, "Λαογραφικαὶ εἰδήσεις παρὰ τῷ θεσσαλονίκης Εὐσταθίω," Ἐπετηρὶς Ἑταιρείας Βυζαντινῶν Σπουδῶν, I (1924), 5–40.

[377] See Vasilievsky's discussion of Theophy-

picture of provincial Byzantine life. They deserve particular attention, and they have not yet been thoroughly studied from the point of view of the internal history of the Empire. His book *On the Errors of the Latins,* was remarkable in its conciliatory tendencies towards the Catholic church.[378]

Michael of Thessalonica lived and wrote during the reign of Manuel. He began his career as deacon and professor of exegesis of the gospels at St. Sophia in Constantinople, then received the honorable title of master of rhetors, and was finally condemned as a follower of the heresy of Soterichus Panteugenus and deprived of his titles.[379] He composed some orations in honor of Manuel, five of which were published; the last one was delivered as a funeral oration a few days after the Emperor's death.[380] Michael's orations give some interesting details of the historical events of the time; the last two orations have not yet been used by any scholar.

In the middle of the twelfth century one of the numerous Byzantine imitations of Lucian's *Dialogues among the Dead, Timarion* was written. Usually, this work is considered as anonymous, but perhaps Timarion was the real name of the author.[381] Timarion narrates the story of his journey to Hades and reproduces his conversations with the dead men whom he met in the underworld. He saw there Emperor Romanus Diogenes, John Italus, Michael Psellus, the iconoclastic emperor, Theophilus, and so on. *Timarion,* without doubt the best Byzantine achievement in the literary field of Lucian's imitations, is full of vigor and humor. But apart from purely literary quality, *Timarion* is important for such descriptions of real life as the famous description of the fair of Thessalonica. Therefore, this piece of work of the Comnenian epoch is a very interesting source for the internal history of Byzantium.[382]

lact of Bulgaria and his works in his essay, "Byzantium and the Patzinaks," *Works,* I, 138. Chalandon, *Alexis Ier Comnène,* I, xxvii (based on Vasilievsky). See also Leib, *Rome, Kiev et Byzance,* 42.

[378] The best piece of work on Theophylact of Bulgaria or of Achrida is Vasilievsky, *Works,* 134–49. Chalandon, *Alexis Ier Comnène,* follows him. See Leib, *Rome, Kiev et Byzance,* 41–50. Krumbacher, *Geschichte der byzantinischen Litteratur,* 133–35, 463–65 (the chronology is incorrect). A. Leroy-Molinghen, "Prolégomènes à une édition critique des lettres de Théophylacte de Bulgarie," *Byzantion,* XIII (1938), 253–62. See S. G. Mercati, "Poesie di Teofilatto de Bulgaria," *Studi Bizantini e neoellenici,* I (1924), 173–94. In 1931 the *Letters of Theophylact of Ochrida* were translated into Bulgarian by the Metropolitan Simeon, of Varna and Preslava, *Sbornik of*

the Bulgarian Academy of Sciences, XXVII (1931); vii–xxxii, for Theophylact's biography.

[379] See Krumbacher, *Geschichte der byzantinischen Litteratur,* 473. Regel, *Fontes rerum byzantinarum,* I (1), xvii. Chalandon, II, xlviii. V. Laurent, "Michel de Thessalonica," *Dictionnaire de théologie et liturgie catholique,* X (2), 1719–20.

[380] Regel, *Fontes rerum byzantinarum,* I (1), 132–82 (three first orations); I (2), 183–228 (the fourth and fifth orations published in 1917).

[381] See J. Dräseke, "Byzantinische Hadesfahrten," *Neue Jahrbücher für das klassische Altertum,* XXIX (1912), 353.

[382] See Krumbacher, *Geschichte der byzantinischen Litteratur,* 467–68. Montelatici, *Storia della letteratura bizantina,* 258–59. H. Tozer, "Byzantine Satire," *Journal of Hellenic*

Another contemporary of the Comneni, John Tzetzes, who died probably at the close of the twelfth century, is of considerable importance from the literary, historical, and cultural point of view, as well as from the point of view of classical antiquity. He received a good philological education in the capital and for some time was a teacher of grammar. Then he devoted himself to literary activity by which he had to earn his living. In his writings John Tzetzes missed no opportunity to speak of the circumstances of his life; he depicted a man of the twelfth century living by literary work who constantly complained of poverty and misery, served the rich and noble, dedicated his writing to them, and often manifested his indignation at the too small recognition of his services. One day he fell into such want that of all his books none was left him but Plutarch. Lacking money, he sometimes lacked necessary books and, relying too much upon his memory, made in his writings a great number of elementary historical errors. In one of his works he wrote, "For me my head is my library; with our complete lack of money we have no books. Therefore I cannot name exactly the writer."[383] In another work he wrote of his memory: "God has shown in life no one man, either formerly or now, who possesses a better memory than Tzetzes."[384] The acquaintance of Tzetzes with ancient and Byzantine writers was indeed very considerable; he was familiar with many poets, dramatists, historians, orators, philosophers, geographers, and literary men, especially Lucian. Tzetzes' works are written in rhetorical style stuffed with mythological and historical references and quotations, are full of self-praise, difficult and rather uninteresting to read. Among his numerous writings is the collection of his 107 letters, which in spite of their literary defects, is of some importance both for the biography of the author and for the biography of the persons addressed. *A Book of Stories* (Βίβλος ἱστοριῶν) written in so-called political, or popular meter,[385] a poetical work of historical and philological character, consists of more than 12,000 lines. Since the time of its first editor, who divided the work, for convenience of quotation, into the first thousand lines, the second, and so on, it is usually called *"Chiliads"* (Thousands). *The Histories* or *Chiliads* of John Tzetzes were described by Krumbacher as, "nothing but a huge commentary in verse on his own letters which, letter after letter, are interpreted in them.

Studies, II (1881), 241–57. Dräseke, "Byzantinische Hadesfahrten," *Neue Jahrbücher*, XXIX (1912), 343–66. An excellent introduction to this work and an interpretation of it is given by M. Hase in *Notices et extraits des manuscrits*, IX (2), 125–268. Charles Diehl, "La Légende de l'empereur Théophile," *Annales de l'Institut Kondakov*, IV (1931), 33–37.

[383] *Argumentum et allegoriae in Iliadem*, XV, 87–89; ed. Matranga, *Anecdota Graeca*, I, 120.

[384] *Chiliades*, I, vss. 277–78; ed. Kiessling, 12.

[385] The chief peculiarity of political verses is the complete disappearance of long and short syllables and the continuous repetition of verses absolutely identical as far as the number of syllables in every verse is concerned.

The relation between his letters and *Chiliads* are so close that the one may be considered as a detailed index to the other."[386] This reason alone deprives *Chiliads* of any great literary significance. Another scholar, V. Vasilievsky, severely remarked "that *Chiliads* are from a literary standpoint complete nonsense, but that sometimes they really explain what remained dark in prose,"[387] that is, in Tzetzes' letters. Another large work by John Tzetzes is *Allegories to the Iliad and Odyssey,* written also in political verse; it is dedicated to the wife of the Emperor Manuel, the German princess Bertha-Irene, who was called by the author the "most Homeric of queens" (ὁμηρικωτάτη),[388] i.e., the greatest admirer of "all-wise Homer, sea of words," "a bright moon of full moon, the light-bringer who appears washed not by the waves of ocean, but by the light-bringer [sun] itself who in its splendor appears from its purple bed."[389] Tzetzes' aim was, by giving the contents of the poems of Homer, one after another, to expound them, especially from the point of view of allegorical interpretation of the world of gods represented by Homer. In the beginning of his *Allegories* Tzetzes said conceitedly, "Thus, I am starting my task, and striking Homer with the staff of my word, I shall make him accessible to all, and his unseen depths will appear before everyone."[390] This work, declared Vasilievsky, also lacks "not only good taste, but also sound sense."[391] Besides these works John Tzetzes left some other writings on Homer, Hesiod, scholia (critical or explanatory marginal notes) to Hesiod, Aristophanes, some poetry, and some others. Not all of the works of John Tzetzes have been published, and some of them seem to have been lost.

In view of these comments, one might question whether John Tzetzes has any importance as a cultural force in the twelfth century. But taking into consideration his extraordinary zeal and assiduity for collecting material, his writings are a rich source of important antiquarian notes of considerable significance for classical literature. Moreover, the method of the author's work and his vast acquaintance with classical literature makes possible some conclusions upon the character of the literary "renaissance" of the epoch of the Comneni.

His elder brother, who worked on philology and metric, Isaac Tzetzes hardly needs to be mentioned, but in philological literature "the brothers

---

[386] Krumbacher, *Geschichte der byzantinischen Litteratur,* 528. Montelatici, *Storia della letteratura bizantina,* 261.

[387] "An Unpublished Funeral Oration of Basil of Ochrida," *Vizantiysky Vremennik,* I (1894), 92.

[388] Longinus, neo-Platonist, philologist and rhetorician of the third century A.D. names Herodotus ὁμηρικώτατος. See J. B. Bury, *The Ancient Greek Historians,* 42, n. 1.

[389] Johannis Tzetzis, *Allegoriae,* prooemium, vss. 1–4, 28; ed. Matranga, *Anecdota Graeca,* I, 1, 2.

[390] *Ibid.,* vss. 32–34; ed. Matranga, *ibid.,* I 2.

[391] "An Unpublished Funeral Oration of Basil of Ochrida," *Vizantiysky Vremennik,* I, 91.

Tzetzae" were often spoken of as if both brothers were of equal importance. In reality Isaac Tzetzes did not distinguish himself in anything, and it would therefore be more accurate to give up referring to "the brothers Tzetzae."

A very interesting and typical personality of the epoch of the first three Comneni, especially of John and Manuel, is the very learned poet, Theodore Prodromus, or Ptochoprodromus (the poor Prodromus), as he sometimes named himself in order to arouse pity, in a rather false spirit of humility. Various works of Prodromus afford much material for study to philologist and philosopher, theologian and historian. Although the published works ascribed with more or less reason to Prodromus are very numerous, nevertheless there is preserved among the manuscripts of different libraries in the West and East not a little material which has not yet been published. At the present time the personality of Prodromus evokes among scholars great divergences of judgment, for it is not clear to whom actually belong the numerous writings ascribed in manuscripts to Prodromus. One group of scholars recognize two writers with the name of Prodromus, another group three, and still a third group only one.[392] The problem has not yet been solved, and probably a solution will be possible only when the whole literary inheritance connected with the name of Prodromus has been published.

The best period of Prodromus' activity was the first half of the twelfth century. His uncle, under the monastic name of John, was a metropolitan of Kiev (John II), in Russia, and a Russian chronicle states under the year 1089 that he was "a man skillful in books and learning, clement to the poor and widows."[393] In all probability, Prodromus died about 1150.

Prodromus belonged, said Diehl, to a degenerate class in Constantinople, the "literary proletariat consisting of intelligent, cultivated, even distinguished men whom life, by its rigors, had peculiarly abased, not counting vice which in connection with misery had sometimes led them strangely astray and misdirected them."[394] Acquainted with court circles and in contact with the imperial family and high and powerful officials, the miserable writers strove with difficulty to obtain protectors whose generosity might render them secure. The whole life of Prodromus passed in search of protectors, in continuous complaints of poverty and sickness, or old age, and in supplications for support. For this purpose he spared no flattery or humiliation, regardless of whom he had to ask for support and whom he had to flatter. But Prodromus must be given credit for remaining almost always faithful to one person, even in his

---

[392] See S. Papadimitriu, *Theodore Prodromus,* xix–xxi and 1 ff. Krumbacher, *Geschichte der byzantinischen Litteratur,* 760.

Montelatici, *Storia della letteratura bizantina,* 197.

[393] *The Laurentian and Ipatian Chronicles.*

[394] Diehl, *Figures byzantines,* II, 140.

disgrace and misfortune; this person was the sister-in-law of Manuel, Irene. The situation of men of letters like Prodromus was at times very hard; for example, in one piece in verse, which was formerly ascribed to Prodromus, the author expressed regret that he was not a shoemaker or tailor, a dyer or baker, for they have something to eat; but the author received irony from the first man he meets: "Eat thy writings and feed upon them, my dear! Chew greedily thy writings! Take off thy ecclesiastic garments, and become a worker!"[395]

A great many writings of very different character have been preserved under the name of Prodromus. Prodromus was a novelist, a hagiographer, and orator, the author of letters and of an astrological poem, of religious poems and philosophical works, of satires and humorous pieces. Many of them are occasional compositions commemorating victories, birth, death, marriage, and the like, and they are very valuable for their allusions to personalities and events as well as for information concerning the life of the lower classes in the capital. Prodromus has often incurred severe censure from scholars who emphasize his "pitiful poverty of themes" and the "disgusting external form of his poetical exercises,"[396] and say that "poetry can not be required from authors who write to get bread."[397] But this adverse judgment may be explained by the fact that for a long time Prodromus was judged by his weakest, though unfortunately best known, writings; for example, by his long bombastic novel in verse, *Rhodanphe and Dosicles,* which some scholars call desperately dull and a real trial to read.[398] This opinion can hardly be regarded as the final word. A survey of his work as a whole, including his prose essays, satiric dialogues, libels and epigrams in which he followed the best examples of antiquity, especially Lucian, calls for a revision in his favor of the general judgment of his literary activity. In these writings are keen and amusing observations of contemporary reality which undoubtedly make them interesting for social history in general and literary history in particular. Prodromus is noteworthy also for one very important contribution. In some of his writings, especially humorous works, he gave up the artificial classic language and had recourse to the spoken Greek of the twelfth century, of which he left very interesting specimens. Great credit is due him for this. The best Byzantine scholars today accordingly acknowledge that in spite of all his defects Prodromus without doubt belongs among the remarkable phenomena of Byzantine litera-

---

[395] E. Miller, *Mélanges de philologie et d'épigraphie,* I, 142; in French, 143. Legrand, *Bibliothèque grecque vulgaire,* I, 106, vss. 140–42. *Poèmes prodromiques en grec vulgaire,* ed. D. Hesseling and H. Pernot, 79, vss. 137–39.

[396] Vasilievsky, "Lives of Meletius the Younger by Nicolaus Bishop of Methone and of Theodore Prodromus," *Pravoslavny Palestinsky Sbornik,* XVII (1886), v.

[397] D. Hesseling, *Byzantium,* 344; in French, 328.

[398] Krumbacher, *Geschichte der byzantinischen Litteratur,* 751.

ture, and is, "as few Byzantines are, a distinctly pronounced cultural and historical figure."[399]

Under the Comneni and Angeli lived also a humanist, Constantine Stilbes, of whom very little is known. He received a very good education, was a teacher at Constantinople, and later received the title of master of literature. Thirty-five pieces, almost all of them in verse, composed by Stilbes, are known, but are not yet published.[400] The best known of his poems is that on the great fire that occurred in Constantinople on July 25, 1197; it was the first mention of this fact. This poem consists of 938 verses and gives much information on the topography, structures, and customs of the capital of the Eastern Empire. In another poem, Stilbes described another fire in Constantinople in the following year, 1198. The literary legacy of Stilbes, preserved in many European libraries, and his personality certainly deserve further investigation.[401]

In the epoch of the Comneni, the dull Byzantine chronicle has also several representatives who began their narrative with the creation of the world. George Cedrenus, who lived under Alexius Comnenus, brought his history down to the beginning of the rule of Isaac Comnenus, in 1057; his narration of the period from 811 on is almost identical with the text of the chronicler of the second half of the eleventh century, John Scylitzes, whose Greek original has not yet been published. John Zonaras wrote in the twelfth century not the usual dry chronicle but "a manual of world history evidently intended for higher requirements,"[402] which rested upon reliable sources; he brought his history down to the accession to the throne of John Comnenus in 1118. The chronicle of Constantine Manasses, written in the first half of the twelfth century in political verses, and dedicated to the enlightened sister-in-law of Manuel, Irene, carries the history down to the ascension to the throne of Alexius Comnenus in 1081. Some years ago a continuation of Manasses' Chronicle was published. It contains seventy-nine verses, covering briefly the time from John Comnenus to the first Latin Emperor in Constantinople, Baldwin; almost half deals with Andronicus I.[403] Manasses also wrote an

[399] *Ibid.*, 750–51. See also Montelatici, *Storia della letteratura bizantina*, 199–200. We must remember that several writings bearing the name of Prodromus did not belong to him personally, but were produced by his literary associates.

[400] See C. Loparev, "On the Byzantine Humanist Constantine Stilbes (of the Twelfth Century) and On his Works," *Vizantiyskoe Obozrenie*, III (1917), 62–64.

[401] The best information on Stilbes is in Loparev, *ibid.* Cf. Krumbacher, *Geschichte der byzantinischen Litteratur*, 762. Apparently Loparev was not familiar with the study of S. Lampros, "Ὁ Μαρκιανὸς Κῶδιξ," Νέος Ἑλληνομνήμων, VIII (1911), 524, where the poem on the fire of July 25, 1197 was published.

[402] Krumbacher, *Geschichte der byzantinischen Litteratur*, 371.

[403] H. Grégoire, "Un Continateur de Constantin Manassès et sa source," *Mélanges offerts à M. Gustave Schlumberger*, I, 272–81. The source of Manasses' Continuator was Nicetas Choniates, *Historia*, Bonn ed., 280.

iambic poem probably entitled Ὁδοιπορικόν (*Itinerarium*), dealing with contemporary events, which was published in 1904.[404] Finally, Michael Glycas wrote in the twelfth century a world chronicle of events down to the death of Alexius Comnenus in 1118.

As far as Byzantine art is concerned, the epoch of the Comneni and Angeli was the continuation of the second Golden Age, the beginning of which many scholars ascribe to the middle of the ninth century, i.e., from the accession of the Macedonian dynasty. Of course, the troubled period in the eleventh century, just before the accession of the Comnenian Dynasty, interrupted for a short time the splendor of artistic achievements under the Macedonian Emperors. But with the new dynasty of the Comneni, the Empire regained some of its former glory and prosperity, and Byzantine art seemed able to continue the brilliant tradition of the Macedonian epoch. But a kind of formalism and immobility may be marked under the Comneni. "In the eleventh century we already mark a decline in the feeling for the antique; natural freedom gives place to formalism; the theological intention becomes more obviously the end for which the work is undertaken. The elaborate iconographical system belongs to this period."[405] In another book Dalton said, "The springs of progress dried up; there was no longer any power of organic growth. . . . As the Comnenian period advanced, sacred art became itself a kind of ritual, memorized and performed with an almost unconscious direction of the faculties. It no longer had fire or fervor; it moved insensibly towards formalism."[406]

But this does not mean that Byzantine art under the Comneni was in a state of decay. Especially in the field of architecture there were many remarkable monuments. At Constantinople the beautiful palace of Blachernae was erected, and the Comneni left the former imperial residence, the so-called Great Palace, and settled in a new palace, at the end of the Golden Horn. The new imperial residence was in no way inferior to the Great Palace, and contemporary writers have left enthusiastic descriptions of it.[407] The abandoned Great Palace fell into decay. In the fifteenth century it was only a ruin and the Turks completed its destruction.

The name of the Comneni is also connected with the construction or recon-

[404] K. Horna, "Das Hodoiporikon des Konstantin Manasses," *Byzantinische Zeitschrift*, XIII (1904), 313–55. See the list of Manasses' editions which have not been included in Krumbacher's *Geschichte*, in P. Maas, "Rhytmisches zu der Kunstprosa des Konstantinos Manasses," *Byzantinische Zeitschrift*, XI (1902), 505, n. 2.

[405] O. M. Dalton, *Byzantine Art and Archaeology*, 18.

[406] Dalton, *East Christian Art*, 18–19.

[407] See Diehl, *Manuel d'art byzantin*, I, 416–18. J. Ebersolt, *Les Arts somptuaires de Byzance*, 16. There is a special monograph on the Palace of Blachernae written in modern Greek by J. Pappadopoulos, and a French translation.

struction of several churches; for example, the Pantocrator at Constantinople, which became the burial place of John II and Manuel I Comneni and in which later on, in the fifteenth century, were to be buried the Emperors Manuel II and John VIII Palaeologi. The famous church of Chora (Qahrieh jami) was reconstructed at the beginning of the twelfth century. Churches were being built not only in the capital, but also in the provinces.[408] In the West, at Venice, the cathedral of St. Mark, reproducing in plan the Church of the Apostles at Constantinople and reflecting in its mosaics Byzantine influence, was solemnly consecrated in 1095. In Sicily, many buildings and mosaics of Cefalù, Palermo, and Monreale, reproducing the best achievements of Byzantine art, belong to the twelfth century. In the East, the mosaics in the Church of the Nativity at Bethlehem are important remains of an elaborate decoration executed by east Christian mosaicists for Emperor Manuel Comnenus in 1169.[409] Thus, in the East as in the West, "the influence of Greek art remained all powerful in the twelfth century, and even where it might be least expected, among the Normans of Sicily and the Latins of Syria, Byzantium continued to initiate and to lead in elegance."[410]

Very important frescoes of the eleventh and twelfth centuries have been discovered in Cappadocia and southern Italy; also in Russia, at Kiev, Chernigov, Novgorod and in its neighborhood, some beautiful frescoes were made by Byzantine artists at the same time. Many artistic specimens of the epoch are to be found in ivory carvings, pottery and glass, metal work, seals, and engraved gems.[411]

But, in spite of all artistic achievements of the epoch of the Comneni and Angeli, the first period of the second Golden Age contemporary with the Macedonian dynasty was more brilliant and more creative. Therefore, one cannot agree with the statement by a French writer: "In the twelfth century the political and military fortune of Byzantium is shaken never to rise again. Nevertheless, the creative power of the Empire and of the Christian Orient reaches, in that epoch, its apogee."[412]

The Byzantine renaissance of the twelfth century is interesting and important not only by itself and for itself; it was an essential part of the general west European renaissance of the twelfth century which has been so well described and expounded by C. H. Haskins in *The Renaissance of the Twelfth Century*. In the first two lines of his preface he said, "The title of this book will appear to many to contain a flagrant contradiction. A renaissance in the twelfth cen-

[408] Diehl, *Manuel d'art byzantin,* I, 463 ff.
[409] See Dalton, *East Christian Art,* 292–93. Diehl, *Manuel d'art byzantin,* II, 561–63. Vincent and Abel, *Bethléem,* 167.
[410] Diehl, *Manuel d'art byzantin,* II, 563 ff.
[411] Detailed information can be found in the two works of Dalton already mentioned, and in the *Manuel d'art* by Diehl.
[412] G. Duthuit, *Byzance et l'art du XIIe siècle,* 96. In spite of its title, this booklet gives very little on the art of the twelfth century.

tury!" There is no contradiction at all. In the twelfth century western Europe witnessed the revival of the Latin classics, of the Latin language, of Latin prose and of Latin verse, of jurisprudence and philosophy, of historical writings; it was the epoch of the translations from Greek and Arabic and of the beginning of the universities. And Haskins was absolutely right when he said, "It is not always sufficiently realized that there was also a notable amount of direct contact with Greek sources, both in Italy and in the east, and that translations made directly from Greek originals were an important, as well as a more direct and faithful, vehicle for the transmission of ancient learning." [413] In the twelfth century direct intercourse between Italy and Byzantium, especially Constantinople, was more frequent and extensive than might be expected at first sight. In connection with the religious plans of the Comneni to draw nearer to Rome, many disputations were held at Constantinople, very often before the emperors, with the participation of the learned members of the Catholic Church who had come to the Byzantine capital for the purpose of a reconciliation between the two churches. These discussions greatly contributed to the transmission of Greek learning to the West. Moreover the trade relations of the Italian commercial republics with Byzantium, and the Venetian and Pisan quarters at Constantinople brought into residence there a number of Italian scholars who learned Greek and transmitted a certain amount of Greek learning to the West. Especially under Manuel Comnenus was there "a steady procession of missions to Constantinople, papal, imperial, French, Pisan, and others, and a scarcely less continuous succession of Greek embassies to the west, reminding us of the Greeks in Italy in the early fifteenth century." [414]

Taking into consideration all this activity the conclusion is that the cultural movement of the epoch of the Comneni and Angeli is one of the brilliant pages in the history of Byzantium. In previous epochs Byzantium had had no such revival, and this revival of the twelfth century becomes of much greater importance when it is compared with the cultural revival at the same time in the West. The twelfth century may certainly be designated as the first Hellenic renaissance in the history of Byzantium.

[413] Haskins, *Studies in Mediaeval Science,* 141. Haskins, "The Greek Element in the Renaissance of the Twelfth Century," *American Historical Review,* XXV (1920), 603–5.

Haskins, *The Renaissance of the Twelfth Century,* 278.
[414] Haskins, *Studies in Mediaeval Science,* 194–95.

CHAPTER VIII: THE EMPIRE OF NICAEA

(1204–61)

NEW STATES FORMED ON BYZANTINE TERRITORY

THE Fourth Crusade, which had ended in the taking and sacking of Constantinople, brought about the disintegration of the Byzantine Empire and the formation, on its territory, of a great number of states, partly Frankish, partly Greek, of which the former received western European feudal organization. The Franks formed the following states: the Latin or Constantinopolitan Empire, the Kingdom of Thessalonica (Salonica), the principality of Achaia in the Peloponnesus (Morea) and the Duchy of Athens and Thebes in middle Greece. The sway of Venice extended over the Byzantine islands of the Aegean and Ionian Seas, the island of Crete, and a number of littoral and inland places. Along with the Latin feudal possessions on the territory of the disintegrated Eastern Empire, three independent Greek centers were formed; the Empire of Nicaea and the Empire of Trebizond in Asia Minor, and the Despotat of Epirus in northern Greece. Baldwin, count of Flanders, became Emperor of Constantinople and master of the greater part of Thrace; Boniface, marquess of Montferrat, became king of Thessalonica (Salonica), with power extending over Macedonia and Thessaly; William of Champlitte and after him Geoffrey de Villehardouin were princes in the Peloponnesus (Morea), and Othon de la Roche took the title of duke (*sire*), or, as he was called by his Greek subjects, *Megaskyr* or "Great Lord" of both Athens and Thebes. In the three Greek states the following princes reigned: at Nicaea (in Bithynia), Theodore I Lascaris; at Trebizond, Alexius I Comnenus; and in the Despotat of Epirus, Michael I Angelus Ducas Comnenus. Moreover, the two foreign states—the Second Bulgarian Empire through the activity of its kings Kalojan and John Asen II, and the Sultanate of Rum or Iconium in Asia Minor—took an active part in the complicated international life which after 1204 was established on the ruins of the Byzantine Empire. This was especially true of Bulgaria.

The whole thirteenth century was full of continuous clashes and strife between these states in the most various combinations: the Greeks struggled against the Frankish newcomers, the Turks and Bulgars; the Greeks strove against the Greeks, introducing in the form of national discord, new elements of dissolution into the life of a country which was already disorganized enough; the Franks fought against the Bulgars; and so forth. All these military conflicts were followed by the making of various and, to a large extent, transient international alliances and understandings, which were easily concluded and equally easily broken.

After the disaster of 1204 the problem of where the political, economic, national, religious, and cultural center should exist, and where the idea of unification and order might be created and strengthened, was extremely important. The feudal states founded in the East on the western models, and commercial factories, where everyone pursued his personal interests, led, under the conditions of general anarchy, to further dissolution; they could neither create a new order nor adequately manage the inheritance which they had received after the Fourth Crusade. "All these Western enclaves in the East reacted not creatively, but destructively," said one historian, "and therefore they were themselves destroyed; but the Orient remained master over the Orient."[1]

Beginnings of the Empire of Nicaea and the Lascarids

In the Empire of Nicaea the idea of Greek national unification and reconstruction of the Byzantine state was formed and strengthened, and it was from this empire that Michael Palaeologus came, the leader who in 1261 took possession of Constantinople and restored, though to much less than its former extent, the Byzantine Empire. For a time it might have been thought that the task of the restoration of the Greek empire would be reserved for another Greek center, the Despotat of Epirus; but for many reasons the despots of Epirus were forced to yield to the increasing importance of Nicaea and to give up the leading role in the Christian East. The third Greek center, the Empire of Trebizond, lay too far away to be able to play the leading part in the process of the unification of the Greeks; therefore the history of Trebizond has its own special interest, political as well as cultural and economic, and deserves a particular investigation of its own.

The founder of the Empire of Nicaea, "an Empire in exile," was Theodore Lascaris, a man about thirty years old, related to the house of the Angeli through his wife Anna, daughter of the former Emperor Alexius III, and to the house of the Comneni through Alexius III. The origin of the Lascarids and the name of Theodore's native city are not known. Under Alexius III he held military command and fought energetically against the crusaders.[2] In all likelihood he had been regarded as a possible emperor of Byzantium by

[1] C. Neumann, "Die byzantinische Marine," *Historische Zeitschrift*, LXXXI (1898), 1–2.

[2] See A. Gardner, *The Lascarids of Nicaea: The Story of an Empire in Exile*, 53–54, A. Meliarakes, Ἰστορία τοῦ βασιλείου τῆς Νικαίας καὶ τοῦ δεσποτάτου τῆς Ἠπείρου, 8. M. A. Andreeva, *Essays on the Culture of the Byzantine Court in the Thirteenth Century*, 82–85.

the Constantinopolitan clergy after the flight of Alexius Ducas Murzuphlus (Mourtzouphlos) and up to the very moment of the taking of the capital by the crusaders; but at that time he fled to Asia Minor. There also sought shelter from the invasion of the crusaders numerous representatives of the Byzantine civil and military nobility, some prominent members of the church, and some other fugitives who did not wish to be under the yoke of the foreign power. The last Greek patriarch of Constantinople, John Camaterus, however, left the capital for Bulgaria and refused to come to Nicaea on Theodore's invitation. The metropolitan of Athens, Michael Acominatus, who had withdrawn into exile before the invading Latins, wrote a letter in which he recommended to the favorable attention of Theodore Lascaris a certain Euboean. He wrote that the latter had gone secretly to Nicaea, preferring the life of an exile at the palace of a Greek (*Romaic*) state to a stay in his native country oppressed by the foreigners; in the same letter Michael emphasized the fact that, if the Euboean found shelter at Nicaea, it would greatly impress the whole population of Greece who "would regard Theodore as a single universal liberator," that is to say, a liberator of the whole of Romania.[3]

After the death of Theodore Lascaris, who ruled from 1204 to 1222, there reigned his son-in-law, his daughter Irene's husband, John III Ducas Vatatzes (1222-1254),[4] the most talented and energetic emperor of Nicaea. After his death the throne was in the power, first of his own son Theodore II (1254-1258), and then of his grandson John IV (1258-1261), who was a minor during his reign. The latter was dethroned by Michael Palaeologus, the restorer of the Byzantine Empire.

The situation of the new state in Bithynia was extremely dangerous: from the east it was threatened by the powerful sultan of Iconium, who occupied the whole interior of Asia Minor and was also master of a part of the Mediterranean shore in the south and of a part of the Black Sea coast in the north; from the west the state of Nicaea was pushed back by the Latin Empire, which set as one of its chief goals the destruction of the new state of Nicaea. A complicated and difficult task devolved upon Theodore Lascaris, who ruled for about the first four years with the title not of emperor, but of despot. Within the country anarchy prevailed; in several parts of the state there arose independent rulers; the city of Nicaea shut its gates to Theodore.

Meanwhile, the Latin knights who had established themselves at Constantinople determined, in the same year, 1204, to conquer Asia Minor. Their military operations there were very successful. It seemed to the Greeks of Asia Minor that all was lost. Villehardouin said, "the people of the country took

---

[3] Michael Acominatus, ed. S. Lampros, II, 276-77.
[4] Historians usually call John Vatatzes John

III, regarding as the first two Johns, John Tzimisces and John Comnenus.

the part of the Franks and began to pay them tributes."[5] At this critical moment for the new state came the sudden news that the Latin emperor, Baldwin, had been captured by the Bulgars.

Since 1196 there had sat upon the Bulgarian throne Kalojan (John, Johannitsa), who, during the time of the Angeli, had been a terrible enemy of Byzantium. The Latin state established in the Balkan peninsula complicated the situation exceedingly. It was absolutely clear that the crusaders and Bulgars would have to raise the question of dominion in the Balkan peninsula. The relations between them became at once very strained, for the crusaders had reacted insultingly to Kalojan's friendly propositions, giving him to understand that he could not regard the Latin emperor as his equal, but must look up to him as a serf looks up to his master; and the Latins warned Kalojan that if he failed in respect, the crusaders would conquer Bulgaria by force of arms and reduce him to his former servile state.[6]

Having thus provoked the anger of the Bulgarian king, the Latins at the same time also irritated the Greek population of Thrace and Macedonia by insulting Greek religious beliefs and rites. The secret relations of the Greeks with King Kalojan prepared in the Balkan peninsula an insurrection in favor of the Bulgars.[7] It may be supposed that the former patriarch of Constantinople, John Camaterus, who is known to have lived in Bulgaria, played an important part in the formation of the Byzantine-Bulgarian alliance in 1204–5.[8] This alliance, Th. Uspensky said, "put an end to Kalojan's hesitations and fixed the plan of his future actions. To come out as a protector of orthodoxy and of the Greco-Bulgarian population against the Catholic Latin predominance and therewith to take upon himself the task of reviving the weakened imperial power in Byzantium became thereafter the chief motive of Kalojan's undertakings against the crusaders."[9] The tsar of Bulgaria longed for the crown of the Byzantine basileus.

The Greco-Bulgarian insurrection which had broken out in the Balkan peninsula, compelled the crusaders to recall to Europe the troops that had been sent to Asia Minor to fight against Theodore Lascaris. In the battle of Hadrianople, on the fifteenth of April, 1205, Kalojan, supported by the Cuman (Polovtzi) cavalry in his army, dealt a decisive defeat to the crusaders. In this battle fell the flower of Western chivalry, and the Emperor Baldwin himself was taken prisoner by the Bulgars. The fate of the captured emperor is not known; but, apparently, by order of the Bulgarian king, Baldwin was

[5] Villehardouin, *La Conquête de Constantinople,* 323; ed. N. Wailly, 193.

[6] Nicetas Choniates, *Historia;* in *Corpus Scriptorum Historiae Byzantinae,* 808–9.

[7] See V. N. Zlatarsky, *The Greek-Bulgarian Alliance in the Year 1204–1205,* 8–11.

[8] See P. Nikov, "Bulgarian Diplomacy from the Beginning of the Thirteenth Century," *Bulgarian Historical Library,* I (1928), 103–4.

[9] *The Formation of the Second Bulgarian Kingdom,* 245–46.

slain in some manner.[10] Because of the lack of information on Baldwin's end, his brother Henry was elected regent of the Latin Empire for the time of Baldwin's absence. More than eight hundred years before, in 378, another Roman emperor, Valens, had been killed near Hadrianople in his conflict with the Goths.

The old doge, Enrico Dandolo, who had also taken part in the battle and conducted the hard night retreat of the remains of the defeated troops, died shortly after this disaster and was buried in St. Sophia. As a widespread tradition states, his corpse remained there till the taking of Constantinople by the Turks, when the Sultan Muhammed II commanded the body of the Venetian hero to be destroyed.[11]

The defeat of Hadrianople placed the crusaders in a desperate situation. It was a blow to the Latin Empire that, at the very beginning of its political existence, undermined its whole future. "The dominion of the Franks over Romania ended on this terrible day,"[12] declared Gelzer, and it is true that "the destiny of the Latin Empire of Constantinople, for a certain period of time, was entirely in the hands of the Bulgarian king."[13]

The battle of Hadrianople had the greatest significance both for the Bulgarian kingdom and for the Empire of Nicaea. The Greeks of Macedonia and Thrace, lacking a national center in Europe and not foreseeing Nicaea's future significance in that connection, considered it possible to come to an agreement and to make common cause with the Bulgars against the Latins; the best possible opportunity was open to Kalojan to carry out his ambitious plan, namely, to establish on the site of the hostile Frankish realm a great Greco-Slavonic state in the Balkan peninsula with its center at Constantinople. But, as V. G. Vasilievsky wrote, "the Slavonic rulers could not succeed in making a representative of the Greco-Slavonic world play an imperial world role. Kalojan's ambition to found a Greco-Bulgarian kingdom in the Balkan peninsula, with the capital at Constantinople, remained in the realm of dreams."[14]

Meanwhile, the unnatural Greco-Bulgarian friendly understanding, which had brought about the victory of Hadrianople, promptly broke down, as soon

---

[10] Gardner, *Lascarids of Nicaea,* 66 (Baldwin is said to have been taken prisoner to Trnovo. He was never seen again). E. Gerland, *Geschichte des lateinischen Kaiserreiches von Konstantinopel,* I, 92 (Kalojan, in a sudden transport of anger, seems to have commanded his captive to be murdered). Nikov, "Bulgarian Diplomacy," *Bulgarian Historical Library,* I (1928), 104 (Baldwin was captured, carried to Trnovo, and there put in prison, where he died); this information is given on the basis of *Innocentii III Gesta;* ed. J. P. Migne, *Patrologia Latina,* CCXIV, 148.

[11] See H. Kretschmayr, *Geschichte von Venedig,* I, 321, 472.

[12] H. Gelzer, *Abriss der byzantinischen Kaisergeschichte,* 1042.

[13] Th. I. Uspensky, *Second Bulgarian Kingdom,* 250.

[14] "The Regeneration of the Bulgarian Patriarchate Under the King John Asen II," *Journal of the Ministry of Public Instruction,* CCXXXVIII (1885), 1, 9.

as the Balkan Greek patriots saw in the sovereign of Nicaea a possible liberator from the Latin conquerors and a spokesman for their national expectations and hopes. In the Balkan peninsula there appeared clearly expressed anti-Bulgarian tendencies, against which the king of Bulgaria opened a merciless and destructive war. According to the statement of a contemporary source, Kalojan was avenging the evils which the Emperor Basil II had inflicted upon the Bulgars. The latter had been given the name of the "slayer of Bulgars" (Bulgaroctonus); Kalojan proudly styled himself the "slayer of Romans" (Romaioctonus, Romaioktonos). The Greeks surnamed him "Dog-John" (in Greek Skyloioannes);[15] in his letter a Latin emperor calls him a "great destroyer of Greece" (magnus populator Graeciae).[16]

"Here manifested itself," stated a Bulgarian historian, "the purely Bulgarian national tendency, which guided the imperialistic policy of the King Kalojan against the Greek element, this sworn enemy of Bulgarian national independence, even in the moment of the alliance with the Greek cities of Thrace against the Latin Empire."[17]

The bloody campaign of John in Thrace and Macedonia ended fatally for him. At the siege of Thessalonica (1207) he died a violent death. A Greek legend inserted into the tales of the miracles of the martyr St. Demetrius, which exist in Greek and Slavonic versions, as well as in the old Russian chronographies, speaks of him as an enemy of the Orthodox church, stricken down by the saintly patron of the city. Thus the king of Bulgaria was unable to take advantage of circumstances which were very favorable to him after the victory of Hadrianople. In his person, Nikov said, there "disappeared from the historical stage one of the greatest diplomatists Bulgaria had ever borne."[18]

But on the other hand, the battle of Hadrianople, which had destroyed the strength of the Frankish dominion at Constantinople, saved the Empire of Nicaea from ruin and gave it hope for a new life. Theodore Lascaris, who had escaped the danger from his western neighbor, set to work actively to organize his state. First of all, when Theodore had succeeded in establishing himself firmly at Nicaea, the question was raised of proclaiming him emperor instead of despot. As the Greek patriarch of Constantinople, who after the Frankish invasion had withdrawn to Bulgaria, refused to come to Nicaea, a new patriarch, Michael Autoreanus, was elected there in 1208; he had his residence at Nicaea and crowned Theodore Emperor in the same year, 1208.[19]

[15] George Acropolita, *Annales*, xiii; in *Opera Omnia*, ed. A. Heisenberg, 23–24.

[16] See J. A. Buchon, *Recherches et matériaux pour servir à une histoire de la domination française*, II, 211.

[17] P. Nikov, *Studies in the Historical Sources of Bulgaria and in the History of the Bulgarian Church*, 8. (Pagination of a reprint.)

[18] "Bulgarian Diplomacy," *Bulgarian Historical Library*, I (1928), 108.

[19] This date, 1208, was established some years ago by A. Heisenberg, *Neue Quellen zur Geschichte des lateinischen Kaisertums und*

This event of 1208 had very great significance for the subsequent history of the state of Nicaea: Nicaea became the center of the Empire, as well as of the Church. By the side of the shaken Latin Empire there grew up this second empire which gradually unified a rather considerable territory in Asia Minor, and by little and little drew the attention and hopes of the European Greeks. In the treaty concluded about 1220 between Theodore Lascaris and the Venetian representative at Constantinople (*podestá*) the official title of the former, apparently acknowledged by Venice, was: "*Theodorus, in Christo Deo fidelis Imperator et moderator Romeorum et semper augustus, Comnenus Lascarus.*"[20] The formation of a new empire caused strained relations with the Empire of Constantinople; the two empires established on the ruins of the single Byzantine Empire could not live on friendly and peaceful terms.

Nicaea, located about forty English miles from Constantinople, became the capital of the new empire. Its position at the intersection of five or six roads, gave it a special political importance. Nicaea had achieved fame in Byzantine history as the site of two ecumenical councils, and its inhabitants boasted of the powerful walls, towers, and gates erected in the Middle Ages. These are still well preserved today. A short time before the First Crusade Nicaea had succumbed to the Seljuq Turks, but the crusaders who had taken the city away from them had been compelled, to their great discontent, to return it to Alexius Comnenus. Magnificent palaces and numerous churches and monasteries, of which now not a trace remains, adorned medieval Nicaea.[21] Speaking of Nicaea and recalling the First Ecumenical Council, an Arabian traveler of the twelfth century, al-Harawy (el-Herewy) wrote: "In the church of this city one may see the image of the Messiah and the portraits of the Fathers enthroned on their seats. This church is the object of particular reverence."[22] The Byzantine and western historians of the thirteenth century point out the vast extent and wealth of Nicaea.[23] A writer of the thirteenth century, Nicephorus Blemmydes, spoke of Nicaea in one of his poems: "Nicaea, a city with wide streets, full of people, well-walled, proud of what it encloses, being the most excellent mark of imperial sympathy."[24] Finally, in the literature of

der Kirchenunion, II, 5-12; the common date was 1206. See also Andreeva, *Culture of the Byzantine Court,* 85, 180-81.

[20] G. L. F. Tafel and G. M. Thomas, *Urkunden zur ältern Handels- und Staatsgeschichte der Republik Venedig,* II, 205.

[21] For very good information on medieval Nicaea, with excellent bibliography, see J. Sölch, "Historisch-geographische Studien über bithynische Siedlungen. Nikomedia, Nikäa, Prusa," *Byzantinisch-neugriechische Jahrbücher,* I (1920), 263-86. See also R. Janin, "Nicée. Étude historique et topogra-

phique," *Échos d'Orient,* XXIV (1925), 482-90. Andreeva, *Culture of the Byzantine Court,* 19-21.

[22] *Indications sur les lieux de Pèlerinage,* trans. C. Schefer, *Archives de l'orient latin,* I, 590.

[23] See, e.g., Nicetas Choniates, *Historia,* Bonn ed., 318. Villehardouin, *Conquête de Constantinople,* par. 304.

[24] Nicephorus Blemmydes, *Curriculum vitae et carmina,* ed. A. Heisenberg, 113, vss. 22-24.

the thirteenth and fourteenth centuries are preserved two panegyrics of Nicaea. The author of one of them, Emperor Theodore II Lascaris, addressed Nicaea: "Thou hast surpassed all the cities, since the Romaeic state, many times divided and crushed by foreign troops . . . has been founded, established, and strengthened only in thee."[25] The second panegyric was written by a very well-known statesman of the fourteenth century, a diplomat, politician and administrator, theologian, astronomer, poet, and artist, Theodore Metochites,[26] whose name is associated with the famous mosaics of the Constantinople monastery Chora (now the mosque Kahrieh Jami), which have been preserved to the present time.

Of the monuments of the Middle Ages to be found in the miserable present-day Turkish city of Isnik (the distorted name of Nicaea) before the First World War, one might have pointed out, in addition to the city walls, the modest small church of the Assumption. This dated probably from the ninth century, and had fine mosaics, important for the study of Byzantine art.[27] But during World War I Nicaea was bombarded, and no single house was left untouched. The Church of the Assumption suffered particularly; during the bombardment it was destroyed, and only the western arch under the dome and the southern part of the narthex have been preserved. The other famous church of Nicaea, the cathedral of Sophia, is also in a deplorable state.[28]

An interesting document has been preserved which shows, to a certain extent, Theodore Lascaris' conception of imperial power. It is called *Silentium* (Σελέντιον, σιλέντιον), the name given at the time of Byzantium to the public imperial speeches delivered by the Emperors in the palace in the presence of the noblest persons of the Empire at the beginning of Lent. The *Silentium* is regarded as the throne speech of Theodore Lascaris delivered in 1208, immediately after his coronation.[29] It was written by his contemporary, the very well-known historian Nicetas Choniates, who, after the sack of Constantinople by the Latins, had found a secure refuge at Nicaea. This rhetorically written speech shows that Theodore, like a Byzantine basileus, considered that his power was granted to him by God. "My Imperial Majesty has been placed by heaven as a father over the universal Roman state; the Will of God has laid upon me the power. . . ." God had granted Theodore for his zeal "the an-

[25] Th. I. Uspensky, "On the Manuscripts of the History of Nicetas Acominatus in the National Library of Paris," *Journal of the Ministry of Public Instruction*, CXCIV (1877), 77.

[26] Printed in C. Sathas, *Bibliotheca graeca medii aevi*, I, 139 ff.

[27] See H. Grégoire, "Le véritable nom et la date de l'église de la Dormition à Nicée. Un texte nouveau et décisif," *Mélanges d'histoire offerts à Henri Pirenne*, I, 171–74. See also

Charles Diehl, *Manuel d'art byzantin*, II, 520–21, 908; Grégoire's article appeared too late to be used by Diehl. O. M. Dalton, *East Christian Art*, 285.

[28] See M. Alpatov and I. Brunov, "A Brief Report of a Journey to the East," *Vizantiysky Vremennik*, XXIV (1923–26), 61. Diehl, *Manuel d'art byzantin*, II, 908.

[29] Heisenberg, *Neue Quellen zur Geschichte des lateinischen Kaisertums*, II, 11–12.

nointment and power of David." The unity of the Empire meant also unity in the church. "There shall be one fold and one shepherd," Theodore declared at the end of the *Silentium*.[30] It is true that this speech does not belong to the pen of the Emperor himself, but it reflects the prevailing opinion of the best-born and best-educated people of the Empire of Nicaea, an opinion based on solid grounds, after Theodore Lascaris, united by ties of parentage with the Angeli and Comneni, became the *"Roman basileus"* at Nicaea and realized that he continued the line of the Byzantine emperors.

FOREIGN POLICY OF THE LASCARIDS AND THE RESTORATION OF THE BYZANTINE EMPIRE

After the defeat of the Latins at Hadrianople, Theodore's situation became temporarily a little easier. Baldwin's successor on the Constantinopolitan throne, however, his brother Henry, an energetic and talented leader and ruler, after his coronation in St. Sophia somewhat recovered from the reverse with the Bulgars and again opened hostilities against Theodore, having it in mind to annex the possessions of Nicaea to the Latin Empire. The Emperor of Nicaea could not, by force of arms, check the successes of the Latins. But the Bulgarian danger to the Latins and the Seljuq danger to Theodore compelled both of them to come to an agreement and to conclude a truce, by the terms of which Theodore had to pull down several fortresses.[31]

The Seljuq Turks

Theodore's war with the Seljuq Sultan, to whom belonged the greater part of Asia Minor, had great importance for the new Empire of Nicaea. The appearance of a new state, the Empire of Nicaea, was, undoubtedly, exceedingly disagreeable to the Turkish Sultanate of Iconium or Rum, for it hindered the Turks in their further advance to the West toward the coast of the Aegean Sea. To this main cause of the strained relations between the two states must be added the fact that Theodore Lascaris' father-in-law, Alexius III Angelus, fled to the sultan and besought him for help to regain his lost throne. Availing himself of the opportunity of Alexius' arrival, the sultan sent to Theodore a threatening demand to deliver the throne to him, concealing under this pretext his real aim of taking possession of the whole of Asia Minor. Hostilities began; they took place particularly at Antioch, on the Maeander river, in Caria. The chief force of Theodore was the eight hundred brave western

[30] Sathas, *Bibliotheca graeca medii aevi*, I, 99, 105, 107.

[31] See E. Gerland, *Geschichte der Kaiser Baldwin I. und Heinrich*, 102–14. After Gerland's book the dissertation of L. Neuhaus, *Die Reichsverwesenschaft und Politik des Grafen Heinrich von Anjou, des zweiten Kaisers im Lateinerreiche zu Byzanz,* has no importance.

mercenaries. In their fight with the Turks, they displayed great heroism and inflicted enormous losses on the enemy, but almost all of them were left dead on the field of battle. By his personal courage and great presence of mind, however, Theodore Lascaris regained control of the situation. In the following clash the sultan was slain, perhaps by Theodore himself. A contemporary source said, the sultan "fell as from a tower," i.e. from the mare on which he was mounted.[32] In the same battle the former emperor, Alexius III, who had taken refuge with the Turks, was captured. He put on the cowl and ended his life in one of the monasteries of Nicaea.

This war seems to have brought about no great territorial changes for Theodore.[33] But the moral significance of the victory of the Greek Christian Emperor of Nicaea over the Muslims was very great: it confirmed the new Empire, revived the former Byzantine traditions of the struggle against Islam, and filled with joy and vigor the hearts of the Greeks, not only the Asiatics, but also the Europeans, who, for the first time, saw in Nicaea a possible center of their future unification. Nicetas Choniates wrote in honor of Theodore's victory a long and bombastic panegyric.[34] Nicetas' brother, Michael Acominatus, the former metropolitan of Athens, from the island of Ceos, where he was spending the last years of his life, sent Theodore a letter of congratulation in which he expressed his wish that Theodore might take possession of the throne of Constantine the Great in the place which our Lord had originally chosen,[35] that is to say, in Constantinople.

The Latin Empire

But if the Greeks rejoiced in Theodore's victory, the Latin emperor, Henry, who feared the brave western mercenaries of Theodore, was also contented with the same victory, however strange it may seem at first sight; since almost all these mercenaries had fallen in the war against the Turks, the victory, in the opinion of Henry, actually weakened the Emperor of Nicaea. A historian of that time said that Henry declared: "Lascaris has been vanquished, and has not vanquished."[36] Henry was mistaken, however, because shortly after the war Theodore had again at his disposal a considerable number of Franks and well-armed Greeks.[37]

---

[32] George Acropolita, *Annales,* chap. 10; ed. Heisenberg, 17.

[33] See G. de Jerphanion, "Les Inscriptions cappadociennes et l'histoire de l'empire grec de Nicée," *Orientalia Christiana Periodica,* I (1935), 242–43. P. Wittek, *Das Fürstentum Mentesche. Studie zur Geschichte Westkleinasiens im 13.–15. Jahrhundert,* 1–23. M. F. Köprülü, *Les Origines de l'Empire Ottoman,* 35–37. P. Wittek, *The Rise of the Ottoman Empire,* 16–32.

[34] Sathas, *Bibliotheca graeca medii aevi,* I, 129–36.

[35] Michael Acominatus, ed. Lampros, II, 353 ff.

[36] George Acropolita, *Annales,* chap. 15; ed. Heisenberg, 27.

[37] Gerland, *Kaiser Baldwin I. und Heinrich,* 216.

The victory over the Turks allowed Theodore to open hostilities against Henry. At that time Theodore's specific goal was to attack Constantinople with the support of his already considerable fleet. A very interesting letter, which Gerland called a manifesto,[38] was written by Henry from Pergamon at the beginning of the year 1212, addressed to "all his friends whom its contents may reach" (*universis amicis suis ad quos tenor presentium pervenerit*). The letter testifies that Henry regarded Theodore as a very dangerous foe; he wrote: "The first and greatest enemy was Lascaris who held the whole land beyond the Strait of Saint George[39] as far as Turkey, and, setting up for an emperor, he often pressed upon us from that part. . . . Lascaris collected a very great number of galleys in order to take possession of Constantinople; therefore the city was trembling in great desolation, so that despairing of our return (from Asia Minor) many of our people were planning to flee across the sea; and a great many passed over to Lascaris promising him help against us. . . . All the Greeks began to murmur against us and promised Lascaris support if he would come to fight Constantinople." The letter ends with an appeal to the Latins to support Henry. "To have full victory and possess our Empire we need a great number of Latins to whom we may give the land which we are acquiring and which we have acquired; for, as you know, it is not enough to acquire the land, but there must be those who can maintain it."[40] This letter shows clearly that Henry was greatly alarmed by the hostilities of Theodore Lascaris, and, furthermore, that the spirit of his new subjects was wavering.

Nevertheless, this first attempt of Nicaea to restore the former capital of the Empire miscarried; the Empire of Nicaea was not yet sufficiently strong nor prepared for this purpose. The success was on the side of Henry, who penetrated rather far into the interior of Asia Minor. In a letter recently published and dated apparently in the year 1213, Henry gives a brief account of his victory over the Greeks, who "with such insolence and abuse rose against the Roman church that they considered all its sons, devoted Latins, as dogs and, because of their contempt of our faith, generally called them dogs."[41]

The peace concluded between the two emperors fixed exactly the borders of the two empires in Asia Minor: the northwestern part of the peninsula remained in the hands of the Latin Empire. In other words, without taking into consideration some insignificant territorial annexations made by the Latin Empire within the country, the Latin possessions in Asia Minor, after that

[38] *Ibid.*, 218.

[39] Brachium Sancti-Georgii is the Bosphorus.

[40] *Recueil des historiens des Gaules et de la France* (2nd ed., 1879), XVIII, 530–33.

[41] See M. P. Lauer, "Une Lettre inédite d'Henri Ier d'Angre, empereur de Constantinople, aux prélats italiens (1213?)," *Mélanges offerts à M. Gustav Schlumberger*, I, 201. I do not know why Lauer ascribed to the year 1213 (p. 194) Henry's dated letter from Pergamon (January 13, 1212).

peace, differed very little from the possessions that the Empire had received in the partition of 1204.[42]

In 1216 the talented and energetic Henry died in the prime of life. He was admired and beloved even by the Greeks, and a Byzantine chronicler of the fourteenth century said that Henry was "a real Ares."[43] The historians of the twentieth century also estimate highly his personality and activities. Gerland declared: "Of the [Latin] Empire Henry became the real founder. His institutions laid the basis upon which the Frankish dominion in Greece developed."[44] "Henry's death," wrote A. Gardner, "was certainly a calamity for the Latins —possibly for the Greeks likewise—since his strong but conciliatory policy might have succeeded, if any policy ever could, in filling up the breach between East and West."[45] In the person of Henry the most dangerous enemy of Nicaea passed away. His successors on the Constantinopolitan throne were distinguished neither for talent nor energy.

In 1222 the founder of the Empire of Nicaea died. Theodore I Lascaris had created a Hellenic center in Asia Minor, unified the state, and attracted to it the attention of the European Greeks. He had laid the foundation upon which his successor was able to build a vast structure. In his eulogistic letters to Theodore Lascaris, Michael Acominatus wrote: "The capital hurled by the barbarian inundation out of the walls of Byzantium to the shores of Asia in the shape of a miserable fragment has been received by thee, guided, and saved. . . . Thou ought to be called forever the new builder and peopler of the city of Constantine. . . . Looking only to thee and calling thee a savior and universal liberator the people wrecked in the universal deluge take refuge in thy state as in a calm harbour. . . . No one of the emperors who reigned over Constantinople I consider equal to thee, except, of those nearer in time, the great Basil Bulgaroctonus, and of the more ancient, the noble Heraclius."[46]

John III Ducas Vatatzes (1222–1254)

After the death of Theodore I Lascaris, John III Ducas Vatatzes, the husband of his daughter Irene, ascended the throne of Nicaea and reigned from

[42] See Gardner, *Lascarids of Nicaea*, 85–86. Gerland, *Kaiser Baldwin I. und Heinrich*, 218–19. Sometimes the statement is given (see, e.g. N. Iorga, *Geschichte des Osmanischen Reiches*, I, 120; and Gerland, *Kaiser Baldwin I. und Heinrich*, I, 246) that Theodore I, in his political activity, also was successful in the south af Asia Minor, where he seized the city of Attalia, on the Mediterranean coast. But this is an error due to the chronological misdating of an inscription found at Attalia, which belongs properly to the year 915–16.

See H. Grégoire, *Recueil des inscriptions grecques chrétiennes d'Asie Mineure*, I, 104. See also A. A. Vasiliev, *Byzantium and the Arabs*, II, 153.

[43] Ephraemius Monachus, *Imperatorum et patriarcharum recensus*, v. 7735; Bonn ed., 312.

[44] Gerland, *Kaiser Baldwin I. und Heinrich*, 251.

[45] *Lascarids of Nicaea*, 93.

[46] Michael Acominatus, ed. Lampros, 150, 151, 276, 354.

1222 to 1254.[47] Although his predecessor had laid some foundation for the further development of the state of Nicaea, nevertheless its international position was such as to require urgently the rule of a decisive and energetic man. This man appeared in the person of John Vatatzes.

At that time four states were contending for mastery over the East: the Empire of Nicaea, the Latin Empire, the Despotat of Epirus, and the Bulgarian Kingdom of John Asen II. John Vatatzes' external policy, therefore, consisted on the one hand of wars, and on the other of alliances with one or another state. By a stroke of good fortune his three rivals in the Balkan peninsula never acted jointly and decisively, but pursued a vacillating and weakening policy of interstate hostilities, or a policy of transient alliances. John Vatatzes thoroughly succeeded in managing the complicated international situation.

The Despotat of Epirus and its relation to the Empire of Nicaea

For the further destiny of the Empire of Nicaea the history of the Despotat of Epirus was extremely important. Epirus was the second Greek center, where, under certain conditions, might have been concentrated the interests of the western Greek patriots and from which might have come the idea of the restoration of the Byzantine Empire. The two Greek states, Epirus and Nicaea, which could not come to a satisfactory compromise in their rivalry to bring about Hellenic unification, were unavoidably to struggle to restore Byzantium.

The founder of the Despotat of Epirus in 1204 was Michael I Angelus. The family of the Epirotic Angeli was related to the families of the Comneni and Ducae, and therefore the names of the rulers of Epirus are sometimes accompanied by a long dynastic title "Angelus Comnenus Ducas." Originally the possessions of the Despotat of Epirus had extended from Dyrrachium (Durazzo) in the north to the Gulf of Corinth in the south; that is to say, they had occupied the territory of ancient Epirus, Acarnania, and Aetolia. The city of Arta became the capital of the new state.

The history of the Despotat of Epirus in the thirteenth century is not yet thoroughly investigated and the sources are far from complete; for this reason, many questions still remain debatable and dark. Much light has been thrown upon the history of the Despotat by the letters of John Apocaucus (Apokaukos), the metropolitan of Naupactus (Lepanto), which were published at the end of the nineteenth century by V. G. Vasilievsky.[48]

[47] The majority of writers regard the year 1254 as that of Vatazes' death. Meliarakes, Ἱστορία τοῦ βασιλείου τῆς Νικαίας καὶ τοῦ δεσποτάτου τῆς Ἠπείρου, 412, and Gardner, *Lascarids of Nicaea*, 192, say that he died on October 13, 1255. In the *Cambridge Medieval History*, IV, 430, the year is given as 1254.

[48] "Epirotica saeculi xiii," *Vizantiysky Vremennik*, III (1896), 233–99.

In its internal administration the Despotat did not differ from the system in use before 1204, when its territory had formed a province of the Byzantine Empire; the name of the form of government changed, but the people continued to live on the basis of the Byzantine administration. Surrounded on all sides by the Latin and Slavonic states, on the east by the feudal Kingdom of Thessalonica, on the northeast by the Bulgarian Kingdom, and on the west by the possessions of Venice which threatened the coast of Epirus, the Despotat was obliged to develop a strong military power that might, in case of need, offer an adequate resistance to external foes. The mountainous and inaccessible nature of the country also served as a great support. The despot Michael I considered himself an absolutely independent ruler and did not recognize any superiority or leadership on the part of Theodore Lascaris of Nicaea. The church in the Despotat was also independent, and Michael I commanded the bishops to be ordained by the local metropolitans.

The original task of the Despot of Epirus was to preserve Hellenism in the western districts of Greece from absorption by the neighboring Franks and Bulgars. Broader aims, which led the Despotat far beyond the narrow limits of its own interests, appeared and developed later.

During the reign of Theodore Lascaris Nicaea seems to have had no conflicts with the Despotat. With the ascension of John Vatatzes to the throne, circumstances changed. At that time the brother of the slain Michael, Theodore, sat on the throne of Epirus. His name is connected with the idea of the expansion of his state at the expense of the Latins and Bulgars.

In his brother's lifetime the new despot, Theodore Angelus, had stayed at the court of the Emperor of Nicaea. When the late Michael I had begged Theodore Lascaris to let his brother go back to Epirus to help the despot in ruling the state, the Emperor of Nicaea granted Michael's request, having previously exacted from Theodore of Epirus an oath of allegiance to him as emperor as well as to his successors. Theodore Lascaris' apprehensions proved well grounded. When Theodore Angelus had become the Despot of Epirus, he paid no attention to the oath he had taken to the Emperor of Nicaea, and when he judged it advisable, he opened hostilities against Nicaea.

The first act that drew attention to Theodore Angelus was his capture of the Latin Emperor of Constantinople, Peter de Courtenay, count of Auxerre. After Henry's death (1216), the barons elected as emperor his brother-in-law, Peter de Courtenay, who had married Yolande, the sister of Baldwin and Henry. At the time of his election he was with his wife in France. Having received the news of the election, he set out with her for Constantinople by way of Rome, where Pope Honorius III crowned Peter with the imperial crown, not in St. Peter's, but in San Lorenzo Fuori le Mura, wishing to emphasize the fact that the Empire of Romania in the East was not the Empire of

Rome in the West,—a distinction which might have been obscured if the coronation of an eastern emperor had taken place in St. Peter's, where the western emperors, beginning with Charlemagne and Otto I, had been crowned.[49] From Italy Peter sent his wife, Yolande, by sea to Constantinople; he and his troops sailed across the Adriatic and landed near Dyrrachium, hoping to reach the capital by land. But Theodore Angelus attacked him from an ambush in the mountains of Epirus, and defeated and captured the greater part of Peter's troops. The Emperor himself, according to one source, fell in battle; according to another, was seized by Theodore and died in Greek captivity.[50] V. G. Vasilievsky said, this "deed of Theodore absolutely in Greek-Byzantine taste"[51] produced a particularly strong impression on the West, where the chroniclers painted in the very darkest colors Theodore's savagery and cruelty.[52] The fate of Peter de Courtenay, like that of the first Latin Emperor, Baldwin, is veiled in mystery; in all likelihood, Peter died in prison. Meanwhile, the widow of Peter, Yolande, who had reached Constantinople, governed the Empire for the two years before her death (1217–19). The death of Peter de Courtenay must be regarded as the first attack of the Despotat of Epirus, that is to say, of the western Hellenic center, upon the Latin newcomers to the Balkan peninsula.

But the anti-Latin policy of Theodore Angelus did not stop there. Soon afterwards there arose the question of the Kingdom of Thessalonica (Salonika) whose king, Boniface of Montferrat, had been killed in 1207 in a fight with the Bulgars. After his death troubles and strife raged in the kingdom. As long as the energetic Latin Emperor, Henry, was alive, he could defend Thessalonica against its two most menacing foes, Bulgaria and Epirus. But after the death of Henry and of the new Latin Emperor, Peter de Courtenay, the Kindom of Thessalonica was unable to resist the aggressive policy of Theodore of Epirus.

Theodore made war against the neighboring Latin kingdom, won the victory and in 1222, without great effort, took possession of Thessalonica, the second city in importance of the former Byzantine Empire and the first fief of the Latin Empire of Constantinople. "Thus, after only eighteen years of existence, this ephemeral Lombard kingdom fell ingloriously—the first of the creations of the Fourth Crusade to succumb."[53] Having seized Thessalonica and extended his dominions from the Adriatic to the Aegean, Theodore

[49] Gardner, *Lascarids of Nicaea*, 93.

[50] Among the more recent books on the death of Peter de Courtenay see, e.g., Gardner, *ibid.*, 94. W. Miller, *The Latins in the Levant*, 82–83. *Cambridge Medieval History*, IV, 427. Nikov, *Historical Sources of Bulgaria*, 40.

[51] "The Regeneration of the Bulgarian Patriarchate," *Journal of the Ministry of Public Instruction*, CCXXXVIII (1885), 21.

[52] See Meliarakes, Ἱστορία τοῦ βασιλείου τῆς Νικαίας καὶ τοῦ δεσποτάτου τῆς Ἠπείρου, 125 and n. 2.

[53] Miller, *Latins in the Levant*, 83.

judged it his right to assume the imperial crown, that is to say, to become emperor of the Romans. This meant that he refused to recognize the title of John Vatatzes, who had just ascended the throne of Nicaea (1222). From the viewpoint of Theodore of Epirus, he himself, as a representative of the glorious families of the Angeli, Comneni, and Ducae, had a great advantage over John Vatatzes, a man of no very noble origin, who had mounted the throne only because he was Theodore Lascaris' son-in-law.

The question of who should crown Theodore at Thessalonica was next raised. The metropolitan of Thessalonica declined the honor, unwilling to violate the rights of the Greek patriarch, who was then living at Nicaea and had already crowned John Vatatzes. Accordingly Theodore turned to another hierarch, who was independent of the Orthodox patriarch of Nicaea, namely, to the autocephalous (independent of archiepiscopal or patriarchal jurisdiction) archbishop of Ochrida (Achrida) and of "all Bulgaria," Demetrius Chomatenus (Chomatianos), whose works, the letters in particular, have great interest for the history of the epoch. He crowned and anointed Theodore who "put on the purple robe and began to wear the red shoes,"[54] distinctive marks of the Byzantine basileus. One of the letters of Demetrius Chomatenus shows that the coronation and anointment of Theodore of Epirus was performed "with the general consent of the members of the senate, who were in the west (that is, on the territory of the state of Thessalonica and Epirus), of the clergy, and of all the large army."[55] Another document testifies that the coronation and anointment were performed with the consent of all the bishops who lived "in that western part."[56] Finally, Theodore himself signed his edicts (*chrysobulls*) with the full title of the Byzantine Emperor: "Theodore in Christ God Basileus and Autocrat of the Romans, Ducas."[57]

Interesting and fresh information on this subject is contained in the precious collection of the letters of the above-mentioned metropolitan of Naupactus, John Apocaucus. From his correspondence, wrote V. G. Vasilievsky, "we learn for the first time what an active part in the Epirotic movement was taken by the Greek clergy and especially by the Greek bishops. The proclamation of Theodore Angelus as the Emperor of the Romans was considered very seriously; Thessalonica, which had passed over into his hands, was contrasted with Nicaea; Constantinople was openly indicated to him as the nearest goal of his ambition and as an assured gain; in speech, thought, and writing, it was the common opinion that he was destined to enter St. Sophia and occupy there

[54] George Acropolita, *Annales,* chap. 21; ed. Heisenberg, 33.

[55] J. B. Pitra, *Analecta sacra et classica spicilegio Solesmensi parata,* VI, ep. 114, 488–90. See M. S. Drinov, "On Some Works of Demetrius Chomatianos as Historical Material,"

Vizantiysky Vremennik, II (1895), 11 and n. 1.

[56] Vasilievsky, "Epirotica saeculi xiii," *Vizantiysky Vremennik,* III (1896), 285.

[57] *Ibid.,* 299.

the place of the Orthodox Roman emperors where the Latin newcomers were sitting illegally. The realization of such dreams did not lie beyond the limits of possibility; it would be even easier to take Constantinople from Thessalonica than from Nicaea."[58]

The proclamation of Theodore's coronation as the Emperor of Thessalonica and his anointment by the archbishop Demetrius Chomatenus must have brought about a political rupture between Thessalonica and Nicaea as well as an ecclesiastical rupture between the western Greek hierarchs and the patriarchate of Nicaea, which was called the patriarchate of Constantinople.

In the course of a rather long period after the fall of the Latin kingdom of Thessalonica, several western European princes related to the family of Montferrat continued to use in the West the extinct title of king of Thessalonica. They were the so-called "titulary" kings of Thessalonica, as, after the fall of the Latin Empire in 1261, there were to be "titulary" Latin emperors in western Europe.

Thus, from 1222,[59] when the Empire of Thessalonica was proclaimed and refused to recognize the Empire of Nicaea, there were in the Christian East three empires: the two Greek Empires of Thessalonica and of Nicaea, and the Latin Empire in Constantinople which was becoming weaker every year.[60] The further history of the thirteenth century is concerned with the relations between these empires, in whose destinies the Bulgarian Kingdom of John Asen II was the decisive factor.

Thessalonica and Nicaea

The two Greek Emperors, John Vatatzes and Theodore Angelus, had one common foe in the Emperor of Constantinople. But the Greek rulers could not come to an agreement concerning the Latin Emperor, for each of them wished at all costs to seize Constantinople for himself. In their opinion, only one of them could be the restorer of the Byzantine Empire. Therefore they had to fight separately against the Latin Empire, and finally clashed with each other.

Tidings of the growth of Nicaea and Epirus reached western Europe and aroused alarm on behalf of the Latin Empire. In a letter (May, 1224) to Blanche, the queen of France, the mother of Louis IX, Pope Honorius III, speaking of the powerful Empire of Romania and the fact "that recently there has been created a sort of new France," warned the queen that "the strength

[58] "The Regeneration of the Bulgarian Patriarchate," *Journal of the Ministry of Public Instruction*, CCXXXVIII (1885), 18–19.

[59] Sometimes the year 1223 is given for the foundation of the Empire of Thessalonica.

[60] We shall not discuss the Empire of Trebizond.

of the French [in the East] has decreased and is decreasing while their adversaries are growing considerably stronger, so that, unless speedy help is given the Emperor, it is to be feared that the Latins may be menaced by irreparable damage to both men and means." Honorius III proceeded to appeal to the king of France, asking him to help the Latin Emperor.[61]

Soon after his ascension to the throne, John Vatatzes opened successful hostilities against the Latins in Asia Minor; then, by means of the fleet which was already at the disposal of the Emperor of Nicaea, he seized some islands of the Archipelago, Chios, Lesbos, Samos, and some others, and after that, having been asked by the inhabitants of Hadrianople to free them from the Latin yoke, he transferred hostilities to Europe. He sent towards Hadrianople an army which seems to have occupied this important point without a battle. To John Vatatzes the possession of Hadrianople might open the gates of Constantinople. One of the rivals seemed to be not far from his cherished goal.

But at the same time, Theodore Angelus set out from Thessalonica and conquered a major part of Thrace; then in 1225, approaching Hadrianople, he caused the army of John Vatatzes to withdraw. To the latter's plans, the loss of Hadrianople was a severe blow. Meanwhile, Theodore seized some other places and with his troops reached the very walls of Constantinople. It was a critical moment for the Latins. The Emperor of Thessalonica was on the point of becoming the real restorer of the Byzantine Empire. His dominions extended from the Adriatic almost to the Black Sea.

But Theodore was compelled to give up hope of further successes in his fight against the Latins, for he himself began to be seriously menaced from the north by John Asen II of Bulgaria, who also had a claim upon Constantinople.

The role of Bulgaria in the Christian East under Tsar John Asen II

John Asen II (1218–1241), the greatest of the Asens, was the son of John Asen I. "Though not himself a conqueror," to quote the well-known historian Jireček, "he expanded the boundaries of the kingdom which he had received in a disorganized state, to limits that it had not reached for several centuries and which it never achieved afterward."[62] Tolerant in religious matters, well educated, and clement, he left a good name not only among the Bulgars, but also among the Greeks. A Greek historian of the thirteenth century, George Acropolita, wrote of him: "All considered him a wonderful and happy man because he did not resort to the sword in his dealings with his subjects and did not stain himself with the murders of Romans, like the Bulgarian kings

[61] Bouquet, *Recueil des historiens des Gaules et de la France*, XIX, 754.

[62] *A History of the Bulgars*, trans. F. Bruun and V. Palauzov, 333. V. Zlararsky, "John Asen II," *Bulgarian Historical Library*, III, 1–55.

who had preceded him. Therefore he was beloved not only by the Bulgars, but also by the Romans and other peoples."[63]

In the history of Byzantium, John Asen II was very important as the representative of the idea of the Great Bulgarian Kingdom which, it seemed, should unify the whole Orthodox population of the Balkan peninsula and establish its capital at Tsargrad (Constantinople). Such plans, undoubtedly, were opposed to the vital interests of both Greek empires and must have brought about hostilities. But the course of events seemed to facilitate the realization of the Bulgarian tsar's plans.

On the death of the Latin Emperor, Robert de Courtenay (1228), the throne was supposed to pass to his brother, Baldwin II, a boy of eleven. The question of regency arose. Some proposed as a regent John Asen, who was related to Baldwin; and to strengthen the ties of friendship between the two countries, the betrothal of Baldwin to Asen's daughter was suggested. Realizing all the advantages of the proposed agreement and hoping to capture Constantinople without bloodshed, Asen accepted the proposition and promised Baldwin that he would free the lands occupied by his enemies, especially Theodore of Epirus. The Latin knights and clergy, however, stubbornly resisted the candidature of a deadly foe of the Latin Empire and insisted upon the election as regent of the Empire a Frenchman, the "titulary" king of Jerusalem, who at that time was in western Europe, John of Brienne, a man of eighty. Thus Asen's first chance of taking Constantinople ended in failure.

After the capture of Hadrianople, the chief role in the Balkan peninsula was played by Theodore of Epirus, Emperor of Thessalonica, who concluded an alliance with Asen. But their friendly relations did not last long. The plan concerning John Asen's regency in Constantinople aroused serious suspicions in Theodore. He treacherously broke his alliance with Asen and opened hostilities against the Bulgars. The decisive battle was fought in 1230 at a place called Klokotinitza (Clocotinitza), now Semidje, between Hadrianople and Philippopolis, and ended in a complete victory for John Asen, who was vigorously supported by the Cuman cavalry.[64] Theodore Angelus was captured. At first mildly treated, he plotted later against Asen's life and, on the discovery of his plot, was blinded.

The battle of Klokotinitza, in 1230, was one of the turning points in the history of the Christian East in the thirteenth century. It destroyed the western Greek Empire and the western Greek center, which seemed to be on the point of restoring the Byzantine Empire. The short-lived western empire (1222–

---

[63] George Acropolita, *Annales,* chap. 25; ed. Heisenberg, 43.

[64] George Acropolita calls this cavalry the Scythians, *ibid.,* chap. 25; ed. Heisenberg,

42. Others think them the Moldo-Wallachs (Vlachs). See O. Tafrali, *Thessalonique des origines au XIVᵉ siècle,* 217–18.

1230) practically ceased to exist, and Manuel, the brother of Theodore Angelus, who was taken prisoner, ruled Thessalonica thereafter, some historians think, not with the title of emperor but with that of despot. But this is doubtful: he continued to sign his decrees with red ink, as befitted the imperial dignity, and called himself in the documents emperor.[65] In the further history of the thirteenth century, Thessalonica and Epirus, two separate dominions, played no role of any importance. From that time on, the struggle for Constantinople was carried on, not between three rivals, but two: John Vatatzes and John Asen.

After the victory over Theodore of Epirus, the tsar of Bulgaria occupied Hadrianople without a struggle, as well as almost the whole of Macedonia and Albania as far as Dyrrachium (Durazzo). Thessalonica, Thessaly, and Epirus remained in the hands of the Greeks.

In an inscription on a white marble column in the Church of the Forty Martyrs at Trnovo (Bulgaria), the tsar of Bulgaria told of the results of his victory in this inflated style: "I, John Asen, in Christ God the faithful Tsar and Autocrat of the Bulgars, son of the old Tsar Asen . . . set forth on a march upon Romania and defeated the Greek troops, and I have captured the Emperor himself, Theodore Comnenus, with all his *boyars* [nobles], and taken all the countries from Hadrianople to Durazzo, the Greek territory, as well as the Albanian and Serbian territories. The Latins [Franks] have kept only the cities round Tsargrad itself, but even they have become subject to the power of my Majesty, for they have no king but myself, and only thanks to me have they continued their existence."[66] From a charter granted by Asen at the same time to the Ragusan merchants concerning the freedom of their commerce in his realm, it is shown that the whole of European Turkey except Constantinople, as it was before World War I, almost all Serbia, and all Bulgaria was under Asen's influence.[67]

The Greco-Bulgarian alliance.—Next, John Asen, irritated by his failure to obtain the regency at Constantinople, took the lead in an alliance of the Orthodox rulers of the East, composed of Asen himself, John Vatatzes of Nicaea, and Manuel of Thessalonica. This new union was directed against the Latins. One cannot help seeing in the formation of this alliance a dangerous step for the interests of the Bulgars in the Balkan peninsula. Thereby, as V. G. Vasilievsky correctly stated, Asen, the soul of the coalition, "contributed to the friendly understanding between Manuel of Thessalonica and the Emperor of Nicaea,

[65] See, e.g., Drinov, "Some Works of Demetrius Chomatianos," *Vizantiysky Vremennik*, II (1895), 3 and n. 1. Tafrali, *Thessalonique*, 219.

[66] See, e.g., A. Pogodin, *A History of Bulgaria*, 87. Jireček, *History of the Bulgars*, 337.

[67] G. Illyinsky, "A Charter of Tsar John Asen II," *Transactions of the Russian Archeological Institute at Constantinople*, VII, 2 (1901), 27. See Pogodin, *History of Bulgaria*, 88.

between the European and Asiatic Greeks, and opened the way to the Nicene master to extend his influence in the former Empire of Thessalonica and even in Asen's own dominions. The restoration of the orthodox Eastern Empire was partly decided by this rapprochement."[68] An important result of this alliance for the internal history of Bulgaria was the recognition there of the autocephalous Bulgarian patriarchate, which was established with the consent of the Nicene and other eastern patriarchs.

The capital of the Latin Empire, surrounded on all sides by enemies, was again in a very dangerous position, which was well realized by contemporaries. The aim of the offensive alliance against the Latins was the complete destruction of Latin domination, the expulsion of the Latins from Constantinople, and the division of their possessions between the allies. The troops of Asen and Vatatzes besieged Constantinople in 1235, by land and sea, but were compelled to withdraw without definite results. In his letter appealing to the West for help for the Emperor of Constantinople, the alarmed Pope Gregory IX declared that "Vatatzes and Asen, schismatics, who had recently concluded an alliance of impiety, had invaded with numerous Greek troops the land of our dearest son in Christ, the Emperor of Constantinople."[69] Driven to despair, Baldwin II, the last Latin Emperor, left Constantinople and traveled through western Europe, begging rulers for help for the Empire in men and money.

For the time Constantinople was saved. One cause for the stopping of the advance of the Orthodox alliance was the gradual withdrawal of John Asen himself, who realized that in the Empire of Nicaea he had a more dangerous enemy than in the dying and weakened Latin Empire. Accordingly the king of Bulgaria changed his policy and came out as a defender of the Latin Emperor. Simultaneously with this change of political combinations, Asen took steps towards reconciliation with the papal throne, announcing his faithfulness to the Catholic church and asking the pope to send a legate for negotiations. Thus the short Greco-Bulgarian alliance of the fourth decade of the thirteenth century came to its end.

Alliance of John Vatatzes and Frederick II Hohenstaufen

With the name of John Vatatzes is connected the interesting question of the friendly relations between the two widely separated rulers, the Emperor of Nicaea and the western Emperor, Frederick II Hohenstaufen.

Frederick II, the most remarkable of all the Germanic kings of the Middle

[68] "The Regeneration of the Bulgarian Patriarchate," *Journal of the Ministry of Public Instruction*, CCXXXVII (1885), 30.

[69] A. Theiner, *Vetera monumenta historica Hungariam sacram illustrantia*, I, 140 (no. CCXLIX). See L. Auvray, *Les Registres de Gregoire IX*, II, 217.

Ages, united under his power Germany and the Kingdom of Sicily. The latter, in the person of the Emperor Henry VI, at the end of the twelfth century had menaced Byzantium with fatal danger. Frederick had spent the years of his childhood and youth under the southern sky of Sicily, at Palermo, where had lived the Greeks, later the Arabs, and then the Normans; he spoke Italian, Greek, and Arabic beautifully and, probably, at least in his youth, he spoke German badly. He regarded religious problems much more coolly than his contemporaries. Under the influence of the eastern scholars, Arabs and Jews, large numbers of whom were at Frederick's court in Sicily, he became an enthusiast about science and philosophy and he founded the University of Naples and patronized the medical school at Salerno, a school famous in the Middle Ages. In a word, in mind and education Frederick greatly surpassed his contemporaries, and they did not always understand him. The time of Frederick II may be designated as a "prologue to the Renaissance." In the middle of the nineteenth century, a French historian wrote that Frederick II "gave the impulse to the Renaissance, which prepared the fall of the Middle Ages and the coming of modern times."[70] He was "a man of creative and daring genius."[71] A few years ago a German historian said: "In his universality, he was a real Renaissance genius on the imperial throne and at the same time an Emperor of genius."[72] A subject of perennial interest to the historian, Emperor Frederick II represents in many respects a riddle which has not yet been solved.[73]

Having inherited the conception of the imperial power as unlimited and granted by God and comprehending supreme sovereignty over the world, Frederick was a sworn enemy of the papacy and of its doctrine of the superiority of the papal power to that of the kings. The struggle of the popes with Frederick II was stubborn; three times the Emperor was excommunicated and he died wearied and exhausted by the persistent struggle, in which the popes, putting aside any spiritual aim, were revenging themselves on their personal enemies, this "viper brood of the Hohenstaufens," which they were determined to exterminate.

In such a nature as Frederick's, political plans and motives were predominant over ecclesiastical. Frederick's hostile attitude toward the papacy extended to all that had the support of the popes. Hence, as to the Latin Empire in the East, in which the papacy saw a means of union between the western and eastern churches, the interests of Frederick and John Vatatzes were the same. Frederick was hostile toward the Latin Empire, because he saw in it one of

---

[70] J. Huillard-Bréholles, *Introduction à l'histoire diplomatique de l'empereur Frédéric II,* DLVII.

[71] M. Amari, *Storia dei Musulmani di Sicilia,* III (2), 616; (2nd ed., 1937), 628.

[72] E. Kantarowicz, *Kaiser Friedrich der Zweite,* 613.

[73] C. H. Haskins, *Studies in the History of Mediaeval Science,* 242.

the elements of papal power and influence; John Vatatzes considered the pope an adversary who, by refusing to recognize the Orthodox patriarchate of Constantinople established at that time at Nicaea, was creating a serious obstacle to Vatatzes' aim of taking possession of Constantinople. Close relations between the two emperors began at the end of the fourth decade of the thirteenth century. Frederick did not hesitate to make an "alliance with the Greeks, deadly enemies both of the papacy and of the Latin Empire."[74]

Even earlier Theodore Angelus of Epirus had held friendly correspondence with the western Emperor and had even received from him financial support, for which Pope Gregory IX had excommunicated and anathematized both Frederick and the Despot of Epirus. It is clear that for Frederick's political combinations, the question of religion, either Orthodox or Catholic, had no importance.

But in their hostility towards the papacy, Frederick and John Vatatzes were pursuing different aims. The former wished the popes to renounce their claim to secular power; the latter wished that, by means of some compromises, the West should recognize the eastern church and that thereby the Latin patriarchate at Constantinople should lose its reason to exist. John Vatatzes could then hope that the Latin Empire would quietly disappear. The pope also differed in his attitude toward the two sudden allies. In Frederick he saw a disobedient son of the Church, who encroached upon the prerogatives of the "vicars of Christ" and the heirs of St. Peter, inalienable from the papal standpoint. John Vatatzes was, in the eyes of the pope, a schismatic, who hindered the fulfillment of the cherished dream of the papacy, that is, the reunion of the churches. The allies came to an agreement. Frederick II promised Vatatzes to free Constantinople from the Latins and return it to the legal emperor; for his part the Emperor of Nicaea pledged himself to become the vassal of the western Emperor and restore the union between the two churches. It is, of course, difficult to say how sincere these promises were.

The relations between Frederick and John Vatatzes were so close that, at the end of the fourth decade of the thirteenth century, the Greek troops fought in Italy in Frederick's army. But the relations of the two antipapal emperors became still closer after the death of the first wife of John Vatatzes, Irene, daughter of Theodore I Lascaris. The widower-Emperor, said a source, "being unable to bear his loneliness"[75] married Constance of Hohenstaufen, the daughter of Frederick II, then only eleven or twelve years old, who, when she joined the Greek church, took the Greek name of Anna. There exists a long poem written by Nicolaus Irenikos (Eirenikos) on the occasion of the nuptial festivities at Nicaea; the first two lines of the poem are:

[74] W. Norden, *Das Papsttum und Byzanz*, 322.

[75] Nicephorus Gregoras, *Historia Byzantina*, II, 7, 3; Bonn ed., I, 45.

Around the lovely cypress-tree, the ivy gently windeth;
The Empress is the cypress-tree, my Emperor is the ivy.[76]

Constance-Anna survived her husband by many years, which were full of vicissitudes and adventures. She ended her days in the Spanish city of Valencia, where, in the little church of St. John-of-the-Hospital, the coffin of the former basilissa (empress) of Nicaea has been preserved. It bears the epitaph: "Here lies the lady Constance, the august Empress of Greece."[77]

Frederick's ecclesiastical ideas, which give some scholars grounds for comparing him to the king of England, Henry VIII, under whom the reformation in England began,[78] are reflected in his correspondence with John Vatatzes. In one of his letters Frederick stated that he was actuated not only by his personal affection for Vatatzes, but also by his general zeal for supporting the principles of monarchic government: "All of us, kings and princes of the earth, especially zealous for the orthodox [orthodoxe] religion and faith, cherish an enmity towards the bishops and an inward opposition to the primates of the Church." Then, inveighing against the abuses of liberty and the privileges of the western clergy, the Emperor exclaimed: "O happy Asia! O happy Powers in the East! they do not fear the arms of their subjects nor dread the interference of the pontiffs."[79] Despite his official allegiance to the Catholic faith, Frederick showed himself remarkably kind to eastern Orthodoxy; in one of his letters to Vatatzes which is preserved both in Greek and in Latin, there is this passage: "How! this so-called great arch-priest [that is, Pope; in Latin *sacerdotum princeps;* in Greek ἀρχιερεύς], excommunicating every day Your Majesty by name in the presence of all men and all your subject Romans (in Latin *Graecos*), shamelessly calling heretics the most orthodox Romans, from whom Christian faith has reached the extreme bounds of the Universe . . ."[80] In another letter to the Despot of Epirus Frederick wrote: "We desire to defend not only our own right, but also that of our friendly and beloved neighbours,

[76] The full text of the poem was published by A. Heisenberg, *Aus der Geschichte und Literatur der Palaiologenzeit,* 100–5. The first eight lines were given by G. Schlumberger in his article "Le Tombeau d'une impératrice byzantine à Valence," *Revue des Deux Mondes,* XVII (March 15, 1902) and reprinted in his *Byzance et croisades. Pages médiévales,* 64. In English in Gardner, *Lascarids of Nicaea,* 308.

[77] See Schlumberger, *Byzance et croisades,* 57–58. Charles Diehl, "Constance de Hohenstaufen, impératrice de Nicée," in *Figures byzantines,* II, 207–25. C. Marinesco, "Du Nouveau sur Constance de Hohenstaufen, impératrice de Nicée," *Byzantion,* I (1924), 451–68

(some new documents from the Archives of Barcelona).

[78] See Huillard-Bréholles, *L'Histoire diplomatique de Frédéric II,* dxvii–dxviii. Huillard-Bréholles, *Vie et correspondance de Pierre de la Vigne ministre de l'empereur Frédéric II,* 241–42. Gardner, *Lascarids of Nicaea,* 172–73.

[79] Huillard-Bréholles, *L'Histoire diplomatique,* vi, 685, 686.

[80] The Greek text in N. Festa, "Le Lettere greche di Federigo II," *Archivio storico italiano,* XIII (1894), 22. F. Miklosich and J. Müller, *Acta et diplomata graeca medii aevi,* II (1865), 72. The Latin text in Huillard-Bréholles, *L'Histoire diplomatique,* VI, 772.

whom pure and sincere love in Christ has united with us, and especially the Greeks, our close friends. . . . [The Pope calls] the most pious and orthodox Greeks most impious and heretics."[81]

The friendly intercourse between Frederick and Vatatzes continued until Frederick's death, though in his last years he was alarmed by the negotiations between Nicaea and Rome and by the exchange of embassies between them. For this reason, in his letter to Vatatzes, Frederick blamed "in a fatherly manner the behavior of the son," who, "without the paternal suggestion, had sent an ambassador to the Pope." Not without irony Frederick wrote further: "We desire to do or undertake nothing without your advice" in the affairs of the East, "for these countries which are your neighbors are better known to your Majesty than to us."[82] Frederick warned Vatatzes that the Roman bishops are "not archpriests of Christ, but rapacious wolves and wild beasts devouring the people of Christ."[83]

After Frederick's death, and especially after his natural son, Manfred, had become king of Sicily, relations changed, and Manfred came out as an enemy of the Empire of Nicaea. In a word, after John Vatatzes' death, in 1254, "the alliance of which Frederick II had dreamt, was nothing but a memory."[84]

It cannot be said that the alliance between the two emperors brought about important results; but it may be pointed out that John Vatatzes, relying on the friendly support of the western Emperor, must have had a surer hope for the final success of his policy, that is, the taking of Constantinople.

The Mongol invasion and the alliance of the rulers of Asia Minor against the Mongols

In the fourth and fifth decades of the thirteenth century there appeared from the East the menacing danger of the invasion of the Mongols, namely, the Tartars (in Byzantine sources, "Tahars, Tatars, Atars"). The hordes of Batu (Baty), one of the descendants of the famous Khan Temuchin, who had assumed the title of Jenghiz Khan, i.e., "Grand Khan," rushed into present-day European Russia and in their destructive and irresistible onslaught seized Kiev in 1240, then crossed the Carpathians, and arrived at Bohemia before they were forced to retrace their march to the Russian steppes. At the same time the other Mongol group, marching in a more southerly direction, conquered all Armenia with Erzerum and invaded Asia Minor, menacing the Sultanate of Rum or Iconium and the weak Empire of Trebizond. Under the pressure of common danger from the Mongols sprang the alliance of the three

[81] Festa, *ibid.,* 15–16. Miklosich and Müller, *ibid.,* 68–69.

[82] Festa, *ibid.,* 27; Miklosich and Müller, *ibid.,* II, 74–75. Huillard-Bréholles, *L'Histoire diplomatique,* 921–22.

[83] Festa, *ibid.,* 25; Miklosich and Müller, *ibid.,* 75.

[84] Diehl, *Figures byzantines,* II, 220.

states of Asia Minor: the Sultanate of Iconium, the Empire of Nicaea, and the Empire of Trebizond. The Seljuqs and the military forces of Trebizond were defeated by the Mongols. After that, the Sultan of Iconium was compelled to relieve himself by paying tribute and supplying annually horses, hunting dogs, and the like. The Emperor of Trebizond, realizing the impossibility of fighting the Mongols, made a speedy peace with them and, on condition of paying an annual tribute, became a Mongol vassal. Fortunately for the Seljuqs and John Vatatzes, the Mongols occupied themselves with other military enterprises and temporarily suspended their onslaught upon the West, which enabled the Emperor of Nicaea to take decisive measures in the Balkan peninsula.

From the example of the alliance mentioned above it is obvious that in the thirteenth century alliances between Christians and infidels did not trouble their participants; before the common danger the Orthodox emperors of Nicaea and Trebizond came to a friendly understanding with the Muhammedan Sultan of Iconium.

In connection with the Tartar invasion two stories given by a western historian of the thirteenth century, Matthew of Paris, reflect some rumors circulating at that time in Europe.[85] In both, Matthew said that in 1248 two Mongol envoys were sent to the papal court and cordially received by Pope Innocent IV, who, like many other members of the Catholic church, hoped to convert the Mongols to Christianity. But in the first version he said also that at that time many supposed that the letter of the Mongol prince to the pope contained the proposition of the prince to make war against John Vatatzes (Battacium), "a Greek, son-in-law of Frederick, schismatic, and disobedient [son] of the papal curia; and this proposition was supposed not to be unpleasant to the Pope." In his *Historia Anglorum* Matthew said that the pope directed the Mongol envoys to notify the king of the Tartars that, if the latter had adopted Christianity, he should march with all his troops upon John Vatatzes, "a Greek, son-in-law of Frederick, schismatic, and rebel against the pope and Emperor Baldwin, and after that upon Frederick himself who had risen against the Roman curia." But the Tartar envoys, not liking to encourage "the mutual hatred of Christians," answered through their interpreters, that they were not authorized to impose such conditions upon their master, and they feared that on receiving this news he would be very angry.

Of course, neither of these versions, especially the second one, which reflects a kind of thirteenth century European gossip, has any real historical value,[86]

---

[85] Matthew of Paris, *Chronica Majora,* ed. H. R. Luard, V, 37–38; the text is also to be found in K. Pertz, *Monumenta Germaniae Historica, Scriptores,* XVIII, 301–2. See *Historia Anglorum,* ed. F. Madden, III, 38–39.

[86] See, e.g., P. Pelliot, "Les Mongols et la Papauté," *Revue de l'oriént chrétien,* XXIV (1924), 330–31; XXVII (1931–32), 3–84. B. Altaner, *Die Dominikanermissionen des 13. Jahrhunderts,* 128. The whole passage of *His-*

and they cannot be treated as historical fact, as W. Miller regarded them. Referring to the second version, Miller wrote: "Having given the Holy Father this lesson in Christianity, the infidels returned to their own savage country."[87] But it is very interesting to emphasize the fact that the political power and importance of John Vatatzes was widely and thoroughly appreciated and played a certain part, at least in the opinion of western European writers, in the negotiations between the pope and the Mongol envoys. The envoys were received with great esteem and attention by Innocent IV, who wrote to "their illustrious king, and to the nobles and to all the princes and barons of the Tartar army" a long letter, in which he urged them to adopt the Christian faith.[88] Of course, the name of John Vatatzes was not mentioned in this papal letter. Meanwhile John Vatatzes, relieved from the danger of Mongol invasion from the East, concentrated all his attention on the Balkan peninsula and obtained brilliant results.

Significance of the external policy of John Vatatzes

With the death of John Asen II, in 1241, the brilliant epoch of the Second Bulgarian Kingdom passed away, and Asen's weak and inexperienced successors could not maintain his conquests. With his death collapsed the second attempt of the Bulgars to found in the Balkan peninsula a great Greco-Slavonic Empire with its center at Constantinople; for both Simeon in the tenth century, and the Asens, Kalojan and John II, in the thirteenth century, this task proved to be too great. The last attempt of this kind conceived and organized on a larger scale by Slavs, that is, by the Serbs, was to be made in the fourteenth century.

Taking advantage of the decline of Bulgaria, John Vatatzes crossed with his army to the European coast and in a few months took away from Bulgaria all the regions of Macedonia and Thrace which had been conquered by Asen II. Pursuing his march, Vatatzes advanced towards Thessalonica, where anarchy prevailed, and in 1246, without difficulty, took possession of this city. The state of Thessalonica ceased to exist. In the ensuing year Vatatzes seized some Thracian cities which were still under Latin rule. The Emperor of Nicaea drew near Constantinople. The Despotat of Epirus submitted to Vatatzes' suzerainty. There were no more rivals in Vatatzes' aspiration for the shores of the Bosphorus.

Towards the end of Vatatzes' reign his dominions, both direct and vassal, extended from the Black Sea to the Adriatic. Leaving out of the question

---

toria Anglorum referring to the secret negotiations between the pope and Mongol envoys is marked in the margin of the manuscript in red letters, "*dubium.*" See Matthew of Paris, *Historia Anglorum,* ed. Madden, III, 39, n. 9.

[87] *The Cambridge Medieval History,* IV, 493.

[88] E. Berger, *Les Registres d'Innocent IV,* II, 113–14 (no. 4682); at Lyons, November 22, 1248.

middle Greece and the Peloponnesus, nothing but Constantinople was lacking for the restoration of the Empire.

In 1254 John Vatatzes died at the age of sixty-two, ending a reign of thirty-three years. With rare unanimity the sources praise him. His son and successor, Theodore II Lascaris, wrote in a panegyric: "He has unified the Ausonian land, which was divided into very many parts by foreign and tyrannic rulers, Latin, Persian, Bulgarian, Scythian and others, punished robbers and protected his land. . . . He has made our country inaccessible to enemies."[89] Byzantine historians unanimously glorify John Vatatzes.[90] Even if there is some exaggeration by the sources in their estimate of the Emperor of Nicaea, John Vatatzes must be considered a talented and energetic politician, and the chief creator of the restored Byzantine Empire.

It is interesting that the name of John Vatatzes was so beloved and esteemed by the people that some time after his death, he became a saint in popular tradition; miracles began to be connected with his memory and *The Life of St. John the Merciful* was composed, a sort of popular canonization. The memory of John Vatatzes has not been officially recognized by the Greek church, and his cult confined itself to the narrow limits of a Lydian city in Asia Minor, Magnesia, where the Emperor was buried. This life of Vatatzes is not to be confused with a biography of a saint of the seventh century, John the Merciful, as sometimes happens, and scholars vary in opinion concerning the place and time of its composition. Even at the present time the clergy and population of Magnesia and its surroundings gather annually on November 4 in the local church and honor the memory of the late Emperor John the Merciful.[91] The Orthodox calendar gives under November 4 the name of "John Ducas Vatadzi."[92]

The external activity of Vatatzes was extremely important because, by eliminating gradually the pretenders to the role of restorer of the Empire—the rulers of Thessalonica, Epirus, and Bulgaria—he brought under his power so much territory as practically to signify the restoration of the Byzantine Empire. The main role in the restoration belonged to John Vatatzes, and in 1261 Michael Palaeologus only profited by the results of the persistence and

[89] Uspensky, "Manuscripts of the History of Nicetas Acominatus," *Journal of the Ministry of Public Instruction,* CXCIV (1877), 76. J. B. Pappadopoulos, *Theodore II Lascaris empereur de Nicée,* 43.

[90] See Nicephorus Gregoras, *Historia,* II, 1, 2; Bonn ed., I, 24. George Acropolita, *Epitaph in Memory of John Vatatzes;* in *Opera Omnia,* ed. Heisenberg, II, 12. Ἀνωνύμου Σύνοψις χρονική, in Sathas, *Bibliotheca graeca medii aevi,* VII, 509.

[91] See A. Heisenberg, "Kaiser Johannes Batatzes der Barmherzige," *Byzantinische Zeitschrift,* XIV (1905), 160, 162. N. Festa, "A propos d'une biographie de St. Jean le Miséricordieux," *Vizantiysky Vremennik,* XIII (1906), 5, 9, 18. Gardner, *Lascarids of Nicaea,* 195–96. Andreeva, *Culture of the Byzantine Court,* 24.

[92] Arch. Sergius, *The Complete Liturgical Calendar (Menologion) of the Orient* (2nd ed., 1901), II, 344.

energy of the best Nicene Emperor. The generations after John Vatatzes looked back upon him as "the Father of the Greeks."[93]

Theodore and John Lascaris and the restoration of the Byzantine Empire

The last rulers of the Empire of Nicaea were the son and grandson of John Vatatzes, Theodore II Lascaris (1254–1258) and John IV Lascaris (1258–1261). Theodore, thirty-three years old, "seated, according to custom, on a shield,"[94] was proclaimed emperor with the consent of the troops and nobility.

In spite of his weak health, Theodore, before ascending the throne, had devoted all his time to studies and literature. His enlightened father had done his best, and Theodore's education had been carefully supervised by the best scholars of the epoch, with Nicephorus Blemmydes and George Acropolita at their head.

On his accession to the throne, Theodore II, like his father, displayed the energetic political activity which made him sometimes forget his studies, even his favorite philosophy. Realizing the importance of external political relations, he turned his chief attention to the forming of a powerful army. Theodore wrote: "I have one truth, one goal, one desire—to gather together the flock of God and protect it from hostile wolves."[95] Believing that the Greeks had to rely on their own strength and not on foreign alliances or on foreign mercenaries, Theodore, perhaps, was almost the only "Byzantine" Emperor who paid attention to the "hellenization" of the army, contrary to the established custom of making use of the mercenary troops of foreign peoples.[96]

In 1258, the young Emperor breathed his last in the prime of life (36 years old), having before death exchanged his imperial robes for those of a monk. He left to his successor the vast conquests of John Vatatzes intact. This active and philosophically educated Emperor lived and worked in the belief that history would pass judgment upon him. In one of his letters he said: "The judgment of history will be passed by the generations to come."[97] The special historian of the time of Theodore II, not without some exaggeration, wrote: "Theodore died very young; otherwise Hellenism might have hoped for better days under the wise rule of the Emperor who had exerted all his energy in order to found the Greek Empire upon a solid and steady basis."[98] But this ambition of Theodore remained a theory. In reality the mercenary troops representing different nationalities took an important part in the life of the

[93] See W. Miller, "The Emperor of Nicaea and the Recovery of Constantinople," *Cambridge Medieval History,* IV, 500.

[94] Nicephorus Gregoras, *Historia,* III, 1, 2; Bonn ed., I, 55. George Acropolita, *Annales,* chap. 53; ed. Heisenberg, I, 105.

[95] Theodore Lascaris, *Epistulae CCXVII;*

ed. N. Festa, 59.

[96] Miller, "The Emperor of Nicaea," *Cambridge Medieval History,* IV, 505.

[97] Theodore Lascaris, *Epistulae XLIV;* ed. Festa, 59, 119–20.

[98] Pappadopoulos, *Théodore II Lascaris,* 180.

Empire of Nicaea in general, and during Theodore's reign in particular.[99]

In external activity, Theodore undertook two hard Bulgarian campaigns. On the news of Vatatzes' death the Bulgarian tsar, Michael Asen, seized the opportunity to recover the provinces lost under Vatatzes, and it was feared that all the latter's European conquests might again become Bulgarian. In spite of many difficulties and the cowardice and treachery of his generals, however, the two Bulgarian campaigns ended successfully for Theodore, and, through the mediation of the Russian prince Rostislav, Michael Asen's father-in-law, a treaty was made. Bulgarians and Greeks received their former frontiers, and one Bulgarian fortress was even ceded to Theodore.[100]

Theodore's relations to the Despot of Epirus in connection with the proposed marriage between the despot's son and Theodore's daughter, resulted in Theodore's receiving the important seaport Dyrrachium (Durazzo), on the Adriatic, and the fortress Serbia (Servia), near the confines of Epirus and Bulgaria. Dyrrachium "was the western outpost of the Nicene Empire, and necessarily a thorn in the side of the despots of Epirus." [101]

In Asia Minor, the Seljuq Turks were seriously menaced by the Mongols, who succeeded in making the sultan their tributary. The situation was delicate and complicated, because Theodore had, though undecidedly, supported the sultan in his struggle against the Mongols, and the sultan, "having the heart of a shy deer,"[102] took refuge as a fugitive with Theodore. But a military conflict between Nicaea and the Mongols was avoided, and a Mongol embassy was sent to Theodore. The reception which took place, probably at Magnesia, was exceptionally brilliant and imposing; Theodore's chief idea was to impress the Tartars, of whom he was afraid. The Emperor received the ambassadors, seated on a lofty throne, sword in hand. Byzantine historians gave a detailed account of the reception.[103]

A recent historian remarked that Theodore "was, in a word, a mass of nerves, an 'interesting case' for a modern mental specialist," and his "brief reign of less than four years did not enable him to make a great mark upon the history of his time."[104] Finally, it has been said lately that "in Theodore was particularly felt what may be called enlightened absolutism."[105] Of course, Theodore's reign was too short for definite judgment to be passed on its sig-

---

[99] Andreeva, *Culture of the Byzantine Court,* 50–54, 105.

[100] George Acropolita, *Annales,* chap. 62; ed. Heisenberg, 126–27.

[101] Gardner, *Lascarids of Nicaea,* 226.

[102] George Acropolita, *Annales,* chap. 69; ed. Heisenberg, 143.

[103] See a very accurate article on this reception by M. Andreeva, "The Reception of the Tartar Ambassadors at the Nicene Court," *Recueil d'études dediées à la mémoire de N. P. Kondakov,* 187–200. Andreeva, *Culture of the Byzantine Court,* 71–72.

[104] Miller, "The Emperor of Nicaea," *Cambridge Medieval History,* 501, 506.

[105] Andreeva, *Culture of the Byzantine Court,* 107.

nificance. But in the history of Nicaea his name will always be honorably remembered for his continuance of his father's successful external policy and for his own breadth of learning.

Theodore's only son and successor, who was not quite eight years old, John IV (1258–61) could not, even with the help of the appointed regent, George Muzalon, master the complicated affairs of the Empire. At this time the crafty and ambitious Michael Palaeologus, John Vatatzes' relative, "a restless intriguer and an infamous hypocrite, but an able officer,"[106] played a decisive role. Several times suspected of plots and treason by Vatatzes and Theodore II, and occupying, nevertheless, high offices, he had in times of danger successfully withdrawn and even fled for a time to the court of the Sultan of Iconium. Stormy times demanded a strong rule. Michael Palaeologus profited skillfully by circumstances and, in 1259, was crowned emperor.

The chief external danger to the Balkan possessions of the Empire of Nicaea arose from the Despot of Epirus, who succeeded in forming an alliance against the Empire consisting of the despot himself, the king of Sicily, Manfred, a relative of the despot and the natural son of Frederick II, and the prince of Achaia, William de Villehardouin. Michael Palaeologus gained some military success against the coalition, and the decisive battle was fought in 1259 in western Macedonia, in the plain of Pelagonia, near the city of Castoria. Turks, Cumans, and Slavs, as well as Greeks, fought in Michael's army. The battle of Pelagonia or Castoria ended in the complete defeat of the allies. The prince of Achaia was captured. The well-armed troops of the western knights fled before the light-armed Bithynian, Slavonic, and eastern troops. "Perhaps it was the first time that Turks fought against Greeks on Greek soil, and on this occasion in Greek service."[107] A contemporary, George Acropolita, gave this judgment of the event: "Under imperial advice our troops have got so great a victory that the fame of it has passed over all the ends of the earth; of such victories the sun has seen but few."[108] In his autobiography, which is preserved, Michael Palaeologus writes concerning this battle: "Along with them [with the traitors to the Roman state, i.e., the Despot of Epirus and his associates] and their allies, who had as their leader the Prince of Achaia, whom have I vanquished? Alamans, Sicilians, and Italians who came from Apulia, the land of the Iapygians and Brundusium, from Bithynia, Euboea, and the Peloponnesus."[109]

[106] G. Finlay, *A History of Greece*, ed. H. F. Tozer, III, 328.

[107] Gardner, *Lascarids of Nicaea*, 248.

[108] *Annales*, chap. 81; ed. Heisenberg, 171.

[109] *De vita sua opusculum*, par. VII, in the *Christianskoe Čtenie*, II (1885), 534; Russian trans., *ibid.*, 554–55; in French in C. Chapman, *Michel Paléologue, restaurateur de l'Empire Byzantin*, 171. M. Dendias disproves the view that Manfred was present at the defeat of the allies at Palagonia: "Le Roi Manfred de Sicile et la bataille de Pélagonie," *Mélanges Charles Diehl*, I, 55–60.

The battle of Castoria had a decisive significance for the restoration of the Byzantine Empire. The dominions of the Despot of Epirus were reduced to his hereditary land in Epirus. The Latin Empire could not rely on the defeated Principality of Achaia, and was itself under the direction of the feeble and apathetic Baldwin II.

Meanwhile, in order to make still more sure the success of the final attack on Constantinople, Michael Palaeologus concluded a treaty with the Genoese. The commercial interests of Genoa and Venice conflicted everywhere in the Levant. After the Fourth Crusade and the formation of the Latin Empire, Venice had gained quite exceptional trade power in the Latin dominions of the Levant, and Genoa could not reconcile herself to this state of affairs. Realizing this, Michael came to an agreement with the Genoese; although they knew that an understanding with the schismatic Greeks would evoke the severe censure of the pope and the West in general, they were so desirous of driving out their Venetian rivals from the East that they concluded the treaty with Michael.

In March, 1261, at Nymphaeum, was signed the very important treaty which granted to the Genoese the commercial supremacy in the Levant so long enjoyed by the Venetians. This was a real offensive and defensive alliance against Venice.[110] Free trade forever was granted the Genoese throughout the present and future provinces of the Empire. Very important grants at Constantinople and in the islands of Crete and Euboea, if Michael "by the mercy of God" should recover them, were included in the treaty; Smyrna, "a city fit for commercial use, having a good port and abounding in all goods," was assigned to the absolute control of the Genoese; commercial stations with churches and consuls were to be established in the islands of Chios and Lesbos, and in some other places; the Black Sea (majus mare) was to be closed to all foreign merchants except the Genoese and Pisans, the faithful subjects of Michael. On their side the Genoese pledged themselves to grant free trade to the Emperor's subjects, and to support him with their fleet, provided that the ships were not employed against the pope and the friends of Genoa. The Genoese fleet was extremely important in Michael Palaeologus' plans to reconquer Constantinople. This treaty was ratified at Genoa a few days before Constantinople was taken by Michael's troops. This was a brilliant victory for Genoa which, after

---

[110] The best text of the treaty is given in C. Manfroni, *Le relazioni fra Genova l'Impero Bizantino e i Turchi*, 791–809. The text is also printed in *Historiae Patriae Monumenta*, VII, *Liber Jurium reipublicae genuensis*, I, cols. 1350–59. See W. Heyd, *Histoire du commerce du Levant au moyen âge*, I, 427–30. G. Caro, *Genua und die Mächte am Mittelmeer, 1257–* *1311*, 105–7. Miller, "The Emperor of Nicaea," *Cambridge Medieval History*, IV, 510–11. Chapman, *Michel Paléologue*, 42. G. Brătianu, *Recherches sur le commerce génois dans la mer Noire au XIIIe siècle*, 81–83. Brătianu, "Etudes pontiques," *Revue historique du sud-est européen*, XXI (1944), 39–52.

Saladin's victories in Syria, had suffered grievous losses. It was a new page in their economic history. "The vigor of the thirteenth century colonial life offers a sharp contrast with the halting, tentative character of that of the twelfth. Naturally this is the result of wide experience, of better organization, and especially of the amazing developments of trade."[111]

On July 25, 1261, without striking a blow, the troops of Michael took possession of Constantinople. Michael himself was at that time in Asia Minor, where he received the news that Constantinople had been taken. He set out immediately and at the beginning of August entered the city, cheerfully greeted by the populace; shortly after, his second coronation was performed in St. Sophia. Baldwin II fled to Euboea (Negroponte). The Latin patriarch and the chief members of the Catholic clergy had time enough to leave the city before it was taken. By Michael's order, the unfortunate John IV Lascaris was blinded. Michael Palaeologus became the restorer of the Byzantine Empire, Michael VIII, the founder of the last Byzantine dynasty of the Palaeologi, by his success in taking advantage of what had been prepared by the emperors of Nicaea. The capital was transferred from Nicaea to Constantinople.

The fugitive Baldwin proceeded from Euboea to Thebes and Athens. There, "on the venerable rock of Athens was played the last pitiful scene in the brief drama of the Latin Empire of Constantinople. Then Baldwin sailed from the Peiraeus for Monemvasia; and leaving behind him not a few of his noble retinue in the Morea, set out for Europe, to solicit aid for his lost cause and to play the sorry part of an emperor in exile."[112]

Thus, the Latin Empire, in the severe judgment of a German historian, Gregorovius, "a creation of western European crusading knights, of the selfish trade-policy of the Venetians, and of the hierarchic idea of the papacy, fell after a miserable existence of fifty-seven years, leaving behind it no other trace than destruction and anarchy. That deformed chivalrous feudal state of the Latins belongs to the most worthless phenomena of history. The sophistical maxim of the German philosopher who asserted that all that exists is rational, becomes here merely an absurdity."[113] Another German historian remarked: "The Latin ignominy belongs to the past."[114]

While Western sources, almost without exception, confine themselves to the mere mention of the taking of Constantinople by Michael and of the expulsion of the Franks, Greek sources express great joy on this occasion. George Acropolita, for example, wrote: "Because of this fact all the Roman people were then in merriment, great cheerfulness, and inexpressible joy; there

[111] E. H. Byrne, "The Genoese Colonies in Syria," *The Crusades and Other Historical Essays Presented to Dana C. Munro*, 160.

[112] Miller, *Latins in the Levant*, 115.

[113] *Geschichte der Stadt Athen im Mittelalter*, I, 412.

[114] Gelzer, *Abriss der byzantinischen Kaisergeschichte*, 1049.

was no one who did not rejoice and exult."[115] Still a discordant note sounded in the words of a high official under Michael Paleologus, a teacher, commentator of Homer, and jurist, Senakherim, who after the taking of Constantinople by the Greeks exclaimed: "What do I hear! This has been reserved to our days! What have we done that we should live through and see such disasters? For the rest, no one can hope for good, since the Romans walk again in the city!"[116]

In summary, most scholars view with condemnation the behavior of the Latins during their domination of Constantinople. Indeed, considering the sack of the capital by the crusaders, the "dispersal" of its numberless treasures throughout Europe, and the oppression of the Greek Orthodox Church, the hostile attitude of contemporary Greek sources and of most modern writers is understandable. Recently, however, a voice has been raised in extenuation of the Latins, that of an eminent American professor, E. H. Swift, who has dealt with the behavior of the Latins in regard to the famous and unique building of the "Great Church" of Saint Sophia.

In 1907 E. M. Antoniades, the Greek author of a detailed monograph on St. Sophia, wrote: "The fifty-seven years of the Latin occupation constituted the worst and most dangerous period of the entire history of the church, which was saved only by the recovery of the city by the Greeks in 1261."[117] Professor Swift questioned this opinion. He believed that it may be inferred from a number of historical sources as well as from archeological evidence observable in the building as it stands today that quite the opposite seems to be the case. A number of earthquakes before 1204 had rendered the structural condition of the church extremely precarious before the crusaders took possession of it. Since they found it in a dangerously weakened state, they shortly took adequate measure to assure the stability of their newly acquired cathedral, repairing it in various ways, particularly by the erection of buttresses. So, Swift concluded, "the Latins were not as black as they usually are painted, but rather . . . became in fact the saviours of one of the greatest monuments of the Greek architectural genius."[118] Swift's observation is an interesting contribution to the history of the building, and it is quite likely that the crusaders contributed appreciably to the preservation of this unique structure. But the fact remains well established that they mercilessly robbed the interior of St. Sophia.

[115] *Annales,* chap. 88; ed. Heisenberg, I, 188.

[116] George Pachymeres, *De Michaele Palaeologo,* I, 149. See P. Yakovenko, *Studies in the Domain of Byzantine Charters. The Charters of the New Monastery in the Island of Chios,* 133–35.

[117] *Hagia Sophia,* I, 25.

[118] "The Latins at Hagia Sophia," *American Journal of Archaeology,* XXXIX (1935), 458–59, 473–74. Swift, *Hagia Sophia,* 87–88, 113–19, especially 118–19.

The taking of Constantinople by the crusaders in 1204 took place against the will of Pope Innocent III. But after the foundation of the Latin Empire the pope clearly realized that the new state of things in the Near East, however disagreeable it might have been at first to the papal dignity, nevertheless had opened wide horizons for the further strengthening of Catholicism and the papacy. The main ecclesiastical problem of the epoch consisted in establishing intercourse between the eastern and western churches in connection with the political changes which had taken place in the Christian East. In the Latin dominions established by the crusaders on the territory of the Byzantine Empire, Catholicism was to be planted. The first task of the papacy was to organize the Catholic church in the regions conquered by the Latins, and then to clear up its relation to the secular power and to the local Greek population, both laic and ecclesiastic. The second task was to render subject to Rome, as far as ecclesiastical matters were concerned, the Greek regions which after 1204 had remained independent and at the head of which stood the state of Nicaea. In a word, the problem of the union with the Greeks became the keystone of all ecclesiastical relations of the thirteenth century.

At the beginning of the political existence of the Latin Empire the position of the pope was very complicated and delicate. According to the treaty concluded between the crusaders and Venice it was stipulated that, if the Emperor had been elected from the Franks, the Latin patriarch should be elected from the Venetian clergy. The interests of the Roman curia were not taken into consideration, for in the treaty there was no suggestion either that the pope should participate in the election of the patriarch or that any revenues should go into the treasury of the curia.

In the letter of the first Latin Emperor to the pope, Baldwin wrote of "the miraculous success" of the crusaders, of the fall of Constantinople, of the lawlessness of the Greeks, "who were producing nausea in God himself," of a hope to go on a crusade to the Holy Land in the future, etc.,[119] but he did not mention the election of the patriarch. And when the new clergy of St. Sophia, consisting of Venetians, had elected to the patriarchate a Venetian noble, Thomas Morosini, the pope, though he at first proclaimed the election uncanonical, nevertheless was forced to yield and, "at his own initiative," confirmed this choice.

The problem of the relation of the papal throne to the Greek clergy who remained within the Latin dominions is also interesting. It is known that a great number of bishops and the majority of the lower clergy did not abandon

---

[119] Tafel and Thomas, *Urkunden zur ältern Handels- und Staatsgeschichte*, I, 508–10.

their places. In this case the pope held a conciliatory policy, allowing the Greek bishops to be ordained in the eparchies with an exclusively Greek population, and granting privileges concerning the preservation of the Greek rites and the church service, conceding, for example, the use of leavened bread for the Eucharist. However, the papal legates appeared in the Balkan peninsula and Asia Minor and tried to persuade the Greek clergy to join the union.

In 1204, a papal legate made the first attempt to obtain the consent of the Greek clergy to the recognition of the pope as the head of their church; the negotiations were held in St. Sophia, at Constantinople, and were of no avail.[120] A very important role in the negotiations of that time was played by Nicholas Mesarites, later bishop of Ephesus, whose personality and activity were first elucidated by A. Heisenberg. In the years 1205–6 the negotiations continued their course. Nicholas of Otranto, abbot of Casole, of southern Italy, took part in them as an interpreter; holding the orthodox opinions, he recognized, like the whole church of southern Italy of that time, the papal primate and was an adherent of the union. Nicholas of Otranto, who has left many poems and prose works, almost all of them unpublished, deserves, as Heisenberg justly remarked, a special monograph.[121] The position of the Greek clergy became more complicated when in 1206 the patriarch of Constantinople, John Camaterus, died in Bulgaria, having fled there before the crusaders. With the permission of Emperor Henry, the Greek clergy of the Latin Empire applied to Innocent III for authorization to elect a new patriarch, and Henry allowed them to choose the patriarch provided they would recognize the overlordship of the pope. But the Greeks wished neither subordination to the Holy See nor reconciliation with it. Therefore nothing came of the disputation held at Constantinople, in the same year, 1206, when at the head of the Latins stood the Latin patriarch, Thomas Morosini and, leading the Greeks, Nicholas Mesarites. The Greeks of the Latin Empire began to turn to Theodore Lascaris.[122] In 1208 a new Orthodox patriarch, Michael Autoreanus, was elected at Nicaea, who crowned Theodore Lascaris the Emperor of Nicaea. This was a fact of great moment not only for Nicaea, but also for the Greeks of the Latin Empire.

The negotiations of 1214 held at Constantinople and in Asia Minor with the participation of Cardinal Pelagius, his delegates, and Nicholas Mesarites broke up without any result. Nicholas Mesarites, at that time metropolitan of Ephesus with the title of the exarch of all Asia, was profoundly discontented with the haughty reception accorded to him by Pelagius in Constantinople.[123]

[120] Heisenberg, *Neue Quellen zur Geschichte des lateinischen Kaisertums*, I, 48–50, par. 37–38 (misprint in Heisenberg's text, par. 32–38); see also pp. 7–8.

[121] *Ibid.*, 8.

[122] *Ibid.*, II, 5–6, 25–35.

[123] *Ibid.*, III, 21–23, par. 16, p. 56. See also Gerland, *Geschichte des lateinischen Kaiserreiches*, 233–43.

From the point of view of influence on the Latin clergy in the East, Innocent III, towards the end of his pontificate, obtained a brilliant victory: the Lateran Council, in 1215, recognized by the western church as an ecumenical council, proclaimed the pope the head of all the eastern Latin patriarchs, that is to say, those of Constantinople, Jerusalem, and Antioch, who from that time on were hierarchically under the jurisdiction of the Holy See.

But Innocent III was entirely disappointed in his idea that Constantinople would engage in the promised crusade. Secular, political, and international interests and problems absorbed the new Latin Empire to such an extent that the Latin rulers entirely put aside the plan of a crusade to the Holy Land and Innocent III began to aim at forming a new crusade from Europe, not through Constantinople.

The papal hopes were not satisfied by the external subjugation of the eastern Church to Rome; for complete victory a religious union was necessary, the spiritual subjugation of the Greek Orthodox population. But this could be attained neither by Innocent III nor by his successors.

The Empire of Nicaea had an Orthodox Greek patriarch of her own, who, residing at Nicaea, continued to bear the title of the patriarch of Constantinople. But the population of Nicaea regarded the patriarchal throne transferred to them as "alien and annexed,"[124] and hoped that it would be later restored to its original place in Constantinople. The first Nicene ruler, Theodore Lascaris, was not recognized by Innocent III as emperor or even as despot and was called in his letter merely "the noble man Theodore Lascaris" (*nobili viro Theodoro Lascari*)."[125] In this letter to Lascaris, the pope, though he does not justify the violence of the crusaders at the taking of Constantinople, nevertheless refers to the fact that the Latins were the tool of Providence in punishing the Greeks for their refusal to accept the headship of the Roman church and that it would be desirable now for the Greeks to become obedient subjects of the Holy See and the Latin Emperor. But this papal admonition was of no avail.

Interest in the ecclesiastical relations in the Empire of Nicaea lies in the attempts by conferences and correspondence to find ways and means of closer intercourse between the two churches. In the very Empire of Nicaea there were men such as the metropolitan of Ephesus, Nicholas Mesarites, who were inclined to establish intercourse and agreement with the Roman church; but the Greek population never wished to accept the union. John III Vatatzes seemed to be particularly favorably disposed towards the recognition of the union, but he was influenced only by political speculations. First, he was alarmed by the election of the brave John of Brienne, formerly king of Jeru-

---

[124] Nicephorus Blemmydes, *Curriculum vitae et carmina*, vii; ed. Heisenberg, 7.

[125] Innocent III, *Epistolae*, XI, 47; ed. Migne, *Patrologia Latina*, CCXV, 1372.

salem, first as regent and then as joint emperor with Baldwin II of Constantinople, at that time a minor. John of Brienne backed by the pope could carry out an aggressive policy against the Empire of Nicaea. Therefore, Vatatzes endeavored to divert the pope from his interest in the Latin Empire.

In 1232 five Franciscan monks (Minorites) arrived in Nicaea from Turkish captivity and opened negotiations with Patriarch Germanus II on the union of the churches. John Vatatzes and Germanus II treated them well, and the Minorites brought to Pope Gregory IX a patriarchal letter, in which the patriarch offered to the pope for consideration the subject of the union.[126] Gregory IX acquiesced willingly in this proposal and in 1234 sent to Nicaea several delegates. The council was held first at Nicaea, and then transferred to Nymphaeum. In the disputation Nicephorus Blemmydes took a leading part.[127] The course of the discussions at the Council of 1234 is very well known, because there is a detailed official report.[128] But the negotiations met with failure, and the papal delegates were forced to withdraw, loaded with the curses of the Greeks gathered there, who shouted: "You are heretics. As we have found you heretics and excommunicated, so we leave you now as heretics and excommunicated!" In their turn the Catholic delegates cried to the Greeks: "You are also heretics!"[129]

At the Council of Lyons, in 1245, Gregory's successor, Pope Innocent IV, announced that he was afflicted "about the schism of Romania, that is to say, of the Greek Church which, in our own days only a few years ago, had arrogantly and foolishly seceded and averted itself from the bosom of its mother as if from its step-mother."[130] "Two states," Luchaire wrote, "two religions,

---

[126] The correspondence between the Pope and Germanus II is to be found in Matthew of Paris, *Chronica Majora,* ed. Luard, III, 448–69, and in J. D. Mansi, *Sacrorum Conciliorum nova et amplissima collectio,* XXIII, 47–62. The Greek text of the two letters is in Sathas, *Bibliotheca graeca medii aevi,* II, 39–49. Matthew of Paris gives the letters incorrectly for the year 1237. See Gardner, *Lascarids of Nicaea,* 165–66. G. Golubovich, *Bibliotheca bio-bibliographica della Terra Sante e dell'Oriente Francescano,* I, 161–62; II, 510–12. Golubovich, "Disputatio Latinorum et Graecorum seu relatio apocrisariorum Gregorii IX de gestis Nicaeae in Bithynia et Nymphaeae in Lydia," *Archivum Franciscanum Historicum,* XII (1919), 418–24. Altaner, *Die Dominikanermissionen,* 16. We have an apparently excellent monograph on the Patriarch Germanus II, in modern Greek. S. N. Logopatis, Γερμανὸς ὁ Β᾽, πατριάρχης Κωνσταντινου-

πόλεως Νικαίας (1222–1240). Βίος, συγγράμματα καὶ διδασκαλία αὐτοῦ (Athens, 1919). See H. Stock's review, *Byzantinisch-neugriechische Jahrbücher,* I (1920), 186–89. I have not seen this book.

[127] Nicephorus Blemmydes, *Curriculum vitae et carmina,* ed. Heisenberg, xl–xlii, 63–71.

[128] See Mansi, *Amplissima collectio conciliorum,* XXIII, 279–319. Golubovich, *Bibliotheca bio-bibliographica,* I, 163–69. The best complete text of "Disputatio Latinorum et Graecorum," in Golubovich, *Archivum Franciscanum Historicum,* XII (1919), 428–65.

[129] Mansi, *Amplissima collectio conciliorum,* XXIII, 306. Golubovich, *Archivum Franciscanum Historicum,* XII, 463–64. See Norden, *Das Papsttum und Byzanz,* 350–52.

[130] Matthew of Paris, *Chronica Majora,* ed. Luard, IV, 434.

and two races, always deeply separated from each other, were maintaining towards each other the same attitude of enmity and distrust."[131] John Vatatzes' alliance with Frederick II Hohenstaufen strained still farther the relations between Nicaea and the papacy, although towards the end of Frederick's reign negotiations between Nicaea and Rome were reopened and an exchange of embassies took place.

But after Frederick's death, in the last years of John Vatatzes' reign, there seemed to come a decisive moment for the union of the Churches. The Emperor had submitted his conditions—the surrender to him of Constantinople, the restoration of the Constantinopolitan patriarchate, and the withdrawal from the city of the Latin Emperor and the Latin clergy—and Innocent IV acceded to them. For the restoration of the unity of the Christian world the pope was ready to sacrifice the state created by the crusaders. For the return of the capital to the Empire Vatatzes was ready to sacrifice the independence of the Greek church. Both sides definitely abandoned their traditional policy. But this agreement remained only a project. A very important letter of the patriarch of Nicaea to Innocent IV, written in 1253, gave to the Greek delegates full power to conclude with the pope the negotiations for union.[132] But in 1254 both John Vatatzes and Innocent IV died, and their agreement, one of the most significant pages in the history of the negotiations for union between the East and West, remained only a project which was never realized.

Theodore II Lascaris, Vatatzes' son and successor, professed to believe that he as Emperor should guide the ecclesiastical policy, take part in church matters, and preside at the ecclesiastical councils. Accordingly he did not desire a patriarch of great energy and strong will. Therefore, the candidature of Blemmydes was finally rejected, and Arsenius was promoted from layman to patriarch in three days.[133] Under Theodore II the relations of Nicaea with the papal curia were closely tied up with the political concerns of the Emperor; as for his father, the union with Rome was for Theodore merely a step to Constantinople.

It is usually related that, in 1256, Pope Alexander IV suddenly sent a bishop of Orvieto, in Italy, to Nicaea to resume the negotiations for union interrupted by Vatatzes' death.[134] This sudden decision of the pope seemed to have no

[131] *Innocent III. La Question d'Orient*, 280.

[132] See this letter in Norden, *Das Papsttum und Byzanz*, 756–59 (appendix, no. XII).

[133] This statement is given by George Acropolita, *Annales*, chap. 53; ed. Heisenberg, 106–7. In his autobiography Blemmydes himself says that he rejected the emperor's offer; *Curriculum vitae et carmina*, ed. Heisenberg, chaps. XLIII–XLV, 41–45. Heisenberg keeps

Acropolita's version (p. xx), which we follow. Barvinok rejects Acropolita and follows Blemmydes, *Nicephorus Blemmydes and His Works*, 49–54.

[134] See, e.g., Norden, *Das Papsttum und Byzanz*, 378–79. L. Bréhier, "Attempts at Reunion of the Greek and Latin Churches," *Cambridge Medieval History*, IV, 609.

particular reason and remained unmotivated. But now, on the basis of some new documents, it is known that the initiative in resuming negotiations belonged not to the pope, but to the Emperor of Nicaea.[135] In 1256, Theodore sent to the pope two nobles who begged Alexander IV to resume negotiations and send a legate to Nicaea. Alexander was overjoyed to acquiesce in the imperial proposal. Both sides wished to hasten matters as much as possible. The papal legate, Constantine, bishop of Orvieto, was to be ready to depart in ten days. It is interesting to note that the proposals made to the curia by the late John Vatatzes were now to serve as the principal basis of the new negotiations.[136] The delegate was supplied with both official and secret instructions. The legate was given some special powers, the most important of which was the right to convoke a council, to preside over it as a vicar of the pope, and to draw up its decisions as he pleased.

This papal mission organized so energetically and hopefully ended in complete failure; the bishop of Orvieto was not even received by the Emperor, who had meantime changed his mind. On his way to Nicaea, in Macedonia, the papal legate was ordered to leave the imperial territory, and forbidden to journey further.[137] Theodore II who, at that time, was taking the field against Bulgaria and was successful in his political enterprises, had come to the conclusion that he had no further need of the papal support. His final aim—the taking of Constantinople—seemed to Theodore entirely realizable without any new attempt to form the union, that is, without losing the independence of the Greek Church.

In 1258 Theodore II died. Michael Palaeologus, who usurped the throne of Nicaea in 1259, was dangerously threatened by the coalition formed against him in the West. The papal support was needed and Michael apparently sent envoys to Pope Alexander IV. But the latter lacked energy and did not take the opportunity of making use of Michael's difficult position.[138] Finally Michael succeeded in seizing Constantinople without any support from the Holy See.

The Empire of Nicaea preserved the Orthodox church and the Orthodox

[135] See F. Schillmann, "Zur byzantinischen Politik Alexanders IV," *Römische Quartalschrift*, XXII (1908), 108–31. From the Vatican archives the author has published twelve new documents referring to the negotiations between Nicaea and Rome in 1256.

[136] Schillmann, *ibid.*, 14–15 (no. II). In these documents the name of Emperor *Caloihannes* (Vatatzes) is mentioned many times.

[137] George Acropolita, *Annales*, chap. 67; ed. Heisenberg, 139–40. Cf. a mistaken statement in the *Cambridge Medieval History* (IV, 505): "After a barren interview with the Papal plenipotentiaries (the Emperor) told Acropolita to get rid of them."

[138] See Norden, *Das Papsttum und Byzanz*, 382–83. See a very interesting article by R. Janin on the various churches and monasteries in Constantinople under the Latin domination; "Les Sanctuaires de Byzance sous la domination latine," *Études byzantines*, II (1945), 134–84.

patriarchate, and restored them to Constantinople. During the Nicene Empire the plan for union had no success.

SOCIAL AND ECONOMIC CONDITIONS IN THE EMPIRE OF NICAEA

The Emperors of Nicaea were always concerned with the problems of the internal life of their state. Economic prosperity was one of their very important aims. In this respect John Vatatzes is especially noticeable; his varied and strenuous external activity did not prevent him from paying adequate attention to the economic wealth of his country. He encouraged agriculture, vineyards, and stock-breeding. To quote a source, "in a short time, all the warehouses have been filled to overflowing with fruits; roads, streets, all stalls, and enclosures have been filled with flocks of cattle and fowls."[139] The famine which at that time befell the adjacent Sultanate of Rum compelled the Turks to crowd into the Nicene dominions to buy, at a high price, the means of subsistence. Turkish gold, silver, Oriental stuffs, jewels, and other articles of luxury poured in abundance into the hands of the Nicene Greeks and filled the imperial treasury. By diminishing taxes Vatatzes succeeded in raising the economic prosperity of the Empire. In times of dearth the large supplies of corn collected in granaries were distributed among the people. Having at his disposal considerable amounts of money Vatatzes erected all over the country forts, and such buildings as hospitals, almshouses, and poorhouses.[140] John Vatatzes was anxious "that, having everything at home he needed, no one should be induced to lay a grasping hand on simple and poor men, and that thereby the state of the Romans might be completely purified from injustice."[141]

Vatatzes himself was a large landowner and many of his nobles also possessed considerable tracts of land, and derived a sufficient living from their estates.[142] These estates seem to have been granted by the Emperor to the members of his officeholding nobility, and resemble the western European *beneficium* or Byzantine *pronoia,* that is to say, land granted by the emperors or, in their name, by their ministers, to subjects for their services to the state on condition that they furnish military service. Perhaps the large landowners were sometimes discontented with Vatatzes' regime and renounced allegiance to him. Towards the close of his reign some confiscations by the Emperor of movable and immovable property took place,[143] and this very interesting phenomenon may be explained by an antagonism between the throne and the

[139] Nicephorus Gregoras, *Historia,* II, 6, 2; Bonn ed., I, 42.

[140] Theodori Scutariotae, *Addimenta ad Georgii Acropolitae Historiam;* ed. A. Heisenberg, 285–86. Nicephorus Gregoras, *Historia,* II, 6, 2; Bonn ed., I, 42.

[141] Nicephoras Gregoras, *ibid.*

[142] *Ibid.*

[143] George Acropolita, *Annales,* chap. 52; ed. Heisenberg, I, 105, lines 3–5.

large landowners, on which there is no information. A recent historian even judged it possible to aver that such risings of the aristocracy against Vatatzes actually took place.[144] From the social standpoint, Vatatzes may be regarded as a protector of the peasantry and urban class; he endeavored, first of all, to raise their wealth and prosperity; and this circumstance might have evoked the dissatisfaction of the landed aristocracy, which brought about severe measures in retaliation against them.

When Theodore II ascended the throne, the officeholding aristocracy persecuted by his father looked upon the new Emperor with confidence, hoping to regain their lost wealth and influence.[145] But they were disappointed in their expectations. Theodore's policy was to diminish the influence of the aristocracy, and severe measures were apparently taken against many of its members; a long list of names of high officials who suffered under Theodore II is given by a contemporary writer.[146] The aristocracy was put down under Theodore II, and men of humble origin surrounded his throne; owing everything to Theodore they were obedient tools in his hands.[147] After Theodore's death, under his son, who was only a child, the aristocracy again increased their influence.

In connection with Theodore's military enterprises the taxes were considerably augmented, and in his letter to Nicephorus Blemmydes, who accused the Emperor of extorting too many taxes from the population, Theodore explained that the reason for his policy was his military activities.[148]

The Emperors of Nicaea were also very much interested in the development of commercial relations with other states, and especially with Venice. In August, 1219, Theodore I Lascaris made an alliance and a commercial treaty with the Venetian podestá in Constantinople, which secured to the Venetian merchants the privilege of trading free of dues on land and sea, all over the Empire of Nicaea (*per totum Imperium meum et sine aliqua inquisitione*).[149]

Western goods imported by the Venetians according to this treaty competed successfully with eastern goods which had to pass through the whole territory of the Sultanate of Iconium. Eastern and Italian stuffs were in special demand, and the population spent enormous amounts of money for their purchase. See-

[144] See Pappadopoulos, *Théodore II Lascaris,* 70. Andreeva, *Culture of the Byzantine Court,* 102–3.

[145] George Acropolita, *Annales,* chap. 52; ed. Heisenberg, I, 105, lines 1–3.

[146] *Ibid.,* chap. 75; ed. Heisenberg, I, 154–55. See also George Pachymeres, *De Michaele Palaeologo,* I, 15; Bonn ed., I, 40.

[147] See Pappadopoulos, *Théodore II Lascaris,* 79–81. Miller, "Emperor of Nicaea," *Cambridge Medieval History,* IV, 504. An-

dreeva, *Culture of the Byzantine Court,* 102, 108–10, 116.

[148] *Epistula XLIV,* ed. Festa, 57–58.

[149] Tafel and Thomas, *Urkunden zur ältern Handels- und Staatsgeschichte,* II, 205–7. See Heyd, *Histoire du commerce,* I, 304–5. A. Schaube, *Handelsgeschichte der Romanischen Völker des Mittelmeergebiets bis zum Ende der Kreuzzuge,* 262–63. Gardner, *Lascarids of Nicaea,* 95, is wrong in stating that this treaty is dated August, 1220.

ing this John Vatatzes, under pain of "dishonor," that is to say, of losing their social position, forbade his subjects to purchase and wear foreign stuffs and ordered them to be satisfied "only with that which the land of the Romans produces and which the hands of the Romans are able to prepare."[150] How long this regulation, which was intended to support local production, remained in force, is not known; probably it was soon forgotten.

The friendly relations with Venice did not last long, and under Vatatzes the Republic of St. Mark was hostile to Nicaea. At that time Vatatzes had some difficulties with the former imperial governor of the island of Rhodes, Leon Gabalas, who, soon after 1204, had styled himself "Lord of the Cyclades," and even "Caesar." When Vatatzes opened hostilities against him, Leon, unable to protect the island with his own forces, made an offensive and defensive alliance with Venice, which broke down the treaty concluded with Theodore I Lascaris. In the treaty of 1234 between Leon Gabalas and Venice the latter was granted vast commercial privileges. In this very interesting document Leon Gabalas called himself *"dominus Rhode et Cicladum insularum Ksserus Leo Gavalla,"* "lord of Rhodes and the Cyclades, Caesar Leo Gavalla."[151] Vatatzes sent an expedition to Rhodes and the island became the possession of the Emperor of Nicaea.[152]

Just before the taking of Constantinople the Genoese gained the upper hand over their Venetian rivals when, in 1261, Michael Palaeologus signed the treaty of Nymphaeum. According to this treaty the Genoese obtained commercial supremacy in the Levant. After the restoration of the Byzantine Empire Michael Palaeologus continued his friendly relations with the Genoese.

EDUCATION, LEARNING, LITERATURE, AND ART

After the ruin of the Empire in 1204 and its division into a certain number of independent Latin and Greek dominions, the state of Nicaea became not only the center for the future political unification of the Hellenes, but also a hotbed of intense cultural life. As George of Cyprus states, in the second half of the thirteenth century, Nicaea was said "to be an ancient Athens in her abundance of scholars" and "a marvelous and greatly loved source of scholarship."[153] Perhaps it may not be amiss to recall that in the West in the Middle Ages Paris was called "a new Athens" and "a city of science." However on his

[150] Nicephorus Gregoras, *Historia,* II, 6, 4; Bonn ed., I, 43; from him in K. E. Zachariä von Lingenthal, *Jus graeco-romanum,* III, 574.

[151] Tafel and Thomas, *Urkunden zur ältern Handels- und Staatsgeschichte,* II, 320; for the text of the treaty, *ibid.,* 320–22.

[152] George Acropolita, *Annales,* chap. 48;

ed. Heisenberg, I, 86–88. See Heyd, *Histoire du commerce,* I, 307. Schaube, *Handelsgeschichte der Romanischen Völker,* 263.

[153] Λόγος τὰ καθ' ἑαυτὸν περιέχων; Migne, *Patrologia Graeca,* CXLII, 21. I. E. Troizky, "An Autobiography of George of Cyprus," *Christianskoe Čtenie,* II (1870), 167, 169–70.

coming to Nicaea George of Cyprus was disappointed in his expectations of Nicaea as a city of scholarship. In one of his works Theodore Lascaris said that Corinth was famous for music, Thessaly for weaving, Philadelphia for shoe-making, and Nicaea for philosophy.[154] All the Lascarids, except the last, the child John IV, were real admirers of learning and education and very well understood that spiritual culture was one of the foundations of a strong state. In spite of the great difficulties in the external and internal relations of his young empire, the first ruler of Nicaea, Theodore I, was interested in the problems of learning. He invited to his court many scholars, especially from the Greek regions occupied or menaced by the Franks. Such an invitation was received, for example, by the metropolitan of Athens, Michael Acominatus, who had fled before the Latin invasion to the island of Ceos, but he was unable to accept it because of his advanced age and poor health. However, Michael's brother, Nicetas Acominatus, an historian, retired to Nicaea after the taking of Constantinople by the Franks. Enjoying leisure and tranquillity at Theodore Lascaris' court, he put into permanent shape his historical works and wrote his theological treatise *A Treasury of Orthodoxy*. Theodore's successor, the famous John III Ducas Vatatzes, despite his vigorous and continued military and international activity, found time enough to satisfy the cultural needs of the Empire. In his cities he founded libraries, particularly of art and sciences, and he sometimes himself sent young men to school to stimulate education in his country. To his time belongs the most eminent representative of the cultural movement of the thirteenth century, Nicephorus Blemmydes, scholar, writer, and teacher. Among his disciples were the enlightened writer on the throne, Vatatzes' successor, Theodore II Lascaris, and a very well known historian and statesman, George Acropolita. Like his father, Theodore was deeply interested in libraries; he collected books and distributed them to different libraries, and he even allowed the books to be taken out by the readers to their homes for reading.[155]

As in the epoch of the Comneni, the educated people of the thirteenth century wrote, with very few exceptions, in the artificial school-Greek tongue. This had broken away from the spoken language, which was not admitted in literature. The Greek classical writers and the Church Fathers were the models under whose yoke the medieval educated Greeks in general, and the Greeks of the thirteenth century in particular, lived and thought.

The most eminent figure in the cultural life of the Nicene Empire was, undoubtedly, Nicephorus Blemmydes. Besides many works of various kinds, he

---

[154] Theodore Lascaris, *De naturali communione,* V, 2. Migne, *Patrologia Graeca,* CXL, 1354. J. Dräseke, "Theodore Laskaris," *Byzantinische Zeitschrift,* III (1894), 500.

[155] Theodori Scutariotae *Additamenta ad Georgii Acropolitae Historiam,* ed. Heisenberg, 297.

left two interesting autobiographies published in 1896 by the German scholar, A. Heisenberg. These give a picture not only of the life of the author, but also of the events and men of his epoch.

Blemmydes was born in Constantinople at the very end of the twelfth century. After the taking of the capital by the Latins the boy Blemmydes and his parents emigrated to Asia Minor, in the dominions of Theodore I Lascaris. There he started his education in the elementary school. Passing from city to city, Blemmydes became gradually acquainted, through various teachers, with poetics, rhetoric, logic, philosophy, natural sciences, medicine, arithmetic, geometry, physics, and astronomy. Then he settled in a monastery and, for the first time, devoted himself entirely to the active study of the Scriptures and the works of the Fathers. In Vatatzes' reign, Patriarch Germanus had a feeling of affection for Blemmydes, kept him at his court, and made him familiar with the broad interests of the Church. But Blemmydes had a tendency to solitary life, abandoned the court in spite of the persuasions of the patriarch, and retired to a monastery on the mountain of Latros, close to Miletus, in Caria, famous for its strict monastic rule, where he devoted himself to the spiritual life. On his return from the monastery, during the negotiations of Vatatzes and the patriarch with the papal legates concerning union, Blemmydes was a strict defender of the Orthodox doctrine; finally, he took refuge in the cowl and established himself in a monastery, where he occupied himself with his scientific works, founded a school, and became a teacher of philosophy. Among other young men entrusted to Blemmydes by the Emperor was the future historian and statesman George Acropolita. Vatatzes, attentive to the progress of learning and art in his Empire, sent Blemmydes on a scientific mission through Thrace, Macedonia, Thessaly, Mount Athos, and other places, to purchase valuable manuscripts of the Scriptures and other works, or, if purchase were impossible, to read them and make extracts and notes. This commission successfully fulfilled, enriched Blemmydes' mind with new knowledge that greatly astonished his contemporaries. The Emperor confided to his care the education of his son and heir, Theodore Lascaris, who later became an enlightened ruler and writer. After having founded a monastery of his own, Blemmydes established himself there. He participated in the religious discussions of his epoch, came near being elected patriarch, devoted most of his time to his literary studies, survived the restoration of·the Byzantine Empire by Michael Palaeologus, and peacefully passed away in his monastery about the year 1272. Blemmydes' contemporaries unanimously pay to him the highest tributes.[156]

---

[156] The best biographies of Blemmydes are: Heisenberg, "Dissertatio de vita et scriptis Nicephori Blemmydae," in his edition of *Curriculum vitae et carmina,* ix–xxv; V. Barvinok, *Nicephorus Blemmydes and His Works,* 1–84. L. Bréhier, "Blemmydes," *Dic-*

Numerous and varied works of Blemmydes have been preserved. The two autobiographies of Blemmydes give much valuable information about both the life and personality of the author and the ecclesiastical history and the political and social conditions of his epoch; in fact, the second is one of the very important sources for the history of Byzantium in the thirteenth century. Blemmydes was the author of a very great number of theological writings in the field of dogmatics, polemics, asceticism, exegetics, liturgics, ecclesiastical poetry, sermons, and lives of the saints. His "version of some psalms," designed for the church service, became later a prescribed part of vespers in the Greek church, appeared afterwards in the south Slavonic churches, and finally reached Russia. Blemmydes' secular works are also of great interest. His political treatise *The Imperial Statue* (Βασιλικὸς ἀνδριάς), dedicated to his pupil, Emperor Theodore II Lascaris, depicts an ideal ruler who is to serve as an example of various dignities and virtues; this emperor is a model of all good, and shines brighter than the celebrated Polycleitus; in his life Theodore must follow such a model. In the opinion of Blemmydes, the ruler is "the highest official ordained by God to care for the people subject to him and to lead them to the highest good." The emperor as "the prop and stay of the people" should have in view the welfare of his subjects, should not give vent to anger, should avoid flatterers, and should care for the army and navy. During peace he must prepare for war, because strong weapons are the best protection; it is necessary for him to care for the internal organization of the state, for religion, and for justice. "May the emperor," Blemmydes said at the end of the treatise, "accept favorably this word of mine, and may he listen to better advice from wiser men which he will collect and keep carefully in the depth of his soul."[157] The starting point of all the speculations of the author on the ideal ruler is this statement: "First of all, the emperor must control himself, and then govern all his people."[158] The exact sources which Blemmydes used for his treatise are not known.

The opinions of scholars vary as to the significance of this treatise. "This work of Blemmydes," a special writer on his life and works said, "has a particular value and significance, chiefly because it perfectly answered the needs and requirements of the Greek people of that time."[159] They had lost Constantinople, found refuge at Nicaea, and they dreamt, through an experienced, strong, energetic, and enlightened monarch, of driving out the foreigners from the shores of the Bosphorus and returning to their fatherland. Such an ideal monarch was portrayed by Blemmydes.

---

tionnaire d'histoire et de géographie ecclésias-tique, IX, 178–182. M. Karapiperes, Νικηφόρος Βλεμμύδης, ὡς παιδαγωγὸς καὶ διδάσκαλος. I have not seen this book.

[157] Migne, *Patrologia Graeca*, CXLII, 633, 657, 659, 667.

[158] *Ibid.*, 613, 659.

[159] Barvinok, *Nicephorus Blemmydes*, 297.

In contradiction to this opinion, another scholar, Th. Uspensky, wrote of the same work: "Blemmydes has no idea of contemporary requirements; he lives in the realm of fairy tales, beyond the limits of reality; he has no realization of contemporary life and the needs of the epoch. Blemmydes' abstract king is wise but lacking in human passions and emotions. He is placed in a setting entirely isolated from life and everyday relations, and therefore his advice and suggestions cannot correspond to real requirements. . . . The misfortune of the medieval Greek was that he was weakened by classical reminiscences; he had no creative force, and real life was veiled from him by books. We imagine Blemmydes to be such a man from his political treatise."[160]

Of course, classical traditions and religious emotions influenced Blemmydes a great deal. Still, in the course of his life, he was several times closely connected with the interests of the Empire and its Emperor, so that, perhaps, he was not always "a dweller in another world, entirely strange to the interests of the sinful earth."[161] Under the rhetorical disguise of his treatise one may distinguish some realistic traits which resemble the personality of Theodore II. It is very probable that when Blemmydes was writing his "imperial statue" the real image of Theodore II was hovering before his eyes, though the real traits in his ideal ruler are overshadowed by his rhetoric and classical erudition.[162]

Of the philosophical writings of Blemmydes based mainly on Aristotle, the best known are *Abridged Physics* and *Abridged Logic,* especially the latter. After the author's death, his *Logic* became known all over the Empire and, little by little, became the basis for teaching and the favorite textbook of philosophy not only in the East, but also in western Europe. The editor of Blemmydes' autobiographies, A. Heisenberg, remarked that these two works "have really created an immortal name for the author."[163]

Blemmydes' *Logic* and *Physics* are also important both from the point of view of understanding the philosophical movements in Byzantium of the thirteenth century, and from the point of view of elucidating the dark problem of the influence of Byzantium on the development of western European thought. There is also a correspondence of Blemmydes with Theodore II Lascaris, which gives much information on the history and culture of the time. Two small geographical writings in the form of textbooks, *A History of the Earth* and *A General Geography,* as well as some poems of secular charac-

---

[160] "The Review of V. I. Barvinok's Work," *Sbornik otcětov o premiyach i nagradach za 1912 god,* 1916, pp. 108, 111.

[161] J. E. Troizky, "Arsenius, Patriarch of Nicaea and of Constantinople, and the Arsenites," *Christianskoe Čtenie,* II (1869), 851.

[162] I formerly held Uspensky's opinion. See A. A. Vasiliev, *The Latin Sway in the Levant,* 45. Now cf. Andreeva, *Culture of the Byzantine Court,* 9–10.

[163] Heisenberg, edition of *Curriculum vitae et carmina,* lxviii.

ter,[164] complete the rich and various literary inheritance left by Blemmydes to subsequent generations. Though it is true that he failed to open up new ways in his works and thoughts, Nicephorus Blemmydes was a brilliant figure in the complicated epoch of the Empire of Nicaea and justly occupies one of the most prominent places in the history of Byzantine culture.

Among the pupils of Blemmydes two became particularly distinguished: George Acropolita and Emperor Theodore II Lascaris. Born at Constantinople, George Acropolita had gone in his youth to Nicaea, during the reign of John Vatatzes. Together with Theodore Lascaris, he had received a good education under Nicephorus Blemmydes. He later even became a teacher of Theodore himself. He reached the highest offices but failed in his military career. Then he accompanied Michael Palaeologus to Constantinople, devoted himself to diplomacy and, by the order of the Emperor, conducted the negotiations at the Council of Lyons in 1274, where he succeeded in accomplishing the union with the western church, against which he had formerly struggled. Acropolita died at the beginning of the ninth decade of the thirteenth century.

The main literary work of Acropolita is the history narrating the events from the capture of Constantinople by the crusaders to the restoration of the Byzantine Empire (1203–1261), which is very important as a source. This work may be called a special history of the epoch of the Nicene Empire and serves as a continuation of the work of Nicetas Choniates. As a contemporary of the events described, who in his official position had taken part in them, Acropolita gave a reasonable and reliable narration of the events of his epoch in clear language. Among the short writings of Acropolita, is the sensitive and beautiful funeral oration on John Vatatzes.

With the name of Blemmydes is also closely connected the name of Emperor Theodore II Lascaris. George Acropolita was the official teacher of Theodore, but Blemmydes had a very strong influence upon the future Emperor, who in his letters called him his teacher and who felt profound reverence for him.[165] Both Blemmydes and Acropolita succeeded in instilling into the soul of their young pupil, during the lifetime of his father John Vatatzes, a real love for knowledge. The correspondence of Theodore published at the end of the last century by the Italian scholar, Festa, affords a new and fresh source of information on this interesting personality. Theodore studied the Greek writers, both ecclesiastical and secular, became acquainted with different sciences, and devoted his chief attention to philosophy, particularly Aristotle.

---

[164] The inscription in hexameter (twenty verses) commemorating the restoration of the walls of Smyrne under John Vatatzes (1222) is justly attributed by H. Grégoire to Blemmydes. *Recueil des inscriptions grecques chré-* *tiennes,* 22–23 and notes 81–82. Grégoire, *Byzantion,* V (1930), 783–84 (in n. 1 on p. 784, n. 81–82 should be read for n. 84).

[165] Andreeva, *Culture of the Byzantine Court,* 100.

Trained in the ideas of Hellenism and classical literature, he beautifully de-scribed, in one of his letters, the profound impression produced upon him by the contemplation of the ancient monuments and ruins of Pergamum.[166] This letter, as far as content and style are concerned, might have been written by an Italian humanist.

Favoring education, he was, like his father, interested in school matters. In one of his letters concerning the pupils who had finished school and been sent to the Emperor for examination, Theodore wrote: "Nothing else rejoices so much the soul of the gardener as to see his meadow in full blossom; if, from the beautiful and flourishing view, he may judge of the bloom of plants, he may, upon the same basis, conjecture that in proper time he will enjoy the fruits of charm and beauty. . . . Although I was terribly oppressed with a great want of leisure on account of my duties as commander, while my mind was distracted by revolts, battles, oppositions, resistance, cunning, changes, menaces . . . nevertheless I have never withdrawn my chief thought from the beauty of the spiritual meadow."[167]

A circle of educated, literary, and scholarly men gathered around Theodore II, who himself was deeply interested in science, art, music, poetry, and the like. He opened many schools, and in one of his letters, he discusses the prob-lem of school organization, programs, and purposes.[168]

Theodore Lascaris wrote several treatises on philosophic and religious sub-jects, and some panegyrics, and left the large collection of letters mentioned above (over two hundred) addressed to various prominent people of his epoch, especially to his tutors, Nicephorus Blemmydes and George Acropolita. In Theodore's writings may be also pointed out his vast knowledge of the natural and mathematical sciences. A more attentive and detailed study of the literary inheritance of Theodore Lascaris, published as well as unpublished,[169] would undoubtedly provide the basis for appreciating the personality of the author—"a sort of Oriental parallel to his great contemporary Frederick II" —as well as for a more profound understanding of the cultural interests of the Christian East in the thirteenth century.[170]

To the second half of the twelfth century and to the first period of the Empires of Nicaea and Constantinople belongs the activity of the two enlight-ened brothers, John and Nicholas Mesaritai, whose very existence came to light only at the beginning of the twentieth century, owing to A. Heisenberg. For

---

[166] Theodore Lascaris, *Epistulae,* lxxx; ed. Festa, 107.

[167] *Ibid.,* ccxvii; ed. Festa, 271–72.

[168] *Ibid.,* 271. See also Theodori Scutariotae *Additamenta ad Georgii Acropolitae Histo-riam,* ed. Heisenberg, 291.

[169] See, e.g., J. B. Pappadopoulos, "La Satire

du Précepteur, oeuvre inédite de Théodore II Lascaris," *Compte-rendu du deuxième Con-grès international des études byzantines* (1929), 27.

[170] Krumbacher, *Geschichte der byzanti-nischen Litteratur,* 478.

this reason, these two names were not mentioned in Krumbacher's famous *History of Byzantine Literature*. The funeral oration delivered by Nicholas Mesarites on the death of his elder brother shows that John had a careful education, held some office under the last two Comneni, and later, under the Angeli, became a professor of the exegesis of the Psalmbook. He wrote a commentary on the Psalms, the authoritative copy of which perished at the capture and sack of Constantinople by the Franks in 1204. John took an active part in the disputes with the papal representatives at Constantinople in the first years of the Latin Empire, and held firmly to the Orthodox standpoint. He died in 1207.[171]

His younger brother, Nicholas, who also held some office about court under the Angeli and agreed with his brother concerning the papal pretensions, went to Nicaea after his brother's death, where he was kindly received by the patriarch and afterwards made bishop of Ephesus. Later he took a leading part in the negotiations for a religious understanding between Nicaea and Rome, about which he left a detailed narrative. Some of the works of Nicholas, though far from all, have been published.

Particularly interesting is the description by Nicholas Mesarites of the Church of the Holy Apostles in Constantinople with its beautiful mosaics.[172] This church, hardly inferior to St. Sophia in luxury and beauty, was the burial place of the Byzantine emperors and the prototype of St. Mark's at Venice, St. John at Ephesus, and St. Front at Périgueux in France. The Church of the Holy Apostles is known to have been destroyed by the Turks in 1453, and on its site the mosque of Muhammed II the Conqueror was constructed. Because of the loss of the important monument itself, the description of Nicholas based upon his personal observation has particular significance. A. Heisenberg, the first to acquaint the scholarly world with Nicholas Mesarites, said that his writings can, to a certain extent, throw new light upon the origin of the Empire of Nicaea and are an important source of information for the period. "Whoever has the courage to prepare an edition of Mesarites' works will render a great service; this task is not easy, but exceedingly valuable, and merits thanks."[173]

One cannot ascribe eminent talents to the brothers Mesaritai, but they belong to those educated and book-loving men who, some in the quiet of monasteries, some at the court of Nicaea, promoted cultural work in the thirteenth century and prepared the way for the spiritual and political regeneration of

[171] A. Heisenberg, *Analecta. Mitteilungen aus italienischen Handschriften byzantinischer Chronographen*, 32–33. Heisenberg, *Neue Quellen zur Geschichte des lateinischen Kaisertums*, I, 5–7; see a complete bibliography of John Mesarites, 3.

[172] Heisenberg, *Analecta*, 24–25. Heisenberg, *Die Apostelkirche in Konstantinopel*, 10 ff.

[173] Heisenberg, *Analecta*, 18, 37.

the state which brought about the Byzantine Empire's restoration in 1261.

The Byzantine chronicle of that period is represented by only one writer, Joel, who wrote, probably in the thirteenth century, a brief universal chronicle having no historical or literary value. It covered the period from Adam to the capture of Constantinople by the Latins in 1204.

All of these works were written in the conventional classic, literary, and artificial tongue that had entirely broken away from the popular spoken language. But there are some examples in the literature of the thirteenth century of the use of the spoken language and popular poetical meters which give interesting specimens of the new currents in literature.

Composed in popular (political) verses on the occasion of the marriage of John Vatatzes to the daughter of Frederick II, the epithalamium (nuptial poem) of Nicholas Irenikos (Eirenikos),[174] was written in the style of the court ceremonial, closely related to the style of the epithalamia of Theodore Prodromus. Nicholas Irenikos' poem gives new information on the splendid ceremonies of the Byzantine court, and therein lies its historical and cultural value.[175] Krumbacher's opinion that this poem resembles the nuptial songs of modern Greek poetry and that the author drew his inspiration directly from the popular poetry of that time, cannot be maintained.[176]

To the epoch of the crusades, especially after the Fourth Crusade, when on the territory of the eastern Empire there were established a number of Latin feudal dominions, belong several poetical works written in the spoken language and presenting a sort of romance which, in a fantastic setting, describes mainly love and chivalrous adventures. One piece of work in the field of Byzantine epic poetry previous to the crusades, namely, the poem of Digenes Akrites, is particularly well known.[177]

The epoch of the crusades created in Byzantium a more complex literary setting. The Frankish conquerors who brought into the East the definitely established institutions of western feudalism, of course made their new subjects acquainted with their western chivalrous literature of the twelfth century, with the Provençal *romans d'aventures* and other works which became widespread at the Latin courts in Greek lands. The medieval French romance which had proved its cosmopolitan character by the fact that it was adopted in Germany, Italy, and England, could certainly take root also in Greece, where the conditions at the beginning of the thirteenth century seemed to be particularly favorable for it. The question has therefore been raised whether the Byzantine romance in verse of the time was a mere imitation of western

[174] On Irenikos, see p. 529.
[175] Heisenberg, *Analecta*, iii. Andreeva, *Culture of the Byzantine Court*, 15.

[176] *Geschichte der byzantinische Litteratur*, 768. Heisenberg, *Analecta*, iii.
[177] See pp. 369–70.

models, or whether the Byzantine *romans d'aventures* were original works created by Byzantine conditions of life, analogous to western conditions, only partly influenced by western literature. Bury suggested that perhaps "their acquaintance with Western romances move the Greeks to produce works impregnated with Western ideas in the same way as the Odes of Horace or the Eclogues and Aeneid of Virgil are charged with the influence of their Hellenic masters."[178] Various opinions of scholars on this problem are based upon the study of literary sources, often anonymous and not to be exactly dated, for style, meter, and literary and historical content.

An anonymous romance in verse, *Belthandros and Chrysantza,* the original version of which is to be dated, probably, in the thirteenth century, is an example of the Byzantine romance. The text bears some traces of a later remodeling and may belong to the fifteenth century.[179]

The plot of the romance is as follows: A certain emperor Rodophilos has two sons, Philarmos and Belthandros. Belthandros, the younger son, distinguished for beauty and courage, cannot bear the persecutions of his father and leaves his country to seek his fortune abroad. Passing by the land bordering on Turkey and entering Armenia (that is to say, lesser Armenia, Cilicia), he reaches Tarsus; near the city he comes to a small stream in the water of which a star is shining. The star leads Belthandros to a magnificent castle full of various miracles, named in the romance a Castle of Love (Ἐρωτόκαστρον). There, from the inscriptions on two statues, he learns of the predestined love between him and Chrysantza, "a daughter of the great king of great Antioch."[180] Deciding to see all "the bitter and sweet beauties of the Castle of Love,"[181] Belthandros, on the invitation of the Lord of the castle, "the king of love who had on his head an imperial crown and held in his hand a huge scepter and a gold arrow,"[182] approaches his throne. On learning the story of Belthandros' life, the king directs him to select, of forty girls, the most beautiful and to give her a rod "of twisted iron, gold, and topaz."[183] Then, in the romance the interesting scene of the competition of beauty is described which resembles the judgment of Paris and reflects the well-known Byzantine custom of the choice of the worthiest bride for the basileus. When Belthandros gives the rod to the most beautiful girl, all that surrounds him, the king himself and the forty girls, suddenly disappear "like a dream."[184] Leaving the

[178] *Romances of Chivalry on Greek Soil,* 5.

[179] E. Legrand, *Bibliothèque grecque vulgaire,* I, 125–68. Legrand's text was reprinted with a detailed study in medieval Greek romance, notes, and a glossary, by G. Meliades, Βέλθανδρος καὶ Χρυσάντζα, Μυθιστόρημα XII

αἰῶνος. See *Byzantinisch-neugriechische Jahrbücher,* VI (1928), 270.

[180] Legrand, *ibid.,* v. 421, p. 139.

[181] *Ibid.,* v. 441, p. 139.

[182] *Ibid.,* vss. 492–94, p. 141.

[183] *Ibid.,* vss. 537–38, p. 142.

[184] *Ibid.,* v. 724, p. 148.

castle, Belthandros, after five days' journey, comes to the outskirts of Antioch, where he meets the king of the city out hunting with his falcons and his court. The master of Antioch offers him a post at his court. Suddenly, in the daughter of the king, Chrysantza, Belthandros recognizes the girl to whom in the Castle of Love he handed the rod. The young couple are inflamed with love for each other and, in spite of all the strictness of women's life in the Orient, a love meeting takes place at night in the royal garden. But the meeting ends badly for Belthandros: at dawn the guard discovers the couple, seizes Belthandros, and throws him into prison. Chrysantza persuades her faithful maidservant to say that Belthandros came to the garden to meet her. When Chrysantza's father hears this he pardons Belthandros and, with the secret consent of Chrysantza, a fictitious marriage between Belthandros and the maidservant is performed. The clandestine meetings between Belthandros and Chrysantza continue. Ten months later the lovers, the maid, and some faithful servants flee from Antioch; while crossing a raging river the maid and the servants perish. The lovers, barely escaping death, reach the seacoast, where they find a Greek vessel sent by Belthandros' father, Rodophilos, in search of his younger son; the beloved elder son has died. Recognizing the son of their emperor, the sailors immediately take Belthandros and Chrysantza on board the ship and bring them speedily to the capital, where Rodophilos, who has despaired of seeing his son again, welcomes them with great joy. The romance ends with a description of the solemn wedding of Belthandros and Chrysantza, at which the bishop performs the ceremony and puts the imperial crown upon the head of Belthandros.

The judgment of scholars on this anonymous romance gives an indication of their general opinion of the Byzantine romance of the epoch of the crusades. One group of scholars thinks that a French romance of chivalry, still unknown or lost, served as a basis for the romance *Belthandros and Chrysantza;* in the Castle of Love, the Greek Erotocastron, they see the *Chateau d'amour* of Provençal poetry; in the proper names of Rodophilos and Belthandros they recognize the popular Hellenized western names of Rodolph and Bertrand;[185] it has even been thought that the whole romance of Belthandros and Chrysantza is nothing but a Greek version of the French tale of a well-known French knight of the fourteenth century, Bertrand du Guesclin, who lived during the Hundred Years' War.[186] Krumbacher, who was inclined to refer to western European sources all that is found in medieval Greek popular poetry on the Castle of Love, Eros, and so on, wrote that the romance of Belthandros and Chrysantza was certainly written by a Greek, but in a land which had been familiar for a long time with Frankish culture; but the chief problem, whether

[185] See Krumbacher, *Geschichte der byzantinischen Litteratur,* 858–59.

[186] See, e.g., T. Warton, *History of English Poetry,* ed. W. C. Hazlitt, II, 302–3.

the kernel of the plot is of Frankish or of Greco-Eastern origin, will remain unsolved till the real prototype of this romance is found.[187] Finally, Bury said that the romance of Belthandros and Chrysantza is Greek from the beginning to the end in its construction, descriptions, and ideas; it has nothing that ought to be referred to western influence. A parallel literary development existed in both Frankish and Greek lands. Just as the French romances of the twelfth century were preceded by a great deal of epic poetry, so the Greek romances of the thirteenth and fourteenth centuries had also as their background an epic basis. In both cases the working out of romantic motives was affected by the influences flowing directly or indirectly from the Hellenistic world: in France, through Latin literature, particularly Ovid; in Greece by means of the literary tradition which was never dead there. . . . The Greeks already possessed, owing to their own experiences, all the ideas, material, and setting for the romances of chivalry, when the western knights were establishing themselves in the East. Therefore the French literature of the twelfth century could exercise no such strong influence on Byzantium as it exercised, for example, on Germany. The romantic literature of the West did not appear as a new revelation to people who in their own literature had motives, ideals, and elements of phantasy similar to those of the West. Of course, some influence from French literature in the epoch of the crusades, through the contact and intermingling of the two cultures in the Christian West, is not to be denied. But, generally speaking, French and Byzantine romances have one common Hellenistic basis, and they developed along parallel lines, independent of each other.[188] As Diehl said, the background of the romance of Belthandros and Chrysantza remains purely Byzantine, and Greek civilization seems to have given the Frankish barons who came as conquerors much more than it received from them.[189] Another "love story" composed in political verses, the story of Callimachos and Chrysorroë, may also be referred to the thirteenth century.[190]

Light has recently been thrown on some eminent personalities of the thirteenth century in the west of the Balkan peninsula connected with the history of the Despotat of Epirus, the second Hellenic center organized on the ruins of the Byzantine Empire. Among the prominent men of this region were: John Apocaucus, metropolitan of Naupactus (the city of Naupactus, in Italian *Lepanto,* at the entrance to the Gulf of Corinth or Lepanto); George Bardanes, metropolitan of Corcyra (the island of Corcyra, Italian Corfù); and De-

[187] See M. Gidel, *Études sur la littérature grecque moderne,* 123–50; the analysis and exposition of the whole romance, 105–50. Krumbacher, *Geschichte der byzantinischen Litteratur,* 860. Bury, *Romances of Chivalry,* 5–10.
[188] Bury, *ibid.,* 10, 21–24.

[189] Diehl, *Figures byzantines,* II, 337.
[190] *Collection de romans grecs en langue vulgaire et en vers,* ed. S. Lampros, 1–109. See Krumbacher, *Geschichte der byzantinischen Litteratur,* 855–57. Montelatici, *Storia della letteratura bizantina,* 191.

metrius Chomatenos (Chomatianos), archbishop of Ochrida (the city of Ochrida or Achrida in western Macedonia, which in the first half of the thirteenth century belonged to the Despotat of Epirus).

In 1897 Krumbacher could only mention John of Naupactus as a polemist against the Latins and as the supposed author of the letters preserved in one of the manuscripts of Oxford which at that time had not been published.[191] But the publication of the correspondence of John, from a manuscript in St. Petersburg, by V. G. Vasilievsky, and the later publication of a portion of John's writings by the French scholar Pétridès, on the basis of the Oxford manuscript, enables students to become acquainted with the interesting personality of this writer.[192] The publication of all the manuscripts referring to John of Naupactus is far from complete.

John Apocaucus, metropolitan of Naupactus, who lived until the thirties of the thirteenth century, received an excellent classical and theological education. He spent some time in Constantinople, perhaps, in his youth, and then as metropolitan of Naupactus, took an active part in the political, public, and ecclesiastical life of the Despotat of Epirus. John appears as a leader of the patriotic portion of the Orthodox Greek clergy, both in independent Epirus and in the regions temporarily conquered, also, perhaps, as a political leader, and finally as the supporter of the Despots in their conflicts with the highest ecclesiastical authority, the patriarch, who was backed by the rival Emperor of Nicaea.[193] E. A. Chernousov wrote: John was "not a gloomy monk confined in his cell, interested only in ecclesiastical affairs, far from the world and men. On the contrary, in his conception and character, in disclosing his own 'Ego,' in the methods of his literary activity, may be noticed the features which, to a certain extent, relate him to the later Italian humanists."[194] In the works of John Apocaucus are evident his love and taste for writing, which has produced his vast correspondence, his love and feeling for nature and, finally, his attitude toward ancient literature, the authority of which, in the persons of the most celebrated writers of antiquity, Homer, Aristophanes, Euripides, Thucydides, Aristotle, and others, he estimated very highly, and which, along with the Bible, gave him a rich mine for parallels and analogies. At present

[191] *Geschichte der byzantinischen Litteratur,* 93, 476.

[192] Vasilievsky, "Epirotica saeculi XIII," *Vizantiysky Vremennik,* III (1896), 233-99. S. Pétridès, "Jean Apokaukos, lettres et autres documents inédits," *Transactions of the Russian Archeological Institute at Constantinople,* XIV, 2-3 (1909), 1-32. Eleven other documents connected with the name of John of Naupactus were published by A. Papadopoulo-Kerameus, "Συνοδικὰ γράμματα Ἰωάννου τοῦ

'Αποκαύκου μητροπλίτου Ναυπάκτου," Βυζαντίς, I (1909), 3-30 (only text of the documents). For a full bibliography on John Apocaucus, of Naupactus, see M. Wellnhofer, *Johannes Apokaukos, Metropolit von Naupaktos in Aetolien (c. 1155-1233),* 1-5.

[193] See Vasilievsky, "Epirotica saeculi XIII," *Vizantiysky Vremennik,* III (1896), 234.

[194] "From a Byzantine Backwoods of the Thirteenth Century," *Essays Presented to V. P. Buzeskul,* 281.

there are in print more than forty of his writings—letters, various canonical works, and epigrams.[195] Among his correspondents were Theodore Comnenus, despot of Epirus, and the famous metropolitan of Athens, Michael Acominatus. As not all the writings of John Apocaucus have been published, a more complete and definite judgment on him as a writer and statesman belongs to the future.[196]

About the second eminent personality of the epoch of the Despotat of Epirus, George Bardanes, metropolitan of Corcyra, there existed for a long time an important misunderstanding. At the end of the sixteenth century, the author of the *Ecclesiastical Annals,* Cardinal Baronius, placed him in the twelfth century on the basis of George's letters to Emperors Frederick and Manual Ducas. Cardinal Baronius thought these letters were addressed to Frederick I Barbarossa and Manuel I Comnenus.[197] Later scholars, realizing that several polemic pieces given under the name of George could not be associated in subject matter with the events of the twelfth century, came to the conclusion that there were two Georges of Corcyra, one who lived in the twelfth century, the other in the thirteenth. This erroneous opinion was accepted in the *History of Byzantine Literature* by Krumbacher, published in 1897.[198] But in 1885 this problem was definitely solved by V. G. Vasilievsky, who proved irrefutably that there was only one George, metropolitan of Corcyra; that he lived in the thirteenth century; and that the two emperors to whom he wrote were Frederick II and Manuel, Despot of Thessalonica, brother of the Emperor of Thessalonica, Theodore Ducas Angelus, who had been captured by the Bulgars. Thus George Bardanes belongs to the thirteenth century.[199]

George was born, probably, at Athens, and was first a pupil and later a friend and correspondent of Michael Acominatus, whose letters give much information about his life. George spent some time at the imperial court of Nicaea, and then returned to the West, where he was ordained bishop of Corcyra by John of Naupactus. The Despot of Epirus, Theodore Angelus, was favorably disposed towards him. George's interesting letters have reached us,

[195] See Pétridès, "Jean Apokaukos," *Transactions of the Russian Archeological Institute at Constantinople,* XIV, 2–3 (1919), 1–3.

[196] See Wellnhofer, *Johannes Apokaukos,* 68–69.

[197] *Annales ecclesiastici,* ed. A. Theiner, XIX, 413–15.

[198] Krumbacher, *Geschichte der byzantinischen Litteratur,* 91, 770.

[199] "The Regeneration of the Bulgarian Patriarchate," *Journal of the Ministry of Public Instruction,* CCXXXVIII (1885), 224–33. E. Kurtz, "Georgios Bardanes, Metropolit von Kerkyra," *Byzantinische Zeitschrift,* XV

(1906), 603–13. In more recent works George Bardanes has been erroneously referred to the twelfth century by Norden, *Das Papsttum und Byzanz,* 112–13; Miller, *Latins in the Levant,* 12 and n. 2; Haskins, *Studies in Mediaeval Science,* 212 and n. 113. Correctly cited Cognasso, *Partiti politici e lotte dinastiche in Bizanzio alla morte di Manuele Comneno,* 293, n. 1. Knowing neither Vasilievsky nor Kurtz's article Golubovich expressed the hope that this complicated problem would be solved in due time, *Bibliotheca bio-bibliografica,* I (1906), 170–75.

and Michael Acominatus on reading them felt the elegance of their style and clearness of their exposition; this, however, did not prevent Michael Acominatus, in his letters, from teaching George and correcting various failures of his style.[200] Besides the letters, George was the author of polemic pieces against the Latins and several iambic poems.

The famous Greek hierarch and canonist of the first half of the thirteenth century, the archbishop of Ochrida (Achrida), ordained by John of Naupactus, Demetrius Chomatenus (Chomatianos), who crowned Theodore of Epirus Emperor of Thessalonica, has left more than 150 writings, letters in which various juridical and ecclesiastical questions were discussed, various canonical messages and replies, judicial decisions, the acts of councils, and so on. These writings are of very great importance for the history of Byzantine law in general and canonic law in particular, and give an interesting source of information on the history of the church, the customs and manners, and the international relations of the first half of the thirteenth century in Epirus, Albania, Serbia, Bulgaria, and the Latin states.

John Apocaucus, metropolitan of Naupactus, George Bardanes, metropolitan of Corcyra, and Demetrius Chomatenus, archbishop of Ochrida, are the most prominent representatives of the cultural movement in the Despotat of Epirus and in the short-lived Empire of Thessalonica.[201]

As far as Byzantine art was concerned, the new Frankish principalities established on the territory of the Byzantine Empire induced many artists from Constantinople and Thessalonica (Salonika) to seek new fields in the now powerful Serbian kingdom, or to join the artists already settled in Venice; "there was a *diaspora* [dispersion] of the painters. These missionaries of Byzantine art gave direction to the Slav schools, the full achievement of which at a rather later time we are now only beginning to understand."[202] But artistic traditions did not die out, and the artistic renaissance under the Palaeologi was, to a certain extent, due to these traditions and achievements of an earlier time which were preserved in the thirteenth century.

The literary movement of the epoch of the Nicene Empire has great importance for the general history of Byzantine culture. The center which had been created at the court of the Emperors of Nicaea became a nursery of culture, which, amid political division, violent international struggle, and internal troubles, saved, protected, and continued the achievements of the first Hellenic renaissance under the Comneni in order to make possible later the

[200] Michael Acominatus, ed. Lampros, II, 282-89, esp. 289.

[201] These three writers are not mentioned at

all in Montelatici, *Storia della letteratura bizantina.*

[202] Dalton, *East Christian Art,* 19-20. Diehl, *Manuel d'art byzantin,* II, 735-36.

appearance of the second cultural Hellenic renaissance under the Palaeologi. Nicaea serves as a bridge from the first renaissance to the second.

The cultural center formed in the thirteenth century in the western part of the Balkan peninsula, in the territory of Epirus, was the link which related the Christian East to western Europe, and to Italy in particular, in the cultural movement of the time. The rise of the culture of Italy in the thirteenth century at the time of Frederick II Hohenstaufen, this "prologue of the Renaissance," although it has not yet been thoroughly studied, has been and is being generally emphasized, discussed, and acknowledged. But the rise of the culture of Nicaea during the same century, and especially the movement in neglected Epirus, have not been taken into consideration. As a matter of fact, these three movements, in Italy, Nicaea, and Epirus, developed more or less actively along parallel lines, and perhaps with some reciprocal influences. Even a phenomenon so modest at first sight as the cultural rise of Epirus in the thirteenth century must lose its exclusively local significance and take its place in the history of general European culture of the thirteenth century.

BYZANTINE FEUDALISM

For a considerable length of time feudalism has been studied as a phenomenon belonging exclusively to medieval western Europe, and indeed as distinguishing the history of this area from the history of other lands.[203] It even has been supposed, not infrequently, that feudalism in all western countries was a homogeneous phenomenon, identical in substance. The fact has been obscured that feudal conditions established in one or another country in the West had their own peculiarities. Recently, however, the meaning of the term feudalism has grown broader; scholars have noted that the presence of feudalizing processes is to be found among different peoples in various parts of the earth and various epochs of history. The comparative historical method has eliminated an important historical prejudice that long dominated: that the complicated political, social, and economic phenomenon conventionally called feudalism belonged exclusively to the Middle Ages in western Europe. Therefore at present the term feudalism is used in two senses, one generic, the other specific. West European feudalism in the Middle Ages is only one species of feudalism and is a concept used in the narrower sense of the word, while in the broader sense feudalism is a stage of culture through which, according to

[203] The original text of the remainder of this chapter was published in my Russian book, *The Latin Sway in the Levant*, 56–74, and was omitted in the English and French editions of this work. It appeared in a revised form in English in *Byzantion*, VIII (1933), 584–604. It appears in this new English edition with slight modifications.

many historians and sociologists, all peoples pass in their historical development. No doubt the feudal process was far from reaching its complete development everywhere; for instance, sometimes the process was limited only to the social aspect and failed to attain political significance. Nevertheless, the transfer of this problem from the limits of western European medieval history into world history has allowed scholars to discover feudalism in ancient Egypt, in the Arab califate, in Japan, in the Islands of the Pacific Ocean, and in Old Russia. In each country where adequate conditions appear, feudalism in one or another stage of development is a phenomenon possible but not necessarily unavoidable.

Striking in its brevity and acumen is the definition of feudalism given by a Russian scholar, P. Vinogradov: "Feudalism is marked by the territorial aspect of political relations and by the political aspect of territorial relations."[204] Obviously this definition does not touch the economic aspect of the problem. But later that aspect was brought up and indeed emphasized by scholars, and now it must be considered.

Many different opinions, sometimes diametrically opposite, have been expressed concerning the origin of western European feudalism. Some scholars derive it from Germanic or Roman conditions existing at the turning-point from ancient to medieval history; some believe it to be the result of the Carolingian legislation; others try to explain this complicated institution by the social conditions of the almost unknown old Germanic life, especially the imaginary conditions of the old Germanic "march." All these theories have now only historical significance and strikingly illustrate the amount of labor and sometimes excessive perspicacity which scholars expend to establish a complicated historical phenomenon, in this case feudalism, on a really scholarly basis.

Many distinctive features of western European feudalism are explained partly by conditions in the Roman Empire during the first three centuries of its existence. Several elements later became constituent parts of feudalism. *Precarium* or benefice (*beneficium*), patronage, and immunity are well known in Roman times. *Beneficium* formerly designated any temporary possessions, sometimes during the life of the possessor; therefore lands given on certain conditions for temporary use, often for life, were also called *beneficia;* among the conditions the possessor's rendering of military service occupied first place, so that *beneficium* usually meant a territorial grant to be held on condition of paying military service. Later when western European feudalism took definite shape, the *beneficium* became a *feodum* (fief), i.e. land given in hereditary possession on definite conditions. The conventional name *feudal-*

<hr />

[204] "The Origin of Feudal Relations in Lombard Italy," *Journal of the Ministry of Public Instruction,* CCVII (1880), 137.

ism comes from this word *feodum,* whose origin has not yet been definitely established. Patronage, i.e. the custom of placing oneself under the protection of a more powerful man, passed from Roman times to the Middle Ages and in the feudal epoch began to be called by a Latin word, *commendatio,* or sometimes by a German word, *mundium.* Finally, *immunitas,* which was known in the Roman period, in the feudal epoch meant giving certain state rights to private individuals; these men were often exempted from certain obligations to the state, and government agents were forbidden to enter the territory of an immunist.

In the West as the central power declined, these three elements, which existed for a considerable time independently of each other, gradually began to concentrate in one person; the same individual, namely the landowner, distributed benefices, received commendations, and used immunities. In other words, the landowner became a sovereign. This process concerned both laity and clergy. Of course this evolution took place in various countries in various ways.

The problem of feudalism in Byzantium has not been much studied; intensive work is still needed, and one must be very cautious in generalizing. But at least it is now quite possible to speak of feudalism and feudalizing processes in Byzantium, whereas not long ago the term "Byzantine feudalism" would have seemed a paradox.

Since Byzantium is the continuation of the Roman Empire, it may be said a priori that the phenomena analogous to benefice, patronage, and immunity are, of course, to be noted in the internal life of Byzantium. The question is only to what extent these phenomena developed in the modified conditions of the eastern provinces of the Empire, and what forms they took.

In the east the Greek word *kharistikion* corresponded in meaning to the Latin word *beneficium,* and the Greek word *kharistikarios* corresponded to *beneficiarius,* i.e. a man granted land on condition of paying military service. But in Byzantium, especially beginning with the tenth century, the system of distribution of land as *kharistikia* was usually applied to monasteries, which were granted both to laymen and to clergy. Possibly this peculiarity of Byzantine *beneficium* (*kharistikion*) should be connected with the iconoclastic epoch, when the government in its struggle against the monks resorted to the secularization of monastery lands, which gave the Emperor a rich source for land grants. This circumstance, in all probability, is the reason why the original meaning of *kharistikion,* a grant of land in general not specifically monasterial, was lost and the term *kharistikion* was used specifically as a monastery grant. A very good authority on the internal life of Byzantium, P. V. Bezobrazov, wrote: "The characteristic feature of the system of *kharistikion* was that the owner of a monastery, whoever he might have been (emperor, bishop, or private individual), gave a monastery for life to someone who thereupon took the name of *kharistikarios*. The *kharistikarios* received all the revenues of the monastery and was obliged to maintain the monks and take care of the buildings, in a word to carry on the whole economy of the monastery. It is evident that the surplus of the revenues belonged to the *kharistikarios*."[205] Another noted Russian Byzantinist, Th. Uspensky, plainly stated that the system of *kharistikion* as a custom of granting monasteries and church lands was an institution which developed within the church itself and was in complete harmony with the customs and opinions existing among the laity as to the right of disposal of land property.[206] If these definitions of *kharistikion,* especially Uspensky's, are accepted, it must also be affirmed that all links with the Roman past were lost; this conclusion is incorrect. The *kharistikion* is a survival of the Roman *precarium-beneficium* which received a special meaning owing to special conditions in the eastern half of the Empire.

In the epoch of the pagan Roman Empire, military landownership existed, the distinctive feature of which was that the land on the borders of the Empire was granted as hereditary property, but on specific condition that the possessors should defend the frontiers and hand down this obligation to their children. The beginning of this measure is usually referred to the period of Emperor Severus Alexander, i.e. to the first half of the third century, when he granted the frontier lands taken from the enemy to the frontier soldiers (*limitanei*) and their chiefs upon condition that they should maintain hereditary military service and not alienate the lands to civilians. Although some scholars categorically state that these frontier lands (*agri limitanei*) have no connection with the later *beneficium* or fief (*feodum*),[207] none the less many eminent historians, not without reason, discover the roots of the *beneficia* of the Middle Ages in the system of the distribution of lands in the pagan Roman Empire.[208] A novel of Theodosius II issued in the first half of the fifth century and included in the Code of Justinian in the sixth century, which was proclaimed binding upon both parts of the Empire, western and eastern, confirms the military service of the frontier soldiers or frontier militia (*limitanei milites*) as a necessary condition for possessing land, and refers the custom to ancient statutes (*sicut antiquitus statutum est*).[209]

[205] *A Byzantine Writer and Statesman, Michael Psellus,* I, 29.

[206] "Opinions and Decrees of Constantinopolitan Local Councils of the Eleventh and Twelfth Centuries Concerning the Distribution of Church Possessions (*Kharistikaria*)," *Transactions of the Russian Archeological Institute at Constantinople,* V (1900), 5.

[207] See, e.g., Fustel de Coulanges, *Les Origines du système féodal,* 1–11, esp. 9.

[208] See C. Jireček, *Staat und Gesellschaft im mittelalterlichen Serbien,* I, 40–41. Cf. P. Mutafčiev, *Vojniški zemi i vojnici v Vizantija prěz XIII–XIV v,* p. 34.

[209] *Novellae Theodosii,* XXIV; in *Theodosiani libri XVI,* ed. T. Mommsen and P. Meyer, II, 63. *Codex Justinianus,* XI, 60, 3.

Beginning with the seventh century, under the menace of the Persian, Arab, Avar, Slavonic, and Bulgarian invasions which often successfully wrested from the Empire important and prosperous frontier provinces, the government strengthened military organization all over the territory of the Empire; so to speak, it applied the former frontier organization to the inland provinces. But many severe military failures which Byzantium suffered from the seventh to the ninth centuries, in addition to the internal troubles of the iconoclastic period and the struggle for the throne, evidently shook the well arranged system of military land holding; the large landowners, the so-called "powerful" men or magnates, took advantage of this new situation and against the law began to buy up military holdings. Therefore when in the tenth century the emperors of the Macedonian dynasty issued their famous novels to defend peasant interests against the encroaching tendencies of the "powerful" men, they were at the same time acting to defend military holdings. The novels of Romanus Lecapenus, Constantine Porphyrogenitus, Romanus II, and Nicephorus Phocas aimed at restoring the firmness and inviolability of military holdings and mainly at securing that such holdings should not be alienated to men who gave no military service; in other words, fundamentally these novels reproduced the provision of the novel of Theodosius II quoted above which passed into the Justinian Code. Th. Uspensky, who regarded the Slavonic influence in Byzantium as one of the most important elements of its internal life, wrote as regards military holdings: "If in the tenth century some traces of community are noted in the organization of military holdings, this of course indicates not Roman origin of the institution but Slavonic, and its first manifestations must be referred to the epoch of the Slavonic settlements in Asia Minor."[210] But this hypothesis of the noted Russian historian cannot be proved. The system of military holdings survived to some extent down to the fall of Byzantium; at least in legislative texts from the eleventh century to the fourteenth the arrangements of the emperors of the tenth century are treated as still in force, although in reality they were not always so.

For a considerable time, as far as the fragmentary and obscure evidence shows, apparently no specific term was generally accepted in Byzantium to designate imperial grants, except possibly the term *kharistikion;* this word has not yet been studied from this particular aspect, so its use may be given only as an hypothesis, although a very plausible one. A special term to designate imperial grants made its appearance in Byzantine sources in the eleventh century; it was a term which was formerly used as an alternative for *kharistikion,* but which later began to be employed specifically in the sense of imperial grant. This term was *pronoia.*

[210] "On the History of Peasant Landownership in Byzantium," *Journal of the Ministry of Public Instruction,* CCXXV (1883), 326.

Some scholars have incorrectly derived this word from the German word *Frohne* (socage, compulsory service); since they discovered it in Serbian documents before they learned it from Byzantine sources, they even believed that the Serbians borrowed it when they were still neighbors of the Goths.[211] It goes without saying that *pronoia* is a Greek word meaning "forethought, care" in the Christian sense, "providence." Of course the word *pronoia* after receiving the special meaning of imperial grant did not lose its original sense, so that in a later period which cannot be exactly dated, Byzantine documents contain both meanings; similarly in the west the feudal term *beneficium* failed to overcome the original use of this word as "favor, benefit."

The man who asked for and received a monastery as a grant (*kharistikion*) pledged himself to take care of it, i.e. in Greek to take "*pronoia*" of it. Therefore the man who received such a grant was sometimes called not only *kharistikarios* but also *pronoetes,* i.e. provider. In the course of time the granted estate itself began to be called *pronoia.* According to Th. Uspensky, in Byzantium the term *pronoia* "means a grant to the office-holding class of populated lands or other revenue-yielding property as a reward for service done and on condition of discharging a certain service from the grant."[212] Military service was especially meant. The *pronoia* was not an hereditary property held unconditionally; the possessor of a *pronoia* could neither sell, bequeath, nor give away the granted land. In other words, the *pronoia* is identified with those military lands which go back to the period of the pagan Roman Empire. The *pronoia* was granted either by the emperors themselves or in their name by their ministers.

As early as the tenth century, there is evidence of the word *pronoia* used in the sense of a land grant on condition of military service. Complete certainty on the special meaning of *pronoia* from documents begins only with the second half of the eleventh century. This circumstance in no way proves that this meaning of *pronoia* could not have existed earlier. Further publication of earlier documents and a study of the published sources from this specific angle may establish the special meaning of *pronoia* for the period previous to the eleventh century. In the epoch of the Comneni the system of granting *pronoias* was already a common thing. In connection with the Crusades and the penetration of western European influence into Byzantium, especially under the latinophile Emperor Manuel I (1143–1180), actual western European feudal terms, though in Greek form, make their appearance in Byzan-

[211] See A. Maïkov, "On Land Property in Old Serbia," *Chteniya of the Society of Russian History and Antiquities,* I (1860), 28–29 and n. 1. In 1902 L. Gumplowicz still derived *pronoia* from the German *Frohne.* See Jireček, *Staat und Gesellschaft,* I, 41, n. 5.

[212] "Significance of Byzantine and South-Slavonic Pronoia," *Collection of Articles on Slavonic Studies for the Twenty-Fifth Anniversary of the Scholarly and Professorial Activities of V. J. Lamansky,* I, 22, 29.

tium, for example *lizios,* which corresponds to the medieval Latin word *ligius,* i.e. a vassal or holder of a fief. It is interesting to note that when the crusaders of the Fourth Crusade, i.e. western European landlords, began to establish themselves on the occupied territories of the Eastern Empire, they found the local land conditions very similar to those of the West and easily adaptable to their own feudal forms. In a document of the beginning of the thirteenth century, the Byzantine emperors' grants are called fiefs (*de toto feudo, quod et Manuel quondam defunctus Imperator dedit patri meo*).[213] Another document of the same period testifies that the western conquerors continued to maintain the conquered population as formerly, exacting from them nothing more than they had been used to under the Greek emperors (*debemus in suo statu tenere, nihil ab aliquo amplius exigentes, quam quod facere consueverant temporibus graecorum imperatorum*).[214] Much material for the study of feudal relations on the territory of Byzantium is contained in the so-called *Chronicle of Morea,* a rich mine of information on this subject. The institution of *pronoia* survived through the Middle Ages till the fall of the Empire.

The study of the problem of *pronoia* in Byzantium, in connection with *kharistikion* and military lots, deserves great attention and may lead to most interesting results,[215] not only for a better and more correct understanding of land conditions and of the internal life of the Empire in general but also for instructive and illuminating analogies with other countries, Western, Slavonic, and Muhammedan, including the later Ottoman Empire.

The term *pronoia* is in common use in Serbian documents. In the history of Russia, *pronoia* is sometimes compared with the Russian *kormlenie* (feeding). This was a custom in Old Russia: the Russian nobles were granted towns or provinces as *kormlenie,* often as reward for service in the field; these nobles were given the opportunity to enrich themselves by *korm* (food), gifts, and fees, legal and administrative, from the local population. But the Russian *kormlenie* was not connected with the possession of a territory and meant only the administration of a town or province with the right to collect revenues for the profit of the administrator. Therefore the Byzantine *pronoia* corresponds rather to the *pomestye* of the State of Moscow, i.e. an estate held temporarily on condition of discharging military service, which speedily assumed an hereditary character.

The Roman patronage (*patrocinium*) or the western European *commendatio-mundium* was also well known in Byzantium. The codes of Theodosius and Justinian contain a considerable number of decrees, beginning with the

[213] Tafel and Thomas, *Urkunden zur älteren Handels- und Staatsgeschichte,* I, 513.

[214] *Ibid.,* II, 57.

[215] On *pronoia* see Mutafciev, *Vojniški zemi i voljnici,* 37–61; Ostrogorsky, *Pronoia* (1951). In Serbian.

fourth century, where patronage (in the codes called *patrocinium*) was very severely punished because poor men who placed themselves under the protection (patronage) of their wealthy and powerful neighbors wished thereby to escape various state obligations, especially burdensome taxation, and this the state could not admit. In the novels of Justinian and later emperors there is a Greek term corresponding to the Latin *patrocinium;* this is *prostasia,* i.e. "acting in behalf of someone, patronage, protection," which in any form whatever was forbidden. But in spite of the prohibitive measures of the central government the large landowners (the "powerful" men) continued their very profitable practice of patronage or *prostasia,* forming a sort of intermediary between the state and the taxable population, and the imperial power was unable to overcome this evil. The novel issued by Romanus Lecapenus in 922 which forbade the "powerful" to acquire any property whatever from the poor, mentions among other means of the rich's oppressing the poor, *prostasia,* i.e. patronage.

The institution of immunity (*immunitas*) was also known in Byzantium as *exkuseia* or *exkusseia* (ἐξκουσσεία), which with the derivative verb (ἐξκουσσεύειν, ἐξκουσσεύεσθαι) is merely the Greek form of the Latin word *excusatio* (verb, *excusare*), with an analogous meaning. Scholars particularly interested in *exkuseia* found the earliest imperial charter (*chrysobull*) granting an *exkuseia* was issued only in the middle of the eleventh century (1045); they accordingly failed to see in this institution, which according to the charter was so far away from Roman times, a survival of the former immunity and therefore they tried to explain its origin by other causes. One scholar, N. Suvorov, traced the origin of the Byzantine immunity-*exkuseia* back to a Western custom which passed to Byzantium in German shape. In his opinion, "it is impossible to establish any historical link between these later Byzantine immunities and the immunities of the Roman Law. Even if we suppose that German immunity has Roman roots, it was already in Frankish form when it passed in Byzantium."[216] Another scholar who made a special study of the problem of *exkuseia,* P. Yakovenko, disagreed with this opinion; he believed that this institution originated and developed in Byzantium independently and he refused to acknowledge any connection between *exkuseia* and the Roman immunity, because there is a strong difference between these two conceptions. "The origin of *exkuseia* is to be sought in the political disorder which broke out in Byzantium because of the degeneration of the Roman state institutions. Along with this, the confusion of the principles of Public Law with those of Private Law also exerted its influence. From these causes the kernel of *exkuseia* originated; the state officials were forbidden to

---

[216] N. Suvorov, in *Vizantiysky Vremennik,* XII (1906), 227–28.

enter granted possessions, and the recipient of the grant of immunity was also granted the right of collecting state revenues."[217]

In Roman legislative documents the Latin terms *immunitas* and *excusatio* are identical in meaning, and the attempts of some learned jurists to establish a definite distinction between them have not led to final results.[218]

In the codes of Theodosius and Justinian there are severe regulations against exemptions from taxation which are called *immunitates* or are expressed by the verb *excusare*.

The documents of the Byzantine period contain grants of immunities-*exkuseias* mostly given to monasteries. According to them the privileges granted by the charters of the Byzantine emperors were chiefly concerned with forbidding imperial officials to enter the privileged localities, with exemptions from taxation, and with the right of jurisdiction; in other words, here was the real medieval immunity on the western feudal model.

It is usually supposed that the earliest charter (*chrysobull*) granting an *exkuseia* was issued in the middle of the eleventh century. But this alone cannot be a proof that no *exkuseia* was granted before, the more so as the style and expressions of the charters of the eleventh and twelfth centuries which are preserved indicate that the idea of *exkuseia* was at that time perfectly common, definite, and well known, requiring no explanation. Nor is this all. The charters of the emperors of the Macedonian dynasty, of the late ninth and of the tenth century, granted to the Athonian monks, show all the traits of *exkuseia*. A charter of Basil I (867–886) protects all those who "have chosen the hermit life on Mount Athos" both from military commanders and imperial officials and from private citizens and peasants so "that no one shall disturb those monks or enter the inner places of Mount Athos."[219] This charter was confirmed by Basil's son, Emperor Leo VI the Philosopher (886–912). Another confirmation of this charter granted by the "earlier reigning" emperors was made in the first half of the tenth century by a charter of Romanus I Lecapenus (919–944).[220] In other Athonian documents on the demarcation of litigable lands on Mount Athos in the tenth century, there are references to the charters of the preiconoclast period, which have survived; these were the charters of the seventh century and the opening of the eighth issued by Constantine IV (668–685), Justinian II Rhinotmetus (685–695 and 705–711), as well as by the first restorer of icon worship, Empress Irene (797–802) and her son Constantine VI (780–797).[221] Of course it is impossible to

[217] *On the History of Immunity in Byzantium,* 38, 48, 63.

[218] *Ibid.,* 6. C. Uspensky, "Exkuseia-Immunity in the Byzantine Empire," *Vizantiysky Vremmenik,* XXIII (1923), 76.

[219] P. Uspensky, *The Christian Orient,* III (1), 37, 295.

[220] *Ibid.,* 45, 49, 298, 299.

[221] *Ibid.,* 51.

tell exactly what these charters contained; but on the basis of the dispute which concerned the possession of land by the Athonian monks it may be supposed that they also dealt with immunities.[222]

The edict of the Emperor Justinian II, which was issued in September, 688, and which exists in an inscription, may be regarded as an example of immunity-*exkuseia* of an earlier period. By this edict Justinian II granted a salina in Thessalonica to the Church of St. Demetrius "for all following and everlasting years," as its exclusive property which was exempted from any previous obligations. In his edict Justinian plainly expressed the purpose of his grant: the entire profit from the salina was to provide for the expenses of the illumination of the church, the daily substance of its clergy, necessary upkeep of the building, and all other needs of the clergy.[223]

The privileged monasteries which are sometimes called "monastery-princedoms"[224] were developing from the period of Justinian the Great (527–565), and these monasterial immunities may be connected with the various privileges established in the fourth century for the Christian clergy by Constantine the Great and his successors.[225] It is true all these fragmentary observations on immunity in Byzantium deal exclusively with monasterial life. But many early charters (*chrysobulls*) have disappeared, and moreover the question of Byzantine immunity has been very little studied in general, especially in its history before the eleventh century. Even various published Byzantine sources, such as histories, chronicles, and lives of saints, have not been adequately estimated from this point of view. When this preparatory work is done, new and important material almost certainly will be available on the problem of lay *exkuseia*-immunity in Byzantium. And it may be inferred that Byzantine *exkuseia* in its origin goes back to the time of Roman immunity and is a part of the complicated social inheritance which the Christian Empire received from the pagan Empire.[226]

Further study of Byzantine *prostasia*-patronage and *exkuseia*-immunity will be exceedingly important both for the better understanding of the internal life of Byzantium itself and for the internal history of the neighboring countries, Muhammedan and Slavonic, Old Russian in particular. The valuable studies on feudalism in Old Russia by N. Pavlov-Silvansky, who compared western patronage with Russian *zakladnichestvo* and western immunity with

[222] C. Uspensky, "Exkuseia-Immunity in the Byzantine Empire," *Vizantiysky Vremennik*, XXIII (1923), 99.

[223] A. A. Vasiliev, "An Edict of the Emperor Justinian II, September, 688," *Speculum*, XVIII (1943), 9.

[224] See C. Uspensky, *Outlines in the History of Byzantium*, 187, 190–91, 195.

[225] For details on monasterial immunity, see C. Uspensky, "Exkuseia-Immunity in the Byzantine Empire," *Vizantiysky Vremennik*, XXIII (1923), 99–117.

[226] Uspensky denied this; he wrote "the exkuseia could not develop from the immunity"; *ibid.*, 115.

bayar samosud (right of jurisdiction among the Russian nobility), would have been still more valuable had the author not limited himself to western analogies but had also made use of Byzantine evidence.

Large landownership, the famous Roman *latifundia,* is also one of the characteristic features of the social structure of the Byzantine Empire. The powerful provincial magnates were at times so dangerous to the central power that the latter was compelled to undertake a stubborn struggle against them, often unsuccessfully.

In this respect the epoch of Justinian the Great, who energetically strove against the large landowners, is exceedingly interesting. The *Secret History* of Procopius as well as Justinian's Novels give the most interesting material on this subject; the *Secret History* is a work of the sixth century, biased and one-sided, obviously reflecting the interests and ideas of the large landowners, but if properly used is an extremely valuable source on the internal history of the Byzantine Empire. This and the Novels reveal the Emperor's struggle against the aristocracy based on landownership, a struggle which not only affected the sixth century but continued far later. One of Justinian's novels addressed to the proconsul of Cappadocia blaming the desperate condition of state and private landownership in the provinces upon the unrestrained conduct of local magnates, contains these significant lines: "News has come to us of such exceedingly great abuses in the provinces that their correction can hardly be accomplished by one person of high authority. And we are even ashamed to tell with how much impropriety the managers of 'landlords' estates promenade about, surrounded by body-guards, how they are followed by large mobs of people, and how shamelessly they steal everything." Then after mentioning a few facts about private property, this novel goes on to say that "state property has almost entirely passed into private ownership, for it was stolen and plundered, including all the herds of horses, and not a single man spoke against it, for all mouths were stopped with gold."[227] From these statements it appears that the Cappadocian magnates had full authority in their provinces, and that they even maintained troops of their own, armed men and bodyguards, and seized private as well as state lands. Similar information about Egypt in the time of Justinian is found in the papyri. A member of the famous Egyptian landowning family of Apions possessed in the sixth century vast landed property in various parts of Egypt. Entire villages were part of his possessions. His household was almost regal. He had his secretaries and stewards, his hosts of workmen, his own assessors and tax collectors, his treasurer, his police, even his own postal service. Many of these magnates had their own prisons and maintained their own troops.[228]

---

[227] *Novella 30,* 5; ed. Schoell-Kroll, 228; ed. Zachariä von Lingenthal, I, 268.

[228] H. I. Bell, "The Byzantine Servile State in Egypt," *Journal of Egyptian Archaeology,*

Against these large landowners Justinian waged a merciless struggle. By various means he consciously and persistently aimed at the destruction of large landownership. He was not completely successful, however, and large landownership remained an undying feature of the Empire in later periods.

A convinced enemy of large landownership by the laity, Justinian at the same time tended to preserve and augment church and monastery property. Justinian's epoch is the most important step in the process of the formation in the Empire of the large church and monastery landownership which in connection with *exkuseias*-immunities created as it were feudal centers, monastery-principalities, or monastery-fiefs, which according to an historian, took in Byzantium the place of the duchies and counties of western Europe.[229] But the distinctive trait of a western European feudal state is first of all the instability, weakness, and sometimes disintegration of the central power. The large landowning Byzantine monasteries, from the feudal standpoint, were created and managed by antifeudal elements, because the abbots (*igumens*) who headed the monasteries possessed full power and were practically monarchs and autocrats in their own possessions. Perhaps this is one of the distinguishing peculiarities of Byzantine feudalism.

In the development of church and monastery landownership in Byzantium, the seventh century is of very great importance. After the conquest by the Arabs of Palestine and Egypt where monasticism was particularly flourishing, a considerable number of monks fled for refuge to the inland provinces of the Empire; old monasteries swarmed with refugees, and new monasteries were built. Therefore the second half of the seventh century and the beginning of the eighth can be justly regarded as the period when monastery landownership reached its climax. Because of many privileges, it undermined the finances of the state and as a great many robust young men entered monasteries and became therefore exempt from military service, it sapped the military power of the Empire. The state could not submit to such a situation. According to Vasilievsky "without much danger of error, it may be inferred that before the beginning of iconoclasm the Eastern Church was in no way inferior in size of land property to the Western Church. The Frankish kings had early begun to complain that their treasury was depleted and their riches had passed to the bishops and clergy; towards the end of the seventh century a whole third of the land in the Frankish state belonged to the Church. We believe that something similar was also the case in Byzantium at the same time."[230]

It may be supposed that the Isaurian emperors who are chiefly famous for

IV (1917), 101–2. A. A. Vasiliev, *Histoire de l'Empire Byzantin*, I, 208. On the Apion family and its estates see E. R. Hardy, *The Large Estates of Byzantine Egypt*.

229 C. Uspensky, *History of Byzantium*, 198.

230 "Materials for the Internal History of the Byzantine State," *Journal of the Ministry of Public Instruction*, CCII (1879), 222; in *Works*, IV, 319–20.

their iconoclastic policy waged their struggle not only against icons but also against monastery landownership or monastery feudalism.[231] In the iconoclastic epoch monastery lands were mercilessly confiscated, and the monks themselves, as well as those attached to the monasteries often not from a religious motive but for exemption from various state obligations, were reduced to lay estate, and thus forced to discharge their state duties.

But with the end of iconoclasm and the accession to the throne of the Macedonian dynasty circumstances changed. The number of monasteries increased again, and the amount of land which passed into monastery possession augmented still more rapidly. Feudalizing processes in the church and monastery domain which had been temporarily stopped by the iconoclastic emperors began to develop again in a direction undesirable and at times dangerous to the central power. The French scholar Charles Diehl wrote on this epoch: "Usurpations continued; the might of the large land aristocracy always grew; feudalism always developed. In the ninth century the crisis took a character of particular acuteness."[232]

In the political life of the Empire a very striking analogy may be drawn between western European feudal lords, dukes (*duces*) and counts (*comites*), and the exarchs of the close of the sixth century, who under Emperor Maurice (582–602) stood at the head of the two vast territorial organizations, the exarchates of Ravenna and of Carthage or Africa. The exarchs or the governors general, first of all military officers, gradually concentrated in their hands the administrative and judicial functions and had the final word in the management of church affairs in the exarchate. Whenever the exarch arrived at Rome, he was accorded an almost imperial reception. The protocol of his entry into Rome became the model of the reception of Frankish kings or German emperors. The reception of Charlemagne in Rome in 774, for instance, was modeled after that of the exarch, and it remained authoritative for all imperial receptions in Rome during the Middle Ages.[233] It is not surprising that from

[231] This point of view was particularly emphasized by C. Uspensky, *History of Byzantium*, 213; see also N. Iorga, "Les Origines de l'iconoclasme," *Bulletin de la section historique de l'Académie roumaine*, XI (1924), 147–48; Iorga, *Histoire de la vie byzantine*, II, 32–43. Charles Diehl and G. Marçais, *Le Monde oriental, de 395 à 1081*, 263 and especially n. 46. This view is energetically refuted by G. Ostrogorsky, "Ueber die vermeintliche Reformtätigkeit der Isaurier," *Byzantinische Zeitschrift*, XXIX (1929–30), 399, n. 2. Cf. Ostrogorsky, "Agrarian Conditions in the Byzantine Empire in the Middle Ages," *Cambridge Economic History of Europe*, I,

[232] Charles Diehl, *Byzance. Grandeur et décadence*, 167.

[233] See L. Duchesne, *Liber Pontificalis*, I, 497: cum adclamationum earundemque laudium vocibus ipsum Francorum susceperunt regem, obviam illi eius sanctitas dirigens venerandas cruces id est signa, sicut nos est exarchum aut patritium suscipiendum, eum cum ingenti honore suscipi fecit (Charlemagne's reception under Pope Hadrian, 772–95). See E. Eichmann, "Studien zur Geschichte der abendländischen Kaiserkrönung, II, Zur Topographie der Kaiserkrönung," *Historisches Jahrbuch*, XLV (1925), 24–25. E.

208–9.

time to time the exarchs raised the banner of revolt both at Carthage and at Ravenna and advanced claims to the imperial throne. At the opening of the seventh century, the revolt of the African exarch Heraclius resulted in the establishment of a new dynasty in Byzantium in the person of his son, also Heraclius.

It is relevant to emphasize the fact that the same Emperor Maurice under whom the two almost independent exarchates were instituted made a will when he was seriously ill several years before his death. This will was apparently not known during his lifetime; it was discovered and opened later, under Heraclius. In it Maurice divided his Empire among his children: he assigned Constantinople and the eastern provinces to his eldest son; Rome, Italy, and the islands to his second son; and distributed the rest of the Empire among his younger sons.[234] This will was not carried into effect because of the revolution of 602 when Maurice was overthrown; but it is interesting as an attempt at a typical feudal division such as often took place in the West in the epoch of the Merovingians and Carolingians as well as in Old Russia in the so-called "appanage period."

The process of formation of a new provincial or, to use the Byzantine term, theme organization may also furnish some material for feudal analogies. In the seventh century in connection with the Persian, Arab, Bulgarian, and Slavonic dangers a reorganization of the provincial administration was carried out by appointing at the head of some vast territories military governors general who gradually obtained complete superiority over the civil authorities. These provincial governors later in the ninth and tenth centuries sometimes handed down their power and functions in their own families from generation to generation; they became as it were hereditary governors in their respective provinces and thus evaded direct control by the imperial power.[235] Their position was analogous to that of the hereditary counts and dukes of the West.

The almost permanent struggle on the eastern frontier in Asia Minor against the Arabs caused the so-called *akritai* to appear. *Akrites* (plural *akritai*) was a name applied during the Byzantine period to the defenders of the outermost borders of the Empire; it is derived from the Greek word *akra*, meaning border. The *akritai* sometimes enjoyed a certain amount of independence from the central government and are with some grounds to be compared with the western European margraves (meaning rulers of the borderland, marches) and with the cossacks of the *ukraina* (also meaning border), in the history of Russia. In these border districts where war was the

---

Kantarowicz, "The 'King's Advent' and the Enigmatic Panels in the Doors of Santa Sabina," *The Art Bulletin*, XXVI (1944), 211 and n. 23.

[234] Theophylact Simocatta, *Historiae*, VIII,

11, 7; ed. C. de Boor, 305–6.

[235] For several examples taken from the lives of saints, see A. Rudakov, *Outlines in Byzantine Culture Based on Data from Greek Hagiography*, 201–2.

normal state of things and security did not exist, "one felt," according to a French historian, A. Rambaud, "far removed from the Byzantine Empire, and one might have been not in the provinces of an enlightened monarchy but in the midst of the feudal anarchy of the West."[236] An English historian, J. B. Bury, says that the continuous strife against the Saracens (Arabs) in the East developed a new type of warrior, the *kavallarios,* i.e. a rider, knight (in German *Ritter*), "whose heart was set on adventure and who was accustomed to act independently of orders from the emperor or a military superior. . . . In the tenth century many of them possessed large domains and resembled feudal barons rather than Roman officers."[237] The famous families in Asia Minor of Phocas, Sclerus, Maleinus, and Philocales, with whom Basil II (976–1025) irreconcilably and continually struggled, are representatives of large landlords in Asia Minor who because of their vast land properties were not only a social anomaly in the Empire but also a serious political danger to the reigning dynasty, for they could group around them their own military forces. A man who received a *pronoia* upon condition of military service had the right or probably even the obligation to maintain a body of troops which, if circumstances allowed, he could bring to a considerable size. The famous Novels of the emperors of the Macedonian dynasty in defense of small landownership point out once more how threatening from the state standpoint was the development of large landownership.

The troubled period of the eleventh century was characterized by a struggle between the large landowners of Asia Minor who relied on their military forces, and the central government. The result was that in 1081 a representative of large landownership, Alexius Comnenus, took possession of the throne and founded a dynasty of long duration (1081–1185). But Alexius was forced to recognize Trebizond as an almost independent state and during his reign he took severe measures against the large landowners among both laity and clergy. A strong reaction against large landownership took place under the last emperor of the Comnenian dynasty, Andronicus I (1182–1185). But the former system triumphed again under the Angeli (1185–1204).

With the epoch of the crusades, western crusaders and other westerners appeared. At first they only passed through the territory of the Empire; then, especially owing to the latinophile policy of Manuel I, they settled in great numbers and penetrated into all branches of Byzantine social and economic life. Finally after the Fourth Crusade they occupied the major part of the Byzantine Empire. By this time feudalizing processes in Byzantium had assumed so definite a shape that the westerners found nothing new to them in the general conditions of the Empire.

A mass of most interesting material for the study of feudalism in the Latin

---

[236] *Études sur l'histoire byzantine,* 73.   [237] *Romances of Chivalry,* 17–18.

states established in the East in the epoch of the Crusades is found in the codes compiled there. The first place belongs to the so-called *Assises of Jerusalem* or the *Letters of the Holy Sepulchre* (*Lettres du Sépulcre*) which, according to later Jerusalemite tradition, were attributed to the first ruler of Jerusalem, Godfrey. Omitting here the complicated and debatable question of the different versions of the *Assises* and all discussion of the relation of the original code to the later *Assises of Jerusalem,* the *Assises,* whatever their origin, were purely thirteenth century law, and "the laws of Jerusalem were based on the feudal customs of eleventh century Europe as brought to the East by the men of the First Crusade."[238] The *Assises* have the most fundamental significance both for better understanding of feudal relations in the Christian Orient in connection with local conditions and for the problem of feudalism in general. A French historian who made a special study of the institutions of the Kingdom of Jerusalem, Gaston Dodu, wrote: "The *Assises de la Haute Cour* [this was the section of the *Assises* treating of the relations between the Latin princes and their vassals] represent the old and the purest expression of French feudalism"; the compilers of the texts which have survived "wrote a complete treatise of feudal holdings superior to anything the Middle Ages have left us on this subject." One must go to the *Assises* "to study the true character of feudalism."[239] Very recently an American historian who wrote a very important book on the feudal monarchy in the Latin Kingdom of Jerusalem, John L. La Monte, emphasized the same idea. He wrote: "The *Assises de la Haute Cour* are in essence French feudal law, and the feudal system of Jerusalem, if the feudal system be taken to mean only the relations between the landholding nobility, was pure western feudalism which the crusaders had brought with them from their western homes. Once established it was preserved. The forces which affected feudalism in the West had but little effect on the slower moving East. For there is truth in the old assertion that in the feudal system of Jerusalem we find an almost ideal system of feudalism. Western institutions of the eleventh and twelfth centuries are transplanted into a semi-virgin field and are retained into a later age when the west itself had largely abandoned them."[240] Thus quite unexpectedly the Christian East has given into the hands of scholars a code of feudal law brought into a definite system, under whose conditions western Europe lived for a long time.

After the Fourth Crusade, the *Assises* of Jerusalem were introduced in Morea, which had been conquered by the crusaders, and in other Latin possessions established at that time on Byzantine territory as well as in the island

[238] J. L. La Monte, *Feudal Monarchy in the Latin Kingdom of Jerusalem 1000 to 1291*, 97.
[239] *Histoire des institutions monarchiques . . . 1099–1291*, 36, 59.

[240] *Feudal Monarchy in the Latin Kingdom*, xx. *Feudal Institutions as Revealed in the Assizes of Romania*, trans. by P. W. Topping (1949).

of Cyprus; for the latter island the *Assises* were translated into Greek. The *Assises* of Antioch, which give a good idea of the laws of this Latin principality in the East, may serve as an excellent supplement to the *Assises* of Jerusalem. The original text of the *Assises* of Antioch has been lost; but their Armenian translation has survived, and in the nineteenth century this was translated into modern French. Thus these Franco-Eastern codes are of great importance for the history both of western European feudalism and of the Latin and Greco-Byzantine Orient, and even for certain sections of the Ottoman law.

The study of feudalism in Byzantium has just begun. In 1879 a Russian historian, V. Vasilievsky, in connection with his discussion on *pronoia,* dropped the remark that only in the epoch of the Comneni and Angeli may one notice in Byzantium "a real embryo of a feudal order, although not the developed system."[241] It is true that Vasilievsky never made any special study of Byzantine feudalism. He could not even imagine that any feudal processes might have existed in Byzantium before the close of the eleventh century, when the Comneni ascended the throne. Of course the well-organized feudal hierarchy which in the feudal society of the West created long lines of suzerains, vassals, and subvassals, was never formed in Byzantium. "But," as Charles Diehl justly remarked, "in the Byzantine Empire the existence of this powerful provincial aristocracy had the same consequences as in the states of the western Middle Ages; especially whenever the central power became weakened, it was a terrible source of troubles and dissolution."[242]

The so-called feudalizing processes in the social, political, and economic aspects may be observed in the Byzantine Empire through the whole course of its history.

[241] "Materials for the Internal History of the Byzantine State," *Journal of the Ministry of Public Instruction,* CCII (1879), 415.

[242] *Byzance. Grandeur et décadence,* 178.

CHAPTER IX: THE FALL OF BYZANTIUM

CONSTANTINOPLE, the Acropolis of the universe, the imperial capital of the Romans, which, by the will of God, was under the power of the Latins, has come again under the power of the Romans—this has been granted them by the will of God through us." These are the words in the autobiography of Michael Palaeologus, the first Emperor of the restored Byzantine Empire.[1]

General situation in the Empire

The territory of Michael's Empire was greatly reduced from the territory of Byzantium in the epoch of the Comneni and Angeli, especially after the First Crusade. In 1261 the Empire comprised the northwestern corner of Asia Minor, the major part of Thrace and Macedonia, Thessalonica, and several islands in the northern part of the Aegean Sea (Archipelago). Accordingly, the Bosphorus and Hellespont, these exceedingly important strategic and commercial waterways, belonged to the restored Empire. The Despotat of Epirus came under the Empire's suzerainty. At the very beginning of his reign Michael received as ransom for the prince of Achaia, William Villehardouin, captured by the Greeks in the battle of Castoria, three strong Frankish fortresses in the Peloponnesus: Monemvasia, situated on the eastern coast, the great rock rising out of the sea near the ancient Epidaurus Limera, which is "not only one of the most picturesque sites of the Peloponnesus, but has a splendid record of heroic independence which entitles it to a high place in the list of the world's fortresses";[2] the well-known fortified castle of Mistra; and Maina, another castle erected by the Franks in the mountains of Taygetus to overawe the Slavs dwelling there. These three strongholds became the strategic bases of support from which the troops of the Byzantine emperors successfully fought the Frankish dukes.

But the rest of the formerly great Empire was menaced on all sides by

---

[1] *De vita sua opusculum*, par. viii, in *Christianskoe Čtenie*, II (1885), 535; in Russian, 556; in French in C. Chapman, *Michel Paléologue, restaurateur de l'Empire Byzantin (1261–1282)*, 172.

[2] W. Miller, *Essays on the Latin Orient*, 231.

peoples politically or economically strong: the Turks threatened from Asia Minor, the Serbs and Bulgars from the north; the Venetians occupied some of the islands of the Archipelago, the Genoese, certain points on the Black Sea, and the Latin knights, the Peloponnesus and a portion of Middle Greece. Michael Palaeologus was not able even to unite all the Greek centers. The Empire of Trebizond continued to live a separate and independent life and the Byzantine possessions in the Crimea—the theme of Cherson (Korsun) with the adjacent country frequently referred to as "the Gothic Klimata"— were in the power of the emperors of Trebizond and paid them tribute. The Despot of Epirus was only to a certain extent dependent upon the restored Empire of Michael. Under Michael Palaeologus the Empire reached the widest limits of the last period of its existence, but these limits were preserved only during his reign, so that "in this respect Michael Palaeologus was the first and also the last powerful emperor of restored Byzantium."[3] The Empire of the first Palaeologus resembled, to the French scholar, Diehl, "a slender, dislocated, miserable body upon which rested an enormous head—Constantinople."[4]

The capital, which had never recovered after the sack of 1204, passed into the hands of Michael in a state of decay and ruin; the best and richest buildings stood as if recently sacked; the churches had been robbed of their precious furnishings; the palace of Blachernae, which, from the time of the Comneni, had been the imperial residence and had dazzled strangers with its rich decorations and mosaics, was completely devastated; inside it was, said a Greek contemporary, "full of Italian smoke and fume"[5] from the carousals of the Latin emperors, and was therefore uninhabitable.

Though the Byzantine Empire of the Palaeologi continued to be of great importance from a cultural standpoint, Constantinople ceased to be one of the centers of European policy. "After the restoration under the Palaeologi the Empire has almost exclusively the local significance of a national Greek medieval kingdom, which, in substance, is the continuation of the Empire of Nicaea, though it established itself in the Blachernae and arrayed itself in the antiquated forms of the old Byzantine Empire."[6] Round this aging organism younger peoples were growing and gathering strength, especially the Serbs of the fourteenth century under Stephen Dušan (Dushan) and the Ottoman Turks. The enterprising commercial Italian republics, Genoa and Venice, especially the former, got control of the whole trade of the Empire, which

[3] T. Florinsky, *The Southern Slavs and Byzantium in the Second Quarter of the Fourteenth Century*, I, 23.

[4] *L'Empire byzantin sous les Paléologues. Études byzantines*, 220.

[5] George Pachymeris *De Michaele Palae-*ologo, II, 31; in *Corpus Scriptorum Historiae Byzantinae*, ed., I, 161.

[6] B. A. Pančenko, "The Latin Constantinople and Pope Innocent III," *The Annals of the Historical-Philological Society at the University of Novorossiya*, XXI (1914), 1.

became wholly dependent on them financially and economically. The only question was which of these peoples would put an end to the Empire of the eastern Christians, seize Constantinople, and become master of the Balkan peninsula. The history of the fourteenth century was to answer this question in favor of the Turks.

But if in the sphere of political international life Byzantium under the Palaeologi played a secondary part, its internal life was of great importance. In the epoch of the Palaeologi one may note the interesting fact of the rise of patriotism among the Greek people, accompanied by a turning back to the glories of ancient Greece. For instance, officially the emperors continued to bear the usual title of "basileus and autocrat of the Romans," but some prominent men of the time tried to persuade the basileus to take the new title of "Emperor of the Hellenes." The former vast Empire, made up of different nationalities, was transformed into a state small in its territorial limits and Greek in its composition. In the manifestation of Hellenic patriotism in the fourteenth and fifteenth centuries and in the profound enthusiasm felt for the glorious Hellenic past one may see, not without reason, one of the elements which in the nineteenth century was to contribute to the regeneration of modern Greece. Moreover, the epoch of the Palaeologi, when in the Empire the elements of East and West were marvelously interwoven, was marked by a powerful spiritual and artistic culture, which, considering the severe external and internal troubles, is at first sight unexpected. At that time Byzantium produced not a few scholars and educated men, writers, sometimes of very original talent, in the most varied fields of knowledge. And such monuments of art as the mosaics in the mosque of Kahrieh jami (Qahriye-jami, the Byzantine church of the Chora), the Peloponnesian Mistra, and the churches of Athos are the basis for appreciation of the importance of artistic creation under the Palaeologi. This artistic flowering has often been compared with the primitive renaissance of art in western Europe, that is to say, the earlier period of Italian Humanism. These phenomena in the field of literature and art and the most important problems which made their appearance in connection with them in the works of many scholars of the nineteenth and twentieth centuries belong to a later section on Byzantine culture in the epoch of the Palaeologi.

To the time of the Palaeologi belong the least investigated problems of Byzantine history. The reason is the extraordinary complexity of the history of the epoch, in external and especially in internal affairs, on the one hand, and on the other, the abundance and variety of the sources, many of which have not yet been published and are preserved in manuscript collections in western and eastern libraries. To date, there exists no complete monograph on any of the Palaeologi which covers all phases of their rule; the existing essays treat of only one side or another of their activity. There is one exception. In 1926 appeared a monograph on Michael Palaeologus by C. Chapman, brief and superficial but of general character.[7]

The dynasty of the Palaeologi belonged to a very well-known Greek family which, beginning with the first Comneni, gave Byzantium many energetic and gifted men, especially in the military field. They became related, in the course of time, to the imperial families of the Comneni, Ducae, and Angeli; on the strength of this relationship the first Palaeologi, Michael VIII always, Andronicus II for the most part, as well as his co-emperor and son, Michael IX, and sometimes, perhaps, Andronicus III, signed four family names, for example, Michael Ducas Angelus Comnenus Palaeologus. Later on the Emperors signed only "Palaeologus."[8]

The dynasty of the Palaeologi occupied the Byzantine throne for one hundred and ninety-two years (1261–1453), the longest dynasty in the whole course of Byzantine history.[9] The first Palaeologus who mounted the throne of the shaken and greatly curtailed Eastern Empire, Michael VIII (1261–82), cunning, cruel, but talented and an artful diplomat, succeeded in saving the Empire from the terrible danger from the West, that is, from the Kingdom of the Two Sicilies, and bequeathed the throne to his son Andronicus II the Elder (1282–1328), whom "nature had intended for a professor of theology but accident had made a Byzantine emperor."[10] Andronicus married twice. His first wife, Anne, was a daughter of the king of Hungary, Stephen V; his second wife, Violanta-Irene, a sister of the north-Italian marquess of Montferrat, after her brother's death, became the heiress to the margravate; unable as a Byzantine empress to accept the margravate, she sent there one of her sons who founded at Montferrat the dynasty of the Palaeologi, which ceased only in the first half of the sixteenth century.[11]

Andronicus in 1295 crowned with the imperial crown his eldest son by his first wife, Michael. Michael died in 1320, before his father, and is often referred to in historical works as his father's co-emperor, Michael IX. Negotiations

[7] *Michel Paléologue.* See also Th. Uspensky, *History of the Byzantine Empire,* III, 607–56.

[8] P. Yakovenko, *Studies in the Domain of Byzantine Charters. The Charters of the New Monastery in the Island of Chios,* 79–80. See also A. Heisenberg, *Aus der Geschichte und Literatur der Palaiologenzeit,* 26 (Andronicus II with two family names) and Plate III (Andronicus II Palaeologus). V. Laurent, "La Généalogie des premiers Paléologues," *Byzantion,* VIII (1933), 125–49. *Stemma* of the first Palaeologi (11th and 12th centuries), ending with Michael VIII and his brothers,

p. 146; slight simplification of the *stemma,* pp. 148–49. See an unreliable account of the Palaeologian genealogy by Theodore Spandugino (died after 1538), in C. Sathas, *Documents inédits relatifs à l'histoire de la Grèce au moyen âge,* IX, v, 175.

[9] The Macedonian dynasty nearest to the Palaeologi in duration reigned for 189 years.

[10] W. Miller, *The Catalans at Athens,* 4. See also Miller, *The Latins in the Levant,* 176.

[11] Violanta-Irene died in 1317. See F. Cognasso, "Una crisobolla di Michele IX Paleologo per Teodoro I di Monferrato," *Studi bizantini,* II (1927), 43.

were entered upon to marry Michael to Catherine de Courtenay, daughter of the titulary Emperor of Romania (of the former Latin Empire), and the pope was greatly interested in this project;[12] but, in the end, Michael married an Armenian princess, Xenia-Maria.

The son of Michael IX and grandson of Andronicus II, young Andronicus, was for many years during his father's lifetime his grandfather's favorite. But Andronicus was frivolous and given to love affairs, and one of his adventures ended in the accidental murder of his brother and as a result the premature death of his father, Michael IX. This entirely changed the grandfather's attitude. Civil war broke out between grandfather and grandson. Against Andronicus the Elder formed a strong party of opponents whose leading spirit was the later famous Cantacuzene. The civil war ended in favor of Andronicus the Younger who, in 1328, suddenly seized Constantinople and induced Andronicus the Elder to abdicate. The old deposed Emperor, whose long reign had been a new period of decay for Byzantium, ended his days as a monk. He died in 1332.

At the head of the government of Andronicus the Younger (1328–1341) stood the chief leader in his rebellion, John Cantacuzene, into whose hands passed the internal administration and the foreign affairs of the Empire. The new Emperor, giving himself up as before to amusements and hunting parties, felt no inclination to occupy himself with state affairs, but nevertheless took a personal part in the many wars fought during his reign. Cantacuzene was not satisfied with the tremendous influence he had obtained, for he aimed at the imperial throne, or at least at an omnipotent regency. This idea possessed him during the thirteen years of Andronicus' government and was the motivating force of all his activity. Andronicus' mother, the widow Xenia-Maria, and his second wife, a western princess, Anne of Savoy,[13] were both hostile to Cantacuzene. But by various intrigues he succeeded in maintaining his position until the very death of Andronicus.

At the death of Andronicus III in 1341, the new Emperor, John V, his eldest son, was hardly eleven years of age (1341–91). A long civil war, in which John Cantacuzene played the chief part, was fought around the throne of the boy Emperor. Against John Cantacuzene there formed a strong party consisting of the widow of the late Emperor, Anne of Savoy, who had been proclaimed regent; her partisan and the former favorite of Cantacuzene, the ambitious and powerful Alexius Apocaucus, the patriarch; and others. The char-

[12] See on this project, G. I. Brătianu, "Notes sur le projet de mariage entre l'empereur Michel IX Paléologue et Catherine de Courtenay (1288–95)," *Revue historique du sud-est européen*, I (1924), 59–63. C. Marinescu, "Ten-

tatives de mariage de deux fils d'Andronic II Paléologue avec des princesses latines," *ibid.*, I, 139–40.

[13] The first marriage of Andronicus III with the German princess Irene was childless.

acteristic feature of the civil strife of the fourteenth century was the participation, now on one side, now on the other, of foreign peoples pursuing their own political aims, Serbs, Bulgars, and especially Seljuq Turks as well as Ottoman Turks. Several months after the death of Andronicus III, Cantacuzene, in one of the cities of Thrace, proclaimed himself Emperor (John VI). Shortly after, the solemn coronation of John V Palaeologus was celebrated in Constantinople. Thus in the Empire there appeared two emperors. Cantacuzene, who had found strong support from the Turks (he had even married his daughter to an Ottoman sultan), gained the upper hand. His chief rival Apocaucus was slain in Constantinople. Cantacuzene was crowned at Hadrianople by the patriarch of Jerusalem, who put on the head of the new emperor a golden crown. Then the capital opened its gates to him. The regent Anne of Savoy was induced to yield, and Cantacuzene was recognized Emperor on a par with John Palaeologus. In 1347, Cantacuzene was crowned for the second time, and his daughter Helena was married to the young Palaeologus. Cantacuzene's ambitious plans were realized.

In the same year there stood for a short time at the head of the government in Rome a famous dreamer imbued with the recollections of the past glory of the Roman Republic, the tribune Cola di Rienzo. Cantacuzene sent him an embassy with a letter of congratulation upon his attainment of power over Rome.[14]

The stormy rule of Cantacuzene, during which John Palaeologus was pushed into the background, was important for the international relations of the epoch. For himself Cantacuzene devoted his energies to superseding Palaeologus; he proclaimed his son Emperor, declared him co-emperor and heir, and forbade the name of John Palaeologus to be mentioned in the churches or at public festivities. But Cantacuzene's influence with the people was gradually declining, and the last blow to his popularity was dealt by the establishment of the Turks in Europe. With the co-operation of the Genoese, John Palaeologus entered Constantinople at the end of 1354. Compelled to abdicate, Cantacuzene took the monastic habit under the name of Ioasaph and spent the rest of his life in writing his important memoirs.[15] In a Greek manuscript in the National Library of Paris are preserved two interesting miniatures of Cantacuzene; in one Cantacuzene is represented twice, in imperial robes and in monastic raiment. His son also abdicated.

John V Palaeologus finally became sole Emperor, but received, especially after the destructive civil war and foreign failures, a pitiful heritage. According to T. Florinsky, "Some islands and one province (Thrace) thoroughly

[14] Cola di Rienzo, *Epistolario,* ed. A. Gabrielli, in *Fonti per la Storia d'Italia. Episto-* *lari,* XIV, no. 6.

[15] Catacuzene died in 1383.

ruined and depopulated, on one side of which, close to the capital, the rapacious Genoese had a footing, while on the other side rose the powerful Turkish state: this was the Empire which he had to govern."[16]

Moreover, John's family troubles were not ended. He had never been intimate with his eldest son Andronicus, who in 1376, with the help of the Genoese, deposed his father, was crowned as Andronicus IV (1376–79), and made his son John co-emperor. The old John V, as well as his favorite son and heir, Manuel, were put in prison. In 1379 John V succeeded in escaping and, with the help of the Turks, regained his throne. John V and Andronicus came to an agreement which lasted until the death of the latter in 1385. After that John V, disregarding his grandson John, crowned as co-emperor his son Manuel. Finally, at the very end of the reign of John V, a rebellion was raised against him by his grandson. In 1390 the young John seized Constantinople and governed it, but only for a few months, under the title of John VII. New documents from the archives of Venice indicate that John's rebellion of 1390 was organized by Sultan Bayazid. The Venetian Senate, as usual very well-informed of the situation in Constantinople through its merchants, apparently judged it probable that Bayazid would be at that time on the Byzantine throne. In any case, in the instructions given the Venetian envoys about to go to Constantinople in 1390, they were admonished: "If you find Murad's son [Bayazid] in Constantinople, you must try to obtain from him the repeal of the sequestration of Venetian vessels."[17] Owing to the activity of Manuel, John V was restored. At the beginning of 1391 John V died after a long, stormy and unhappy reign. His son Manuel became Emperor (1391–1425).

A short time before his ascension to the throne the new Emperor had married Helena, daughter of the ruler of Northern Macedonia, Constantine Dragosh (Dragases), a Slav, or, as C. Jireček said, "the only Serbian who became Empress of Byzantium."[18] She gave birth to six sons, of whom two became the last Byzantine emperors, John VIII and Constantine XI; the latter is often given the Slavonic name of his grandfather on his mother's side, Dragosh (Dragases). The two last Palaeologi on the imperial throne were accordingly half-Slav. A picture of Helena, surnamed Palaeologina, is on a beautiful miniature in a precious Greek manuscript at the museum of the Louvre in Paris. In this miniature are Emperor Manuel, his wife Helena, and three of their sons, crowned by the Virgin Mary. This manuscript, one of the jewels of the Louvre,

[16] Florinsky, *The Southern Slavs and Byzantium*, I, 135.

[17] See M. Silberschmidt, *Das orientalische Problem zur Zeit der Entstehung des Türkischen Reiches*, 66–68.

[18] "Die Wittwe und die Söhne des Despoten Esau von Epirus," *Byzantinisch-neugriechische Jahrbücher*, I (1920), 4; geneological table, 6. Towards the end of her life Helena took refuge in the cowl under the name of Hypomene. Several historians call the mother of Constantine XI not Helena but Irene.

containing the works of St. Dionysius the Areopagite, was sent to Paris by Manuel as a present some years after his return to Constantinople from Paris.[19] Another portrait of Helena has been preserved on a lead seal or *molybdobullon*.[20]

Manuel, handsome, noble, very well educated, and endowed with literary talent, even as a youth during his father's lifetime felt sharply all the horror of the situation of the Empire and all the humiliating burden of his heritage. When the government of Thessalonica was confided to him by his father, he entered into negotiations with the population of a Macedonian city captured by the troops of the Sultan Murad with the aim of annihilating the Turkish garrison and freeing the city from the Turkish yoke. The sultan learned of the plan and determined to punish severely the governor of Thessalonica. Unable to make an adequate resistance, Manuel, after a fruitless attempt to take refuge with his frightened father, set out directly to the residence of Murad and expressed to him his repentance for his behavior. "The impious but reasonable sultan," said a historian of the fifteenth century, "favorably kept him as a guest for several days, and, supplying him when he took his leave, with food for his journey and rich presents, sent him back to his father with a letter in which he begged John V to pardon his son for what he had done in ignorance." In his valedictory address to Manuel, Murad said: "Govern peacefully what belongs to you and do not seek for foreign lands. But if you have need of money or any other support, I shall always be glad to fulfill your request."[21]

Later, Murad's successor Bayazid required that John V send him, with the stipulated tribute, his son Manuel and some Greek auxiliaries. Manuel was compelled to yield and take part in a predatory Turkish expedition through various regions of Asia Minor. His humiliation, complete impotence, and the privations of the expedition are clearly felt in Manuel's letters. Having described famine, cold, fatigue, and the crossing of the mountains, "where even wild beasts could not feed," Manuel made a tragic remark: "all this is being suffered jointly by the whole army; but one thing is unbearable for us: we are fighting with them [the Turks] and for them, and it means that we increase their strength and decrease ours."[22] In another letter Manuel wrote an account of the destroyed cities which he had seen during the expedition: "To

[19] This miniature has been reproduced rather often. See, e.g., S. Lampros, "Εἰκόνες Ἰωάννου Η' τοῦ Παλαιολόγου," Νέος Ἑλληνομνήμων, IV (1907), between 386–87. Lampros, *Empereurs byzantins. Catalogue illustré de la collection de portraits des empereurs de Byzance*, 53. G. Schlumberger, *Byzance et croisades*, 145 and Plate IV.

[20] B. A. Pančenko, *A Catalogue of the Molybdobulla of the Collection of the Russian Archeological Institute in Constantinople*, I, 133 (no. 380).

[21] George Phrantzes, *Annales*, I, ch. 11; Bonn ed., 48–49.

[22] *Lettres de l'empereur Manuel Paléologue*, ed. E. Legrand, 28–29 (letter no. 19).

my question what was the name of those cities, those whom I asked, answered: 'As we have destroyed them, so time has destroyed their names'; and immediately sorrow seized me; but I sorrow silently, being still able to conceal my feelings."[23] Such humiliation and subserviency towards the Turks Manuel had been forced to suffer before he ascended the throne.

His nobility was manifest when he redeemed his father John V from the Venetians who, on the Emperor's return from Italy, had arrested him at Venice on account of his failure to pay back borrowed money. While the eldest son of John, Andronicus, who ruled the Empire in his father's absence, was deaf to John's prayers to collect the sum due, Manuel obtained it at once and, going to Venice in person, redeemed his father from his humiliating captivity.

After his long and painful reign Manuel, in the last years of his life, withdrew from state affairs, which he entrusted to his son John, and devoted all his time to the study of the Scriptures. Shortly after, Manuel was struck with apoplexy; two days before his death he took holy orders under the name of Matthias (Matthew).

His son and successor, John VIII, reigned from 1425 to 1448. The new Emperor was married three times, and all three wives belonged to different nationalities. His first wife was a young Russian princess, Anna, daughter of the grand prince of Moscow, Vasili I; she lived in Constantinople only three years, but in that short time she became very popular in the capital. She fell a victim to the plague. John's second wife was an Italian, Sophia of Montferrat, a woman of lofty spiritual qualities but so unattractive in appearance that John felt only repulsion for her; the Byzantine historian Ducas, who describes her appearance, gave a popular proverb of his time: "Lent in front and Easter behind."[24] She could not bear her humiliating position at court, and, with the help of the Genoese of Galata and to the satisfaction of her husband, fled to Italy, where she ended her days in monastic retirement. His third wife John found in a princess of Trebizond, Maria (Mary), of the house of the Comneni, "who was distinguished for her beauty and good manners."[25] The attractiveness of this charming lady is remarked both by a Byzantine historian, and by a French pilgrim to the Holy Land, who was enraptured by the beauty of the basilissa when he saw her leaving St. Sophia.[26] She possessed great influence over the Emperor, who outlived her. There stands today in one of the Princes Islands (near Constantinople) a small chapel of the Holy Virgin erected by the beautiful Empress of Trebizond.

John VIII had no children by any of his three wives. When he died in the autumn of 1448, the question of an heir arose. The Empress mother, Manuel

[23] *Ibid.*, 23 (letter no. 16).

[24] Michael Ducas, *Historia bizantina,* chap. xx; Bonn ed., 100.

[25] *Ibid.;* Bonn ed., 102.

[26] Bertrandon de la Broquière, *Le Voyage d'outremer,* ed. C. Schefer, 155.

II's wife, who was still alive; the brothers of the late Emperor; and the highest officials of Constantinople fixed their choice upon Constantine, one of the brothers of John VIII, who at that time was the Despot of Morea. The sultan was informed of the choice of the new Emperor and approved the candidate. A deputation was sent to Morea, which notified Constantine of his election to the tottering throne of the once great Empire of Byzantium. At the beginning of 1449, from medieval Sparta, that is from the residence of the Despot at Mistra, he sailed at once for Constantinople in a Catalonian vessel and was solemnly received by the people. It was long believed that Constantine XI was crowned by a layman. But it is now known, since the publication of the works of John Eugenicus by Sp. Lampros, that the coronation of Constantine XI was never performed officially at all. The Church demanded that it should be performed by the patriarch, but it was probably postponed because of the tense antagonism between the partisans of the union of the churches and their opponents.[27] Constantine had been twice married, both of his wives belonging to Latin families which had established themselves in the Christian East —one to the family of Tocco, the other to the Genoese dynasty in the island of Lesbos, of Gattilusio—but both had died before Constantine's election to the Byzantine throne. The negotiations concerning a third wife for the new Emperor, in the West and East, at Venice, Portugal, Trebizond, and Iberia (Georgia), came to nothing. The fall of Constantinople and Constantine's death prevented the fulfillment of these matrimonial plans. His intimate friend, a diplomat and historian of the epoch of the Palaeologi, George Phrantzes, preserved in his *History* an interesting description of his mission to find a bride for the Emperor in Trebizond and Iberia.[28] The French historian Diehl remarked that, despite continued matrimonial intercourse between the Byzantine emperors and western princesses, at the critical moment the eyes of the last Emperor, in search of a bride, turned to the near, congenial, and kindred East.[29]

Constantine XI was killed in May 1453, at the taking of Constantinople by the Turks. On the site of the Christian eastern monarchy was founded the strong military empire of the Ottoman Turks.

Of the brothers who survived Constantine, Demetrius Palaeologus was captured by Muhammed II, to whom his daughter was married, and died at Hadrianople as a monk, under the name of David. Another brother, Thomas,

---

[27] See P. Charanis, "The Crown Modiolus Once More," *Byzantion*, XIII (1938), 379, 381–82. Sources and literature are given. In 1938 F. Dölger wrote that Constantine XI was crowned by a layman; *Byzantinische Zeitschrift*, XXXVIII (1938), 240. In 1940 G. Ostrogorsky said that Constantine was crowned emperor in Morea; *Geschichte des byzantinischen Staates*, 408.

[28] George Phrantzes, *Annales*, III, 1; Bonn ed., 206 ff.

[29] Charles Diehl, *Figures byzantines*, II, 289–90.

ended his days in Italy dreaming of a crusade against the Turks, receiving from the pope his means of subsistence. His son Andreas (Andrew), who had already become a Catholic, was the only legitimate representative of the dynasty of the Palaeologi who possessed rights to the lost Byzantine throne. An interesting document exists in which Andreas Palaeologus transmitted his rights to the Empires of Constantinople and Trebizond as well as to the Despotat of Serbia to the king of France, Charles VIII. When the latter at the end of the fifteenth century undertook his expedition against Naples, he considered it only as the steppingstone to eventual conquest of Constantinople and Jerusalem. In other words, at the end of the fifteenth century dreams of a crusade still existed. Andreas' transmission of his rights to Charles VIII seems never to have been fully carried out, for later Andreas again transmitted his rights to the Byzantine throne to Ferdinand and Isabella of Spain (Castile).[30] This act, of course, had no practical result.

Zoë, the daughter of Thomas Palaeologus and the sister of Andreas, was married to the far distant Grand Prince of Moscow, Ivan (John) III, and is known in Russian sources as Sophia Palaeologina. A Russian historian, Kluchevsky, said: "As heiress to the declining house of Byzantium, the new Tsarina of Russia had transferred the supreme rights of the Byzantine house to Moscow, as to a new Tsargrad, and there shared them with her husband."[31]

Moscow began to be compared with "seven-hilled Rome" and called "the third Rome." The Grand Prince of Moscow became "Tsar of all Orthodoxy," and Moscow as the capital of the Russian state became "the new city of Constantine" (i.e., a new Constantinople-Tsargrad).[32] A Russian scholar of the beginning of the sixteenth century, the monk Philotheus, wrote: "Two Romes have fallen, and the third stands, while a fourth is not to be."[33] The pope called the attention of the successor of Ivan III to his right to defend his "patrimony of Constantinople."[34] Thus, the fall of Constantinople and the marriage of Ivan III to Sophia Palaeologina brought up the problem of the rights of the rulers of Moscow, those representatives and defenders of eastern Orthodoxy, to the throne of the Byzantine Empire which was seized by the Ottoman Turks in 1453.

[30] See A. A. Vasiliev, "The Transmission by Andreas Palaeologus of the Rights to Byzantium to the King of France, Charles VIII," *Papers Presented to N. I. Kareev*, 273–74. For the text of the document see Foncemagne, in the *Mémoires de l'Academie royale des inscriptions et belles-lettres*, XVII (1751), 572–77. The Russian translation in Vasiliev, 275–78.

[31] *A History of Russia*, II, 150; in English, trans. C. J. Hogarth, II, 19.

[32] See H. Schaeder, *Moskau das Dritte Rom. Studien zur Geschichte der politischen Theorien in der slavischen Welt*, 36–37. The author is very familiar with the Russian sources.

[33] V. Malinin, *The Old Monk of the Monastery of Eleazar, Philotheus, and His Works*, appendices, 42, 45.

[34] See, e.g., L. P. Pierling, *La Russie et le Saint-Siège*, I, 221–39. See also an interesting text in N. Iorga, *Byzance après Byzance*, 26 and n. 5.

The external policy of Michael VIII

Byzantium and the Kingdom of the Two Sicilies, Charles of Anjou, and the Sicilian Vespers.—The attitude of Michael VIII towards the Kingdom of the Two Sicilies is the keystone to his external policy. In connection with this attitude were developing and shaping his relations with the Italian republics, Genoa and Venice, as well as with the papal curia. His relations with the Turks in the East also depended upon his western policy.

At the close of the twelfth century, the king of Germany, Henry VI Hohenstaufen, Frederick Barbarossa's son, owing to his marriage with the Norman princess Constance, heiress to the Norman state in southern Italy and Sicily, gained control of the Kingdom of the Two Sicilies and inherited the stubborn enmity of the Normans for Byzantium and their aggressive plans. The union of the Kingdom of the Two Sicilies with Germany lasted till 1250, when, at the death of Frederick II Hohenstaufen, his natural son Manfred became king of Sicily. The legitimate son of Frederick, Conrad, began to rule in Germany and reigned for a short time. Under the rule of Manfred, who took care not only of the material but also of the spiritual interests of his kingdom, Sicily enjoyed a period of peace. His court was the most brilliant of that time; foreign rulers esteemed him highly; and the last Latin Emperor, Baldwin II, who had fled from Constantinople, appealed to him for help in regaining his lost throne. With regard to Byzantium, Manfred adopted the policy of his predecessors which must have seriously alarmed Michael VIII, especially from the point of view of possible Latin re-establishment at Constantinople. Baldwin II, deprived of his throne, appeared at Manfred's court with definite plans and requests for help. Moreover, the podestá (the chief representative) of the Genoese who lived at Constantinople and possessed at that time exceptionally favorable trade conditions in Byzantium, entered into negotiations with Manfred. He proposed to him a plan for the sudden capture of Constantinople and the restoration of Latin dominion there. Informed of this, the infuriated Michael VIII sent the Genoese away from the capital and opened negotiations with Venice, the result of which was a new treaty with the Republic of St. Mark restoring and confirming the previous privileges of the Venetians, and binding them, along with the Greeks, to fight against the Genoese if they opened hostilities against the Empire.

But Manfred had no time to take actual steps against Byzantium; he fell a victim to papal intrigue. The pope, seeing that after the death of Frederick II, the irreconcilable enemy of the papacy, the strength of the Hohenstaufens was weakened, determined to deal a death blow to the hated dynasty by destroying Manfred. Charles of Anjou, brother of the king of France, Louis IX (St. Louis), became the executor of the papal plans. In inviting Charles to take the Kingdom of Sicily, the pope had in view not only the destruction of the Hohenstaufens, but also the help which Charles would furnish for the restoration of the Latin Empire in the East. At least, in 1265, Pope Clement IV expressed the hope that with the aid of Charles "the position of the Roman Empire would be restored" (*imperii Romani status reformabitur*).[35] Accepting the pope's proposal to interfere in south-Italian affairs, Charles of Anjou opened the era of French expeditions to Italy—an era very destructive to the essential interests and needs of France which, for several centuries, was to spend her energy and means on Italy, instead of turning her forces and attention to her nearest neighbors, for example, to the Netherlands and the Rhinelands.

Few prominent figures of history have been portrayed by historians so darkly as Charles of Anjou, and perhaps they have not been quite just. Recent works on Charles have put aside forever the legend which made him a real tyrant, "covetous, cunning, and wicked, always ready to drown in blood the smallest resistance."[36] In their appeals to Charles the popes seem not to have taken into consideration the distinctive features of his character which entirely precluded the possibility of his becoming a mere tool in the hands of another. He was a well-trained, energetic, at times severe, even cruel, ruler, but not without cheerfulness, a love of tournaments, and an interest in poetry, art, and science; above all he was unwilling to become a puppet in the hands of the pope who had invited him to Italy.

On his coming to Italy with an army, Charles crushed Manfred at Beneventum in 1266. With Manfred's death, Sicily and Naples came under French sway. Charles of Anjou became the new king of the Two Sicilies. The French began to leave their country in masses and emigrate into Charles' new dominions, where general conditions were excellent.[37]

Shortly after, Charles' attitude toward Byzantium was clearly shown. With the consent and in the presence of the pope, at Viterbo, a small Italian city north of Rome, he made a treaty with the expelled Latin Emperor, Baldwin II, in which the latter transmitted to Charles his right to the supreme power over all Frankish dominions in the former Latin Empire, reserving to himself only Constantinople and several islands in the Archipelago, which Charles was to help him reconquer from the Greeks. The Norman claims to Byzantium thus revived again in full measure under the French sway in the Kingdom of the Two Sicilies.

[35] See E. Martene and U. Durand, *Thesaurus novus anecdotorum*, II, 197. See E. Jordan, *Les Registres de Clément IV* (1265–1268), 61–62 (no. 224). W. Norden, *Das Papsttum und Byzanz*, 444, n. 1.

[36] E. Jordan, *Les Origines de la domination angevine en Italie*, 410, 414–15.

[37] See the enthusiastic description of Charles' realm in Italy by F. Carabellese, *Carlo d'Angiò nei rapporti politici e commerciali con Venezia e l'Oriente*, xxviii–xxx. It is the author's posthumous work.

Realizing fully the approaching danger, Michael VIII had recourse to skillful diplomacy. On the one hand, by means of negotiations with the pope concerning the union between the eastern and western churches, Michael diverted him from close co-operation with Charles, and made him wish for a conciliatory policy regarding Byzantium. On the other hand, Michael decided to make peace with the Genoese who, as has been mentioned above, had established relations with Manfred of Sicily, planned to hand Constantinople over to the Latins, and thereupon had been expelled from the capital. The Genoese were allowed to return to Constantinople, where some quarters were allotted to them not in the city itself, but in its suburb of Galata, across the Golden Horn. This distance did not prevent the Genoese from regaining all their former trade privileges, expanding their commercial activity, and forcing the Venetians, their rivals, into the background. A Genoese of the family of Zaccaria, for example, who obtained from the Emperor the right to work and exploit rich deposits of alum in the mountains of Asia Minor, near the city of Phocaea (in Italian, *Fogia, Foglia*) at the entrance into the Gulf of Smyrna, made a colossal fortune.[38] Finally, all over the Byzantine East, under the Palaeologi, Genoa took the place of Venice.

Meanwhile, Charles of Anjou seized the island of Corfù, which was the first step in carrying out his plan of invading Byzantium. Michael VIII, hoping to be more successful in his conciliatory policy towards the pope and to imitate the aggressive policy of Charles of Anjou, appealed to the latter's brother, the king of France, Louis IX, who was the most pious, just, and esteemed ruler of that time. Shortly before Michael's appeal to him, England had begged him to be arbiter and to settle some complicated problems of her internal life. Circumstances tended to involve Louis also in the history of Byzantium. Michael sent Louis IX a manuscript of the New Testament adorned with miniatures. When at the close of the seventh decade the Byzantine envoys arrived in France "in view of the reunion of the Greek and Roman churches," Michael proposed to the king of France that he should "settle as an arbiter the conditions of the union of the two churches, and assured him in advance of his full concurrence."[39]

At the outset, Louis IX disapproved of the decision of his brother Charles to conquer southern Italy and only later does he seem to have become reconciled to the *fait accompli,* probably because he was persuaded of its utility for a future crusade. Moreover, Charles' plan of conquering Byzantium also met with Louis' serious objection, because, if the main forces of Charles were di-

---

[38] S. W. Heyd, *Histoire du commerce du Levant,* I, 438. W. Miller, "The Zaccaria of Phocaea and Chios (1275–1329)," in his *Essays on the Latin Orient,* 284–85. See also an important book by R. Lopez, *Genova marinara nel duecento. Benedetto Zaccaria ammiraglio e mercante,* II, 23–61.

[39] J. Ebersolt, *Orient et Occident. Recherches sur les influences byzantines et orientales en France pendant les Croisades,* 34.

verted to Constantinople, they would be unable to take an adequate part in the crusade to the Holy Land, an idea which strongly influenced Louis. Besides, Michael's decision, with which Louis had been acquainted through the embassy, to beg him to be arbiter in the problem of the church union, and the Emperor's promise to submit entirely to his decision, inclined the king of France, a zealous Catholic, to the side of the Byzantine Emperor.

It could hardly be expected that pressure from Louis would really persuade his warlike brother to give up his aggressive plans against the Empire. But Charles was somewhat delayed in his hostilities against Byzantium by Louis' second crusade to Tunis, which encroached upon the policy of Charles in the West. The question of Charles' attitude as to the origin of this crusade, is one on which scholars' opinions vary.[40] The sudden death of Louis in Tunis in 1270 destroyed Michael's hopes of his co-operation. The Byzantine envoys, who had arrived in Tunis for negotiations a short time before Louis' death, went back, said a Greek source, "with hands empty of promises."[41] Charles made his appearance in Tunis and after two brilliant victories compelled the emir of Tunis to make peace on his terms, that the emir should indemnify Charles for his military expenses and pay him an annual tribute. Charles then decided to carry out his plan of invading Byzantium. But on his way back from Tunis a terrible storm destroyed a major part of his fleet, so that, at least for a time, he was unable to undertake the offensive against Byzantium on such a large scale as he had planned.

At the beginning of the seventies, however, Charles was able to send a considerable number of auxiliaries to the Peloponnesus, into Achaia, where they fought successfully against the imperial troops. At the same time Charles succeeded in establishing himself in the Balkan peninsula. He seized several fortified places, the most important of which was Dyrrachium (Durazzo, Drač), on the east coast of the Ionian Sea; the Albanian mountaineers became Charles' subjects, and the Despot of Epirus took the oath to him. Accordingly, the king of the Two Sicilies began to style himself the king of Albania (*regnum Albaniae*).[42]

In a document he names himself "by the Grace of God the King of Sicily and Albania" (*Dei gratia rex Sicilie et Albanie*.)[43] In a letter Charles writes that the Albanians "elected us and our heirs kings and perpetual masters of

[40] See, e.g., E. Lavisse, *Histoire de France*, III (2), 101–2. Norden, *Das Papsttum und Byzanz*, 468.

[41] George Pachymeris *De Michaele Palaeologo*, V, 9; Bonn ed., I, 364.

[42] C. Jireček, "The Situation and Past of the City of Drač," *Transactions of the Geographical Society of Serbia*, I, 2 (1912), 6 (in Serbian); in German in L. von Thalloczy, *Illyrisch-albanische Forschungen*, 161.

[43] P. Durrieu, *Les Archives angevines de Naples. Étude sur les registres du roi Charles Ier*, I, 191, n. 5. *Acta diplomata res Albaniae mediae aetatis illustrantia*, ed. L. von Thalloczy, C. Jireček, and E. de Sufflay, I, 77 (no. 270).

the said kingdom" (*nos et heredes nostros elegerunt in reges et dominos perpetuos dicti Regni*).[44] An Italian historian of the twentieth century remarks: "When Charles' work is better studied and known, he will appear in his true light, as a dim precursor of the political and civil autonomy of the Albanian people that, even at the beginning of the twentieth century, seems a dream and a vague and indetermined aspiration."[45] But Charles was not satisfied. He addressed the Serbs and Bulgars and found in them zealous allies. The envoys of *"imperatoris Vulgarorum et regis Servie"* appeared at his court.[46] The southern Slavs began to crowd into his service and to emigrate into his Italian dominions. A Russian scholar, who was well acquainted with the Italian archives and from them drew a great deal of information on the Slavs, V. Makushev, wrote that, in spite of the incomplete and laconic material, "one may form an idea of the course of the Slavonic settlements in southern Italy and of the great number of Slavs pouring from all quarters of the south-Slavonic world into the service of the Angevins. . . . The Slavonic settlements in southern Italy, from the thirteenth to the fifteenth century, are constantly increasing: new ones are being founded, the old ones are growing."[47] In a document of 1323 at Naples is mentioned "a quarter called Bulgarian" (*vicus qui vocatur Bulgarus*).[48] The Serbian and Bulgarian envoys arrived in Naples for negotiations. Obviously serious danger threatened Byzantium from the Slavo-French allies. Moreover, Venice, which occupied a most important place in the political, economic, and commercial life of Charles' realm, was also on a friendly footing with him and for the time being supported his imperialistic policy in the East.[49] In addition, the last Emperor of Nicaea, John IV Lascaris, deposed and blinded by Michael VIII, escaped from his Byzantine prison and, at Charles' invitation, appeared at his court.

Thus, around Charles of Anjou gradually assembled all those who were dissatisfied with and offended by the Byzantine Emperor; the Serbs and Bulgars, Baldwin II and John IV Lascaris, even cautious Venice, became tools in the hands of the ambitious and skillful king. The marriage between Baldwin's son and Charles' daughter gave Baldwin the hope, with the aid of his new relative, of restoring the Latin Empire. Such was the general international situation in Italy and the Balkan peninsula, which must have roused extreme fear in Michael VIII for Constantinople and his throne.[50]

[44] J. A. Buchon, *Nouvelles recherches historiques sur la Principauté Française de Morée*, II, 317.

[45] Carabellese, *Carlo d'Angiò*, xl. These lines were written in 1911.

[46] See C. Jireček, *Geschichte der Serben*, I, 323.

[47] *The Italian Archives and Material on the History of the Slavs Preserved in Them*, II, 67–68.

[48] *Ibid.*, 69. Jireček, *A History of the Bulgars*, 363.

[49] On Venice, see Carabellese, *Carlo d'Angiò*, xxxiv–xxxviii, 106–42.

[50] Unfortunately Carabellese's book does not deal systematically with the relations be-

But the skillful politician Charles faced in Michael VIII a politician no less skillful, who concentrated his chief attention upon the papal curia, to which he promised the union of the churches. Pope Gregory X willingly inclined to the desire of the Emperor, not only from fear of the increasing power of Charles, which could not but alarm him, but because of his sincere desire to establish ecclesiastical peace and unity and to further the liberation of Jerusalem. In his peaceful policy of coming to an understanding with the eastern church Gregory X undoubtedly met many obstacles from Charles, who was planning the forcible subjugation of the Emperor. But the pope succeeded in persuading Charles to postpone for a year the expedition against Byzantium already decided on, and within that time he accomplished the union with the eastern church.

The envoys of Michael Palaeologus to the council, which was to be held in the French city of Lyons, passed safely through the dominions of Charles, who provided them with special safe conducts and provisions.[51] At Lyons in 1274, the union was achieved between the pope and the representatives of Michael VIII. According to newly studied Vatican documents, this union led at once to negotiations between Gregory X and Michael VIII concerning a new anti-Turkish league. A cardinal of high rank went to Constantinople in the depth of winter. The date and place for a personal conference of the pope and the Emperor were immediately fixed: the two venerable personages were to meet on Easter Monday, 1276, at Brindisi or at Valona. But at the very beginning of that year, on January 6, the pope suddenly died, and the project came to nothing.[52] Michael, however, felt that the union gave him the right to hope for papal support in his plans to reconquer the regions of the Balkan peninsula, which had formerly been under the power of the Empire. Accordingly he opened hostilities against the troops of Charles and his allies and met with great success, because Charles was at the time diverted by some difficulties with Genoa.

But after some friction with the pope, evoked by the union of Lyons, Charles succeeded in seating upon the papal throne one of his best friends, a Frenchman, Martin IV, who supported entirely the policy of the Sicilian king and broke the union with Michael. Then in 1281 a treaty was concluded between Charles, the titulary Latin Emperor, and Venice "for the recovery of the Empire of Romania which is under the sway of the Palaeologus" (*ad recupera-*

---

tween Charles and Michael Palaeologus. *Ibid.,* xxix, the author said: "but of the great number of documents, published or unpublished, which refer to the Palaeologus, we will speak at a later time." I think the author did not have time enough to fulfill his intention.

[51] *Ibid.,* 23–24.

[52] V. Laurent, "Grégoire X (1271–1276) et le projet d'une ligue anti-turque," *Échos d'Orient,* XXXVII (1938), 257–73, especially, 269. This article is from Laurent's projected book, *The Second Council of Lyons and the Religious Policy of Michael VIII Palaeologus.*

tionem ejusdem Imperii Romaniae, quod detinetur per Paleologum).[53] A vast coalition formed against Byzantium: the troops of the Latin possessions on the former territory of the Byzantine Empire, the troops of Italy and of Charles' native France, the Venetian fleet, the papal forces, and the armies of the Serbs and Bulgars. The Byzantine Empire seemed to be on the brink of ruin, and Charles of Anjou, the "forerunner of Napoleon in the thirteenth century,"[54] had world power in his grasp. A Greek author of the fourteenth century, Gregoras, wrote that Charles "was dreaming, if he took possession of Constantinople, of the whole monarchy of Julius Caesar and Augustus."[55] Sanudo, a western chronicler of the same time, said that Charles "was aspiring to world monarchy" (*asperava alla monarchia del mondo*).[56] It was the most critical moment in Michael's external policy. In 1281 Michael VIII opened negotiations with the Egyptian Sultan Qala'un concerning the military alliance "against the common enemy," to wit against Charles of Anjou.[56a]

Deliverance to Byzantium came suddenly from the West, from Sicily, where on March 31, 1282 a revolt against French domination burst out; it spread rapidly all over the island and has become known in history as the Sicilian Vespers.[57] Michael VIII had some part in this rebellion.

The Sicilian Vespers, one of the most important events in the early history of the political unification of Italy, always brings to mind a work of the famous Italian historian and patriot, Michele Amari, *The War of the Sicilian Vespers*. This book, written at the beginning of the fifth decade of the nineteenth century, has been edited many times and has formed the basis for scientific study of this problem. Of course, in Amari's lifetime many of the sources were inaccessible, and Amari himself, gradually becoming acquainted with new discoveries in the field, made changes and corrections in the later editions of his book. A new stimulus to the study of this problem was given by the celebration in Sicily, in 1882, of the six hundredth anniversary of the Sicilian Vespers, when a great number of new publications appeared. An enormous mass of fresh and important documents has already been published, and more are still being published from the Angevin archive at Naples and the Vatican at Rome, as well as from the Spanish archives. The Sicilian Vespers, which at first sight seems to be an event of western European history, has its part also in the history of Byzantium.

[53] G. L. F. Tafel and G. M. Thomas, *Urkunden zur ältern Handels- und Staatsgeschichte der Republik Venedig*, III, 289.
[54] Norden, *Das Papsttum und Byzanz*, 604.
[55] Nicephorus Gregoras, *Historia*, V, 1, B; Bonn ed., I, 123.
[56] *Historia del regno di Romania*, in C.

Hopf, *Chroniques grèco-romanes inédites ou peu connues*, 138.
[56a] See below, n. 73.
[57] The very name of this event, "The Sicilian Vespers," probably appeared in literature not earlier than the end of the fifteenth century, after the first great French expedition against Italy.

Before Amari's work came out, it was usually thought that the chief creator and leader of the Sicilian revolution of 1282 was a Sicilian exile, Giovanni Procida (Prochida, Prochyta) who, motivated by personal revenge, entered into negotiations with Peter of Aragon, the Byzantine Emperor, Michael VIII, the representatives of the Sicilian nobility, and others; that he won all of them over to his side and thus raised the revolt. The great humanist of the fourteenth century, Petrarca, regarded Procida as the chief mover of the revolution.[58] But on investigation of the sources Amari showed that this account is a legendary development of historical fact, which, among the causes of the Sicilian revolution, has only secondary significance.[59]

The Sicilian people felt bitter anger against the severe French domination. The arrogant attitude of the French to the subject population and the terrible taxes which were levied, especially in connection with Charles' expensive and difficult expedition against Byzantium, were the chief causes of the revolt of March 31. The two best politicians of that time, exclusive of Charles, Michael VIII and Peter of Aragon, skillfully used the discontent of the Sicilian population. Peter, related to the former king of Sicily, Manfred, the natural son of Frederick II Hohenstaufen, could not become reconciled to the excessive power of Charles, and felt he was within his rights in taking possession of Sicily. Michael VIII made use of Peter's ambition, and promised him a subsidy if he opened hostilities against Charles. In Italy the imperial party, the Ghibellines, and a portion of the Sicilian nobility sided with Peter. Giovanni Procida was an intermediary in all these negotiations, but no more than that.

The revolt was crowned with success. Upon the invitation of the Sicilians, in August of the same year, Peter of Aragon landed on the island and was crowned with Manfred's crown at Palermo. The attempts of Charles, who had returned from the East where hostilities against Byzantium were going on, to reconquer Sicily and to expel Peter of Aragon were unsuccessful. Charles was forced to give up his plans against the Empire of Michael VIII. Thereafter Charles was king only of southern Italy. The importance to Byzantium of the Sicilian Vespers, which deprived Charles of Sicily and saved the Eastern Empire from fatal danger, is obvious. In addition, the events connected with the revolution of 1282 laid the foundation for friendly relations between the Byzantine emperors and the kings of Aragon. Since Michael had supported Peter of Aragon with subsidies, he accordingly took part in the settlement of the Sicilian problem. In his autobiography Michael VIII, speaking of Charles' expedition against his Empire, remarked, "The Sicilians disdaining the rest of Charles' force as despicable, dared to raise arms and free themselves from

[58] F. Petrarca, *Itinerarium Syriacum*, in *Opera Omnia*, 559. G. Lumbroso, *Memorie italiane del buon tempo antico*, 34.

[59] See Lopez, *Genova Marinara nel duecento*, 69–71, 88, n. 28.

slavery; therefore, if I said that God who granted freedom to them, granted it through us, I should tell the truth."[60]

The Sicilian Vespers greatly affected the position of Pope Martin IV. It was not only an unheard-of innovation that, as the historian Ranke wrote, "the people, despite the commands of Rome, had dared to set a king over themselves,"[61] but the events of 1282 undermined the foundations of the Byzantine policy of this pope, who had broken with the Union of Lyons, sided wholly with the eastern plans of Charles of Anjou, and hoped for the Latin occupation of Constantinople. The Sicilian Vespers made that impossible, for it dismembered and weakened the south-Italian kingdom of Charles which hitherto had been the chief basis for the western aggressive policy against Byzantium.

The revolution of 1282 had a repercussion on the policy of Venice who, a year before, had bound herself by an alliance with Charles against Byzantium. Learning of the rising in Sicily and foreseeing the fall of Charles' power and the defeat of his eastern plans, the Republic of St. Mark rapidly changed her policy; realizing that Charles could be of no more use to her, she broke with him, formed closer relations with Byzantium, and three years later concluded a treaty of friendship with Michael's successor, Andronicus the Elder. Moreover, Venice also established relations with Peter of Aragon.

Thus the international relations of the times and the discontent of Sicily, of which Michael VIII took advantage, saved Byzantium from the fatal danger that menaced her from the powerful Charles of Anjou.

Eastern policy of Michael VIII.—The Emperors of Nicaea and, after the restoration of Constantinople, Michael VIII, turned their main forces to the West for the recovery of the Balkan peninsula, and to the exhausting struggle with Charles of Anjou, which practically decided the destiny of the restored Empire. The eastern border was somewhat neglected, and the Byzantine government seems sometimes to have forgotten the threatening danger there. A Byzantine historian of the fifteenth century, George Phrantzes, wrote: "Under Michael Palaeologus, because of the wars in Europe against the Italians, the Roman Empire has been exposed to dangers in Asia from the Turks."[62] Of course, the Turkish danger to Byzantium had begun much earlier; but this observation of the historian well emphasizes a distinct feature of the eastern policy under Michael VIII. It was fortunate for the Empire that in the thirteenth century the Turks themselves were living through a troubled epoch owing to the military successes of the Mongols.

In the thirties and forties of the thirteenth century the threatening danger

---

[60] Michael Palaeologus, *De vita sua opusculum,* par. ix; in *Christianskoe Čtenie,* II (1885), 537–38; in Russian, 558; in French, ed. Chapman, 145, 174.

[61] *Weltgeschichte,* VIII, 538.

[62] George Phrantzes, *Annales,* I, 3; Bonn ed., 23.

of the Mongol invasion appeared from the East. The Seljuq Sultanate of Rum or Iconium, bordering on the eastern part of the Empire of Nicaea, had been defeated by the Mongols. In the second half of the thirteenth century, at the time of Michael VIII, the last Seljucids were the mere deputies of the Mongols of Persia, whose dominions extended from India to the Mediterranean, and at whose head stood Hulagu, acknowledging the khan of the eastern Mongols as his overlord. In 1258 Hulagu took Bagdad, where the last Abbasid caliph suffered a violent death. After that he invaded and devastated Syria, Mesopotamia, and the surrounding lands, and meditated a march on Jerusalem and then probably a campaign against Egypt. But the news of the death of the Mongol Great Khan Mangu forced him to give up his aggressive plans in the south. The Mongol dynasty established in Persia was, in the last decades of the thirteenth century, an ally of the Christians against the Muhammedans. As a recent historian said, "Hulagu led the Nestorian [i.e., Christian] Turks of Central Asia on a real *Yellow Crusade (Croisade Jaune)* against Islam."[63] Finally, in 1260, the Mongol army was crushed by the Egyptian Mamluks, at Ain-Jalut. Another very powerful Mongol state was at that time established in the north, in Russia. This was the Golden or Kipchak Horde with its capital at Sarai, on the lower Volga. Realizing the great importance of this new Mongol factor in the international life of his epoch, Michael Palaeologus tried to make use of it several times in his external policy.[64]

In this connection it is important to remember that the Mamluk (Mameluke) dynasty established in Egypt in 1250 was united ethnographically with south Russia. The word *Mamluk* means "owned," "belonging to," "slave," and the Mamluks in Egypt were originally the bodyguard of Turkish slaves first formed there under the successors of Saladin; in 1260 these "slaves" seized the throne, and they reigned over Egypt from 1260 to 1517, when Egypt was conquered by the Ottoman Turks. From the third decade of the thirteenth century on, the chief contingent of the Mamluk bodyguard consisted of the Turkish tribe of Cumans (Polovtzi) from southern Russia, who had fled before the Mongol invasion or had been taken captives and sold into slavery.[65] A Byzantine historian says that the Mamluks were drawn from "the European Scythians dwelling near the Maeotis (the Sea of Azov) and the river of Tanais (Don)."[66]

Thus, owing to the Cuman origin of many Mamluks, they were interested

[63] R. Grousset, *Histoire d'Asie,* III, 100.

[64] Two interesting Russian articles on this subject have been published: Th. I. Uspensky, "Byzantine Historians on the Mongols and Egyptian Mamluks," *Vizantiysky Vremennik,* XXIV (1923-26), 1-16; and G. Vernadsky, "The Golden Horde, Egypt, and Byzantium in Their Mutual Relations in the Reign of Michael Palaeologus," *Annales de l'Institut Kondakov,* I (1927), 73-84.

[65] Vernadsky, *ibid.,* 76.

[66] Nicephorus Gregoras, *Historia,* IV, 7, 1; Bonn ed., I, 102.

in maintaining and developing relations with their compatriots of south Russia, where, even after the Mongol conquest, a considerable number of Cumans (Polovtzi) were left. Besides, the khan of the Golden (Kipchak) Horde had embraced Islam, and the sultan of Egypt, Mameluk Beybars, was also a Muslim, while Hulagu was a Shamanist, i.e., a pagan,[67] and an enemy of Islam. Deadly rivalry, not only political but also religious, existed between Hulagu and Berke (Bereke), khan of the Golden Horde.

The land route between the Mamluks and Kipchaks was blocked by the dominions of Hulagu. Communication by sea between Egypt and south Russia was possible only through the Hellespont, Bosphorus, and Black Sea; but both straits were in the power of the Byzantine Emperor, so that the Mamluks needed special permission from Michael Palaeologus to use them.[68] Accordingly the sultan of Egypt, "willing to be a friend of the Romans and to have permission for the Egyptian merchants to sail through our straits [the Hellespont and Bosphorus] once a year," sent his envoys to Michael Palaeologus.[69] The difficulty was that at that time Michael was on friendly terms with Hulagu, head of the Mongols in Persia; therefore the Egyptian ambassadors were from time to time retained at Constantinople. In 1265 the Kipchak Khan Berke declared war against Michael, and in this war the Bulgarian Tsar Constantine Tech (Tich) took part on the side of the Mongols, under Berke's general Nogai. The Mongols (Tartars) and Bulgarians vanquished the Byzantine troops. After this defeat Michael was forced to abandon Hulagu and to join the Kipchak-Egyptian combination.[70] To win over the powerful Nogai Michael gave him his illegitimate daughter to wife, and in the following war with the Bulgarian king, Constantine Tech, Michael was so actively supported by his son-in-law that the Bulgarian king was forced to stop hostilities.[71] Diplomatic relations between the Golden Horde, Egypt, and Byzantium existed during Michael's whole reign.[72] The friendly relations between Michael Palaeologus towards the end of his reign and the sultan of Egypt, Mamluk Qala'un (1279–90) are very interesting. A common danger urged both monarchs to come to an agreement, for the ambitious plans of Charles of Anjou menaced both empires. These relations were apparently to lead to the conclusion of a formal treaty of friendship and commerce, which according to

[67] Shamanism is one of the religions of the Ural-Altaic peoples.

[68] George Pachymeres, *De Michaele Palaeologo*, III, 3; Bonn ed., I, 176–77.

[69] Nicephorus Gregoras, *Historia*, IV, 7, 1; Bonn ed., I, 101.

[70] Vernadsky, "The Golden Horde," *Annales de l'Institut Kondakov*, I (1927), 79. P. Nikov, *The Tartaro-Bulgarian Relations in*

the Middle Ages, 6–11. Cf. Chapman, *Michel Paléologue*, 74–75. G. I. Brătianu, *Recherches sur le commerce génois dans la mer Noire au XIIIe siècle*, 207–8.

[71] See Nikov, *Tartaro-Bulgarian Relations*, 11–12.

[72] See, e.g., S. Lane-Poole, *A History of Egypt in the Middle Ages*, 266.

the French scholar M. Canard was actually concluded in 1281 but according to the German scholar F. Dölger did not go beyond the stage of diplomatic negotiations. The fall of Charles of Anjou and the Sicilian Vespers entirely altered the situation both in the West and in the East.[73]

In Asia Minor Michael Palaeologus was not particularly menaced. Although he had broken with Hulagu, the Persian Mongols were too much preoccupied with their internal troubles to take any decisive steps against Byzantium. As for the sultanate of Rum, it was a mere dependency of the Mongol Empire. Still, separate Turkish bodies of troops, sometimes real predatory bands, regardless of any treaties formerly concluded between the emperors and sultans, ceaselessly invaded the Byzantine territory, and penetrated into the interior of the country, sacking cities, hamlets, and monasteries, and murdering and taking captive the people.

Beginning with the time of the Arabian power, Byzantium had established on the eastern border of Asia Minor a line of fortified places, especially in the mountain passes (*clisurae*), and, besides the regular troops, had organized a peculiar sort of defenders of the outermost borders of the Empire, called *akritai*. Gradually, along with the advance of the Turks toward the west, the border line with its defenders, *akritai*, was also being pushed back to the west, so that in the thirteenth century they were concentrated chiefly in the mountains of the Bithynian Olympus, that is to say, in the northwestern corner of Asia Minor. In the epoch of Nicaea these border settlers, provided with land, exempted from taxes and contributions, and enjoying great wealth, had had only to render military service and to defend the border from enemies, and, as far as one may judge from the sources, they had defended it courageously and energetically. But after the capital was transferred from Nicaea to Constantinople, the *akritai* ceased to receive the support formerly given by the government, which, in its new center, felt itself less dependent upon the eastern border. Moreover Michael Palaeologus, attempting financial reform, took an official census of the wealth of the *akritai* and confiscated to the treasury the greater part of their land, from which they drew their incomes. This measure undermined the economic prosperity of the Bithynian *akritai*, on which their

[73] M. Canard, "Le Traité de 1281 entre Michel Paléologue et le sultan Qalâ'ûn," *Byzantion*, X (1935), 669–80. Canard, "Un Traité entre Byzance et l'Egypt au XIIIe siècle et les relations diplomatiques de Michel VIII Paléologue avec les sultans Mamlûks Baibars et Qalâ'ûn," *Mélanges Guadefroy-Demombynes*, 197–224. F. Dölger's doubts and criticisms in *Byzantinische Zeitschrift*, XXXVI (1936), 467; XXXXVII (1937), 537–38. See Dölger, *Corpus der griechischen Urkunden*, III, 74 (no. 2052), which refers to 1281; III, 75 (no. 2062), which refers to the year 1282. Here Dölger did not use Canard's Arabic source, the work of Qalqashandi (who died in 1418). But see now Dölger, *Der Vertrag des Sultans Qalâ'un von Aegypten mit dem Kaiser Michael VIII Palaiologus. Serta Monacensia*. (Leiden, 1952), 68; 78–79.

military readiness depended, and who were "the nerves of war,"[74] and left the eastern border of the Empire almost defenseless. The government quelled the revolt raised by the *akritai* and refrained from exterminating them completely only from fear of opening the way to the Turks. Influenced by the Russian scholar, V. I. Lamansky, several other scholars have considered the Bithynian *akritai* Slavs.[75] But more probably they were representatives of various peoples among whom may have been the descendants of the Slavs who had long ago settled in Bithynia. The external policy of Michael VIII, so strongly influenced by the imperialistic policy of Charles of Anjou, had a bad effect upon the eastern border.

The results of Michael's enforced eastern policy were felt when the Turks, after a period of troubles and disintegration, were unified and strengthened by the Ottoman Turks; they were to deal the final blow to Byzantium and destroy the eastern Christian Empire.

The external policy of Byzantium during the reigns of the Andronicoi

The external policy of Andronicus II and Andronicus III, grandfather and grandson, differed from that of their predecessor, Michael VIII. A great danger had menaced Michael from the West, from Charles to Anjou; but the Sicilian Vespers had removed that danger forever in the year of Michael's death. The Turks had been prevented by their own troubles from making adequate use of their advantageous position on the eastern border of the Empire.

Andronicus II and Andronicus III had to face two new and strong foes: Serbia in the Balkan peninsula and the Ottoman Turks in Asia Minor. Like Charles of Anjou, the rulers of these two peoples had set as their definite goal in the struggle with Byzantium, the complete destruction of the Empire and the formation on its site of either a Greco-Slavonic or a Greco-Turkish Empire. Charles' plan to establish the Greco-Latin Empire had failed. In the fourteenth century the great king of Serbia, Stephen Dushan (Dušan), seemed to be on the point of establishing a great Slavonic empire. But for many reasons only the Ottoman Turks were to succeed in carrying out this plan: in the middle of the fifteenth century they were to establish an enormous empire, not only Greco-Turkish, but Greco-Slavo-Turkish, controlling both the Serbs and the Bulgars.

The Ottoman Turks.—The rise of the Ottoman Turks was the chief phenomenon in the East in the epoch of the two Andronicoi. Advancing toward

[74] George Pachymeres, *De Michaele Palaeologo*, I, 5; Bonn ed., I, 18.

[75] V. I. Lamansky, *The Slavs in Asia Minor, Africa, and Spain*, 11–14. Th. I. Uspensky, "On the History of the Peasant Landholding in Byzantium," *Journal of the Ministry of Public Instruction*, CCXV (1883), 342–45. P. Mutafčiev, *Military Lands and Soldiers in Byzantium in the Thirteenth and Fourteenth Centuries*, 67.

Asia Minor, the Mongols had pushed back to the West, from the Persian province of Khorasan (Khurasan), a Turkish horde of the tribe of Ghuzz, who had come into the territory of the sultanate of Iconium, and been allowed by the sultan to stay and pasture their herds. After the defeat inflicted by the Mongols the Kingdom of the Seljuqs divided into several independent possessions (emirates) with separate dynasties, which harassed the Empire severely. Along with this disintegration of the Empire of the Seljuqs, the Turkish horde of Ghuzz also became independent. At the very end of the thirteenth century their leader was Osman (Othman), who began the dynasty of the Ottomans and gave his name to the Turks who were under his control; from that time on they were called the Ottoman Turks. The dynasty founded by Osman ruled in Turkey until 1923.[76]

From the end of the thirteenth century on, the Ottoman Turks began to harass seriously the small possessions in Asia Minor which still remained in the power of Byzantium. The imperial troops held with difficulty the three most important points in Asia Minor: Brusa, Nicaea, and Nicomedia. The co-emperor Michael IX was sent against the Turks and defeated. Constantinople itself seemed in danger, and the Emperor "seemed to sleep or be dead."[77]

The Spanish (Catalan) companies in the East.—Andronicus could not master the situation without foreign aid, and he got such aid from the Spanish mercenary bands, the so-called "Catalan companies," or "almughavars."[78] Mercenary bands of various nationalities, under the name of "companies," which lived only for war and would fight for pay for anyone against anyone, were very well known in the latter half of the Middle Ages. "The Catalan companies," which consisted not only of Catalans, but also of the inhabitants of Aragon, Navarre, the island of Majorca, and other places, fought as mercenaries on the side of Peter of Aragon during the war which burst out after the Sicilian Vespers. When at the very beginning of the fourteenth century a peace was concluded between Sicily and Naples, the Catalans were out of work. Such allies, accustomed to war, pillage, and violence, became in time of peace dangerous to those who had invited them, and who now tried to get rid of them. Moreover, the companies themselves, finding no satisfaction in peaceful living conditions, sought new opportunities for activity. The Catalans

---

[76] See H. A. Gibbons, *The Foundation of the Ottoman Empire.* F. Giese, "Das Problem der Entstehung des osmanischen Reiches," *Zeitschrift für Semitistik,* II (1923), 246–71. For valuable information of general critical and bibliographical character see E. L. Langer and R. P. Blake, "The Rise of the Ottoman Turks and Its Historical Background," *American Historical Review,* XXXVII (1932), 468–

505. M. F. Köprülü, *Les Origines de l'Empire Ottoman,* 5–32. P. Wittek, *The Rise of the Ottoman Empire,* 33–51.

[77] George Pachymeres, *De Andronico Palaeologo,* V, 21; Bonn ed., II, 412.

[78] "Almughavars" is the Arabic word borrowed from the Spanish Arabs, literally meaning "making an expedition," hence "light cavalry," scouts.

chose for leader Roger de Flor, a German by origin, whose father's surname, Blum (i.e. a flower), was translated into Spanish as "Flor."

With the consent of his companions Roger, who spoke Greek fluently, offered his services to Andronicus II for his struggle with the Seljuq and Ottoman Turks and extorted from the hard pressed Emperor unheard-of conditions: the insolent adventurer demanded the consent of Andronicus to his marriage with the Emperor's niece, the granting of the title of *megadukas* (admiral), and a large sum of money for his company. Andronicus was compelled to yield, and the Spanish companies took ship and sailed for Constantinople.

The participation of the Spaniards in the destinies of Byzantium is narrated in detail both in the Spanish (Catalan) sources and in the Greek. But while a participant of the expedition, the Catalan chronicler Muntaner[79] described Roger and his companions as courageous and noble fighters for a right cause, a credit to their country, Greek historians consider the Catalans pillagers and insolent ruffians, and one of them exclaimed: "Would that Constantinople had never seen the Latin Roger!"[80] Historians of the nineteenth century devoted much attention to the Catalan expedition. A Spanish investigator of the problem compared their deeds with those of the famous Spanish conquerors of Mexico and Peru in the sixteenth century, Cortez and Pizarro; he does not know "what other people may plume themselves on such a historical event as our glorious expedition to the East," and he considered the expedition an eternal testimony to the glory of the Spanish race.[81] The German historian Hopf declared that "the Catalan expedition is the most attractive episode in the history of the Empire of the Palaeologi," especially on account of its dramatic interest.[82] Finlay wrote that the Catalans "guided by a sovereign like Leo III or like Basil II, might have conquered the Seljuq Turks, strangled the Ottoman power in its cradle, and carried the double-headed eagle of Byzantium victorious to the foot of Mount Taurus and to the banks of the Danube."[83] Elsewhere the same historian remarked: "The expedition of the Catalans in the East is a wonderful instance of the success which sometimes attends a career of rapacity and crime, in opposition to all the ordinary maxims of hu-

[79] *Chronica o descripcio fets e hazanyes del inclyt rey Don Jaume;* in Buchon, *Chroniques étrangères;* ed. K. Lanz. On Muntaner see N. Iorga, "Ramón Muntaner et l'empire byzantin," *Revue historique du sud-est européen,* IV (1927), 325–55.

[80] George Pachymeres, *De Andronico Palaeologo,* V, 12; Bonn ed., II, 393.

[81] A. Rubió y Lluch, *La expedición y dominación de los Catalanes en Oriente,* 6, 7, 10. Rubió y Lluch, *Los Catalanes en Grecia.* Últi-

mos años de su dominación. *Cuadros históricos,* 6. C. Banús y Comas, *Expedición de Catalanes y Aragoneses en Oriente en principio del siglo XIV,* 43, 46: Roger de Flor went to the Orient looking for glory and booty.

[82] C. Hopf, *Geschichte Griechenlands vom Beginne des Mittelalters bis auf die neuere Zeit,* I, 380.

[83] *A History of Greece,* ed. H. F. Tozer, III, 388.

man prudence."[84] The Spanish archives still afford much new information on this expedition.

At the very beginning of the fourteenth century Roger de Flor with his company arrived in Constantinople.[85] There were almost ten thousand members of the expedition; but this number included wives, mistresses, and children. The marriage of Roger to the Emperor's niece was celebrated at Constantinople with great pomp. After some serious conflicts in the capital between the Catalans and Genoese, who, jealous for their exceptional privileges in the Empire, felt the newcomers their rivals, the company was finally transported into Asia Minor, where the Turks were besieging the large city of Philadelphia, east of Smyrna. Supported by a band of imperial troops the small Hispano-Byzantine army, under Roger de Flor, freed Philadelphia from the Turkish siege. The victory of the western mercenaries was enthusiastically received in the capital; some men thought that the Turkish danger to the Empire was over forever. The first success was followed by others against the Turks in Asia Minor. But the unbearable extortions and arbitrary cruelties of the Catalans towards the local population, on one hand, and the clearly expressed intention of Roger to establish in Asia Minor a principality of his own, though under the Emperor's suzerainty, on the other, strained the relations between the mercenaries, the people of Asia Minor, and the government of Constantinople. The Emperor recalled Roger to Europe, and the latter with his company crossed the Hellespont and occupied first an important fortress on the straits of Gallipoli, and then the whole peninsula of Gallipoli. The new negotiations between Roger and the Emperor ended in Roger's obtaining the title next to the Emperor's, that of Caesar, never till then borne by a foreigner. Before marching again to Asia Minor the new Caesar went with a small band to Hadrianople, where the eldest son of Andronicus, the co-emperor Michael IX, resided. On Michael's instigation, Roger and his companions were slain during a festival. When these tidings spread among the population of the Empire, the Spaniards in the capital and other cities were also murdered.

The Catalans, who were concentrated at Gallipoli, inflamed and thirsty for revenge, broke their obligations as allies of the Empire and set out to the West, ravaging with fire and sword the regions through which they passed. Thrace and Macedonia were terribly devastated. Not even monasteries on Mount Athos were spared. An eyewitness, a pupil of Daniel, igumen (abbot) of the

[84] *Ibid.,* IV, 147. A general sketch of the study of the Catalan problem in Greece can be found in Rubió y Lluch, *Los Catalanes en Grecia,* 19–50.

[85] In the palace of the Senate in Madrid a picture by a nineteenth century Spanish painter, José Moreno Carbonero (1888–) presents the entrance of Roger de Flor into Constantinople. The picture is described in Banús y Comas, *Expedición de Catalanes y Aragoneses en Oriente,* 48; a reproduction is given.

Serbian monastery of Chilandarion, on Mount Athos, wrote: "It was horror to see then the desolation of the Holy Mountain by the hands of enemies."[86] The Catalans also burned the Russian monastery of St. Panteleemon, on Mount Athos, but their assault on Thessalonica failed. In retaliation for the Catalan devastations Andronicus commanded the merchandise of some Catalan vessels in the Byzantine waters seized and the merchants themselves arrested.[87]

After having stayed some time in Thessaly, the Catalans marched to the south, through the famous pass of Thermopylae, into middle Greece to the territory of the Duchy of Athens and Thebes, which had been founded after the Fourth Crusade and was under French control. In the spring of 1311 there took place a battle in Boeotia, at the river of the Cephisus, near the Lake of Copais (near the modern village of Skripù). The Catalans won a decisive victory over the French troops. Putting an end to the flourishing French duchy of Athens and Thebes, they established there Spanish control which lasted for eighty years. The church of the Holy Virgin, the ancient Parthenon on the Acropolis, passed into the hands of the Catalan clergy, who were impressed by its sublimity and riches. In the second half of the fourteenth century a Spanish duke of Athens called the Acropolis "the most precious jewel that exists in the world, and such as all the kings of Christendom together would imitate in vain."[88]

The Athenian Duchy of the Catalans established by mere accident in the fourteenth century and organized upon Spanish or Sicilian models, has generally been considered a harsh, oppressive, and destructive government, which at Athens and in Greece in general has left very few material traces of its domination. On the Acropolis, for instance, the Catalans carried out some changes, especially in the disposition of the fortifications, but no traces of them remain. But in Greek popular tradition and in the Greek tongue there still linger reminiscences of the cruelty and injustice of the Spanish invaders. Even today, in some regions of Greece, for example, in the island of Euboea, a man in condemnation of illegal or unjust action may say: "Not even the Catalans would have done that." In Acarnania to the present day the word "Catalan" is the synonym for "savage, robber, criminal." At Athens the word "Catalan" is considered an insult. In some cities of the Peloponnesus, when one wishes

---

[86] P. Uspensky, *The Christian Orient, Athos*, III (2), 118.

[87] See *Acta Aragonensia. Quellen zur deutschen, italienischen, franzöischen, spanischen, zur Kirchen- und Kulturgeschichte aus der diplomatischen Korrespondenz Jaymes II. (1291–1327)*, ed. H. Finke, II, 741 (no. 458). In this edition the text is dated May 2, 1293. But in the document itself the year is obliter-

ated. I think that it should be assigned to the beginning of the fourteenth century, for in 1293 the Catalan companies had not yet taken any part in the history of Byzantium.

[88] Miller, *The Catalans at Athens*, 14. Miller, *Essays on the Latin Orient*, 129. Setton, *Catalan Domination of Athens 1311–1388*, 17, 187, 257.

to say that a woman possesses a bad character, one says, "She must be a Catalan woman."[89]

But recently much new material, especially in the Archives of Barcelona (the archives *de la Corona d'Aragó*), has come to light which shows that the conception of former historians on this subject was biased. The years of the Catalan domination in middle Greece in the fourteenth century were not only troubled and destructive; they were productive. The Acropolis, which was called in Catalan *Castell de Cetines,* was fortified; for the first time since the closing of the Athenian school by Justinian the Great, a university was established at Athens.[90] Catalan fortifications were also erected in middle and northern Greece.[91] A modern Catalan historian, the best recent authority on the Catalan problem in Middle Greece, A. Rubió y Lluch, declared, "The discovery of a Catalan Greece is, in our opinion, one of the most unexpected surprises the modern investigators have had in the history of medieval political life."[92] Of course, the full story of the Catalan dominion in Greece remains to be learned; but we must realize that the older works and former opinions on this problem of many very eminent scholars must be rectified, and that a new history of the Catalan dominion in Greece must be told on the basis of new material.[93] The Navarrese invasion in 1379 dealt a death blow to the Catalan dominion in Greece.

Successes of the Turks in Asia Minor.—At the very beginning of the fourteenth century the Catalan company fought successfully against the Ottoman Turks. But these military successes did not last long. The bloody advance of the Catalan companies through the Balkan peninsula, after Roger de Flor's murder, and the internal strife between the two Andronicoi, grandfather and grandson diverted the forces and attention of the Empire from the eastern border. The Ottomans seized their advantage, and in the last years of Andronicus the Elder and in the reign of Andronicus the Younger won some important successes in Asia Minor. The sultan Othman (Osman) and after him his son Orkhan conquered there the chief Byzantine cities, Brusa, Nicaea, and

[89] Rubió y Lluch, *La expedición y dominación de los Catalanes,* 14–15. G. Schlumberger, *Expédition des "Almugavares" ou routiers catalans en Orient,* 391–92.

[90] See A. Rubió y Lluch, "Atenes en temps dels Catalans," *Anuari de l'Institut d'Estudis Catalans,* II (1907), 245–46.

[91] Rubió y Lluch, "Els Castells Catalans de la Grecia continental," *ibid.,* III (1908), 362–425.

[92] Rubió y Lluch, "La Grecia Catalana des de la mort de Roger de Lluria fins a la de Frederic III de Sicilia (1370–1377)," *ibid.,* V

(1913–14), 393. See also Rubió y Lluch, "Une Figure Athénienne de l'époque de la domination catalane. Dimitri Rendi," *Byzantion,* II (1925), 194.

[93] Rubió y Lluch, "La Grecia Catalana de la mort de Frederic III fins a la invasió navarresa (1377–1379)," *ibid.,* VI (1915–20), 199. See his *Diplomatari de l'Orient català* (Barcelona, 1948), a posthumous work. See also his *Los Catalanes en Grecia,* 13. For a list of many publications of Rubió y Lluch see *Cambridge Medieval History,* IV, 862 and particularly Setton, 286–91.

Nicomedia, and then reached the coast of the Sea of Marmora. Several cities of the western coast of Asia Minor began to pay tribute to the Turks. In 1341, when Andronicus III died, the Ottoman Turks had already become the real masters of Asia Minor, with the obvious intention of transferring hostilities into the European territory of the Empire and even threatening Constantinople itself; Thrace was exposed to continuous incursions from them. Meanwhile, the Seljuq emirates, fearing danger from the Ottomans, entered into friendly relations with the Empire in order to struggle against both the Latins and the Ottomans.

Byzantium and the rise of Serbia; Stephen Dushan (Dušan).—The possessions of Byzantium in the Balkan peninsula, at the end of the thirteenth century, embraced the whole of Thrace and southern Macedonia with Thessalonica; but the lands lying farther to the west and south—Thessaly, Epirus, and Albania—only partially recognized the power of the Empire, and not in equal degree. In the Peloponnesus the Empire under Michael Palaeologus had reconquered from the Franks Laconia in the southeast of the peninsula, and then the central province, Arcadia. In the rest of the Peloponnesus and middle Greece the Latins continued to rule. As to the Archipelago, Byzantium possessed only a few islands in the northern and northeastern portion of the sea.

Parallel with the Ottoman danger in the East, another threatening danger to Byzantium was growing up in the Balkan peninsula, in the first half of the fourteenth century, from Serbia.

The Serbs and the closely related, perhaps even identical, Croats made their appearance in the Balkan peninsula in the seventh century at the time of Emperor Heraclius and occupied the western part of the peninsula. While the Croats dwelling in Dalmatia and in the region between the rivers Sava and Drava began to enter into closer relations with the West, adopted Catholicism, and in the eleventh century lost their independence and came under the power of the Hungarian (Magyar) Kingdom, the Serbs remained faithful to Byzantium and the eastern church. For a long time, that is, up to the second half of the twelfth century, in contrast to the Bulgars the Serbs failed to form one unified state. They lived in independent districts or *župy,* at the head of which were *župans.* A tendency towards unification did not appear among the Serbs until the twelfth century, and coincided chronologically with the Bulgarian movement towards the foundation of the second Bulgarian Kingdom. Just as the Asen family led the movement in Bulgaria, so the family of the Nemanjas played a similar role in Serbia.

The founder of the Serbian monarchy in the second half of the twelfth century was Stephen Nemanja, proclaimed "Great *Župan,*" the first to unify the Serbians by the power of his family. Thanks to successful wars with Byzan-

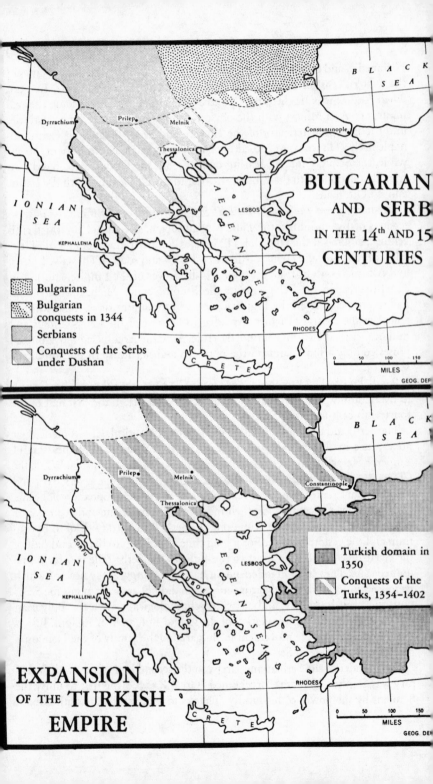

BULGARIAN AND SERB IN THE 14th AND 15 CENTURIES

Bulgarians

Bulgarian conquests in 1344

Serbians

Conquests of the Serbs under Dushan

EXPANSION OF THE TURKISH EMPIRE

Turkish domain in 1350

Conquests of the Turks, 1354–1402

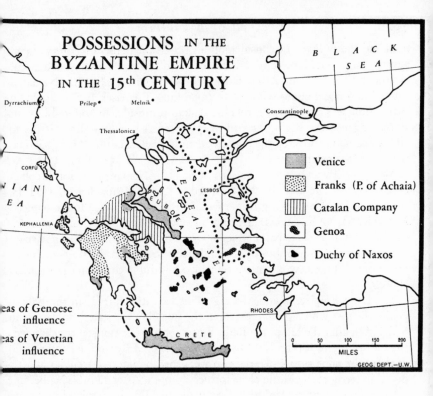

POSSESSIONS IN THE
BYZANTINE EMPIRE
IN THE 15th CENTURY

Venice

Franks (P. of Achaia)

Catalan Company

Genoa

Duchy of Naxos

eas of Genoese
influence

eas of Venetian
influence

The Decline of the Byzantine Empire
in the Fourteenth and Fifteenth Centuries

The map at top left shows the territory occupied by the Serbs and Bulgarians in the fourteenth century, and the invasions they made into the Byzantine Empire during that century. The expansion of the Turks westward from 1354 to 1402 is illustrated in the map at lower left. The map above shows the areas controlled in the fifteenth century by the Venetians, Genoese, Franks, and Catalans and shows the boundaries of the Duchy of Naxos. Studied together with the boundaries of the Byzantine Empire in 1340, 1350, and 1402 (see endpaper map), these maps show the gradual limitation of territory which preceded the fall of the Empire in 1453. The general areas in these maps are modified from the maps in Ostrogorsky, *Geschichte des byzantinischen Staates.*

tium and the Bulgars, he considerably increased the Serbian territory; then, having carried out his political task, he abdicated and ended his days as a monk in a monastery on Mount Athos. During the Third Crusade Stephen Nemanja entered into negotiations with the German king, Frederick Barbarossa, who at that time was on his way across the Balkan peninsula, and offered him an alliance against the Byzantine emperor, if Frederick would allow Serbia to annex Dalmatia and keep the regions taken from Byzantium. These negotiations came to nothing.

After a civil war between the sons of Stephen Nemanja, his son Stephen became ruler of the state and was crowned in 1217 by a papal legate. After the coronation he became King of Serbia and is known as the "first-crowned" King (Kral), "of all Serbia." During his reign, the Serbian church received from the hands of the papal representative an independent head in the person of a Serbian archbishop. But the dependence of Serbia on the Roman church was short, and the new Kingdom remained faithful to the Eastern Orthodox church.

The Latin Empire, in endeavoring to increase its influence in the Balkan peninsula, met with a great obstacle in the two Slavonic states, Bulgaria and Serbia. But after the fall of the Latin Empire in 1261 circumstances changed; the Latin Empire was replaced by the weak restored Byzantine Empire, and at about the same time Bulgaria, also weakened by internal troubles and reduced in territory, had little of its former strength. After 1261 Serbia became the most important state in the Balkan peninsula. But the Serbian kings committed a strategic error in failing to annex the western Serbian (Croatian) land; without having achieved national unification, they turned their attention to Constantinople.

During the civil war between the two Andronicoi, the Serbian "Kral" (King) supported the grandfather. The victory of the Serbs in 1330 over the Bulgars, who were allies of Andronicus III, near Velbužd (now Köstendil), in Upper Macedonia, had great significance for the future of Serbia. The young prince, Stephen Dushan (Dušan), destined to be the famous king of Serbia, is believed, despite some discrepancy of sources,[94] to have had a decisive share in the victory. In his flight the Bulgarian king was unhorsed and slain. The results of the battle at Velbužd were of great importance to the young Serbian Kingdom. The Greco-Bulgarian alliance was dissolved, and any possibility that Bulgaria might restrain the further rise of Serbia was destroyed forever. Thereafter the Kingdom of Serbia played the leading role in the Balkan peninsula.

But Serbia reached the climax of her power under Stephen Dushan, 1331–55.

[94] See Florinsky, *The Southern Slavs and Byzantium*, II, 55. Jireček, *Geschichte der Serben*, I, 362.

Ten years before he mounted the throne, Stephen and his father had been crowned together with the benediction of the archbishop. Sources call him, therefore, "Stephen, the young *Kral* (King)," *"rex juvenis,"* in opposition to "the old *Kral," "rex veteranus."* T. Florinsky commented, "this simultaneous coronation of father and son was a new and remarkable phenomenon in the history of Serbia. It showed clearly the influence of Byzantium, where it was an old custom of the emperors to appoint their co-rulers and have them crowned with the imperial title."[95]

During the first ten years of his rule, while Andronicus III reigned in Byzantium, Stephen Dushan took advantage of the fact that the Emperor and John Cantacuzene were occupied in the east by the Ottoman danger, to open his aggressive policy, on one hand, by the annexation of northern Macedonia, and on the other, by the occupation of the major part of Albania, where Andronicus' troops had recently fought with success. Before the death of the Emperor in 1341, Stephen Dushan, though he had not fully developed his plans against Byzantium, nevertheless had already shown how strong an enemy he was to prove to the Empire.

Advance of the Albanians to the south.—In the first half of the fourteenth century, the Albanians for the first time began to play a considerable part in the history of the Balkan peninsula. Both Andronicus III and Stephen Dushan fought with them.

Albania had never, from the time of classical antiquity, been able to form a single unified nation, and the history of the Albanians had always been a part of the history of some foreign people. Internally they were divided into small principalities and autonomous mountain tribes, and their interests were exclusively local. "Albania abounds in ancient remains which as yet have been unexplored. The history of Albania cannot, therefore, be written in its proper and final form without reference to the precious relics the Albanian soil has jealously guarded for centuries. It is only when these archeological treasures come to light that a really scientific history of Albania can be written."[96]

The ancestors of the Albanians were the ancient Illyrians, who dwelled along the eastern coast of the Adriatic Sea, from Epirus as far north as Pannonia. The Greek geographer of the second century A.D., Ptolemy, mentioned an Albanian tribe with a city of Albanopolis. The name of these Albanians was in the eleventh century extended to the rest of the ancient Illyrians. This people was called in Greek, *Albanoi, Arbanoi,* or *Albanitai, Arbanitai;* in Latin, *Arbanenses* or *Albanenses;* from the Latin or Roman form comes the Slavonic *Arbanasi,* in modern Greek *Arvanitis,* in Turkish *Arnaut.* The Albanians also

[95] *The Southern Slavs and Byzantium,* II, 45–46. See Jireček, *Geschichte der Serben,* I, 355–56.

[96] C. A. Chekrezi, *Albania—Past and Present,* 8.

call themselves *Arber* or *Arben*. Later on there appeared a new name for the Albanians, *Shkipetars,* the etymological origin of which has not been definitely fixed.[97] The Albanian language is now full of Roman elements, beginning with the ancient Latin language and ending with the Venetian dialect, so that some specialists call the Albanian tongue "a half-Romance mixed-language" (*halbromanishe Mischsprache*).[98] Of old the Albanians were a Christian people. In the earlier Byzantine time, Emperor Anastasius I, who came from the chief Illyrian coast city of Dyrrachium (Durazzo), may have been Albanian. An Albanian origin for the family of Justinian the Great is also possible.

Great ethnographic changes occurred in the Albanian population in the epoch of the so-called barbarian invasions of the fourth and fifth centuries, and of the gradual occupation of the peninsula by the Slavs. Later, the Albanians (not yet called in the sources by this name) were subject first to Byzantium, then to the Great Bulgaria of Simeon. For the first time, Albanian, as a general name for the whole people, appeared in the Byzantine sources of the eleventh century, after the Normano-Byzantine conflicts in the Balkan peninsula.[99] In the epoch of the Latin Empire and of the first Palaeologi the Albanians were successively controlled by the Despotat of Epirus, the second Bulgarian Empire, the Emperor of Nicaea John Ducas Vatatzes, and finally, by Charles of Anjou, who styled himself "by the grace of God the King of Sicily and Albania." In the fourth decade of the fourteenth century, not long before Andronicus' death, the Serbian king Stephen Dushan conquered the major part of Albania.

At this time a strong movement of the Albanians towards the south began, at first into Thessaly, but extending later, in the second half of the fourteenth and in the fifteenth century, all over middle Greece, the Peloponnesus, and many islands of the Aegean Sea. This powerful stream of Albanian colonization is felt even today. A German scholar of the first half of the nineteenth century, Fallmerayer, came out with the astounding theory that the Greeks had been completely exterminated by the Slavs and Albanians; "not a single drop of pure Hellenic blood flows in the veins of the Christian population of modern Greece." He wrote in the second volume of his *History of the Peninsula of Morea in the Middle Ages,* that, beginning with the second quarter of

---

[97] C. Jireček, "Albanen in der Vergangenheit," in *Oesterreichische Monatschrift für den Orient,* no. 1–2 (1914), 2; reprinted in Thallóczy, *Illyrisch-albanische Forschungen,* I, 66. On the word *Shkipetars,* see A. C. Chatziz, Πόθεν τὸ ἐθνικὸν Σκιπετάρ in the Πρακτικά *of the Academy of Athens,* IV (1929), 102–4. H. Gregoire, *Byzantion,* IV

(1929), 746–48: in modern Greek σκιππέττο = Italian *shiopetto* = French *escopette,* meaning "gun," "the armed people." The problem has not yet been definitely solved.

[98] Jireček, *ibid.,* 2. Thallóczy, *ibid.,* I, 67. G. Gröber, *Grundriss der romanischen Philologie* (2nd ed., 1904–6), 1039.

[99] Michael Attaliates, *Historia,* 9, 18.

the fourteenth century, the Greek-Slavs who inhabited Greece were displaced and crushed by Albanian settlers, so that, in his opinion, the Greek revolution of the nineteenth century which freed Greece from the Turkish yoke, was in reality the work of Albanian hands. Fallmerayer journeyed through Greece and found in Attica, Boeotia, and the major part of the Peloponnesus a very great number of Albanian settlers, who sometimes did not even understand Greek. If one calls this country a new Albania, wrote the same author, one gives it its real name. Those provinces of the Greek Kingdom are no more closely related to Hellenism than the Scottish Highlands are to the Afghan regions of Kandahar and Kabul.[100]

Although Fallmerayer's theory as a whole is rejected, it is true that even today many islands of the Archipelago and almost all Attica as far as Athens are Albanian. According to the approximate statistics made by scholars, the Albanians in the Peloponnesus number now more than twelve per cent of the whole population (about 92,500 souls).[101] In 1854 J. G. Hahn, the author of a German work *Albanian Studies,* estimated that "of a total of one million inhabitants of Greece, about 173,000 were Albanians," and a modern writer remarked: "No changes have occurred in the meantime to alter their position."[102]

Thus, the time of Andronicus III was marked by the beginning of Albanian colonization to the south in Greece as far as the Peloponnesus, and of an important ethnographical alteration among the population of the Greek peninsula.

Venice and Genoa.—Michael VIII's government gave undoubted preference to Genoa in the rivalry between the two western commercial republics, Venice and Genoa. In connection with political conditions, he then restored friendly relations with Venice, making skillful use of the antagonism between the two republics. Andronicus II continued his father's policy of privileges for Genoa, so that causes for conflict between Genoa and Venice continued to exist.

Towards the end of the thirteenth century all Christian possessions in Syria were lost. In 1291 the Muhammedans took away from the Christians their last important coast city, Acre (Acca, ancient Ptolemaïs); all the rest of the coast cities surrendered to the Muhammedans almost without struggle.

[100] J. P. Fallmerayer, *Geschichte der Halbinsel Morea während des Mittelalters,* II, xxiv–xxvii.

[101] See, e.g., Phillipson, "Zur Ethnographie des Peloponnes," *Petermann's Mitteilungen,* XXXVI (1890), 35. Phillipson, *Das Byzantinische Reich als Geographische Ercheinung,* 131. D. A. Zakythinos, *Le Despotat Grec de Morée,* 102–5.

[102] J. Hahn, *Albanesische Studien,* I, 32 (this figure is approximate); cf. II, 1 (almost half of the population of Greece); see also preface, vi. See Chekrezi, *Albania—Past and Present,* 25, n. 1; 205. Finlay (*History of Greece,* IV, 32) counted about 200,000 Albanians in Greece.

All Syria and Palestine passed into the possession of the Muhammedans.

This event was a terrible blow to Venice, for by it she lost the whole south-east Mediterranean, where her trade for a long time had been predominant. On the other hand, the Genoese, with a solid footing on the Bosphorus, extended their influence in the Black Sea, where apparently they hoped for a trade monopoly. This was of particular importance in the Crimea, where both Venetians and Genoese colonies had already been established. Realizing the threatening danger to her commercial power Venice declared war on Genoa. Many of the hostilities took place on the territory or in the waters of the Byzantine Empire. The Venetian fleet breaking through the Hellespont and the Marmora sea pillaged and burnt the shores of the Bosphorus and the suburb of Galata, where the Genoese dwelt. The Genoese colony found safety behind the walls of Constantinople, whose Emperor actively supported the Genoese. The Venetians who lived in the capital were murdered. The Genoese obtained from Andronicus II an authorization to surround Galata with a wall and moat. Soon after, their quarters were embellished with many public and private buildings. At the head of the colony stood a podestá appointed from Genoa, who governed on the basis of certain regulations and had charge of the interests of all the Genoese who lived on the territory of the Empire. Thus, said T. Florinsky, "along with the orthodox Tsargrad there arose a small, but well fortified, Latin city with a Genoese podestá, republican organization, and Latin churches and monasteries. Genoa, besides its commercial significance, acquired great political importance in the Empire."[103] Towards the time of the ascension of Andronicus III Galata became a sort of state within the state, and by the end of his reign this situation was very strongly felt. No real peace between Genoa and Venice was possible.

Besides these two most powerful commercial republics there was considerable trade activity at Constantinople, at the end of the thirteenth and in the fourteenth century on the part of some other western cities which had their colonies there—for example, of Italy, Pisa, Florence, and Ancona—of the Adriatic Sea the Slavonic Ragusa (Dubrovnik),[104] and several south-French cities, like Marseilles.

The reigns of the two Andronicoi, grandfather and grandson, came to sad conclusions. In the east the Ottoman Turks had become the masters of the situation in Asia Minor; in the Balkan peninsula Stephen Dushan had already obtained some real successes, which indicated his still broader plans for

[103] *The Southern Slavs and Byzantium,* I, 32–33.

[104] See N. Iorga, "Une ville 'romane' devenue slave: Raguse," *Bulletin de la section historique de l'Académie roumaine,* XVIII (1931), 32–100. P. Skok, "Les Origines de Raguse," *Slavia,* X (1931), 449–500. A brief popular sketch by M. Andreeva, "Dubrovnik," *Revue internationale des études balkaniques,* II (1935), 125–28.

the future. The Catalan companies had terribly devastated many regions of the Empire in their march to the west. Finally, Genoese Galata, economically strong and politically almost independent, had established and fortified itself side by side with Constantinople.

John V (1341–1391), John VI Cantacuzene (1341–1354) and the apogee of Serbian power under Stephen Dushan

Under Andronicus III, John V's predecessor, Stephen Dushan had already taken possession of northern Macedonia and the major part of Albania. With the ascension to the throne of the boy John V, when a devastating civil war began to tear the Empire, Dushan's aggressive plans widened and took definite form against Constantinople itself. A Byzantine historian of the fourteenth century, Nicephorus Gregoras, put into the mouth of John Cantacuzene these words: "The great Serb (Stephen Dushan)[105] like an overflowing river which has passed far beyond its banks, has already submerged one part of the Empire of Romania with its waves, and is threatening to submerge another."[106] Stephen Dushan came to an agreement, now with Cantacuzene, now with John V, as it seemed advantageous to him. Taking advantage of the desperate situation of the Empire, whose forces were occupied by internal troubles, Stephen conquered all of Macedonia except Thessalonica without difficulty and after a siege took Seres, an important fortified place in eastern Macedonia, lying on the way from Thessalonica to Constantinople. The surrender of Seres was of great importance; Dushan gained a fortified and purely Greek city, only slightly inferior to Thessalonica, which might serve as a key to Constantinople. From this time on, broader plans against the Empire developed in the mind of the Serbian leader.

Contemporary Byzantine sources connect with the capture of Seres Dushan's assumption of the title of tsar and the open display of his claims to the Eastern Empire. John Cantacuzene, for example, wrote, "The Kral [King] approached Seres and took possession of it. . . . After that, becoming excessively conceited and seeing himself master of the major part of the Empire, he proclaimed himself Tsar of the Romans and Serbs,[107] and upon his son he conferred the title of Kral."[108] In his letter to the Doge of Venice from Seres, Dushan, among other titles, glorifies himself as "the master of almost all the Empire of Romania" [*et fere totius imperii Romaniae dominus*].[109] His Greek

---

[105] Nicephorus Gregoras called him "the Great Triball." By this name, really that of an ancient Thracian tribe, Gregoras meant the Serbs.

[106] *Historia*, XIV, 4; Bonn ed., II, 817.

[107] Like Nicephorus Gregoras, Cantacuzene

in his memoirs called the Serbs by the name of the old Thracian tribe of the Triballs.

[108] *Historiae*, III, 89; Bonn ed., II, 551–52.

[109] Florinsky, *The Southern Slavs and Byzantium*, II, 108, 111. Jireček, *Geschichte der Serben*, I, 386.

decrees Dushan signed in red ink "Stephen in Christ God the faithful Kral and autocrat of Serbia and Romania."[110]

Dushan's broad plans concerning Constantinople differed from the plans of the Bulgarian kings of the ninth and thirteenth centuries, Simeon and the Asens. The chief aim of Simeon had been the liberation of the Slavonic lands from the power of Byzantium and the formation of one great Slavonic Empire; "his very attempt," wrote T. Florinsky, "to take possession of Constantinople was due to the same tendency to destroy the power of the Greeks and replace it by that of the Slavs. . . ."[111] "He wished to possess Tsargrad and to exert power over the Greeks, not as emperor of the Romans, but as tsar of Bulgaria."[112] Similar aims were pursued by the Asens, who aspired to the liberation and complete independence of the Bulgarian people and wished to found a Bulgarian Empire which should include Constantinople.

In assuming the title of emperor (basileus) and autocrat Stephen Dushan was guided by different aims. The question was not only the liberation of the Serbian people from the influence of the eastern emperor. There is no doubt that Dushan set himself the goal of creating a new empire instead of Byzantium, not Serbian, but Serbian-Greek, and that "the Serbian people, the Serbian kingdom, and all the Slavonic lands annexed to it were to become only a part of the Empire of the Romans, whose head he proclaimed himself."[113] Proposing himself as an aspirant to the throne of Constantine the Great, Justinian, and other Byzantine emperors, Dushan wished, first of all, to become emperor of the Romans, and then of the Serbs, that is, to establish in his person a Serbian dynasty on the Byzantine throne.

It was important for Dushan to draw to his side the Greek clergy of the conquered regions; he realized that, in the eyes of the people, his proclamation as tsar of the Serbs and Greeks would be legal only if sanctioned by the higher authority of the Church. The archbishop of Serbia, dependent upon the patriarch of Constantinople, was not sufficient; even though the complete independence of the Serbian church had been proclaimed, the archbishop or patriarch of Serbia could crown the kral (king) only as tsar of Serbia. In order to sanctify the title of the "Tsar of the Serbs and Romans," which might help him to the Byzantine throne, something more was needed. The patriarch of Constantinople, naturally, would not consent to such a coronation. Dushan began to plan to sanctify his new title by the approbation of the highest Greek clergy of the conquered regions as well as by the monks of the Greek monasteries of the famous Mount Athos.

---

[110] See C. Sathas, *Bibliotheca graeca medii aevi*, I, 239. Florinsky, *The Athonian Acts and Photographs of Them in the Collections of Sevastyanov*, 96.

[111] *The Southern Slavs and Byzantium*, II, 109.

[112] *Ibid.*, 110.

[113] *Ibid.*

For this purpose he confirmed and widened the privileges and increased the endowments of the Greek monasteries in conquered Macedonia, where many estates (μετόχια) which belonged to Athos also came under his power. The peninsula of Chalcidice itself with the Athonian monasteries came into Dushan's hands, and the monks could not fail to understand that the protection of the monasteries had passed from the Byzantine emperor to a new master, upon whom their further welfare would depend. The charters (*chrysobulls*) written in Greek granted by Dushan to the Greek monasteries of Athos testify not only to his confirmation of their former privileges, exemptions, and possessions, but to the granting of new ones. Besides the charters given to separate monasteries there is a general charter granted to all the Athonian monasteries; in this charter he said: "Our Majesty, having received (into our power) all the monasteries situated on the Holy Mountain of Athos, which from all their hearts have had recourse to us and have become subject to us, has granted and accorded to them by this general edict (*chrysobull*) a great benefaction in order that the monks dwelling therein may fulfil peacefully and without disturbance their pious work."[114]

Easter 1346 brought a momentous day in the history of Serbia. At Scopia (Skoplje, Uskub, in northern Macedonia), Dushan's capital, there assembled the noble princes of the whole kingdom of Serbia, all the higher Serbian clergy with the archbishop of Serbia at their head, the Bulgarian and Greek clergy of the conquered regions, and, finally, the *protos,* the head of the council of igumens (abbots), which administered Athos, and the igumens and hermits of the Holy Mountain of Athos. This large and solemn council was "to ratify and sanctify the political revolution achieved by Dushan: the foundation of a new Empire."[115]

First of all, the Council established a Serbian patriarchate entirely independent from the Constantinopolitan patriarchate. Dushan needed an independent Serbian patriarch for his coronation as emperor. As the choice of that patriarch took place without the participation of the ecumenical patriarchs of the East, the Greek bishops and the hermits of Mount Athos had to substitute for the patriarch of Constantinople. The Serbian patriarch was elected, and the patriarch of Constantinople, who refused to recognize the acts of this council as regular, excommunicated the Church of Serbia.

After the election of the patriarch the solemn coronation of Dushan with the imperial crown was performed. This event had probably been preceded by the ceremony of the proclamation of Dushan as tsar at Seres, soon after this city was taken. In connection with those events Dushan introduced at his court pompous court dignities and adopted Byzantine customs and man-

[114] Florinsky, *The Athonian Acts,* 95. Uspensky, *The Christian Orient,* III (2), 156.

[115] Florinsky, *The Southern Slavs and Byzantium,* II, 126.

ners. The new basileus turned to the representatives of the Greek nobility; the Greek language seems to have become officially equal to the Serbian tongue, for many of Dushan's charters were written in Greek. "The privileged classes in Serbia, large landowners and clergy, who had exerted enormous influence and power and limited the freedom of action of the Serbian kings, were now forced to yield to the higher authority of the Tsar, as an absolute monarch."[116] In accordance with Byzantine custom, Dushan's wife was also crowned, and their ten year old son was proclaimed "Kral of all Serbian lands." After the coronation, by means of many charters (*chrysobulls*) Dushan expressed his gratitude and favor to the Greek monasteries and churches, and with his wife visited Athos, where he stayed about four months, praying in all the monasteries, generously endowing them, and receiving everywhere "the benediction of the saintly and holy fathers, who led angelic lives."[117]

After the coronation Stephen's sole dream was to reach Constantinople; after his victories and coronation he could see no impediment to the attainment of this goal. Although in the last period of his reign his campaigns against Byzantium were not so frequent as before, and his attention was distracted now by hostilities in the west and north, now by internal affairs, nevertheless, as Florinsky said, "to all this Dushan's attention only turns aside, no more: his eyes and thoughts are as before concentrated upon the same alluring extreme southeast corner of the peninsula. The desire of taking possession of this southeast corner, or, properly speaking, of the world city situated there, now holds still more firmly all the Tsar's thoughts, becomes the leading motive of his activity, and characterizes the whole time of his reign."[118]

Powerfully affected as he was by the dream of an easy conquest of Constantinople, Dushan did not immediately grasp the fact that some serious obstacles to the realization of his plan already existed. First, there was the growing power of the Turks, who were also aiming at the Byzantine capital and whom the badly organized Serbian troops could not overcome; besides, in order to take Constantinople it was necessary to have a fleet, which Dushan had not. To increase his maritime force he planned to enter into alliance with Venice, but this step was from the beginning doomed to failure. The Republic of St. Mark, unreconciled to the return of Constantinople to the Palaeologi, would never have consented to support Dushan in his conquest of the city for himself; if Venice conquered Constantinople, it would be for her own sake. The attempt of Dushan to form an alliance with the Turks also miscarried, due to the policy of John Cantacuzene; in any event the interests of

---

[116] Florinsky, *The Monuments of Dushan's Legislative Activity*, 13.

[117] Florinsky, *The Southern Slavs and Byzantium*, II, 134.

[118] *Ibid.*, 141.

Dushan and the Turks must undoubtedly have collided. Nor could interference in the internal strife of the Empire materially help Dushan's plans. In the last years of his reign a body of Serbian troops fighting on the side of John V Palaeologus was slain by the Turks. Dushan was doomed to disappointment; it became obvious that the way to Constantinople was closed to him.

The statement in the later chronicles of Ragusa (Dubrovnik) that Dushan undertook a vast expedition against Constantinople in the very year of his death, which alone prevented its being carried into effect, is not confirmed by any contemporary information, and the best scholars do not consider it true.[119] In 1355 the Great Master of Serbia died without realizing his ambition. Thus, Dushan failed to create a Greco-Serbian Empire to replace the Byzantine Empire; he managed to form only the Empire of Serbia, which included many Greek lands,[120] but which after his death fell, as John Cantacuzene said, "into a thousand pieces."[121]

The existence of Dushan's monarchy was of such short duration, that, as Florinsky says, "in it, properly speaking, only two moments may be observed: the moment of formation during the whole time of Dushan's reign, and that of disintegration, starting immediately after the death of its founder."[122] "Ten years after," another Russian scholar wrote, "the grandeur of the Serbian Empire seemed to belong to a remote past."[123] Thus, the most grandiose attempt of the Slavs, their third and last, to create in the Balkan peninsula a great Empire, with Constantinople at its head, ended in failure. The Balkan peninsula was open and almost defenseless to the aggressive plans of the warlike Ottoman Turks.

The policies of Byzantium in the second half of the fourteenth century

The Turks.—Toward the end of the reign of Andronicus the Younger the Turks were almost in complete control of Asia Minor. The eastern portion of the Mediterranean and the Archipelago were continuously threatened by the vessels of Turkish pirates, both Ottomans and Seljuqs. The situation of the Christian population of the peninsula, coastlands, and islands became unbearable; trade died away. Turkish attacks on the Athonian monasteries forced one of the monks, Athanasius, to leave Athos and emigrate to Greece, to Thessaly, where he founded the famous monasteries "in air," "the weirdly fantastic Metéora, which crown the needle-like crags of the grim valley of Kalabaka."[124] The king of Cyprus and the Master of the military order of

[119] *Ibid.,* 200–201, 206–7.

[120] *Ibid.,* 208.

[121] John Cantacuzene, *Historiae,* IV, 43; Bonn ed., III, 315.

[122] *The Southern Slavs and Byzantium,* II, 1.

[123] A. Pogodin, *A History of Serbia,* 79.

[124] See N. A. Bees, "Geschichtliche Forschungsresultate und Mönchs- und Volkssagen über die Gründer der Meteorenklöster," *Byzantinisch-neugriechische Jahrbücher,* III (1922), 364–69. Miller, *Latins in the Levant,*

the Hospitalers, or of St. John, who had held Rhodes since the beginning of the fourteenth century, besought the pope to rouse the western European states to take arms against the Turks. But the small relief expeditions which answered the papal appeals, though not altogether unsuccessful, could not accomplish much. The Turks were resolved to establish themselves firmly on the European coast; and this was facilitated by the civil war in the Empire, in which John Cantacuzene involved the Turks.

The first establishment of the Ottoman Turks in Europe is usually connected with the name of John Cantacuzene, who often called upon their support in his struggle with John Palaeologus. Cantacuzene even married his daughter to Sultan Orkhan. On the invitation of Cantacuzene the Turks as his allies devastated Thrace several times. Nicephorus Gregoras remarked that Cantacuzene hated the Romans as he loved the barbarians.[125] It is quite possible that the first settlements of the Turks in the peninsula of Gallipoli took place with the knowledge and consent of Cantacuzene. The same Byzantine historian wrote that while a Christian service was being celebrated in the imperial church, the Ottomans who had been admitted into the capital were dancing and singing near the palace, "crying out in incomprehensible sounds the songs and hymns of Muhammed, and thereby attracting the crowd to listen to them rather than to the divine Gospels."[126] To satisfy the financial claims of the Turks Cantacuzene even handed over to them the money sent from Russia by the Great Prince of Moscow, Simeon the Proud, for the restoration of the Church of St. Sophia, at that time in a state of decay.

Although some private settlements of the Turks in Europe, namely in Thrace and the Thracian (Gallipoli) peninsula, had existed, in all likelihood, from the first years of the reign of Cantacuzene, they did not seem dangerous, for they were, of course, under Byzantine authority. But at the beginning of the fifties, a small stronghold near Callipolis (Gallipoli), Zympa, fell into the hands of the Turks. Cantacuzene's attempt to bribe the Turks to evacuate Zympa failed.

In 1354 almost the whole southern coast of Thrace was struck by a terrible earthquake, which destroyed many cities and fortresses. The Turks fortified Zympa, and seized several cities in the peninsula which were abandoned by the population after the earthquake, among them Callipolis. There they constructed walls, erected strong fortifications and an arsenal, and set a large garrison, so that Callipolis became an extremely important strategic center and a base of support for their further advance in the Balkan peninsula. The people of Constantinople immediately realized their danger, and the news of

294–95. I. Boghiatzides, "Τὸ χρονικὸν τῶν Μετεώρων," Ἐπετηρὶς Ἑταιρείας Βυζαντινῶν Σπουδῶν, II (1925), 149–82.

[125] Nicephorus Gregoras, *Historia*, XXVIII, 2; Bonn ed., III, 177.
[126] *Ibid.*, 40; Bonn ed., 202–3.

the capture of Callipolis by the Turks threw them into despair. A prominent writer of the epoch, Demetrius Cydones, testified that clamors and lamentations resounded all over the whole city.

"What speeches," he wrote, "were more heard then in the city? Have we not perished? Are not all of us within the walls [of the city] caught as if in the net of the barbarians? Is he not happy who, before these dangers, has left the city?" "In order to escape slavery" all were hastening to Italy, Spain, and even farther "towards the sea beyond the Pillars,"[127] that is to say, beyond the Pillars of Hercules (present day Straits of Gibraltar), perhaps to England. Of these events a Russian chronicler remarked, "In the year 6854 [ab. 1346] the Ismailites [i.e., the Turks] crossed on this side, into the Greek land. In the year 6865 [ab. 1357] they took Callipolis from the Greeks."[128]

At that time the Venetian representative at Constantinople notified his government of the danger from the Turks, their possible capture of the remnants of the Empire, the general discontent in Byzantium with the Emperor and government, and finally, the desire of the majority of the population to be under the power of the Latins, particularly of Venice. In another report the same official wrote that the Greeks of Constantinople, wishing to be protected against the Turks, desired first of all, the domination of Venice, or, if that was impossible, that of "the King of Hungary or Serbia."[129] To what extent the point of view of the Venetian representative reflected the real spirit in Constantinople is difficult to say.

Historians usually call John Cantacuzene the sole cause of the first establishment of the Turks in the Balkan peninsula; he called on them for aid during his personal struggle for power with John Palaeologus. The impression was that the whole responsibility for the subsequent barbaric behavior of the Turks in Europe was Cantacuzene's. But, of course, it is not he alone who is responsible for this event, fatal to both Byzantium and Europe. The chief cause lies in the general conditions in Byzantium and the Balkan peninsula, where no serious obstacles could be opposed to the unrestrainable onslaught of the Turks to the west. If Cantacuzene had not called them to Europe, they would have come there in any case. As T. Florinsky said, "By their continuous incursions the Turks had paved the way for the conquest of Thrace; the miserable internal conditions of the Greco-Slavonic world had greatly contributed to the success and impunity of their invasions; finally, the political leaders of various states and peoples . . . had not the least idea of the threatening danger from the advancing Muhammedan power; on the con-

---

[127] Demetrius Cydones, Συμβουλευτικὸς ἕτερος; Migne, *Patrologia Graeca,* CLIV, 1013.
[128] Voskresenskaya lietopis (The Annals of Voskresensk), *The Complete Collection of Russian Annals,* VII, 251.

[129] See N. Iorga, "Latins et Grecs d'Orient et l'établissement des Turcs en Europe (1242–1362)," *Byzantinische Zeitschrift,* XV (1906), 217. Hopf, *Geschichte Griechenlands,* I, 448.

trary, all of them sought to compromise with it for their own narrow, egoistic goals; Cantacuzene was no peculiar exception." Like Cantacuzene, the Venetians and Genoese, "these privileged defenders of Christianity against Islam," were at that time occupied with the idea of an alliance with the Turks. The great "Tsar of the Serbs and Greeks," Dushan, was also seeking for the same alliance. "No one, of course, will absolutely justify Cantacuzene; he cannot be entirely cleared of blame for the unfortunate events which led to the establishment of the Turks in Europe; but we must not forget that he was not the only one. Stephen Dushan would perhaps have brought the Turks into the peninsula, as Cantacuzene had done, if the latter had not anticipated him and prevented him from coming to an agreement with Orkhan."[130]

Having established themselves at Callipolis the Turks, taking advantage of the unceasing internal troubles in Byzantium and the Slavonic states, Bulgaria and Serbia, began to extend their conquests in the Balkan peninsula. Orkhan's successor, Sultan Murad I, captured many fortified places very near Constantinople, took possession of such important centers as Hadrianople and Philippopolis, and advancing to the west, began to menace Thessalonica. The capital of the Turkish state was transferred to Hadrianople. Constantinople was being gradually surrounded by Turkish possessions. The Emperor continued to pay tribute to the sultan.

These conquests brought Murad face to face with Serbia and Bulgaria, which had already lost their former strength due to their internal troubles. Murad marched upon Serbia. The Serbian prince Lazar set out to meet him. In the summer of 1389 the decisive battle took place in the central part of Serbia on the field of Kossovo. At the outset the victory seemed to be on the side of the Serbs. The story goes that a noble Serb, Milosh (Miloš) Obilić or Kobilić, contrived to force a passage into the Turkish camp, presented himself as a deserter to the Turks, and entering Murad's tent killed him with a stab from a poisoned dagger. The confusion among the Turks was rapidly quelled by Bayazid, the son of the slain Murad. He surrounded the Serbian army and inflicted a crushing defeat upon it. Lazar was taken prisoner and slain. The year of the battle of Kossovo may be considered the year of the fall of Serbia. The miserable remnants of the Serbian Empire which continued to exist for seventy years more, do not deserve the name of a state. In 1389 Serbia became subject to Turkey.[131] Four years later, in 1393 (i.e., after the death of John V), the capital of Bulgaria, Trnovo, was also captured by the Turks, and a short time later the whole territory of Bulgaria came under the power of the Turkish Empire.

[130] Florinsky, *The Southern Slavs and Byzantium*, II, 192–93.

[131] For the Greek sources on the battle of Kossovo, see N. Radojčić, "Die griechischen Quellen zur Schlacht am Kossovo Polje," *Byzantion*, VI (1931), 241–46. H. Gregoire, "L'Opinion byzantine et la bataille de Kossovo, *Byzantion*, VI (1931), 247–51.

The old and ill John V had to suffer a new humiliation which accelerated his death. To protect the capital against danger from the Turks John set about restoring the city walls and erecting fortifications. On learning of this the sultan commanded him to destroy what had been built and, in case of refusal, threatened to blind the Emperor's son and heir, Manuel, who was at that time at Bayazid's court. John was compelled to yield, and fulfill the sultan's demand. Constantinople entered upon the most critical epoch of its existence.

Genoa, the Black Death of 1348, and the Venetian-Genoese War.— Toward the end of the reign of Andronicus III, the Genoese colony of Galata had obtained a powerful economic and political position and was a sort of state within the state. Taking advantage of the absence of the Byzantine fleet, the Genoese sent their vessels to all the ports of the Archipelago and seized the whole import trade in the Black Sea and in the Straits. A contemporary source, Nicephorus Gregoras, stated that the income from custom duties of Galata amounted annually to 200,000 gold coins, while Byzantium received barely 30,000.[132] Realizing the danger to Byzantium from Galata, Cantacuzene, notwithstanding the internal strife that was wasting the country, started, as far as the disordered finances of the Empire permitted, to build vessels for military and commercial use. The alarmed population of Galata determined to resist Cantacuzene's plans by force; they occupied the heights commanding Galata and there erected walls, a tower, and various earthen fortifications, and took the initiative against Cantacuzene. The first attack of the Genoese upon Constantinople itself was a failure. The vessels built by Cantacuzene entered the Golden Horn to fight the Genoese, who at sight of the strength of the new Byzantine fleet were on the point of making peace. But the inexperience of the Greek commanders and the outbreak of a storm led to the crushing of the Greek fleet. The Genoese at Galata decorated their vessels and sailed triumphantly by the imperial palace, mocking the imperial flag which had been taken from the defeated Greek ships. According to the conditions of peace, the debatable heights over Galata remained in the hands of the Genoese, and Galata became increasingly dangerous to Constantinople.

This increase in Genoese influence, already great, could not fail to affect the position of Venice, Genoa's chief commercial foe in the East. The interests of both republics clashed acutely in the Black Sea and in the Maeotis (the Sea of Azov), where the Genoese had established themselves at Kaffa (Caffa, present-day Theodosia in the Crimea) and Tana, at the mouth of the River Don (near present-day Azov). The Bosphorus, the entrance into the Black Sea, was also in the hands of the Genoese, who, also possessing Galata, had organized on the shore of the Straits a sort of customs house which took commercial tolls from all vessels not Genoese, especially Venetian and Byzantine,

[132] Nicephorus Gregoras, *Historia*, XVII, i, 2; Bonn ed., II, 842.

sailing into the Black Sea. Genoa's goal was the establishment of a trade monopoly in the Bosphorus. The interests of Venice and Genoa also came into collision in the islands and on the coast of the Aegean Sea.

An immediate clash between the two republics was temporarily averted by the plague of 1348 and the following years, which paralyzed their forces. This terrible plague, the so-called Black Death, which had been carried from the interior of Asia to the coast of the Maeotis (the Sea of Azov) and to the Crimea, spread from the pestiferous Genoese trade-galleys sailing from Tana and Kaffa all over Constantinople, where it carried off, according to the probably exaggerated statements of the western chronicles, two-thirds or eight-ninths of the population.[133] Thence the plague passed to the islands of the Aegean Sea and the coast of the Mediterranean. Byzantine historians have left a detailed description of the disease showing the complete impotence of the physicians in their struggle against it.[134] In his description of this epidemic John Cantacuzene imitated the famous description of the Athenian plague in the second book of Thucydides. From Byzantium, as western chroniclers narrated, the Genoese galleys spread the disease through the coast cities of Italy, France, and Spain. "There is something incredible," remarked M. Kovalevsky, "in this uninterrupted wandering of the pestiferous galleys through the Mediterranean ports."[135] From these the plague spread to the north and west, and affected Italy, Spain, France, England, Germany, and Norway.[136] At this time, in Italy, Boccaccio was writing his famous *Decameron* which begins "with a description of the Black Death classical in its picturesqueness and measured solemnity,"[137] when many brave men, fair ladies, and gallant youths "in the soundest of health, broke fast with their kinsfolk, comrades, and friends in the morning, and when evening came, supped with their forefathers in the other world."[138] Scholars compare the description of Boccaccio with that of Thucydides, and some of them hold the humanist in higher estimation even than the classic writer.[139]

From Germany through the Baltic Sea and Poland the plague penetrated into Pskov, Novgorod, and Moscow, in Russia, where the great prince, Simeon the Proud, fell its victim in 1353, and then it spread all over Russia. In some

---

[133] Chronicon Estense; see Muratori, *Scriptores rerum italicarum*, XV, 448. Bartholomaeus della Pugliola, *Historia miscella Bononiensis, ibid.*, XVIII, 409.

[134] Nicephorus Gregoras, *Historia*, XV, i, 5; Bonn ed., II, 797–98. John Cantacuzene, *Historiae*, IV, 8; Bonn ed., III, 49–53.

[135] *The Economic Growth of Europe*, III, 191; trans. M. Kupperberg, V, 236. A. A. Vasiliev, *The Goths in the Crimea*, 175–77; bibliography is given.

[136] On Norway, see e.g., K. Gjerset, *History of the Norwegian People*, I, 202.

[137] A. N. Veselovsky, "Boccaccio, his Environment and Contemporaries," *Works of A. N. Veselovsky*, V, 448, 451; *idem*, in *Sbornik Otdeleniya Russkago Yazyka i Slovesnosti*, LII, 444, 447.

[138] *The Decameron*, first day, introduction.

[139] See, e.g., M. Korelin, *The Earlier Italian Humanism and Its Historiography*, 495.

cities, according to the statement of a Russian chronicle, no single man was left alive.[140]

Venice was actively preparing for war. After the horrors of the plague were somewhat forgotten, the Republic of St. Mark made an alliance with the King of Aragon. The latter was discontented with Genoa and consented, by his attacks upon the shores and islands of Italy, to distract the Genoese and thereby to facilitate the advance of Venice in the east. After some hesitation John Cantacuzene joined the Aragon-Venetian alliance against Genoa; he accused the "ungrateful nation of the Genoese" of forgetting "the fear of the Lord," devastating the seas "as if they were seized with a mania for pillaging," and of endeavoring permanently "to disturb the seas and navigators by their piratical attacks."[141]

The chief battle, in which about 150 Greek, Venetian, Aragonese, and Genoese vessels took part, was fought in the beginning of the sixth decade, in the Bosphorus. It had no decisive result; each side claimed victory. The friendly relations between the Genoese and Ottoman-Turks forced John Cantacuzene to give up his alliance with Venice and become reconciled with the Genoese, to whom he gave his promise not to support Venice henceforth. He also consented to give more territory to the Genoese colony of Galata. But after some clashes Venice and Genoa, exhausted by the war, made peace. Since it failed to solve the chief problem in the conflict, the peace lasted only a short time; again a war broke out, the war of Tenedos. Tenedos, one of the few islands of the Archipelago still in the hands of the Byzantine emperors, possessed, owing to its position at the entrance into the Dardanelles, the greatest significance for the states which had commercial relations with Constantinople and the countries around the Black Sea. Since both shores of the straits were in the hands of the Ottoman Turks, Tenedos was an excellent observation point of their actions. Venice, which had already for a long time dreamed of occupying this island, after long negotiations with the Emperor at last got his consent. But the Genoese could not acquiesce in the cession of Tenedos to Venice; in order to prevent its accomplishment, they succeeded in raising a revolution at Constantinople which deposed John V and set his eldest son, Andronicus, upon the throne for three years. The war which had broken out between the two republics exhausted both of them and ruined all the states which had commercial concerns in the East. At last, in 1381, the war ended with the peace made at Turin, the capital of the Duchy of Savoy.

A detailed and voluminous text of the conference of Turin exists.[142] With

[140] Nikonovskaya letopis, *The Complete Collection of Russian Annals,* X, 224.

[141] See N. Iorga, "Latins et Grecs d'Orient," *Byzantinische Zeitschrift,* XV (1906), 208.

[142] *Liber jurium reipublicae Genuensis,* II, 858–906; in *Monumenta Historiae Patriae,* IX. *Monumenta spectantia historiam slavorum meridionalium,* IV, 199–263.

the personal participation of the count of Savoy, the conference discussed various general problems of international life, which was already very complicated at that time, and worked out the conditions of peace; of the latter, only those are interesting here which put an end to the dispute between Venice and Genoa and which referred to Byzantium. Venice was to evacuate the island of Tenedos, the fortifications of which were leveled to the ground; the island itself was on a set date to pass into the hands of the Count of Savoy (*in manibus prefati domini Sabaudie comitis*), who was related to the Palaeologi (on the side of Anne of Savoy, wife of Andronicus III). Thus neither Venice nor Genoa gained this important strategic point, to whose possession they had so eagerly aspired.

A Spanish traveler, Pero Tafur, who visited Constantinople in 1437 gave a very interesting description of Tenedos:

We came to the island of Tenedos, where we anchored and disembarked. While the ship was being refitted we set out to see the island, which is some eight or ten miles about. There are many conies, and it is covered with vineyards, but they are all spoilt. The harbour of Tenedos looks so new that it might have been built to-day by a masterhand. The mole is made of great stones and columns, and here the ships have their moorings and excellent anchorage. There are other places where ships can anchor, but this is the best, since it is opposite the entrance to the Straits of Romania [Dardanelles]. Above the harbour is a great hill surmounted by a very strong castle. This castle was the cause of much fighting between the Venetians and Genoese until the Pope sentenced it to be destroyed, that it might belong to neither. But, without doubt, this was very ill-advised, since the harbour is one of the best in the world. No ship can enter the straits without first anchoring there to find the entrance, which is very narrow, and the Turks, knowing how many ships touch there, arm themselves and lie in wait and kill many Christians.[143]

As for the acute question of the trade-monopoly of the Genoese in the Black Sea and Maeotis, especially in the colony of Tana, Genoa, according to the conditions of the peace of Turin, was obliged to give up her intention of closing the Venetian markets of the Black Sea and of shutting off access to Tana. The commercial nations resumed their intercourse with Tana, which, situated at the mouth of the river Don, was one of the very important centers of trade with eastern peoples. Peaceful relations between Genoa and the elderly John V, who had regained the throne, were restored. Byzantium had again to steer a way between the two republics, whose commercial interests in the East, despite the terms of peace, continued to collide. However, the peace of Turin,

[143] *Andanças é viajes de Pero Tafur por diversas partes del mundo avidos (1435–1439)*, 135–36; ed. Malcolm Letts, 113–14. See A. A. Vasiliev, "Pero Tafur, a Spanish Traveler of the Fifteenth Century and his Visit to Constantinople, Trebizond, and Italy," *Byzantion*, VII (1932), 75–122. Charles Diehl, "Un Voyageur espagnol à Constantinople," *Mélanges Glotz*, I (1932), 319–27.

which ended a great war caused by the economic rivalry of Venice and Genoa, was of great importance because it allowed the nations which maintained intercourse with Romania to resume their trade, which had been interrupted for many years. But their further destiny depended upon the Ottoman Turks, to whom, as was already obvious at the end of the fourteenth century, belonged the future of the Christian East.

Manuel II (1391–1425) and the Turks

In one of his essays, Manuel II wrote: "When I had passed my childhood and not yet reached the age of man, I was encompassed by a life full of tribulation and trouble; but according to many indications, it might have been foreseen that our future would cause us to look at the past as a time of clear tranquility."[144] Manuel's presentiments did not deceive him.

Byzantium, or rather, Constantinople, was in a desperate and humiliating position in the last years of the reign of John V. At the moment of John's death, Manuel was at the court of Sultan Bayazid. When tidings of his father's death reached him, he succeeded in fleeing from the sultan and arrived in Constantinople, where he was crowned emperor. According to Ducas, Bayazid, feared the popularity of Manuel and regretted not having murdered him during his stay at his court. Bayazid's envoy sent to Constantinople to Manuel, as Ducas related, gave the new Emperor these words from the sultan: "If you wish to execute my orders, close the gates of the city and reign within it; but all that lies outside belongs to me."[145] Thereafter Constantinople was practically in a state of siege. The only relief for the capital lay in the unsatisfactory condition of the Turkish fleet; for that reason the Turks, though possessing both sides of the Dardanelles, were unable for the time being to cut off Byzantium from intercourse with the outside world through this strait. Especially terrible to the Christian East was the moment when Bayazid, by craftiness, gathered together in one place the representatives of the families of the Palaeologi with Manuel at their head, and the Slavonic princes; he seems to have intended to do away with them at once, "in order that," to quote the Sultan's words given in a writing of Manuel, "after the land had been cleared of thorns, by which he meant us [that is to say, the Christians], his sons might dance in the Christian land without fearing to scratch their feet."[146] The representatives of the ruling families were spared, but the severe wrath of the sultan struck many nobles of their retinue.

In 1392 Bayazid organized a maritime expedition in the Black Sea ostensibly

[144] Berger de Xivrey, "Mémoire sur le vie et les ouvrages de l'empereur Manuel Paléologue," *Mémoires de l'Institut de France,* XIX (2), 25–26.

[145] Michael Ducas, *Historia byzantina,* XIII; Bonn ed., 49.

[146] Manuel Palaeologus, *Oratio funebris in proprium ejus fratrem despotam Theodorum Palaeologum;* ed. Migne, *Patrologia,* CLVI, 225.

against Sinope. But the sultan put the Emperor Manuel at the head of the Turkish fleet. Therefore Venice thought that this expedition was directed not against Sinope, but against the Venetian colonies, south of the Dardanelles, in the Archipelago—not a Turkish expedition, but a disguised Greek expedition, supported by Turkish troops. As a recent historian said, the Oriental problem of the end of the fourteenth century might have been solved by the formation of a Turko-Greek Empire.[147] This interesting episode, evidence of which is in the archives of Venice, had no important results. Shortly after, the friendly relations between Byzantium and Bayazid came to an open break, and Manuel again turned to the West which for some time had been neglected.

Hard pressed, Manuel opened friendly negotiations with Venice. Bayazid tried to cut off Constantinople from its food supply. Such acute need was felt in the capital that, as a Byzantine chronicler said, the people pulled down their houses in order to get wood for baking bread.[148] At the request of Byzantine envoys, Venice sent some corn to Constantinople.[149]

The crusade of Sigismund of Hungary and the Battle of Nicopolis.— Meanwhile, the successes of the Turks in the Balkan peninsula again raised the question of immediate danger to western Europe. The subjugation of Bulgaria and the nearly complete conquest of Serbia had led the Turks to the borders of the Kingdom of Hungary. The king of Hungary, Sigismund, feeling complete impotence against the threatening Turkish danger with only his own forces, appealed to the European rulers for help. France answered the appeal with the greatest enthusiasm. In obedience to the voice of his people, the king of France sent a small body of troops, the duke of Burgundy at their head. Poland, England, Germany, and some smaller states also sent troops. Venice joined the campaign. Just before Sigismund's crusade started, Manuel seems to have formed a league with the Genoese of the Aegean islands, namely Lesbos and Chios, and with the Knights of Rhodes, in other words, with the Christian outposts in the Aegean Sea.[150] As for Manuel's relation to Sigismund's crusade, perhaps he pledged himself to share in the expenses of the campaign.

The crusading enterprise ended in complete failure. In 1396, the crusaders were crushed by the Turks in the battle of Nicopolis (on the right shore of the lower Danube) and compelled to return to their homes. Sigismund, who had

---

[147] Silberschmidt, *Das orientalische Problem*, 78–79. The author used a misleading term, "Griechisches Reich türkischer Nation" (p. 79). See R. Salomon's review, *Byzantinische Zeitschrift*, XXVIII (1928), 144. See also Peter Charanis, "The Strife Among the Palaeologi and the Ottoman Turks, 1370–1402," *Byzantion*, XVI, 1 (1944), 286–314.

Among other sources, the author used the correspondence of Demetrius Cydones.

[148] Michael Ducas, *Historia byzantina*, XII; Bonn ed., 50.

[149] Silberschmidt, *Das orientalische Problem*, 87.

[150] *Ibid.*, 119.

barely escaped capture, sailed in a small vessel by way of the mouth of the Danube and the Black Sea to Constantinople, whence, by a roundabout way through the Archipelago and the Adriatic Sea, he returned to Hungary.[151] A participator in the battle of Nicopolis, the Bavarian soldier Schiltberger, who had been taken prisoner by the Turks, and spent some time at Gallipoli, described as an eyewitness Sigismund's passage through the Dardanelles which the Turks could not prevent. According to his statement, the Turks put all their Christian captives in line along the shore of the straits and mockingly shouted to Sigismund to leave his vessel and free his people.[152]

After the defeat of the western crusaders at Nicopolis, the victorious Bayazid, planning to strike a final blow to Constantinople, decided to ruin the few regions that still belonged, though almost nominally, to the Empire, from which the besieged capital could get some help. He devastated Thessaly, which submitted to him, and, according to Turkish sources, even seized Athens for a short time;[153] his best generals inflicted terrible destruction on Morea, where Manuel's brother was ruling under the title of Despot.

Meanwhile, popular dissatisfaction was growing in the capital; the tired and exhausted populace were murmuring, accusing Manuel of their misery, and beginning to turn their eyes to his nephew John, who had in 1390 deposed for some months Manuel's old father, John V.

The expedition of Marshal Boucicaut.—Realizing that with his own forces he would not be able to overcome the Turks, Manuel decided to appeal for help to the most powerful rulers of western Europe and to the Russian great prince Vasili I Dmitrievich. The pope, Venice, France, England, and possibly Aragon replied favorably to Manuel's appeal. His request seemed especially flattering to the king of France, because, declared a contemporary western chronicler, "it was the first time that the ancient emperors of the whole world had appealed for help to such a remote country."[154] Manuel's appeal to western Europe gained him a certain, but an insufficient, amount of money, and the hope of getting from France aid in men.

Manuel's request for help from the Great Prince of Moscow, supported by a request to the same purpose from the patriarch of Constantinople, was favorably received in Moscow. There seems to have been no question at the court of Moscow of sending troops to Constantinople; it was only a question of grant-

[151] Aziz Suryal Atiya, *The Crusade of Nicopolis.* H. L. Savage, "Enguerrand de Coucy VII and the Campaign of Nicopolis," *Speculum,* XIV (1939), 423–42.

[152] H. Schiltberger, *Reisebuch,* ed. V. Langmantel, 7.

[153] See J. H. Mordtmann, "Die erste Eroberung von Athen durch die Türken zu Ende des 14 Jahrhunderts," *Byzantinisch-neugriechische Jahrbücher,* IV (1923), 346–50. R. Loenertz, "Pour l'histoire du Péloponèse au XIVᵉ siècle (1382–1404)," *Études byzantines,* I (1944), 185–86.

[154] *Chronique du Religieux de Saint-Denys,* ed. Bellaguet, II, 562.

ing "alms to those who are in such need and misery, besieged by the Turks."[155] Money was sent to Constantinople, where it was accepted with great gratitude. But money contributions could not help Manuel substantially.

The king of France, Charles VI, fulfilled his promise and sent in support of Constantinople 1200 men-at-arms, at whose head he placed Marshal Boucicaut. Boucicaut was one of the most interesting men of France at the end of the fourteenth and the beginning of the fifteenth century. A man of extraordinary valor and determination, he had spent all his life in long journeys and dangerous adventures. As a young man, he had set out to the East, to Constantinople, traveled all over Palestine, reached Sinai, and for several months had been captive in Egypt. On his return to France, hearing of the appeal of the king of Hungary, Sigismund, Boucicaut had hastened to him, fought with astounding valor in the fatal battle of Nicopolis, and had fallen prisoner to Bayazid. Escaping death almost by a miracle, and ransomed, Boucicaut returned to France in order, in the ensuing year, with all readiness and energy, to take the head of the body of troops sent by Charles VI to the East.

Members of the most eminent families of the French chivalry were included among the men-at-arms of Boucicaut. He set out by sea. Notified of the approach of his vessels to the Dardanelles, Bayazid attempted to prevent the Marshal from passing through the straits. But Boucicaut, after many dangers and with much effort, succeeded in breaking through the Dardanelles, and arriving in Constantinople, where his fleet was received with the greatest joy. Boucicaut and Manuel made many devastating raids along the Asiatic coast of the Marmora Sea and the Bosphorus, and even penetrated into the Black Sea. But these successes did not change the situation; they could not free Constantinople from her approaching fall. Seeing the critical position of Manuel and his capital, as regards both finances and provisions, Boucicaut determined to return to France, but only after he had persuaded the Emperor to go with him to the West in order to make a stronger impression there and induce the western European rulers to take more decisive steps. Such modest expeditions as that of Boucicaut evidently could not help the desperate situation of Byzantium.

The journey of Manuel II in Western Europe.—When Manuel's journey to the West was decided, his nephew John consented to take the reins of government during the Emperor's absence. Late in the year 1399, accompanied by a retinue of clerical and lay representatives, Manuel and Boucicaut left the capital for Venice.[156]

---

[155] Nikonovskaya letopis, *Complete Collection of Russian Annals,* XI (1897), 168.

[156] For the most detailed description of Manuel's journey see A. A. Vasiliev, "The Journey of the Byzantine Emperor Manuel II Palaeologus in Western Europe (1399-1403)," *Journal of the Ministry of Public Instruction,* N.S. XXXIX (1912), 41-78, 260-304. See also

The Republic of St. Mark was in a difficult position when asked to lend Byzantium a helping hand. Her important commercial interests in the East caused Venice to regard the Turks, especially after their brilliant victory at Nicopolis, not only from the point of view of a Christian state, but also from that of a trading state. Venice had even made some treaties with Bayazid. Then commercial rivalry with Genoa in the East, and the attitude of Venice towards the other Italian states, also kept her forces from Manuel's aid. They were needed at home. But Venice and the other Italian cities visited by Manuel received him with honor and showed him great compassion. Whether the Emperor saw the pope or not is doubtful. When Manuel was leaving Italy, encouraged by the promises of Venice and the Duke of Milan and the papal bulls, and planning a visit to the greatest centers of western Europe, Paris and London, he still believed in the importance and effectiveness of his long journey.

The Emperor arrived in France at a complex and interesting time, the epoch of the Hundred Years' War between France and England. The armistice which existed at his arrival might be broken at any moment. In France there was going on a very real and active polemic struggle between the Pope of Avignon and the University of Paris, which had reduced the papal power in France and caused the recognition of the final authority of the king in ecclesiastical affairs. Finally King Charles VI himself was subject to frequent fits of insanity.

A solemn reception and a richly adorned residence in the palace of the Louvre were prepared in Paris for Manuel. A Frenchman who was an eyewitness of the Emperor's entrance into Paris describes his appearance: he was of average stature and solid constitution, with a long and already very white beard, had features which inspired respect and, in the opinion of the French, was worthy of being Emperor.[157]

His stay in Paris of more than four months afforded modest results: the king and Royal Council decided to support him by a body of men-at-arms, at whose head Marshal Boucicaut was to be placed. Satisfied with that promise, the Emperor went to London, where he was also received with great honor and given many promises, but he was soon disappointed. In one of his letters from London, Manuel wrote: "The King gives us help in warriors, marksmen, money, and vessels to carry the troops where we need."[158] But this promise

---

G. Schlumberger, "Un Empereur de Byzance à Paris et à Londres," *Revue des Deux Mondes,* XXX (December 15, 1915); reprinted in his *Byzance et croisades,* 87–147. M. Jugie, "Le Voyage de l'Empereur Manuel Paléologue en Occident," *Échos d'Orient,* XV (1912), 322–32. H. C. Luke, "Visitors from the East to the Plantagenet and Lancastrian Kings," *Nineteenth Century,* CVIII (1930), 760–69. Brief note on Manuel's visit.

[157] *Chronique de Religieux de Saint-Denys,* XXI, 1; ed. Bellaguet, 756.
[158] *Lettres de Manuel Paléologue,* ed. Legrand, I, 52.

was not fulfilled. After a stay of two months in London, Manuel, loaded with presents and overwhelmed with attention and honor, but without the promised military support, returned to Paris. An English historian of the fifteenth century, Adam Usk, wrote: "I thought within myself, what a grievous thing it was that this great Christian prince from the farther East, should perforce be driven by unbelievers to visit the distant islands of the West, to seek aid against them. My God! What dost thou, ancient glory of Rome? Shorn is the greatness of thine empire this day; and truly may the words of Jeremy be spoken unto thee: 'Princess among the provinces, how is she become tributary, (Lament. I:i).' Who would ever believe that thou shouldst sink to such depth of misery, that, although once seated on the throne of majesty thou didst lord it over all the world, now thou hast no power to bring succour to the Christian faith?"[159]

Manuel's second stay in Paris lasted about two years. Information on this visit is scanty. He became, apparently, a matter of course to the French, and contemporary chroniclers who note many details concerning Manuel's first stay in Paris, say very little of his second visit. The little information on this subject comes from his letters. Those which refer to the beginning of his second stay are marked by high spirits; but these spirits gradually fell as he began to understand that he could not count upon any important support from either England or France. Of the last period of his stay in France, there are no imperial letters.

But some interesting records exist describing the way the Emperor spent his leisure time in Paris. In the beautifully decorated castle of the Louvre, for example, where Manuel had his residence, the Emperor turned his attention, among other decorations, to a magnificent tapestry, a kind of Gobelin, with a reproduction of spring. In his leisure time, the Emperor made a fine description written in a rather jocose style of this reproduction of spring on "a royal woven curtain." This essay of Manuel exists today.[160]

The battle of Angora and its significance to Byzantium.—Meanwhile, the fruitless stay of Manuel in Paris began to seem endless. At this time an event which had taken place in Asia Minor induced the Emperor to leave France at once and to return to Constantinople. In July, 1402, was fought the famous battle of Angora, by which Timur (Tamerlane) defeated Bayazid and thereby relieved Constantinople from immediate danger. The news of this exceedingly important event reached Paris only two and a half months after the battle. The Emperor prepared quickly for his return journey and came back

---

[159] *Chronicon Adae de Usk*, ed. E. M. Thompson (2nd ed., 1904), 57; in English, 220.

[160] Migne, *Patrologia Graeca*, CLVI, 577–

80. Russian translation of this essay in A. A. Vasiliev, "The Journey of Manuel II Palaeologus," *Journal of the Ministry of Public Instruction*, XXXIX (1912), 58–60.

to the capital via Genoa and Venice after three years and a half of absence. The Slavonic city on the Adriatic, Ragusa (Dubrovnik), hoping that the Emperor would stop there on his way home, made elaborate preparations to welcome him. But he passed by without stopping.[161] In memory of his stay in France, he presented to the abbey of St. Denis near Paris an illuminated manuscript of Dionysius the Areopagite, preserved today in the Louvre. Among the miniatures of this manuscript is the picture of the Emperor, his wife, and their three sons. Manuel's picture is of great interest, because the Turks found and admired in his features a strong resemblance to Muhammed, the founder of Islam. Bayazid, reported the Byzantine historian Phrantzes, said of Manuel: "One who does not know that he is Emperor would say from his appearance that he is Emperor."[162]

The fruitlessness of Manuel's journey to western Europe, as far as the substantial needs of the Empire were concerned, is evident; both historians and chroniclers of the time recognized the lack of result and pointed it out in their annals.[163] But this journey is of great interest examined from the point of view of the information acquired by western Europe about the Byzantine Empire in the period of its fall. This journey is an episode in the cultural intercourse between West and East at the end of the fourteenth and beginning of the fifteenth century, in the epoch of the Italian Renaissance.

The battle of Angora had great importance for the last days of the Byzantine Empire. Towards the end of the fourteenth century, the Mongol empire, which had fallen into pieces, was unified again under the power of Timur or Tamerlane (Timur-Lenk, which means in translation "iron-lame," Timur the Lame). Timur had undertaken on a large scale many devastating expeditions into southern Russia, northern India, Mesopotamia, Persia, and Syria. His marches were accompanied by atrocious cruelties. Thousands of men were slain, cities ruined, fields destroyed. A Byzantine historian wrote: "When Timur's Mongols left one city to go to another, they left it so deserted and abandoned, that in it was heard neither barking of dog, nor cackling of fowl, nor cry of child."[164]

Entering Asia Minor after his Syrian expedition, Timur clashed with the Ottoman Turks. Sultan Bayazid hastened from Europe to Asia Minor to meet Timur, and there, at the city of Angora (Ancyra), in 1402, was fought a bloody battle, which ended in the complete defeat of the Turks. Bayazid himself fell a prisoner to Timur; he shortly after died in captivity. Timur did not remain in Asia Minor. He undertook an expedition against China, and on his way

[161] See M. Andreeva, "Zur Reise Manuels II. Palaiologos nach West-Europa," *Byzantinische Zeitschrift*, XXXIV (1934), 37–47.

[162] George Phrantzes, *Annales*, I, 39; Bonn ed., 117.

[163] *Ibid.*, I, 15; Bonn ed., 62. *Chronicon Tarvisinum*, in Muratori, *Scriptores rerum italicarum*, XIX, 794.

[164] Michael Ducas, *Historia byzantina*, XVII; Bonn ed., 76–77.

there died. After his death, the whole huge Mongol Empire fell to pieces and lost its significance. But after their defeat at Angora, the Turks were so weakened that for a time they were unable to take decisive steps against Constantinople; thereby the existence of the dying Empire was prolonged for another fifty years.

In spite of Manuel's poor success, he did not give up his plans after his return from western Europe but continued to seek for the help of the West against the Turks. There are two very interesting letters addressed by Manuel to the kings of Aragon, Martin V (1395–1410) and Ferdinand I (1412–1416). In the first, which was transmitted to Martin through the agency of the famous Byzantine humanist Manuel Chrysoloras, who was at that time in Italy, Manuel informed Martin that he was sending him, at his request, some precious relics, and begged him to convey to Constantinople the money which had been collected in Spain to help the Empire.[165] Chrysoloras' mission, however, came to nothing. Later, during a voyage to Morea, Manuel wrote another letter from Thessalonica, this time addressed to Ferdinand I. It shows that Ferdinand had promised Manuel's son Theodore, the despot of Morea, to come there with a considerable army to aid the Christians in general and Manuel in particular. Manuel wrote to express his hope of meeting Ferdinand in Morea, but Ferdinand never came.[166]

The situation in the Peloponnesus.—In the last fifty years of the existence of the remains of the Byzantine Empire, the Peloponnesus, rather unexpectedly, attracted the attention of the central government. As the territory of the Empire was reduced to Constantinople, the adjoining portion of Thrace, one or two islands in the Archipelago, Thessalonica, and the Peloponnesus, obviously next to Constantinople the Peloponnesus was the most important part of the Greek possessions. Contemporaries discovered that it was an ancient and purely Greek country, that the inhabitants were real Hellenes and not Romans, and that nowhere else could be created a basis for continuing the struggle against the Ottomans. While northern Greece had already fallen a prey to the Turks and the rest of ancient Greece was on the point of succumbing to the Turkish yoke, in the Peloponnesus there arose a center of Greek national spirit and Hellenic patriotism, which was powerfully affected by a dream, delusive from the historical point of view, of regenerating the Empire and opposing the might of the Ottoman state.

[165] See C. Marinescu, "Manuel II Paléologue et les rois d'Aragon. Commentaire sur quatre lettres inédites en latin, expediées par la chancellerie byzantine," *Bulletin de la section historique de l'Académie roumaine,* XI (1924), 194–95, 198–99.

[166] *Ibid.,* 195–96, 200–201: "Vestra Excellen-tia illustri filio nostro, despoti Moree Porfirogenito, notificaverat qualiter accedere intendebat pro communi utilitate christianorum et specialiter nostra ad dictas partes Moree cum potencia maxima." See D. A. Zakythinos, *Le Despotat Grec de Morée,* 168.

After the Fourth Crusade, the Peloponnesus (or Morea) passed into the power of the Latins. At the beginning of the reign of the restorer of the Byzantine Empire, Michael VIII Palaeologus, the prince of Achaia, William Villehardouin, was captured by the Greeks and gave as ransom three strongholds: Monembasia, Maina, and the recently built Mistra. Since the Greek power in the Peloponnesus was slowly but continuously increasing at the expense of the Latin possessions, the Byzantine province which had been formed there became by the middle of the fourteenth century so important that it was reorganized as a separate despotat and made the appanage of the second son of the Constantinopolitan emperor, who became a sort of viceroy of the emperor in the Peloponnesus. At the end of the fourteenth century the Peloponnesus was mercilessly devastated by the Turks. Having lost all hope of defending the country with his own forces, the Despot of Morea proposed to yield his possessions to the Knights of the Order of Hospitalers of St. John, who at that time held the island of Rhodes, and only the popular insurrection at Mistra, capital of the Despotat, which burst out at this proposal, prevented him from doing so. The weakness of the Ottoman Turks after the defeat of Angora made it possible for the Peloponnesus to recover a little and to hope for better times.[167]

The chief city of the Despotat of Morea, Mistra, medieval Sparta, residence of the Despot, was in the fourteenth century and at the beginning of the fifteenth a political and cultural center of reviving Hellenism. Here were the tombs of the Despots of Morea. Here John Cantacuzene died at a very advanced age, and here he was buried. While the condition of the country people made a contemporary, Mazaris, afraid that he himself would become a barbarian,[168] at the court of the Despot, in his castle of Mistra, was a cultural center which was attracting educated Greeks, scholars, sophists, and courtiers. It is related that in the fourteenth century, at Sparta, there existed a school for copiers of ancient manuscripts. Gregorovius justly compared the court of Mistra with some courts of Italian princes of the Renaissance.[169] The famous Byzantine scholar, humanist, and philosopher, Gemistus Plethon, lived at the court of the Despot of Morea during the reign of Manuel II.

In 1415, Manuel himself visited the Peloponnesus, where his second son Theodore was Despot at the time. The Emperor's first measure to protect the peninsula against future invasions was the construction of a wall with numerous towers on the Isthmus of Corinth. The wall was erected on the site of the rampart which in the fifth century B.C. the Peloponnesians had raised on the approach of Xerxes; this was restored in the third century A.D. by the

---

[167] Zakythinos, *ibid.,* is a very fine work.
[168] Mazari Ἐπιδημία Μάζαρι ἐν Ἅιδου; A.

Ellissen, *Analekten der mittel- und neugriechischen Litteratur,* IV, 230.
[169] *Geschichte der Stadt Athen,* II, 240–83.

Emperor Valerian when he fortified Greece against the Goths; and finally it was constructed again by Justinian the Great when Greece was threatened by the Huns and Slavs.[170] In preparation for this same Turkish danger in the fifteenth century, the predecessor of Theodore had established numerous colonies of Albanians in some desert regions of the Peloponnesus, and Manuel II, who delivered his funeral oration,[171] praised him for this precaution.

The projected reforms of Gemistus Plethon.—In Peloponnesian affairs in that time there were two interesting contemporary writers, quite different in character. One was the Byzantine scholar and humanist, Gemistus Plethon, a philhellenist obsessed by the idea that the Peloponnesian population was of the purest and most ancient Hellenic blood and that from the Peloponnesus had come the noblest and most famous families "of the Hellenes," who had achieved "the greatest and most celebrated deeds."[172] The other was Mazaris, author of the *Sojourn of Mazaris in Hades,* "undoubtedly," as K. Krumbacher said, perhaps not without exaggeration, "the worst of the hitherto known imitations of Lucian,"[173] a kind of libel, in which the author describes sarcastically the customs and manners of the Peloponnesus-Morea, deriving the latter name in the form of *Mora* (μώρα) from the Greek word *moria* (μωρία)[174] meaning silliness, folly. In contrast to Plethon, Mazaris distinguished seven nationalities in the population of the Peloponnesus: Greeks (in Mazaris, Lacedaemonians and Peloponnesians), Italians (i.e. the remains of the Latin conquerors), Slavs (Sthlavinians), Illyrians (i.e. Albanians), Egyptians (Gipsies), and Jews.[175] These statements of Mazaris are historical truth. Although both writers, the learned utopian Plethon as well as the satirist Mazaris, must be used with caution, both of them afford rich and interesting cultural data on the Peloponnesus of the first half of the fifteenth century.

To the time of Manuel II should be referred two interesting "accounts" or "addresses" written by Gemistus Plethon on the urgency of political and social reform for the Peloponnesus. One of these pamphlets was addressed to the Emperor, and the other to the Despot of Morea, Theodore. The German historian, Fallmerayer, was the first, in his *History of the Peninsula of Morea,* to draw the attention of scholars to the importance of those schemes of the Hellenic dreamer.[176]

[170] See Miller, *Latins in the Levant,* 377.

[171] Manuel Palaeologus, *Oratio funebris;* Migne, *Patrologia Graeca,* CLVI, 212–13.

[172] Gemistus Plethon, *Oratio prima,* 2–3; ed. Ellissen, *Analekten,* IV (2), 42.

[173] *Geschichte der Byzantinischen Litteratur,* 494.

[174] Mazari, ’Επιδημία Μάζαρι ἐν ″Αιδου, 2, Ellissen, *Analekten,* IV (7), 192.

[175] Mazari, *ibid.,* 22. Ellissen, *ibid.,* 239.

[176] *Halbinsel Morea,* II, 300–66. See H. F. Tozer, "A Byzantine Reformer (Gemistus Plethon)," *Journal of Hellenic Studies,* VII (1886), 353–80. J. Dräseke, "Plethons und Bessarions Denkschriften über die Angelegenheiten im Peloponnes," *Neue Jahrbücher für das klassische Altertum,* XXVII (1911), 102–19.

Plethon had in view the regeneration of the Peloponnesus, and for this purpose he drew up a plan for a radical change in the social system and the treatment of the land problem.[177] According to Plethon, society should be divided into three classes: (1) the cultivators of the soil (ploughmen, diggers, for example, diggers for vineyards, and shepherds); (2) those who provide instruments of work (i.e. those who care for oxen, cattle, and so on);[178] and (3) those who have the care of safety and order, i.e., the army, government, and state officials; at the head of all should be an emperor—basileus. Opposed to mercenary troops, Plethon advocated the formation of an indigenous Greek army; and that the army may devote all their time and attention to performing their proper duties, Plethon divided the population into two categories: tax-payers, and those who render military service; the soldiery should not be liable to taxation. The portion of the taxable population which takes no part in administration and defense was called by Plethon the Helots. Private land ownership was abolished; "the whole land, as it seems to have been established by nature, should be the common property of the population; every one who will may plant and build a home where he would, and till the soil as much as he would and could."[179] These were the chief points of Plethon's report. His scheme shows the influence of Plato, whom the Byzantine humanist greatly admired. It will remain an interesting cultural document of the Byzantine renaissance of the epoch of the Palaeologi. Several scholars indicate in Plethon's scheme some points of analogy with parts of the *Social Contract* of Jean Jacques Rousseau, and with the ideas of Saint-Simon.[180]

Thus, on the eve of the final catastrophe, Plethon was proposing to Manuel II a plan of reforms for regenerated Hellas. The French Byzantinist, Ch. Diehl, wrote: "While Constantinople is weakened and falling, a Greek state tries to be born in Morea. And however vain these aspirations may seem and however sterile these wishes may appear, nevertheless this recovery of the consciousness of Hellenism and this conception of and obscure preparation for a better future is one of the most interesting and remarkable phenomena of Byzantine history."[181]

The siege of Constantinople in 1422.—Until the beginning of the third decade of the fifteenth century, the relations between Manuel and Bayazid's successor, Muhammed I, a noble representative of the Ottoman state, were

---

[177] Gemistus Plethon, *De Rebus Peloponnesiacis Orationes duae,* ed. Ellissen, *Analekten,* IV (2); ed. Migne, *Patrologia Graeca,* CLX, 821–66.

[178] *Ibid.,* Oratio I, par. 12, Oratio II, par. 13; ed. Migne, *Patrologia Graeca,* CLX, 829, 853. See Tozer, "Gemistus Plethon," *Journal of Hellenic Studies,* VII (1886), 370; he called the second class "those employed in trade and manufactures," or "the trading class" (372).

[179] Gemistus Plethon, *Oratio I,* par. 18; ed. Ellissen, *Analekten,* IV (2), 53; ed. Migne, *Patrologia Graeca,* CLX, 833.

[180] See Ellissen, *Analekten,* IV (2), 143, n. 3. Tozer, "Gemistus Plethon," *Journal of Hellenic Studies,* VII (1886), 379.

[181] *Études byzantines,* 232.

marked, in spite of some errors on the part of the Emperor, by confidence and peace. Once, with the Emperor's knowledge, the sultan passed through a suburb of Constantinople, where he was met by Manuel. Each sovereign remained on his own galley, and conversing from the galleys in a friendly manner, crossed the straits to the Asiatic coast where the sultan pitched his tents; but the Emperor did not descend from his galley. During dinner, the monarchs sent each other their most delicate dishes from their tables.[182] But under Muhammed's successor, Murad II, circumstances changed.

In the last years of his life, Manuel withdrew from state affairs and entrusted them to his son, John, who had neither experience nor the poise and noble character of his father. John insisted on supporting one of the Turkish pretenders to the sultan's throne; an attempt at revolt failed and the infuriated Murad II decided to besiege Constantinople and crush at once this long-coveted city.

But the Ottoman forces, which had not had time enough to recover after the defeat of Angora and which were weakened by internal complications, were not yet ready to deal such a blow. In 1422, the Turks besieged Constantinople. In Byzantine literature there is a special work on this siege written by a contemporary, John Cananus, entitled, "A narrative of the Constantinopolitan wars of 6930 (= 1422), when Amurat-bey attacked the city with a great army and would have taken it if the Blessed Mother of God had not preserved it."[183] A strong Muhammedan army equipped with various war machinery attempted to take the city by storm but it was repulsed by the heroic efforts of the population of the capital. Some complications within the Ottoman Empire compelled the Turks to give up the siege. The capital's relief from danger was, as always, connected in popular tradition with the intercession of the Mother of God, the constant protectress of Constantinople. Meanwhile, the Turkish troops were not satisfied to attack the capital; after an unsuccessful attempt to take Thessalonica, they marched south into Greece where they destroyed the wall on the Isthmus of Corinth built by Manuel, and devastated Morea.[184] Manuel's co-emperor John VIII spent about a year in Venice, Milan, and Hungary in search of aid. According to the peace made with the Turks, the Emperor pledged himself to continue to pay the sultan a definite tribute, and delivered to him several cities in Thrace. The territory of Constantinople was growing still more limited. After this siege, the capital dragged out a pitiful existence for about thirty years in anxious expectation of its unavoidable ruin.

[182] George Phrantzes, *Annales*, I, 37; Bonn ed., 111–12.

[183] John Cananus, *De Constantinopoli anno 1422 oppugnata narratio*, Bonn ed., 457.

[184] Gemistus as an eyewitness described Turkish atrocities in Greece. His lengthy poem, "Ad S. D. N. Leonem X. Pont. Maximi Ioannis Gemisti Graeci a secretis Anconae Protrepticon et Promosticon," is given by C. Sathas, *Documents inédits relatifs a l'histoire de la Grèce au moyen âge*, VIII, 546–91, especially 548–50. See also *ibid.*, IX, vii.

In 1425, the paralyzed Manuel passed away. With a feeling of profound mourning the mass of the population of the capital followed the hearse of the dead Emperor. Such a crowd of mourning people had never been seen at the burial of any of his predecessors.[185] A special investigator of Manuel's activity, Berger de Xivrey, wrote: "This feeling will seem sincere to whoever will remember all the trials which this sovereign shared with his people, all his endeavors to help them, and the deep sympathy of thought and feeling he always had for them."[186]

The most important event of the time of Manuel was the battle of Angora, which delayed the fall of Constantinople for fifty years. But even this brief relief from the Ottoman danger was attained not by the strength of the Byzantine emperor, but by the Mongol power accidentally created in the east. The chief event upon which Manuel had relied, the rising of western Europe in a crusade, had not taken place. The siege and storm of Constantinople by the Turks in 1422 was only a prologue to the siege and storm of 1453. In estimating relations with the Turks in Manuel's time one must not lose sight of the personal influence which the Emperor had with the Turkish sultans and which several times delayed the final doom of the perishing Empire.

John VIII (1425–48) and the Turkish menace.—Under John VIII the territory of the Empire was reduced to the most modest extent. Shortly before his father's death John had been forced to cede several cities of Thrace to the sultan. After John had become sole ruler of the Empire, his power extended, properly speaking, over Constantinople and the nearest surrounding country. But the rest of the Empire, for example, the Peloponnesus, Thessalonica, and some scattered cities in Thrace, were under the power of his brothers as separate principalities almost entirely independent.

In 1430, Thessalonica was conquered by the Turks. One of the brothers of John VIII, who was governing Thessalonica with the title of despot, realized that with his own forces he could not contend with the Turks, and sold the city to Venice for a sum of money. Venice in taking possession of this important commercial point pledged herself, according to Ducas, "to protect and nourish it, raise its prosperity, and make it a second Venice."[187] But the Turks, who already possessed the surrounding country, could not tolerate the establishment of Venice at Thessalonica. Under the personal leadership of the sultan, they laid siege to Thessalonica; the course and result of the siege are well described in a special work, *On the last capture of Thessalonica,* written by a contemporary, John Anagnostes (i.e., Reader).[188] The Latin garrison

[185] George Phrantzes, *Annales,* I, 40; Bonn ed., 121.

[186] "Mémoire sur Manuel Paléologue," *Mémoires de l'Institut de France,* XIX (2), 180.

[187] Michael Ducas, *Historia byzantina,* XXIX; Bonn ed., 197.

[188] *De extremo Thessalonicensi excidio,* Bonn ed., 481–528.

of Thessalonica was small and the population of the city regarded the new Venetian masters as aliens. They could not resist the Turks who, after a short siege, took the city by storm and exposed it to terrible destruction and outrage. The people were murdered without distinction of sex or age. Churches were turned into mosques, but the Church of St. Demetrius of Thessalonica, the chief patron of the city, was temporarily left to the Christians, though in a state of complete desolation.

The taking of Thessalonica by the Turks was also described in Greek verse by a high church official in Constantinople in his Chronicle on the Turkish Empire.[189] Some Greek folk songs were composed on this disastrous event.[190] The loss of Thessalonica impressed deeply both Venice and western Europe. The nearness of the decisive moment was of course also felt in the city of Constantinople.

An interesting description of Constantinople was written by a pilgrim returning from Jerusalem, a Burgundian knight, Bertrandon de la Broquière, who visited the capital of the Palaeologi at the beginning of the thirties, shortly after the fall of Thessalonica. He praised the good state of the walls, the land-walls in particular, but noticed some desolation in the city; he spoke for example of the ruins and remnants of two beautiful palaces destroyed, according to a tradition, by an Emperor at the command of a Turkish sultan. The Burgundian pilgrim visited the churches and other monuments of the capital, attended the solemn church services, saw in the church of St. Sophia the performance of a mystery on the subject of the three youths cast by Nebuchadnezzar into the fiery furnace, was charmed with the beauty of the Byzantine Empress, who came from Trebizond, and told the Emperor, who was interested in the fate of Joan of Arc, who had just been burnt at Rouen, "the whole truth" about the famous "Maid of Orléans."[191] The same pilgrim, from his observations of the Turks, believed it possible to expel them from Europe and even to regain Jerusalem. He wrote: "It seems to me that the noble people and the good government of the three nations I have mentioned, i.e., the French,

---

[189] Ἱέρακος χρονικὸν περὶ τῆς τῶν Τούρκων βασιλείας. Sathas, *Bibliotheca graeca medii aevi*, I, 256–57, lines 360–88; the same fragment is given in "Ἡ ἐν Θεσσαλονίκῃ μονὴ τῶν Βλαταίων καὶ τὰ μετόχια αὐτῆς," *Byzantinische Zeitschrift*, VIII (1899), 421; a brief Greek note on the fall of Thessalonica on pp. 403–4. S. Lampros, "Τρεῖς ἀνέκδοτοι μονῳδίαι εἰς τὴν ὑπὸ τῶν Τούρκων ἅλωσιν τῆς Θεσσαλονίκης," *Νέος Ἑλληνομνήμων*, V (1908), 369–91 (two pieces in verse, and one in prose).

[190] See Florence McPherson, "Historical Notes on Certain Modern Greek Folk-songs,"

Journal of Hellenic Studies, X (1889), 86–87.

[191] La Broquière, *Voyage d'outremer*, ed. Schefer, 150–65. See A. A. Vasiliev, "La Guerre de Cent Ans et Jeanne d'Arc dans la tradition byzantine," *Byzantion*, III (1926), 249. Some news of Joan of Arc penetrated to Ragusa. See N. Iorga, *Notes et extraits pour servir à l'histoire des Croisades*, II, 272: "on parle 'd'una mamoleta virgine, la qual gli è (al rè Carlo) apparuta maravigliosamente, la qual rege et guida lo suo exercito,'" (from the Archives of Ragusa, April 30–December 28, 1430, Nouvelles de France).

English, and German, are rather formidable, and, if they are united in sufficient number, will be able to reach Jerusalem by land."[192]

Realizing the coming danger to the capital from the Turks, John VIII undertook the great work of restoring the walls of Constantinople. Many inscriptions on the walls preserved today with the name of "John Palaeologus
Autocrat in Christ," testify to the Christian Emperor's difficult last attempt to
restore the fortifications of Theodosius the Younger, which had once appeared
inaccessible.

But this did not suffice for the struggle with the Ottomans. Like his predecessors, John VIII hoped to receive real help against the Turks from the West,
with the co-operation of the pope. For this purpose the Emperor himself with
the Greek patriarch and a brilliant retinue sailed for Italy. The result of this
journey was the conclusion of the famous Union of Florence. As far as real
help to Byzantium was concerned, however, the imperial journey to Italy was
of no avail.

Pope Eugenius IV preached a crusade and succeeded in arousing to war
against the Turks the Hungarians, Poles, and Roumanians. A crusading army
was formed under the command of the king of Poland and Hungary, Vladislav, and the famous Hungarian hero and chief, John Hunyadi. In the battle at
Varna, in 1444, the crusaders were crushed by the Turks. Vladislav fell in
battle. With the remnants of the army, John Hunyadi retreated to Hungary.
The battle of Varna was the last attempt of western Europe to come to the
help of perishing Byzantium. Thereafter Constantinople was left to its fate.[193]

Some documents from the archives of Barcelona, comparatively recently
published, have revealed the aggressive plans of the famous Maecenas of the
epoch of the Renaissance, the king of Aragon, Alfonso V the Magnanimous,
who died in 1458. Having reunited Sicily and Naples under his power for a
short time in the middle of the fifteenth century, he was planning to carry
on a vast aggressive campaign in the East, which was similar to the grandiose
plans of Charles of Anjou. Constantinople was one of Alfonso's goals, and
the idea of a crusade against the Turks never left him. For a long time he had
realized that, if the growing might and "insolent prosperity" of the Ottomans
were not put down, he would have no security for the maritime confines of
his realm. But Alfonso's ambitious plans were not realized and the Turks were
never seriously menaced by this talented and brilliant humanist and politician.[194]

---

[192] *Ibid.*, 230.

[193] Aziz Suryal Atiya, *Crusade in the Later
Middle Ages;* see a review by O. Halecki, *Byzantion*, XV (1940–41), 473–83. Halecki, *The
Crusade of Varna. A Discussion of Controversial Problems,* 96. A fine monograph.

[194] See F. Cerone, "La politica orientale di
Alfonso d'Aragona," *Archivio storico per le
provincie Napolitane,* XXVII (1902), 425–56,
555–634; XXVIII (1903), 167. Norden, *Das

After the victory of the Turks at Varna, John VIII, who had taken no part in the crusading expedition, entered immediately into negotiations with the sultan, whom he endeavored to soften with presents, and he succeeded in keeping peaceful relations with him up to the end of his reign.

Although in relations with the Turks, Byzantium under John VIII suffered continuous and bitter failures, the Greek arms gained a considerable victory, though of short duration, in the Peloponnesus (Morea), an appanage nearly independent from the central government. Besides the Byzantine possessions, there were in the Peloponnesus the remnants of the principality of Achaia and some other places, especially in the very south of the peninsula which belonged to Venice. At the beginning of the fifteenth century Venice set herself the goal of subduing the portion of the Peloponnesus which was still in Latin hands; for this purpose she entered into negotiations with the different rulers in the peninsula. On one hand, the Republic of St. Mark wanted to take possession of the wall on the Isthmus of Corinth, which had been built under Manuel II, in order to offer adequate resistance to the Turkish invasions. On the other, Venice was attracted by her commercial interests, because, according to the information gathered by the representative of the Republic, the resources of the country in gold, silver, silk, honey, corn, raisins, and other things promised great advantages. During the reign of John VIII, however, the troops of the Greek despotat in Morea opened hostilities against the Latins, quickly gained the Latin part of the Peloponnesus, and thereby put an end to Frankish power in Morea. From then to the time of the Turkish conquest, the whole peninsula belonged to the family of the Palaeologi; Venice maintained only the points in the south, which she had possessed before.

One of the Despots of Morea, Constantine, John VIII's brother, who was to be the last emperor of Byzantium, took advantage of some difficulties of the Turks in the Balkan peninsula to march north with his troops across the Isthmus of Corinth into middle and northern Greece, where the Turks were already making their conquests. After his victory over the Christians at Varna, Sultan Murad II considered the invasion of Constantine into northern Greece as an insult to him; he marched south, broke through the fortified wall on the Isthmus of Corinth, terribly devastated the Peloponnesus, and carried away into captivity a great number of Greeks. The horrified Despot Constantine was glad to make peace on the sultan's terms; he remained Despot of Morea and pledged himself to pay a tribute to the sultan.

Papsttum und Byzanz, 731–33. C. Marinescu is preparing, on the basis of the rich store of unpublished documents of the *Archivios de la Corona de Aragon* in Barcelona, a work especially devoted to the relations of Alfonso V and the Orient. See "Manuel II Paleologue et les rois d'Aragon," *Bulletin de la section historique de l'Académie roumaine,* XI (1924), 197. See also *Compte-rendu du deuxième Congrés international des études byzantines* (1929), 162.

Under Constantine Palaeologus the famous traveler, archeologist, and merchant of that time, Cyriacus of Ancona, visited Mistra, where he was graciously received by the despot (*Constantinum cognomento Dragas*) and his dignitaries. At his court Cyriacus met Gemistus Plethon, "the most learned man of his age," and Nicholas Chalcocondyles, son of his Athenian friend George, a young man very well versed in Latin and Greek.[195] Nicholas Chalcocondyles can have been none other than the future historian Laonikos Chalcocondyles, for the name Laonikos is merely Nicolaos, Nicholas, slightly changed. During his first stay at Mistra, under the Despot Theodore Palaeologus, in 1437, Cyriacus had visited ancient monuments at Sparta and copied Greek inscriptions.[196]

Constantine XI (1449–53) and the capture of Constantinople by the Turks.—The territory which recognized the power of the last Byzantine emperor was confined to Constantinople with its nearest environs in Thrace, and the major part of the Peloponnesus or Morea at some distance from the capital, and governed by the Emperor's brothers.

Honesty, generosity, energy, valor, and love of country were Constantine's characteristics, vouched for by many Greek sources of his time and by his own conduct during the siege of Constantinople. An Italian humanist, Francesco Filelfo, who during his stay at Constantinople, knew Constantine personally before his ascension to the throne, in one of his letters calls the Emperor a man "of pious and lofty spirit (*pio et excelso animo*)."[197]

The strong and terrible adversary of Constantine was Muhammed II, twenty-one years old, who combined rude outbursts of harsh cruelty, bloodthirstiness, and many of the baser vices, with an interest in science, art, and education, energy, and the talents of a general, statesman, and organizer. A Byzantine historian relates that he occupied himself enthusiastically with the sciences, especially astrology, read the tales of the deeds of Alexander of Macedon, Julius Caesar, and the emperors of Constantinople, and spoke five languages besides Turkish.[198] Oriental sources praise his piety, justice, clemency, and protection of scholars and poets. Historians of the nineteenth and

[195] See Cyriacus' description of the Peloponnesus, first published by R. Sabbadini, "Ciriaco d'Ancona e la sua descrizione autografa del Peloponneso trasmessa da Leonardo Botta," *Miscellanea Ceriani*, 203–4. On Cyriacus of Ancona see G. Castellani, "Un Traité inédit en Grec de Cyriaque d'Ancône," *Revue des études grecques*, IX (1896), 225–28. E. Ziebarth, "Κυριακὸς ὁ ἐξ Ἀγκῶνος ἐν Ἠπείρῳ," Ἠπειρωτικὰ Χρονικά, II (1926), 110–19; some additions and corrections by Δ. Καμπουρογλοῦ, *ibid.*, III (1928), 223–24; he gives an exact date for Cyriacus' death: 1452 (p. 224). F. Pall, "Ciriaco d'Ancona e la crociata contro i Turchi," *Bulletin de la section historique de l'Académie roumaine*, XX (1937), 9–60. See also Zakythinos, *Le Despotat Grec*, 231–35.

[196] See *Epigrammata reperta per Illyricum a Cyriaco Anconitano apud Liburniam*, xxxvii. Zakythinos, *Le Despotat Grec*, 236.

[197] Iorga, *Notes et extraits pour servir à l'histoire des Croisades*, IV, 83.

[198] George Phrantzes, *Annales*, I, 32; Bonn ed., 93, 95.

twentieth centuries vary in their estimation of Muhammed II; they range from denying him all positive qualities[199] to acknowledging him as a man of genius.[200] The desire to conquer Constantinople was an obsession with the young sultan, who, as the historian Ducas said, "by night and day, going to bed and getting up, within his palace and without, turned over and over in his mind the military actions and means by which he might take possession of Constantinople." He spent sleepless nights drawing on paper the plan of the city and its fortifications, pointing out the places where it could be most easily attacked.[201]

The pictures of both these adversaries survive, those of Constantine Palaeologus on seals and in some later manuscripts,[202] and those of Muhammed II on the medals struck by Italian artists in the fifteenth century in honor of the sultan and in some portraits, particularly one painted by the famous Venetian artist, Gentile Bellini, who spent a short time (in 1479–80) at Constantinople at the end of the reign of Muhammed.[203]

Having decided to deal the final blow to Constantinople, Muhammed set to work with extreme circumspection. First of all, north of the city, on the European shore of the Bosphorus, at its narrowest point, he built a powerful stronghold with towers, the majestic remnants of which are still to be seen (Rumeli-Hisar); the guns placed there hurled stone cannon balls which were enormous for the time.

When the erection of the stronghold on the Bosphorus was known, there came from the Christian population of the capital, Asia, Thrace, and the islands, from all directions, as Ducas said, exclamations of despair. "Now the end of the city has come; now we see the signs of the ruin of our race; now the days of Antichrist are at hand; what is to become of us or what have we to do? . . . Where are the saints who protect the city?"[204] Another contemporary and eyewitness, who lived through all the horrors of the siege

[199] For example, Ellissen, *Analekten*, III, 87–93. On Muhammed's interest in science, poetry, and art, see J. Karabaček, *Abendländische Künstler zu Konstantinopel im XV. und XVI. Jahrhundert*, 2.

[200] N. Iorga, *Geschichte des Osmanischen Reiches*, II, 3.

[201] Michael Ducas, *Historia byzantina*, XXXV; Bonn ed., 249, 252.

[202] See Lampros, "Αἱ εἰκόνες Κωνσταντίνου τοῦ Παλαιολόγου," Νέος Ἑλληνομνήμων, III (1906), 229–42; Lampros, "Νέαι εἰκόνες Κωνσταντίνου τοῦ Παλαιολόγου," *ibid.*, IV (1907), 238–40; VI (1909), 399–408. S. Lampros, *Empereurs byzantins. Catalogue illustré*

de la collection de portraits des empereurs de Byzance, 57–58.

[203] See L. Thuasne, *Gentile Bellini et Sultan Mohammed II. Notes sur le séjour du peintre vénitien à Constantinople (1479–1480)*, 50–51; in this book Muhammed's pictures and medals are reproduced. Karabaček, *Abendländische Künstler zu Konstantinopel*, I, 24–49; this work has many illustrations. Before World War I the famous picture of Bellini was in the private collection of Lady Enid Layard at Venice; during the war it was transferred to London. See Karabaček, *ibid.*, 44.

[204] *Historia byzantina*, XXXIV; Bonn ed., 238.

of Constantinople, the author of the precious *Journal of the Siege,* a Venetian, Nicolò Barbaro, wrote, "This fortification is exceedingly strong from the sea, so that it is absolutely impossible to capture it, for on the shore and walls are standing bombards in very great number; on the land side the fortification is also strong, though less so than from the sea."[205] This stronghold put an end to the communication of the capital with the north and the ports of the Black Sea, for all foreign vessels, both on entering and leaving the Bosphorus, were intercepted by the Turks; in case of siege Constantinople would be deprived of the supply of corn from the ports of the Black Sea. It was very easy for the Turks to carry out these measures, because, opposite the European stronghold, there towered on the Asiatic shore of the Bosphorus the fortifications which had been built at the end of the fourteenth century by the Sultan Bayazid (Anatoli-Hisar). Next Muhammed invaded the Greek possessions in Morea, in order to prevent the Despot of Morea from coming to the aid of Constantinople in case of emergency. After these preliminary steps Muhammed, this "pagan enemy of the Christian people,"[206] to quote Barbaro, began the siege of the great city.

Constantine made every possible effort adequately to meet his powerful adversary in the unequal struggle whose result, one may say, was foreordained. The Emperor had all possible corn supplies from the environs of the capital brought into the city and some repairs made on the city walls. The Greek garrison of the city numbered only a few thousands. Seeing the coming fatal danger, Constantine appealed to the West for help; but instead of the desired military support, a Roman cardinal, Greek by origin, Isidore, the former metropolitan of Moscow and participator in the Council of Florence, arrived in Constantinople, and in commemoration of the restored peace between the Eastern and Western churches, celebrated a union service in St. Sophia, which aroused the greatest agitation in the city population. One of the most prominent dignitaries of Byzantium, Lucas Notaras, uttered his famous words, "It is better to see in the city the power of the Turkish turban than that of the Latin tiara."[207]

The Venetians and Genoese took part in the defense of the capital. Constantine and the population of the city relied especially on a Genoese noble of great military reputation, John (Giovanni) Giustiniani, who arrived in Constantinople with two large vessels bringing seven hundred fighting men. Access to the Golden Horn was barred, as had already happened several times at dangerous moments in the past, by a massive iron chain. The remains of this

[205] *Giornale dell'assedio di Constantinopoli,* ed. E. Cornet, 2.
[206] *Ibid.,* 18.

[207] Michael Ducas, *Historia byzantina,* XXXVII; Bonn ed., 264.

chain, it was supposed, could be seen until recently in the Byzantine church of St. Irene, where the Ottoman Military-Historical Museum is now established.[208]

The military forces of Muhammed on land and sea which consisted, besides the Turks, of the representatives of different peoples whom he had conquered, largely exceeded the modest number of the defenders of Constantinople, the Greeks and some Latins, particularly Italians.

One of the most important events in all world history was imminent.

The very fact of Turkish siege and capture of the "City protected by God," Constantinople, left a deep mark in the sources, which, in various languages and from different points of view, described the last moments of the Byzantine Empire and allow one to follow, sometimes literally by days and hours, the development of the last act of this thrilling historical drama. The sources which exist are written in Greek, Latin, Italian, Slavonic, and Turkish.

The chief Greek sources vary in their estimation of the event. George Phrantzes, who participated in the siege, an intimate friend of the last Emperor, and a very well-known diplomat, who held high offices in the Empire, was full of boundless love for his Emperor-hero and for the house of the Palaeologi in general, and was opposed to the union of the Churches; he described the last days of Byzantium in order to restore the honor of the vanquished Constantine, his abused country, and the insulted Greek Orthodox faith. Another contemporary writer, the Greek Critobulus, who had passed over to the Turks and wished to prove his devotion to Muhammed II, dedicated his history, which shows strongly the influence of Thucydides, to the "greatest emperor, king of kings, Mehemet";[209] he related the last days of Byzantium from the point of view of a subject of the new Ottoman Empire, though he did not attack his Greek countrymen. A Greek of Asia Minor, Ducas, a supporter of the union, in which he saw the only means of security for the Empire, wrote from a standpoint favorable to the West, especially stressed the services and merits of the Genoese commander, Giustiniani, rather belittled the role of Constantine, but at the same time wrote not without love and pity for the Greeks. Finally, the fourth Greek historian of the last period of Byzantium, the only Athenian in Byzantine literature, Laonikos Chalcocondyles (or Chalcondyles), choosing as the main topic of his history not Byzantium, but the Turkish Empire, took a new and vast theme to describe— "the extraordinary evolution of the might of the young Ottoman Empire which was rising on the ruins of the Greek, Frankish, and Slavonic states";[210]

[208] At the present time this chain is believed to be a portion of the chain from the harbor of the island of Rhodes, which was brought to Constantinople by the Turks after the conquest of Rhodes.

[209] C. Müller, *Fragmenta historicorum graecorum*, V, 52.

[210] Krumbacher, *Geschichte der byzantinischen Litteratur*, 302. See also W. Miller, "The Last Athenian Historian: Laonikos

in other words, his work is general in character. Since, in addition to that, Laonikos was not an eyewitness of the last days of Constantinople, it has only secondary significance.

Among the most valuable sources written in Latin were several by authors who lived through the whole time of the siege at Constantinople. One was the appeal *To All the Faithful of Christ* (*Ad universos Christifideles de expugnatione Constantinopolis*) written by Cardinal Isidore, who narrowly escaped Turkish captivity. He begged all Christians to rise up in arms to defend the perishing Christian faith. The report to the pope of the archbishop of Chios, Leonard, who also escaped Turkish captivity, interpreted the great distress which had befallen Byzantium as a punishment for the Greeks' secession from the Catholic faith. Finally, a poem in verse, in four stanzas, "Constantinopolis," was composed by an Italian, Pusculus, who spent some time in Turkish captivity. He was an imitator of Virgil and to a certain extent of Homer. A zealous Catholic, he dedicated his poem to the pope and was, like Leonard, convinced that God had punished Byzantium for its schism.

Italian sources have given us the priceless *Journal of the siege of Constantinople,* written in the old Venetian dialect in a dry business style, by a noble Venetian, Nicolò Barbaro. He enumerated day by day the conflicts between the Greeks and Turks during the siege, and his work is therefore of the greatest importance for the reconstruction of the chronology of the siege.

In old Russian an important history of the capture of Tsargrad, "this great and terrible deed," was written by the "unworthy and humble Nestor Iskinder (Iskander)."[211] Probably a Russian by origin, he fought in the sultan's army and described truthfully and, as far as possible, day by day, the actions of the Turks during the siege and after the fall of the city. The story of the fall of Constantinople is also related in various Russian chronicles.

Finally, there are Turkish sources estimating the great event from the point of view of triumphant and victorious Islam and its brilliant representative, Muhammed II the Conqueror. Sometimes Turkish sources offer a collection of Turkish popular legends about Constantinople and the Bosphorus.[212]

Chalkokondyles," *Journal of Hellenic Studies,* XLII (1922), 38.

[211] *The Tale of Tsargrad* by Nestor-Iskander, ed. Abbot Leonides, *Pamyatniki drevney pismennosti,* LXII (1886), 43. For other Slavic accounts, see *Cambridge Medieval History,* IV, 888. A Russian text of the Tale, from the edition of 1853, is reprinted by N. Iorga, "Origines et prise de Constantinople," *Bulletin de la section historique de l'Académie roumaine,* XIII (1927), 89–105. The question now arises whether the original text of this tale is not Greek and whether the Slavic ac-

count of it may belong not to a Russian but to a Serbian. See N. Iorga, "Une Source négligée de la prise de Constantinople," *ibid.,* 65. B. Unbegaun, "Les Relations vieux-russes de la prise de Constantinople," *Revue des études slaves,* IX (1929), 13–38: on the Russian version of Iskander and on the old Russian translation of the account of Aeneas Sylvius of the capture of Constantinople by the Turks.

[212] See F. Babinger, *Geschichtsschreiber der Osmanen und ihre Werke,* 23–45 and *passim.*

This enumeration of the chief sources shows what rich and various information exists for the study of the problem of the siege and capture of Constantinople by the Turks.

At the beginning of April, 1453, the siege of the great city began. It was not only the incomparably greater military forces of the Turks that contributed to the success of the siege. Muhammed II, called by Barbaro, "this perfidious Turk, dog-Turk,"[213] was the first sovereign in history who had at his disposal a real park of artillery. The perfected Turkish bronze cannons, of gigantic size for that time, hurled to a great distance enormous stone shots, whose destructive blows the old walls of Constantinople could not resist. The Russian tale of Tsargrad states that "the wretched Muhammed" conveyed close to the city walls "cannons, arquebuses, towers, ladders, siege machinery, and other wall-battering devices."[214] The contemporary Greek historian, Critobulus, had a good understanding of the decisive role of artillery when he wrote that all the saps made by the Turks under the walls and their subterraneous passages "proved to be superfluous and involved only useless expense, as cannons decided everything."[215]

In the second half of the nineteenth century, in several places of Stamboul, one might still see on the ground the huge cannon shots which had hurtled over the walls and were lying in nearly the same places in which they had fallen in 1453. On April 20 the only piece of good fortune for the Christians in the whole siege took place: the four Genoese vessels which had come to the aid of Constantinople, defeated the Turkish fleet in spite of its far superior numbers. "One may easily imagine," wrote a recent historian of the siege and capture of the Byzantine capital, Schlumberger, "the indescribable joy of the Greeks and Italians. For a moment Constantinople considered itself saved."[216] But this success, of course, could have no real importance for the outcome of the siege.

On April 22 the city with the Emperor at its head was struck by an extraordinary and terrifying spectacle: the Turkish vessels were in the upper part of the Golden Horn. During the preceding night the sultan had succeeded in transporting the vessels from the Bosphorus by land into the Golden Horn; for this purpose a kind of wooden platform had been specially made in the valley between the hills, and the vessels were put on wheels and dragged over the platform by the exertions of a great number of "canaille," according to Barbaro,[217] who were at the sultan's disposal. The Greco-Italian fleet stationed

---

[213] *Giornale dell'assedio di Constantinopoli,* ed. Cornet, 20, 21.

[214] *Tale of Tsargrad,* ed. Leonides, 27. See also *The Tales of Tsargrad,* ed. V. Yakovlev, 92, 93. Iorga, "Origines et prise de Constantinople," *Bulletin de la section historique de l'Académie roumaine,* XIII (1927), 99.

[215] Critobulus, I, 31, 3; ed. C. Müller, 80.

[216] *Le Siège, la prise, et le sac de Constantinople par les Turcs en 1453,* 140.

[217] Barbaro, *Giornale dell'assedio di Constantinople,* ed. Cornet, 28.

in the Golden Horn beyond the chain was thereafter between two fires. The condition of the city became critical. The plan of the besieged garrison to burn the Turkish vessels in the Golden Horn at night was treacherously revealed to the sultan and prevented.

Meanwhile the heavy bombardment of the city, which did not cease for several weeks, brought the population to the point of complete exhaustion; men, women, children, priests, monks, and nuns were compelled, day and night, under cannon fire, to repair the numerous breaches in the walls. The siege had already lasted for fifty days. The tidings which reached the sultan, perhaps especially invented, of the possible arrival of a Christian fleet to aid the city, induced him to hasten the decisive blow to Constantinople. Imitating the famous orations in the history of Thucydides, Critobulus even gave the speech of Muhammed to the troops appealing to their courage and firmness; in this speech the sultan declared, "There are three conditions for successful war: to want (victory), to be ashamed(of dishonor, defeat), and to obey the leaders."[218] The assault was fixed for the night of May 29.

The old capital of the Christian East, anticipating the inevitable catastrophe and aware of the coming assault, spent the eve of the great day in prayer and tears. Upon the Emperor's order, religious processions followed by an enormous multitude of people singing "O Lord, have mercy on us," passed along the city walls. Men encouraged one another to offer a stubborn resistance to the Turks at the last hour of battle. In his long speech quoted by the Greek historian, Phrantzes,[219] Constantine incited the people to a valorous defense, but he clearly realized their doom when he said that the Turks "are supported by guns, cavalry, infantry, and their numerical superiority, but we rely on the name of the Lord our God and Saviour, and, secondly, on our hands and the strength which has been granted us by the power of God."[220] Constantine ended his speech thus: "I persuade and beg your love to accord adequate honor and obedience to your chiefs, everyone according to his rank, his military position, and service. Know this: if you sincerely observe all that I have commanded you, I hope that, with the aid of God, we shall avoid the just punishment sent by God."[221] In the evening of the same day service was celebrated in St. Sophia, the last Christian ceremony in the famous church. On the basis of Byzantine sources an English historian, E. Pears, gave a striking picture of this ceremony:

The great ceremony of the evening and one that must always stand out among the world's historic spectacles was the last Christian service held in the church of Holy Wisdom. . . . The emperor and such of the leaders as could be spared were

[218] Critobulus, I, 50, 2; ed. Müller, 91.
[219] George Phrantzes, *Annales.* III, 6; Bonn ed., 271–79.
[220] *Ibid.,* 273.
[221] *Ibid.,* 278.

present and the building was once more and for the last time crowded with Christian worshippers. It requires no great effort of imagination to picture the scene. The interior of the church was the most beautiful which Christian art had produced, and its beauty was enhanced by its still gorgeous fittings. Patriarch and cardinal, the crowd of ecclesiastics representing both the Eastern and Western churches; emperor and nobles, the last remnant of the once gorgeous and brave Byzantine aristocracy; priests and soldiers intermingled; Constantinopolitans, Venetians and Genoese, all were present, all realizing the peril before them, and feeling that in view of the impending danger the rivalries which had occupied them for years were too small to be worthy of thought. The emperor and his followers partook together of "the undefiled and divine mysteries," and said farewell to the patriarch. The ceremony was in reality a liturgy of death. The empire was in its agony and it was fitting that the service for its departing spirit should be thus publicly said in its most beautiful church and before its last brave emperor. If the scene so vividly described by Mr. Bryce of the coronation of Charles the Great and the birth of an empire is among the most picturesque in history, that of the last Christian service in St. Sophia is surely among the most tragic.[222]

Phrantzes wrote: "Who will tell of the tears and groans in the palace! Even a man of wood or stone could not help weeping."[223]

The general assault began on Tuesday night between one and two o'clock of May 28–29. At the given signal, the city was attacked simultaneously on three sides. Two attacks were repulsed. Finally, Muhammed organized very carefully the third and last attack. With particular violence the Turks attacked the walls close to the St. Romanus gate (or Pempton) where the Emperor was fighting. One of the chief defenders of the city, the Genoese Giustiniani, seriously wounded, was forced to abandon the battle; he was transported with difficulty to a vessel which succeeded in leaving the harbor for the Island of Chios. Either there or on the journey there Giustiniani died. His tomb is still preserved in Chios, but the Latin epitaph formerly in the church of S. Dominic in the citadel has apparently disappeared.[224]

The departure and death of Giustiniani was an irreparable loss to the besieged. In the walls more and more new breaches opened. The Emperor fought heroically as a simple soldier and fell in battle. No exact information exists about the death of the last Byzantine Emperor; for this reason his death soon became the subject of a legend which has obscured the historical fact.

[222] *The Destruction of the Greek Empire and the Story of the Capture of Constantinople by the Turks,* 330–31. A French paraphrase of Pear's account is given by Schlumberger, *Le Siège, la prise et le sac de Constantinople,* 269–70. R. Byron, *The Byzantine Achievement. An Historical Perspective A.D. 330– 1453,* 295–98.

[223] George Phrantzes, *Annales;* Bonn ed.,

279.

[224] See F. W. Hasluck, "The Latin Monuments of Chios," *Annual of the British School at Athens,* XVI (1909–10), 155 and fig. 18. The text of the inscription is given. The author remarked: "This is the tomb of the famous Giovanni Giustiniani, whose wound was the immediate cause of the fall of Constantinople" (p. 155).

After Constantine's death, the Turks rushed into the city inflicting terrible devastation. A great multitude of Greeks took refuge in St. Sophia, hoping for safety there. But the Turks broke in the entrance gate and poured into the church; they murdered and insulted the Greeks who were hiding there, without distinction of sex or age. The day of the capture of the city, or perhaps the next day, the sultan solemnly entered conquered Constantinople, and went into St. Sophia, where he offered up a Muhammedan prayer. Thereupon Muhammed took up his residence in the imperial palace of Blachernae.

According to the unanimous indication of the sources, the pillage of the city, as Muhammed had promised his soldiers, lasted for three days and three nights. The population was mercilessly murdered. The churches, with St. Sophia at the head, and the monasteries with all their wealth were robbed and polluted; private property was plundered. In these fatal days an innumerable mass of cultural material perished. Books were burnt or torn to pieces, trodden upon or sold for practically nothing. According to the statement of Ducas, an enormous number of books were loaded upon carts and scattered through various countries; a great number of books, the works of Aristotle and Plato, books of theology, and many others, were sold for one gold coin; the gold and silver which adorned the beautifully bound Gospels was torn off, and the Gospels themselves were either sold or thrown away; all the holy images were burnt, and the Turks ate meat boiled on the fire.[225] Nevertheless, some scholars, for example Th. Uspensky, believe that "the Turks in 1453 acted with more mildness and humanity than the crusaders who had seized Constantinople in 1204."[226]

A popular Christian tradition relates that at the moment of the appearance of the Turks in St. Sophia the liturgy was being celebrated; when the priest who held the holy sacrament saw the Muslims rush into the church, the altar wall miraculously opened before him and he entered it and disappeared; when Constantinople passes again into the hands of the Christians, the priest will come out from the wall and continue the liturgy.

About sixty years ago the local guides used to show tourists, in one of the remote places of Stamboul, a tomb purporting to be that of the last Byzantine Emperor, over which a simple oil lamp was burning. But of course this nameless tomb is not really that of Constantine; his burial place is unknown. In 1895 E. A. Grosvenor wrote, "Today, in the quarter of Abou Vefa in Stamboul, may be seen a lowly, nameless grave which the humble Greeks revere as that of Constantine. Timid devotion has strewn around it a few rustic ornaments. Candles were kept burning night and day at its side. Till eight years ago it

---

[225] Michael Ducas, *Historia byzantina,* XLII; Bonn ed., 312.

[226] "The Start and Development of the Eastern Problem," *Transactions of the Slavonic Charitable Society,* III (1886), 251.

was frequented, though secretly, as a place of prayer. Then the Ottoman Government interposed with severe penalties, and it has since been almost deserted. All this is but in keeping with the tales which delight the credulous or devout."[227]

It has usually been said that two days after the fall of Constantinople a western relief fleet arrived in the Archipelago, and learning the tidings of the fall of the city immediately sailed back again. On the basis of some new evidence, at the present time this fact is denied: neither papal vessels nor Genoese nor Aragonese sailed to the East in support of Constantinople.[228]

In 1456 Muhammed conquered Athens from the Franks;[229] shortly after all Greece with the Peloponnesus submitted to him. The ancient Parthenon, in the Middle Ages the church of the Holy Virgin, was, on the sultan's order, turned into a mosque. In 1461 the far-off Trebizond, capital of the once independent Empire, passed into the hands of the Turks. At the same time they took possession of the remnants of the Despotat of Epirus. The orthodox Byzantine Empire ceased to exist, and on its site the Muhammedan Ottoman (Othman) Empire was established and grew. Its capital was transferred from Hadrianople to Constantinople, which was called by the Turks Istamboul (Stamboul).[230]

Ducas, imitating the "lamentation" of Nicetas Acominatus after the sack of Constantinople by the Latins in 1204, bewailed the event of 1453. He began his lamentation:

O, city, city, head of all cities! O, city, city, center of the four quarters of the world! O, city, city, pride of the Christians and ruin of the barbarians! O, city, city, second paradise planted in the West, including all sorts of plants bending under the burden of spiritual fruits! Where is thy beauty, O, paradise? Where is the blessed strength of spirit and body of thy spiritual Graces? Where are the bodies of the Apostles of my Lord? . . . Where are the relics of the saints, where are the relics of the martyrs? Where is the corpse of the great Constantine and other Emperors. . . .[231]

Another contemporary, the Polish historian Jan Dlugosz, wrote in his *History of Poland:*

[227] *Constantinople,* I, 47.

[228] See G. B. Picotti, "Sulle navi papali in Oriente al tempo della caduta di Costantinopoli," *Nuovo Archivio Veneto,* N.S. XXII (1911), 416, 436.

[229] This is the correct date. Sometimes the year 1458 is given. See, e.g., Gregorovius, *Geschichte der Stadt Athen,* II, 381.

[230] The Arabian geographer al-Masudi, of the tenth century, said that the Greeks in his day spoke of their capital as Bulin (i.e. the Greek word Polin), also as Istan-Bulin (Greek στὴν πόλιν, *stinpolin*), and did not use the name of Constantinople. See G. LeStrange, *The Lands of the Eastern Caliphate,* 138, n. A. Andreadès, "De la population de Constantinople sous les empereurs byzantins," *Metron,* I (1920), 69, n. 2. Thus Istamboul (Stamboul) is the Greek *stinpolin,* "to the city."

[231] *Historia byzantina,* XLI; Bonn ed., 306. See nine texts, six in prose and three in verse, of different Monodies and Laments on the fall of Constantinople in S. Lampros, "Μονῳδίαι καὶ θρῆνοι ἐπὶ τῇ ἁλώσει τῆς Κωνσταντινουπόλεως," Νέος Ἑλληνομνήμων, V (1908), 190–269.

This Constantinopolitan defeat, both miserable and deplorable, was the enormous victory of the Turks, the extreme ruin of the Greeks, the infamy of the Latins; through it the Catholic faith was wounded, religion confused, the name of Christ reviled and oppressed. One of the two eyes of Christianity was plucked out; one of the two hands was amputated, since the libraries were burnt down and the doctrines of Greek literature destroyed, without which no one considers himself a learned man.[232]

A far-off Georgian chronicler remarked piously, "On the day when the Turks took Constantinople, the sun was darkened."[233]

The fall of Constantinople made a terrible impression upon western Europe, which first of all was seized with dismay at the thought of the future advances of the Turks. Moreover, the ruin of one of the chief centers of Christianity, schismatic though it was from the point of view of the Catholic Church, could not fail to arouse among the faithful of the West anger, horror, and zeal to repair the situation. Popes, sovereigns, bishops, princes, and knights left many epistles and letters portraying the whole horror of the situation and appealing for a crusade against victorious Islam and its representative, Muhammed II, this "precursor of Antichrist and second Sennacherib."[234] In many letters the ruin of Constantinople was lamented as that of a center of culture. In his appeal to Pope Nicholas V the western emperor, Frederick III, calling the fall of Constantinople "a general disaster to the Christian faith," wrote that Constantinople was "a real abode [*velut domicilium proprium*] of literature and studies of all humanity."[235] Cardinal Bessarion, mourning the fall of the city, called it "a school of the best arts" (*gymnasium optimarum artium*).[236] The famous Enea Silvio Piccolomini, the future Pope Pius II, calling to mind numberless books in Byzantium which were still unknown to the Latins, styled the Turkish conquest of the city the second death of Homer and Plato.[237] Some writers named the Turks Teucrians (Teucri), considering them the descendants of the old Trojans, and warned Europe of the sultan's plans to attack Italy, which allured him "by its wealth and by the tombs of his Trojan ancestors."[238] On one hand, various epistles of the fifth decade of the fifteenth century said that "the Sultan, like Julian the Apostate, will be finally forced to recognize the victory of Christ"; that Christianity, doubtless, is strong enough to have no fear of the Turks; that "a strong expedition [*valida expeditio*]" will be ready and the Christians will be able to defeat the Turks and "drive them out of Europe (*fugare extra Europam*)." But, on the

---

[232] The Latin text of Dlugosz is reproduced by O. Halecki, "La Pologne et l'Empire Byzantin," *Byzantion*, VII (1932), 65.

[233] See M. Brosset, *Histoire de la Géorgie*, I, 683.

[234] See G. Voigt, *Enea Silvio Piccolomini*, II, 95.

[235] Baronii *Annales ecclesiastici*, ed. A. Theiner, XXVIII, 598.

[236] See Iorga, *Geschichte des Osmanischen Reichs*, II, 41.

[237] Voigt, *Enea Silvio Piccolomini*, II, 94.

[238] Iorga, *Notes et extraits pour servir à l'histoire des Croisades*, IV, 74.

other hand, some epistles anticipated the great difficulties in the coming struggle with the Turks and the chief cause of these difficulties—the discord among the Christians themselves, "a spectacle which inspires the Sultan with courage."[239] Enea Silvio Piccolomini gave in one of his letters an excellent and true picture of the Christian interrelations in the West at that time. He wrote:

I do not hope for what I want. Christianity has no longer a head: neither Pope nor Emperor is adequately esteemed or obeyed; they are treated as fictitious names and painted figures. Each city has a king of its own; there are as many princes as houses. How might one persuade the numberless Christian rulers to take up arms? Look upon Christianity! Italy, you say, is pacified. I do not know to what extent. The remains of war still exist between the King of Aragon and the Genoese. The Genoese will not fight the Turks: they are said to pay tribute to them! The Venetians have made a treaty with the Turks. If the Italians do not take part, we cannot hope for maritime war. In Spain, as you know, there are many kings of different power, different policy, different will, and different ideas; but these sovereigns who live in the far West can not be attracted to the East, especially when they are fighting with the Moors of Granada. The King of France has expelled his enemy from his kingdom; but he is still in trouble, and will not dare to send his knights beyond the borders of his kingdom for fear of a sudden landing of the English. As far as the English are concerned, they think only of taking revenge for their expulsion from France. Scotch, Danes, Swedes, and Norwegians, who live at the end of the world, seek nothing beyond their countries. The Germans are greatly divided and have nothing to unify them.[240]

Neither the appeals of popes and sovereigns, nor the lofty impulse of individuals and groups, nor the consciousness of common danger before the Ottoman menace could weld disunited western Europe for the struggle with Islam. The Turks continued to advance, and at the end of the seventeenth century they threatened Vienna. That was the climax of the might of the Ottoman Empire. They were turned back from Europe, but Constantinople, it is well known, even today is in the hands of the Turks.

ECCLESIASTICAL PROBLEMS UNDER THE PALAEOLOGI

The ecclesiastical history of the time of the Palaeologi is extremely interesting both from the point of view of the relations between the Greek Eastern church and the papal throne, and from the point of view of the religious movements in the internal life of the Empire. The relations with Rome, which took the form of attempts to achieve union with the Catholic church, were, except the Union of Lyons, closely connected with the ever-growing Turkish danger, for in the opinion of the Byzantine Emperor this danger could be prevented

[239] *Ibid.*, 64, 76, 82, 84, 90.   [240] Voigt, *Enea Silvio Piccolomini,* II, 118–

only by the intervention of the pope and the western European sovereigns. The readiness of the pope to favor the proposition of the eastern monarch very often depended upon international conditions in the West.

The Union of Lyons.—The popes of the second half of the thirteenth century, in their eastern policy wished no repetition of the Fourth Crusade, which had failed to solve the extremely important problem of the Greek schism, and merely had served to postpone the other important question of a crusade to the Holy Land. Now it seemed desirable to the popes to achieve a peaceful union with the Greeks, which would put an end to the old schism and give grounds to hope for the liberation of Jerusalem. The recapture of Constantinople by the Greeks in 1261 was a heavy blow to the pope. Papal appeals to save what the Latins had accomplished in the East were sent to many sovereigns. But the papal attitude depended upon affairs in Italy: the popes, for example, did not wish to act with the Hohenstaufen Manfred, whom they hated. Yet when Manfred's power in southern Italy was destroyed by Charles of Anjou, though the latter had been invited by the pope, his aggressive policy against Byzantium found no favor with the papacy. The popes realized that the power of Charles, increased by the conquest of Byzantium, would be hardly less dangerous to the world position of the papacy than the Hohenstaufen sway in Byzantium. It is interesting to note that the first union at Lyons under Michael Palaeologus was achieved not under the pressure of the eastern Turkish danger, but under the menace of the aggressive policy of Charles of Anjou.

Since the Comneni, the attitude of the eastern Emperor towards the union had greatly changed. Under the Comneni, especially in the epoch of Manuel, the emperor had sought for union not only under pressure of the external Turkish danger but also in the hope, already merely an illusion, that with the aid of the pope he might gain supreme power over the West, i.e. restore the former Roman Empire. This aspiration clashed with the similar aspiration of the popes to attain supreme temporal power over the West, so that no union took place. The first Palaeologus, in his negotiations for union, had much more modest pretensions. He had in mind not the expansion of the Byzantine Empire in the West, but its defense, with the help of the pope, against the West in the person of the powerful and menacing Charles of Anjou. The papal curia met his proposals favorably, realizing that the ecclesiastical submission of Byzantium to Rome would bring about a political submission also even if the Sicilian danger were averted. But the possibility of such an increase of the temporal power of the pope met with definite resistance from western European rulers. In his turn, on his way to the reconciliation with the Roman church, the eastern Emperor met with stubborn opposition among the Greek clergy who, in an overwhelming majority, remained faithful to Greek Orthodoxy. The historian Norden said that Pope Gregory X "influenced the King of Sicily with spiritual reasons, Palaeologus his prelates with political arguments."[241]

One of the prominent representatives of the Greek church, the future patriarch John Beccus (Veccus), "a wise man, master of eloquence and science,"[242] according to Gregoras, had been opposed to union and was therefore imprisoned. During his confinement he became a partisan of the union and an active supporter of the Emperor in his project of reconciliation with Rome, an event of great importance for Michael's aim.

The council was held in 1274 in the French city of Lyons. Michael sent a solemn embassy headed by the former patriarch Germanus and the historian George Acropolitas, the grand logothete and the Emperor's friend. It was intended that Thomas Aquinas, the most famous representative of medieval Catholic scholarship, should take the leading part at the council on behalf of Rome, but he died on his way to Lyons. His place was taken by the no less brilliant Cardinal Bonaventura. A Mongol bishop also attended the council.[243] The author of the *Vita* of Saint Bonaventura, Petrus Galesinius (Pietro Galesino) in the sixteenth century, and some other writers of the fifteenth and sixteenth centuries asserted that at the invitation of the pope Emperor Michael Palaeologus himself went to Lyons to attend the council. But this error was caught and refuted by Leo Allatius in the seventeenth century.[244]

The Union of Lyons was achieved on condition that the Emperor should recognize *filioque, azyme* (unleavened bread), and the supreme authority of the pope; to all these stipulations, in the name of Michael, George Acropolitas took oath.[245] Michael also expressed to the pope his readiness to support by troops, money, and provisions the proposed joint crusade for the liberation of the Holy Land, but he stipulated that peace be established with Charles of Anjou so that the Emperor, in diverting all his forces to the East, need not fear attack from the West.[246]

[241] Norden, *Das Papsttum und Byzanz*, 505.

[242] *Historia*, V, 2, 5; Bonn ed., I, 128.

[243] L. Bouvat, *L'Empire Mongol*, 1.

[244] On Michael's journey to Lyons see, e.g., Theodore Spandugino, patritio Constantinopolitano (died after 1538), "De la origine deli imperatori Ottomani," in Sathas, *Documents inédits relatifs à l'histoire de la Grèce*, IX, 143. *Chronicon Carionis a Casparo Peucero expositi et aucti*, V, part 3, 874–75. There are also several old editions of this chronicle. Also Flavius Blondus (Biondo), who died in 1463. On the refutation of this story see Leo Allatius, *De ecclesiae occidentalis atque orientalis perpetua consensione*, II, chap. XV, 753. Allatius quoted several other names.

[245] See the profession of faith read at the Council on behalf of Michael Palaeologus, in the very interesting article by F. Vernet, "Le IIe concile oecumenique de Lyon, 7 mai–17 juillet, 1274," *Dictionnaire de théologie catholique*, IX, 1384–86. See also V. Grumel, "Le IIe concile de Lyon et la réunion de l'église grecque," *ibid.*, 1391–1410. Both articles afford information on the sources and literature of the Union of Lyons. See also Norden, *Das Papsttum und Byzanz*, 520–615.

[246] On the Union of Lyons there is an old Russian work, accurate but written strictly from the Greek Orthodox point of view:

Neither side was pleased with the results of the union. As was to be expected, Michael met with stubborn resistance among the great majority of the Greek clergy. An antiunion council against Michael Palaeologus and John Beccus was held in Thessaly.[247] Moreover, the idea of a crusade could not be agreeable to the Emperor, who was unable to forget the warning of the Fourth Crusade. There was the additional difficulty that Michael Palaeologus was on good terms with the sultan of Egypt, the sworn enemy of the Latins of Syria.

From 1274 to 1280, five papal embassies came to Constantinople in order to confirm the union.[248] But in 1281 the new pope, the Frenchman Martin IV, whom Charles of Anjou set upon the papal throne, broke the union and gave entire support to Charles' aggressive plans against Byzantium. But Michael regarded himself as formally bound by the Union of Lyons to the day of his death.

The Arsenites.—Besides the question of union Byzantium was agitated during the reign of Michael by the struggle of religious-political parties, the most important of which was concerned with the so-called Arsenites.

Beginning with the twelfth century, there were two irreconcilably opposing parties in the Byzantine church which were struggling for influence and power in ecclesiastical administration. One of those parties is called in Byzantine sources the "zealots" (ζηλωταί), the other the "politicians" (πολιτικοί) or moderates;[249] church historian A. Lebedev styled this party "by the modern French parliamentary term of *opportunists.*"[250]

The zealots, champions of the freedom and independence of the church, were opposed to state interference in church affairs, a point of view which brought them into continual collision with the emperor. In this respect the zealots' ideas resembled those of the famous Theodore of Studion who in the ninth century openly spoke and wrote against imperial interference with

Vladimir Nikolsky, "The Union of Lyons. An Episode from Medieval Church History, 1261–1293," *Pravoslavnoe Obozrenie,* XXIII (1867), 5–23, 116–44, 352–78; XXIV (1867), 11–33. According to Nikolsky, "the union was a heavy burden, a shameful spot on Michael Palaeologus' conscience. Of course it collapsed, covering its builder with infamy and leaving behind it piles of hideous rubbish—those fatal consequences which his successors were destined to suffer" (XXIII, 377–78).

[247] V. Grumel, "En Orient après le II⁰ concile de Lyon," *Échos d'Orient,* XXIV (1925), 321–22. See G. Rouillard, "La Politique de Michel VIII Paléologue à l'égard des monastères," *Études byzantines,* I (1944), 73–84. Michael VIII and the monasteries of Mount Athos.

[248] See V. Grumel, "Les Ambassades pontificales à Byzance après le II⁰ concile de Lyon (1274–1280)," *Échos d'Orient,* XXIII (1924), 446–47; in this article there are some important corrections of the chronology given by W. Norden. Cf. M. Viller, "La Question de l'union des églises entres Grecs et Latins depuis le concile de Lyon jusqu'à celui de Florence (1274–1438)," *Revue d'histoire ecclésiastique,* XVI (1921), 261.

[249] Nicephorus Gregoras, *Historia,* VI, 1, 7; Bonn ed., I, 165. George Pachymeres, *De Andronico Palaeologo,* IV, 12; Bonn ed., I, 280.

[250] *Historical Essays on the Situation of the Byzantine-Eastern Church* (2nd ed., 1902), 296–97.

church affairs. The zealots would not make any concession to the imperial power; they wished to submit the Emperor to severe ecclesiastical discipline, and were fearless of any collision with the government or society that might arise from their ideas. Accordingly, they became involved at various times in political troubles and disorders and gained the reputation of a party political as well as ecclesiastical. They could not boast of much education and took no care to have an educated clergy, but they faithfully observed the rules of strict morality and austerity. In the struggle with their opponents they were often supported by the monks, and in the moments of their triumph they opened to the monks the way to power and activity. A historian of that time, Gregoras, noted that one patriarch "could not even read correctly."[251] Describing the spirit prevailing among the monks when a zealot became patriarch the same historian wrote: "It seemed to these malignant monks that after storm and troubles calm had come, and after winter, spring."[252] Strict supporters of Orthodoxy, the zealots were stubbornly opposed to Michael's inclination to the union, and they had great influence with the mass of the people.

The politicians or moderates were directly opposed to the zealots. They stood for state support of the church and co-operation between church and state; accordingly they did not object to the exerting of state influence on the church. They believed that a strong temporal power unrestrained by external interference was essential for the well-being of a nation; therefore they were ready to make considerable concessions to the imperial power. They followed the so-called theory of "economy," which stated that the church in its relation to the state should accommodate itself to circumstances; to justify the theory of economy the politicians usually referred to the life of the Apostles and the Holy Fathers. Recognizing the importance of education, they tried to fill the ecclesiastical offices with cultured and educated men. As they interpreted the rules of strict morality rather liberally and lacked sympathy with severe asceticism, the politicians sought support not among the monks, but among the secular clergy and the educated classes of society.

Naturally, the activities of both parties greatly differed. The Russian church historian A. Lebedev, said: "When the politicians were acting on the church stage, they put their theories into effect smoothly and with comparative peace; on the contrary, when the zealots had the reins of government, relying upon so changeable an element in Byzantium as the monks and, to some degree, the mob, they always acted noisily, often stormily, and sometimes even seditiously."[253] The majority of the politicians were in favor of the Union of Lyons, giving their support to the religious policy of Michael Palaeologus.

The struggles between the zealots and politicians, the origin of which some

[251] *Historia*, VIII, 12, 1; Bonn ed., I, 360.
[252] *Ibid.*, VI, 7, 4; Bonn ed., 193.

[253] *Essays on the Byzantine-Eastern Church*, 298.

scholars trace back to the epoch of iconoclasm and the disputes between the Ignatians and Photians in the ninth century, were felt, of course, by the people and aroused great agitation. Sometimes matters came to such a pass that one house and one family held representatives of both parties; a historian of that time said: "The church schism has reached such a point that it separates the dwellers of one house: father is opposed to son, mother to daughter, sister-in-law to mother-in-law."[254]

Under Michael Palaeologus the zealots, or, as they were sometimes called at the end of the thirteenth and beginning of the fourteenth century, the Arsenites, displayed intensive activity. The word Arsenite comes from the name of Patriarch Arsenius, who twice mounted the patriarchal throne, the first time at Nicaea, the second time at Constantinople after the restoration of the Empire. A man of little scholarship, Arsenius was chosen patriarch by the Emperor of Nicaea, Theodore II Lascaris, who hoped that Arsenius, exalted beyond his merits, would be a mere tool in the Emperor's hands. But Theodore's expectations were not fulfilled. The administration of Arsenius was marked by severe collisions with the Emperor and led to the formation first of the party and then of the schism of the "Arsenites," which agitated the Greek church for several decades. Arsenius did not hesitate to excommunicate Michael Palaeologus, who, contrary to his oath, had dethroned and blinded the unfortunate John IV Lascaris, the last Emperor of Nicaea. The infuriated Emperor deposed Arsenius and sent him into exile, where he died. Arsenius considered his deposition and the ordination of the new patriarchs of Constantinople misdeeds which were bringing about the ruin of the church. Arsenius' ideas roused the people and found not a few partisans among both clergy and laymen. The result was the formation of the schism of the "Arsenites," who chose as their motto a sentence of the Apostle Paul: "Touch not; . . . handle not" (Coloss., 2:21), i.e. touch not those whom Arsenius has condemned. Eager guardians of Eastern Orthodoxy, the Arsenites are distinguished from the zealots only by their position in regard to the Patriarch Arsenius.

The Arsenites gained strong support from the people, among whom they sent secret agents, pilgrims and vagrants, called by the populace "godly men" and by a historian, Pachymeres, "wearers of sackcloth" ($\sigma\alpha\kappa\kappa o\phi\acute{o}\rho o\iota$),[255] who made their way into many families and sowed there the seeds of schism. A Russian church historian, J. E. Troizky, described the situation as follows:

There was in the Byzantine Empire a force, dark and unrecognized. It was a strange force. It had no name, and revealed itself only in moments of emergency. It was complicated, intricate, and of doubtful origin and character. It consisted of the most

[254] George Pachymeres, *De Michaele Palae-*   [255] *Ibid.,* IV, 11; Bonn ed., I, 277.
ologo, IV, 28; Bonn ed., I, 314.

manifold elements. Its members were beggars, "wearers of sackcloth," pilgrims, simpletons, obscure wanderers, madmen, and other disreputable people—men of unknown origin, without settled homes. For various reasons they were joined by disgraced dignitaries, deposed bishops, interdicted priests, monks expelled from their monasteries, and sometimes even by dishonored members of the imperial family. The spirit of this party was determined by its origin and composition. Created by abnormal social conditions, it offered a secret opposition, in general passive but effective, to these conditions and to the power responsible for them, that is, the imperial power. This opposition was usually expressed by spreading rumors which more or less compromised persons in government authority. This force seldom ventured openly to provoke political punishment, but it often seriously affected the government, whose fear was the greater, because, on the one hand, the secret activity was very difficult to trace, and, on the other hand, it had a great effect on the social organization. The people, miserable, depressed, and ignorant, and therefore credulous and superstitious, constantly persecuted both by external enemies and state officials, burdened with exorbitant taxes, and crushed under the pressure of the privileged classes and foreign merchant monopolists—the people were very easily influenced by the insinuations coming from the out-of-the-way places where lived the representatives of the secret force. This was the more true because the force, formed from the people and subject to the conditions under which they lived, had the secret of playing upon their feelings at the decisive moment. The populace of the capital itself was particularly affected by these insinuations. . . . This force in its opposition to the government used different slogans; but its opposition was particularly dangerous to the head of the state, when upon its banner was exhibited the magic word "Orthodoxy."[256]

Under Michael Palaeologus the partisans of the blinded ex-Emperor John Lascaris joined the Arsenites.

The government of Michael Palaeologus resorted to measures of compulsion and severity and the Arsenites were forced to flee from the capital, where their activity had been almost exclusively concentrated. The provinces were now open to their propaganda, and the provincial population, in huge crowds, thronged to listen to their inflammatory speeches condemning the Emperor and exalting the deposed patriarch. Arsenius' death failed to put an end to the schism, and the struggle continued. As J. Troizky said, the struggle of the parties under Michael, "by its feverish animation and unscrupulousness, reminds us of the stormiest times of the heresy struggles in the fourth, fifth, and sixth centuries."[257]

The Union of Lyons changed in many respects the position of the Arsenite party. The question of union presented a broader interest, for it touched the main foundation of the Greek church—Orthodoxy. The Arsenites with their narrow interests and biased speculations were pushed temporarily into the

---

[256] *Arsenius and the Arsenites,* 99–101. See also I. Sykutres, "Περὶ τὸ σχίσμα τῶν Ἀρσενιτῶν," Ἑλληνικά, II (1929), 267–332; III (1930), 15–44. The author said that the book of the Russian theologian Ivan Troizky, was absolutely inaccessible to him (II, 269).

[257] Troizky, 178.

background; the attention of the government and people was turned almost exclusively to the problem of the union. This fact explains the almost complete silence of the sources upon the activity of the Arsenites from the time of the Union of Lyons to the death of Michael VIII. There is a rather hazy indication that in 1278 an Arsenite council was held in Thessaly or Epirus; its chief aim was to secure the triumph of the Arsenite cause and to glorify Arsenius' memory.[258]

Feeling this stubborn opposition, open and secret, to his plans for union, Michael behaved with great cruelty in the last years of his reign.

His successor and son Andronicus II inherited from his father two difficult problems in the ecclesiastical life of the Empire: the union, and the strife between the Arsenites and the official church. First of all, the new Emperor solemnly renounced the union and restored Orthodoxy. A historian of that time wrote: "Envoys were sent everywhere carrying the imperial decrees which announced the settlement of the church disorders, free return to all those who had been exiled for their zeal in church affairs, and an amnesty to those who had suffered in any other way."[259] The carrying out of this measure presented no great difficulties, because the great majority of the Eastern clergy and population was opposed to the union with the Roman church. The Union of Lyons lasted formally for eight years (1274–82).

The abolition of the union meant the triumph of the ideas of the zealots and Arsenites, who were the convinced enemies of union, the "uniates," and of everything Latin. But the Arsenites were not satisfied. They took part on the side of Lascaris in a political plot against the Emperor, hoping, in the case of success, to obtain exclusive influence in the state. But the conspiracy was disclosed in time and put down; thereafter the Arsenite schism gradually disappeared and did not survive Andronicus the Elder, who, in spite of many troubles from the Arsenites, finally consented to their solemn reconciliation with the church. After the reconciliation, a few of the schismatic Arsenites "seceded from the agreement and began to live apart in schism again";[260] but J. Troizky, said this was "the last convulsion before the death of the out-of-date movement, which at that time found no support anywhere, and soon disappeared, leaving no trace, along with its last followers, giving place to new civil and ecclesiastical troubles."[261]

Towards the end of the thirteenth century, in connection with the abolition of the union and triumph of the Orthodox policy, the party of the zealots, who placed their reliance upon the monks and monastic ideals, increased in power.

[258] See Grumel, "En Orient après le IIᵉ concile de Lyon," *Échos d'Orient,* XXIV (1925), 324–25.

[259] Nicephorus Gregoras, *Historia,* VI, 1, 2; Bonn ed., I, 160.

[260] *Ibid.,* VII, 9, 4; Bonn ed., I, 262.

[261] *Arsenius and the Arsenites,* 445.

In the fourteenth century they showed vigorous activity not limited to church problems, but extended to politics and social movements. For example, the zealots took an active part in the troubles of Thessalonica in the fourteenth century, pursuing some political aims which have not yet been satisfactorily elucidated, and they sided with Emperor John V Palaeologus against Cantacuzene; for this reason Iorga called the zealots "legitimists."[262] An interesting attempt to expound the political ideology of the zealots, on the basis of an unpublished oration of the famous Byzantine mystic Nicholas Cabasilas has been recently made by the Roumanian scholar Tafrali.[263]

In the first half of the fourteenth century the zealots and monks gradually got the upper hand of the secular clergy. This movement ended in the complete triumph of the Athonian monks over the patriarchate of Constantinople in the epoch of the so-called Hesychast controversies. This period saw the last patriarch elected from the state officials and the last patriarch elected from the secular clergy. "From this time on the highest posts in the hierarchy are exclusively occupied by monks, and the patriarchal throne of Constantinople becomes for a long time the property of the representatives of Mt. Athos."[264]

Under Andronicus II the Elder an important change in the administration of Athos took place. At the end of the eleventh century Alexius Comnenus had freed Athos from submission to any outside ecclesiastical or civil power and placed the monasteries of Athos under the control of the Emperor alone. He ordained the *protos,* that is to say, the head of the council of abbots (igumens), to whom the administration of the monasteries was entrusted. Andronicus the Elder renounced direct power over Mount Athos and handed the monasteries over to the patriarch of Constantinople, who was to ordain the *protos.* In the imperial charter (*chrysobull*) granted on this occasion, the *protos* of Mount Athos, this "second paradise or starry heaven or refuge of all virtues," was to be "under the great spiritual power of the Patriarch."[265]

With the name of Andronicus the Elder is connected the last important reform of the ecclesiastical organization in the history of Byzantium, a new distribution of the eparchies in accordance with the reduced territory of the Empire. In spite of some changes under the Comneni and Angeli, the distribution of the eparchies and episcopal sees at the end of the thirteenth century corresponded nominally to the distribution usually ascribed to Leo the Wise in about 900. But in the thirteenth century circumstances completely changed. The territory of the Empire was reduced: Asia Minor was almost entirely lost; in Europe, the Slavonic and Latin states occupied the major part of the land

262 "Latins et Grecs d'Orient," *Byzantinische Zeitschrift*, XV (1906), 185. We shall discuss later the troubles of Thessalonica.

263 *Thessalonique au quatorzième siècle,* 225–72.

264 Troizky, *Arsenius and the Arsenites,* 522.

265 P. Uspensky, *The Christian Orient,* III (2), 140, 141, 144, 633, 651. P. Meyer, *Die Haupturkunden für die Geschichte der Athosklöster,* 191, 193.

which had belonged before to the Empire. Nevertheless "the list of the metropoles submitted to the Apostolic and Patriarchal throne of the city protected by God, Constantinople,"[266] which was drawn up under Andronicus the Elder, entirely disregards the modest extent of the territory of the Empire: the list enumerates a long line of cities in foreign regions and lands, which in ecclesiastical respects were subject to the patriarch of Constantinople. Of the more distant points indicated in this list one may notice several metropoles in the Caucasian regions, in the Crimea, Russia, Galich, and Lithuania. The distribution of the metropoles under Andronicus the Elder is also important, because with some changes which were introduced later, it is still in force in Constantinople. "The list at present in force of the metropoles of the Oecumenical throne," wrote a Russian specialist in the field of the Christian East, J. Sokolov, "goes back to ancient times and in one part is a direct and undoubted continuation from the Byzantine epoch."[267]

The Hesychast movement.—In the first half of the fourteenth century the interesting Hesychast movement, mystical and religious, made its appearance in Byzantium and gave rise to eager controversies and vigorous polemic. Hesychasts (Greek word ἡσυχασταί), i.e. "those who live in quiet," or quietists, was the name given to the men whose goal was indivisible and full unity with God, and who chose as the only way to its attainment complete seclusion from the world, *hesychia* (ἡσυχία) which meant "silence, speechlessness."

The quarrel of the Hesychasts, which greatly disturbed the inner life of the state, originated in the troubled and complicated period when the Empire was struggling for its existence, first against invasion by the Turks and later the Serbs, and second, against severe internal troubles arising from the stubborn conflict of the two Andronicoi, grandfather and grandson, and of John Palaeologus and John Cantacuzene. Only a short time had elapsed since the schism of the Arsenites, which had greatly disturbed church and state affairs.

A Greek monk, Barlaam, who arrived from south Italy (Calabria), began the quarrel. He distorted and ridiculed the Hesychast doctrine prevalent chiefly in the Athonian monasteries, which was communicated erroneously to him by an uneducated Byzantine monk. A report presented to the patriarch contains these lines: "Until the most recent time we had lived in peace and stillness, receiving the word of faith and piety with confidence and cordial simplicity, when, through the envy of the devil and insolence of his own mind a certain Barlaam was raised against the Hesychasts who, in the simplicity of their heart, live a life pure and near to God."[268] Athos, which had always

---

[266] See H. Gelzer, *Ungedruckte und ungenügend veröffentlichte Texte der Notitae Episcopatuum. Ein Beitrag zur byzantinischen Kirchen- und Verwaltungsgeschichte*, 595, 597, 599–600, 605.

[267] *The Eparchies of the Constantinopolitan Church of the Present Time*, 66.

[268] Th. I. Uspensky, *Essays on the History of Byzantine Civilization*, 327. The best accounts of the Hesychast doctrine are The Monk

been the guardian of the purity of Eastern Orthodoxy and monastic ideals, was painfully affected by this quarrel and, of course, took a leading part in its development and solution.

Scholars consider this quarrel a very important event of the fourteenth century. The German Byzantinist Gelzer rather exaggerated when he said this ecclesiastical struggle "belongs to the most remarkable and, in its cultural and historical aspect, the most interesting phenomena of all times."[269] Another scholar, the more recent investigator of the problem, a Greek who received his education in Russia, Papamichael, considered the Hesychast movement the most important cultural phenomenon of the epoch, deserving attentive study.[270] Scholars vary greatly concerning the inner conception of the Hesychast movement. Troizky saw in this movement the continuation of the struggle between the zealots and the politicians,[271] or, in other words, the monks and the secular clergy, a struggle which, during the Hesychast quarrel, ended in complete triumph for the monks. Th. Uspensky came to the conclusion that the Hesychast quarrel was a conflict between two philosophical schools, the Aristotelian, whose doctrines had been adopted by the Eastern church, and the Platonic, whose followers were anathematized by the Church. Later the conflict was transferred into the theological sphere. The historical significance of the chief spokesmen for the Hesychast doctrine comes from the fact that they were not only the spokesmen for the Greek national ideas in the struggle with the West, but, still more important, stood at the head of the monastic movement and had the support of Athos and the monasteries in the Balkan peninsula which depended upon the Holy Mountain.[272] A more recent investigator of this problem, Papamichael, whose book came out in 1911, did not deny that the struggle of the monks (the party of the zealots) with the politicians, and some philosophical speculation, were secondary factors in the movement; but he believed that the correct interpretation of the Hesychast quarrel lies primarily in the purely religious domain. On the one hand it is found in that intense mysticism prevalent at that time, not only in the West but also in the East, especially in Athos; on the other hand, in the attempt of the western Greek monk Barlaam to Latinize the Orthodox Byzantine East,

Vasiliy (Krivoshein), "The Ascetic and Theological Doctrine of St. Gregorius Patamas," *Seminarium Kondakovianum,* VIII (1936), 99–151, and Archimandrite Cyprian, *The Anthropology of Saint Gregory Palamas* (Paris, s.d. [1951]).

[269] Gelzer, *Abriss der byzantinischen Kaisergeschichte,* 1058.

[270] G. Papamichael, Ὁ ἅγιος Γρηγόριος Παλαμᾶς ἀρχιεπίσκοπος Θεσσαλονίκης, 14–15. See the detailed exposition of this work by

J. Sokolov in *Journal of the Ministry of Public Instruction,* N.S. XLIV (1913), 381. A very fine study of Gregory Palamas and the Palamite controversy by M. Jugie, "Palamas et Controverse palamite," *Dictionnaire de théologie catholique,* XI (2), 1735–1818.

[271] Troizky, *Arsenius and the Arsenites,* 521.

[272] Uspensky, *Byzantine Civilization,* 273, 364, 366.

by rationalistic and sarcastic attacks, which shook monastic authority in Byzantium.[273]

Barlaam's Latin proselyting is not yet satisfactorily proved. Putting that aside, the Hesychast movement, though primarily religious, became still more interesting in connection with the prevailing mysticism in western and eastern Europe, and with some cultural phenomena of the epoch of the Italian renaissance. The study of this aspect of the Hesychast movement belongs to the future.

The most prominent of the Hesychasts in the fourteenth century and the man who best reduced to a system the doctrine of *hesychia* was the archbishop of Thessalonica, Gregorius Palamas, a well-educated man and an able writer, a sworn adversary of Barlaam and the head of the party of the Palamites, named from him. At the same time many other Hesychasts were explaining and interpreting the doctrine of *hesychia,* especially a Byzantine mystic, unfortunately very little known, Nicholas Cabasilas, whose ideas and works deserve careful study.

According to the above-mentioned work of Papamichael and its exposition by J. Sokolov, the Hesychasts devote themselves entirely to the knowledge and contemplation of God, and the attainment of unity with Him, and concentrate all their strength for this purpose. They retire "from the whole world and all that reminds them of the world," and isolate themselves "by means of the concentration and gathering of the mind in themselves." To attain this concentration the Hesychast has to detach himself from all imagination, all conceptions, all thoughts, and free his mind from all knowledge, in order to be able freely, by an absolute independent flight, to merge easily into the truly mystic darkness of ignorance. The highest, most sincere, and most perfect prayer of the perfect Hesychasts is an immediate intercourse with God, in which there exist no thoughts, ideas, images of the present or recollection of the past. This is the highest contemplation—the contemplation of God one and alone, the perfect ecstasy of mind and withdrawal from matter. No thought is more perfect or higher than such a prayer. It is a state of ecstasy, a mystic unity with God, deification (apotheosis; $\dot{\eta}$ $\theta\epsilon\omega\sigma\iota\varsigma$). In this state the mind wholly transcends the limits of matter, frees itself from all thought, requires a complete insensibility to outward impressions and becomes deaf and mute. Not only is the Hesychast entirely cut off from outward impressions, but he also transcends his individuality and loses consciousness of himself, being wholly absorbed in the contemplation of God. Therefore he who has reached ecstasy no longer lives a personal and individual life; his spiritual and corporeal life stops, his mind remains immovable, attached

[273] Papamichael, Ὁ ἅγιος Γρηγόριος Παλα-μᾶς ἀρχιεπίσκοπος Θεσσαλονίκης, 18. J. Soko-lov, in *Journal of the Ministry of Public Instruction,* N.S. XLIV (1913), 382.

to the object of contemplation. Thus, the basis and center of *hesychia* is the love of God from soul, heart, and mind, and the desire for divine contemplation through the abnegation of everything, however small and remote, which might recall the world and its contents. The goal of the Hesychasts is attained by absolute isolation and silence, by "the care of the heart" and mortification of the mind, continuous penitence, abundant tears, the memory of God and death, and the constant repetition of an "inner" prayer: "Lord Jesus Christ, have mercy upon me; oh, Son of God, help me." The consequence of this prayerful spirit is a blissful humility. Later the doctrine of the sacred *hesychia* was more systematized, especially among the Athonian monks, where the way to attaining the more perfect "hesychia" was divided into several categories and composed of definite "schemes" and "ladders," in one of which, for example, are "the four deeds of the speechless": the beginners, progressives, successful, and perfect. Very few became perfect, i.e. attained the highest degree of *hesychia*, "contemplation." The majority of ascetics reached only the first degrees.[274]

The leader of the Hesychast movement was the archbishop of Thessalonica Gregorius Palamas. Under the protection of Andronicus II, he had received a broad and many-sided education at Constantinople, and he had been inclined from his youth to the study of the problems of monastic life. At twenty he took the monastic habit on Mount Athos. Then, dwelling in Athos, Thessalonica, and some isolated places in Macedonia, he excelled all his fellows on the Holy Mountain in asceticism and devoted all his strength to endeavoring to reach "contemplation." He worked out a definition of his own of the so-called "contemplation" ($\theta\epsilon\omega\rho\iota\alpha$), and proceeded to devote his literary talents to the interpretation of his ascetic ideas. His intention to withdraw into complete solitude in order to devote himself wholly to the "inner" prayer was defeated by the outbreak on Athos of the troubles aroused by Barlaam.

The plans with which Barlaam came to Byzantium have not yet been satisfactorily elucidated. He inspired there such confidence that he was appointed igumen (abbot) of a monastery at Constantinople. Defeated in a discussion with an eminent Byzantine scholar, Nicephorus Gregoras, Barlaam fled to Thessalonica and thence to Athos. There through an ignorant monk he became acquainted with the doctrine of *hesychia*. He accused the Hesychasts who attained the highest degree of perfection "of seeing with their corporeal eyes, the divine and uncreated light shining around them"; thus, the monks destroy the dogmas of the church, if they affirm that they see the divine light with their corporeal eyes, for thereby they declare the divine blessing created and the divine being apprehensible.

The literary dispute which arose on this point between Palamas and Bar-

[274] Sokolov, *ibid.*, 384–86; N.S., XLIV (1913), 171–72, 181–82.

laam and created the parties of the Palamites and Barlaamites, had no definite result. The matter was transferred to Constantinople, where it was decided to convoke a council. The council was to deal with the problem of the nature of the light of Thabor, that is to say, of the light which had shone on Christ and which His disciples had seen on the mountain of Thabor during the Transfiguration. Was that light created or uncreated? In the doctrine of Palamas, the light or shining which the perfect Hesychasts were deemed worthy to attain was in truth a light identical with the light of Thabor; the divine light was uncreated, and the light of Thabor was also uncreated.

At the council summoned in the church of St. Sophia, Palamas gained the upper hand of Barlaam, who was forced publicly to express repentance for his error. However, the sources on that council are rather contradictory, and Th. Uspensky, for example, was inclined to be doubtful about whether, as a result of the council, Barlaam was condemned or pardoned. In any case, Palamas was dissatisfied with the decision of the council.[275]

Church troubles continued, debatable questions were discussed at other councils, and the representatives of the church were entangled in the political complications of the strife between John Palaeologus and John Cantacuzene. Palamas lived an agitated life; for a time he was even confined in prison by the patriarch for his religious ideas. At this time he met with an active opponent in Nicephorus Gregoras, who had formerly acted with such energy against Barlaam and then gone over to the side of the reconciliation with Rome. Finally Palamas' cause triumphed, and his doctrine was recognized by the council as the true doctrine of the whole Orthodox church. The decree of the council listing "Barlaam's blasphemies" proclaimed that "he has been cut off from intercourse with Christians as much for his numerous faults as for the fact that he called the light of the Transfiguration of the Lord, which appeared to His blessed disciples, who ascended the mountain with Him created and describable and differing in nothing from the light perceived by the sense."[276] But the struggle and many misfortunes of Palamas had undermined his strength, and after a severe illness he died in 1360. On a beautiful miniature in a manuscript containing John Cantacuzene's works in the National Library of Paris, John Cantacuzene is portrayed seated upon the throne at the council solving the problem of the nature of the light of Thabor.

The Hesychast quarrel of the middle of the fourteenth century resulted in a decisive victory for strict Orthodoxy in general and for the monastic ideals of Athos in particular. The monks dominated both the church and the state. The dead body of Palamas' chief opponent, Nicephorus Gregoras, was exposed to insults and dragged along the streets of the city, according to another

---

[275] Uspensky, *Byzantine Civilization*, 336.   [276] Migne, *Patrologia Graeca*, CLI, 718–19.

opponent, John Cyparissiotes surnamed "the Wise."[277] At this moment, according to L. Bréhier, a dark future was beginning for the Empire.[278] But the German Byzantinist Gelzer drew a rather idyllic picture of the life of the Athonian monks of the period. He wrote:

The Holy Mountain proved to be the Zion of the true faith. In the horrible crisis of the death of the whole nation, when the Ottomans were mercilessly treading down the Roman people, Athos became a refuge, whose stillness was sought by broken souls, and many strong hearts, which had been led astray in their earthly life, preferred in isolation from the world to live through their moral strife in union with God. In those sad times monastic life offered the unfortunate nation the only permanent and real consolation.[279]

The role of the Hesychasts in the political struggle of their epoch has not yet been clearly determined, but the leaders of the political parties, such as Palaeologus and Cantacuzene, realized plainly the significance and strength of the Hesychasts and turned to them more than once for help in purely secular problems. But the threatening political situation, such as the ever present Turkish danger, for instance, compelled the Emperors—even those who sought for the support of the Hesychasts—to deviate from the strict Orthodoxy of the triumphant Palamas and his partisans, and seek for reconciliation with the Roman church, which, in the opinion of the Eastern emperors, alone could rouse western Europe to defend Christianity. This leaning to the West grew particularly strong, when, after Cantacuzene's deposition, there established himself on the throne John V Palaeologus, half-Latin on his mother's side, who himself became Catholic.

The conversion to Catholicism of Emperor John V.—Towards the seventh decade of the fourteenth century the Turks were the masters of Asia Minor and the peninsula of Gallipoli in Europe, and were beginning to advance through the Balkan peninsula and threatening to encircle Constantinople. John V Palaeologus put all his trust in the pope.

The fourteenth century was the epoch of the so-called "Babylonian Captivity"; from 1305 to 1378 the seven popes consecutively occupying the throne of St. Peter had a more or less permanent residence on the Rhone, at Avignon, and were practically dependent on the French kings. The papal appeals to the western rulers for aid against the Turks were fruitless or brought about only small expeditions, sometimes temporarily successful, but of no permanent help. There was no longer any crusading enthusiasm in the West. Also, in the opinion of the west Europeans of that time, the schismatic Greeks were

---

[277] John of Cyprus, *Palamiticarum Transgressionum Liber,* chap. X; ed. Migne, *Patrologia Graeca,* CLII, 733–36. See R. Guilland, *Essai sur Nicéphore Grégoras,* 54. L. Bréhier, "La Renovation artistique sous les Paléologues et le mouvement des idées," *Mélanges Diehl,* I, 9.

[278] Bréhier, *ibid.*

[279] Gelzer, *Abriss der byzantinischen Kaisergeschichte,* 1059–60.

more repulsive than the Muslim Turks. Petrarca wrote: "The Turks are enemies, but the Greeks are schismatics and worse than enemies."[280]

In 1367 Pope Urban V decided to move from Avignon to Rome. On his way to the Eternal City he was met by Byzantine envoys who notified him that the Emperor was anxious to adopt Catholicism and for this purpose was ready to come to Rome. John V arrived in Rome by sea, via Naples.[281] That John in his decision to adopt Catholicism had no support from the Byzantine church is clear from the fact that among the high officials who accompanied him to Rome there was not a single representative of the Byzantine clergy. In October 1369, in Rome, he solemnly read aloud his confession of faith in full accordance with the dogmas of the Roman Catholic church. In the temple of St. Peter the pope celebrated a solemn service during which John V once more read the confession of faith and confirmed again the dogma that the Holy Spirit proceeded from the Father and Son, and that the pope was the head of all Christians. On the same day the Emperor dined with the pope; all the cardinals were invited to the table. Through Naples and Venice, the Emperor returned to Constantinople. His stay at Venice ended in humiliation. He was arrested by the Venetians as an insolvent debtor and released only when his noble and energetic son, the future Emperor Manuel, came in person to Venice and redeemed his father. Shortly after the Emperor's departure, Pope Urban V returned to Avignon.

In his encyclical letter the pope expressed his joy at John's return to the Catholic faith and abjuration of the schism, and declared his hope that this example would be imitated by "the numberless peoples who followed the schism and the errors of the Greeks." At the same time, however, the patriarch of Constantinople Philotheus, sent messages not only to the population of the Empire but also to the Orthodox Christians beyond its confines, in Syria, in Egypt, in the South-Slavonic countries, and in far-off Russia, urging them to be constant to the Orthodox faith. There was to be a stubborn resistance to John's religious policy. His conversion in Rome had no real results, and he could receive from the pope nothing but attention, presents, and promises. Despite the papal appeals, western Europe sent no help against the Turks. John's conversion, so solemnly proclaimed, was merely a personal affair; the overwhelming majority of the population of the Empire remained faithful to the Eastern Orthodox church.[282] Nevertheless this journey of the Emperor

[280] F. Petrarca, *Rerum senilium, liber VII*, in *Opera Omnia*, 912. Baronii *Annales ecclesiastici*, ed. Theiner, XXVI, 135.

[281] H. Gelzer is wrong in saying that in 1369 John was determined to go to Avignon (*Abriss der byzantinischen Kaisergeschichte*, 1060).

[282] In my study on John's journey to Rome and his conversion to Catholicism I have erroneously referred to his conversion as "the Union of Rome in 1369." See "Il viaggio dell 'Imperatore Bizantino Giovanni V Paleologo in Italia (1369–1371) e l'Union e di Roma del 1369," *Studi bizantini e neoellenici*, III (1931),

is of interest as an episode in the history of cultural intercourse between Byzantium and western Europe in the epoch of the Renaissance.

The Union of Florence.—The most celebrated church union was the Union of Florence in 1439. At this time the political atmosphere in the Christian East was much more critical than at the time of John's conversion. The sack of Serbia and Bulgaria by the Turks, the defeat of the crusaders at Nicopolis, the fruitless journey of Manuel II through western Europe, and finally the conquest of Thessalonica by the Turks in 1430, had put the Eastern Empire in a situation too critical to be saved by the Mongol defeat of the Turks at Angora. The Turkish successes were already a serious menace to Europe also; this was the reason why at the Council of Florence the necessity of a common Latin-Greek struggle against the Turks was so strongly felt. But in spite of the desperate situation, the Orthodox nationalistic party in Byzantium opposed the idea of union, not only from the fear of losing the purity of Greek Orthodoxy, but also from the feeling that western aid bought by the price of union would result in the political supremacy of the West over the East: in other words, the impending domination of the Turks might be replaced by that of the Latins. At the beginning of the fifteenth century, a Byzantine polemist, Joseph Bryennius, wrote: "Let no one be deceived by delusive hopes that the Italian allied troops will sooner or later come to us. But if they do pretend to rise to defend us, they will take arms in order to destroy our city, race, and name."[283] In the fifteenth century, this apprehension was justified by the political plans of Alfonso the Magnanimous against the East.

About the same time in the West, after the Councils of Pisa and Constance, there was convoked the third great council of the fifteenth century, the Council of Basel, which announced as its program the reform of the Church in its head and members, and the settlement of the Hussite movement which, after the death of John Huss, had spread very widely. Pope Eugenius IV was not in sympathy with the council. The Council of Basel and the pope, at the same time and independently of each other, opened negotiations with Emperor John VIII. The Council of Basel and Constantinople exchanged embassies, and among the Greek envoys was the igumen (abbot) of a Constantinopolitan monastery, Isidore, the future metropolitan of Moscow. He delivered a speech in favor of church union which, he said, "would create a great monument vying with the Colossus of Rhodes, whose top would reach

---

151–93. John's conversion was personal and received no support whatever from the Byzantine clergy. See a very fine and amply documented study by O. Halecki, *Un Empereur de Byzance à Rome*, especially 188–234. See also Ostrogorsky, *Geschichte des byzantinischen Staates*, 388–89.

[283] Kalogeras, Μάρκος ὁ Εὐγενικὸς καὶ Βησσαρίων ὁ Καρδινάλις, 70 (on the basis of a rare edition of the works of Joseph Bryennius published in Leipzig, 1768). See also Norden, *Das Papsttum und Byzanz*, 731.

the sky and whose brilliancy would be seen in East and West."[284] After fruit-less disputes concerning the place of a future council, the Fathers of the Council of Basel decided they would settle the Hussite quarrel, and then consider the Greek problem. The Byzantine Greeks, representatives of true Orthodoxy, were deeply offended at being put on the same footing with the "heretic" Hussites. "A real storm burst out" at Constantinople.[285] Meanwhile, the Emperor was nearing agreement with the pope, who was taking over the leadership in the union negotiations. Fearing the reformatory tendencies of the Council of Basel, Eugenius IV transferred the council to the north-Italian city of Ferrara, and when the plague broke out there, to Florence. Some of the members of the council, however, in disobedience to the papal orders, re-mained at Basel and even elected another pope.

The meetings of the Council of Ferrara-Florence were held with unusual solemnity. Emperor John VIII with his brother; Joseph, the patriarch of Con-stantinople; Mark (Marcus), the metropolitan of Ephesus, a convinced op-ponent of the union; Bessarion, the gifted and highly educated supporter of the union; and a great number of other representatives of the clergy and laity arrived at Ferrara by way of Venice. The Grand Prince of Moscow, Vasili II the Dark (or Blind), sent to the council Isidore, metropolitan of Moscow, who was favorably inclined to the union; a numerous retinue of the Russian clergy and laity accompanied him. This was the time of the very flower of the Italian Renaissance. Ferrara under the House of Este and Flor-ence under the House of Medici were brilliant centers of artistic and intel-lectual activity.

The quarrels and debates at the Council, which were reduced to the two chief problems, the *filioque* and the primacy of the pope, dragged on for a long time. Not all the Greeks were willing to recognize these dogmas, and the weary Emperor was on the point of leaving Florence. Patriarch Joseph, who was opposed to the union, died at Florence before its official promulga-tion. But Isidore, the metropolitan of Moscow, worked very actively in favor of the union. Finally, the decree of union drawn up in two languages was solemnly promulgated in the presence of the Emperor on July 6, 1439, in the cathedral of Florence, Santa Maria del Fiore. Several Greeks, however, with Mark of Ephesus at their head, refused to sign the decree.

In Italy there exist today a number of marks of the union of Florence. A very interesting contemporary copy of the decree of union, written in three languages, Latin, Greek, and Slavonic, is preserved and exhibited in one of the libraries of Florence, Biblioteca Laurenziana; besides the Greek and Latin

---

[284] See Pierling, *La Russie et le Saint-Siège* (2nd ed., 1906), I, 11.

[285] *Ibid.,* 12, 15.

signatures to this document, there is the Russian signature "of the humble bishop Abramius of Suzdal," who was present at the council. The cathedral of Florence, Santa Maria del Fiore, where the union was promulgated, still exists. In another church of Florence, Santa Maria Novella, one may see today the funeral monument of Patriarch Joseph, who died during the council, with his life-size picture in fresco. Finally, in the Palazzo Riccardi, also at Florence, there has been preserved a fresco by the fifteenth century Italian painter, Benozzo Gozzoli, representing the procession of the Magi, who go to Bethlehem to adore the newborn Christ; in the persons of the Magi the painter portrayed, though rather fantastically, John Palaeologus and Patriarch Joseph, whose entrance into Florence he might have personally observed. Rome also has some relics of the Union of Florence. Between the big bas-reliefs, fifteenth century work with the pictures of the Savior, the Holy Virgin, and St. Peter and St. Paul on the well-known entrance gates into the temple of St. Peter, are some small bas-reliefs relating to the Council of Florence: the Emperor's sailing from Constantinople, his arrival in Ferrara, a meeting of the Council of Florence, the Emperor's departure with his retinue from Venice. Finally, in one of the museums of Rome there is preserved a beautiful bronze life-size bust of John Palaeologus wearing a pointed hat. This bust, which is often reproduced, was perhaps made from life during the Emperor's stay at Florence.[286]

Like the Union of Lyon, the Union of Florence was not accepted in the East, and on his return to Constantinople John very soon realized that his enterprise had miscarried. A numerous Orthodox party gathered around Mark of Ephesus, who had refused to sign the decree of union; many of those who had signed withdrew their signatures. At Moscow, Isidore ordered the decree of union to be solemnly read in the Cathedral of the Assumption (Uspenski Cathedral), but he found no support. The Grand Prince called him no longer the shepherd and teacher of his flock but a ravening wolf, and he was placed under arrest in a monastery, from which he escaped to Rome. The eastern patriarchs of Alexandria, Antioch, and Jerusalem also declared against the union, and at the Council of Jerusalem, in 1443, the Council of Florence was called "impure ($\mu\iota\alpha\rho\acute{\alpha}$)."[287]

The Catholic church, however, still recognizes the validity of the decree of the Council of Florence, and as late as the nineteenth century Pope Leo XIII in his encyclical concerning the union of the churches appealed to the Orthodox to return to the decree of union.

---

[286] The authenticity of this bust is now sometimes contested. See, e.g., Byron, *The Byzantine Achievement*, 318: "The bust in the Museo di Propaganda at Rome may be considered a nineteenth century forgery."

[287] Leo Allatius, *De ecclesiae occidentalis atque orientalis perpetua consensione*, III (4), 939.

The last Byzantine emperor, Constantine XI, like his brother John VIII, believed that the salvation of the perishing Empire lay in union with the western church.

The question of the Council of St. Sophia.—Some scholars assume that in 1450 in the church of St. Sophia, a council was summoned which was attended by numerous representatives of the Orthodox clergy who had come to Constantinople, among them the patriarchs of Antioch, Alexandria, and Jerusalem; this council condemned the union and its partisans and announced the restoration of Orthodoxy. Leo Allatius, a very well-known scholar in Italy in the seventeenth century, was the first to publish the fragments of the acts of this council but he considered them spurious. Since then the opinions of scholars have been divided: some, following the example of Allatius, regarded the acts of the council as spurious and affirmed that the council itself never existed; others, Greek theologians and Greek scholars in particular, who were exceedingly interested in such a council, considered the published acts genuine and the convocation of the Council of St. Sophia a historical fact. In more recent times, the tendency has been to consider the acts of the Council of St. Sophia false and to deny the very fact of the convocation of the council,[288] although some scholars still aver that the council really took place.[289] There is not enough evidence to affirm that under Constantine there was an open break from the union confirmed by a council. On the contrary, when he saw fatal danger approaching the city, Constantine again appealed for aid to the West. Instead of the desired military aid, only the former metropolitan of Moscow, Isidore, who had participated in the Union of Florence, now a cardinal in the Roman Catholic church, arrived in Constantinople and in December 1452, five months before the fall of the city, read in St. Sophia the solemn promulgation of union and celebrated the union liturgy, including the name of the pope. This act at such a crisis aroused the greatest agitation among the population of the city.

After the fall of Constantinople, the religion and religious institutions of the Greeks were preserved under the Turkish sway. In spite of the occasional violence of the Turkish government and the Muhammedan people against the representatives of the Greek church and the Orthodox population, under Muhammed II and his immediate successors the religious rights which had been granted the Christians were strictly observed. The patriarch, bishops,

---

[288] On this problem see K. Papaioannu, "The Acts of the So-called Council of Sophia (1450) and their Historical Significance," *Vizantiysky Vremennik*, II (1895), 394, 413. Lebedev, *Essays on the Byzantine-Eastern Church* (2nd ed., 1902), 294. Both declare the acts spurious.

[289] See, e.g., J. Dräseke, "Zum Kircheneinigungsversuch des Jahres 1439," *Byzantinische Zeitschrift*, V (1896), 580. L. Bréhier, "Attempts at Reunion of the Greek and Latin Churches," *Cambridge Medieval History*, IV, 624–25.

and priests were proclaimed inviolable. The clergy was exempted from taxes, while all the rest of the Greeks were obliged to pay an annual tribute (charadj). Half of the churches in the capital were converted into mosques, and the other half remained in use by the Christians. The church canons remained in force in all matters concerning the inner church administration, which was in the hands of the patriarch and bishops. The sacred patriarchal synod continued to exist, and the patriarch along with the synod carried on the matters of church administration. All religious services could be freely celebrated; in all cities and villages, for instance, Easter might be solemnly celebrated. This religious toleration in the Turkish Empire has been preserved to the present day,[290] although in the course of time, cases of Turkish violation of the religious rights of the Christians became more frequent, and the position of the Christian population was from time to time very difficult.

The first patriarch of Constantinople under the new rule was elected by the clergy soon after the capture of the city by the Turks, and he was recognized by the sultan. The choice fell on Gennadius (George) Scholarius. He had accompanied John VIII to the Council of Ferrara and Florence and had been then a partisan of union, but later he changed his mind and became a zealous defender of Orthodoxy. With his accession, the Greco-Roman union entirely ceased to exist.

POLITICAL AND SOCIAL CONDITIONS IN THE EMPIRE

The problem of the internal conditions of the Empire under the Palaeologi is among the least studied and most complicated problems of Byzantine history. The sources on this subject, numerous and manifold, have not yet been satisfactorily examined or adequately estimated. Much precious material, especially imperial *chrysobulls* and monastic and private charters, is still preserved unpublished among manuscript treasures of different libraries in the East and West; in this respect the manuscripts of the Athonian monasteries are of the greatest importance. But the Orthodox monks of Mount Athos were too watchful guards of their libraries, and in the eighteenth century and the first half of the nineteenth, the Athonian manuscripts were practically inaccessible to scholars who were not of the Orthodox faith. For this reason in the earlier study of Athonian manuscripts the Russian Orthodox scholars played a very important part.

In the eighteenth century, a Russian traveler, V. G. Barsky, visited the Athonian monasteries twice (in 1725–26 and in 1744). He was the first to become acquainted with the hidden archives and, through his detailed description, he threw light on a rich mine of historical sources preserved

290 The Turkish Empire was changed to a republic in 1923.

in the Athonian libraries.[291] In the nineteenth century, the Russian scholars, Bishop Porphyrius (Uspensky), P. Sevastyanov, T. Florinsky, and V. Regel, worked assiduously in the monasteries of the Holy Mountain and published a long series of very important documents on the internal situation of the Byzantine Empire. Especially important are the charters published in the supplements to several volumes of the Russian Byzantine review, *Vizantiysky Vremennik,* which have not yet been thoroughly studied. At the very end of the nineteenth century, a Greek scholar, Sp. Lampros, published a catalogue of the Greek manuscripts on Mount Athos. But owing to circumstances beyond his control, Lampros could not include in his catalogue the two most important collections of manuscripts preserved in the monasteries of the Laura and of Vatopedi. The catalogue of the Greek manuscripts in the library of the monastery of Vatopedi came to light in 1924.[292] In 1915, the French scholar G. Millet was sent on a mission to Mount Athos, where he collected a series of documents from the archives of the Laura, which is, according to a *chrysobull,* "the head and Acropolis of the whole monastic republic."[293]

In the preface to the Vatopedi catalogue, the authors declared: "The Holy Mountain has preserved and saved intact Byzantine civilization and the spiritual forces of the Hellenic people."[294]

Rich material on the Palaeologian epoch is also to be found in other libraries. Of great importance is the collection published by Miklosich and Müller, *Acta et diplomata graeca medii aevi,* as well as numerous editions of Greek texts by a Greek scholar, C. Sathas. Finally, the acts of the monastery of Vazelon, near Trebizond, recently published, give new and rich material for the history of peasant and monastery landownership, not only in the Empire of Trebizond, but in Byzantium in general from the thirteenth to the fifteenth century.[295]

As the territory of the restored Empire of the Palaeologi was small and was continually being reduced and constantly menaced by the Normans, Turks, Serbs, Venetians, and Genoese, the Empire under the Palaeologi passed into the secondary rank and was no longer a normal and well-organized state. Disorganization in all parts of the state machinery and decay of the central imperial power are the characteristic traits of the period. The

[291] See *Travels of V. G. Barsky in the Holy Places of the East from 1723 to 1747,* ed. N. Barsukov, I, xxxiii.

[292] S. Eustratiades and Arcadios of Vatopedi, *Catalogue of the Greek Manuscripts in the Library of the Monastery of Vatopedi on Mt. Athos.*

[293] See G. Rouillard, "Les Archives de Lavra (Mission Millet)," *Byzantion,* III (1926), 253.

G. Rouillard and P. Collomp, *Actes de Lavra* (1937), I.

[294] Eustratiades and Arcadios, *Catalogue of Greek Manuscripts,* i.

[295] Th. I. Uspensky and V. Beneševič, *The Acts of Vazelon. Materials for the History of Peasant and Monastery Landownership in Byzantium from the Thirteenth to the Fifteenth Century.*

long dynastic strife of the two Andronicoi, grandfather and grandson, and of John V Palaeologus and John Cantacuzene; submission to the popes with the view of achieving union and in connection with this, the sometimes humiliating voyages to western Europe of the emperors (John V, who was arrested at Venice for debt, Manuel II, and John VIII, similar abasement and humiliation before the Turkish sultans in various forms), the payment of tribute, forced stays at the Turkish court, and the giving of the imperial princesses in marriage—all this weakened and degraded the power of the Byzantine basileus in the eyes of the people.

Constantinople itself, which had passed into the hands of the Palaeologi after sack and pillage by the Latins, was a ruin of the city it had been before. Greek writers and various foreign travelers and pilgrims, who visited Constantinople at that time, all testify to the decay of the capital.

At the beginning of the fourteenth century, an Arab geographer, Abulfeda, after briefly enumerating the most important monuments of Constantinople, remarked: "Within the city there are sown fields and gardens, and many destroyed houses."[296] At the very beginning of the fifteenth century a Spanish traveler, Ruy Gonzales de Clavijo, wrote: "Everywhere throughout the city there are many great palaces, churches and monasteries, but most of them are now in ruin. It is, however, plain that in former times when Constantinople was in its pristine state it was one of the noblest capitals of the world." In contrast with Constantinople, when Clavijo visited the Genoese settlement across the Golden Horn, at Pera, he noted: "The city of Pera is only a small township, but very populous. It is surrounded by a strong wall and has excellent houses, all well built."[297] At the same time, an Italian, Buondelmonti of Florence, wrote that one of the most famous churches of Constantinople, the Church of the Holy Apostles, was in a state of decay (*ecclesia jam derupta*).[298] None the less, pious pilgrims from different countries, who visited Constantinople in the fourteenth and fifteenth centuries, among them seven Russian pilgrims, were amazed and spellbound by the decorations and relics of the Constantinopolitan church.[299] In 1287, the monk Rabban Sauma, an envoy of the king of the Mongols, after meeting the Emperor, Andronicus II, and with his special permission, piously visited the churches and relics of the city.[300] Under Manuel II, in 1422, a Burgundian traveler, diplomat, and

[296] *Géographie d'Aboulféda,* trans. J. T. Reinaud, II (1), 315–16.

[297] *A Diary of the Journey to the Court of Timur (Tamerlane), to Samarqand in 1403–1406,* ed. J. Sreznevsky, 87–88; ed. G. Le Strange, 88–89.

[298] *Description des îles de l'Archipel,* ed. E. Legrand, 88; Bonn ed. (with the works of Cinnamus), 181.

[299] See J. Ebersolt, *Constantinople byzantine et les voyageurs du Levant,* 41–43. J. Ebersolt, *Les Arts somptuaires de Byzance,* 118–19.

[300] J. B. Chabot (ed.), "Histoire de Mar Jabalaha III, patriarche des Nestoriens (1281–1317), et du moine Rabban Cauma, ambassadeur du roi Argoun en Occident (1287)," *Re-*

moralist, Ghillebert de Lannoy, was kindly received by the Emperor and by his young son and heir, who allowed him to visit "the marvels and antiquities of the city and of the churches."[301]

In 1437, a Spanish traveler, Pero Tafur, was graciously treated at Constantinople by Emperor John VIII. When, on his way back from the Crimea and Trebizond, Pero Tafur visited Constantinople again, the "Despot Dragas," John's brother, was governing there, for John himself at that time was in Italy. Tafur remarked that "the church they called Valayerna [Blachernae] is today so burnt that it cannot be repaired"; that "the dockyard must have been magnificent; even now it is sufficient to house the ships." "The Emperor's Palace must have been very magnificent, but now it is in such state that both it and the city show well the evils which the people have suffered and still endure. . . . The city is sparsely populated. . . . The inhabitants are not well clad, but sad and poor, showing the hardship of their lot which is, however, not so bad as they deserve, for they are a vicious people, steeped in sin." Perhaps it would not be amiss to add this statement of Tafur: "The Emperor's state is as splendid as ever, for nothing is omitted from the ancient ceremonies, but, properly regarded, he is like a Bishop without a See."[302]

After the Turkish and Serbian conquests in the Balkan peninsula in the second half of the fourteenth century, Constantinople with its nearest possessions in Thrace was surrounded by the dominions of the Turks and could hardly maintain by sea, relations with the territories which still composed a part of the Empire: Thessalonica, Thessaly, and the Despotat of Morea. These territories therefore became almost independent of the central government. Under these new conditions, when the sea route from the northern shore of the Black Sea, very important for the corn supply of the capital, was cut off by the Turks, the island of Lemnos, in the north of the Archipelago, became for a time a granary for Constantinople.[303]

Owing to the feudalizing processes within the Empire which had begun before the Palaeologi, the skillfully organized central state machinery gradually weakened; at times, the central departments had almost nothing to do, for the Empire was disunited and disorganized to an extreme degree. Under the Palaeologi, finances, which had been undermined at the root by the Latin regime, became absolutely exhausted. The taxes from the few devastated

vue de l'orient latin, II (1894), 82–87; in separate ed., 54–59. *The History of Yaballaha III Nestorian Patriarch and of his Vicar Bar Sauma,* ed. J. A. Montgomery, 52–54.

[301] *Oeuvres de Ghillebert de Lannoy, voyageur, diplomate, et moraliste,* ed. C. Potvin, 65. See Petras Klimas, *Ghillebert de Lannoy in Medieval Lithuania,* 80.

[302] *Andanças é viajes de Pero Tafur,* 176, 181, 184. Pero Tafur, *Travels,* 142, 145, 146. A. A. Vasiliev, "Pero Tafur, a Spanish Traveler of the Fifteenth Century and his Visit to Constantinople, Trebizond and Italy," *Byzantion* (1932), 111–13.

[303] See Rouillard, "Les Archives de Lavra," *Byzantion,* III (1926), 255–56, 257.

provinces which still remained in the hands of the Emperor were not paid; all the balances of the funds were spent; the imperial jewelry was sold; soldiers could not be fed; misery reigned everywhere.[304] A historian of the fourteenth century, Nicephorus Gregoras, described the wedding festivities of John V:

At that time, the palace was so poor that there was in it no cup or goblet of gold or silver; some were of pewter, and all the rest of clay . . . at that festival most of the imperial diadems and garb showed only the semblance of gold and jewels; [in reality] they were of leather and were but gilded, as tanners do sometimes, or of glass which reflected in different colors; only seldom, here and there, were precious stones having a genuine charm and the brilliancy of pearls, which does not mislead the eyes. To such a degree the ancient prosperity and brilliance of the Roman Empire had fallen, entirely gone out and perished, that, not without shame, I tell you this story.[305]

The cities particularly threatened by the Turks began to be deserted by their population. After the taking of Callipolis (Gallipoli) by the Turks a number of inhabitants of Constantinople left for the West.[306] In 1425 many people emigrated from Thessalonica, and some of them went to Constantinople in the hope that the capital was more secure than Thessalonica.[307] This was the critical time when Thessalonica was occupied by the Venetians, and the Turks were about to seize the city, which actually happened in 1430.

The reduced territory of the Empire and the very small population made it impossible for the Palaeologian government to keep a large local army, so that the army was composed of mercenaries of various nationalities. Under the Palaeologi appeared the Spanish (Catalan) companies, Turks, Genoese, and Venetians, Serbs and Bulgars. There were also, as before, Anglo-Saxon mercenaries, the so-called Varangians or Anglo-Varangians, and Vardariots, of Turkish stock.[308] Unable to pay its mercenaries well, the government was forced sometimes to tolerate their arrogant restlessness and their devastation of entire provinces and large centers, as, for example, the bloody passage of the Catalans through the Balkan peninsula. Having a weak and disorganized land army, the Palaeologi endeavored in vain to restore the navy, which was in a state of complete decay. Michael Palaeologus accomplished something.

[304] See John Cantacuzene, *Historiae,* IV, 5; Bonn ed., III, 33.

[305] Nicephorus Gregoras, *Historia,* XV, ii, 4; Bonn ed., II, 788–89.

[306] See pp. 622–23.

[307] See S. Kugéas, "Notizbuch eines Beamten der Metropolis in Thessalonike aus dem Anfang des XV. Jahrhunderts," *Byzantinische Zeitschrift,* XXIII (1914–19), 152 (par. 82), 158. Tafrali, *Thessalonique,* 16.

[308] See the decree of Michael Palaeologus, 1272, in Heisenberg, *Aus der Geschichte und Literatur der Palaiologenzeit,* 39, lines 49–50, 61–62. E. Stein, "Untersuchungen zur spätbyzantinischen Verfassungs- und Wirtschaftsgeschichte," *Mitteilungen zur osmanischen Geschichte,* II (1924), 47–49. The Varangians and Vardariots are mentioned several times in Codinus (Kodinus); references are given by Heisenberg, 61–62.

But his successor, Andronicus II, neglected the fleet again, so that the islands of the Archipelago which were under the control of the Empire could no longer be protected against the aggressions of the pirates.[309] The navy could do nothing against the well equipped and strong fleets of the Genoese and Venetians, or even against the Turkish fleet, which had just made its appearance. The Black and Aegean Seas passed entirely out of the control of Byzantium, and in the fourteenth century and the first half of the fifteenth the fleets of the Italian commercial republics were masters there.

The provincial or theme organization had been broken up by the Latin dominion and could not function normally under the Palaeologi. For the earlier type of provincial administration the Empire had not enough territory. The former title of the governor of a theme, *strategus,* wholly disappeared under the Comneni and was replaced by the more modest title of *dux.*[310] The term *theme* has sometimes been used by modern scholars for the province of Macedon and Thessaly in the fourteenth century.[311] But a province separated from the capital by the Turkish and Serbian dominions became a sort of despotat whose ruler was almost independent of the central government. Usually, a member of the imperial family was at the head of such a new state. At the end of the fourteenth century Thessalonica received as her despot one of the sons of the Emperor John V. The Despotat of Morea was also ruled by sons or brothers of the imperial dynasty.

Social relations between the higher and lower classes were very strained under the Palaeologi. Agriculture, always considered the real basis of the economic welfare of the Empire, fell into decay. Many fertile provinces were lost; the rest were devastated by the almost continuous civil strife and by the fatal passage of the Catalan companies. In Asia Minor the economic prosperity of the border settlers (*akritai*), also based on agriculture, was thoroughly undermined by the repressive measures of Michael VIII and the victorious advance of the Turks.

Large landownership was a distinctive feature of the Palaeologian epoch. The ruined peasants were in the power of their landlords. Quite a number of Greeks became powerful landowners in Thessaly after 1261. In the western part of Thessaly, which was seized by the Despot of Epirus, and in the northeastern part of Thessaly, which belonged to the Byzantine Emperor, the wealthy landlords played a most important role, and established feudal relations with smaller landowners. But owing to the Catalan devastations at the

---

[309] See a very interesting passage on the fleet under Andronicus II in George Pachymeres, *De Andronico Palaeologo,* I, 26; Bonn ed., II, 69–71; also in Nicephorus Gregoras, *Historia,* VI, 3; Bonn ed., I, 174–75. See Yakovenko, *Studies in Byzantine Charters,* 180–81.

[310] See Stein, "Untersuchungen zur spätbyzantinischen Verfassungs- und Wirtschaftsgeschichte," *Mitteilungen zur Osmanischen Geschichte,* II (1924), 21.

[311] See Tafrali, *Thessalonique,* 44–50.

beginning of the fourteenth century and the invasions of the Albanians, the land system of Thessaly fell into a chaotic condition. Many Albanians became large landowners. Some improvement in the administration of the land was made, when in 1348 the king of Serbia, Stephen Dushan, took possession of Thessaly.[312] In some mountainous parts of Thessaly there were to be found some individual peasant landownership and free peasant communities.[313]

On the power and wilfulness of the large landowners (*archonts*) in the Peloponnesus important information is given by Mazaris.[314] Earlier in the fourteenth century, John Cantacuzene wrote that the internal decay of the Peloponnesus was the effect not of the Turkish or Latin invasions, but of internal strife, which made "the Peloponnesus more desert than Scythia." When Manuel, son of John V, was appointed Despot of Morea, he more or less restored agriculture, so that "the Peloponnesus became in a short time cultivated," and the population began to come back to their homes.[315] But the Turkish conquest put an end to the Byzantine work in Morea.

Under the pressure of the all-powerful, large landholders, the villages and the peasantry endured great hardships. The peasantry was ruined. It is sometimes stated that the position of the peasants, for example, in the district of Thessalonica in the fourteenth century, at least on the estates of large land-owners, was not very bad.[316] But, even if this was true, the misery of the peasants in general is not to be doubted. Class struggles and the hatred of the lower classes for the wealthy was felt not only in the provinces, but also in the chief cities of the Empire. During the revolution of 1328 the populace of Constantinople sacked the magnificent palace of Theodore Metochites.[317]

From the point of view of the social antagonism between aristocratic and democratic elements, the revolutionary attempt in Thessalonica which broke out in the middle of the fourteenth century is exceedingly interesting and important. The revolutionary movement rose in 1341 at Hadrianople in connection with the proclamation of John Cantacuzene as Emperor, and manifested

---

[312] See J. Sokolov, "Large and Small Landlords in Thessaly in the Epoch of the Palaeologi," *Vizantiysky Vremennik*, XXIV (1923-26), 35-42. I. Boghiatzides, "Τὸ χρονικὸν τῶν Μετεώρων," Ἐπετηρὶς Ἑταιρείας Βυζαντινῶν Σπουδῶν, I (1924), 146-56. Uspensky and Beneševič, *The Acts of Vazelon*, xcii-xciii. A. V. Solovjev, "The Thessalian Archonts in the Fourteenth Century. Traces of Feudalism in the Byzantino-Serbian Order," *Byzantino-Slavica*, IV, 1 (1932), 159-74.

[313] See Sokolov, "Large and Small Land-

lords in Thessaly," *Vizantiysky Vremennik*, XXIV (1923-26), 42.

[314] See J. Dräseke, "Byzantinische Hadesfahrten," *Neue Jahrbücher für das klassische Altertum*, XXIX (1912), 364-65.

[315] John Cantacuzene, *Historiae*, IV, 13; Bonn ed., III, 85-86.

[316] See P. Yakovenko, in *Vizantiysky Vremennik*, XXI, 3-4 (1914), 183.

[317] See R. Guilland, "Le Palais de Théodore Métochite," *Revue des études grecques*, XXXV (1922), 82, 92-93. Ebersolt, *Les Arts somptuaires de Byzance*, 109.

itself in sedition, successful at first, of the populace against the rich classes (δυνατοί); then it spread to the other cities of the Empire.[318] The revolution of the zealots at Thessalonica, in the fifth decade of the fourteenth century, is particularly interesting.[319]

The sources distinguish three classes at Thessalonica: (1) the wealthy and noble; (2) the middle class or *bourgeoisie*, "the middle" (οἱ μέσοι), to whom belonged merchants, manufacturers, rich craftsmen, small landowners and professional men; and, finally, (3) the populace—the small farmers, small craftsmen, sailors, and workers. While the significance and influence of the wealthy class was becoming more and more powerful, the position of the lower class, especially that of the farmers near the city, whose lands were continuously ruined by the enemy, was going from bad to worse. All the commerce of this important economic center and the advantages connected with it were in the hands of the higher class. Resentment was growing, and any casual incident might provoke a clash. Then John Cantacuzene was proclaimed Emperor with the support of the nobility; immediately the democratic elements came to the defense of the Palaeologi. Tafrali wrote: "It was no longer a struggle of the ambitions of two persons who contested with each other for the supreme power, but a struggle between two classes, of which one wanted to maintain its privileges and the other was attempting to throw off its yoke."[320] One contemporary source wrote that "Thessalonica was regarded as the teacher of the other cities in the uprisings of the populace against the aristocracy."[321]

At the head of the democracy of Thessalonica stood the zealots who in 1342 expelled the nobles from the city, pillaged their rich houses, and established a sort of republican government by the members of the zealot party. Complications within the city led to a bloody massacre of the nobility in 1346. Nicholas Cabasilas was one of the few who escaped death. Even after Cantacuzene had come to an agreement with John V Palaeologus, the zealot government at Thessalonica continued to exist and "in certain respects resembled a real republic."[322] The zealots paid no attention to orders from Constantinople, and Thessalonica was governed as an independent republic until in 1349 John V and Cantacuzene finally succeeded, by their united efforts, in putting an end to the democratic regime of the zealots.

The real causes of the revolution of Thessalonica are not yet quite clear.

[318] See John Cantacuzene, *Historiae*, III, 28; Bonn ed., II, 175–79.

[319] We have now a well-documented study on these turbulent years in the history of Thessalonica: P. Charanis, "Internal Strife in Byzantium in the Fourteenth Century," *By-zantion*, XV (1940–41), 208–30.

[320] *Thessalonique*, 224.

[321] Demetrius Cydones, in Charanis, "Internal Strife in Byzantium," *Byzantion*, XV (1940–41), 217.

[322] Tafrali, *Thessalonique*, 249.

The Roumanian historian, Tafrali, considered the chief cause the deplorable economic situation of the population, and saw in the zealots the champions of freedom and better social conditions for the future.[323] Diehl wrote: "The struggle of the classes, rich against poor, aristocrats against plebeians, and the atrocity of the struggle manifest themselves in the interesting, tragic and bloody history of the commune of Thessalonica in the fourteenth century"; this struggle "betrays a vague tendency towards a communistic movement."[324] On the other hand, another historian maintained that in the revolt of Thessalonica the political element, that is, the struggle against the partisans of John Cantacuzene, prevailed over the social element.[325] This problem deserves further study, but it appears that the social background occupied the first place in the revolution of Thessalonica; however, the social problem was intermingled with the political interests of that time, with the civil war between John V and John Cantacuzene. As an example of class struggle the revolution at Thessalonica is one of the most interesting phenomena in the general history of medieval social problems.

Owing to the external and internal conditions of the Empire, Byzantium lost control of her trade. Yet before the Turks definitely cut off all connection, Constantinople, as before, remained a center where merchandise came from various quarters and where one might meet merchants of different nationalities.

Francesco Balducci Pegolotti, a Florentine merchant and writer of the first half of the fourteenth century, a factor in the service of the mercantile house of the Bardi, gave valuable information about the merchandise for sale at Constantinople itself and at Galata or Pera, and about western merchants there.[326] Pegolotti mentions Genoese, Venetians, Pisans, Florentines, Provençals, Catalans, Anconans, Sicilians, and "all other strangers" (*e tutti altri strani*).[327] A Burgundian pilgrim of the first half of the fifteenth century, Bertrandon de la Broquière, wrote that he saw in Constantinople many merchants of various nations, but the Venetians "had more authority"; in

---

[323] *Ibid.*, 255, 259–72. Charanis, "Internal Strife in Byzantium," *Byzantion*, XV (1940–41), 221.

[324] *Byzance. Grandeur et décadence*, 20. Charles Diehl, "Byzantine Civilization," *Cambridge Medieval History*, IV, 760.

[325] Yakovenko, in *Vizantiysky Vremennik*, XXI, 3–4 (1914), 184.

[326] On Pegolotti see W. Heyd, *Histoire du commerce du Levant au moyen âge*, I, xvii–xviii. C. R. Beazley, *The Dawn of Modern Geography*, III, 324–32. An article in the *Encyclopaedia Brittanica* is based on Beazley. H. J.

Yule, *Cathay and the Ways Thither*, II, 278–308; ed. H. Cordier, III, 137–42. E. Friedmann, *Der mittelalterliche Welthandel von Florenz in seiner geographischen Ausdehnung (nach der Pratica della mercatura des Balducci Pegolotti)*, 3–5.

[327] Francesco Balducci Pegolotti, *La pratica della mercatura della decima e delle altre gravezze*, III, 24; ed. Allan Evans, xv–xxvi, and on Pegolotti's sources, xxvi–l. Of course, the best general guide on Byzantine commerce under the Palaeologi is Heyd, *Histoire du commerce du Levant*, I, 427–527 and II.

another place he mentioned Venetians, Genoese, and Catalans.[328] Of course, in addition there were in Constantinople many other merchants both from the west, for example from Ragusa on the Adriatic Sea, and from the east. Commercial intercourse in Constantinople was truly international.

But trade itself was no longer carried on by Byzantines; it passed entirely into the hands of the western merchants, mainly those of the Venetians and Genoese but to some extent those of the Pisans, Florentines, and others. From the reign of Michael VIII on, Genoa occupied the first place in the economic life of Byzantium. The Genoese were exempt from taxes, were allowed to build up and fortify Galata, and organized their factories and colonies not only in the islands of the Aegean Sea and in Asia Minor but also on the shores of the Black Sea, at Trebizond, in Caffa (Theodosia) in the Crimea, and at Tana at the mouth of the Don River.[329] Caffa especially was a flourishing and well-organized city with powerful fortifications and a detailed statute (1449) of administration.[330] A Byzantine historian, Pachymeres, admired the Genoese because the winter storms could not prevent them from navigating with their vessels in the Black Sea.[331] Venice was also free from trade taxes, and the permanent political and economic rivalry between the two powerful republics, Genoa and Venice, sometimes resulted in violent wars. The position of Byzantium in these wars was extremely delicate. At the end of the thirteenth century, when in 1291 St. Jean d'Acre, the last stronghold of the crusaders in Syria, fell to the sultan of Egypt, Venice was deprived of her trade in the southeast Mediterranean basin; thereafter she devoted all her energy to a violent struggle with Genoa in the north to regain her economic position in Byzantium, in the Aegean and Black Seas. New evidence on commercial relations between Florence and Constantinople show that this trade was very active and was carried on chiefly in corn.[332]

[328] *Voyage d'autremer,* ed. Schefer, 150, 164.

[329] See an interesting chapter on Genoese commerce in the Byzantine Empire in the thirteenth century in Brătianu, *Recherches sur le commerce génois,* 108–54. On commercial treaties between Venice and Trebizond in the fourteenth century, see D. A. Zakythinos, *Le Chrysobulle d'Alexis III Comnène empereur de Trébizonde en faveur des Vénetiens,* 4–12.

[330] See the text of this exceptionally interesting statute of 1449, published by V. Yurguevich in *Transactions of the Historical and Archeological Society of Odessa,* V (1865), 631–837 and by P. Vigna, in *Atti della Società Ligure di Storia Patria,* VII (2), 567–680. On the Genoese inscriptions at Caffa see the accurate book of Elena Skrzinska, "Inscriptions latines des colonies genoises en Crimée," in *ibid.,* LVI (1928), 1–180. On the statute of 1449 see A. A. Vasiliev, *The Goths in the Crimea,* 226–27.

[331] George Pachymeres, *De Andronico Palaeologo,* Bonn ed., I, 419–20.

[332] Some documents of the thirteenth and fourteenth century, which were inaccessible to W. Heyd, are given by R. Davidson, *Forschungen zur Geschichte von Florenz,* III, 69–70 (no. 315), 135 (no. 686), 193 (no. 974). See Friedmann, *Der Mittelalterliche Welthandel von Florenz,* 26. Of course, some documents of the fifteenth century are to be found in J. Müller, *Documenti sulle relazioni delle città toscane coll' Oriente Cristiano e coi Turchi,* 149–50, 162–63, 169–77, 283–84.

But all the profit from the commercial activity of the many western merchants in Byzantium went to them, not to Byzantium; the economic dependence of the Palaeologi upon the wealthy and striving western republics and cities was complete. Economically the Palaeologi had no control over the Empire.

Italian influence may also be noticed on Byzantine coins. In the fourteenth century, under Andronicus II, Andronicus III, and John V, there was an attempt at monetary reform in connection with which the Florentine type of coin was introduced. The Venetian type may also be noted. The last golden coin of the Byzantine Empire was minted under Manuel II, perhaps for his coronation, and on it the Holy Virgin surrounded by the walls of Constantinople was reproduced. No coins of the last Byzantine emperor, Constantine XI, are known.[333] The theory exists that under Manuel II and John VIII a reform took place which placed Byzantium under the regime of silver monometallism.[334] But this theory is not proved.

The economic might of the west in Byzantium was ended by the victorious advance of the Ottoman Turks; gradually they took possession of Constantinople and the rest of the Empire, of Trebizond, and the northern shores of the Black Sea.

In view of the general deplorable position of the Empire, both external and internal, it is strange to read an anonymous treatise concerning court offices attributed to the fourteenth century and often, though wrongly, ascribed to Kodinus (Codinus). In this treatise are described in detail the gorgeous raiment of the court dignitaries, their various coverings for the head, their shoes, and their decorations; meticulous descriptions are given of the court ceremonial, coronations, and promotions to one or another rank. This treatise serves as a supplement to the well-known work of the tenth century which described ceremonies of the Byzantine court. In the tenth century, at the time of the greatest brilliance and power of the Empire, such a work was comprehensible and necessary. But the appearance of an analogous treatise in the fourteenth century, on the eve of the final collapse of the Empire, is puzzling and reveals the blindness that apparently reigned at the court of the Byzantine Emperors of the last dynasty. Krumbacher, also puzzled by the appearance of this treatise in the fourteenth century, remarked, not without irony: "The answer is, perhaps, given by a medieval Greek proverb: 'the world was perish-

---

[333] See W. Wroth, *Catalogue of the Imperial Byzantine Coins in the British Museum*, I, lxviii–lxxiii; II, 635–43. A. Blanchet, "Les dernières monnaies d'or des empereurs de Byzance," *Revue Numismatique*, IV, 4 (1910), 89–91. See some interesting pages on the By-

zantine coinage under the Palaeologi in Stein, "Untersuchungen zur spätbyzantinischen Verfassungs- und Wirtschaftsgeschichte," *Mitteilungen zur Osmanischen Geschichte*, II (1924), 11–14.

[334] Blanchet, *ibid.*, 14–15.

ing and my wife was still buying new clothes' (ὁ κόσμος ἐποντίζετο καὶ ἡ ἐμὴ γυνὴ ἐστολίζετο)."[335]

LEARNING, LITERATURE, SCIENCE, AND ART

In political and economic respects the Empire under the Palaeologi was living through critical times, receding step by step before the Ottoman Turks, gradually reduced in territory until it was confined to Constantinople with its surroundings, and Morea. Apparently there would be neither place nor time nor suitable conditions for cultural development. In reality, however, the perishing Empire of the fourteenth and fifteenth centuries, especially the city of Constantinople, was a center of ardent culture, both intellectual and artistic. The schools of Constantinople flourished as they had in her most brilliant past, and students came not only from the far-off Greek regions, like Sparta or Trebizond, but even from Italy, at that time in the height of the Renaissance. Philosophers, headed by Gemistus Plethon, explained Aristotle and Plato. Rhetoricians and philologists, who had studied the best specimens of classical antiquity and endeavored to equal them in their style, attracted enthusiastic groups of auditors and disciples and in their activity and interests presented a striking analogy to the Italian humanists. A great number of historians described the last days of the Empire. An active ecclesiastical life marked by the Hesychast movement and the problem of the union with the Roman church left its trace in literature, dogmatic, ascetic, mystic, and polemic. A revival may also be noted in poetry. Finally, this literary renaissance was followed by an artistic renaissance which has left monuments of great value. Besides Constantinople, Mistra-Sparta was also remarkable for a vivid intellectual movement. The fourteenth century was the golden age of Thessalonica (Salonica) in art and letters.[336]

In a word, at the time of its political and economic decay, Hellenism seemed to gather all its strength to show the viability of classical culture and to give grounds for hope for the future Hellenic renaissance of the nineteenth century. One historian said, "on the eve of her definite ruin, all Hellas was reassembling her intellectual energy to throw a last splendid glow."[337]

[335] *Geschichte der byzantinischen Litteratur,* 425.

[336] See Miller, *Essays on the Latin Orient,* 278–79. Tafrali, *Thessalonique,* 149–69.

[337] E. Lavisse and A. Rambaud, *Histoire générale du IVe siècle à nos jours,* III, 819. Charles Diehl, *Manuel d'art byzantin,* II, 750. Cf. a gloomy and biased picture of the culture of the Palaeologian age based only on the opinion of the Byzantine polemicist of the beginning of the fifteenth century, Joseph Bryennius, by L. Oeconomos, "L'État intellectuel et moral des Byzantins vers le milieu du XIVe siècle d'après une page de Joseph Bryennios," *Mélanges Diehl,* I, 225–33; see especially 226: the progressive decline of the intellectual and moral level. See a fine remark by N. H. Baynes, in *Journal of Hellenic Studies,* LII (1932), 159.

Many members of the imperial families, Palaeologus and Cantacuzene, were distinguished for their learning. Michael VIII was the author of some essays in favor of union and some canons dedicated to important martyrs; he has also left his interesting autobiography,[338] the manuscript of which was found at the Synodal Library of Moscow, and he founded a grammar school at Constantinople. Andronicus the Elder admired letters and art and was a patron of scholars and artists. Some scholars assume that his protection developed the artistic atmosphere which produced such remarkable monuments of art as the mosaics of the monastery Chora (present-day mosque Qahriyejami) at Constantinople.[339] Manuel II was particularly renowned for his education and literary talent. A fine theologian, an authority in the classics, a skillful dialectian, and an excellent stylist, he left many writings: a treatise on the Procession of the Holy Ghost, an attack against Islam, a number of orations on various subjects, the "Description of spring on a regal woven curtain," in a rather jocose style, and, finally, a large collection of important letters to many prominent men of his epoch, written either during his forced stay at the Turkish court or on his journey through western Europe. Altogether there exist about 109 essays and letters from the pen of Manuel.[340]

But from the point of view of literary activity, the first place among the emperors must be attributed to John VI Cantacuzene, who after his forced abdication ended his days as a monk under the name of Ioasaph and devoted the time of his solitude to scientific work and literature. His chief literary work is the *Histories,* in four books, or, perhaps, *Memoirs,* which covers the period from 1320 to 1356 and makes some references to later periods. The author announced in the introduction that he would write nothing but the truth,[341] but he deviated, perhaps unconsciously, from his intention, in dealing with the events in which he took part. He endeavored to free himself from blame and to praise himself and his friends and partisans; at the same time he tried to abase, ridicule, and blacken his adversaries. Cantacuzene was the only Byzantine Emperor to write detailed memoirs and, in spite of his prejudiced statements, they constitute a rich mine of very important information on the troubled history of the fourteenth century in the Balkan peninsula, and on the Slavs and the geography of the Balkan regions in particular. Cantacuzene also wrote some theological essays of which the greater part are not yet published. Examples of these are the polemic essays against Barlaam,

[338] Parts of this autobiography are translated into French by Chapman, *Michel Paléologue,* 167–77.

[339] D. Aïnalov, *The Byzantine Painting of the Fourteenth Century,* 132–33.

[340] Berger de Xivrey, "Mémoire sur Manuel Paléologue," *Mémoires de l'Institut de France,* XIX (2), 1. L. Petit, "Manuel II Paléologue," *Dictionnaire de théologie catholique,* IX (2), 1925–32. Not all of Manuel's writings are published. Some fragments of his letters and essays have already been cited.

[341] *Historiae,* preface; Bonn ed., I, 10.

the Jews, and the Muhammedans. John Cantacuzene transmitted his literary interests to his son Matthew who, after his father's fall, was also forced to take refuge in the cowl. He wrote some theological and rhetorical treatises.

The epoch of the Palaeologi produced a group of important and gifted historians who endeavored to describe and to explain the tragic events of the time. The historian Pachymeres (1242–1310), who, after the expulsion of the Latins, had come from Nicaea to Constantinople, was a very well-educated man. Owing to his high official position, Pachymeres could supplement his own observation by reliable official documents. He was an earnest spokesman for national Greek spirit and therefore opposed to the idea of union. Besides some rhetorical and philosophical essays, his autobiography written in hexameter, and some letters, he was the author of a very important historical work which embraces the period from 1261 to the beginning of the fourteenth century (1307–1308). This is the chief source for the reign of Michael VIII and for a part of the rule of Andronicus the Elder. Pachymeres was the first Byzantine historian whose main interest lay in the subtle and complicated dogmatic disputes of the time. "It seems," Krumbacher wrote, "as if those men, turning with horror from the distressing events of the political life of the Empire, sought for consolation and relief in abstract investigation of the religious dogmatic problems which were then agitating all minds."[342] One of the most interesting portions of Pachymeres' history is his narration of Roger de Flor's Catalan expedition, which is important in comparison with the account of the Catalan chronicler Muntaner.[343] Pachymeres' writing, where Homeric phrases are intermingled with theological declamation and foreign and popular expressions, is permeated with pedantic imitation of antique style; with an evident loss of clearness, Pachymeres even used the little known Attic names for the months instead of the common Christian names. Some of Pachymeres' writings are not yet published, and even his chief historical work needs a new critical edition.[344]

In the beginning of the fourteenth century, Nicephorus Kallistus Xanthopulos compiled his *Ecclesiastical History.* His original plan may have been to

---

[342] *Geschichte der byzantinischen Litteratur,* 288.

[343] See the excellent characterization of Pachymeres given by A. Rubió i Lluch, "Paquimeres i Muntaner," *Secció historico arqueologica del Institut d'Estudis Catalans, Memories,* I (1927), 33–60.

[344] See A. Heisenberg, "Eine Handschrift des Georgios Pachymeres," in his *Aus der Geschichte und Literatur der Palaiologenzeit,* 3–13. For a manuscript of Pachymeres to be found in a Jerusalem library see *Byzantinisch-*

neugriechische Jahrbücher, II (1921), 227. See also Krumbacher, *Geschichte der byzantinischen Litteratur,* 288–91, and Montelatici, *Storia della letteratura bizantina,* 224–25. More recently written, V. Laurent, "Les Manuscrits de l'Histoire Byzantine de Georges Pachymère," *Byzantion,* V (1929–30), 129–205: the history of the edition and description and citation of ten manuscripts. Laurent, "Deux nouveaux manuscrits de l'Histoire Byzantine de Georges Pachymère," *Byzantion,* XI (1936), 43–57; two additional manuscripts.

bring the *History* up to his own time, but he stopped at the year 911. Only the part of his work which covers the time from the birth of Christ to the beginning of the seventh century exists today in full. He also wrote church poems, epigrams, and some other writings.[345]

In the fourteenth century also lived one of the greatest scholars and writers of the two last centuries of Byzantium, Nicephorus Gregoras, who participated in the Hesychast quarrel. In variety and extent of knowledge, in skill in dialectic, and in strength of character he was superior to almost all the eminent men in Byzantium of the Palaeologian epoch and may be freely compared with the best representatives of the western Renaissance. He received an excellent education, was familiar with classic literature, and was so enthusiastic about astronomy that he even proposed to the Emperor a calendar reform. Gregoras, after several years of successful teaching, took an active part in the stormy theological quarrels of the epoch and wrote many works, of which a considerable part are not yet published.[346] He began as a violent opponent of the Calabrian monk Barlaam, but gradually came over to the side of union; for this he was severely persecuted by the authorities and even confined in prison. Gregoras ended his stormy life, in all probability, about 1360. He wrote in almost all fields of Byzantine scholarship—theology, philosophy, astronomy, history, rhetoric, and grammar. The most important is his large Roman history in thirty-seven books, covering the period from 1204 to 1359, the epoch of the Nicene and Latin Empires and the time of the first four Palaeologi and John Cantacuzene. The events previous to 1204 are sketched briefly, and the detailed account, especially of the dogmatic quarrel of his epoch, begins with this year. Gregoras could not help giving full details of the religious disputes in which he was one of the leading participants; therefore his history clearly reflects his sympathies and is not free from prejudice. Perhaps it is better classed as a sort of memoir than as a history. It may be called "a subjectively painted picture of an imposing ecclesiastical process of fermentation."[347] Scholars vary in their estimation of Gregoras' importance. Krumbacher called him "the greatest polyhistor of the last two centuries of Byzantium";[348] Montelatici described him as "the greatest scholar of his time."[349] The most recent biographer of Gregoras, Guilland, disagreed with

---

[345] See Krumbacher, *Geschichte der byzantinischen Litteratur*, 291–93. Montelatici, *Storia della letteratura bizantina*, 226. See also M. Jugie, "Poésies rhythmiques de Nicéphore Calliste Xanthopoulos," *Byzantion*, V (1929–30), 357–90. Jugie published ten church poems.

[346] See R. Guilland, *Essai sur Nicéphore Grégoras*, xxxii–xxxiii. Guilland, *Correspondance de Nicéphore Grégoras*, xii–xviii.

[347] Krumbacher, *Geschichte der byzantinischen Litteratur*, 293–96. Guilland, *Essai sur Nicéphore Grégoras*, 236–38.

[348] *Geschichte der byzantinischen Litteratur*, 288. Learned men acquainted with various realms of knowledge were called "polyhistors."

[349] *Storia della letteratura bizantina*, 225: "il più grande erudito del suo tempo."

Krumbacher. He wrote: "Is Gregoras the greatest polyhistor of the time of the Palaeologi, as Krumbacher likes to call him? No. He is one of the most eminent writers of Byzantium in the fourteenth century, but he is not the greatest . . . Gregoras is not the greatest, but one of the greatest writers of the century, which is still too little known though very important in the history of Byzantine civilization and even of European civilization."[350] In any event, the universality of Gregoras' knowledge is amazing, and it is difficult to find in Byzantium an adequate parallel to this brilliant representative of the Byzantine renaissance.

The important political events of the fifteenth century left considerable trace in the historical literature of the time. John Cananus wrote a special essay on the unsuccessful siege of Constantinople by the Turks in 1422. Cananus, who wrote in language very close to the spoken tongue, attributed the rescue of the capital to the miraculous intercession of the Holy Virgin. Perhaps John Cananus was also the author of a very brief account usually ascribed to Cananus Lascaris, on his voyage to Germany, Sweden, Norway, Livonia, and even to the far-off island of Iceland.[351]

John Anagnostes is the author of a trustworthy account of the capture of Thessalonica by the Turks in 1430. Unlike Cananus, Anagnostes followed strictly the rules of literary art and was very anxious to maintain the purity of his Greek.

Finally, the historians of the fatal event of 1453, which so deeply and painfully struck its contemporaries, are represented by four men whose works differ in point of view and value. They have already been discussed. But these four—George Phrantzes, Ducas, Laonikos Chalcocondyles (or Chalcocandyles), and Critobulus—are sources not only for the fall of Constantinople but also for the Palaeologian epoch in general.

The *Chronicle* of Phrantzes has been preserved in two forms, one abridged, the other more detailed. The briefer, which is often called *minus,* deals with the years 1413–78 only, whereas the longer (*maius*), or Phrantzes' *History,* covers the time from 1258 to 1478; it begins with the last years of the Empire of Nicaea and ends in the time of the Turkish sway at Constantinople. He was within the capital during the siege, so that his detailed account is that of an eyewitness. After the fall of Constantinople he was captured by the Turks. Later he was ransomed and escaped for a time to Mistra, which the Turks had not then taken. Before they conquered the Peloponnesus, Phrantzes fled to the island of Corfù, which at that time belonged to Venice. There in a mon-

[350] *Essai sur Nicéphorus Grégoras,* 296.
[351] Laskaris Kananos, *Reseanteckningar från nordiska länderna. Smärre Byzantinska skrifter,* ed. V. Lundstrom, 14–17; ed. A. A. Vasiliev, "Laskaris Kananos, Byzantine Traveler of the Fifteenth Century Through Northern Europe and to Iceland," *Essays Presented to V. P. Buzeskul,* 397–402. Krumbacher, *Geschichte der byzantinischen Litteratur,* 422.

astery where he took holy orders under the name of Gregorius, he wrote his history at the request of some noble Corfiotes.[352] Wholly indebted for his official career to the Palaeologi, with whom his relations were close, Phrantzes was their special historian and he often exaggerated their merits and suppressed their defects. Hatred of the Turks, faithfulness and devotion to Orthodoxy, and loyalty to the Palaeologi are the distinctive traits of Phrantzes' work. In spite of his prejudices, his work, written by an eyewitness close to the events, is of great importance, especially from the reign of John VIII on. Phrantzes' style is simple and easy; it contains a number of Turkish and a few Italian words. A biographer of Phrantzes remarked: "Essentially a man of affairs—and this constitutes the value of his history—he yet, like most Byzantine historians, had a good knowledge of literature."[353] "A man of affairs" means that Phrantzes was closely connected with the state and personal affairs of Constantine XI and the real situation of the empire.

Ducas (Doukas), a Greek of Asia Minor, wrote "in slightly polished spoken Greek"[354] a history from 1341 to 1462, i.e., from the accession of John V to the conquest of the island of Lesbos by the Turks. In the opening pages of his work he gave a brief chronological introduction beginning with Adam; the reigns of the last three Palaeologi are treated in great detail. Inwardly Orthodox, he accepted the compromise with Rome as the only way to save the perishing Empire. Ducas spent almost all his life in the service of a Genoese ruler of Lesbos, but he did not break with the Greek people. He looked with deep sorrow upon their fatal destiny, and his account of the fall of Constantinople ends with the "lament," from which a fragment already has been quoted. Ducas' history has been preserved not only in its original Greek text, but also in an old Italian version, which in some places supplements passages lacking in the original Greek.[355] One of Ducas' biographers said: "Sober, modest, well-educated, truthful, and, in spite of all his patriotism, comparatively impartial, Ducas serves as an excellent guide for understanding the real situation of persons and events."[356] A more recent biographer of Ducas remarked: "Ducas is an author worthy of study; for he was truthful and in several instances an eyewitness—qualities which, in the opinion of historians,

[352] W. Miller, "The Historians Doukas and Phrantzes," *Journal of Hellenic Studies*, XLVI (1926), 70.

[353] *Ibid.*, 71. On the basis of a comparison of Phrantzes' two versions, the question has recently been raised as to whether Phrantzes really was the author of the great chronicle which bears his name. J. B. Faller-Papadopoulos, "Phrantzès est-il réellement l'auteur de la grande chronique qui porte son nom?" *Bulletin de la l'Institut Archéologique Bulgare,* IX (1935), 177–89.

[354] Krumbacher, *Geschichte der byzantinischen Litteratur,* 306. Montelatici, *Storia della letteratura bizantina,* 231.

[355] The Italian version of Michael Ducas is published in the Bonn edition of his Greek text, 347–512.

[356] E. Chernousov, "Ducas, One of the Historians of the Fall of Byzantium," *Vizantiysky Vremennik,* XXI (1914), 221.

far outweigh the barbarism of his style, which so much offended his super-cilious editor in the defective Bonn edition."[357]

Laonikos Chalcocondyles (or Chalcocandyles), or in its abbreviated form, Chalcondyles,[358] Athenian by origin, centered his work, not in Constantinople or at the court of the Palaeologi, but in the young and vigorous Ottoman Empire. He wrote a *History* in ten books, from 1298 to 1463 or, to be more exact, early in 1464;[359] he related not the history of the Palaeologian dynasty but the history of the Ottomans and their rulers. Laonikos was forced to flee from Athens, spent the time up to the Turkish conquest in the Peloponnesus, and then went to Italy, or more probably to Crete, where he composed his work. Following Herodotus and Thucydides, Laonikos was a good example of how a Greek could study the ancient language in the letter, without being able to grasp the spirit. Like Thucydides, he put speeches into the mouths of his characters, which were, of course, works of pure imagination. A good deal of information, often not very exact, is given by Laonikos on the peoples and countries of western Europe.[360] His recent biographer declared, "With an impartiality rare in a part of the world where racial hatred burns so fiercely, he describes the origin, organization, and triumph of his nation's great enemy, while he extends his narrative beyond the borders of the Greek Empire, to the Serbs, the Bosniaks, the Bulgarians and the Roumanians, with interesting and curious digressions, quite in the style of Herodotus, about the manners and customs of countries beyond southeastern Europe—Hungary, Germany, Italy, Spain, France, and England. This great variety justifies the remark of a critic, that 'he has the gift of arousing our attention, by inspiring us with curiosity, and of not letting us fall asleep over his book.' "[361]

Finally, Critobulus, unsuccessfully imitating Thucydides, composed a eulo-gistic history of Muhammed II, in the years from 1451 to 1467.

The epoch of the Palaeologi, represented by a number of historians, pro-duced almost no chroniclers. In the fourteenth century there was only one, a certain Ephraim, who wrote a chronicle in verse (about 10,000 lines) embrac-ing the time from Julius Caesar to the restoration of the Empire by Michael Palaeologus in 1261. It is quite useless from the historical point of view.

[357] Miller, "The Historians Doukas and Phrantzes," *Journal of Hellenic Studies*, XLVI (1926), 63.

[358] *Chalcondyles* means "the man with the brazen pen," and *Chalcocandyles*, "the man with the brazen candlestick." His first name Laonikos is nothing other than Nikolaos, Nicholas.

[359] See Miller, "The Last Athenian Histo-rian," *Journal of Hellenic Studies*, XLII (1922), 37. See also D. Kampouroglou, Οἱ Χαλκοκον-δύλαι. Μονογραφία, 104–71.

[360] See E. Darkó, "Neuere Beiträge zur Bi-ographie des Laonikos Chalkokondyles," *Compte-rendu du deuxième Congrès interna-tional des études byzantines, 1927*, 25–26. See, e.g., K. Dieterich, *Quellen und Forschungen zur Erd- und Kulturkunde*, II, 124–25. Vasiliev, "La Guerre de Cent Ans et Jeanne d'Arc," *Byzantion*, III (1926), 242–48.

[361] Miller, "The Last Athenian Historian," *Journal of Hellenic Studies*, XLII (1922), 38.

The problem of union, which became especially pressing in the epoch of the Palaeologi and led twice to the formal achievement of union, as well as the long and stormy Hesychast quarrel, evoked intense activity in dogmatic and polemic literature. The latter produced a number of writers among both partisans and opponents of the union and the Hesychasts; some of these writers have already been discussed.

Three writers and men of affairs may be mentioned among the most eminent partisans of the union: John Beccus who died at the end of the thirteenth century, Demetrius Cydones who lived in the fourteenth century, and the famous learned theologian of the fifteenth century, Bessarion of Nicaea.

John Beccus, a contemporary of Michael Palaeologus, was originally opposed to the reconciliation with Rome and resisted Michael's union policy. He therefore incurred the Emperor's anger and in spite of his high church office was put in prison. According to the sources, Beccus was a man of conspicuous intellect and education. According to a Greek historian, he was distinguished "by scholarship, long experience, and eloquence which could put an end to schism."[362] Another historian of the fourteenth century called him "a clever man, master of eloquence and learning, endowed with such gifts of nature as no one of his contemporaries possessed. . . . In sharpness of mind, fluency of speech, and knowledge of church dogmas, all others, compared with him, seemed children."[363] The writings of Nicephorus Blemmydes, of the epoch of Nicaea, made him change his religious ideas and sympathies. He became a partisan of the union. Michael VIII elevated him to the patriarchal throne, which he occupied up to the beginning of the reign of Andronicus II. The latter broke the union, deposed Beccus, and confined him in prison, where he died. The longest work of Beccus is a treatise, *On the Union and Peace Between the Churches of Old and New Rome,* in which the author attempted to prove that the Greek Church Fathers already recognized the Latin dogma, but that the later Greek theologians, with Photius at their head, corrupted their doctrine. Beccus similarly treated the subject of the Procession of the Holy Ghost. He wrote some other theological essays of the same character. For the partisans of union who succeeded him, Beccus' works were a rich source from which they were able to draw needed material.[364]

Demetrius Cydones belongs among the talented writers in theology and rhetoric of the Palaeologian epoch. He was born at Thessalonica at the very beginning of the fourteenth century and died at the beginning of the fifteenth century, so that his life lasted an entire century.[365] At Milan he became thor-

[362] George Pachymeres, *De Michaele Palaeologo,* V, 24; Bonn ed., I, 403.

[363] Nicephorus Gregoras, *Historia,* V, 2, 5; Bonn ed., I, 128–29.

[364] A. D. Zotos, Ἰωάννης ὁ Βέκκος πατ- ριάρχης Κωνσταντινουπόλεως Νέας Ῥώμης.

[365] See G. Cammelli, "Demetrio Cidonio: Brevi Notizie della vita e delle opere," *Studi Italiani di filologia classica,* N.S. I (1920), 144–45; Cydones was born between 1300

oughly acquainted with Latin language and literature. He lived successively in Thessalonica, Constantinople, and Crete, was granted citizenship of Venice,[366] and ended his days in a monastery. Cydones took an active part in the religious disputes of his time, favoring reconciliation with Rome. In his literary works he had the great advantage over the majority of his contemporaries of knowing Latin, and could make use of the most eminent western writers and scholars. He was the author of numerous essays on different problems in theology, rhetoric, and philosophy.[367] A treatise on *The Procession of the Holy Ghost,* published among Cydones' works, apparently does not belong to him, but to one of his disciples, Manuel Calecas.[368] Cydones translated from Latin into Greek, among other things, the famous work of Thomas Aquinas, *Summa Theologiae.* This translation has not yet been published. A Catholic writer remarked: "These laborious translations which make St. Thomas speak in the tongue of St. Jean Damascene have been buried for four centuries in the dust of libraries. Is this their destiny for the future? Will there not be found somewhere a theologian, an apostle, both Thomist and Hellenist, to spread and circulate in the Greek Church the doctrinal riches that Cydones has preserved for future times?" May this translation not be "the doctrinal guide to union"?[369]

Among Cydones' orations may be noted two "deliberative" orations (συμβουλευτικοί) which picture the depressed mood of the people of Constantinople before the Turkish danger, speak of the emigration to western Europe, and urge the Greeks and Latins to unite their forces against the common enemy.[370]

But of greatest importance for the cultural history of the fourteenth century is Cydones' voluminous correspondence. Most of his letters are as yet unpublished; of 447 only 51 have been printed. Among his correspondents may be noted Manuel II (32 letters), John Cantacuzene, with whom he was on very

and 1310, and he lived until between 1403 and 1413. Guilland, *Correspondance de Nicéphore Grégoras,* 325–27, dates death at beginning of 1400. M. Jugie, "Démétrius Cydonès et la théologie latine à Byzance aux XIVᵉ et XVᵉ siècles," *Échos d'Orient,* XXXI (1928), 386–87, states he was born between 1310 and 1320 and died in 1399–1400. A recent and most detailed biography by G. Cammelli, *Démétrius Cydonès. Correspondance,* v–xxiv.

[366] On Cydones' Venetian citizenship see R. Loenertz, "Démétrius Cydonès, citoyen de Venise," *Échos d'Orient,* XXXVII (1938), 125–26.

[367] See Guilland, *Essai sur Nicéphore Grégoras,* 327–31.

[368] This discovery has been recently made by an Italian scholar, G. Mercati. See M. Jugie, "Démétrius Cydonès," *Échos d'Orient,* XXXI (1928), 385.

[369] See E. Bouvy, "Saint Thomas. Ses traducteurs byzantins," *Revue augustinienne,* XVI (1910), 407–8. See also M. Rackl, "Demetrios Kydones als Verteidiger und Uebersetzer des hl. Thomas von Aquin," *Der Katholik. Zeitschrift für Katholische Wissenschaft und Kirchliches Leben,* XV (1915), 30–36. Jugie, "Démétrius Cydonès," *Échos d'Orient,* XXXI (1928), 148.

[370] See G. Cammelli, "Demetrii Cydonii orationes tres adhuɔ ineditae," *Byzantinisch-neugriechische Jahrbücher,* III (1922), 67–76; IV (1923), 77–83, 282–95.

friendly terms (11 letters), and a great many other eminent persons of his epoch.[371]

Until all his letters are available for study neither Cydones' biography nor a full list of his works can be attempted. Moreover, without attentive and detailed study of this new material the history of Greek civilization during the last centuries of Byzantium cannot be fully known or adequately appreciated. This study would not only concern Greek civilization, but also throw new light on the cultural relations between Byzantium and the Italian Renaissance, with which Cydones was so closely associated. One of the best representatives of the Italian Renaissance at the end of the fourteenth century, Coluccio Salutati, wrote Cydones a long and eulogistic letter.[372]

The unpublished correspondence of the patriarch of Constantinople, Athanasius I, who under Andronicus II Palaeologus twice occupied the patriarchal throne (1289–1293 and 1304–1310), apparently may supply much interesting material for the political, religious, and social conditions of the Empire of his day. This may be deduced from some specimens of his letters already published.[373]

To the partisans of union belonged also the famous Bessarion of Nicaea, member of the Council of Florence and later cardinal of the Roman church. But the significance of his activity and personality goes far beyond theological literature, where he is represented by some dogmatic treatises, written from the Latin point of view, and therefore will be discussed and estimated in the section on the problem of Byzantium and the Renaissance.

The opponents of the union had their writers too, but they cannot be compared with such eminent partisans of the union as Cydones or Bessarion. Gregory of Cyprus (his secular name was George), patriarch under Andronicus II, the chief although not always a successful adversary of John Beccus,

[371] See G. Cammelli, "Personaggi bizantini dei secoli XIV–XV attraverso le epistole di Demetrio Cidonio," *Bessarione*, XXIV, 151–54 (1920), 77–108. For a preliminary list of Cydones' published and unpublished works see Cammelli, "Demetrio Cidonio," *Studi Italiani di filologia classica*, N.S. I (1920), 157–59. In 1930 Cammelli published fifty letters with a French translation and gave a complete list of 447 dated and undated letters; see *Démétrius Cydonès. Correspondance*. See a detailed review of this edition by V. Laurent, "La Correspondance de Démétrius Cydonès," *Échos d'Orient*, XXX (1931), 339–54. Laurent, "Manuel Paléologue et Démétrius Cydonès. Remarques sur leur correspondance," *Échos d'Orient*, XXXVI (1937), 271–87, 474–87; XXXVII (1938), 107–24. G. Mercati, "Per

L'Epistolario di Demetrio Cidone," *Studi bizantini e neoellenici*, III (1931), 201–30. P. Charanis, "The Greek Historical Sources of the Second Half of the Fourteenth Century," *The Quarterly Bulletin of the Polish Institute in America* (Jan. 1944), 2–5.

[372] See *Epistolario di Coluccio Salutati*, ed. F. Novati, III, 105–19; the letter was written in 1396.

[373] R. Guilland, "La Correspondance inédite d'Athanase, patriarche de Constantinople (1289–1293; 1304–1310)," *Mélanges Diehl*, I, 121–40. N. Banescu, "Le Patriarche Athanase Ier et Andronic II Paléologue. Etat religieux, politique et social de l'Empire," *Bulletin de la section historique de l'Académie roumaine*, XXIII, 1 (1942), 1–29.

a man, to quote a contemporary source, "known by his scholarship,"[374] left some writings of dogmatic character, in which he attempted to solve from the Greek point of view the problem of the Procession of the Holy Ghost. Gregory's rhetorical essays are of great importance. Marcus (Mark) Eugenicus, metropolitan of Ephesus, who refused to sign the act of the union at the Council of Ferrara-Florence, wrote some small compilations of polemic character, for example an essay against Bessarion, which justify including him among the spokesmen for the Greek national standpoint concerning the union.[375]

Finally, the last great polemist of the Byzantine church and the first patriarch of Constantinople under the Turkish power, Gennadius Scholarius (his secular name was George), was a good scholar in theology and philosophy. He also took part in the Council of Ferrara-Florence, where he first advocated union but eventually, particularly influenced by Marcus of Ephesus, went over to the antiunionists. He was a very productive writer, a versatile theologian and scholar whose numerous works embraced almost all branches of literature. He wrote a number of polemic essays. His philosophical works, which originated from his dispute with Gemistus Plethon on Aristotelianism and Platonism, relate him to the humanists and caused a Greek scholar, Sathas, to call him "the last Byzantine and the first Hellene."[376] His *Lament on the Misfortunes of My Life* contains historical details on the life and works of the author and the situation of the Greek Church in the first years of the Muhammedan domination. He wrote also a brief historical essay, a *Chronography,* published for the first time in 1935 from his own autograph manuscript. Though the *Chronography* occupies only nine pages of printed text, it covers all the years from the time of Adam to the year 1472.[377]

The Hesychast movement also produced a number of writers on both sides, beginning with its founder, Gregorius of Sinai. The leading spirit of the Hesychasts, Gregorius Palamas, was also the author of some dogmatic essays and many orations, sixty-six of which were found in one of the Meteora monasteries in Thessaly.[378] The literary activity of Nicephorus Gregoras, a violent opponent of the Hesychasts, has already been discussed. Another opponent

[374] Nicephorus Gregoras, *Historia,* VI, 1, 5; Bonn ed., I, 163.

[375] On Marcus of Ephesus see a very fine article by L. Petit in *Dictionnaire de théologie catholique,* IX, 2 (1927), 1968–86.

[376] *Documents inédits relatifs à l'histoire de la Grèce,* IV, vii and n. 7.

[377] Gennadius' works recently were published in eight vols. *Oeuvres complètes de Gennade Scholarios,* ed. L. Petit, X. A. Siderides, M. Jugie. Among recent essays on Gennadius, see M. Jugie, "Georges Schola-

rios, professeur de philosophie," *Studi bizantini e neoellenici,* V (1939), 482–94. A detailed study of Gennadius' biography, activities, and literary achievements is urgently needed.

[378] Owing to the untiring energy of N. A. Bees the manuscripts of the Meteora monasteries are now known and described. See J. Dräseke, "Die neuen Handschriftenfunde in den Meteoraklöstern," *Neue Jahrbücher für das klassische Altertum,* XXIX (1912), 552.

of Palamas, John Cyparissiotes, who lived in the second half of the fourteenth century, may be mentioned as the author of Ἔκθεσις στοιχειώδης ῥήσεων θεολογικῶν, or *Expositio materiaria eorum quae de Deo a theologis dicuntur*. the first attempt at dogmatics according to the pattern of western Scholasticism.[379]

One of the great theologians, one of the best Byzantine writers of the fourteenth century, and one of the very talented mystics of the eastern church, Nicholas Cabasilas, also belongs to the fourteenth century. The basis of Cabasilas' ideas was, as in western European mysticism, the works of the so-called Dionysius Pseudo-Areopagite, who wrote probably at the end of the fifth and the beginning of the sixth century. Byzantine mysticism passed through an important evolution in the seventh century, thanks to Maximus Confessor, who freed the mysticism of the Pseudo-Areopagite from its neo-Platonic elements and reconciled it with the doctrine of the Eastern Orthodox church. Maximus' influence was still felt by the mystic writers of the fourteenth century, with Nicholas Cabasilas at their head.

Nicholas Cabasilas belongs to the writers who are very little known and unsatisfactorily studied, for many of his writings are unpublished. Quite a number of these, especially orations and letters, are preserved in several manuscripts of the National Library of Paris, one of which has been used by the Roumanian historian Tafrali in his monograph on Thessalonica.[380] In a study of Cabasilas' doctrine two essays are important: "Seven words on the Life in Christ" (*De vita in Christo*), and "The Interpretation of the Sacred Liturgy" (*Sacrae liturgiae interpretatio*).[381] A discussion of Cabasilas' doctrine with its thesis "To live in Christ is the very union with Christ" would go far afield; but one may certainly say that Cabasilas' literary work in Byzantine mysticism, on its own merits as well as in connection with the Hesychast movement and the western European mystic movements, deserves an honorable place in the cultural history of Byzantium in the fourteenth century, and should attract the attention of scholars, who have hitherto quite wrongly neglected this interesting writer. Scholars vary in their definition of Cabasilas' mysticism, and some of them even declare that he cannot be recognized as a mystic at all.[382] Cabasilas' correspondence deserves publication. According

[379] Krumbacher, *Geschichte der byzantinischen Litteratur*, 106–7 (Ehrhard). The text in Migne, *Patrologia Graeca*, CLII, 741–992.

[380] See Tafrali, *Thessalonique*, iv and *passim*. In the English and French editions of my *History of the Byzantine Empire*, following other scholars I erroneously called Nicholas Cabasilas "metropolitan of Thessalonica." He was never metropolitan of any city.

[381] Migne, *Patrologia Graeca*, CL, 367–492, 493–726. See S. Salaville, "Deux manuscrits du 'De vita in Christo' de Nicholas Cabasilas," *Bulletin de la section historique de l'Académie roumaine*, XIV (1928); *Compte-rendu du deuxième Congrès international des études byzantines, 1927*, 79.

[382] See P. Anikiev, "On the Problem of Orthodox-Christian Mysticism," *Pravoslavno-russkoye Slovo*, no. 13 (1913), 200–17. Monte-

to the French scholar Guilland his letters are written in an easy and elegant, though sometimes over-refined, style, and contain new and interesting data.[383]

Philosophy is represented in the Palaeologian epoch by the famous George Gemistus Plethon.[384] Filled with enthusiasm for ancient Hellenism, an admirer of Plato, whom he knew thoroughly through neo-Platonism, a dreamer who thought to create a new religion by means of the gods of ancient mythology, Plethon was a real humanist and intimately connected with Italy. Interest in ancient philosophy, especially in Aristotle and, beginning with the eleventh century, in Plato, had never been discontinued in Byzantium. In the eleventh century Michael Psellus, in the twelfth John Italus, in the thirteenth Nicephorus Blemmydes had devoted a considerable part of their time to philosophy, Psellus particularly to Plato, the others to Aristotle. The struggle between the two philosophical movements, Aristotelian and Platonic, which is so characteristic of the Middle Ages in general, was strongly felt in Byzantium during the Hesychast quarrel. Therefore the way was well prepared for the extremely interesting personality of Gemistus Plethon.

Plethon received his elementary education at Constantinople and spent the greater part of his life, almost a century long, at Mistra, the cultural center of the Despotat of Morea. He accompanied Emperor John VIII to the Council of Ferrara-Florence. Plethon died at Mistra, probably in 1450. In 1465 an Italian general and patron of letters, of the famous family of Malatesta, captured Sparta from the Turks and transported Plethon's ashes to the small Italian city of Rimini, where they now repose in the church of San Francisco.[385]

The aim of Plethon's philosophical works was to explain the significance of Platonic philosophy as compared with Aristotelian. Plethon opened a new phase in the struggle between Aristotelianism and Platonism. He brought to Italy his knowledge of Plato and his enthusiasm and produced a striking impression upon Cosimo Medici and other Italian humanists. Indeed he initiated the idea of founding the Platonic Academy at Florence.

latici, *Storia della letteratura bizantina*, 251–52. F. Vernet, "Nicholas Cabasilas," *Dictionnaire de théologie catholique*, II (2), 1292–95.

[383] "La Correspondance inédite de Nicolas Cabasilas," *Byzantinische Zeitschrift*, XXX (1929–30), 98. See S. Salaville, *Nicolas Cabasilas: Explication de la divine liturgie* (Paris, 1943). A French translation of this essay with a lengthy introduction contains Cabasilas' biography. See a very favorable review of this book by V. Grumel, *Études byzantines*, II (1945), 265–67.

[384] His real name was George Gemistus;

Plethon is identical with Gemistus, both meaning "full." Gemistus began calling himself Plethon in the desire to replace the common Greek name of Gemistus by the more Hellenic word Plethon. Cf. Desiderius-Erasmus. See H. Tozer, "A Byzantine Reformer: Gemistus Plethon," *Journal of Hellenic Studies*, VII (1886), 354.

[385] See F. Schultze, *Geschichte der Philosophie der Renaissance*, I, 23–109. J. W. Taylor, *Georgius Gemistus Pletho's Criticism of Plato and Aristotle*, 1–2.

In this city Plethon wrote the treatise "On the difference between Aristotle and Plato," in which he endeavored to prove the superiority of his favorite philosopher over Aristotle. The stay of the Byzantine philosopher at Florence is one of the most important episodes in the history of the transplantation of Greek classical learning to Italy and especially of the revival of Platonic philosophy in the West.[386] Plethon's chief piece of work was a kind of Utopia, "A Treatise on the Laws" (Νόμων συγγραφή), which unfortunately does not exist in full. On the one hand, it was an attempt, interesting as indicating a tendency of the epoch but of course doomed to failure, to restore paganism on the ruins of Christianity by establishing neo-Platonic philosophy; on the other hand, it was designed to give mankind ideal living conditions. In order to find in what men's happiness consists, Plethon judged it necessary to understand as thoroughly the nature of man himself as the system of the universe of which man forms part. Plethon also submitted plans to Manuel II for the restoration of the Peloponnesus.

In his significance and influence Plethon goes far beyond the confines of the cultural history of Byzantium, and if only for this reason deserves the deepest attention. As his activity and importance have not yet been fully estimated, the significance of Gemistus Plethon is one of the most fascinating themes for the historian interested in the cultural history of the later Byzantine Empire.[387]

In rhetoric, which is often connected with philosophy, several writers may be specially remembered. Gregorius (George) of Cyprus, a patriarch under Andronicus the Elder, composed an interesting and beautifully written autobiography.[388] Nicephorus Chumnos, a contemporary and disciple of Gregorius of Cyprus, wrote a number of theological, philosophical, and rhetorical essays and left a collection of 172 letters. In his philosophical essays he is one of the most ardent and skillful defenders of Aristotle. Chumnos was in correspondence with almost all the personalities of his epoch who were known in politics, religion, or literature. Though inferior in intelligence, originality, and knowledge to his master, Gregorius of Cyprus, Chumnos is not without distinct significance for the Byzantine and Italian Renaissance of his epoch. "By his love of antiquity, passionate, though a little servile, and by the variety

[386] Ellissen, *Analekten,* IV (2), 11.

[387] See E. Stephanou, "Études récentes sur Pléthon," *Échos d'Orient,* XXXI (1932), 207–17. Fine bibliography, especially 217. It would be out of place here to discuss the enormous literature on Gemistus Plethon. The most recent substantial study is by Milton V. Anastos, "Pletho's Calendar and Liturgy," *Dumbarton Oaks Papers,* IV (1948), 183–305. Excellent bibliography.

[388] G. Misch, "Die Schriftsteller-Autobiographie und Bildungsgeschichte eines Patriarchen von Konstantinopel aus dem XIII. Jahrhundert. Eine Studie zum byzantinischen Humanismus," *Zeitschrift für Geschichte der Erziehung und des Unterrichts,* XXI (1931), 1–16.

of his knowledge Chumnos heralds Italian humanism and the western Renaissance."[389]

Finally, the works of Mazaris—the imitation of Lucian, *The Sojourn of Mazaris in Hades,* and *A Dream After the Return to Life,* as well as his letters on Peloponnesian affairs of the early fifteenth century—afford, in spite of the small literary talent of their author, important material on the problem of the imitation of Lucian in Byzantine literature, and give interesting details on the Byzantine culture of the time.

In philology the Palaeologian epoch produced not a few interesting writers who, in their tendencies and ideas, are forerunners of a new intellectual era and are, as Krumbacher said, less closely connected with their Byzantine predecessors, for example Photius or Eustathius of Thessalonica, than they are with the first representatives of the classic renaissance in the west.[390] But there is one side of the work of the philologists of the Palaeologian epoch for which they are reproached, and not without reason, by classical scholars. This is their treatment of classical texts. While the commentators and copyists of the eleventh and twelfth centuries preserved the manuscript tradition of the Alexandrian and Roman time almost intact, the philologists of the Palaeologian epoch began to remodel the text of ancient authors according to their preconceived ideas of the "purity" of Hellenic language or sometimes in the style of new meters. This tendency has caused classical scholars to refer, when it was possible, to manuscripts of the pre-Palaeologian epoch. However vexatious this practice may have been, it must be judged by the conditions of the time. The philologists were beginning to be dissatisfied with the purely mechanical methods of their predecessors and were seeking, though rudely and awkwardly, to express their own creative tendencies.

Among the philologists was the monk Maximus Planudes (his secular name was Manuel), a contemporary of the two first Palaeologi, who devoted his leisure to science and teaching. He visited Venice as a Byzantine envoy, and was closely related to the cultural movement then rising in the West, especially owing to his knowledge of the Latin language and literature. An assiduous teacher, Planudes was the author of some grammatical essays, and the collection of more than 100 of his letters portrays his intellectual personality as well as his scholarly interests and occupations. Besides historical and geographical extracts compiled from the works of ancient writers, Planudes left translations of Latin authors such as Cato the Elder, Ovid, Cicero, and Caesar. He is perhaps best known in western Europe for his edition of selections from Greek

---

[389] See Guilland, *Correspondance de Nicéphore Grégoras,* 324; a chapter on Chumnos, 317–24. See also Georgios Chumnos, *Old Testament Legends from a Greek Poem on Genesis and Exodus,* ed. F. H. Marshall.

[390] *Geschichte der byzantinischen Litteratur,* 541.

authors. The vast number of existing manuscripts of his translations shows that, in the earlier days of humanism, they often served as texts for the teaching of Greek in the West. At the same time, his numerous translations from Latin into Greek greatly contributed to the cultural rapprochement between East and West in the Renaissance epoch.[390a]

Planudes' disciple and friend, Manuel Moschopulus (Moschopulos), a contemporary of Andronicus II, is, like his teacher, of great significance in determining the characteristics of Byzantine learning at the end of the thirteenth and beginning of the fourteenth centuries as well as for the transmission of classical studies in the West. His *Grammatical Questions* and Greek *Dictionary* were, along with Planudes' translations, favorite textbooks for the study of Greek in the West; in addition, his commentaries on a number of classical writers and his collected letters afford interesting material, which has not yet been adequately studied or estimated.

A contemporary of Andronicus II, Theodore Metochites, is sometimes remembered in the history of Byzantine literature in connection with philology.[391] But his wide and many-sided activities go far beyond the modest confines of philology. In the section on the Empire of Nicaea he has been mentioned as the author of a panegyric on Nicaea. Well-educated, an authority on the classical authors, an admirer of Plutarch and Aristotle and especially of Plato, whom he called "Olympus of wisdom," "a living library," and "Helicon of the Muses,"[392] a talented statesman, and first minister under Andronicus II, Theodore Metochites is an exceedingly interesting type of Byzantine humanist of the first half of the fourteenth century. This man of learning and distinguished statesman had exceptional influence in state affairs, and he enjoyed the complete confidence of the Emperor. His contemporary Nicephorus Gregoras wrote: "From morning to evening he was wholly and most eagerly devoted to public affairs, as if scholarship were absolutely irrelevant to him; but late in the evening, after having left the palace, he became absorbed in science to as high a degree as if he were a scholar with absolutely no connection with any other affairs."[393] On the basis of his political opinions, which he sometimes expressed in his works, Sathas drew an interesting conclusion: inclined neither to democracy nor aristocracy, he had a political ideal of his own, a sort of constitutional monarchy. Diehl remarked: "It is not the least mark of originality in this Byzantine of the fourteenth century that he cherished such dreams under the absolute regime of the *basileus* pledged to the

[390a] The most recent and exhaustive study on Planudes is C. Wendel in *Paulys Real-Encyclopädie. Neue Bearbeitung.* XX (1950), 2202–53.

[391] Krumbacher, 350–53. Krumbacher called Theodore Metochites one of the most promi-nent polyhistors of the Byzantine Renaissance.

[392] Nicephorus Gregoras, *Historia,* VII, 2, 2; Bonn ed., I, 272. Sathas, *Bibliotheca graeca medii aevi,* I, introduction, 60–61.

[393] Nicephorus Gregoras, *Historia,* VII, II, 3; Bonn ed., I, 272–73.

theory of divine right."[394] Of course the history of Byzantine political theory has not yet been told. But this example plainly shows that "the history of political ideas in Byzantium is not a tedious repetition of the same things. It had life and it had development."[395] More recent investigation, however, makes it probable that Metochites' statement was not a practical political theory but an interpretation of a Platonic idea in the spirit of neo-Platonism.[396]

During the revolution which dethroned Andronicus II, Theodore lost position, money, and home, and was confined in prison. On account of a dangerous illness he was allowed to end his days in the Constantinopolitan monastery of the Chora (the present-day mosque Qahriye-jami). When he was still in power, he had restored the monastery, which was old and in a state of decay, supplied it with a library, and adorned it with mosaics. Today, among other beautiful mosaics preserved in the mosque, one may see, over the main door from the inner narthex to the church, a representation of the enthroned Christ and at His feet the kneeling figure of Theodore Metochites in the gorgeous dress of one of the highest Byzantine dignitaries holding a model of the church in his hand; his name is on the mosaic. He died there in 1332.

The famous Nicephorus Gregoras, who was among his pupils, in his writings has portrayed the personality of his master in a detailed and enthusiastic fashion.[397] His numerous and various works of which many are unpublished and very little studied—philosophical and historical essays, rhetorical and astronomical writings, poetry and numerous letters to eminent contemporaries—place Theodore Metochites along with Nicephorus Gregoras and Demetrius Cydones as one of the most brilliant Byzantine humanists of the fourteenth century. The most recent investigator defined the work of Metochites as prodigious and various, and styles him "probably the greatest writer of the fourteenth century and one of the greatest writers of Byzantine literature."[398] His philosophical studies cause some scholars (for example, Sathas and later Th. Uspensky) to consider Metochites a forerunner of the Byzantine Platonists of the fifteenth century in general and of Gemistus Plethon in particular.[399]

Of all his works, the best known is *Commentaries and Moral Judgments,* usually known as *Miscellanies* (*Miscellanea philosophica et historica*). It is a

[394] *Études byzantines,* 401. See also Guilland, *Correspondance de Nicéphore Grégoras,* 361.

[395] See V. Valdenberg, "An Oration of Justin II to Tiberius," *Bulletin of the Academy of Science of the Union of Soviet Socialistic Republics,* no. 2 (1928), 140.

[396] D. C. Hesseling, "Een Konstitutioneel Keizerschap," *Hermeneus,* XI (1938–39), 89–93. See *Byzantinische Zeitschrift,* XXXIX (1939), 263.

[397] See St. Bezdeki, *Le Portrait de Théodore Métochite par Nicéphore Grégoras. Mélanges d'histoire générale,* 57–67.

[398] See R. Guilland, "Les Poésies inédites de Théodore Métochite," *Byzantion,* III (1927), 265. Guilland, *Correspondance de Nicéphore Grégoras,* 358.

[399] Sathas, *Bibliotheca graeca medii aevi,* I, introd., 64. Uspensky, *Byzantine Civilization,* 263–64.

sort of encyclopedia, "an inestimable mine of Metochites' ideas," which gives the reader grounds to admire his vast and profound erudition. Metochites cited and, in all probability, had read over seventy Greek writers. Synesius seems to have been his principal source and his favorite author.[400] In his works are scattered many very important historical records on the history not only of Byzantium, but also of neighboring peoples; an example is his detailed account of his embassy to the tsar of Serbia in 1298 to negotiate for the marriage of one of the daughters of Andronicus II.[401]

Metochites wrote twenty poems, of which only two are published. The first one, of 1355 lines, is a long description of his own life and of the monastery of Chora; the second poem is another description of that monastery;[402] the other eighteen poems, which are not yet published, have been analyzed, and they contain a great deal of information on the author's life and on the historical events of his time.[403] In the nineteenth poem Metochites gave a detailed description of his palace with its riches, comfort, and beauty,[404] which he lost during the revolution of 1328. His poems are written in a polished style which is sometimes not easy to understand. But this was not his peculiarity alone; many Byzantine writers, both of prose and poetry, wrote in a style which lacked clarity and needed commentaries. From their point of view the subtlest style had most value.

Metochites also left some letters; only four of them exist, and they are of no great importance. In all likelihood his other letters were destroyed by his enemies.[405] Metochites' role in art is also very important; this importance is due particularly to the mosaics of the Chora. He was right when he expressed the hope that his work in the field of art would secure to him "a glorious memory among posterity until the end of the world."[406]

Without doubt, one of the most important problems for research in the history of the Palaeologian renaissance is the whole work of Theodore Metochites. There is still much to be done. His greatness as a man and his impor-

[400] See Guilland, *Correspondance de Nicéphore Grégoras*, 360–62. Krumbacher, *Geschichte der byzantinischen Litteratur*, 551–52.

[401] See Sathas, *Bibliotheca graeca medii aevi*, I, 22; the text of the "Embassy" on 154–93. Guilland, *Correspondance de Nicéphore Grégoras*, 364. The text is reprinted and estimated by Nikov, *Tartaro-Bulgarian Relations*, 54–95.

[402] See M. Treu, *Dictungen des Gross-Logotheten Theodoros Metochites*, 1–54.

[403] Guilland, "Les Poésies inédites de Théodore Métochite," *Byzantion*, III (1927), 265–302. Krumbacher, *Geschichte der byzanti-*

nischen Litteratur, 552–53. Recently the manuscript tradition of the poems was discussed by I. Ševčenko, "Observations sur les recueils des discours et des poèmes de Th. Metochite," *Scriptorium*, II (1951), 279–88.

[404] See R. Guilland, "Le Palais de Théodore Métochites," *Revue des études grecques*, XXXV (1922), 82–95; on 86–93 he published a part of the Greek text of the poem with a French translation. Ebersolt, *Les Arts somptuaires de Byzance*, 109.

[405] See Guilland, *Correspondance de Nicéphore Grégoras*, 368.

[406] See Diehl, *Études byzantines*, 401.

tance in the cultural movement of the fourteenth century is just beginning to be recognized. His writings must first be completely published and studied, and only then will it be possible to estimate adequately a great man in a great cultural epoch.

Among the philologists under Andronicus II may be mentioned Thomas Magister, who came from the literary circle of Moschopulus, Theodore Metochites, and Gregoras, and was the author of many scholia on ancient writers, orations, and letters, and whose literary work deserves to be better known than it is now.[407] Another philologist of the same time was Demetrius Triklinius, an excellent text critic, who, as Krumbacher said,[408] may be placed on a level with some modern editors, and a high authority on ancient authors, such as Pindar, Aeschylus, Sophocles, Euripides, Aristophanes, and Theocritus.

In jurisprudence there belongs to the epoch of the Palaeologi the last important juridical work which has preserved its vital significance to the present. It is a great compilation written by a jurist and judge of Thessalonica in the fourteenth century, Constantine Harmenopulus, known by the title of *Hexabiblos* (ἐξάβιβλος), for it is divided into six books, or "Promptuarium" (πρόχειρον νόμων, manuale legum). This compilation contains civil and criminal law with some supplements, for example, the very well-known Rural Code. The author used the earlier legislative works, the Prochiron, the Basilics, the Novels, as well as the Ecloga, Epanagoge, and some others.[409] In connection with the question of the sources of the *Hexabiblos,* there has been pointed out a very important problem which has not yet been satisfactorily elucidated. It was shown that Harmenopulus used several sources in very old versions, without the additions and alterations that were made by the legislative commission of Justinian the Great;[410] in other words, the *Hexabiblos* offers valuable material for critical study on the sources of the Justinian Code, the original form of altered texts, and the traces of the so-called classical Roman Law in the juridical works of Byzantium. After 1453 the *Hexabiblos* of Harmenopulus became widespread in the West, and the humanists studied attentively and carefully that juridical work of fallen Byzantium. The compilation of Harmenopulus is still in use in judicial practice in present-day Greece and Bessarabia.[411]

Several medical treatises showing Arabic influence belong to the period of the Palaeologi. A medical manual of the end of the thirteenth century had considerable influence even on western medicine and was used as a textbook

[407] See Guilland, *Correspondance de Nicéphore Grégoras*, 348–53.

[408] Krumbacher, *Geschichte der byzantinischen Litteratur*, 554.

[409] See P. Collinet, "Byzantine Legislation," *Cambridge Medieval History*, IV, 722–23.

[410] See L. Siciliano, "Dirritto bizantino," *Enciclopedia Giuridica Italiana*, IV (5), 72. Collinet, "Byzantine Legislation," *Cambridge Medieval History*, IV, 723.

[411] L. Kasso, *Byzantine Law in Bessarabia*, 42–49.

by the faculty of medicine in Paris until the seventeenth century. The complete lack of originality in Byzantine medicine, however, has been repeatedly pointed out. A French professor of medicine who was particularly interested in Byzantine times remarked: "If one wished to deal with original works [on medicine], he would have nothing to record, and the page devoted to this more than millenarian period would remain blank."[412] The study of mathematics and astronomy also flourished under the Palaeologi, and many of the versatile and encyclopaedic men already mentioned devoted part of their time to the exact sciences, drawing their material from the ancient works of Euclides and Ptolemy as well as from Persian and Arabic writings, the greater part of which, in their turn, were based upon Greek sources.

Poetry was represented under the Palaeologi by Manuel Holobolus and Manuel Philes. Holobolus' poetry has usually been estimated as artificial and unoriginal, seeking its subjects in the sphere of court interests, and therefore conventional and sometimes unpardonably fulsome and subservient.[413] But more recent investigation shows that this judgment is erroneous; the poems, it is true, describe the magnificence and brilliance of court ceremonies, but show no personal flattery or subservience towards the emperor.[414] Holobolus was also the author of an encomium of the Emperor Michael VIII.[415] Manuel Philes, whose life was one of extreme misery, was forced to use his literary talent to get daily bread; sometimes, accordingly, he stooped to every kind of flattery and sycophancy. In this respect he may be compared with Theodore Prodrome of the twelfth century.

The last great literary figure of the fourteenth century is Theodore Meliteniotes. Several persons of this name are known who lived at the end of the thirteenth and at the beginning of the fourteenth century; therefore it is rather difficult to distinguish who among them wrote a work ascribed only to Meliteniotes.[416] However, it is certain that Theodore Meliteniotes, who lived in the fourteenth century, was the author of an astronomical work, the most vast and most scientific of the entire Byzantine epoch, as well as of a long allegori-

[412] E. Jeanselme, "Sur un aide-mémoire de thérapeutique byzantine contenu dans un manuscrit de la Bibliothèque Nationale de Paris (Supplement grec, 764): traduction, notes et commentaire," *Mélanges Diehl*, I, 170.

[413] See M. Treu, "Manuel Holobolos," *Byzantinische Zeitschrift*, V (1896), 538–59. Krumbacher, *Geschichte der byzantinischen Litteratur*, 770–72; Krumbacher's essay on Manuel Holobolus is based on Treu.

[414] See Heisenberg, *Aus der Geschichte und Literatur der Palaiologenzeit*, 112–32.

[415] X. Siderides, Μανουὴλ Ὁλοβώλου Ἐγκώμιον εἰς Μιχαὴλ Η΄ Παλαιολόγον," Ἐπετηρὶς Ἑταιρείας Βυζαντινῶν Σπουδῶν, III (1926), 168–91.

[416] See Krumbacher, *Geschichte der byzantinischen Litteratur*, 782. F. Dölger, "Neues zu Alexios Metochites und zu Theodorus Meliteniotes," *Studi e testi*, CXXIII (1946), 238–51. Cf. M. Miller, "Poème allégorique de Méliténiote, publié d'après un manuscrit de la Bibliothèque Impériale," *Notices et extraits des manuscrits de la Bibliothèque Nationale*, XIX, 2 (1858), 2–11.

cal poem in 3062 "political" verses, entitled *Concerning Prudence* (Εἰς τὴν σωφροσύνην).[417] A very interesting question has recently been raised as to whether or not Meliteniotes' poem was composed under the direct influence of Boccaccio's *L'Amorosa Visione*.[418] This example may illustrate once more the importance of cultural exchanges between Byzantium and Italy in the epoch of the Palaeologi. Some parallels between *Concerning Prudence* and the famous legendary *Pèlerinage de Charlemagne* have recently been pointed out.[419]

Some very interesting literary documents written in the spoken language of the Palaeologian epoch have been preserved. The Greek version of the *Chronicle of Morea,* more than nine thousand verses in length, which has already been evaluated from the historical point of view in connection with the conquest of the Peloponnesus by the Latins, gives an interesting specimen of the Greek spoken language of the time, which had already absorbed a number of words and phrases from the tongues of the Roman conquerors. The problem of the original language of the *Chronicle* is still under debate: some scholars hold to the French version as the original, others to the Greek; more recently the opinion has been expressed that the original text was Italian, probably in the Venetian dialect.[420] In my own opinion, the original text is Greek. The author of the Greek version is usually regarded as a Hellenized Frank who lived at about the time of the events described and who was well acquainted with Peloponnesian affairs.

To the same epoch belongs a romance in verse (about four thousand verses) "Lybistros and Rhodamne," which strongly resembles, in plot and ideas, the romance, "Belthandros and Chrysantza." The plot is briefly: Lybistros learns in a dream that Rhodamne is his predestined wife; he finds her in the person of an Indian princess, seeks for her love, and finally, victorious in single combat over his rival, wins her as his wife. Thanks to magic charms, the rival car-

[417] *Ibid.,* 11–138. Montelatici, *Storia della letteratura bizantina,* 269, failed to mention this poem. Fragments from his astronomical work, in Migne, *Patrologia Graeca,* CXLIX, 988–1001. A better text and more fragments in *Catalogus codicum astrologicorum graecorum,* V, 3 (1910), 133–47 (excerpta ex codice 21, Vatic. 1059); XI, 1 (1932), 54 (codices escorialenses).

[418] See F. Dölger, "Die byzantinische Literatur und Dante," *Compte-rendu du deuxième Congrès international des études byzantines, 1927,* 47–48. At the Congress Dölger sustained the thesis that Theodore's poem was composed under the influence of Dante's *Divina Comedia,* but later, following the sugges-

tion of S. G. Mercati, he changed his view in favor of Boccaccio. During the Renaissance some of Boccaccio's works were translated into Greek. A translation into spoken Greek of his *Theseis* "begins the series of romantic epics which had a brilliant career in Italy." J. Schmitt, "La 'Théséide' de Boccace et la 'Théséide' grecque," *Études de philologie néogrecque,* ed. J. Psichari, 280. See also Krumbacher, *Geschichte der byzantinischen Litteratur,* 870.

[419] M. Schlauch, "The Palace of Hugon de Constantinople," *Speculum,* VII (1932), 505, 507–8.

[420] J. Longnon, *Livre de la Conquête de la Princée de l'Amorée,* lxxxiii–lxxxiv.

ries off Rhodamne, who at last, after many adventures, is safely reunited to Lybistros.[421] In this romance the blending of Frankish culture with Eastern living conditions is to be emphasized. While in "Belthandros and Chrysantza" the Frankish culture is still quite distinct from the Greek, in "Lybistros" the Frankish culture has deeply penetrated the Byzantine soil; but, in turn, it is beginning to yield to Greek influence. Nevertheless, despite the Latin influence, this poem is much more than an imitation of a Western model. Diehl said: "If the society described seems to be penetrated with certain Latin elements, it keeps, as a whole, a clearly Byzantine color."[422] The original version of the romance belongs to the fourteenth century. The romance "Lybistros and Rhodamne" exists in a later revised version.

Probably to the fifteenth century belongs the Greek version of a Tuscan poem *The Romance of Fiorio and Biancifiore* (*Il cantare di Fiorio e Biancifiore*), dating from the fourteenth century. The Greek version contains about 2000 lines in popular Greek and in "political" meter. The Greek text does not give any indication as to the Greek poet. Krumbacher thought that the author of the version was a Hellenized Frank,[423] that is to say, a member of the Catholic religion. But this statement is now regarded as erroneous, and probably the anonymous author of the Greek version was an Orthodox Greek.[424] The Greek version of the "Romance of Phlorias and Platzia Phlore" (Φλωρίου καὶ Πλάτζια Φλώρης) is of great interest as far as the popular Greek of the Palaeologian epoch is concerned.

Probably at the beginning of the fifteenth century originated the poem, *The Byzantine Achilleid,* also written in political meter. In spite of the classical title calling to mind the Trojan war and Homer, the poem has very little to do with Homer. The scene is laid in a setting of Frankish feudalism. The personality of the hero of the poem, Achilles, is influenced by another Byzantine epic hero, Digenes Akrites. "Achilles is Digenes baptised under a classical name."[425] It is not clear whether the author of the *Achilleid* was acquainted with one of the versions of the Byzantine epic, or whether he drew his similar episodes from the sources common to both poems, i.e. popular songs. The question cannot be definitely decided; but some parallels in both texts make the first assumption more probable.[426] The poem ends with the death of

[421] The Greek text in W. Wagner, *Trois poèmes du moyen âge,* 242–349; detailed analysis of the romance, M. Gidel, *Études sur la littérature grecque moderne,* 151–96. New ed. by J. A. Lambert, 545. J. B. Bury, *Romances of Chivalry on Greek Soil,* 11–12.

[422] Diehl, *Figures byzantines,* II, 348.

[423] Krumbacher, *Geschichte der byzantinischen Litteratur,* 868.

[424] *Le roman de Phlorios et Platzia Phlore,* ed. D. C. Hesseling, 9, 13–14; see also 104, line 1794.

[425] *L'Achilléide Byzantine,* ed. D. C. Hesseling, 9.

[426] *Ibid.,* 3–15. Cf. Krumbacher, *Geschichte der byzantinischen Litteratur,* 848–49. Montelatici, *Storia della letteratura bizantina,* 192–93.

Achilles in Troy at the hands of Paris and Deiphobos, and the sack of the city by the Hellenes in revenge for his death.

A striking rise in art, at first sight rather unexpected considering the general situation of the Empire under the Palaeologi, must also be emphasized. The revival of Byzantine art under the Palaeologi, which produced such work as the mosaics of Qahriye-jami, Mistra, Athos, and Serbia, was so sudden and incomprehensible that scholars have advanced various hypotheses to explain the sources of the new forms of art. The followers of the so-called "western" hypothesis, taking into consideration western influence on Byzantine life in all its aspects since the Fourth Crusade, compared the Byzantine monuments with the Italian frescoes of *trecento* in general and with those of Giotto and some other artists in particular, who were living in Italy when the first productions of art of the eastern renaissance under the Palaeologi appeared. They came to the conclusion that the Italian masters of *trecento* might have influenced Byzantine art, and that this was the explanation of the new forms in the East. The western hypothesis, however, cannot be accepted, because an exactly opposite situation, that is, Byzantine influence upon Italian art, rather than Italian influence upon the art of the Byzantine Empire, has now been proved to exist.

The second or "Syrian" hypothesis, advanced at the beginning of the twentieth century by Strzygowski and Th. Schmidt, consists of the assumption that the best achievements of Byzantine art under the Palaeologi were mere copies of old Syrian originals, i.e. of originals which, in truth, from the fourth century to the seventh, furnished not a few new forms adopted by Byzantine art. If one accepts this theory, there is no renaissance of Byzantine art in the fourteenth century, or any originality, or any creative power of Byzantine masters of that epoch; in this case all is reduced to good copies from some good old models very unsatisfactorily known. This theory, which N. Kondakov called "archaeological sport,"[427] has found a few adherents.[428]

In the first edition of his *Manual of Byzantine Art,* published in 1910, Ch. Diehl rejected both these theories and saw the roots of the renaissance of art under the Palaeologi in the general cultural rise so characteristic of their epoch, and in the awakening of a very vivid feeling of Hellenic patriotism, as well as in the gradual rising of new currents in Byzantine art which had appeared in Byzantium as early as the eleventh century, i.e. beginning with the time of the Comnenian dynasty. Therefore, "for him who examines the matter attentively, the great artistic movement of the fourteenth century is no sudden and unexpected phenomenon; it owed its being to the natural evolution of art in conditions particularly favorable and vigorous; and if foreign influences

[427] *Macedonia. An Archaeological Journey,* 280.

[428] See Diehl, *Manuel d'art byzantin* (2nd ed., 1926), II, 744–45.

partially contributed to its brilliant flowering, it drew from itself, from the deep roots embedded in the past, its strong and original qualities."[429]

In 1917 D. Aïnalov criticized Diehl's solution from the point of view of method. Diehl did not base his conclusions upon direct analysis of the works of art, but drew it indirectly from data on the development of literature, science, and so on. Aïnalov believed that the problem of the origin of the new forms of Byzantine painting in the thirteenth and fourteenth centuries could be solved only by the comparative method. Examination of the geographical and architectural peculiarities of the mosaics of Qahriye-jami at Constantinople and of the Church of St. Mark at Venice caused Aïnalov to emphasize a remarkable relationship between these forms and those of the landscape painting of the primitive Italian Renaissance. He came to the conclusion that Byzantine painting of the fourteenth century cannot be considered a genuine phenomenon of Byzantine art; it is only the reflection of a new development in Italian painting, which in its turn was based on earlier Byzantine art. "Venice is one of the intermediary centers of this retro-action of the art of the earlier Renaissance upon the later Byzantine art."[430]

Th. Schmidt maintained that amid the general economic and political decay of the Empire under the Palaeologi a real renaissance of art in the fourteenth century was impossible.[431] In this connection Diehl justly remarked: "This hypothesis may seem ingenious; but it is a matter of affirmation rather than of proof."[432] In 1925 Dalton, independently of Aïnalov, wrote of the fourteenth century: "The new things out of Italy which appear in Serbia, at Mistra, or in Constantinople are very largely old Greek things returning home, superficially enhanced by a Sienese attractiveness. This being so, we cannot properly regard the painting either of the Slavs or of the Byzantine Greeks in the fourteenth century as dominated by Western influence. Italy had touched with animation and grace an art essentially unchanged."[433] Finally, taking into consideration the recent works of Millet, Bréhier, and Aïnalov, Diehl in the second edition of his *Manual of Byzantine Art* summed up the matter by calling the fourteenth century a true renaissance. It developed with magnificent fullness and complete continuity the trends of the eleventh and twelfth centuries, so that between the past and the fourteenth century there is no break. At this point Diehl repeated the passage of his first edition already quoted.[434]

[429] *Ibid.*, 751; this passage is repeated from the 1st ed. (1910), 702.

[430] Aïnalov, *Byzantine Painting*, 86, 89, 96.

[431] "La 'Renaissance' de la peinture byzantine au XIVe siècle," *Revue archéologique*, II (1912), 127–28.

[432] *Manuel d'art byzantin*, II, 748.

[433] Dalton, *East Christian Art*, 240.

[434] *Manuel d'art byzantin*, II, 751. The whole chapter on the renaissance of Byzantine art in the fourteenth century (pp. 735–51) was reprinted in *Byzantion*, II (1926), 299–316. In his second edition Diehl was unable to make use of Dalton's work, but a short time later he published a detailed review of it in *Byzantinische Zeitschrift*, XXVI (1926), 127–33.

In 1930 L. Bréhier wrote: "The Byzantine art of the epoch of the Palaeologi appears as a synthesis between the two spiritual forces which dominate the history of Byzantium: classicism and mysticism."[435] In 1938 A. Grabar stated that the progress (*l'essor*) of Byzantine art under the Palaeologi was particularly remarkable; under them the last renaissance of arts, specifically of painting, manifested itself both within the Empire which was finally reduced to Constantinople and its suburbs, and in the autonomous Greek principalities (Sparta, Trebizond) and the Slavonic kingdoms which followed the example of Byzantium.[436] After all that has been said, the following statement seems incomprehensible: "The story of Byzantine art really ends with the sack of Constantinople by the Franks in 1204."[437] On the contrary, the Byzantine Renaissance is a rich, fruitful field, worthy of more investigation.[438]

Many monuments of the renaissance of Byzantine art under the Palaeologi survive. Among the buildings, the churches are most notable, in particular seven in Peloponnesian Mistra, several on Mount Athos, many in Macedonia, which in the fourteenth century was under the power of Serbia, and a number in Serbia itself. The brilliant flowering of mosaic work and fresco painting under the Palaeologi resulted in a remarkable legacy: the mosaics of Qahriye-jami in Constantinople, already referred to, and many frescoes of Mistra, Macedonia, and Serbia. On Mount Athos are mosaics and frescoes of the late thirteenth, the fourteenth, and fifteenth centuries, but the full flower of Athonian art belongs to the sixteenth century. The famous Byzantine painter Manuel Panselinos of Thessalonica (Salonika), the "Raphael" or "Giotto of Byzantine painting," probably lived in the first half of the sixteenth century; some of his work is perhaps still to be seen on Mount Athos, but on this point some uncertainty exists.[439]

Many icons and illuminated manuscripts dating from the epoch of the Palaeologi have also been preserved. An example is a famous manuscript of Madrid of the fourteenth century containing the chronicle of John Scylitzes with about 600 interesting miniatures reflecting the history of Byzantium from 811 to the middle of the eleventh century—the period Scylitzes covered.[440] Two Parisian manuscripts, one belonging to the fourteenth century with a

---

[435] "La Rénovation artistique," *Mélanges Diehl,* II, 10.

[436] *L'Art byzantine,* 7, 10.

[437] H. Pierce and R. Tyler, *Byzantine Art,* 15.

[438] See, e.g., a review by Charles Diehl of the work of G. Millet, *Recherches sur l'iconographie de l'Evangile* in *Journal des Savants,* N.S. XV (1917), 376. See also G. Soteriou, "Die byzantinische Malerei des XIV. Jahrhundert in Griechenland. Bemerkungen zum

Stilproblem der Monumentalmalerei des XIV. Jahrhundert," Ἑλληνικά, I (1928), 95–117.

[439] See Diehl, *Manuel d'art byzantin,* II, 840–44; on the problem of Panselinos' dates, see 842 and n. 1. Dalton, *East Christian Art,* 238.

[440] A complete set of those miniatures photographed may be found in the photograph collection of the Ecole des Hautes-Études in Paris. See also J. Ebersolt, *La Miniature byzantine,* 59.

miniature of John Cantacuzene presiding at the Hesychast council, and the other to the beginning of the fifteenth century with a miniature of Manuel II, have already been mentioned.[441]

The art of the Palaeologian epoch and its reflections in the Slavonic countries in general and Russia in particular have not yet been thoroughly studied; the evidence on this period has not yet been completely collected or studied, and in some cases not even discovered. Discussing the study of icon painting of the thirteenth and fourteenth centuries N. P. Kondakov wrote in 1909: "To speak generally, we enter a dark forest in which the paths are unexplored."[442] A more recent scholar of Byzantine painting of the fourteenth century, D. V. Aïnalov, added: "In this forest, however, some pioneers have already beaten paths in various directions and made some important positive observations."[443] In 1919 G. Millet, in his book on the medieval Serbian churches, endeavored to refute the common opinion that Serbian art was nothing but a branch of Byzantine art and to prove that Serbian art had an original character of its own.[444]

Summarizing what has been said of the cultural movement under the Palaeologi, one must first of all certify to a great strength, activity, and variety not present in earlier times, when the general situation of the Empire seemed much more favorable to cultural achievement. This rise, of course, must not be considered sudden, without roots in the past. These roots are to be seen in the cultural rise of Byzantium in the epoch of the Comneni; and the connecting link between these two periods, separated from each other by the fatal Latin domination, is the cultural life of the Empire of Nicaea with Nicephorus Blemmydes and the enlightened emperors of the Lascarid dynasty. In spite of all the difficulties of the political situation the Nicaean emperors succeeded in sheltering and developing the best intellectual spirit of the epoch to transmit it to the restored Empire of the Palaeologi. Under the latter the cultural life flowered abundantly, especially at the end of the thirteenth and in the fourteenth century. Thereafter, under the pressure of Turkish danger, it began to decline in Constantinople, and the best minds of the fifteenth century, such as Bessarion of Nicaea and Gemistus Plethon, transferred their activity to the Peloponnesus, to Mistra, the center resembling some of the smaller Italian centers of the Renaissance and apparently less exposed to Turkish conquest than Constantinople or Thessalonica.

Several times Byzantine cultural interests and problems have been compared with analogous interests and problems of the epoch of the earlier Italian Renaissance. Both Italy and Byzantium were living through a time of intense cul-

---

[441] On the miniatures of the epoch of the Palaeologi see Diehl, *Manuel d'art byzantin,* II, 872-84.

[442] *Macedonia,* 285.

[443] *Byzantine Painting,* 68.

[444] *L'Ancient art serbe. Les églises,* 9. Millet, "La Renaissance byzantine," *Compte-rendu du deuxième Congrès international des études byzantines, 1927,* 19-21.

tural activity with many common traits and a common origin arising from the economic and intellectual revolution achieved by the crusades. This was not the epoch of an Italian Renaissance or a Byzantine Renaissance but, to use the word in its broad sense and not to limit it to a single nation, the epoch of the Greco-Italian or, generally speaking, southern European Renaissance. Later, in the fifteenth century, in southeastern Europe this rise was ended by the Turkish conquest; in the west, in Italy, general conditions shaped themselves in such a way that the cultural life could develop further and spread to other countries.

Of course, Byzantium had no Dante. The Byzantine Renaissance was bound by the traditions of its past, in which creative spirit and independence had been subdued by the strict authority of church and state. Formalism and conventionalism were the characteristics of the Byzantine past. Taking into consideration these conditions of Byzantine life, one is amazed by the intensive cultural activity of the Palaeologian period and by the energetic efforts of its best minds to enter the new way of free and independent investigation in literature and art. But the fatal destiny of the Eastern Empire prematurely crushed this literary, scientific, and artistic ardor.[445]

BYZANTIUM AND THE ITALIAN RENAISSANCE

In considering what influence was exerted on the Italian Renaissance by the medieval Greek tradition in general and by the Byzantine Greeks in particular, it is important to remember that it was not interest in and acquaintance with classical antiquity that called forth the Renaissance in Italy. On the contrary, the conditions of Italian life which evoked and developed the Renaissance were the real cause of the rise of interest in antique culture.

In the middle of the nineteenth century some historians thought that the Italian Renaissance was called forth by the Greeks who fled from Byzantium to Italy before the Turkish danger, especially at the fall of Constantinople in 1453. For example, a Russian Slavophile of the first half of the nineteenth cen-

[445] In his very interesting article, "Das Problem der Renaissance in Byzanz," *Historische Zeitschrift*, CXXXIII (1926), 393–412, A. Heisenberg, generally speaking, denied the existence of the Byzantine Renaissance, but he ended his article: "It was only some centuries later that the leading class [in Byzantium] began to feel that, under the covering of antique tradition imposed rather ostentatiously by state and church, forces of a new, richer, and deeper life lay hidden. But at that moment, through the avarice of western Europe, the strength of the Byzantine world was forever broken down; a real Renaissance was destined neither to the Byzantine people, nor to the rest of the Orthodox World in eastern Europe" (p. 412). See also F. Dölger, in *Deutsche Literaturzeitung*, XLVII (1926), 1142–43, 1445. "A real Renaissance" in Byzantium of the fourteenth century was emphasized by R. Guilland, *Essai sur Nicéphore Grégoras*, 294–95 and *passim*. Cf. a brilliant although one-sided article by C. Neumann, "Byzantinische Kultur und Renaissancekultur," *Historische Zeitschrift*, XCI (1903), 215–32.

tury, J. V. Kireyevsky, wrote: "When after the capture of Constantinople the fresh and pure air of Hellenic thought blew from the East to the West, and the thinking man in the West breathed more easily and freely, the whole structure of scholasticism collapsed at once."[446] Obviously, such a point of view is quite untenable if only for no other reason than elementary chronology: the Renaissance is known to have embraced the whole of Italy by the first half of the fifteenth century, and the chief leaders of the so-called Italian humanism, Petrarca and Boccaccio, lived in the fourteenth century.

There are, then, two problems: the influence of the medieval Greek tradition upon the Renaissance and the influence of the Byzantine Greeks upon the Renaissance. Considering the latter first, what sort of Greeks were those whose names are connected with the epoch of the earlier Renaissance, i.e. the fourteenth century and the very beginning of the fifteenth?

Chronologically, the first to be named is a Greek of Calabria, in southern Italy, Barlaam, who died about the middle of the fourteenth century, who participated in the Hesychast quarrel. He put on the monastic habit in Calabria, changed his name from Bernardo to Barlaam, and spent some time in Thessalonica, on Mount Athos, and in Constantinople. The Emperor, Andronicus the Younger, sent him on an important mission to the West concerning the crusade against the Turks and the union of the churches. After a fruitless journey he returned to Byzantium, where he took part in the religious movement of the Hesychasts, and then went back to the West, where he ended his days. Barlaam is a personality of whom the first humanists often speak, and the scholars of the nineteenth century vary in their opinion of him. At Avignon Petrarca met Barlaam and began to learn Greek with him in order to be able to read Greek authors in the original. In one of his letters Petrarca spoke of Barlaam as follows: "There was another, my teacher, who, having aroused in me the most delightful hope, died and left me at the very beginning of my studies [*in ipso studiorum lacte*]." In another letter Petrarca wrote: "He [i.e. Barlaam] was most excellent in Greek eloquence, and very poor in Latin; rich in ideas and quick in mind, he was embarrassed in expressing his emotions in words."[447] In a third letter he said: "I always was very anxious to study all of Greek literature and if Fortune had not envied my beginnings and deprived me of an excellent teacher, now I might be something more than an elementary Hellenist."[448] Petrarca never succeeded in reading Greek litera-

[446] *Works*, II, 252. This opinion was even given in the first edition of J. Kulakovsky, *History of Byzantium*, I, 12; in the second edition (1913) it was omitted.

[447] F. Petraeca, *Epistolae de rebus familiaribus et Variae*, XVIII, 2, and XXIV, 12; ed. G. Fracassetti, II, 474, III, 302. See Uspensky,

Byzantine Civilization, 301–2. A. Veselovsky, "Boccaccio, His Surroundings and Contemporaries," *Works*, V, 86.

[448] *Variarum epistolarum*, XXV; ed. Fracassetti, II, 369. Uspensky, *Essays on Byzantine Civilization*, 303.

ture in the original. Barlaam also had some influence on Boccaccio, who in his work *The Genealogy of the Gods* (*Genealogia deorum*) calls Barlaam a man "with a small body but enormous knowledge," and who puts entire confidence in him in all matters pertaining to Greek scholarship.[449]

The theological and mathematical essays, notes, and orations of Barlaam which are accessible afford no sufficient reason to call him a humanist. In all probability, his writings were unknown to Petrarca; and Boccaccio distinctly says that he "has seen no single one of his works."[450] Neither is there enough data to testify to his wide education or exceptional knowledge of literature, in other words, no reason to believe that Barlaam possessed enough talent or cultural force to exert a great influence on his most talented and educated Italian contemporaries, the leading spirits of the epoch, such as Petrarca and Boccaccio. Therefore we cannot agree with the exaggerated estimation of Barlaam's influence upon the Renaissance which appears sometimes in excellent works. For example, a German scholar, G. Körting, observed: "When Barlaam, by his hasty departure from Avignon, had deprived Petrarca of the possibility of deeper knowledge of the Greek tongue and civilization, he destroyed thereby the proud structure of the future and decided for centuries the destiny of the European peoples. Small causes, great effects!"[451] A Russian scholar, Th. Uspensky, wrote on the same subject: "The vivid conception of the idea and importance of Hellenic studies with which the men of the Italian Renaissance were filled, must be wholly attributed to the indirect and direct influence of Barlaam. Thus, great merit in the history of medieval culture belongs to him. . . . On the basis of real facts, we may strongly affirm that he combined the best qualities of the scholarship then existing."[452]

The role of Barlaam in the history of the Renaissance was in reality much more modest. He was nothing but a rather imperfect teacher of the Greek language, who could impart the elements of grammar and serve as a dictionary, "containing," said Korelin, "very inexact information."[453] The most correct estimation of Barlaam's significance was given by A. Veselovsky: "The role of Barlaam in the history of earlier Italian humanism is superficial and casual. . . . As a medieval scholastic and enemy of Platonic philosophy, he could share with his Western friends only the knowledge of the Greek language and some fragments of erudition; but he was magnified by virtue of the hopes and expectations in which the genuine evolution of humanism expressed itself and to which he was unable to respond."[454]

The second Greek who played a considerable role in the epoch of the earlier

[449] *De genealogia deorum*, XV, 6; 1532 ed., 389. M. Korelin, *The Early Italian Humanism and Its Historiography*, 993.

[450] *De genealogia deorum*, XV, 6; 1532 ed., 390: hujus ego nullum vidi opus.

[451] *Petrarca's Leben und Werke*, 154.

[452] *Essays on Byzantine Civilization*, 308.

[453] *Early Italian Humanism*, 998.

[454] *Works*, V, 100–1.

Renaissance was a pupil of Barlaam, Leontius Pilatus, who like his teacher came from Calabria and who died in the seventh decade of the fourteenth century. Moving from Italy to Greece and back again, passing in Italy for a Greek of Thessalonica and in Greece for an Italian and living nowhere without quarrels, he stayed for three years at Florence with Boccaccio, to whom he taught Greek and gave some information for his *Genealogy of the Gods*. Both Petrarca and Boccaccio spoke of Leontius in their writings, and depict in a similar way the refractory, harsh, and impertinent character and repulsive appearance of this "man of such bestial manners and strange customs."[455] In one of his letters to Boccaccio, Petrarca wrote that Leontius, who left him after many insolent remarks against Italy and the Italians, on his journey sent him a letter "longer and more disgusting than his beard and hair, in which he exalts to the skies hated Italy and vilifies and blames Greece and Byzantium, which he greatly exalted before; then he asks me to call him back to me and supplicates and beseeches more earnestly than the Apostle Peter besought Christ commanding the waters." In the same letter are the following interesting lines: "And now listen and laugh: among other things, he asks me to recommend him by letter to the Constantinopolitan Emperor, whom I know neither personally nor by name; but he wants this and therefore imagines that [that Emperor] is as benevolent and gracious to me as the Roman Emperor; as if the similarity of their title identified them, or because the Greeks call Constantinople the second Rome and dare to regard it not only as equal to the ancient, but even as surpassing it in population and wealth."[456] In his *Genealogy of the Gods* Boccaccio described Leontius as horribly ugly, always absorbed in his thoughts, rough and unfriendly, but the greatest living authority on Greek literature and an inexhaustible archive of Greek legends and fables.[457] While he was with Boccaccio, Leontius made the first literary Latin translation of Homer. However, this translation was so unsatisfactory that later humanists judged it desirable to replace it by a new one. Taking into account the fact that Leontius, as Boccaccio stated, was indebted to his teacher Barlaam for much of his knowledge, Th. Uspensky said that "the importance of the latter must rise even higher in our eyes."[458]

Fully recognizing the considerable influence of Leontius Pilatus on Boccac-

[455] Petrarca, *Lettere sinili di Petrarca*, V, 3; ed. Fracassetti, I, 299; also III, 6, ed. Fracassetti, I, 73: "è certamente una gran bestia." See *Lettere di Petrarca*, ed. Fracassetti, IV, 98. Boccaccio, *De genealogia deorum*, XV, 6, 1532 ed., 389. See Veselovsky, "Boccaccio," *Works*, VI, 364.

[456] Petrarca, *Lettere sinili*, III, 6; ed. Fracassetti, I, 174–75. *Lettere*, ed. Fracassetti, IV, 98.

See Veselovsky, "Boccaccio," *Works*, VI, 362–63.

[457] *De genealogia deorum*, XV, 6; 1532 ed., 390. See Veselovsky, "Boccaccio," *Works*, VI, 351–52.

[458] *Essays on Byzantine Civilization*, 308. See Boccaccio, *De genealogia deorum*, XV, 6; 1532 ed., 390: "Leontium . . . ut ipse asserit, praedicti Barlaae auditorem."

cio in the study of Greek, nevertheless, in the general history of the Renaissance, the role of Pilatus is reduced to the spreading of the knowledge of the Greek language and literature in Italy by means of lessons and translations. Moreover, the immortality of Boccaccio does not rest upon the material afforded him by Greek literature, but upon an entirely different basis.

Thus, the role in the history of the early humanistic movement of these Greeks who were in origin not Byzantines, but south Italians (Calabrians), is reduced to the mere transmission of technical information on language and literature.

Stress has several times been laid on the fact that Barlaam and Leontius Pilatus came from Calabria, from southern Italy, where the Greek language and tradition continued to live all through the Middle Ages. Regardless of the ancient "Magna Graecia" in southern Italy, whose Hellenic elements had not been entirely absorbed by Rome, the conquests of Justinian in the sixth century had introduced to Italy in general and to southern Italy in particular not a few Greek elements. The Lombards, who shortly after Justinian conquered the greater part of Italy were themselves affected by Greek influence, became to some extent the champions of Hellenic civilization. It is important to examine the evolution of Hellenism in southern Italy and Sicily, the Greek population of which gradually increased. In the sixth and seventh centuries many Greeks were forced to leave their country for southern Italy and Sicily under pressure of Slavonic invasions into Greece.[459] In the seventh century a huge Greek emigration to Sicily and southern Italy took place from the Byzantine regions conquered and devastated by the Persians and Arabs. In the eighth century a vast number of Greek monks came to Italy, escaping the persecution of the iconoclastic emperors. Finally, in the ninth and tenth centuries Greek refugees from Sicily, then being conquered by the Arabs, inundated southern Italy. This was probably the main source of the Hellenization of Byzantine southern Italy, because Byzantine culture there began to flourish only in the tenth century, "as if it were but the continuation and inheritance of the Greek culture of Sicily."[460] A. Veselovsky wrote: "Thus, in southern Italy there formed densely populated Greek ethnic islands as well as a people and society united by one language and religion and by a cultural tradition, which was represented by the monasteries. The bloom of that culture embraces the period from the second half of the ninth century to the second half of the tenth; but it also continues later, in the epoch of the Normans. . . . The founding of the most important Greek monasteries in southern Italy belongs to the twelfth century. Their history is the history of south Italian Hellenism.

[459] P. Charanis, "On the Question of the Hellenization of Sicily and Southern Italy," *American Historical Review,* LII (1946–47), 74–86.

[460] P. Batiffol, *L'Abbaye de Rossano,* ix.

They had had their heroic period, that of anchorites living in caves and preferring contemplation to reading and writing, as well as the period of well-
organized cenobitic institutions with schools of copyists, libraries, and literary
activity."[461] Greek medieval southern Italy produced a number of writers who
devoted themselves to composing not only lives of the saints, but also religious
poetry; they "were also preserving the traditions of learning."[462] In the second
half of the thirteenth century Roger Bacon wrote the Pope concerning Italy,
"in which, in many places, the clergy and people were purely Greek."[463] An
old French chronicler stated of the same time that the peasants of Calabria
spoke nothing but Greek.[464] In the fourteenth century, in one of his letters,
Petrarca spoke of a certain youth who, on his advice, is to go to Calabria: he
wished to go directly to Constantinople, "but learning that Greece abounding
once in great talents now lacks them, he believed my words . . . ; hearing
from me that in our time in Calabria there were some men thoroughly acquainted with Greek literature . . . he determined to go there."[465] Thus,
the Italians of the fourteenth century did not need to appeal to Byzantium
for elementary technical acquaintance with the Greek language and the beginnings of Greek literature; they had a nearer source, in southern Italy, the
source which gave them Barlaam and Leontius Pilatus.

The real influence of Byzantium upon Italy begins at the end of the fourteenth century and continues during the fifteenth century, the time of the real
Byzantine humanists, Manuel Chrysoloras, Gemistus Plethon, and Bessarion
of Nicaea.

Born in Constantinople about the middle of the fourteenth century, Manuel
Chrysoloras enjoyed in his native country the renown of an eminent teacher,
rhetorician, and philosopher. A young Italian humanist, Guarino, went to
Constantinople on purpose to hear Chrysoloras; the latter taught him Greek,
and Guarino began to study Greek authors. Chrysoloras, by order of the Emperor, came on a special political mission to Italy, where his fame had already
reached and where he was enthusiastically received. The Italian centers of
humanism, in eager rivalry, showered the foreign scholar with invitations.
For several years he taught at the University of Florence, where a great group
of humanists attended his classes. At the request of Emperor Manuel II, who
was at that time in Italy, he removed for a short time to Milan and later on
became a professor at Pavia. After a short stay in Byzantium Chrysoloras re-

---

[461] "Boccaccio," *Works*, V, 22.

[462] *Ibid.*, V, 23.

[463] Nec multum esset pro tanta utilitate ire
in Italiam, in qua clerus et populus sunt pure
Graeci in multis locis; Roger Bacon, *Compendium studii philosophiae*, chap. vi; Bacon,
Opera quaedum hactenus inedita, 434.

[464] Et par toute Calabre li païsant ne parlent
se grizois non. P. Meyer, "Les Premières compilations françaises d'histoire ancienne," *Romania*, XIV (1885), 70, n. 5.

[465] *De rebus senilibus*, XI, 9; ed. Fracassetti, II, 164.

turned to Italy, and then, in behalf of the Emperor, made a long journey to England, France, and, possibly, Spain, finally entering into close relation with the papal curia. Sent by the pope to Germany to negotiate about the coming council, he arrived at Constance, where the Council was held, and died there in 1415. Chrysoloras' chief importance was apparently due to his teaching and to his ability to transmit to his auditors his vast knowledge of Greek literature. His writings in the form of theological treatises, Greek grammar, translations (for example, a literary translation of Plato), and letters, do not justify attributing to him a really great literary talent. But his influence on the humanists was enormous, and they showered upon the Byzantine professor the highest praise and most sincere enthusiasm. Guarino compared him with the sun illuminating Italy which had been sunk in deep darkness, and expressed a wish that thankful Italy should erect in his honor triumphal arches along his way.[466] He is sometimes called "the prince of Greek eloquence and philosophy."[467] The most eminent men of the new movement were among his pupils. A French historian of the Renaissance, Monnier, recalling the judgments of the humanists on Barlaam and Pilatus, wrote: "Here is no dull intellect, no lousy beard, no coarse Calabrian ready to laugh bestially at the admirable flashes of wit of a Terence. Manuel Chrysoloras is a veritable Greek; he is from Byzantium; he is noble; he is erudite; besides Greek he knows Latin; he is grave, mild, religious, and prudent; he seems to be born for virtue and glory; he is familiar with the latest achievements of science and philosophy; he is a master. This is the first Greek professor who renewed the classical tradition by occupying a chair in Italy."[468]

But Italy of the fifteenth century was influenced much more deeply and widely by the famous leaders of the Byzantine Renaissance, Gemistus Plethon and Bessarion of Nicaea. The former was the initiator of the Platonic Academy at Florence and the regenerator of Platonic philosophy in the West, and Bessarion was a man of first importance in the cultural movement of the time.

Bessarion was born at the very beginning of the fifteenth century at Trebizond, where he received his elementary education. He was sent to Constantinople for further advance in knowledge, and then he began to study thoroughly the Greek poets, orators, and philosophers. A meeting with the Italian humanist, Filelfo, who was then attending lectures in Constantinople, made Bessarion acquainted with the humanistic movement in Italy, and with the deep interest in ancient literature and art which was then making its appear-

[466] See P. Monnier, *Le Quattrocento. Essai sur l'histoire littéraire du XVᵉ siècle italien*, II, 6.

[467] See Korelin, *Early Italian Humanism*, 1002.

[468] Monnier, *Le Quattrocento*, II, 4: "Quis enim praestantiorem Manuele virum, aut vidisse aut legisse meminit, qui ad virtutem ad gloriam sine ulla dubitatione natus erat? . . ." Decembrio declares "that as to his knowledge of letters, he did not seem to be a man but rather an angel."

ance there. After taking the monastic habit Bessarion continued his studies in the Peloponnesus, at Mistra, under the guidance of the famous Plethon himself. As the archbishop of Nicaea he accompanied the Emperor to the Council of Ferrara-Florence and greatly influenced the course of the negotiations toward union. Bessarion wrote during the council, "I do not judge it right to separate from the Latins in spite of all plausible reasons."[469]

During his stay in Italy, he plunged into the intense life of the Renaissance and, not inferior himself to the Italian humanists in talent and education, he came into close contact with them, and, thanks to his opinion on the problem of union, he had also an intimate connection with the papal curia. On his return to Constantinople, Bessarion soon realized that, because of the hostility of the great majority of the Greek population, the union could not be accomplished in the East. At this time he received news from Italy that he had been appointed a cardinal of the Roman church. Feeling the ambiguity of his position in his own country, he yielded to his desire to return to Italy, the center of humanism, and left Byzantium for Italy.

At Rome the house of Bessarion became a center of humanistic intercourse. The most eminent representatives of humanism, such as Poggio and Valla, were his friends. Valla in reference to Bessarion's excellent knowledge of both classical languages called him "the best Greek of the Latins and the best Latin of the Greeks" (*latinorum graecissimus, graecorum latinissimus*).[470] Purchasing books or ordering copies made, Bessarion collected an excellent library comprising the works of the Fathers of the Eastern and Western churches and works of theological thought in general, as well as humanistic literature. Towards the end of his life he bestowed his very rich library upon the city of Venice, where it became one of the chief foundations of the famous present-day library of St. Mark (Bibliotheca Marciana); at the entrance door the portrait of Bessarion may be still seen.

Another idea in which he was greatly interested was that of a crusade against the Turks. At the news of the fall of Constantinople, Bessarion wrote immediately to the Doge of Venice calling his attention to the danger threatening Europe from the Turks and for this reason appealing to him to take arms against them.[471] At that time Europe was unable to understand any other reason. Bessarion died at Ravenna in 1472, whence his body was transported to Rome for a solemn burial.

Bessarion's literary activity was carried on in Italy. Besides numerous works of theological character concerning union, *A Dogmatic Oration*, the refuta-

[469] *Oratio dogmatica pro unione;* ed. Migne, *Patrologia Graeca,* CLXI, 612.

[470] H. Vast, *Le Cardinal Bessarion* (*1403–1472*), title page. R. Rocholl, *Bessarion. Studie zur Geschichte der Renaissance,* 105.

L. Mohler, *Kardinal Bessarion als Theologe, Humanist und Staatsmann,* 406.

[471] See A. Sadov, *Bessarion of Nicaea,* 276. Mohler, *Kardinal Bessarion,* 275–76; concerning Bessarion's library, 408–15.

tion of Marcus Eugenicus (Mark of Ephesus), and works of polemic and exegesis, Bessarion left translations of some classical authors, among them Demosthenes and Xenophon, and of the metaphysics of Aristotle, works much more characteristic of him as a humanist. An admirer of Plato, Bessarion in his work *Against Plato's Calumniator* (*In calumniatorem Platonis*), succeeded in remaining more or less objective, which cannot be said of the other champions of Aristotelianism and Platonism. Only a short time ago was published Bessarion's long *Encomium* (*Eulogy*) of his native city, Trebizond, which is of great importance from the historical point of view.[472]

Bessarion presents, as his French biographer said, better than anyone else among the eminent men of his time an example of the fusion of the Greek genius with the Latin genius, from which the Renaissance sprang forth. "Bessarion lived on the threshold between two ages. He is a Greek who becomes Latin, . . . a cardinal who protects scholars, a scholastic theologian who breaks lances in favor of Platonism, an enthusiastic admirer of antiquity who has contributed more than anyone to originating the modern age. He is connected with the Middle Ages by the ideal which he endeavors to realize in the Christian union and the crusade; and he predominates over his age and urges it with ardor into the new ways of progress and the Renaissance."[473] One of the contemporaries of Bessarion, Michael Apostolius (Apostolios), full of enthusiasm for Bessarion's personality and talent, made him almost a demigod. In his funeral oration for Bessarion he wrote: "[Bessarion] was the reflection of divine and true wisdom."[474] Many of Bessarion's writings are still not published. An interesting modern tribute is that at the end of the nineteenth century Italy began issuing a Catholic periodical pursuing the aim of the union of the churches, under the title *Bessarione*.

But Byzantium contributed greatly to the history of the Renaissance not only by implanting the knowledge of the Greek language and literature by lessons and lectures and by the activity of such talented men as Plethon or Bessarion, who opened new horizons to Italy; Byzantium also gave the West a vast number of earlier Greek manuscripts, which contained the best classical authors, not to mention Byzantine texts and the works of the Fathers of the Greek Church.

Italian humanists, guided by the well known bibliophile Poggio, traveled through Italy and western Europe about the fourth decade of the fifteenth century, i.e. the epoch of the Council of Florence, and gathered together almost all the Latin classics now known. After Manuel Chrysoloras, who aroused an enthusiastic veneration for ancient Hellas in Italy, there was evi-

[472] Ed. S. Lampros, Νέος Ἑλληνομνήμων, XIII (1916), 146–94; also published separately.

[473] Vast, *Le Cardinal Bessarion*, ix, xi.

[474] *Laudatio funebris Bessarionis;* Migne, *Patrologia Graeca*, CLXI, 140.

dent an intensive movement for the acquisition of Greek books. For this purpose the Italians hoped to use the Byzantine libraries. The Italians who had gone to Byzantium to learn Greek wisdom returned to Italy bringing Greek books. The first of these was an auditor of Chrysoloras in Constantinople, Guarino. What Poggio did for collecting the works of Roman literature, Giovanni Aurispa did for Greek literature: he went to Byzantium and brought from Constantinople, the Peloponnesus, and the islands no less than 238 volumes, in other words, a whole library comprising the best classical writers.

As, in connection with the Turkish conquest, living conditions in Byzantium were growing harder and more dangerous, the Greeks emigrated in large numbers to the West and carried with them the works of their literature. The accumulation in Italy of the treasures of the classical world owing to conditions in Byzantium, created in the West exceptionally favorable conditions for acquaintance with the remote past of Hellas and her eternal culture. By transmitting classical works to the West and thereby saving them from destruction at the hands of the Turks, Byzantium performed great service for the future destinies of mankind.

APPENDIX

APPENDIX

EMPERORS OF THE BYZANTINE EMPIRE

324–1453

Constantine the Great (sole emperor), 324–337.
Constantine, 337–340.
Constans, 337–350.
Constantius, 337–361.
Julian the Apostate, 361–363.
Jovian, 363–364.
Valens, 364–378.
Theodosius the Great, 379–395.
Arcadius, 395–408.
Theodosius II the Younger, 408–450.
Marcian, 450–457.
Leo I the Great, 457–474.
Leo II, 474.
Zeno, 474–491.
Anastasius I, 491–518.
Justin I, 518–527.
Justinian I the Great, 527–565.
Justin II, 565–578.
Tiberius II, 578–582.
Maurice, 582–602.
Phocas, 602–610.
Heraclius, 610–641.
Constantine II, 641.
Heraclonas (Heracleon), 641.
Constantine III (Constans II), 641–668.
Constantine IV, 668–685.
Justinian II Rhinotmetus, 685–695.
Leontius, 695–698.
Tiberius III (Apsimar), 698–705.
Justinian II (for the second time), 705–711.
Philippicus Bardanes, 711–713.
Anastasius II (Artemius), 713–715.
Theodosius III, 715–717.
Leo III, 717–741.
Constantine V Copronymus, 741–775.
Leo IV the Khazar (Chazar), 775–780.
Constantine VI, 780–797.
Irene, 797–802.
Nicephorus I, 802–811.
Stauracius, 811.

Michael I Rangabé, 811–813.
Leo V the Armenian, 813–820.
Michael II the Stammerer, 820–829.
Theophilus, 829–842.
Michael III, 842–867.
Basil I, 867–886.
Leo VI the Philosopher (the Wise), 886–912.
Alexander, 912–913.
Constantine VII Porphyrogenitus, 913–959.
Romanus I Lecapenus (co-emperor), 919–944.
Stephen and Constantine, Romanus Lecapenus' sons, Dec. 944–Jan. 945.
Romanus II, 959–963.
Nicephorus II Phocas, 963–969.
John I Tzimisces, 969–976.
Basil II Bulgaroctonus, 976–1025.
Constantine VIII, 1025–1028.
Romanus III Argyrus, 1028–1034.
Michael IV the Paphlagonian, 1034–1041.
Michael V Calaphates, 1041–1042.
Theodora and Zoë, 1042.
Constantine IX Monomachus, 1042–1055.
Theodora, 1055–1056.
Michael VI Stratioticus, 1056–1057.
Isaac I Comnenus, 1057–1059.
Constantine X Ducas, 1059–1067.
Romanus IV Diogenes, 1067–1071.
Michael VII Ducas Parapinakes, 1071–1078.
Nicephorus III Botaniates, 1078–1081.
Alexius I Comnenus, 1081–1118.
John II, 1118–1143.
Manuel I, 1143–1180.
Alexius II, 1180–1183.
Andronicus I, 1182–1185.
Isaac II Angelus, 1185–1195.
Alexius III, 1195–1203.
Isaac (for the second time) and Alexius IV, 1203–1204.
Alexius V Ducas Mourtzouphlos, 1204.
Theodore I Lascaris, 1204–1222.

John III Ducas Vatatzes, 1222–1254.
Theodore II Lascaris, 1254–1258.
John IV, 1258–1261.
Michael VIII Palaeologus, 1261–1282.
Andronicus II, 1282–1328.
Michael (IX), 1295–1320.
Andronicus III, 1328–1341.

John V, 1341–1391.
John VI Cantacuzene, 1341–1354.
Andronicus (IV), 1376–1379.
John (VII), 1390.
Manuel II, 1391–1425.
John VIII, 1425–1448.
Constantine XI, 1449–1453.

GENEALOGICAL TABLES
OF THE BYZANTINE DYNASTIES

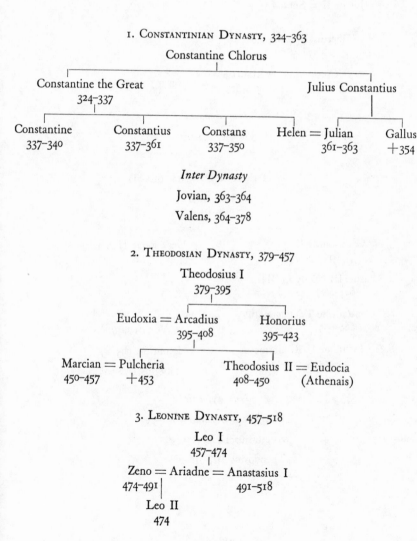

1. CONSTANTINIAN DYNASTY, 324–363

Constantine Chlorus

Constantine the Great
324–337

Julius Constantius

Constantine
337–340

Constantius
337–361

Constans
337–350

Helen = Julian
361–363

Gallus
+354

Inter Dynasty

Jovian, 363–364

Valens, 364–378

2. THEODOSIAN DYNASTY, 379–457

Theodosius I
379–395

Eudoxia = Arcadius
395–408

Honorius
395–423

Marcian = Pulcheria
450–457   +453

Theodosius II = Eudocia
408–450   (Athenais)

3. LEONINE DYNASTY, 457–518

Leo I
457–474

Zeno = Ariadne = Anastasius I
474–491 | 491–518

Leo II
474

4. JUSTINIANIAN DYNASTY, 518–602

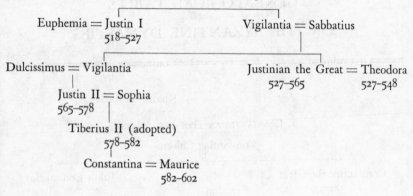

Euphemia = Justin I
518–527

Vigilantia = Sabbatius

Dulcissimus = Vigilantia

Justinian the Great = Theodora
527–565   527–548

Justin II = Sophia
565–578

Tiberius II (adopted)
578–582

Constantina = Maurice
582–602

Non-dynastic

Phocas, 602–610

5. HERACLIAN DYNASTY, 610–711

Heraclius
610–641

Constantine II
641

Heraclonas (Heracleon)
641

Constantine III (Constans II)
641–668

Constantine IV Pogonatus
668–685

Non-dynastic

Justinian II Rhinotmetus
685–695 & 705–711

Leontius, 695–698

Tiberius, 698–705

Non-dynastic

Philippicus Bardanes, 711–713

Anastasius II, 713–716

Theodosius III, 716–717

6. ISAURIAN OR SYRIAN DYNASTY, 717–802

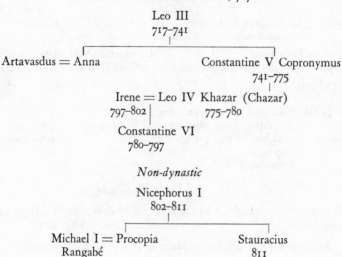

Leo III
717–741

Artavasdus = Anna   Constantine V Copronymus
741–775

Irene = Leo IV Khazar (Chazar)
797–802 | 775–780

Constantine VI
780–797

Non-dynastic

Nicephorus I
802–811

Michael I = Procopia   Stauracius
Rangabé   811
811–813

8. AMORIAN OR PHRYGIAN DYNASTY, 820–867

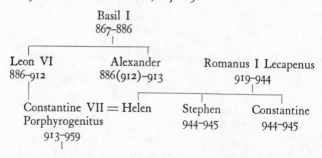

Michael the Stammerer
820–829

Theophilus = Theodora
829–842 |

Michael III the Drunkard
842–867

9. MACEDONIAN DYNASTY, 867–1056

Basil I
867–886

Leon VI   Alexander   Romanus I Lecapenus
886–912   886(912)–913   919–944

Constantine VII = Helen   Stephen   Constantine
Porphyrogenitus   944–945   944–945
913–959

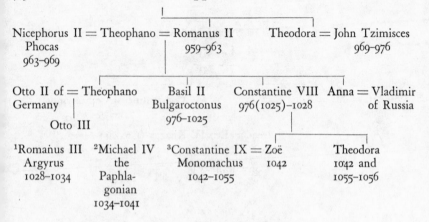

Nicephorus II = Theophano = Romanus II   Theodora = John Tzimisces
Phocas   959–963   969–976
963–969

Otto II of = Theophano   Basil II   Constantine VIII   Anna = Vladimir
Germany   Bulgaroctonus   976(1025)–1028   of Russia
      Otto III   976–1025

¹Romanus III   ²Michael IV   ³Constantine IX = Zoë   Theodora
Argyrus   the   Monomachus   1042   1042 and
1028–1034   Paphla-   1042–1055   1055–1056
           gonian
          1034–1041

10. Ducas Dynasty, 1059–1081

Constantine X = Eudocia Macrembolitissa = Romanus IV Diogenes
1059–1067   1067–1071

Michael VII Parapinakes = Maria = Nicephorus III Botaniates
1071–1078   1078–1081

11. Comnenian Dynasty, 1081–1185

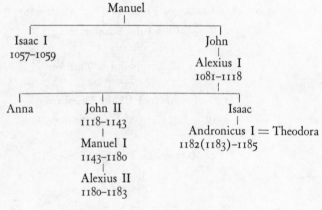

Manuel

Isaac I   John
1057–1059

                            Alexius I
                            1081–1118

Anna   John II   Isaac
        1118–1143
                  Andronicus I = Theodora
       Manuel I   1182(1183)–1185
       1143–1180

       Alexius II
       1180–1183

12. Dynasty of the Angeli, 1185–1204

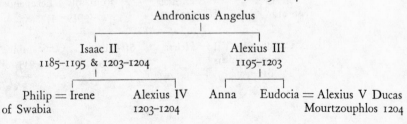

Andronicus Angelus

Isaac II   Alexius III
1185–1195 & 1203–1204   1195–1203

Philip = Irene   Alexius IV   Anna   Eudocia = Alexius V Ducas
of Swabia   1203–1204   Mourtzouphlos 1204

13. DYNASTY OF THE LASCARIDS, 1204–1261

Theodore I = Anna (d. of Alexius III)
1204–1222

Irene = John III Ducas Vatatzes
1222–1254

Theodore II
1254–1258

John IV
1258–1261

14. DYNASTY OF THE PALAEOLOGI, 1261–1453

Michael VIII
1261–1282

[1]Anna of Hungary = Andronicus II = [2]Irene of Montferrat
1282–1328

Michael IX = Xenia-Maria
1295–1320

John VI Cantacuzene   Andronicus III = Anna of Savoy
1341–1354   1328–1341

Helen ⟶ John V   Constantine Dragosh
1341–1391   (Dragases) of Macedon

Andronicus IV   Manuel II = Helen
1376–1379   1391–1425

John VII   John VIII   Constantine XI   Demetrius   Thomas
1390   1425–1448   1449–1453

Andreas   Zoë-Sophia = John III
                                                           of Russia

BIBLIOGRAPHY AND INDEX

BIBLIOGRAPHY

Abel, R. P. F. M. "L'île de Jotabe," *Revue biblique*, XLVII (1938), 520–24.

Aboulféda. *Géographie d'Aboulféda*. Trans. from Arabic by Reinaud, J. T. Vol. II. Paris, 1848.

L'Achilléide Byzantine. Ed. Hesseling, D. C. Amsterdam, 1919.

Acquis, Fr. J. da. *Della Chonaca Dell' Imagine del Mondo*. (*Monumenta Historiae Patriae. Scriptorum*, Vol. III, intro. and cols. 1457–1626.) Turin, 1848.

Acropolita, George. *Opera*. Ed. Heisenberg, August. (*Bibliotheca Scriptorum Graecorum et Romanorum Teubneriana*.) Leipzig, 1903.

Acta Aragonensia. Quellen zur deutschen, italienischen, franzöischen, spanischen, zur Kirchen- und Kulturgeschichte aus der diplomatischen Korrespondenz Jaymes II. (1291–1327). Ed. Finke, H. 2 vols. Berlin and Leipzig, 1908–22.

Acta 42 martyrum Amoriensium. Ed. Vasilievsky, V. G. and Nikitin, P. *Transactions of the Imperial Academy of Sciences*, VIII ser. VII, 2 (1905). In Greek and Russian.

Adam, Paul. *Princesses byzantines*. Paris, 1893.

Adamek, O. *Beiträge zur Geschichte des byzantinischen Kaisers Maurikios*. Graz, 1890–91.

Adonz, N. "L'âge et l'origine de l'empereur Basile I (867–86)," *Byzantion*, IX (1934), 223–60.

———. *Armenia in the Epoch of Justinian*. St. Petersburg, 1908. In Russian.

———. "Samuel l'Armenien, Roi des Bulgares," *Memoires de l'Académie royale de Belgique*, XXXIX (1938).

Agapius (Mahboub) de Menbidg. *Histoire Universelle*. Ed. Vasiliev, A. A. in *Patrologia Orientalis*, VIII (1912), 399–550.

Agathias Scholasticus. *Historiarum*. Ed. Dindorf, L. A. (*Historici Graeci Minores*, Vol. II. Pp. 132–432.) Leipzig, 1870–71. Ed. Niebuhr, B. G. (*Corpus Scriptorum Historiae Byzantinae*.) Bonn, 1828.

Aïnalov, D. *The Byzantine Painting of the Fourteenth Century*. (*Zapiski klassicheskago otdeleniya Russkago Archeologicheskago Obschestwa*. Vol. IX.) Petrograd, 1917. In Russian.

———. "La Chronique de George Hamartolus," *Compte-rendu du deuxième congrés international des études byzantines, Belgrade, 1927*. Belgrade, 1929.

Albertoni, A. *Per una esposizione del diritto bizantino*. Imola, 1927.

Albornez, A. Crillo de. *Juan Chrisostomo y su influencia social en el imperio bizantino*. Madrid, 1934.

Alexandre, C. Pléthon. *Traité de lois*. Paris, 1858.

Alföldi, A. *The Conversion of Constantine and Pagan Rome*. Oxford, 1948.

———. "Hoc signo victor eris. Beiträge zur Bekehrung Konstantins des Grossen," *Pisciculi. Studien zur Religion und Kultur des Altertums*. Munich, 1939.

Allard, P. *Julien l'Apostat*. 3 vols. 3rd. ed., Paris, 1906–10.

Allatius, Leo. *De ecclesiae occidentalis atque orientalis perpetua consensione*. Cologne, 1648.

Allen, W. E. D. *A History of the Georgian People*. London, 1932.

Alpatov, M. and Brunov, I. "A Brief Report of a Journey to the East," *Vizantiysky Vremennik*, XXIV (1923–26).

Altaner, B. *Die Dominikanermissionen des 13. Jahrhunderts*. Habelschwerdt, 1924.

Alvari Cordubensis. *Opera. Indiculus luminosus*. Ed. Florenz, F. H. *España Sagrada*, XI (Madrid, 1753), 219–75.

Amantos, K. Ἱστορία τοῦ Βυζαντινοῦ Κράτους. 2 vols. Athens, 1939–47.

Amari, M. *Storia dei musulmani di Sicilia*. Vols. I–III. Florence, 1854–72. Ed. Nallino, C. A. Vols. I–III. Catania, 1933–37.

Amélineau, E. "La Conquête de l'Égypte par les Arabes," *Revue historique*, CXIX (1915), 273–310.

Anastasijević, D. "A Hypothesis of Western Bulgaria," *Bulletin de la Société Scientifique de Skoplje*, III (1927), 1–12. In Serbian.

Anastasius. *Chronographia tripertita*. Ed. de Boor, C. Leipzig, 1885. (Volume two of *Theophanis Chronographia*, ed. de Boor, C.).

Anastos, M. "Plethos' Calendar and Liturgy," *Dumbarton Oaks Papers*, IV (1948), 183–305.

Andreadès, A. "De la population de Constantinople sous les empereurs byzantins," *Metron*, I (1920).

Andreev, I. *Germanus and Tarasius, the Patriarchs of Constantinople: Their Life and Activity in Connection with the History of Iconoclastic Troubles*. Sergiev Posad, 1907. In Russian.

Andreeva, M. A. "Dubrovnik," *Revue internationale des études balkaniques*, II (1935), 125–28.

———. *Essays on the Culture of the Byzantine Court in the Thirteenth Century*. Prague, 1927. In Russian. Good piece of work.

———. "The Reception of the Tartar Ambassadors at the Nicene Court," *Recueil d'études dédiées à mémoire de N. P. Kondakov*. Prague, 1926. In Russian.

———. "Zur Reise Manuels II. Palaiologos nach Westeuropa," *Byzantinische Zeitschrift*, XXXIV (1934), 37–47.

Andriotes, N. "Κριτόβουλος ὁ Ἴμβριος καὶ τὸ Ἱστορικό του ἔργο," Ἑλληνικά, II (1929), 167–200.

Anecdota Bruxellensia. I. *Chroniques byzantines du Manuscrit 11.376*. Ed. Cumont, Franz. Gand., 1894.

Anikiev, P. "On the Problem of Orthodox-Christian Mysticism," *Pravoslavnoye-Russkoye Slovo*, No. 13 (August, 1903), 200–17. In Russian.

Annales Colonienses Maximi, s. a. 1185. Ed. Pertz, K. (*Monumenta Germaniae Historica. Scriptores*, XVII, 723–847.) Hanover, 1861.

Annales Marbacenses. Ed. Pertz, K. (*Monumenta Germaniae Historica. Scriptores*, XVII, 142–80.) Hanover, 1861.

Annales Stadenses. Ed. Pertz, K. (*Monumenta Germaniae Historica. Scriptores*, XVI, 349 ff.) Hanover, 1861.

Anonymous Valesianus. Ed. Gardhausen, V. (Vol. II of his edition of Ammianus Marcellinus.) Leipzig, 1875. Ed. Mommsen, T. (*Monumenta Germaniae Historica. Auctorum Antiquissimorum*, IX. *Chronica Minora*, I.) Berlin, 1892. Ed. Cessi (*Rerum Italicarum Scriptores*.) Bologna, 1913.

Ansbertus. *Historia de expeditione Frederici Imperatoris.* (*Fontes rerum Austriacarum. Scriptores,* V, 1–90.) Vienna, 1863.

Antiochus Strategus. *The Capture of Jerusalem by the Persians in the Year 614.* Trans. from the Georgian by Marr, N. St. Petersburg, 1909. Trans. into English by Conybeare, F. C. *The English Historical Review,* XXV (1910), 502–17.

Antoniades, E. M. *Hagia Sophia.* Athens, 1907. In Greek.

Apostoli, M. *Laudatio funebris Bessarionis.* Ed. Migne, J. P. (*Patrologia Graeca,* CLXI, cols. 140 ff.) Paris, 1866.

Arnakes, G. Georgiades. "Captivity of Gregory Palamas by the Turks and Related Documents as Historical Sources," *Speculum* (January, 1951), 104–18.

———. Οἱ πρῶτοι Ὀθωμάνοι. Συμβολὴ εἰς τὸ πρόβλημα τῆς πτώσεως τοῦ Ἑλληνισμοῦ τῆς Μικρᾶς Ἀσίας (1282–1337). (*Texte und Forschungen zur byz. neugr. Philologie.* No. 41) Athens, 1947.

Ashburner, W. "The Farmer's Law," *Journal of Hellenic Studies,* XXX (1910), 85–108; XXXII (1912), 68–83.

———. *The Rhodian Sea Law.* Oxford, 1909.

Assemani, Joseph Simeon. *Kalendaria Ecclesiae Universae.* 4 vols. Rome, 1755.

Atiya, Aziz Suryal. *The Crusade in the Later Middle Ages.* London, 1938.

———. *The Crusade of Nicopolis.* London, 1934.

Attwater, S. *St. John Chrysostom.* Milwaukee, 1939.

Auvray, L. *Les Registres de Gregoire IX.* Paris, 1907.

Babinger, F. *Geschichtsschreiber der Osmanen und ihre Werke.* Leipzig, 1927.

Bach, E. "Les Lois agraires byzantines du Xe siècle," *Classica et Mediaevalia,* V (1942), 70–91.

Bacon, R. "Compendium studii philosophiae," *Opera quaedum hactenus inedita.* London, 1859.

Baker, G. P. *Justinian.* New York, 1931. Illustrated military narrative. Unimportant and superficial.

Balsamonis, Theodori. *In canonem XVI concilii Carthaginiensis.* Ed. Migne, J. P. (*Patrologia Graeca,* CXXXVIII, cols. 83–95.) Paris, 1865.

Bănescu, N. *Un Problème d'histoire médiévale: Création et caractère du Second Empire Bulgare.* Bucharest, 1943. Important.

Banús y Comas, C. *Expedicion de Catalanes y Aragoneses en Oriente en principio del siglo XIV.* Madrid, 1929.

Barbaro, Nicolò. *Giornale dell' assedio di Constantinopoli.* Ed. Çornet, E. Vienna, 1856.

Bardenhewer, O. *Geschichte der altkirchlichen Literatur.* 5 vols. Freiburg, 1912–32. Fine bibliography.

———. *Patrologie.* 3rd ed., Freiburg, 1910. English trans. Shahan, T. J. Freiburg and St. Louis, 1908.

Barlone, Daniel. *Une Fiancée de Charlemagne Irène imperatrice de Byzance.* Algiers and Paris, 1945. Historical fiction; no historical value.

Baronii, Caesare. *Annales ecclesiastici.* Ed. Theiner, A. 37 vols. Paris and Brussels, 1864–83.

Barsky, V. G. *Travels of V. G. Barsky in the Holy Places of the East from 1723 to 1747.* Ed. Barsukov, N. St. Petersburg, 1885. In Russian.

Barth, W. *Kaiser Zeno.* Basil, 1894.

Barthold, V. "Charlemagne and Harun al-Rashid," *Christiansky Vostok,* I (1912), 69–94. In Russian.

———. "The Orientation of the First Muslim Mosques," *Annual Publications of the Russian Institute of Art History,* I (1922). In Russian.

———. Review, *Transactions of the Oriental College,* I (1925). In Russian.

Barvinok, V. *Nicephorus Blemmydes and His Works.* Kiev, 1911. In Russian.

Basset, René. "Berbères: Religion, langue et litterature," *Encyclopédie de l'Islam,* I (1913), 721–23.

Batiffol, P. *L'Abbaye de Rossano.* Paris, 1891.

———. *La Paix constantinienne et le catholicisme,* 3rd ed., Paris, 1914.

Baur, P. C. *Der heilige Johannes Chrysostomus und seine Zeit.* Munich, 1929–30.

Baynes, N. H. "Alexandria and Constantinople: A Study in Ecclesiastical Diplomacy," *Journal of Egyptian Archaeology,* XII (1926), 145–56.

———. "Athanasiana," *Journal of Egyptian Archaeology,* XI (1925), 58–69.

———. *A Bibliography of the Works of J. B. Bury.* Cambridge, 1929.

———. "Bibliography: Papyri on Social Life in Graeco-Roman Egypt," *Journal of Egyptian Archaeology,* XVIII (1932), 90–91.

———. "Byzantine Civilization," *History,* X (1926), 289–99.

———. *The Byzantine Empire.* New York and London, 1926.

———. and Moss, H. St. L. B. (Eds.) *Byzantium. An Introduction to East Roman Civilization.* Oxford, 1948.

———. *Constantine the Great and the Christian Church.* (*Proceedings of the British Academy,* XV.) London, 1929.

———. "The Date of the Avar Surprise, a Chronological Study," *Byzantinische Zeitschrift,* XXI (1912), 110–28.

———. "The Death of Julian the Apostate in a Christian Legend," *Journal of Roman Studies,* XXVII (1937), 22–29.

———. "The Early Life of Julian the Apostate," *Journal of Hellenic Studies,* XLV (1925), 251–54.

———. *The Historia Augusta: Its Date and Purpose.* Oxford, 1926.

———. "The Historia Augusta: Its Date and Purpose. A Reply to Criticism," *The Classical Quarterly,* XXII (1928), 166–71.

———. "Review: *Melanges Charles Diehl,*" *Journal of Hellenic Studies,* LII (1932), 157–61.

———. "Review: Stein, *Geschichte des spätrömischen Reiches,* vol. I," *Journal of Roman Studies,* XVIII (1928), 217–25.

———. "The Vita S. Danielis Stylitae," *The English Historical Review,* XL (1925), 397–402.

Beazley, C. *The Dawn of Modern Geography.* 4 vols. London, 1897–1906.

Becker, C. "The Expansion of the Saracens—the East," *The Cambridge Medieval History,* II (1913), 329–64.

———. *Vom Werden und Wesen der Islamischen Welt: Islamstudien.* Vol. I. Leipzig, 1924.

Bees, A. "Bambacoratius, ein Beiname des Kaisers Alexios III. Angelos (1195–1203)," *Byzantinisch-neugriechische Jahrbücher,* III (1922), 285–86.

———. "Eine unbeachtete Quelle über die Abstammung des Kaisers Basileios I., des Mazedoniers," *Byzantinisch-neugriechische Jahrbücher,* IV (1923), 76.

———. "Geschichtliche Forschungsresultate und Mönchs- und Volkssagen über die

Gründer der Meteorenklöster," *Byzantinisch-neugriechische Jahrbücher,* III (1922), 364–403.

Beladsori (Baladhuri). *Liber expugnationum regionum.* Ed. de Goeje, M. J. Leyden, 1866.

——. *The Origins of the Islamic State.* Trans. Hitti, P. (Columbia University Studies in History, Economics and Public Law, LXVIII, part I.) New York, 1916.

Belin, M. A. *Histoire de la Latinité de Constantinople.* 2nd ed., Paris, 1894. Brief and very superficial sketch of the history of the Catholic Church in Byzantium in the thirteenth century.

Bell, H. I. "The Decay of a Civilization," *Journal of Egyptian Archaeology,* X (1924), 201–16.

——. *Egypt from Alexander the Great to the Arab Conquest. A Study in the Diffusion and Decay of Hellenism.* Oxford, 1948.

——. "An Epoch in the Agrarian History of Egypt," *Recueil d'études égyptologiques dédiées à la mémoire de Jean-François Champollion.* Paris, 1922.

——. "The Byzantine Servile State in Egypt," *Journal of Egyptian Archaeology,* IV (1917), 86–106.

Beneševič, V. and Uspensky, Th. I. *The Acts of Vazelon.* Leningrad, 1927. In Russian and in Greek.

——. "Die byzantinischen Ranglisten nach dem Kletorologion Philothei (De Cer. I, II c. 52) und nach den Jerusalemer Handschriften zusammengestellt und revidiert," *Byzantinisch-neugriechische Jahrbücher,* V (1926), 97–167.

——. "Sur la date de la mosaïque de la Transfiguration au Mont Sinaï," *Byzantion,* I (1924), 145–72.

Benjamin, Rabbi, of Tudela. *Oriental Travels.* Trans. Grunhüt, L. and Adler, M. N. Jerusalem, 1903. In German. Ed. Komroff, Manuel. New York, 1928. Trans. Adler, M. N. London, 1907.

Berger, A. and Schiller, A. A. *Bibliography of Anglo-American Studies in Roman, Greek, and Greco-Egyptian Law and Related Sciences.* (An annual extraordinary number of *The Jurist.*) Washington, D.C., 1945.

Berger, A. "Tipoukeitos: The Origin of a Name," *Traditio,* III (1945), 394–402.

Berger, E. *Les Registres d'Innocent IV.* Paris, 1887.

Bergkamp, J. U. *Dom Jean Mabillon and the Benedictine Historical School of Saint-Maur.* Washington, D.C., 1928.

Berthelot, M. *La Chimie au moyen âge.* Vol. I. Paris, 1893.

Besta, E. *La cattura dei Veneziani in Oriente.* Feltre, 1920.

Bezdeki, St. *Le Portrait de Théodore Métochite par Nicéphore Grégoras. Mélanges d'histoire générale.* Cluj, 1927.

Bezobrazov, P. V. *A Byzantine Writer and Statesman, Michael Psellus.* I. *The Biography of Michael Psellus.* Moscow, 1890. In Russian.

——. "Comptes rendus," *Vizantiysky Vremennik,* XVIII (1911), 33–36; III (1896). In Russian.

——. "Craft and Trade Corporations," in Hertzberg, G. *History of Byzantium.* Ed. Bezobrazov, P. V. Moscow, 1896. In Russian.

——. "The Empress Zoë," *Historical Articles.* Vol. I, 225–51. Moscow, 1893. Popular article. In Russian.

Bikélas, D. *La Grèce byzantine et moderne.* Paris, 1893.

————. *Seven Essays on Christian Greece*. Trans. John, Marquess of Bute. London, 1890.

Biondi, B. *Guistiniano Primo Principe e Legislatore Cattolico*. Milan, 1936. Justinian's religious policy and his relations with the Papacy.

Bizilli, P. "The Version of Novgorod of the Fourth Crusade," *Istoricheskiya Izvestiya*, 3, 4 (1916). In Russian.

Blake, R. P. "The Monetary Reforms of Anastasius I and its Economic Implications," *Studies in the History of Culture, the Disciplines of the Humanities*. Menasha, Wisconsin, 1942.

————. "Note sur l'activité littéraire de Nicéphore, Ier patriarche de Constantinople," *Byzantion*, XIV (1939), 1–15.

Blanchet, A. "Les dernières monnaies d'or des empereurs de Byzance," *Revue numismatique*, IV, 4 (1910), 78–90.

Blemmydes, Nicephorus. *Curriculum vitae et carmina*. Ed. Heisenberg, A. Leipzig, 1896.

Boak, A. E. R. "Byzantine Imperialism in Egypt," *The American Historical Review*, XXXIV (1928), 1–8.

Bobtchev, S. *History of the Ancient Bulgarian Law*. Sofia, 1910. In Bulgarian.

Boccaccio, G. *De genealogia deorum*. Basil, 1532.

Boghiatzides, I. "Τὸ χρονικὸν τῶν Μετεώρων," *Ἐπετηρὶς Ἑταιρείας Βυζαντινῶν Σπουδῶν*, I (1924), 146–56.

Bogišič, V. *Pisani zakoni na slovenskom jugu*. Zagreb, 1872.

Böhmer, J. F. *Acta imperii selecta*. Innsbruck, 1870.

Bois, J. "Gregoire le Sinaite et l'Hésychasme à l'Athos au XIVe siècle," *Échos d'Orient*, V (1901).

Boissier, G. *La Fin du paganisme; étude sur les dernières luttes religieuses en Occident au quatrième siècle*. Paris, 1891.

Boïves, K. Ἀκολουθία ἱερὰ τοῦ ὁσίου καὶ θεοφόρου πατρὸς ἡμῶν Χριστοδούλου. 3rd. ed. Athens, 1884.

Bolotov, V. *Lectures on the History of the Ancient Church*. III. *A History of the Church in the Period of the Ecumenical Councils*. St. Petersburg, 1913. Very important. In Russian.

Bon, A. *Le Péloponnèse byzantin jusqu'en 1204*. Paris, 1951.

de Boor, C. "Der Angriff der Rhos auf Byzanz," *Byzantinische Zeitschrift*, IV (1895), 449–53.

Bouchier, E. *Spain Under the Roman Empire*. Oxford, 1914.

Bouvat, L. *L'Empire Mongol*. Paris, 1927.

Bouvy, E. "Saint Thomas. Ses traducteurs byzantins," *Revue augustinienne*, XVI (1910), 407 ff.

Brătianu, G. I. *Actes des notaires génois de Péra et de Caffa de la fin du XIIIe siècle*. Bucharest, 1927.

————. "Charles Diehl et la Roumanie," *Revue historique du sud-est européen*, XXII (1945), 5–36.

————. *Études byzantines d'histoire économiques et sociale*. Paris, 1938.

————. "Études pontiques," *Revue historique du sud-est européen*, XXI (1944), 39–52.

————. "La Fin du regimes des partis à Byzance et la crise antisemite du VIIe siècle," *Revue historique du sud-est européen*, XVIII (1941), 49–57.

———. "Notes sur le projet de mariage entre l'empereur Michel IX Paléologue et Catherine de Courtnay (1288–95)," *Revue historique du sud-est européen,* I (1924), 59–63.

———. "La Politique fiscale de Nicéphore Ier ou Ubu Roi à Byzance," *Études byzantines d'histoire économique et sociale.* Paris, 1938. Interesting.

———. *Recherches sur le commerce génois dans la mer Noire au XIIIe siècle.* Paris, 1929.

———. *Recherches sur Vicina et Cetatea Alba.* Bucharest, 1943.

———. "Vicina. I. Contribution à l'histoire de la domination byzantine et du commerce génois en Dobrogea," *Bulletin de la section historique de l'Académie roumaine,* X (1923).

Bréhier, L. "Andronic I (Comnène)," *Dictionnaire d'histoire et de géographie ecclésiastiques.* Ed. Baudrillart, A. II (1914–20), cols. 1776–82.

———. "Attempts at Reunion of the Greek and Latin Churches," *The Cambridge Medieval History,* IV (1923), 594–626.

———. "Constantin et la fondation de Constantinople," *Revue historique,* CXIX (1915), 241–72.

———. *L'Église et l'orient au moyen âge; les croisades.* Paris, 1907. 5th ed., Paris, 1928.

———. "Les Empereurs byzantins dans leur vie privée," *Revue historique,* CLXXXVIII–IX (1949), 193–217.

———. "The Greek Church: Its Relations with the West up to 1054," *The Cambridge Medieval History,* IV (1923), 246–73.

———. *Un héros de roman dans la littérature byzantine.* Clermont-Ferrand, 1904.

———. "Iconoclasme," *Histoire de l'Église.* Ed. Fliche, A. and Martin, V. Vol. V (1938), 431–70. Very important; has an excellent bibliography.

———. *Le Monde byzantin.* 3 vols. Paris, 1947–50.

———. "Notes sur l'histoire de l'enseignment supérieur à Constantinople," *Byzantion,* III (1927), 72–94; IV (1929), 13–28.

———. *La Querelle des images, VIIIe-IXe siècles.* Paris, 1904. Important.

———. "La Rénovation artistique sous les Paléologues et le mouvement des idées," *Mélanges Diehl: Études sur l'histoire et sur l'art de Byzance.* Paris, 1930.

———. *La Schisme oriental du XIe siècle.* Paris, 1899. Important.

———. "La Transformation de l'empire byzantine sous les Héraclides," *Journal des Savants,* N.S. XV (1917), 401–15.

Brilliantov, A. *The Emperor Constantine the Great and the Edict of Milan, 313 A.D.* Petrograd, 1916. An excellent work, analyzing the period on the basis of original sources and later literature, including the extensive literature of 1913. In Russian.

———. *The Influence of Eastern Theology upon Western as Evidenced by the Works of John the Scot Eriugena.* St. Petersburg, 1898. In Russian.

Brion, M. *Crowned Courtesan. The Tale of Theodora, Empress of Byzantium.* Trans. from French by Wells, W. B. London, 1936.

Brooks, E. W. "The Arab Occupation of Crete," *The English Historical Review,* XXVIII (1913), 431–43.

———. "Arabic Lists of the Byzantine Themes," *Journal of Hellenic Studies,* XXI (1901), 67–77.

——. "Byzantines and Arabs in the Time of the Early Abbasids," *English Historical Review*, XV (1900), 728–47.

——. "The Campaign of 716–18, from Arabic Sources," *Journal of Hellenic Studies*, XIX (1899), 19–31.

——. "The Eastern Provinces from Arcadius to Anastasius," *The Cambridge Medieval History*, I (1911), 456–86.

——. Ed. and trans. John of Ephesus. *Lives of the Eastern Saints*. Syriac text and trans. *Patrologia Orientalis*, XVII (1923), 1–307.

——. "Review: Vasiliev, *Lektsii po Istorii Vizantii*," *The English Historical Review*, XXXIV (1919), 117.

——. "Who was Constantine Pogonatus?" *Byzantinische Zeitschrift*, XVII (1908), 460–62.

Brosset, M. *Histoire de la Géorgie*. Vol. I. St. Petersburg, 1849.

Brown, H. F. "The Venetians and the Venetian Quarter in Constantinople to the Close of the Twelfth Century," *Journal of Hellenic Studies*, XL (1920), 68–88.

Bruns, K. G. and Sachau, E. (Eds.) *Syrisch-Römisches Rechtsbuch aus dem fünften Jahrhundert*. Leipzig, 1880.

Bryanzev, D. "John Italus," *Vera i Razum*. Vol. II, part 1. St. Petersburg, 1904. In Russian.

Bryce, James. *The Holy Roman Empire*. New York, 1919.

——. "Life of Justinian by Theophilus," *Archivio della Reale Società Romana di Storia Patria*, X (1887), 137–71; also in *The English Historical Review*, II (1887), 657–84.

Bubnov, N. *The Collection of Gerbert's Letters as a Historical Source*. St. Petersburg, 1890. In Russian.

Buchon, J. A. *Chroniques étrangères relatives aux expéditions françaises pendant le XIIIe siècle*. Ed. Lanz, K. (*Bibliothek des literarischen Vereins in Stuttgart*, VIII, 1844.) Stuttgart, 1844.

——. *Nouvelles recherches historiques sur la principauté française de Morée et ses hautes baronnies fondées à la suite de la quatrième croisade, pour servir de complément aux éclaircissements historiques, généalogiques et numismatiques sur la principauté française de Morée*. Paris, 1843–45.

——. *Recherches et matériaux pour servir à une histoire de la domination française*. Paris, 1840.

Buckler, Georgiana. *Anna Comnena: A Study*. Oxford, 1929. The best detailed monograph, abundantly documented.

Buondelmonti, Chr. *Description des îles de l'Archipel*. Ed. Legrand, E. Paris, 1897. Ed. Meineke, A. (*Corpus Scriptorum Historiae Byzantinae*.) Bonn, 1836.

Burckhardt, J. *Die Zeit Constantins des Grossen*. 1st ed., Leipzig, 1853. 3rd ed., Leipzig, 1898. Trans. into English by Moffat, J. London, 1904. 4th ed., enlarged and revised, in the original German. Leipzig, 1925.

Bury, J. B. *The Ancient Greek Historians*. New York, 1909.

——. "The Bulgarian Treaty of A.D. 814 and the Great Fence of Thrace," *The English Historical Review*, XXV (1910), 276–87.

——. "The Ceremonial Book of Constantine Porphyrogennetos," *The English Historical Review*, XXII (1907), 209–27; 417–39.

——. "Charles the Great and Irene," *Hermathena*, VIII (1893), 17–37.

——. *The Constitution of the Later Roman Empire*. Cambridge, 1910.

——. *A History of the Eastern Roman Empire from the Fall of Irene to the Accession of Basil I (802–67)*. London, 1912. The best work on this epoch.

——. *A History of the Later Roman Empire from Arcadius to Irene (395–800)*. 2 vols. London, 1889. New ed. covering period A.D. 395–565. 2 vols. London, 1923.

——. *The Imperial Administrative System in the Ninth Century, with a revised text of the Kletorologion of Philotheos. (British Academy Supplemental Papers, I.)* London, 1911.

——. "The Notitia Dignitatum," *Journal of Roman Studies*, X (1920), 131–54.

——. "The Provincial Lists of Verona," *Journal of Roman Studies*, XIII (1923), 127–51.

——. "Roman Emperors from Basil II to Isaac Komnênos," *The English Historical Review*, IV (1889), 41–64; 251–85. A fine study of Psellus' work.

——. *Romances of Chivalry on Greek Soil*. Oxford, 1911.

——. *Selected Essays*. Ed. Temperley, H. Cambridge, 1930.

——. "The Struggle with the Saracens; summary," *The Cambridge Medieval History*, IV (1923), 151–52.

——. "The Treatise *De Administrando Imperio*," *Byzantinische Zeitschrift*, XV (1906), 517–77.

Byrne, E. H. "The Genoese Colonies in Syria," *Crusades and Other Historical Essays Presented to Dana C. Munro by his Former Students*. New York, 1928.

Byron, R. *The Byzantine Achievement: An Historical Perspective A.D. 330–1453*. London, 1929.

Butler, M. *The Arab Conquest of Egypt*. Oxford, 1902.

Caetani, L. *Annali dell' Islam*. Vols. I–X. Milan, 1905–26. A very important work for the relations between Byzantium and the Arabs in the time of the first califs.

——. *Studi di storia orientale*. Vols. I and III. Milan, 1911–14. Important for the primitive history of Islam.

Cahen, C. "La Campagne de Mantzikert d'après les sources musulmanes," *Byzantion*, IX (1934), 613–42.

——. "La première pénétration turque en Asie Mineure (seconde moitré du XIe siècle)," *Byzantion*, XVIII (1948), 5–67.

——. *La Syrie du Nord à l'époque des croisades*. Paris, 1940.

Callistus, Nicephorus. *Historia ecclesiastica*. Ed. Migne, J. P. *(Patrologia Graeca, CXLV, CXLVI.)* Paris, 1865.

The Cambridge Medieval History. XII. *The Imperial Crisis and Recovery A.D. 193–324*. Cambridge, 1929. Important; copious bibliography.

Cammelli, G. "Demetrii Cydonii orationes tres, adhuc ineditae," *Byzantinisch-neugriechische Jahrbücher*, III (1922), 67–76; IV (1923), 77–83, 282–95.

——. "Demetrio Cidonio: Brevi notizie della vita e delle opere," *Studi Italiani di filologia classica*, N.S. I (1920), 140–61.

——. *Démétrius Cydonès Correspondance*. Paris, 1930.

——. "L'inno per la nativita de Romano il Melode," *Studi Bizantini*. Rome, 1925.

——. "Personaggi bizantini dei secoli XIV–XV attraverso le epistole di Demetrio Cidonio," *Bessarione*, XXXVI (1920), 77–108.

——. *Romano il Melode*. Florence, 1930.

Cananus, John. *De Constantinopoli anno 1422 oppugnata narratio*. Ed. Bekker, I. *(Corpus Scriptorum Historiae Byzantinae.)* Bonn, 1838.

Canard, M. "Les Expéditions des arabes contre Constantinople dans l'histoire et dans la légende," *Journal asiatique,* CCVIII (1926), 61–121.

———. "La Guerre sainte dans le monde islamique et dans le mond chrétien," *Revue africaine,* LXXIX (1936), 605–23.

———. *Sayf al Daula.* (*Bibliotheca Arabica,* publiée par La Faculté des Lettres d'Alger, VIII.) Algiers, 1934. Arab text only; no translation.

———. "Le Traité de 1281 entre Michel Paléologue et le sultan Qalâ'ûn," *Byzantion,* X (1935), 669–80.

———. "Un Traité entre Byzance et l'Egypt au XIIIᵉ siècle et les relations diplomatiques de Michel VIII Paleologue avec les sultans Mamlûks Baibars et Qalâ'ûn," *Mélanges Guadefroy-Demombynes.* Cairo, 1937.

Carabellese, F. *Carlo d'Angiò nei rapporti politici e commerciali con Venezia e l'Oriente.* Bari, 1911. Not much material on Byzantium.

Caro, G. "Die Berichterstattung auf dem ersten Kreuzzuge," *Neue Jahrbücher für das klassische Alterum,* XXIX (1912), 50–62.

———. *Genua und die Mächte am Mittelmeer,* 1257–1311. Halle, 1895.

Carpenter, M. "The Paper that Romanos Swallowed," *Speculum,* VII (1932), 3–22.

———. *Romanos and the Mystery Play of the East.* (*The University of Missouri Studies,* XI, 3.) Columbia, Mo., 1936.

Caspar, E. *Geschichte des Papsttum.* Vols. I–II. Tübingen, 1930–33.

———. "Letters of Gregory II," *Zeitschrift für Kirchengeschichte,* LII (1933), 29–89.

———. *Roger II. (1101–1154) und die Gründung der normannish-sicilischen Monarchie.* Innsbruck, 1904.

Castellani, G. "Un Traité inédit en Grec de Cyriaque d'Ancône," *Revue des études grecques,* IX (1896), 225–28.

Cedrenus, George. *Historiarum compendium.* Ed. Bekker, I. (*Corpus Scriptorum Historiae Byzantinae.*) Bonn, 1838.

Cerone, F. "Il Papa ed i Veneziani nella quarta crociata," *Archivio Veneto,* XXXVI (1888), 57–70; 287–97.

———. "La Politica orientale di Alfonso d'Aragona," *Archivio storico per le provincie Napolitane,* XVII (1902), 425–56, 555–634; XVIII (1903), 167 ff.

Chabot, J. "Un Épisode de l'histoire des croisades," *Mélanges offerts à M. Gustave Schlumberger.* Vol. I. Paris, 1924.

Chalandon, F. *Les Comnène: Études sur l'empire byzantin au XIᵉ et au XIIᵉ siècles.* 2 vols. Paris, 1900–12.

———. "The Earlier Comneni," *The Cambridge Medieval History,* IV (1923), 318–50.

———. *Histoire de la domination normande en Italie et en Sicile.* Paris, 1907.

———. *Histoire de la première croisade jusqu'à l'election de Godefroi de Bouillon.* Paris, 1925.

Chamberlin, William. "On Rereading Gibbon," *The Atlantic Monthly,* CLXXIV (1944), 65–70.

Chapman, C. *Michael Paléologue restaurateur de l'empire byzantin (1261–82).* Paris, 1926. Useful; too brief.

Charanis, P. "Byzantium, the West and the Origin of the First Crusade," *Byzantion,* XIX (1949), 17–37.

————. "The Chronicle of Monemvasia and the Question of the Slavonic Settlements in Greece," *Dumbarton Oaks Papers*, V (1950), 139–67.

————. *Church and State in the Later Roman Empire. The Religious Policy of Anastasius the First, 491–518.* Madison, Wisconsin, 1939. Very accurate study.

————. "The Crown Modiolus Once More," *Byzantion*, XIII (1938), 337–81.

————. "Internal Strife in Byzantium in the Fourteenth Century," *Byzantion*, XV (1940–41), 208–30.

————. "The Monastic Properties and the State in the Byzantine Empire," *Dumbarton Oaks Papers*, IV (1948), 51–119.

————. "On the Question of the Hellenization of Sicily and Southern Italy during the Middle Ages," *The American Historical Review*, LII (1946–47), 74–86.

————. "The Strife among the Palaeologi and the Ottoman Turks, 1370–1402," *Byzantion*, XVI (1942–43), 286–314.

Chatzes, A. C. " Ἱστορία τοῦ Βυζαντινοῦ Κράτους," Πρακτικά *of the Academy of Athens*, IV (1929), 746–48.

Chekrezi, C. *Albania: Past and Present*. New York, 1919.

Chernousov, E. "Ducas, One of the Historians of the Fall of Byzantium," *Vizantiysky Vremennik*, XXI (1914), 171–221. In Russian.

————. "From a Byzantine Backwoods of the Thirteenth Century," *Essays Presented to V. P. Buzeskul*. Kharkov, 1913–14. In Russian.

————. "The Roman and Byzantine Guilds," *Journal of the Ministry of Public Instruction*. 1914. A Russian article on Stöckle's book.

Cheronis, N. D. "Chemical Warfare in the Middle Ages. Kallinikos Prepared Fire," *Journal of Chemical Education*, XIV, 8 (1937), 360–65.

Chiliades. Ed. Kiessling, Th. Leipzig, 1826.

Christ, W. *Geschichte der griechischen Litteratur*. 6th ed., Munich, 1924.

The Christian Roman Empire and the Foundation of the Teutonic Kingdom. (*The Cambridge Medieval History*, I.) Cambridge, 1911.

Chronica Minora. Trans. Guidi, I. (*Corpus Scriptorum Christianorum Orientalium*.) Paris, 1903–5.

Chronicle of John, bishop of Nikiu. Trans. from the Ethiopian by Zotenberg, M. *Notices et extraits des manuscrits de la Bibliothèque Nationale*, XXIV (1883). Trans. into English by Charles, R. London, 1916.

The Chronicle of Morea. Ed. Schmitt, J. London, 1904. Ed. Kalonares, P. Athens, 1940. In Greek.

The Chronicle of Novgorod. St. Petersburg, 1888. In Russian. Latin trans. Hopf, C. *Chroniques gréco-romanes inédites ou peu connues*. Berlin, 1873.

Chronicon Adae de Usk. Ed. Thompson, E. M. 2nd ed., London, 1904. Latin text and English trans.

Chronicon Estense. Ed. Muratori, L. A. (*Scriptores Rerum Italicarum*, XV.) Milan, 1729.

Chronicon Magni Presbyteri (*Annales Reicherspergenses*). Ed. Pertz, G. H. (*Monumenta Germaniae Historica. Scriptores*, XVII, cols. 439–534.) Hanover, 1861.

Chronique de Michel le Syrien. Trans. Chabot, J. B. Vols. I–III. Paris, 1899–1910.

Chronique du Religieux de Saint-Denys. Published by Bellaguet, M. L. 6 vols. Paris, 1839–52.

Chrysostom, John. *Epistolae*. Ed. Migne, J. P. (*Patrologia Graeca,* LII.) Paris, 1862.
———. *Oeuvres complètes de saint Jean Chrysostome*. Trans. into French by Jeannin, M. Arras, 1887.
Chumnos, Georgios. *Old Testament Legends from a Greek Poem on Genesis and Exodus*. Ed. Marshall, F. H. Cambridge, 1925.
Cinnamus, John. *Historia*. Ed. Meineke, A. (*Corpus Scriptorum Historiae Byzantinae*.) Bonn, 1838.
Clavijo, Ruy Gonzales de. *A Diary of the Journey to the Court of Timur (Tamerlane), to Samarqand in 1403–6*. Spanish text, Russian trans. and commentary by Sreznevsky, J. St. Petersburg, 1881. English trans. by Le Strange, Guy. London, 1928.
Clement of Alexandria. *Stromata*. Ed. Migne, J. P. (*Patrologia Graeca,* VIII, cols. 717–20.) Paris, 1891; ed. Stählin, O. Leipzig, 1939.
Codellas, P. S. "The Pantocrator, the Imperial Byzantine Medical Center of the Twelfth Century A.D. in Constantinople," *Bulletin of the History of Medicine,* XII, 2 (1942), 392–410.
Cognasso, F. "Una crisobolla di Michele IX Paleologo per Teodoro I di Monferrato," *Studi bizantini,* II (Rome, 1927).
———. "Un imperatore bizantino della decadenza Isacco II Angelo," *Bessarione,* XXXI (1915), 29–60, 246–89. Reprinted separately. Rome, 1915.
———. *Partiti politici e lotte dinastiche in Bizanzio alla morte di Manuele Comneno*. (*Reale Accademia delle scienze di Torino,* 1911–12.) Turin, 1912.
Cohn. "Eustathius," *Real-Encyclopädie der Classischen Altertumswissenschaft*. Ed. Pauly, A. F., Wissowa, G. and others. 1 ser. VI (1909), cols. 1452–89.
Coleman, C. B. *Constantine the Great and Christianity*. (*Columbia University Studies in History, Economics and Public Law,* LX.) New York, 1914. Very good bibliography, pp. 243–54.
Collectio Avellana. Ed. Günther, Otto (*Corpus Scriptorum Ecclesiasticorum Latinorum,* XXXV.) Vienna, 1895.
Collinet, P. "Byzantine Legislation from the Death of Justinian (565) to 1453," *The Cambridge Medieval History,* IV (1923), 707–23.
———. *Études historiques sur le droit de Justinien*. Vol. I. Paris, 1912. Interesting and important.
———. *Histoire de l'école de droit de Beyrouth*. Paris, 1925.
Comnena, Anna. *The Alexiad*. Ed. Reifferscheid, A. 2 vols. Leipzig, 1884. Trans. Dawes, Elizabeth A. S. London, 1928.
Complete Collection of Russian Chronicles. Arkheograficheskaia Komissiia, *Polnoe Sobranie Russkikh Lietopisei*. St. Petersburg, 1846–1926.
Condurachi, E. "Factions et jeux de cirque à Rome au début du VIᵉ siècle," *Revue historique du sud-est européen,* XVIII (1941), 95–102.
———. "Les Idées politiques de Zozime," *Revista Clasică,* XIII–XIV (1941–42).
———. "La Politique financière de l'Empereur Julien," *Bulletin de la section historique de l'Académie roumaine,* XXII, 2 (1941), 1–59.
Constantinescu, N. A. "Réforme sociale ou réforme fiscale?" *Bulletin de la section historique de l'Académie roumaine,* XI (1924), 95–96.
Constantinus Porphyrogenitus. *De administrando imperio*. Ed. Moravcsic, G. and trans. Jenkins, R. J. H. Budapest, 1949.

——. *De ceremoniis aulae bizantinae.* Ed. Reiske, J. J. and Bekker, I. (*Corpus Scriptorum Historiae Byzantinae.*) Bonn, 1829–40.

——. *Excerpta historica jussu imp. Constantini Porphyrogeniti confecta.* Ed. de Boor, C. Berlin, 1903.

——. *De thematibus.* Ed. Bekker, I. (*Corpus Scriptorum Historiae Byzantinae.*) Bonn, 1840.

Constitutio Imperatoriam majestatem. Ed. Krüger, P. Berlin, 1892.

Corripus, Flavius. *De laudibus Justini.* Ed. Bekker, I. (*Corpus Scriptorum Historiae Byzantinae.*) Bonn, 1836.

Cosmas (Indicopleustes). *Topographia christiana.* Ed. Migne, J. P. (*Patrologia Graeca,* CLXXXVIII, cols. 51–476.) Paris, 1864. Ed. Winstedt, E. *The Christian Topography of Cosmas Indicopleustes.* Cambridge, 1909. Trans. McCrindle, J. W. *The Christian Topography of Cosmas, an Egyptian Monk.* (*Hakluyt Society Publications,* no. 98.) London, 1897.

Coster, C. H. "Synesius, a Curialis of the Time of the Emperor Arcadius," *Byzantion,* XV (1940–41), 10–38.

Critobulus. Ed. Müller, C. (*Fragmenta historicorum graecorum,* V.) Paris, 1870.

Cross, S. H. *The Russian Primary Chronicle.* (*Harvard Studies and Notes in Philology and Literature,* XII.) Cambridge, 1930.

Crump, C. and Jacob, E. (Eds.) *The Legacy of the Middle Ages.* Oxford, 1926.

Curtis, E. *Roger of Sicily and the Normans in Lower Italy, 1016–1154.* New York and London, 1912.

Cydones, Demetrius. Συμβουλευτικὸς ἕτερος. Ed. Migne, J. P. *Patrologia Graeca,* CLIV.

Cyprian, Archimandrite. *The Anthropology of Saint Gregory Palamas.* Paris, n.d. (1951). In Russian.

Cyriacus of Ancona. *Epigrammata reperta per Illyricum a Cyriaco Aconitano,* Rome, 1747.

Dahn, F. *Procopius von Cäsarea.* Berlin, 1865.

Dalton, O. M. *Byzantine Art and Archaeology.* Oxford, 1911.

——. *East Christian Art.* Oxford, 1925.

The Damascus Chronicle of the Crusaders. Extracted and trans. from the *Chronicle of Ibn al-Qalanisi.* Gibb, H. A. R. London, 1932.

Danduli, Andrae. *Chronicon.* Ed. Muratori, L. A. (*Rerum Italicarum Scriptores,* XII, 1–523.) Milan, 1728.

Daniel, igumen of Russia. "Life and Pilgrimage of Daniel," *Pravoslavny Palestinsky Sbornik.* Number 3 (1885). In original old Russian. French trans. *Vie et pèlerinage de Daniel, hégoumene russe. Itinéraires russes en Orient.* Ed. Khitrovo, B. de. Geneva, 1889.

Danstrup, J. "Manuel's coup against Genoa and Venice in the Light of Byzantine Commercial Policy," *Classica et Mediaevalia,* X (1949), 195–219.

——. *Recherches critiques sur Andronic I.* Arsbok, 1944 and Lund, 1945.

——. "The State and Landed Property in Byzantium to 1250," *Classica et Mediaevalia,* VIII (1946), 221–62.

Darkó, J. "La militarizatione dell' Impero Bizantino," *Studi bizantini e neoellenici,* V (1939), 88–99.

——. "Neuere Beiträge zur Biographie des Laonikos Chalkokondyles," *Compte-*

rendu du deuxième Congrès international des études byzantines à Belgrade, 1927. (Belgrade, 1929), 25–29.

———. "Zum Leben des Laonikos Chalkondyles," *Byzantinische Zeitschrift,* XXIV (1923), 29–39.

Davidson, R. *Forschungen zur Geschichte von Florenz.* Berlin, 1901.

Dawkins, R. M. "Greeks and Northmen," *Custom is King: Essays Presented to Dr. R. R. Marett.* Oxford, 1936.

Declareuil, T. *Rome et l'organisation du droit. (Bibliothèque de synthèse historique. L'évolution de l'humanité.* Ed. Berr, H.) Paris, 1924. See especially Book II, *Le droit du Bas-Empire et les réformes Justiniennes.*

Delarue, F. *Albrégé de l'histoire de Bas-Empire de Lebeau.* Lyon, 1847.

Delehaye, H. *Les Saints Stylites.* Brussels, 1923.

———. "La vie de Saint Paul le jeune et la chronologie de Metaphraste," *Revue des questions historiques,* N.S. X (1893), 49–85.

——— (Ed.) "Life of Daniel the Stylite," *Analecta Bollandiana,* XXXII (1913), chap. 31.

Dendias, M. "Le Roi Manfred de Sicile et la bataille de Pélagonie," *Mélanges Charles Diehl: Études sur l'histoire et sur l'art de Byzance.* Paris, 1930.

Destunis, G. "Essay on the biography of George Phrantzes," *Journal of the Ministry of Public Instruction,* CCLXXXVIII (1893), 427–97. In Russian.

Devreesse. *Le Patriarcat d'Antioche depuis la paix de l'église jusqu'à la conquête Arabe.* Paris, 1945.

Dewing, H. B. (Ed. and trans.) *Procopius of Caesarea.* 7 vols. 1914–40.

Dictionnaire de théologie catholique. Ed. Vacant, A., Mangenot, E., and Amann, E. 15 vols. Paris, 1931–(cont.).

Diehl, Charles. *L'Afrique byzantine.* Paris, 1896.

———. *Byzance. Grandeur et décadence.* Paris, 1920.

———. "Byzantine Civilization," *The Cambridge Medieval History,* IV (1923), 745–77.

———. "La dernière renaissance de l'art Byzantin," *Journal des Savants,* N.S. XV (1917), 361–76.

———. "L'empereur au nez coupé," *Revue de Paris,* January 1, 1923. Reprinted in his *Choses et gens de Byzance.* Paris, 1926.

———. *Études byzantines: Introduction a l'histoire de Byzance, les études d'histoire byzantine en 1905, ...* Paris, 1905.

———. *Études sur l'administration byzantine dans l'exarchat de Ravenne (568–751).* Paris, 1888.

———. Guilland, R., Oeconomos, L., and Grousset, R. *L'Europe Orientale de 1081 à 1453.* Paris, 1945.

———. *Figures byzantines.* 2 series. Paris, 1906–8. 4th ed., Paris, 1909. The biography of Theodora (Vol. I, 4th ed., 1909, 51–75) is the best on the subject. The essay on Andronic Comnene (2nd ser., 1908, 86–133) is brilliantly written. English trans. Bell, H. *Byzantine Portraits.* New York, 1927.

———. "The Fourth Crusade and the Latin Empire," *The Cambridge Medieval History,* IV (1923), 415–31.

———. *Les Grands Problèmes de l'histoire byzantine.* Paris, 1943.

———. *Histoire de l'empire byzantin.* Paris, 1930. English trans. Ives, G. B. Princeton, 1925.

————. *Justinien et la civilization byzantine au VIe siècle.* Paris, 1901.

————. "La Légende de l'empereur Théophile," *Annales de l'Institut Kondakov,* IV (1931), 33–37.

————. "Leo III and the Isaurian Dynasty (717–802)," *The Cambridge Medieval History,* IV (1923), 1–26.

————. *Manuel d'art byzantin.* Paris, 1910. 2nd ed., Paris, 1925–26.

———— and Marçais, G. *Le Monde oriental de 395 à 1018.* Paris, 1936.

————. "L'Origine du régime des thèmes dans l'empire byzantin," *Études byzantines.* Paris, 1905. First edition of this article in *Les Études d'histoire du moyen âge dédidées à G. Monod.* Paris, 1896.

————. *Ravenne.* Paris, 1907.

————. *Une République patricienne. Venise.* Paris, 1915. 2nd ed., Paris, 1928. Beautifully written.

————. "Review: Runciman, *Byzantine Civilization," Byzantinische Zeitschrift,* XXXIV (1934), 127–30. Diehl indicates some mistakes but concludes by pronouncing the work excellent.

————. "La Société byzantine à l'époque des Comnènes," *Revue historique du sudest européen,* VI (1929), 198–280. Separate ed., Paris, 1929. Very interesting.

————. *Théodora, impératrice de Byzance.* 3rd ed., Paris, 1904. Reprint in 1937.

Diener, Bertha. *Imperial Byzantium.* Boston, 1938.

Dieterich, K. *Quellen und Forschungen zur Erd- und Kulturkunde.* Leipzig, 1912.

Dirr, A. "Géorgie," *Encyclopédie de l'Islam,* II (1927), 139–40.

"Disputatio Latinorum et Graecorum," *Archivum Franciscanum Historicum,* XII (1919).

Dmitrievsky, A. *The Description of the Liturgical Manuscripts Preserved in the Libraries of the Orthodox East.* Kiev, 1895. In Russian and Greek.

Dobiache-Rojdestvensky, O. *The Epoch of the Crusades; the West in the Crusading Movement.* Petrograd, 1918. In Russian.

Dobroklonsky, A. *Blessed Theodore the Confessor and Abbot of Studion.* Odessa, 1913. In Russian.

Dodu, G. *Histoire des institutions monarchiques dans le royaume latin de Jérusalem 1099–1291.* Paris, 1894.

Dölger, Franz. *Beiträge zur Geschichte der byzantinischen Finanzverwaltung besonders des 10 und 11 Jahrhunderts.* Leipzig and Berlin, 1927. Important.

————. "Bulgarisches Cartum und byzantinisches Kaisertum," *Actes du IVe congrès international des études byzantines.* Sofia, 1934.

————. "Die byzantinische Literatur und Dante," *Compte-rendu du deuxième congrès international des études byzantines, Belgrade, 1927.* Belgrade, 1929.

————. *Corpus der griechischen Urkunden des Mittelalters und der neueren Zeit. Regesten I. Regesten der Kaiserurkunden des oströmischen Reiches.* 3 vols. Munich and Berlin, 1924–32.

————. "Die neuentdeckte Quelle zur Helenaszene in Goethes Faust. Die Prophyläen," *Beilage zur Münchner Zeitung,* XXVIII (1931), 289–90.

————. "Reviews and comments," *Deutsche Literaturzeitung,* XLVII (1926), cols. 1440–45. *Historisches Jahrbuch,* XLVII (1927), 760–66. *Historische Zeitschrift,* CXLI (1930), 110–13. *Byzantinische Zeitschrift,* XXVI (1926), 95–101; XXXVI (1936), 467–68; XXXVII (1937), 542–47.

――――. *Der Vertrag des Sultans Qala'un von Aegypten mit dem Kaiser Michael VIII Palaiologus. Serta Monacensia.* Leyden, 1952.

Dopsch, A. *Wirtschaftliche und soziale Grundlagen der europäischen Kulturentwicklung.* Vol. I. Vienna, 1918. 2nd ed., Vienna, 1923. Very interesting and important, especially for the West.

Dräseke, J. "Byzantinische Hadesfahrten," *Neue Jahrbücher für das klassische Altertum,* XXIX (1912), 343–66.

――――. "Die neuen Handschriftenfunde in den Meteoraklöstern," *Neue Jahrbücher für das klassische Altertum,* XXIX (1912), 542–53.

――――. "Plethons und Bessarions Denkschriften 'Ueber die Angelegenheiten im Peloponnes,'" *Neue Jahrbücher für das klassische Altertum,* XXVII (1911), 102–19.

――――. "Theodoros Lascaris," *Byzantinische Zeitschrift,* III (1894), 498–515. Especially Theodore II's literary activity.

――――. "Zu Johannes Kantakuzenos," *Byzantinische Zeitschrift,* IX (1900), 72–84.

――――. "Zum Kircheneinigungsversuch des Jahres 1439," *Byzantinische Zeitschrift,* V (1896), 572–86.

Drapeyron, L. *L'Empereur Héraclius et l'empire byzantin au VIIe siècle.* Paris, 1869. Out of date.

Drinov, M. S. "On Some Works of Demetrius Chomatianos as Historical Material," *Vizantiysky Vremennik,* I (1894), 319–40; II (1895), 1–23. In Russian.

――――. *The Slavic Occupation of the Balkan Peninsula.* Moscow, 1873. In Russian.

――――. *The Southern Slavs and Byzantium in the Tenth Century.* Moscow, 1875. Reprinted in *Works of M. S. Drinov.* Ed. Zlatarsky, V. N. Vol. I. Sofia, 1909. A very important work on the Bulgaro-Byzantine relations. In Russian.

Ducas, Michael. *Historia byzantina.* Ed. Bekker, I. (*Corpus Scriptorum Historiae Byzantinae.*) Bonn, 1834. Greek text and Italian version.

Duchataux, V. *Eustathe, Archevêque de Thessalonique. Sa Vie, ses oeuvres, son histoire du siège et de la prise de Thessalonique par les Normands Siciliens.* (*Travaux de l'Académie Nationale de Reims,* CVIII.) Reims, 1902.

Duchesne, L. *Liber Pontificalis.* Paris, 1886.

Dudden, F. *Gregory the Great: His Place in History and Thought.* London, 1905.

Dulaurier, E. "Chronique de Matthieu d'Edesse," *Bibliothèque historique arménienne.* (Paris, 1858), 16–24.

Duncalf, F. "The Pope's Plan for the First Crusade," *The Crusades and Other Historical Essays Presented to D. C. Munro by his former Students.* New York, 1928.

Dupuy. "Eloge de Lebeau," *Histoire du Bas-Empire.* Ed. de Saint-Martin, M. Vol. I. Paris, 1824.

Durrieu, P. *Les Archives angevines de Naples. Études sur les registres du roi Charles Ier.* (Bibliothèque des écoles françaises d'Athènes et de Rome, XLVI.) Paris, 1886.

Duruy, V. *Histoire des Romains.* Vols. VI–VII. Paris, 1883–85. English trans. Ripley, M. M. Boston, 1883–86.

Dussaud, R. *Les Arabes en Syrie avant l'Islam.* Paris, 1907.

Duthuit, G. *Byzance et l'art du XIIe siècle.* Paris, 1926.

Dvornik, F. *Les Légendes de Constantin et de Méthode vues de Byzance.* Prague, 1933. Very important.

———. *The Making of Central and Eastern Europe*. London, 1949.

———. *The Photian Schism, History and Legend*. Cambridge, 1948. In French, Paris, 1950. Very important.

———. *Les Slaves, Byzance et Rome au IXe siècle*. Paris, 1926. Important.

———. *La Vie de saint Grégoire de Décapolite et les slaves macédoniens au IXe siècle*. Paris, 1926.

Dyakonov, A. P. "The Byzantine Demes and Factions (τὰ μέρη) in the Fifth to the Seventh Centuries," *Vizantiysky Sbornik* (Moscow and Leningrad, 1945).

———. *John of Ephesus and his Ecclesiastical-Historical Works*. St. Petersburg, 1908. Very important. In Russian. E. W. Brooks says: "All studies of John of Ephesus have now been thrown into the shade by the great work of A. Dyakonov." (*Patrologia Orientalis*, XVII [1923], iii.)

Ebersolt, J. *Les Arts somptuaires de Byzance*. Paris, 1923.

———. *Constantinople byzantine et les voyageurs du Levant*. Paris, 1918.

———. *La Miniature byzantine*. Paris and Brussels, 1926.

———. *Orient et occident*. 2 vols. Paris, 1928–29.

Ecloga ad Procheiron mutata founded upon the *Ecloga* of Leo III and Constantine V of Isauria and on the *Procheiros nomos* of Basil I of Macedonia, including the Rhodian maritime law edited in 1166 A.D. Ed. Freshfield, E. H. *A Manual of Later Roman Law*. Cambridge, 1927.

Eichmann, E. "Studien zur Geschichte der abenländischen Kaiserkrönung. II. Zur Topographie der Kaiser Kaiserkrönung," *Historisches Jahrbuch*, XLV (1925), 21–56.

Eichner, W. "Die Nachrichten über den Islam bei den Byzantinern," *Der Islam*, XXIII (1936), 133–62; 197–244.

Elderkin, G. W. and Stillwell, R. (Eds.) *Antioch-on-the-Orontes*. (*Publications of the Committee for the Excavation of Antioch and its vicinity*.) Princeton, 1934–41.

Ellissen, A. *Analecten der mittel-und neugriechischen Litteratur*. IV. Leipzig, 1860.

———. *Michael Akominatos von Chonä*. Göttingen, 1846.

Emereau, C. "Notes sur les origines et la fondation de Constantinople," *Revue archéologique*, XXI (1925), 1–25.

Ensslin, W. "Leo I., Kaiser 457–74," *Real-Encyclopädie der Classischen Altertumwissenschaft*. Ed. Pauly, A. F., Wissowa, G. and others. 1 ser. XII (1925), cols. 1947–61.

———. "Maximus und sein Begleiter der Historiker Priskos," *Byzantinisch-neugriechische Jahrbücher*, V (1926), 1–9.

———. *Theoderich der Grosse*. Munich, 1947.

Ephraemius Monachus. Ed. Bekker, I. (*Corpus Scriptorum Historiae Byzantinae*.) Bonn, 1840.

Epifanovich, S. *The Blessed Maximus Confessor and Byzantine Theology*. Kiev, 1915. In Russian.

Erdmann, C. *Die Entstehung des Kreuzzugsgedankens*. Stuttgart, 1935.

Ermoni, V. *Saint Jean Damascène*. Paris, 1904.

Ertov, I. *History of the Eastern Roman or Constantinopolitan Empire*. St. Petersburg, 1837. In Russian.

Eusebius of Caesarea. *De laudibus Constantini*. Ed. Heikel, I. von. *Eusebius Werke*. Leipzig, 1902. Ed. Schaff, P., Wace, H., and others. *A Select Library of Nicene and Post-Nicene Fathers of the Christian Church*. 2nd ser. Vol. I. New York, 1890.

———. *Historia Ecclesiastica.* Ed. Schaff, P., Wace, H. *A Select Library of Nicene and Post-Nicene Fathers of the Christian Church.* 2nd ser. Vol. I. New York, 1890.

———. *Vita Constantini.* Ed. Heikel, I. *Eusebius Werke.* Leipzig, 1902. Ed. Schaff, P., Wace, H. and others. *A Select Library of Nicene and Post-Nicene Fathers of the Christian Church.* 2nd ser. Vol. I. New York, 1890.

Eustathius of Thessalonica. *De Thessalonica a Latinis capta.* Ed. Bekker, I. (*Corpus Scriptorum Historiae Byzantinae.*) Bonn, 1842.

———. *Manuelis Comneni Laudatio funebris.* Ed. Migne, J. P. (*Patrologia Graeca,* CXXXV.) Paris, 1887.

Eustratiades, S. and Arcadios of Vatopedi. *Catalogue of the Greek Manuscripts in the Library of the Monastery of Vatopedi on Mt. Athos.* (Harvard Theological Studies, XI.) Cambridge, 1924.

Eutropius. *Breviarium Historiae Romanae ad Valentem Augustum.* Ed. Rühl, F. Leipzig, 1919.

Eutychius of Alexandria. *Annales.* Ed. Cheikho, L., Carra de Vaux, B. and Zayyat, H. (*Corpus Scriptorum Christianorum Orientalium. Scriptores Arabici.*) Beirut and Paris, 1906–12. In Arabic. Latin trans. ed. Migne, J. P. (*Patrologia Graeca,* CXI, cols. 889–1156.) Paris, 1863.

Evagrius (Scholasticus). *Historia Ecclesiastica.* Ed. Bidez, J. and Parmentier, L. London, 1898.

Evangelides, T. Ἡράκλειος ὁ αὐτοκράτωρ τοῦ Βυζαντίου. Odessa, 1903. Brief compilation.

Every, G. *The Byzantine Patriarchate (451–1204).* London, 1948.

Excerpta e Theophanis Historia. Ed. Bekker, I. (*Corpus Scriptorum Historiae Byzantinae.*) Bonn, 1829.

Excerpta historica jussu imperatoris Constantini Porphyrogeniti confecta. Ed. de Boor, C. Berlin, 1903.

Falcandus, Hugo. *Historia sicula.* Ed. Muratori, L. A. (*Scriptores Rerum Italicarum,* VII, cols. 249–344.) Milan, 1751.

Falier-Papadopoulos, J. B. "Phrantzès est-il réellement l'auteur de la grande chronique qui porte son nom?" *Bulletin de l'institut archéologique bulgare,* IX (1935), 177–89.

Fallmerayer, J. P. *Geschichte der Halbinsel Morea während des Mittelalters.* Stuttgart, 1830–36. Biased.

Faral, E. "Geoffroy de Villehardouin. La question de la sincérité," *Revue historique,* CLXXVII (1936), 530–82.

Ferrini, C. "Edizione critica del νόμος γεωργικός," *Byzantinische Zeitschrift,* VII (1898), 558–71.

———. *Opera di Contardo Ferrini.* Vol. I. Milan, 1929.

Festa, Nicola. "A Propos d'une biographie de St. Jean le Miséricordieux," *Vizantiysky Vremennik,* XIII (1906).

———. "La Lettere greche di Federigo II," *Archivio storico italiano,* Ser. 5 XIII (1894), 1–34.

Feugère, L. *Étude sur la vie et les ouvrages de Ducange.* Paris, 1852.

Fialon, E. *Étude historique et littéraire sur saint Basile.* 2nd ed., Paris, 1869.

Finlay, G. *History of the Byzantine Empire from DCXIV to MLVII.* 2nd ed., Edinburgh and London, 1856. Ed. Tozer, H. F. Oxford, 1877.

———. *A History of Greece.* Ed. Tozer, H. F. Oxford, 1877.

Fischer, W. *Studien zur byzantinischen Geschichte des 11. Jahrhunderts.* Plauen, 1883.

Fitzgerald, A. *The Essays and Hymns of Synesius of Cyrene.* Oxford and London, 1930.

———. *The Letters of Synesius of Cyrene.* London, 1926.

Fletcher, W. *Ante-Nicene Christian Library.* Edinburgh, 1871.

Florinsky, T. D. "Andronicus the Younger and John Cantacuzene. Sketch on the History of Byzantium in the Second Quarter of the Fourteenth Century (1328–1355)," *Journal of the Ministry of Public Instruction,* CCIV–CCV (1879). Important. In Russian.

———. *The Athonian Acts and Photographs of Them in the Collections of Sevastyanov.* St. Petersburg, 1880.

———. *The Monuments of Dushan's Legislative Activity.* Kiev, 1888. In Russian.

———. *The Southern Slavs and Byzantium in the Second Quarter of the Fourteenth Century.* Vols. I–II. St. Petersburg, 1882. Very good survey of the Empire's external relations under Andronicus III, John Cantacuzene and Stephen Dushan.

Foakes-Jackson, F. J. "Anna Comnena," *Hibbert Journal,* XXXIII (1934–35), 430–42. Vividly written popular sketch.

Fontes rerum byzantinarum. Ed. Regel, W. St. Petersburg, 1892. Vol. 2. Petrograd, 1917.

Fotheringham, J. K. "Genoa and the Fourth Crusade," *The English Historical Review,* XXV (1910), 20–57.

———. *Marco Sanudo, Conqueror of the Archipelago.* Oxford, 1915.

Freeman, E. A. *Historical Essays.* Vol. III, ser. 2, 2nd ed. London, 1892.

———. *The History of the Norman Conquest of England.* Oxford, 1870.

Freshfield, E. (Ed.) *A Manual of Eastern Roman Law. The Procheiros Nomos published by the Emperor Basil I at Constantinople between 867 and 879 A.D.* Cambridge, 1928.

———. (Ed.) *A Manual of Roman Law—the Ecloga—Published by the Emperors Leo III and Constantine V of Isauria at Constantinople A.D. 726.* Cambridge, 1926.

———. *A Revised Manual of Roman Law founded upon the Ecloga of Leo III and Constantine V, of Isauria. Ecloga privata aucta.* Cambridge, 1927.

———. (Ed.) *Roman Law in the Later Roman Empire. Byzantine Guilds. Professional and Commercial Ordinances of Leo VI. c. 895 from the Book of the Eparch* rendered into English. Cambridge, 1938. Introduction and English translation.

Freytag, G. *Regnum Saahd-Aldaulae in oppido Halebo.* Bonn, 1820. Also in the volume with Leo the Deacon (Diaconus), *Historiae.* Ed. Hasii, C. B. (*Corpus Scriptorum Historiae Byzantinae.*) Bonn, 1828.

Friedländer, P. *Johannes von Gaza und Paulus Silentiarius.* Leipzig and Berlin, 1912.

Friedmann, E. *Der mittelalteriche Welthandel von Florenz in seiner geographischen Ausdehnung (nach der Practica della mercatura des Balducci Pegolotti).* (*Abhandlungen der Kaiserlichen Königlichen Geographischen Gesellschaft in Wien,* X.) Vienna, 1912.

Fuchs, F. *Die höheren Schulen von Konstantinopel im Mittelalter.* Leipzig and Berlin, 1926. Important.

Fulgentii Ferrandi *Epistolae*. Ed. Migne, J. P. (*Patrologia Latina,* LXVII.) Paris, 1848.

Fuller, G. T. *Andronicus, or the Unfortunate Politician.* London, 1646. R. Byron, in *The Byzantine Achievement* (London, 1929) notes this work, perhaps the earliest English Byzantine study.

Fustel de Coulanges, Numa Denis. *Histoire des institutions politiques de l'ancienne France.* 2nd ed., Paris, 1904.

———. *Les Origines du système féodal.* Paris, 1890.

Gabotto, F. *Eufemio il movimento separatista nella Italia bizantina.* Turin, 1890.

Gardner, A. *The Lascarids of Nicaea: The Story of an Empire in Exile.* London, 1922. An interesting and reliable monograph on the Empire of Nicaea.

———. *Theodore of Studion, His Life and Times.* London, 1905.

Gasquet, A. *L'Empire byzantin et la monarchie franque.* Paris, 1888.

Gass, W. *Die Mystik des Nikolaus Kabasilas vom Leben in Christo.* Greisswald, 1849.

Gay, I. *L'Italie méridionale et l'empire byzantin depuis l'avènement de Basile Ier jusqu'à la prise de Bari par les normands, 867–1071.* Paris, 1904. Important.

———. *Les Papes du XIe siècle et la chrétienté.* Paris, 1926.

Geffcken, J. *Kaiser Julianus.* Leipzig, 1914.

Gelzer, H. *Abriss der byzantinischen Kaisergeschichte.* Munich, 1897.

———. *Die Genesis der byzantinischen Themenverfassung.* Leipzig, 1899.

———. (Ed.) *Georgii Cyprii Descriptio Orbis Romani.* Leipzig, 1890.

———. "Kosmas der Indienfahrer," *Jahrbücher für protestantische Theologie,* IX (1883), 105–41.

———. *Leontius' von Neapolis Leben des heiligen Johannes des Barmherzigen Erzbischof von Alexandrien.* Freiburg and Leipzig, 1893.

———. *Ungedruckte und ungenügend veröffentlichte Texte der Notitiae Episcopatuum, ein Beitrag zur byzantinischen Kirchen- und Verwaltungsgeschichte. (Abhandlungen der philologische-philosophischen Klasse der Akademie der Wissenschaften zu München,* XII.) Munich, 1901.

Gelzer, M. *Studien zur byzantinische Verwaltung Äegyptens.* Leipzig, 1909.

Genesius, Joseph. *Regna.* Ed. Lachmann, C. (*Corpus Scriptorum Historiae Byzantinae.*) Bonn, 1834.

Gennadius Scholarios. *Oeuvres complètes de Gennade Scholarios.* Ed. Petit, L., Siderides, X. A., Jugie, M., and others. 8 vols. Paris, 1928–36.

George of Cyprus. Ed. Migne, J. P. (*Patrologia Graeca,* CXLII.) Paris, 1885.

George Monachus Hamartolus. *Chronicle.* Ed. Muralt, E. St. Petersburg, 1859. Ed. de Boor, C. 2 vols. Leipzig, 1904.

George of Pisidia. *De expeditione persica.* Ed. Bekker, I. (*Corpus Scriptorum Historiae Byzantinae*) Bonn, 1836.

Gercke, A. and Norden, E. *Einleitung in die Altertumswissenschaft.* Vol. III. 2nd ed., Leipzig and Berlin, 1914.

Gerland, E. "Byzantion und die Gründung der Stadt Konstantinopel," *Byzantinisch-neugriechische Jahrbücher,* X (1933), 93–105.

———. *Geschichte der Frankenherrschaft in Griechenland.* II. *Geschichte des lateinischen Kaiserreiches von Konstantinopel.* Hamburg, 1905. A detailed account of the external history of the Latin Empire from 1204 to 1216, made on the basis of the manuscripts of K. Hopf.

————. *Konstantin der Grosse in Geschichte und Sage*. (*Texte und Forschungen zur byzantinisch-neugriechischen Philologie*, no. 23. Athens, 1937. Gerland's post-humous tentative study, of no importance, which has not been worked out. See H. Grégoire's criticism in *Byzantion*, XII (1937), 698–99.

————. "Die Quellen der Helenaepisode in Goethes Faust," *Neue Jahrbücher für das klassische Altertum*, XXV (1910), 735–39.

————. *Das Studium der byzantinischen Geschichte vom Humanismus bis zur Jeztheit*. Athens, 1934.

————. "Der vierte Kreuzzug und seine Probleme," *Neue Jahrbücher für das klassische Altertum*, XIII (1904), 505–14.

Gesta Dagoberti I regis Francorum. (*Monumenta Germaniae Historica Scriptores. Rerum Merovingicarum*, II, 396–425.) Hanover, 1888.

Gesta regis Henrici Secundi. Ed. Stubbs, W. (*Rerum Britannicarum Medii Aevi Scriptores*, vol. XLIX.) London, 1867.

Gfrörer, A. *Byzantinische Geschichten*. Vols. II–III. Graz, 1873–77. Sketches of the rules of the emperors, from John Tzimisces to Romanus Diogenes, inclusive.

Ghines, D. "Τὸ ἐπαρχικὸν βιβλίον καὶ οἱ νόμοι Ἰουλιανοῦ τοῦ Ἀσκαλωνίτου," Ἐπετηρὶς Ἑταιρείας Βυζαντινῶν Σπουδῶν, XIII (1937), 183–91.

Gibbon, Edward. *The Autobiographies of Edward Gibbon*. Ed. Murray, J. London, 1896.

————. *The History of The Decline and Fall of the Roman Empire*. Ed. Bury, J. B. 7 vols. London, 1897–1902.

Gibbons, H. A. *The Foundation of the Ottoman Empire*. Oxford, 1916.

Gidel, M. *Études sur la littérature grecque moderne*. Paris, 1866.

Giese, F. "Das Problem der Entstehung des Osmanischen Reiches," *Zeitschrift für Semitistik*, II (1923), 246–71.

Gildersleeve, B. L. "Paulus Silentiarius," *American Journal of Philology*, XXXVIII (1917), 42–72.

Ginnis, D. "Das promulgationsjahr der Isaurischen Ecloge," *Byzantinische Zeitschrift*, XXIV (1924), 346–58.

Gjerset, K. *History of the Norwegian People*. New York, 1915.

de Goeje, M. J. "Harun-ibn-Yahya," *Bibliotheca Geographorum Arabicorum*, VII (1892), 119–32.

————. *Mémoire sur la conquête de la Syrie*. 2nd ed., Leyden, 1900.

Görres, F. "Die byzantinischen Besitzungen an den Küsten des spanisch-west-gothischen Reiches (554–624)," *Byzantinische Zeitschrift*, XVI (1907), 530–32.

————. "Justinian II. und das römische Papsttum," *Byzantinische Zeitschrift*, XVII (1908), 440–50.

Goldziher, I. *Muhammedanische Studien*. Halle, 1890.

————. "Die Religion des Islams, in Die Kultur der Gegenwart . . . von P. Hinne-berg," *Die Religionen des Orients*, III (1913).

————. *Vorlesungen über den Islam*. Heidelberg, 1910.

Golubinsky, E. E. *History of the Russian Church*. Vol. I. 2nd ed., Moscow, 1901. Ex-cellent book for the early relations between Byzantium and Russia. In Rus-sian.

Golubovich, G. "Disputatio Latinorum et Graecorum," *Archivum Franciscanum Historicum*, XII (1919), 428–65.

Goubert, P. "L'Administration de l'Espagne Byzantine," *Études byzantines,* III (1945), 127–43; IV (1946), 71–135.

———. "Byzance et l'Espagne wisigothique (554–711)," *Revue des études byzantines,* II (1945), 5–78.

Grabar, André. *L'Art byzantine.* Paris, 1938.

Granovsky, T. N. "The Latin Empire; a Review of Medovikov's Work," *Complete Works of T. N. Granovsky.* 4th ed., Moscow, 1900. In Russian.

Grégoire, Henri. "An Armenian Dynasty on the Byzantine Throne," *Armenian Quarterly,* I (1946), 4–21.

——— and Keyser, R. "La chanson de Roland et Byzance; ou de l'utilité du grec pour les romanistes," *Byzantion,* XIV (1939), 265–301.

———. "Un Continateur de Constantin Manassès et sa source," *Mélanges offerts à M. Gustav Schlumberger,* Vol. I. Paris, 1924.

———. "La 'Conversion' de Constantin," *Revue de l'Université de Bruxelles,* XXXVI (1930–31) 231–72. Very important.

———. *Digenis Akritas. The Byzantine Epic in History and Poetry.* New York, 1942. Fundamental work in modern Greek.

———. "Du Nouveau sur la chronographie byzantine; le 'Scriptor incertus de Leone Armenio' est la dernier continuateur le Malalas," *Bulletin de la classe des lettres de l'Académie royale de Belgique,* XXII (1936), 420–36.

———. "Du nouveau sur le Patriarche Photius," *Bulletin de la classe des lettres de l'Académie royale de Belgique,* XX (1934), 36–53.

———. "L'Etymologie de 'Labarum,'" *Byzantion,* IV (1929), 477–82.

———. "Eusèbe n'est pas l'auteur de la 'Vita Constantini' dans sa forme actuelle et Constantin ne s'est pas 'converti' en 312," *Byzantion,* XIII (1938), 561–83.

———. "La Légende d'Oleg et l'expédition d'Igor," *Bulletin de la classe des lettres de l'Académie royale de Belgique,* XXIII (1937), 80–94.

——— and Kugener, M. A. (Eds.) *Marc le Diacre, vie de Porphyre évêque de Gaza.* Paris, 1930.

———. "M. Charles Diehl, M. G. Ostrogorsky et M. Stein ou 'Slavica non leguntur,'" *Byzantion,* XIII, 2 (1938), 749–57.

———. "Notules epigraphique," *Byzantion,* XIII (1938).

———. "Un Nouveau Fragment du 'Scriptor incertus de Leone Armenio,'" *Byzantion,* XI (1936), 417–28.

———. L'Opinion byzantine et la bataille de Kossovo," *Byzantion,* VI (1931), 247–51.

———. "Le Peuple de Constantinople," *Byzantion,* XI (1936), 617–716.

———. "Les Pierres qui crient," *Byzantion,* XIV (1939), 317–21.

———. "Le Problème de la version 'originale' de l'Epopée Byzantine de Digenis Akritas," *Revue des études byzantines,* VI, 1 (1948), 27–35. Very useful for the whole question of Digenis Akritas, as well as for its most recent bibliography.

———. "The Question of the Diversion of the Fourth Crusade," *Byzantion,* XV (1941), 158–66.

——— and Goossens, R. "Les Recherches récentes sur l'epopée byzantine," *L'Antiquité Classique,* I (1932), 419–39; II (1933), 449–72. The second study is by R. Goossens alone. Excellent introduction to the epic of Digenes Akritas.

———. *Recueil des inscriptions grecques chrétiennes d'Asie Mineure.* Paris, 1922.

———. "Review: Ostrogorsky, *Geschichte des Byzantinischen Staates*," *Byzantion*, XIV, 2 (1944), 545–55.

———. "Review: Ostrogorsky, *Studien zur Geschichte des byzantinischen Bilderstreites*," *Byzantion*, IV (1929), 765–71.

———. "Une Source byzantine du second Faust," *Revue de l'Université de Bruxelles*, XXXVI (1930–31), 348–54.

———. "Le tome II du Vasiliev," *Byzantion*, V (1930), 779–84.

———. "Le Véritable nom et la date de l'église de la dormition à Nicée. Un texte nouveau et décisif," *Mélanges d'histoire offerts à Henri Pirenne*. Vol. I. Paris and Brussels, 1926.

——— and Kugener, M. A. "La Vie de Porphyre, evêque de Gaza, est-elle authentique?" *Revue de l'Université de Bruxelles*, XXXV (1929–30), 53–60.

Gregoras, Nicephorus. *Historia Byzantina*. Ed. Schopen, L. (*Corpus Scriptorum Historiae Byzantinae*.) Bonn, 1829–35.

Gregorii Magni *Epistolae*. Ed. Hartmann, L. M. (*Monumenta Germaniae Historica Epistolarum*, I–II.) Berlin, 1891–99. Ed. Migne, J. P (*Patrologia Latina*, LXXV–LXXIX.) Paris, 1849. Ed. Schaff, P. and others. *A Select Library of Nicene and Post-Nicene Fathers of the Christian Church*. 2nd ser., XI–XIII. New York, 1895–98. Ed. Mansi, J. D. (*Conciliorum Nova et Amplissima Collectio*, IX, cols. 1023–1240.) Florence, 1763.

Gregorii Turonensis Episcopi *Historia Francorum*. Ed. Omont, H. and Collon, G. Vol. II. Paris, 1913.

Gregorius Nyssenus. *Oratio de Deitate Filii et Spiritus Sancti*. Ed. Migne, J. P. (*Patrologia Graeca*, XLVI.) Paris, 1845.

Gregorovius, F. A. *Geschichte der Stadt Athen im Mittelalter von der zeit Justinian's bis zur türkischen Eroberung*. Stuttgart, 1889.

Grimbert, E. *Theodora. Die Tanzerin auf dem Kaiserthron*. Munich, 1928.

Grimme, H. *Mohammed. I. Das Leben*. Münster, 1892.

Gröber, G. *Grundriss der romanischen Philologie*. 2nd ed., Strassburg, 1904–6.

Groh, K. *Geschichte des oströmischen Kaisers Justin II, nebst den Quellen*. Leipzig, 1889.

Grossu, N. *The Attitude of the Byzantine Emperors John II and Manuel I Comneni Towards Union with the West*. (*Transactions of the Spiritual Academy of Kiev*, 1912.) Kiev, 1912. In Russian.

———. *The Blessed Theodore of Studion; His Times, Life and Works*. Kiev, 1907. In Russian.

———. *The Church and Religious Activity of the Byzantine Emperor Alexius I Comnenus (1081–1118)*. (*Transactions of the Spiritual Academy of Kiev*, 1912.) Kiev, 1912. In Russian.

———. *The Edict of Milan*. (*Transactions of the Spiritual Academy of Kiev*, 1913). Kiev, 1913. In Russian.

Grosvenor, E. A. *Constantinople*. Boston, 1895.

Grot, C. *Account of Constantine Porphyrogenitus on the Serbians and Croatians and their Settlement in the Balkan Peninsula*. St. Petersburg, 1880. In Russian.

———. *From the History of Ugria (Hungary) and the Slavs in the Twelfth Century*. Warsaw, 1889. In Russian.

———. *Moravia and Magyars from the Ninth until the Beginning of the Tenth Centuries*. St. Petersburg, 1881. In Russian.

Grousset, R. *L'Empire des steppes. Attila, Gengiz-Kahn, Tamerlan.* Paris, 1939.
———. *L'Empire du Levant. Histoire de la question d'Orient.* Paris, 1949.
———. *Histoire d'Asie.* III. *Le Monde mongol.* Paris, 1922.
———. *Histoire de l'Arménie des origines à 1071.* Paris, 1947.
———. *Histoire des croisades et du Royaume Franc de Jérusalem.* 3 vols. Paris, 1934–36. Important from the point of view of the history of Byzantium.
Gruhn, A. *Die Byzantinische Politik zur Zeit der Kreuzzüge.* Berlin, 1904.
Grumel, V. "L'Affaire de Léon de Chalcedoiné. Le chrysobulle d'Alexis Ier sur les objets sacrés," *Études byzantines,* II (1945), 126–33.
———. "Les Ambassades pontificales à Byzance après le IIe Concile de Lyon (1274–80)," *Échos d'Orient,* XXIII (1924), 437–47.
———. La Date de la promulgation de l'Eclogue de Leon III," *Echos d'Orient,* XXXIV (1935), 331 ff.
———. "En Orient après le IIe concile de Lyon," *Échos d'Orient,* XXIV (1925), 321 ff.
———. "Michel Glykas," *Dictionnaire de théologie catholique,* X, 2 (1928), 1705–7.
———. "Review: Lemerle, Histoire de Byzance," *Études byzantines,* II (1945), 275.
Grupe, E. *Kaiser Justinian, aus seinem Leben und aus seiner Zeit. (Wissenschaft und Bildung,* no. 184.) Leipzig, 1923. On the basis of the books of Diehl and Holmes.
Gsell, S. *Les Monuments antiques de l'Algérie.* Paris, 1901.
Güldenpenning, A. *Geschichte des oströmischen Reiches unter den Kaisern Arcadius und Theodosius II.* Halle, 1885.
——— and Ifland, J. *Der Kaiser Theodosius der Grosse.* Halle, 1878.
Guérard, L. "Les Lettres de Grégoire II à Léon l'Isaurien," *Mélanges d'archéologie et d'histoire,* X (1890), 44–60.
Güterbock, K. *Byzanz und Persien in ihren diplomatisch-völkerrectlichen Beziehungen im Zeitalter Justinians.* Berlin, 1906.
———. *Der Islam im Lichte der byzantinischen Polemik.* Berlin, 1912.
———. "Laonikos Chalkondyles," *Zeitschrift für Völkerrecht und Bundesstaatsrecht,* IV (1910), 72–102.
Guilland, R. *Correspondance de Nicéphore Grégoras.* Paris, 1927.
———. "La Correspondance inédite d'Athanase, Patriarche de Constantinople (1289–93; 1304–10)," *Mélanges Diehl: Études sur l'histoire et sur l'art de Byzance.* Paris, 1930.
———. "La Correspondance inédite de Nicolas Cabasilas," *Byzantinische Zeitschrift,* XXX (1929–30), 96–102.
———. *Essai sur Nicéphore Grégoras. L'homme et l'Oeuvre.* Paris, 1926.
———. "Le Palais de Théodore Métochite," *Revue des études grecques,* XXXV (1922), 82–95.
———. "Les Poésies inédites de Théodore Métochite," *Byzantion,* III (1927), 265–302.
———. "Le Protovestiarite George Phrantzès," *Revue des études byzantines,* VI, 1 (1948), 48–57.
Guldencrone, Baronne Diane de. *L'Achaie féodale. Étude sur le moyen âge en Grèce (1205–1456).* Paris, 1886. Popular book with references to some sources.
———. *L'Italie byzantine. Étude sur le haut moyen âge, 400–1050.* Paris, 1914.

Gwatkin, H. M. "Arianism," *The Cambridge Medieval History*, I (1911), 118–42.
———. *Studies on Arianism.* 2nd ed., Cambridge, 1900. Excellent work.
Hagenmeyer, H. "Der Brief des Kaisers Alexios I Komnenos an den Grafen Robert I von Flandern," *Byzantinische Zeitschrift*, VI (1897), 1–32.
———. *Die Kreuzzugsbriefe aus den Jahren 1088–1100.* Innsbruck, 1901.
Hahn, J. *Albanesische Studien.* Jena, 1854.
Halecki, O. *The Crusade of Varna. A Discussion of Controversial Problems.* New York, 1943.
———. *Un Empereur de Byzance à Rome.* Warsaw, 1930.
———. "La Pologne et l'empire Byzantin," *Byzantion*, VII (1932), 41–67.
Haller, J. "Kaiser Heinrich VI," *Historische Zeitschrift*, CXIII (1914), 473–504.
Halphen, L. *Les Barbares; des grandes invasions aux conquêtes turques de XIe siècle.* Paris, 1926.
———. "La Conquête de la Méditerranée par les Europeens au XIe et au XIIe siècles," *Mélanges d'histoire offerts à H. Pirenne.* Brussels and Paris, 1926.
Hamid, Mustafa. "Das Fremdenrecht in der Türkei," *Die Welt der Islam*, VII (1919), 26–27.
Hanotaux, G. "Les Vénitiens ont-ils trahi la chrétienté en 1202?" *Revue historique*, IV (1887), 74–102.
Harnack, A. *Geschichte der altchristlichen Litteratur bis Eusebis.* II. *Die Chronologie der altchristlichen Litteratur bis Eusebis.* Leipzig, 1904.
———. *Lehrbuch der Dogmengeschichte.* Vol. II. 4th ed., Tübingen, 1909. English trans. Speirs, E. and Millar, J. Vol. IV. London, 1898. (Trans. from the 3rd German edition.)
———. *Die Mission und Ausbreitung des Christentums in den ersten drei Jahrhunderten.* 4th revised ed., Leipzig, 1924.
Harrison, F. *Among My Books: Centenaries, Reviews, Memoirs.* London, 1912.
Hase, M. *On Timarion, Notices et extraits des manuscrits de la Bibliothèque Nationale*, IX (1813), 125–68.
Haskins, C. H. "The Greek Element in the Renaissance of the Twelfth Century," *The American Historical Review*, XXV (1920), 603–15.
———. *The Renaissance of the Twelfth Century.* Cambridge, 1927.
———. "The Spread of Ideas in the Middle Ages," *Speculum*, I (1926), 19–30.
———. *Studies in the History of Mediaeval Science.* Cambridge, 1924.
Hasluck, F. W. "The Latin Monuments of Chios," *The Annual of the British School at Athens*, XVI (1909–10), 137–84.
Hasset, M. "The Reign of Justinian," *The American Catholic Quarterly Review*, XXXVIII (1912), 266–85. Strict Catholic point of view.
Havet, T. *Lettres de Gerbert (983–97).* Paris, 1889.
Hefele, K. J. von. *Conciliengeschichte.* 9 vols. Freiburg, 1873–95. In English: *A History of the Councils of the Church.* 5 vols. Edinburgh, 1876–96. In French: *Histoire des conciles.* Ed. Leclercq, C. Paris, 1907–ff. The last volume was published in 1949.
Hegel, G. W. F. *Vorlesungen über die Philosophie der Geschichte.* Trans. Sibree, J. London, 1890.
Heichelheim, Fritz. *Wirtschaftsgeschichte des Altertums vom Paläolitikum bis zur Völkerwanderung der Germanen, Slaven und Araber.* 2 vols. Leyden, 1938.
Heimbach, G. *Basilicorum Libri LX.* Leipzig, 1870.

——. "Ueber die angebliche neueste Redaction der Basiliken durch Constantinus Porphytogeneta," *Zeitschrift für Rechtsgeschichte,* VIII (1869), 417 ff.

Heisenberg, A. *Analecta: Mittelungen aus italienischen Handschriften byzantinischer Chronographen.* Munich, 1901.

——. *Die Apostelkirche in Konstantinopel.* Leipzig, 1908.

——. *Aus der Geschichte und Literatur der Palaiologenzeit.* Munich, 1920.

——. "Dissertatio de vita et scriptis Nicephori Blemmydae," *Nicephori Blemmydae Curriculum vitae et carmina.* Leipzig, 1896.

——. "Dissertatio de vita scriptoris Georgii Acropolitae," *Opera Georgii Acropolitae.* Leipzig, 1903.

——. "Kaiser Johannes Batatzes der Barmherzige," *Byzantinische Zeitschrift,* XIV (1905), 160–233.

——. *Neue Quellen zur Geschichte des lateinischen Kaisertums und der Kircheunion. I. Der Epitaphios des Nikolaos Mesarites auf seinen Bruder Johannes. II. Die Unionsverhandlungen vom 30. August 1206. Patriarchenwahl und Kaiserkrönung in Nikaia 1208.* Munich, 1923.

——. *Nicolaos Mesarites. Die Palastrevolution des Johannes Komnenos.* Würzburg, 1907.

——. "Das Problem der Renaissance in Byzanz," *Historische Zeitschrift,* CXXXIII (1926), 393–412.

——. *Studien zu Georgios Akropolites. (Sitzungsberichte der philosophischphilologisch und der historische Klasse der Akademie der Wissenschaften,* II.) Vienna, 1899.

Henderson, B. *The Life and Principate of the Emperor Hadrian.* London, 1923.

Herewy (Harewy), Aboul Hassan Aly el. *Indications sur les lieux de Pèlerinage.* Trans. Schefer, C. *Archives de l'Orient Latin.* Paris, 1881.

Hergenröther, J. *Photius, Patriarch von Constantinopel: Sein Leben, seine Schriften und das griechische Schisma.* Vols. I–III Regensburg, 1867–69. Very important for the discussion of the separation of the churches up to 1054. Catholic point of view.

Hertzberg, G. F. *Geschichte der Byzantiner und des Osmanischen reiches bis gegen ende des 16. Jahrhunderts.* Berlin, 1883. Russian trans. Bezobrazov, P. V. Moscow, 1896.

Herzen, A. *The Past and Thoughts. Venezia la Bella.* Geneva, 1879. In Russian.

Hesseling, D. *Byzantium.* Haarlem, 1902. French ed. *Essai sur la civilization byzantine.* Paris, 1907.

——. "Een Konstitutioneel Keizershap," *Hermenuns,* XI (1938–39), 89–93.

——. *La Plus ancienne rédaction du poème épique sur Digenis Akritas. (Mededeelingen der Koninklijke Akademie van Wetenschappen, Afdeeling Letterkunde,* Vol. LXIII, ser. A, no. 1.) Amsterdam, 1927.

—— and Pernot, N. (Eds.) *Poemès prodromiques en grec vulgaire.* Amsterdam, 1910.

Heyd, W. *Histoire du commerce du Levant au moyen âge.* Leipzig, 1885. Reprint, 1936.

Hierax, I. Χρονικὸν περὶ τῆς τῶν Τούρκων βασιλείας. Ed. Sathas, K. (*Bibliotheca Graeca Medii Aevi,* Vol. I, 256–57.) Venice, 1872.

Hieronymi. *Opera Omnia.* Ed. Migne, J. P. (*Patrologia Latina,* Vols. XXII–XXX). Paris, 1845–46.

Higgins, M. J. "International Relations at the Close of the Sixth Century," *The Catholic Historical Review,* XXVII (1941), 279–315.

———. *The Persian War of the Emperor Maurice.* I. *The Chronology, with a Brief History of the Persian Calendar.* Washington, D. C., 1939.

Hill, G. A. *A History of Cyprus.* 3 vols. Cambridge, 1948.

Hime, H. W. L. *The Origin of Artillery.* London, 1915.

Hirsch, F. *Kaiser Constantin VII Porphyrogennetos.* Berlin, 1873. Brief sketch on the basis of Rambaud's work.

Histoire de l'église depuis les origines jusqu'à nos jours. Ed. Fliche, A. and Martin, V. Vol. I. Paris, 1936.

"Historia belli sacri (Tudebodus imitatus et continuatus)," *Recueil des historiens des croisades.* Ed. Bouquet, D. Vol. III. Paris, 1833. 2nd ed., Paris, 1879.

Hitti, P. K. *History of the Arabs.* London, 1937. 3rd ed. 1951. 5th ed. *The Arabs. A Short History.* Princeton, 1943. Very good.

Hodgkin, T. *Italy and Her Invaders, 376–744.* Vol. I. 2nd ed., 1892.

Hodgson, F. C. *The Early History of Venice from the Foundation to the Conquest of Constantinople, A.D. 1204.* London, 1901.

Höfer, F. *Histoire de la chimie.* Paris, 1842.

Hönn, K. *Konstantin der Grosse. Leben einer Zeitwende.* Leipzig, 1940. 2nd ed., Leipzig, 1945.

Hofler, K. R. von. *Abhandlungen aus dem Gebiete der slavischen Geschichte.* I. *Die Walachen als Begründer des zweiten bulgarischen Reiches der Asaniden, 1186–1257. (Sitzungsberichte der philosophische-historische Klasse der Akademie der Wissenschaften,* XCV, 229–49.) Vienna, 1879.

Holmes, W. G. *The Age of Justinian and Theodora.* 2 vols. 2nd ed., London, 1912.

Holtzmann, W. "Die Unionsverhandlungen zwischen Alexios I. und Papst Urban II. im Jahre 1089," *Byzantinische Zeitschrift,* XXVIII (1928), 38–67.

Homo, L. *Essai sur le règne de l'empereur Aurélien.* Paris, 1904.

Honigmann, E. "La Liste originale des Pères de Nicée," *Byzantion,* XIV (1939), 17–76.

———. "The Original Lists of the Members of the Council of Nicaea, the Robber-Synod and the Council of Chalcedon," *Byzantion,* XVI, 1 (1944), 20–80.

Hopf, K. *Geschichte Griechenlands vom Beginne des Mittelalters bis auf die neuere Zeit.* Leipzig, 1867. (In Ersch and Gruber, *Allgemeine Encyclopädie der Wissenschaften und Künste,* 85, 86.)

Horma, K. "Das Hodiporikon des Konstantin Manasses," *Byzantinische Zeitschrift,* XIII (1904), 313–55.

Houedene, Roger de. *Chronica.* Ed. Stubbs, W. (*Rerum Britannicarum Medii Aevi Scriptores,* LI.) London, 1869.

Houssaye, Henri. *1815.* Vol. I. *La Première Restauration; le retour de l'isle d'Elbe; les cent jours.* Paris, 1905.

Huart, C. *Histoire des Arabes.* Paris, 1912. Useful.

Huillard-Bréholles, J. *Introduction à l'histoire diplomatique de l'empereur Frédéric II.* Paris, 1858.

———. *Vie et correspondance de Pierre de la Vigne ministre de l'empereur Frédéric II.* Paris, 1865.

Hussey, J. "Michael Psellus," *Speculum,* X (1935), 81–90.

Hussey, J. M. "The Byzantine Empire in the Eleventh Century: Some Different

Interpretations," *Transactions of the Royal Historical Society,* ser. 4, XXXII (1950), 71–85.

——. *Church and Learning in the Byzantine Empire 867–1185.* London, 1937. Important.

Huttmann, M. A. *The Establishment of Christianity and the Proscription of Paganism.* (*Columbia University Studies in History, Economics and Public Law,* LX, no. 2.) New York, 1914. Good bibliography.

Illyinsky, G. "A Charter of Tsar John Asen II," *Transactions of the Russian Archaeological Institute at Constantinople,* VII (1901). In Russian.

Imperatorum Basili Constantini et Leonis Prochiron. Ed. Zachariä von Lingenthal, Karl Eduard. Heidelberg, 1837.

Innocent III. *Epistolae.* Ed. Migne, J. P. (*Patrologia Latina,* CCXV–CCXVII.) Paris, 1855.

Inostrantzev, K. *Hunnu and Huns. Examination of the Theories of the Origin of the People Hunnu of Chinese Annals, of the Origin of the European Huns, and of the Mutual Relations of These Two Peoples.* 2nd ed. Leningrad, 1926. In Russian.

Iorga, N. *Byzance après Byzance.* Bucharest, 1935.

——. *Choses d'Orient et de Roumanie.* Bucharest and Paris, 1924.

——. "Deux siècles d'histoire de Venise," *Revue historique du sud-est européen,* IX (1932), 1–59.

——. *Geschichte des Osmanischen Reiches.* Vol. II. Gotha, 1909.

——. *Histoire de la vie byzantine. Empire et civilization.* 3 vols. Bucharest, 1934.

——. "Latins et Grecs d'Orient et l'établissement des Turcs en Europe (1342–1362)," *Byzantinische Zeitschrift,* XV (1906), 179–222.

——. *Notes et extraits pour servir à l'histoire des croisades au XVᵉ siècle.* Bucharest, 1915.

——. "Les Origines de l'iconoclasme," *Bulletin de la section historique de l'Académie roumaine,* XI (1924), 143–55.

——. (Ed.) "Origines et prise de Constantinople," *Bulletin de la section historique de l'Académie roumaine,* XIII (1927), 88–128.

——. "Ramón Muntaner et l'empire byzantin," *Revue historique du sud-est européen,* IV (1927), 325–55.

——. "Une ville 'romane' devenue slave : Raguse," *Bulletin de la section historique de l'Académie roumaine,* XVIII (1931), 32–100.

Isambert, F. A. *Histoire de Justinien.* 2 vols. Paris, 1856. Out of date.

Isidori, Hispalensis Episcopi. *Chronica Majora.* Ed. Migne, J. P. (*Patrologia Latina,* LXXXIII.) Paris, 1850. Ed Mommsen, T. (*Monumenta Historiae Germanica. Auctorum Antiquissima,* XI. *Chronica Minora,* II.) Berlin, 1894.

——. *Opera Omnia.* Ed. Migne, J. P. (*Patrologia Latina,* LXXXI–LXXXIV). Paris, 1850.

Istrin, V. M. *The Chronicle of George Hamartolus in its Old Sloveno-Russian Version.* 3 vols. Petrograd, 1920–30. In Russian.

Ites, M. "Zur Bewertung des Agathias," *Byzantinische Zeitschrift,* XXVI (1926), 273–85.

Ivanov, J. "The Origin of the Family of the Tsar Samuel," *Essays in Honour of V. N. Zlatarsky.* Sofia, 1925. In Bulgarian.

Jähns, Max. *Handbuch einer Geschichte des Kriegswesens von der Urzeit bis zur Renaissance.* Leipzig, 1880.

Jaffé, P. *Regesta Pontificum Romanorum.* Leipzig, 1885.

Jager, M. *Histoire de Photius.* 2nd ed., Paris, 1845.

Janin, R. *Constantinople Byzantine. Développement urbain et répertoire topographique.* Paris, 1950. (*Institut Français d'Études byzantines.*)

———. "Nicée. Étude historique et topographique," *Échos d'Orient,* XXIV (1925), 482–90.

———. "Les Sanctuaires de Byzance sous la domination latine," *Études byzantines,* II (1945), 134–84.

Jean Catholicos. *Histoire d'Arménie.* Trans. Saint-Martin, A. J. Paris, 1841.

Jeanselme, E. and Oeconomos, L. *Les Oeuvres d'assistance et les hôpitaux byzantins au siècle des Comnènes.* Anvers, 1921.

——— and Oeconomos, L. "La Satire contre les Higoumènes," *Byzantion,* I (1924), 317–39.

———. "Sur un aide-mémoire de thérapeutique byzantine contenu dans un manuscrit de la Bibliothèque Nationale de Paris (Supplément grec, 764): traduction, notes et commentaire," *Mélanges Diehl: Études sur l'histoire et sur l'art de Byzance,* Vol. I. Paris, 1930.

Jeffrey, A. "Ghevond's Text of the Correspondence between Umar II and Leo III," *The Harvard Theological Review,* XXXVII (1944), 269–332.

Jerphanion, G. de. "Les Inscriptions cappadociennes et l'histoire de l'empire grec de Nicée," *Orientalia Christiana Periodica* (1935), 237–56.

———. *Une Nouvelle Province de l'art byzantine. Les églises rupestres de Cappadoce.* Paris, 1925.

Jireček, C. "Albanien in der Vergangenheit," *Oesterreichische Monatsschrift für den Orient,* No. 1–2 (1914). Reprinted in *Illyrisch-albanische Forschungen.* Ed. Thallóczy, L. von. Munich and Leipzig, 1916.

———. *Geschichte der Bulgaren.* Prague, 1876. Russian revised ed. Bruun, F. and Palauzov, V. Odessa, 1878. Bulgarian trans. Zlatarsky, V. Sofia, 1929.

———. *Geschichte der Serben.* Vol. 1. Gotha, 1911. Vol. II, part 1. Gotha, 1918. Excellent work.

———. "The Situation and Past of the City of Drač," *Transactions of the Geographical Society of Serbia,* I (1912), part 2. In Serbian.

———. *Staat und Gesellschaft in mittelalterlichen Serbien.* (*Denkschriften der Wissenschaften in Wien, philosophisch-historische Klasse,* LVI.) Vienna, 1912.

———. "Die Wittwe und die Söhne des Despoten Esau von Epirus," *Byzantinisch-neugriechische Jahrbücher,* I (1920), 1–16. Geneological table, p. 6.

John Anagnostes. *De extremo Thessalonicensi excidio.* Ed. Bekker, I. (*Corpus Scriptorum Historiae Byzantinae.*) Bonn, 1838.

John Cantacuzene. *Historiae.* Ed. Schopen, L. (*Corpus Scriptorum Historiae Byzantinae.*) Bonn, 1828–32.

John of Cyprus. *Palamiticarum transgressionum liber.* Ed. Migne, J. P. (*Patrologia Graeca,* CLII, cols. 663–738.) Paris, 1865.

John Damascene, Saint. *Barlaam and Joasaph.* English trans. Woodward, G. R. and Mattingly, H. London and New York, 1914.

John of Ephesus. *Ecclesiastical History.* English trans. Payne-Smith, R. Oxford, 1860. Latin trans. Brooks, E. W. Louvain, 1936.

———. Lives of the Eastern Saints. Syriac text and English trans. Brooks, E. W. *Patrologia Orientalis,* XVIII (1924). Latin trans. van Douwen, W. J. and Land, J. P. N. Amsterdam, 1889.

John the Lydian. *De magistratibus.* Ed. Bekker, I. (*Corpus Scriptorum Historiae Byzantinae.*) Bonn, 1837. Ed. Wuensch, R. (*Bibliotheca Scriptorum Graecorum et Romanorum Teubneriana.*) Leipzig, 1903.

Jones, A. H. M. *Constantine and the Conversion of Europe.* London, 1948. "Constantine hardly deserves the title of Great." No Russian publications used.

Joranson, E. "The Alleged Frankish Protectorate in Palestine," *The American Historical Review,* XXXII (1927), 241–61.

———. "The Great German Pilgrimage of 1064–1065," *The Crusades and Other Historical Essays Presented to Dana C. Munro by His Former Students.* New York, 1928. Excellent article with a full bibliography.

———. "The Problem of the Spurious Letter of Emperor Alexis to the Count of Flanders," *American Historical Review,* LV, 4 (1950), 811–32.

Jordan, E. *Les Origines de la domination angevine en Italie.* Paris, 1909.

———. *Les Registres de Clément IV (1265–1268).* Paris, 1893.

Jordanis. *Getica.* Ed. Mommsen, T. (*Monumenta Germaniae Historica. Auctores antiquissimi,* V, 1.) 1882.

Joshua, the Stylite. *The Chronicle of Joshua the Stylite.* Trans. Wright, W. Cambridge, 1882.

Jugie, M. "Démétrius Cydonès et la théologie latine à Byzance au XIVᵉ et XVᵉ siècles," *Échos d'Orient,* XXXI (1928).

———. "Georges Scholarios, professeur de philosophie," *Studi bizantini e neoellenici,* V (1939), 482–94.

———. "Michael Psellus," *Dictionnaire de théologie catholique,* XIII (1936), 1149–58.

———. "Palamas et controverse palamite," *Dictionnaire de théologie catholique,* XI (1932), 1735–1818.

———. "Poésies rhythmiques de Nicèphore Calliste Xanthopoulos," *Byzantion,* V (1929–30), 357–90.

———. *Le Schisme byzantin. Aperçu historique et doctrinal.* Paris, 1941.

———. "Le Schisme de Michel Cérulaire," *Echos d'Orient,* XXXVI (1937), 440–73.

———. "Sur la Vie et les procédés littéraires de Symeon Métaphraste," *Échos d'Orient,* XXII (1923), 5–10.

———. "La vie de S. Jean Damascène," *Échos d'Orient,* XXIII (1924), 137–61.

———. "Le Voyage de l'Empereur Manuel Paléologue en Occident," *Échos d'Orient,* XV (1912), 322–32.

Julian the Apostate, Emperor. *Juliani Opera.* II. *Epistolae.* Ed. with English trans. Wright, W. C. 3 vols. London, 1913–23.

———. *Quae supersunt.* Ed. Hertlein, F. C. Leipzig, 1875–76.

Justinian. *Corpus juris civilis. Institutiones.* Intro. and English trans. Abdy, J. T. and Walker, B. Cambridge, 1876. Justinian's *Institutiones* were trans. into Russian in 1859 and in 1888. *Constitutiones.* Ed. Zachariä von Lingenthal, K. E. Leipzig, 1884–91. *Edicta.* Ed. Zachariä von Lingenthal, K. E. Leipzig, 1884–85. *Digest of Justinian.* Trans. Monro, C. H. Cambridge, 1904. *Institutiones und Digesta.* Ed. Krueger, P. and Mommsen, T. Berlin, 1889. *Codex.* Ed. Krueger, P. Berlin, 1892. *Novellae.* Ed. Kroll, G. Berlin, 1928.

Kadlec, C. "The Empire and Its Northern Neighbors," *The Cambridge Medieval History,* IV (1923), 183–215. See also the very good bibliography for the problem of Byzantium and ancient Russia, pp. 819–21.

Kaestner, T. *De imperio Constantini III. 641–68.* Leipzig, 1907. Brief and accurate dissertation.

Kahle, P. "Zur Geschichte des mittelalterlichen Alexandria," *Der Islam,* XII (1922), 29–83.

Kalligas, P. Μελέται βυζαντινῆς ἱστορίας ἀπὸ τῆς πρώτης μέχρι τῆς τελευταίας ἁλώσεως *(1205-1453).* Athens, 1894.

Kalogeras. Μάρκος ὁ Εὐγενικὸς καὶ Βησσαρίων ὁ Καρδινάλις. Athens, 1893.

Kampouroglou, D. Οἱ Χαλκοκονδύλαι. Μονογραφία. Athens, 1926.

Kananos, Laskaris. *Reseanteckningar från nordiska länderna. Smärre Byzantinska skrifter.* Ed. Lundström, V. Upsala and Leipzig, 1902. A Russian translation with commentary by Vasiliev, A. A. "Laskaris Kananos, Byzantine Traveler of the Fifteenth Century Through Northern Europe and to Iceland," *Essays Presented to V. P. Buzeskul.* Kharkov, 1914. In Russian.

Kantarowicz, E. *Kaiser Friedrich der Zweite.* Berlin, 1927. English trans. London, 1931.

———. "The 'King's Advent' and the Enigmatic Panels in the Doors of Santa Sabina," *The Art Bulletin,* XXVI (1944), 207–31.

Kap-Herr, H. von. *Die Abenländische Politik Kaiser Manuels.* Strassburg, 1881. An accurate dissertation.

Karabaček, J. *Abenländische Künstler zu Konstantinopel im XV. und XVI. Jahrhundert. (Denkschriften der philosophische-historischen Klasse der Akademie der Wissenschaften in Wien, LXII.)* Vienna, 1918.

Karapiperes, M. Νικηφόρος Βλεμμύδης, ὡς παιδαγωγὸς καὶ διδάδκαλος. Jerusalem, 1921. I have not seen this book.

Karolidis, P. Ὁ αὐτοκράτωρ Διογένης ὁ 'Ρωμανός. Athens, 1906. In Modern Greek. Popular sketch of the reign of Romanus IV Diogenes.

Kasso, L. *Byzantine Law in Bessarabia.* Moscow, 1907. In Russian.

Kaufmann, C. M. *Die Menasstadt.* Leipzig, 1910.

Khomiakov, A. S. "The Voice of a Greek in Defense of Byzantium," *Works of A. S. Khomiakov.* Vol. III. 4th ed., Moscow, 1914. In Russian.

Khrysostomica. *Studie ricerche intorno a S. Giovanni Crisostomo a cura del Comitato per il XVᵉ centenario della sua morte (407–1907).* Rome, 1908.

Khvostov, M. *History of the Commerce in Greco-Roman Egypt.* Kazan, 1907. In Russian.

Kidd, B. J. *A History of the Church to A.D. 461.* 3 vols. Oxford, 1922.

Kingsley, C. *Hypatia, or New Foes with an Old Face.* 2 vols. Ed. and abridged Goddard, Mabel. New York, 1929.

Kireyevsky, J. *Works.* Moscow, 1861. In Russian.

Kleinclausz, A. *L'Empire Carolingien: Ses origines et ses transformations.* Paris, 1902.

———. "La Legende du protectorat de Charlemagne sur la Terre Sainte," *Syria,* VII (1926), 211–33.

Klimas, Petras. *Ghillebert de Lannoy in Medieval Lithuania.* New York, 1945.

Kluchevsky, V. O. *A History of Russia.* 2nd ed., Moscow, 1906. In Russian. English trans. Hogarth, C. J. 5 vols. New York and London, 1911–31.

Knappen, M. M. "Robert II of Flanders in the First Crusade," *The Crusades and Other Historical Essays Presented to Dana C. Munro by His Former Students.* New York, 1928.

Knecht, A. *Die Religions-Politik Kaiser Justinians.* Wurzburg, 1896.

Knipfing, J. R. von. "Das Angebliche 'Mailänder Edikt' v. J. 313 im Lichte der neueren Forschung," *Zeitschrift für Kirchengeschichte,* XL (1922), 206–18.

Körting, G. *Petrarca's Leben und Werke.* Leipzig, 1878.

Kokovtzov, P. C. *A Hebrew-Khazar Correspondence of the Tenth Century.* Leningrad, 1932. In Russian.

———. "A New Jewish Document on the Khazars and the Khazaro-Russo-Byzantine Relations in the Tenth Century," *Journal of the Ministry of Public Instruction,* XLVIII (1913), 150–72. A Russian trans. of the Jewish text with a brief commentary also written in Russian.

———. "A Note on the Judeo-Khazar Manuscripts at Cambridge and Oxford," *Comptes rendus de l'Académie des Sciences de l'Union des Républiques Soviétiques Socialistes* (1926), 121–24. In Russian.

Kondakov, N. P. *An Archeological Journey Through Syria and Palestine.* St. Petersburg, 1904. In Russian.

———. *Histoire de l'art byzantin considéré principalement dans les miniatures.* Paris, 1886. This was published originally in Odessa in Russian, 1876.

———. *Iconography of the Holy Virgin.* Petrograd, 1915. In Russian.

———. *Macedonia. An Archaeological Journey.* St. Petersburg, 1909. In Russian.

———. *Sketches and Notes on the History of Mediaeval Art and Culture.* Prague, 1929. In Russian. Posthumous.

"Konstantin der Grosse und seine Zeit," *Gesammelte Studien.* Ed. Dölger, F. Freiburg, 1913.

Köprülü, M. F. *Les Origines de l'empire Ottoman.* Paris, 1935.

Koran. Trans. Palmer, E. H. Oxford, 1880. Trans. Sale, G. London and New York, 1891. 9th ed., Philadelphia and London, 1923. Trans. Rodwell, J. M. New York, 1915.

Korelin, M. *The Earlier Italian Humanism and Its Historiography.* Moscow, 1892. In Russian.

Kornemann, E. *Römische Geschichte.* Vol. II. Stuttgart, 1939. 2nd ed., 1941.

Kougéas, S. B. Ὁ Καισαρείας Ἀρέθας Καὶ τὸ ἔργον αὐτοῦ. Athens, 1913.

Koukoules, Ph. "Λαογραφικαὶ εἰδήσεις παρὰ τῷ Θεσσαλονίκης Εὐσταθίῳ," Ἐπετηρὶς Ἑταιρείας Βυζαντινῶν Σπουδῶν, I (1924), 5–40.

Kovalevsky, M. *The Economic Growth of Europe.* Moscow, 1903. In Russian. German trans. Kupperburg, M. *Die ökonimische Entwicklung Europas.* Berlin, 1911.

Kratchkovsky, J. *The Arab Culture in Spain.* Moscow and Leningrad, 1937. In Russian.

Kraus, R. *Theodora. The Circus Empress.* New York, 1938. Of no historical value.

Kreller, H. "Lex Rhodia. Untersuchungen zur Quellengeschichte des römischen Seerechtes," *Zeitschrift für das Gesamte Handelsrecht und Konkursrecht,* XXV (1921), 257–367.

Kremer, A. *Culturgeschichte des Orients.* 2 vols. Vienna, 1875–77

Kretschmayr, H. *Geschichte von Venedig.* Vol. I. Gotha, 1905. Important.

Krey, A. C. "A Neglected Passage in the Gesta and Its Bearing on the Literature of the First Crusade," *The Crusades and Other Historical Essays Presented to Dana C. Munro by His Former Students.* New York, 1928.

Krivoshein, V. "The Ascetic and Theological Doctrine of the Saint Gregorius Palamas," *Annales de l'Institut Kondakov,* VIII (1936), 99–151. A very fine piece of work; ample bibliography. In Russian. A résumé in French, pp. 152–54. German trans. Wassilij, Mönch. "Die asketische und theologische Lehre des Whl. Gregorius Palamas," *Das östliche Christentum,* VIII (1939). In English, in *Eastern Churches Quarterly,* III (1938), nos. 1–4.

Krumbacher, K. *Geschichte der byzantinischen Litteratur von Justinian bis zum ende des oströmischen reiches (527–1453).* Munich, 1891. 2nd ed., 1897.

——. *Die Griechische Literatur des Mittelalters. Die Kultur des Gegenwart ihre Entwicklung und ihre Ziele.* 3rd ed., Leipzig and Berlin, 1912.

——. *Kasia. (Sitzungsberichte der philosophish-phililogischen und der historischen Klasse der bayerischen Akademie der Wissenschaften,* III, 305–70.) Munich, 1897.

——. *Michael Glykas. (Sitzungsberichte der philosophish–philologischen und historischen Klasse der bayerischen Akademie der Wissenschaften,* 1894.) Munich, 1894.

Krymsky, A. *A History of Muhammedanism.* Moscow, 1903–4. In Russian.

Kuchuk-Ioannesov, C. "The Letter of Emperor John Tzimisces to the Armenian King Ashot III," *Vizantiysky Vremennik,* X (1903), 93–101. In Russian.

Kugéas, S. "Notizbuch eines Beamten der Metropolis in Thessalonike aus dem Anfang des XV. Jahrhunderts," *Byzantinische Zeitschrift,* XXIII (1914–19), 143–63. *See also* Kougéas.

Kugler, B. *Geschichte der Kreuzzüge.* Berlin, 1880. 2nd ed., Berlin, 1891.

——. "Kaiser Alexius und Albert von Aachen," *Forschungen zur deutschen Geschichte,* XXIII (1883).

——. *Studien zur Geschichte des zweiten Kreuzzuges.* Stuttgart, 1866.

Kulakovsky, J. *History of Byzantium.* 3 vols. Kiev, 1910–15. 2nd ed., Vol. I. Kiev, 1913. In Russian.

——. *The Past of the Tauris.* 2nd ed., Kiev, 1914. In Russian.

Kulischer, J. *Russische Wirtschaftsgeschichte.* Jena, 1925.

Kunik, A. *On the Report of the Toparchus Gothicus.* St. Petersburg, 1874. In Russian.

Kupperberg, M. *Die ökonimische Entwicklung Europas.* Berlin, 1911. See Kovalevsky, M.

Kurtz, E. *Die Gedichte des Christophoros Mytilenaios.* Leipzig, 1903. Russian trans. Shestakov, D. "Three Poets of the Byzantine Renaissance," *Transactions of the University of Kazan,* LXXIII (1906).

——. "Georgios Bardanes, Metropolit von Kerkyra," *Byzantinische Zeitschrift,* XV (1906), 603–13.

Kyriakides, S. ʻΟ Διγένης ʼΑκρίτας. Athens, 1926.

Labbé, Ph. *De byzantinae historiae scriptoribus ad omnes per orbem eruditos* προτρεπτικόν. Paris, 1648.

Labourt, J. *Le Christianisme dans l'empire perse sous la dynastie Sassanide.* 2nd ed., Paris, 1904.

Lā Broquière, B. de. *Le Voyage d'outremer*. Ed. Schefer, C. (Recueil de voyages et de documents pour servir à l'histoire de la géographie, XII.) Paris, 1892.

Lactantius. *De mortibus persecutorum*. Migne, *P.L.* VII. Corpus Ser. Eccles. Latin., 27.

Ladner, G. B. "Origin and Significance of the Byzantine Iconoclastic Controversy," *Medieval Studies,* II (1940), 127–49.

Lamansky, V. I. *The Slavs in Asia Minor, Africa and Spain*. St. Petersburg, 1859. In Russian.

Lammens, P. H. *Études sur le règne du calife Omaiyade Moawia I*. Paris, 1908.

———. "La Mecque à la veille de l'hégire," *Mélanges de l'Université de Saint-Joseph,* IX (1924), 97–439.

———. "Les Sanctuaires pré-islamiques dans l'Arabie Occidentale," *Mélanges de l'Université de Saint-Joseph,* XI (1926).

La Monte, John J. *Feudal Monarchy in the Latin Kingdom of Jerusalem 1100 to 1291*. Cambridge, Mass., 1932.

———. "To What Extent Was the Byzantine Empire the Suzerain of the Latin Crusading States?" *Byzantion* VII (1932), 253–64.

Lampridius. *Antonini Heliogabali Vita*.

Lampros, Sp. "Αἱ εἰκόνες Κωνσταντίνου τοῦ Παλαιολόγου," Νέος Ἑλληνομνήμων, III (1906), 229–42.

———. (Ed.) "Bessarion's *Encomium,*" Νέος Ἑλληνομνήμων, XIII (1916), 146–94. Also published separately.

———. (Ed.) *Collection de romans grecs en langue vulgaire et en vers*. Paris, 1880.

———. "Εἰκόνες Ἰωάννου Η τοῦ παλαιολόγου," Νέος Ἑλληνομνήμων, IV (1907).

———. *Empereurs byzantins. Catalogue illustré de la collection de portraits des empereurs de Byzance*. Athens, 1911.

———. "Leo und Alexander als Mitkaiser von Byzance," *Byzantinische Zeitschrift,* IV (1895), 92–98.

———. "Mazaris und seine Werke," *Byzantinische Zeitschrift,* V (1896), 63–73.

———. "Μονῳδίαι καὶ θρῆνοι ἐπὶ τῇ ἁλώσει τῆς Κωνσταντινουπόλεως," Νέος Ἑλληνομνήμων, V (1908), 190–269.

———. "Νέαι εἰκόνες Κωνσταντίνου τοῦ Παλαιολόγου," Νέος Ἑλληνομνήμων, IV (1907), 238–40; VI (1909), 399–408.

———. "Ὁ Μαρκιανὸς Κώδιξ 524," Νέος Ἑλληνομνήμων, VIII (1911).

———. "Τρεῖς ἀνέκδοτοι μονῳδίαι εἰς τὴν ὑπὸ τῶν Τούρκων ἅλωσιν τῆς Θεσσαλονίκης," Νέος Ἑλληνομνήμων, V (1908), 369–91.

Lane-Poole, Stanley. *A History of Egypt in the Middle Ages*. London, 1901.

Langen, J. *Johannes von Damaskus*. Gotha, 1879.

Lannoy, G. de. *Oeuvres de Ghillebert de Lannoy, voyageur diplomate et moraliste*. Ed. Potvin, C. Louvin, 1878.

Laqeur, R. *Eusebius als Historiker seiner Zeit*. Berlin and Leipzig, 1929.

Lascaris, Theodore Ducas. *De naturali communione*. Ed. Migne, J. P. (*Patrologia Graeca,* CXL.) Paris, 1887.

———. *Epistulae* CCXVII. Ed. Festa, N. (*Publicazioni del R. Istituto di studi superiori pratici e di perfezionamento. Sezione di filiosofia e lettere,* no. 29.) Florence, 1898.

Laskin, G. *Heraclius. The Byzantine State in the First Half of the Seventh Century*. Kharkov, 1889. New sources. In Russian.

Lathoud, D. "La Consécration et la dédicace de Constantinople," *Échos d'Orient,* XXIII (1924), 289–94.

Latyshev, V. V. "Two Orations of Theodore Daphnopates with an introduction on his Life and his Literary Work and a Russian Translation," *Provoslavny Palestinsky Sbornik,* LIX (1910). In Russian.

Lauer, M. P. "Une Lettre inédite d'Henri Ier d'Angre, empereur de Constantinople, aux prélats italiens (1213?)," *Mélanges offerts à M. Gustav Schlumberger.* Vol. I. Paris, 1924.

Laurent, J. *L'Arménie entre Byzance et l'Islam depuis la conquête arabe jusqu'en 886. (Bibliothèque des Ecoles Françaises d'Athènes et de Rome, CXVII.)* Paris, 1919.

———. *Byzance et les Turcs Seljoucides dans l'Asie occidentale jusqu'en 1081. (Annales de l'Est publiées par la Faculté des Lettres de l'Université de Nancy, XXVII–XXVIII.)* Paris, 1913–14.

———. "Byzance et l'origine du sultanat de Roum," *Mélanges Charles Diehl: Études sur l'histoire et l'art de Byzance.* Paris, 1930.

Laurent, V. "Charles Diehl, historien de Byzance," *Revue historique du sud-est européen,* XXII (1945), 5–26.

———. "La Correspondance de Démétrius Cydonès," *Échos d'Orient,* XXX (1931), 339–54.

———. "Deux nouveaux manuscrits de l'histoire byzantine de Georges Pachymère," *Byzantion,* XI (1936), 43–57.

———. "La généalogie des premiers Paléologues," *Byzantion,* VIII (1933), 125–249.

———. "Gregoire X (1271–76) et le projet d'une ligue anti-turque," *Échos d'Orient,* XXXVII (1938), 257–73.

———. "Manuel Paléologue et Démétrius Cydonès. Remarques sur leur correspondance," *Échos d'Orient,* XXXVI (1937), 271–87; 474–87; XXXVII (1938), 107–24.

———. "Les Manuscrits de l'Histoire Byzantine de Georges Pachymère," *Byzantion,* V (1929–30), 129–205.

———. "Michel de Thessalonica," *Dictionnaire de théologie et liturgie catholique,* X, 2 (1928), 1719–20.

The Laurentian and Ipatian Chronicles. In *Complete Collection of Russian Annals (Polnoe Sobranie Russkikh Letopisey).* Vols. I–II. St. Petersburg, 1841 and ff. New ed. *Laurentian Chronicle* by Karsky, E. F. Leningrad, 1926. English trans. this chronicle by Cross, S. H. Cambridge, Mass., 1930.

Lavisse, E. *Histoire de France depuis les origines jusqu'à la révolution.* Paris, 1900–11.

——— and Rambaud, A. *Histoire générale du IVe siècle à nos jour.* Paris, 1893–1901.

Lawson, F. H. "The Basilica," *The Law Quarterly Review,* XLVI (1930), 486–501.

Le Barbier, E. *Saint Christodule et la réforme des couvents grecs au XIe siècle.* 2nd ed., Paris, 1863.

Lebeau, Charles. *Histoire du Bas-Empire.* Ed. Saint-Martin, M. de and Brosset, M. 21 vols. Paris, 1824–36.

Lebedev, A. *The Ecumenical Councils of the Sixth, Seventh and Eighth Centuries.* 3rd ed., St. Petersburg, 1904. In Russian.

———. *The Epoch of Christian Persecutions.* 3rd ed., St. Petersburg, 1904. In Russian.

———. *Historical Essays on the Situation of the Byzantine-Eastern Church from the End of the Eleventh Century to the Middle of the Fifteenth Century.* 2nd ed., Moscow, 1902. In Russian.

———. *A History of the Greek-Eastern Church under the Sway of the Turks.* 2nd ed., St. Petersburg, 1904. In Russiaɩ. Very useful.

———. *History of the Separation of the Churches in the Ninth, Tenth and Eleventh Centuries.* 2nd ed., Moscow, 1905. In Russian.

Lebedev, N. S. "Vasilievsky and the Importance of His Work," *Istoricesky Journal,* Leningrad (1944). In Russian.

Lebon, J. *Le monophysisme sévérien. Étude historique, littéraire et théologique sur la résistance monophysite au Concile de Chalcédonien jusqu'à la constitution de l'église jacobite.* Louvain, 1909. Very important.

Leclercq, H. *L'Afrique chrétienne.* Paris, 1904.

———. "Constantin," *Dictionnaire d'archéologie chrétienne et de liturgie,* III, 2 (1914), cols. 2622–95.

———. "Constantine Porphyrogenétè et le livre des cérémonies de la cour de Byzance," *Dictionnaire d'archéologie chrétienne et de liturgie,* III, 2 (1914), cols. 2695–2713.

———. "Culte et querelle des images," *Dictionnaire d'archéologie chrétienne et de liturgie,* VII, 1 (1926), cols. 180–302. Excellent bibliography.

———. "Julien l'Apostat," *Dictionnaire d'archéologie chrétienne et de liturgie,* VIII, 1 (1928), cols. 305–99. Good bibliography.

———. "Justinien," *Dictionnaire d'archéologie chrétienne et de liturgie,* VIII, 1 (1928), cols. 507–604. Very good bibliography.

———. "Kosmas Indicopleustès," *Dictionnaire d'archéologie chrétienne et de liturgie,* VIII, 1 (1928), cols. 819–49.

Lefebvre, G. *Recueil des inscriptions grecques chrétiennes d'Egypte.* Cairo, 1907.

Lefort, L. T. "La Littérature égyptienne aux derniers siècles avant l'invasion arabe," *Chronique d'Egypte,* VI (1931), 315–23.

Legrand, E. *Bibliothèque grecque vulgaire.* Paris, 1880.

Leib, Bernard. "Les Idées et les faits à Byzance au XIe siècle. Aperçus d'histoire religieuse d'après un témoin, Anne Comnène," *Orientalia Christiana Periodica,* I (1935), 164–203. This study in an enlarged form has been published as a general introduction to Leib's edition of the *Alexiad* (vol. I, [Paris, 1937], pp. ix–clxxxi). Interesting.

———. *Rome, Kiev et Byzance à la fin du XIe siècle.* Paris, 1924.

Lemerle, P. *Philippe et la Macédoine Orientale à l'époque chrétienne et byzantine. Recherches d'histoire et d'archéologie.* Paris, 1945.

———. *Histoire de Byzance.* Paris, 1948.

Leo the Deacon. *Historiae.* Ed. Hasius, C. B. (*Corpus Scriptorum Historiae Byzantinae.*) Bonn, 1828.

Leo the Grammarian. *Chronographia.* Ed. Bekker, I. (*Corpus Scriptorum Historiae Byzantinae.*) Bonn, 1842.

Leonhardt, W. *Der Kreuzzugsplan Kaiser Heinrichs VI.* Borna and Leipzig, 1913.

Leroy-Mohinghen, A. "Prolégomènes à une édition critique des Lettres Théophylacte de Bulgarie," *Byzantion,* XIII (1938), 253–62.

Le Strange, G. *Bagdad during the Abbasid Caliphate*. Oxford, 1900.

Levchenko, M. V. *History of Byzantium*. Moscow and Leningrad, 1940. In Russian. Bulgarian trans. Sofia, 1948. French trans. Paris, 1949.

Lewis, A. R. *Naval Power and Trade in the Mediterranean A.D. 500–1100*. Princeton, 1951.

Libanii. *Oratio*. Ed. Förster, R. (*Bibliotheca Scriptorum Graecorum et Romanorum Teubneriana*.) 7 vols. Leipzig, 1903–13.

Liber jurium reipublicae Genuensis. Ed. Riccotius, H. (*Monumenta Historiae Patriae*, IX.), Turin, 1857.

Liber Pontificalis. Ed. Duchesne, L. 2 vols. Paris, 1884–92.

Lipshitz, E. "The Byzantine Peasantry and Slavonic Colonization (particularly upon the data of the Rural Code)," *Vizantiysky Sbornik*, 1945. In Russian.

Liudprandi. *Legatio*. Ed. Becker, J. 3rd ed. 1915.

Le Livre du préfet ou l'édit de l'empereur Léon le Sage sur les corporations de Constantinople. Ed. Nicole, J. Geneva, 1893. Greek text and Latin trans. French trans. Nicole, J. Geneva and Basel, 1894. English trans. Boak, A. E. R. *The Journal of Economic and Business History*, I (1929), 600–19. English trans. Freshfield, E. H. *Roman Law in the Later Roman Empire. Byzantine Guilds Professional and Commercial Ordinances of Leo VI c. 895 from the Book of the Eparch*. Cambridge, 1938. From Nicole's edition the Greek text was reprinted in Zepos, J. and R. *Jus Graeco Romanum*, II (1931), 371–92.

Loenertz, R. "Démétrius Cydonès, citoyen de Venise," *Échos d'Orient*, XXXVII (1938), 125–26.

———. "Manuel Paléologue et Démétrius Cydonès," *Échos d'Orient*, XXXVI (1937), 271–87; 476–87; XXXVII (1938), 107–24.

———. "Pour l'histoire du Péloponnèse au XIVᵉ siècle (1382–1404)," *Études byzantines*, I (1944).

Loewe, H. M. "The Seljūqs," *The Cambridge Medieval History*, IV· (1923), 299–317, 836.

Logopatis, S. N. Γερμανὸς ὁ Β, πατριάρχης Κωνσταντινουπόλεως-Νικαίας (1222–40). Βίος, συγγράμματα καὶ διδασκαλία αὐτοῦ, Athens, 1919.

Lombard, A. *Études d'histoire byzantine: Constantin V, empereur des Romains (740–75)*. Paris, 1902.

Longnon, J. *L'Empire Latin de Constantinople et la Principauté de Morée*. Paris, 1949.

———. *Livre de la conqueste de la Princée de l'Amorée. Chronique de Morée*. Paris, 1911.

Loofs, F. *Leontius von Byzanz*. Leipzig, 1887.

Loparev, C. "Concerning the Unitarian Tendencies of Manuel Comnenus," *Vizantiysky Vremennik*, XIV (1907), 334–57.

———. "Hagiography of the Eighth and Ninth Centuries as a Source of Byzantine History," *Revue byzantine*, II (1916), 167–76. In Russian.

———. "On the Byzantine Humanist Constantine Stilbes (of the Twelfth Century) and His Works," *Vizantiyskoe Obozrenie*, III (1917), 57–88. In Russian.

Lopez, R. *Genova Marinara nel duecento. Benedetto Zaccaria, ammiraglio e mercante*. Messina and Milan, 1933.

———. "Mohammed and Charlemagne: A Revision," *Speculum*, XVIII (1943), 14–38.

Lopez, R. S. "Byzantine Law in the Seventh Century and Its Reception by the Germans and the Arabs," *Byzantion*, XVI, 2 (1944), 445–61.

———. "Le Problème des relations Anglo-byzantines du septième au dixième siècle," *Byzantion*, XVIII (1948), 139–62.

———. "Silk Industry in the Byzantine Empire," *Speculum*, XX (1945), 1–42.

Lot, F. *La Fin du monde antique et le début du moyen âge*. Paris, 1927. Important.

Luchaire, A. *Innocent III: La Question d'Orient*. Paris, 1907. Interesting book which covers the period up to 1216. No reference to sources.

Luke, H. C. "Visitors from the East to the Plantagenet and Lancastrian Kings," *Nineteenth Century*, CVIII (1930), 760–69.

Lumbroso, G. *Memorie italiane del buon antico*. Turin, 1889.

Lupton, J. H. *St. John of Damascus*. London, 1882.

Maas, P. "Die Chronologie der Hymnen des Romanos," *Byzantinische Zeitschrift*, XV (1906), 1–44.

———. "Das Hodoiporikon des Konstantin Manasses," *Byzantinische Zeitschrift*, XIII (1904), 313–55.

———. "Die ikonoclastiche Episode im Briefe des Epiphanios an Johannes," *Byzantinische Zeitschrift*, XXX (1929–30), 279–86.

———. "Metrische Akklamationen der Byzantiner," *Byzantinische Zeitschrift*, XXI (1912), 28–51.

———. "Die Musen des Kaisers Alexios I," *Byzantinische Zeitschrift*, XXII (1913), 348–69.

———. "Rhytmisches zu der Kunstprosa des Konstantinos Manasses," *Byzantinische Zeitschrift*, XI (1902), 505–12.

Macartney, C. A. "The Greek Sources for the History of the Turcs in the Sixth Century," *Bulletin of the School of Oriental and African Studies*, XI (1944), 226–75.

McCabe, J. *The Empresses of Constantinople*. Boston, n.d.

McPherson, Florence. "Historical Notes on Certain Modern Greek Folk Songs," *Journal of Hellenic Studies*, X (1889), 86–89.

Macri, C. M. *L'Organization de l'économie urbaine dans Byzance sous la dynastie de Macédoine, 867–1057*. Paris, 1925. No new findings.

Madler, H. *Theodora, Michael Stratiotikos, Isaak Komnenos. Ein Stüch byzantinischer Kaisergeschichte*. Plauen, 1894. Summary with the indication of sources and general sketches of the reigns of Theodora, Michael Stratioticus, and Isaac Comnenus.

Maïkov, A. "On Land Property in old Serbia," *Chteniya of the Society of Russian History and Antiquities*, I (1860). In Russian.

Makushev, V. *Historical Studies on the Slavs in Albania in the Middle Ages*. Warsaw, 1871. In Russian.

———. *The Italian Archives and Material on the History of the Slavs Preserved in Them*. (Addition to the *Transactions of the Academy of Sciences*, XIX, no. 3.) St. Petersburg, 1871. In Russian.

Malafosse, J. de. *Les Lois agraires à l'époque Byzantine. Tradition et Exégèse*. (*Recueil de l'Académie de Législation*, XIX.) Toulouse, 1949.

Malalas, John. *Chronicle*. Books 8–18. Trans. from Church Slavonic by Spinka, M. and Downey, G. Chicago, 1940.

Malinin, V. *The Old Monk of the Monastery of Eleazar, Philotheus and His Works.* Kiev, 1901. In Russian.

Manasses, Constantine. *Breviarium historiae metricum.* Ed. Bekker, I. (*Corpus Scriptorum Historiae Byzantinae.*) Bonn, 1837.

Manfroni, C. "Le relazioni fra Genova l'Impero Bizantino e i Turchi," *Atti della Società Ligure di Storia Patria,* XXVIII (1896), 575–858.

Mann, H. K. *The Lives of the Popes in the Early Middle Ages.* 2nd ed., London, 1925.

Manojlović, Gauro. "Memoirs," *Compte-rendu du deuxième congrès international des études byzantines, Belgrade, 1927.* Belgrade, 1929.

———. "Le Peuple de Constantinople," *Byzantion,* XI (1936), 617–716.

———. "Studije o spisu 'De administrando imperio' cara Konstantina VII Porfirogenita," *Publications of the Academy of Zagreb,* CLXXXII (1910–11), 1–65; CLXXXVI (1910–11), 35–103; 104–84; CLXXXVII (1910–11), 1–132.

Mansi, Joannes Dominicus. (Ed.) *Sacrorum Consiliorum Nova et Amplissima Collectio.* 31 vols. Florence and Venice, 1758–98.

Manuel Palaeologus. *Oratio funebris.* Ed. Migne, J. P. (*Patrologia Graeca,* CLVI, cols. 181–308.) Paris, 1866. *See also* Palaeologus, Manuel.

Marcellini, Comitis. *Chronicon, ad annum 517.* Ed. Mommsen, T. (*Monumenta Germaniae Historica. Auctorum Antiquissimorum,* XI. *Chronica Minora,* II.) Berlin, 1894.

Marcellinus, Ammianus. *Res Gestae.* Ed. Rolfe, J. I–III (1935–39).

Marin, E. *Saint Théodore, 759–826.* Paris, 1906.

Marinescu, C. "Manuel II Paléologue et les rois d'Aragon. Commentaire sur quatre lettres inédites en latin, expediées par la chancellerie byzantine," *Bulletin de la section historique de l'Académie roumaine,* XI (1924), 192–206.

———. "Tentatives de mariage de deux fils d'Andronic II Paléologue avec des princesses latines," *Revue historique du sud-est européen,* I (1924), 139–40.

Marquart, J. *Osteuropäische und ostasiaische Streifzüge.* Leipzig, 1903.

Marr, N. "The Caucasian Cultural World and Armenia," *Journal of the Ministry of Public Instruction,* LVII (1915).

———. "John Petritzi, Iberian (Gruzinian) Neoplatonic of the Eleventh-Twelfth Century," *Accounts of the Oriental Section of the Russian Archeological Society,* XIX (1909). In Russian.

Martène, E. and Durand, U. *Thesaurus novus anecdotorum.* Paris, 1717.

Martin, E. J. *A History of the Iconoclastic Controversy.* London, 1930. Important.

Martin, Pope. *Epistolae.* Ed. Migne, J. P. (*Patrologia Latina,* LXXXVII.) Paris, 1851.

Marzemin, G. "Il Libro del Prefetto. Sistema corporativo romano di Costantinopoli e di Venezia," *Atti del Reale Istituto Veneto di scienze, lettere ed arti,* XCIV (1934–35), 381–406.

Masefield, John. *Basilissa, A Tale of the Empress Theodora.* New York, 1940.

Mas Latrie, M. L. de. *Histoire de l'île de Chypre sous le règne des princes de la maison de Lusignan.* 3 vols. Paris, 1852–61.

Maspero, J. "Un dernier Poète grec d'Egypte: Dioscore, fils d'Apollôs," *Revue des études grecques,* XXIV (1911), 426–81.

———. *Histoire des patriarches d'Alexandrie.* Paris, 1923.

———. *Organization militaire de l'Egypte byzantine*. Paris, 1912.

Matranga, P. *Anecdota Graeca*. Rome, 1850.

Mattern, J. "À Travers les villes mortes de Haute-Syrie," *Mélanges de l'Université Saint-Joseph*, XVII, 1 (1933). 2nd ed., *Villes mortes de Haute-Syrie*. Beirut, 1944.

Matthew of Paris. *Chronica Majora*. Ed. Luard, H. R. 7 vols. (*Rerum Britannicarum Medii Aevi Scriptores*, LVII.) London, 1880.

———. *Historia Anglorum*. Ed. Madden, F. 3 vols. (*Rerum Britannicarum Medii Aevi Scriptores*, XLIV.) London, 1866–69.

Maurice, J. *Constantin le Grand: L'Origine de la civilization chrétienne*. Paris, 1925.

———. *Numismatique constantinienne*. Paris, 1908–12. Vols. I–III are very important.

———. *Les Origines de Constantinople*. (*Centenaire de la Société Nationale des Antiquaires de France*.) Paris, 1904.

Mednikov, N. *Palestine from its Conquest by the Arabs to the Crusades, based upon Arabic Sources*. Vols. I–IV. St. Petersburg, 1897–1902. A Russian translation of Arabic sources, with notes and citations of special monographs.

Medovikov, P. *The Latin Emperors in Constantinople and Their Relations to the Independent Greek Rulers and to the Local Population in General*. Moscow, 1849. In Russian. Out of date.

Meliades, G. Βέλθανδρος καὶ Χρυσάντζα, Μυθιστόρημα XII αἰῶνος. Athens, 1925.

Meliarakes, A. Ἱστορία τοῦ Βασιλείου τῆς Νικαίας καὶ τοῦ Δεσποτάτου τῆς Ἠπείρου (1204–61). Athens, 1898. An important book which emphasizes the history of Nicaea and Epirus.

Menander. *Excerpta ex historia*. Ed. Niebuhr, B. G. (*Corpus Scriptorum Historiae Byzantinae*.) Bonn, 1829.

Mercati, S. G. "Per l'epistolario di Demetrio Cidone," *Studi bizantini e neoellenici*, III (1930), 201–30.

———. "Poesie de Teofilatto de Bulgaria," *Studi bizantini e neoellenici*, I (1924), 173–94.

Mercier, E. *Histoire de l'Afrique septentrionale*. Paris, 1888.

Merejkowski, D. *Christ and Antichrist*. I. *The Death of the Gods: Julian the Apostate*. Trans. Trench, H. New York, 1929. A novel. Interesting reading.

Meyer, L. *S. Jean Chrysostome, maître de perfection chrétienne*. Paris, 1933.

Meyer, P. *Die Haupturkunden für die Geschichte der Athosklöster*. Leipzig, 1894.

———. "Les premières compilations françaises d'histoire ancienne," *Romania*, XIV (1885), 1–81.

Michael Acominatos (Choniates). *Works*. Ed. Lampros, S. Athens, 1879.

Michael Attaliates. *Historia*. Ed. Bekker, I. (*Corpus Scriptorum Historiae Byzantinae*.) Bonn, 1853.

Michel, A. *Humbert und Kerullarios. Studien*. Vols. I–II. Paderborn, 1925–30.

Mickwitz, G. *Die Kartellfunktionen der Zünfte*. Helsingfors, 1936.

———. "Die Organizationsformen zweier byzantinischer Gewerbe im X. Jahrhundert," *Byzantinische Zeitschrift*, XXXVI (1936), 63–76. Important.

———. Review: Christophilopoulos, Τὸ ἐπαρχικὸν βιβλίον Λέοντος τοῦ Σοφοῦ, *Byzantinisch-neugriechische Jahrbücher*, XII (1936), 368–74.

Miklosich, F. and Müller, J. *Acta et diplomata graeca medii aevi*. 6 vols., Vienna, 1860–90.

Miller, E. *Mélanges de philologie et d'épigraphie.* Paris, 1876.

Miller, M. "Poème allégorique de Méliténiote, publié d'après un manuscrit de la Bibliothèque Impériale," *Notices et extraits des manuscrits de la Bibliothèque Nationale,* XIX, 2 (1858), 11–138.

Miller, W. *The Catalans at Athens.* Rome, 1907.

——. "The Emperor of Nicaea and the Recovery of Constantinople," *The Cambridge Medieval History,* IV (1923), 478–516.

——. *Essays on the Latin Orient.* Cambridge, 1921. Articles and monographs of the author published between 1897 and 1921, revised and brought up to date. A very useful book.

——. "The Finlay Library," *The Annual of the British School at Athens,* XXVI (1923–25), 46–66.

——. "The Finlay Papers, George Finlay as a Journalist and the Journals of Finlay and Jarvis," *The English Historical Review,* XXXIX (1924), 386–98, 552–57; XLI (1926), 514–25.

——. "The Historians Doukas and Phrantzes," *Journal of Hellenic Studies,* XLVI (1926), 63–71.

——. "The Last Athenian Historian: Laonikos Chalkokondyles," *Journal of Hellenic Studies,* XLII (1922), 36–49.

——. *The Latins in the Levant. A History of Frankish Greece (1204–1566).* London, 1908. The best general work on the Frankish sway in Greece and in the islands.

Millet, G. *L'ancient Art serbe. Les Églises.* Paris, 1919.

——. *Recherches sur l'iconographie de l'Evangile.* Paris, 1916.

——. "La Renaissance byzantine," *Compte-rendu du deuxième congrès international des études byzantines, Belgrade, 1927.* Belgrade, 1929.

Minorsky, V. "Roman and Byzantine Campaigns in Atropatene," *Bulletin of the School of Oriental and African Studies, University of London,* XI, 2 (1944).

Mioni, E. *Romano il Melode. Saggio critico e dieci inni inediti.* Turin, 1937.

Miracula S. Wulframni. Ed. Mabillon, D. T. (*Acta Sanctorum ordina S. Benedicti in saeculorum classes distributa,* III.) Paris, 1668–1701.

Misch, G. "Die Schriftsteller-Autobiographie und Bildungsgeschichte eines Patriarchen von Konstantinopel aus dem XIII. Jahrhundert. Eine Studie zum byzantinischen Humanismus," *Zeitschrift für Geschichte der Erziehung und des Unterrichts,* XXI (1931), 1–16.

Mitchison, Naomi. "Anna Comnena," *Representative Women.* London, 1928.

Mitrofanov, P. "The Change in the Direction of the Fourth Crusade," *Vizantiysky Vremennik,* IV (1897), 461–523. In Russian.

Mohler, L. *Kardinal Bessarion als Theologe, Humanist und Staatsmann.* (*Quellen und Forschungen, herausgegeben von der Görres-Gesellschaft,* XX.) Paderborn, 1923.

Monnier, H. "Études du droit byzantine," *Nouvelle revue historique de droit,* XVI (1892), 497–542, 637–72.

Monnier, Ph. *Le Quattrocento. Essai sur l'histoire littéraire du XVe siècle italien.* Paris, 1912.

Montelatici, G. *Storia della letteratura bizantina (324–1453).* Milan, 1916.

Montesquieu, Ch. Louis, Baron de. *Considérations sur les causes de la grandeur des Romains et de leur décadence.* Trans. Baker, J. New York, 1882.

Monumenta Germaniae Historica. Epistolarum. III–IV. *Epistolae Merowingici et Karolini aevi.* Ed. Dümmler, E. Berlin, 1892–95.

Moravcsik, G. *Byzantinoturcica.* 2 vols. Budapest, 1942–43.

——. "L'Edition critique du 'De administrando imperio,'" *Byzantion,* XIV (1939), 353–60.

——. "Zur Geschichte der Onoguren," *Ungarische Jahrbücher,* X (1930), 68–69.

——. "Zur Quellenfrage der Helenaepisode in Goethes Faust," *Byzantinisch-neugriechische Jahrbücher,* VIII (1931), 41–56.

Mordtmann, J. H. "Die erste Eroberung von Athen durch die Türken zu Ende des 14 Jahrhunderts," *Byzantinisch-neugriechische Jahrbücher,* IV (1923), 346–50.

Morey, C. R. *East Christian Paintings in the Freer Collection.* (*University of Michigan Studies, Humanities Series,* XII.) New York, 1914.

——. *The Mosaics of Antioch.* New York, 1932.

Moshin, V. A. "Again on the Newly Discovered Khazar Document," *Publications of the Russian Archeological Society in the Kingdom of the Serbs, Croats and Slovenes* (Jugoslavia), I (1927), 41–60. In Russian.

Müller, A. *Der Islam im Morgen- und Abendland.* Vol. I–II. Berlin, 1885.

Müller, C. *Fragmenta historicorum graecorum.* Paris, 1870.

Müller, J. *Documenti sulle relazioni della città toscane coll' Oriente Cristiano e coi Turchi.* Florence, 1879.

Munro, Dana C. "Did the Emperor Alexius I Ask for Aid at the Council of Piacenza, 1095?" *The American Historical Review,* XXVII (1922), 731–33.

——. "Speech of Pope Urban II at Clermont, 1095," *The American Historical Review,* XI (1906), 231–42.

Muntaner, Ramon. *Chronica o descripcio fets e hazanyes dell inclyt rey Don Jaume.* Ed. Buchon, J. A. in *Chroniques étrangères relatives aux expéditions pendant le XIIIe siècle.* Paris, 1840–60. Ed. Lanz, Karl. *Chronik des edlen En Ramon Muntaner.* (*Bibliothek des Litterarischen vereins in Stuttgart,* VIII.) Stuttgart, 1844. Trans. Goodenough, Lady. *The Chronicle of Muntaner.* (*Publications of the Hakluyt Society,* L.) Oxford, 1921.

Murnu, G. "L'Origine des Comnènes," *Bulletin de la section historique de l'Académie roumaine,* XI (1924), 212–16.

Mutafčiev, P. *Military Lands and Soldiers in Byzantium in the Thirteenth and Fourteenth Centuries.* Sofia, 1923. In Bulgarian.

——. *The Rulers of Prosek.* Sofia, 1913. In Bulgarian.

——. *Vojniški zemi i vojnici v Vizantija préz XIII–XIV v.* Sofia, 1932. (Offprint from the *Spisanije na Bulgaska Akademija,* XXVII). In Bulgarian.

Nasir-i-Khusrau. *A Diary of a Journey Through Syria and Palestine.* Trans. le Strange, Guy. (Palestine Pilgrim's Text Society, IV.) London, 1896.

Negri, G. *L'Imperatore Giuliano l'Apostata.* 2nd ed., Milan, 1902. English trans. Litta-Visconti-Arese, Duchess. 2 vols. New York, 1905.

Nersessian, Sirarpie der. *Armenia and the Byzantine Empire.* Cambridge, Mass., 1945.

——. "Remarks on the Date of the Menologium and the Psalter Written for Basil II," *Byzantion,* XV (1940–41), 104–25.

Nestor-Iskander. *The Tale of Tsargrad.* Ed. Leonides, Abbot. (*Pamyatiki drevney pismennosti,* LXII, no. 43.) St. Petersburg, 1886. In Old Russian. For other slavic accounts see *The Cambridge Medieval History,* IV (1923), 888. Russian text of the *Tale,* from the edition of 1853, is reprinted by N. Iorga, "Origines et prise de Constantinople," *Bulletin de la section historique de l'Académie roumaine,* XIII (1927), 89–105. The question now arises whether the original text of this tale is not Greek and whether the Slavic account of it may belong, not to a Russian, but to a Serbian. See N. Iorga, "Une source négligée de la prise de Constantinople," *Bulletin de la section historique de l'Académie roumaine,* XIII (1927), 65. B. Unbegaun, "Les relations vieu-russes de la prise de Constantinople," *Revue des études slaves,* IX (1929), 13–38. On the Russian version of Iskander and on the Old Russian translation of the account of Aeneas Sylvius of the capture of Constantinople by the Turks.

Neuhaus, L. *Die Reichsverwesenschaft und Politik des Grafen Heinrich von Anjou, des zweiten Kaisers im Lateinerreiche zu Byzanz.* Leipzig, 1904. Has no importance.

Neumann, C. "Byzantinische Kultur und Renaissancekultur," *Historische Zeitschrift,* XCI (1903), 215–32. This article was also published separately. Berlin and Stuttgart, 1903.

——. "Die byzantinische Marine," *Historische Zeitschrift,* N.S. XLV (1898), 1–23.

——. *Griechische Geschichtschreiber und Geschichtsquellen im zwölften Jahrhundert. Studien zu Anna Comnena, Theodor Prodromus, Johannes Cinnamus.* Leipzig, 1888.

——. *Die Weltstellung des Byzantinischen Reiches vor den Kreuzzügen.* Leipzig, 1894. French trans. "La Situation mondiale de l'empire byzantin avant les croisades." *Revue de l'orient Latin,* X (1905), 37–171. Extremely interesting for the general conditions of the empire in the eleventh century.

Nicetas Choniates. *Historia.* Ed. Bekker, I. (*Corpus Scriptorum Historiae Byzantinae.*) Bonn, 1835.

Nicholas Mysticus. *Epistolae.* Ed. Migne, J. P. (*Patrologia Graeca,* CXI.) Paris, 1863.

Nickles, H. G. "The Continuatio Theophanis," *Transactions of the American Philological Association,* LXVIII (1937), 221–7.

Niederle, L. *Manuel de l'antiquité slave.* 2 vols. Paris, 1923–26.

Nikolsky, V. "The Union of Lyons. An Episode from Medieval Church History 1261–1293," *Pravoslavnoe Obozrenie,* XXIII (1867), 5–23, 116–44, 352–78; XXIV (1867), 11–33. Accurate but written strictly from the Greek-Orthodox point of view.

Nikonovskaya letopis. The Complete Collection of Russian Chronicles. Vols. IX–XIII. St. Petersburg, 1762 ff. In Old Russian.

Nikov, P. "Bulgarian diplomacy from the Beginning of the Thirteenth Century," *Bulgarian Historical Library,* I (1928). In Bulgarian.

——. *The Second Bulgarian Empire 1186–1936.* Sofia, 1937. Popular sketch. In Bulgarian.

——. *Studies in the Historical Sources of Bulgaria and in the History of the Bulgarian Church.* (Reprint from the *Transactions of the Bulgarian Academy of Sciences,* XX.) Sofia, 1921. In Bulgarian.

——. *Tartaro-Bulgarian Relations in the Middle Ages.* Sofia, 1921. Text and Bulgarian translation.

Nöldeke, T. *Aufsätze zur persischen Geschichte.* Leipzig, 1887.

————. *Geschichte der Perser und Araber zur Zeit der Sasaniden.* Leyden, 1879.

————. "Ueber Mommsen's Darstellung der römischen Herrschaft und römischen Politik im Orient," *Zeitschrift der deutschen morgenländischen Gesellschaft,* XXXIX (1885).

Nomiku, X. A. "Τὸ πρῶτο τ᾿ϳαμὶ τῆς Κωνσταντινουπόλεως," Ἐπετηρὶς Ἑταιρείας Βυϳαντινῶν Σπουδῶν, I (1924), 199–209.

Norden, E. *Einleitung in die Altertumswissenschaft.* 2nd ed., Leipzig and Berlin, 1914.

Norden, W. *Das Papsttum und Byzanz. Die Trennung der beiden Mächte und das Problem ihrer Wiedervereinigung bis zum Untergange des byzantinischen Reichs (1453).* Berlin, 1903. This book contains much that is new and very important on the Norman-Byzantine relations.

————. *Der vierte Kreuzzug im Rahmem der Beziehungen des Abendlandes zu Byzanz.* Berlin, 1898.

"Nuova serie di documenti sulle relazioni di Genova coll' Impero Bizantino," ed. Sanguineti, A. and Bertolotto, G. *Atti della Società ligure di storia patria,* XXVIII (1896–98), 351–60.

O'Conner, John B. "John Damascene," *Catholic Encyclopedia,* VIII (1910), 459–61.

Oeconomos, L. "L'État intellectuel et moral des Byzantins vers le milieu du XIVᵉ siècle d'après une page de Joseph Bryennios," *Mélanges Diehl: Études sur l'histoire et sur l'art de Byzance.* Paris. 1930.

————. *La Vie religieuse dans l'empire byzantin au temps des Comnènes et des Anges.* Paris, 1918. Important.

Olmstead, A. T. "Review: Spinka and Downey (eds.) *The Chronicle of John Malalas,*" *Chicago Theological Seminary Register,* XXXI, 4 (1942), 22–23.

Oman, C. *A History of the Art of War in the Middle Ages.* 2nd ed. London, 1924.

Omont, H. "Le Glossaire grec de Du Cange. Lettres d'Anisson à Du Cange relatives à l'impression du Glossaire (1682–1688)," *Revue des études grecques,* V (1892), 212–49.

Orderici Vitalis. *Historia ecclesiastica.* Ed. Migne, J. P. (*Patrologia Latina,* CLXXXVIII, cols. 17–986.) Paris, 1855.

Orosius, Paul. *Historiae adversum paganos.* VII.

Oster, E. *Anna Komnena.* I–III. Rastatt, 1868–71.

Ostrogorsky, G. "Agrarian Conditions in the Byzantine Empire in the Middle Ages," *The Cambridge Economic History,* I (1941), 194–223. Important.

————. "The Athonian Hesychasts and their Opponents," *Transactions of the Russian Scientific Institute in Belgrade,* V (1931), 349–70. Very clear presentation. In Russian.

————. "A Byzantine Treatise on Taxation," *Recueil d'études dediées à la mémoire de N. P. Kondakov.* Prague, 1926. In Russian.

————. "L'Expédition du prince Oleg contre Constantinople," *Annales de l'Institut Kondakov,* XI (1940), 47–62.

————. *Geschichte des byzantinischen Staates.* Munich, 1940.

————. "Die ländliche Steuergemeinde des byzantinischen Reiches im X. Jahrhundert," *Vierteljahrschrift für Sozial- und Wirtschaftsgeschichte,* XX (1927).

————. "Die Perioden der byzantinischen Geschichte," *Historische Zeitschrift,* CLXIII (1941), 229–54.

————. "Das Projekt einer Rangtabelle aus der Zeit des Caren Fedor Alekséevič," *Jahrbuch für Kultur und Geschichte der Slaven*, IX (1933), 86–148.

————. "Relation Between the Church and the State in Byzantium," *Annales de l'Institut Kondakov*, IV (1931), 121–23. In Russian.

————. "A Slavonic Version of the Chronicle of Symeon Logothete," *Annales de l'Institut Kondakov*, V (1932), 17–36. In Russian. Important.

————. *Studien zur Geschichte des byzantinischen Bilderstreites*. Breslau, 1929. Important.

————. "Theophanes," *Real-Encyclopädie der Classischen Altertumswissenschaft*. Ed. Pauly, A. F., Wissowa, G., and others. 2nd ser. X (1934), cols. 2127–32.

————. Über die vermeintliche Reformtätigkeit der Isaurier," *Byzantinische Zeitschrift*, XXX (1029–30), 394–400.

————. "V. G. Vasilievsky as Byzantinologist and Creator of Modern Russian Byzantology," *Annales de l'Institut Kondakov*, XI (1940), 227–35. In Russian.

————. "Die wirtschaftlichen und sozialen Entwicklungs-grundlagen des byzantinischen Reiches," *Vierteljahrschrift für Sozial- und Wirtschaftsgeschichte*, XXII (1929).

Otto of Freising. *Gesta Friderci I. imperatoris*. Ed. Waitz, G. (*Scriptores Rerum Germanicarum in Usum Scholarum*, XXXIII).

Pachymeres, George. *De Michaele Palaeologus* and *De Andronico Palaeologo*. Ed. Bekker, I. (*Corpus Scriptorum Historiae Byzantinae*.) Bonn, 1835.

Palaeologus, Manuel. *Lettres de l'empereur Manuel Paléologue*. Ed. Legrand, E. Paris, 1893. *See also* Manuel Palaeologus.

Palaeologus, Michael. *De vita sua opusculum*. Greek text and Russian translation in *Christianskoe Čtenie*. St. Petersburg, 1885, II. French trans. in Chapman, C. *Michel Paléologue, restaurateur de l'Empire Byzantin (1261–1282)*. Paris, 1926.

Palanque, J. R. *Essai sur la préfecture du prétoire du Bas-Empire*. Paris, 1933.

————. "Sur la Liste des préfets du prétoire du IVᵉ siècle. Réponse à M. Ernest Stein," *Byzantion*, IX (1934), 703–13.

Palgrave, F. *The History of Normandy and of England*. London, 1864.

Pall, P. "Ciriaco d'Ancona e la crociata contro i Turchi," *Bulletin de la section historique de L'Académie roumaine*, XX (1937), 9–60.

Pančenko, B. *A Catalogue of the Molybdobulla of the Collection of the Russian Archaeological Institute in Constantinople*. (*Transactions of the Institute*, VIII, IX). Sofia, 1903, 1904. In Russian.

————. "The Latin Constantinople and Pope Innocent III," *The Annals of the Historical-Philological Society at the University of Novorossiya*, XXI, 1 (1914). In Russian.

————. "On the Secret History of Procopius," *Vizantiysky Vremennik*, II (1895), 300–16; III (1896), 461–527; IV (1897), 402–51. In Russian.

————. *Peasant Property in the Byzantine Empire. The Rural Code and Monastic Documents*. Sofia, 1903. In Russian.

————. "The Slavonic Monument in Bithynia of the Seventh Century," *Transactions of the Russian Archeological Institute in Constantinople*, VIII, 1-2 (1902). In Russian.

Papadimitriu, T. D. *Theodore Prodromus*. Odessa, 1905. In Russian.

Papadopoulos-Kerameus, A. *Fontes Historiae Imperii Trapezuntini*. Petropolis, 1897.

Papaioannu, K. "The Acts of the So-Called Council of Sophia (1450) and Their Historical Significance," *Vizantiysky Vremennik*, II (1895), 394–415. In Russian.

Papamichael, G. Ὁ ἅγιος Γρηγόριος Παλαμᾶς ἀρχιεπίσκοπος Θεσσαλονίκης. Alexandria, 1911. Interesting book on the history of the religious and mystical movement of the Hesychasts in the fourteenth century.

Paparrigopoulo, K. *Histoire de la civilisation hellénique*. Paris, 1878.

———. *History of the Greek People*. Athens, 1871–77. Ed. Karolides, P. 8 vols. Athens, 1925. In Greek.

Pappadopoulos, J. B. Ἡ Κρήτη ὑπὸ τοὺς Σαρακητοὺς 824–961. Athens, 1948.

———. "La Satire du précepteur, oeuvre inédite de Théodore II Lascaris," *Compte-rendu du deuxième congrès international des études byzantines, Belgrade, 1927*. Belgrade, 1929.

———. *Theodore II Lascaris empereur de Nicée*. Paris, 1908. A rather thin sketch of Theodore II's reign. See the severe review by N. Festa in *Byzantinische Zeitschrift*, XVIII (1909), 213–17.

Paris, G. "La Légende de Saladin," *Journal des Savants* (1893), 7–34.

Parisot, V. *Cantacuzène homme d'état et historien*. Paris, 1845. An old but interesting and good monograph which gives a general idea of John Cantacuzene's epoch. Shows a tendency in favor of Cantacuzene.

Pascal, P. "Le 'Digenis' slave ou la 'Geste de Devgenij,'" *Byzantion*, X (1935), 301–34. From Speransky's edition.

"Pauli Diaconi." *Historia Langobardorum*. Ed. Bethmann, L. and Waitz, G. (*Monumenta Germaniae Historica. Scriptores rerum Langobardicarum et Italicarum*.) Hanover, 1878.

Pears, E. *The Destruction of the Greek Empire and the Story of the Capture of Constantinople by the Turks*. London and New York, 1903. Good book.

Peeters, P. "La Prise de Jérusalem par les Perses," *Mélanges de l'Université de Saint-Joseph*, IX (1923).

———. "S. Romain le néomartyr († 1 Mai 780) d'après un document géorgien," *Analecta Bollandiana*, XXX (1911), 393–427.

Pegolotti, Francesco Balducci. *La pratica della mercatura. Della decima e delle altre gravezze*. Lisbon and Lucca, 1766. Ed. Evans, Allan. (*The Medieval Academy of America Publications*, no. 24.) Cambridge, Mass., 1936.

Pelliot, P. "Les Mongols et la Papauté," *Revue de l'orient chrétien*, XXIV (1924), 330–31; XXVII (1931–32), 3–84.

Pernice, A. *L'Imperatore Eraclio*. Florence, 1905. The best monograph.

Pernot, H. *Études de littérature grecque moderne*. Paris, 1916.

———. "Le Poème de Michel Glykas sur son emprisonnement," *Mélanges Charles Diehl: Études sur l'histoire et sur l'art de Byzance*. Paris, 1930.

Perrier. *Jean Damascène: Sa Vie et ses écrits*. Strasbourg, 1863.

Pervanoglu, J. *Historische Bilder aus dem byzantinischen Reiche. I. Andronik Comnenus*. Leipzig, 1879. Of no importance.

Peter the Venerable. *Opera Omnia*. Ed. Migne, J. P. (*Patrologia Latina*, CLXXXIX, cols. 61–1054.) Paris, 1890.

Petit, L. "Manuel II Paléologue," *Dictionnaire de théologie catholique*, IX, 2 (1926), cols. 1925–32. Very good article with bibliography.

———. "Marcus of Ephesus," *Dictionnaire de théologie catholique*, IX, 2 (1927), cols. 1968–86.

Petrarca, Francesco. *Epistolae de rebus familiaribus et variae*. Ed. Fracassetti, G. Florence, 1859–63.

——. *Itinerarium Syriacum*. In *Opera Omnia*. 2 vols. Basil, 1554.

——. *Lettere di Francesco Petrarca*. Ed. Fracassetti, G. Florence, 1892.

——. *Lettere sinili di Francesco Petrarca*. Ed. Fracassetti, G. Florence, 1869–70.

——. *Rerum sinilium lib. VII*. In *Opera Omnia*, 2 vols. Basil, 1554.

Pétridès, S. "Jean Apokaukos, lettres et autres documents inédits," *Transactions of the Russian Archaeological Institute at Constantinople*, XIV, 2–3 (1909), 1–32.

Petrovsky, N. M. "On the Problem of the Genesis of Fallmerayer's Theory," *Journal of the Ministry of Public Instruction*, 1913, 104–49. In Russian.

Pfister, Kurt. *Der Untergang der Antiken Welt*. Leipzig, 1941.

Philippson, A. E. *Das Byzantinische Reich als Geographische Ercheinung*. Leyden, 1939.

——. "Zur Ethnographie des Peloponnes," *Petermann's Mitteilungen*, XXXVI (1890).

Philostorgius of Borissus. *Historia Ecclesiastica*. Ed. Bidez, Joseph. Paris and Brussels, 1913.

Phoropoulos, I. D. Εἰρήνη ἡ ʽΑθηναία αὐτοκράτειρα ʽΡωμαίων. Leipzig, 1887.

Phrantzes, George. *Annales*. Ed. Bekker, I. (*Corpus Scriptorum Historiae Byzantinae*.) Bonn, 1839. Ed. Pappadopoulos, J. B. I. Leipzig, 1935.

Pichon, R. *Lactance. Étude sur le movement philosophique et religieux sous le règne de Constantin*. Paris, 1901.

Picotti, G. B. "Sulle navi papali in Oriente al tempo della caduta di Costantinopoli," *Nuovo Archivio Veneto*, N.S. XXII (1911).

Pierce, H. and Tyler, R. *Byzantine Art*. New York, 1926.

Pierling, L. P. *La Russie et le Saint-Siège*. Paris, 1896. 2nd ed., Paris, 1906.

Piganiol, A. *L'Empereur Constantin le Grand*. Paris, 1932.

——. *L'Empire Chrétien 325–395*. Paris, 1947.

——. "L'État actuel de la question constantinienne 1939–1949," *Historia*, I, 1 (1950).

Pipe Rolls. Vols. XXVI, XXVIII. (*The Great Roll of the Pipe for the Reign of King Henry the Second*. Published by the Pipe Roll Society.) London, 1905, 1907.

Pirenne, Henri. "À propos de la lettre d'Alexis Comnène à Robert le Frison, comte de Flandre," *Revue de l'instruction publique en Belgique*, L (1907), 217–27.

——. "Mahomet et Charlemagne," *Revue belge de philologie et d'histoire*, I (1922). English trans. New York, 1949.

——. *Medieval Cities*. Princeton, 1925. French trans. *Les villes du moyen âge*. Brussels, 1927.

Pitra, J. B. *Analecta sacra et classica spicilegio Solesmensi parata*. Paris and Rome, 1891.

Plethon, George Gemistos. "Ad. Sanctissimum Dominum Nostrum Leonem Decimum Pontificem Maximum, Ioannis Gemisti Graeci, secretarii Ancone, Protrepticon et Pronosticon." Ed. Sathas, C. *Documents inédits relatifs à l'histoire de la Grèce au moyen âge*, VIII (1888), 545–91.

——. *De Rebus Peloponnesiacis Orationes duae*. Ed. Ellissen, A. *Analekten der mittel- und neugriechischen Litteratur*, IV, 2 (1860).

———. *Oratio prima.* Ed. Ellissen, A. *Analekten der mittel- und neugriechischen Litteratur,* IV, 2 (1860).

Pniower, O. "Review: Schmitt, *Die Chronik von Morea," Deutsche Literaturzeitung,* XXV (1904), 2739–41.

Pogodin, A. *History of Bulgaria.* St. Petersburg, 1910. In Russian.

———. *A History of Serbia.* St. Petersburg, 1909. In Russian.

Pogodin, P. "Survey of the Sources on the History of the Siege and Capture of Byzantium by the Turks in 1453," *Journal of the Ministry of Public Instruction,* CCLXIV (1889), 205–58. In Russian. Very good.

Pokrovsky, I. A. *History of Roman Law.* 2nd ed., Petrograd, 1915. In Russian.

Popov, N. *The Emperor Leo VI the Wise and His Reign from an Ecclesiastical Standpoint.* Moscow, 1892. In Russian.

———. *Outlines in the Secular History of Byzantium in the Time of the Macedonian Dynasty.* Moscow, 1916. A course of lectures.

Porphyrius, A. *History of Athos.* Kiev, 1877. In Russian.

Preobrazhensky, V. "The Blessed Theodore of Studion and His Time, 759–826," *Pastyrsky Sobesednik* (1895). In Russian.

Procopius. *Opera Omnia.* Ed. Haury, J. (*Bibliotheca Scriptorum Graecorum et Romanorum Teubneriana.*) Munich, 1913. Vols. I, II, *De bellis libri i–viii* (1905); Vol. III, 1, *Historia arcana* (1906); Vol. III, 2, *VI libri* Περὶ κτισμάτων *sive De aedificius* (1913). English trans. Dewing. 7 vols. London and New York, 1914–40.

Prutz, H. *Kulturgeschichte der Kreuzzüge.* Berlin, 1883.

Psellus, Michael. *Chronographia.* Ed. Sathas, C. (*Bibliotheca Graeca Medii Aevi,* IV.) Paris, 1874. Ed. and trans. into French by Renauld, E. 2 vols. Paris, 1926–28.

Puigi i Cadafalch, J. "L'Architecture religieuse dans le domaine byzantin en Espagne," *Byzantion,* I (1924), 519–33.

Rackl, M. "Demetrios Kydones als Verteidiger und Uebersetzer des hl. Thomas von Acquin," *Der Katholik. Zeitschrift für Katholische Wissenschaft und Kirchliches Leben,* XV (1915), 30–36.

Radojčić, N. "Die Griechischen Quellen zur Schlacht am Kossovo Polje," *Byzantion,* VI (1931), 241–46.

———. *Dva posljednja Komnena na carigradskom prijestolu.* Zagreb, 1907. In Croatian. Discussion of the last Comneni on the Byzantine throne. Brief but good.

Radonić, J. "Critobulus, a Byzantine Historian of the Fifteenth Century," *Glas of the Royal Academy of Belgrad,* CXXXVIII (1930), 59–83. In Serbian.

Rambaud, A. *L'Empire grec au dixième siècle. Constantin Porphyrogénète.* Paris, 1870. An excellent work.

———. *Études sur l'histoire byzantine.* Paris, 1912.

Ramsay, W. M. "The Attempts of the Arabs to Conquer Asia Minor (641–694 A.D.) and the Causes of Its Failure," *Bulletin de la section historique de l'Académie roumaine,* XI (1924).

———. *The Cities and Bishoprics of Phrygia.* Oxford, 1895.

———. *Historical Geography of Asia Minor.* London, 1890.

———. "The War of Moslem and Christian for the Possession of Asia Minor," *Contemporary Review,* XC (1906), 1–15.

Ranke, Leopold von. *Weltgeschichte.* Vol. VIII. Leipzig, 1887.

Rappaport, B. *Einfälle der Goten in das Römische Reich bis auf Constantin.* Leipzig, 1899.

Rasovsky, D. A. "Polovtzi, IV. Military History of Polovtzi," *Annales de l'Institut Kondakov,* XI (1940). In Russian.

Rauschen, G. *Jahrbücher der christlichen Kirche unter dem Kaiser Theodosius dem Grossen.* Freiburg, 1897.

Recueil des historiens des Gaules et de la France. Ed. Bouquet, D. Paris, 1833. 2nd ed., Paris, 1879.

Redin, K. *The Christian Topography of Cosmas Indicopleustes from Greek and Russian Versions.* Ed. Aïnalov, D. Moscow, 1916. Contains many illustrations and plates. In Russian.

Reinach, S. *Cultes, mythes et religions.* Vol. I. 3rd ed., Paris, 1922.

Renaudin, R. P. "Christodoule, higoumene de Saint-Jean, à Patmos (1020–1101)," *Revue de l'orient chrétien,* V (1900), 215–46.

Renauld, E. *Étude de la langue et du style de Michel Psellos.* Paris, 1920.

———. *Lexique choisi de Psellos.* Paris, 1920.

———. *Michel Psellos Chronographie ou histoire d'un siècle de Byzance, 976–1077.* Vols. I–II. Paris, 1926–28.

Reverdy, G. "Les Relations de Childebert II et de Byzance," *Revue historique,* CXIV (1913), 61–85.

Riant, P. E. *Alexii I Comneni ad Robertum I Flandriae comitem epistola spuria.* Geneva, 1879.

———. "Le Changement de direction de la quatrième croisade d'après quelques travaux recents," *Revue des questions historiques,* XXIII (1878), 71–114.

———. *Exuviae sacrae constantinopolitanae.* 2 vols. Geneva, 1876.

———. "Innocent III, Philippe de Souabe et Boniface de Montferrat," *Revue des questions historiques,* XVII (1875), 321–74; XVIII (1875), 5–75.

———. "Inventaire critique des lettres historique de croisades," *Archives de l'orient latin,* I (1881), 1–224.

Rienzi, Cola di. *Epistolario.* Ed. Gabrielli, A. (*Fonti per la Storia d'Italia. Epistolari,* XIV, no. 6.) Rome, 1890.

Roby, H. J. *Introduction to Justinian's Digest.* Cambridge, 1884. Useful.

Rocholl, R. *Bessarion. Studie zur Geschichte der Renaissance.* Leipzig, 1904.

Röhricht, R. *Geschichte der Kreuzzüge im Umriss.* Innsbruck, 1898.

———. *Geschichte des Königreichs Jerusalem, 1100–1291.* Innsbruck, 1898.

Le Roman de Phlorios et Platzia Phlore. Ed. Hesseling, D. C. Amsterdam, 1917.

Romance of Lybistros and Rhodamne. Greek text. Wagner, W. *Trois poèmes du moyen âge.* Berlin, 1881. Detailed analysis by Gidel, M. *Études sur la littérature grecque moderne.* Paris, 1866. New ed., Lambert, J. A. Amsterdam, 1935.

Romanos, I. A. Περὶ τοῦ Δεσποτάτου τῆς Ἠπείρου ἱστορικὴ πραγματεία. Corfù, 1895. An important and reliable posthumous monograph on the Despotat of Epirus.

Romein, Jan. *Byzantium. An Historical Review of the State and Civilization in the Eastern Roman Empire.* Zutphen, 1928. In Dutch.

Rose, A. *Die byzantinische Kirchenpolitik unter dem Kaiser Anastasius I.* Wohlau, 1888.

———. *Kaiser Anastasius I.* I. *Die äussere Politik des Kaisers.* Halle, 1882.

Rosen, V. R., Baron. *The Emperor Basil Bulgaroctonus. Selections from the*

Chronicle of Yahya of Antioch. St. Petersburg, 1883. In Russian. Very important work largely used by Schlumberger.

Rosenberg, A. *Einleitung und Quellenkunde zur römischen Geschichte.* Berlin, 1921.

Rosseykin, T. M. *The First Rule of Photius, Patriarch of Constantinople.* Sergiev Posad, 1915. An important work. In Russian.

Rossini, C. *Storia d'Etiopia.* Bergamo, 1928.

Rostovtzeff, M. *The Social and Economic History of the Roman Empire.* Oxford, 1926.

Roth, K. *Studie zu den Briefen des Theophylactos Bulgarus.* Ludwigshafen am Rhein, 1900.

Rouillard, Germaine. *L'Administration civile de l'Egypte byzantine.* 2nd ed., Paris, 1928.

——. "À propos d'un ouvrage récent sur l'histoire de l'état byzantin," *Revue de philologie,* XIV (1942), 169–80.

——. "Les Archives de Lavra (Mission Millet)," *Byzantion,* III (1926), 253–64.

——. "La politique de Michel VIII Paléologue à l'égard des monastères," *Études byzantines,* I (1944), 73–84.

—— and Collomp, P. (Eds.) *Actes de Lavra.* Paris, 1937.

Royou, M. *Histoire du Bas-Empire.* Paris, 1803. 5th ed., Paris, 1836. 7th ed., Paris, 1844.

Rubió y Lluch, A. "Atenes en temps dels Catalans," *Anuari de l'Institut d'Estudis Catalans,* I (1907), 225–54.

——. "Els Castells catalans en la Grecia continental," *Anuari de l'Institut d'Estudis Catalans,* II (1908), 364–425.

——. *Los Catalanes en Grecia: Ultimos años de su Dominación: Cuadros históricos.* Madrid, 1927.

——. *La expedición y Dominación de los Catalanes en Oriente, Juzgadas por los Griegos. Memorias de la Real Academia de Buenas Letras de Barcelona,* IV (1883).

——. "Une figure athénienne de l'époque de la domination catalane: Dimitri Rendi," *Byzantion,* II (1925), 193–229.

——. "La Grecia catalana des de la mort de Frederic III fins a la invasió navarresa (1377–1379)," *Anuari de l'Institut d'Estudis Catalans,* VI (1915–20), 127–99.

——. "La Grecia catalana des de la mort de Roger de Lluria fins a la de Frederic III de Sicilia (1370–1377)," *Anuari de l'Institut d'Estudis Catalans,* V (1913–14), 393–485.

——. "Paquimeres i Muntaner," *Secció Historico-Arqueologica del Institut d'Estudis Catalans, Memòries,* I (1927), 33–66.

Rudakov, A. P. *Outlines in Byzantine Culture Based on Data from Greek Hagiography.* Moscow, 1917. In Russian.

Rügamer, P. W. *Leontius von Byzanz.* Würzburg, 1894.

Runciman, S. *Byzantine Civilization.* London, 1933.

——. "Charlemagne and Palestine," *The English Historical Review,* L (1935), 606–19.

——. *The Emperor Romanus Lecapenus and His Reign. A Study of Tenth Century Byzantium.* Cambridge, 1929. Important.

——. *A History of the Crusades.* Vol. I. Cambridge, 1951.

——. *A History of the First Bulgarian Empire.* London, 1930. Important.

The Russian Chronography. (Version of the year 1512). St. Petersburg, 1911. In Russian.

Sabbadini, R. "Ciriaco d'Acona e la sua descrizione autografa del Peloponneso trasmessa de Leonardo Botta," *Miscellanea Ceriani* (1910), 203–4.

Sadov, A. *Bessarion of Nicaea, His Activity at the Council of Ferrara-Florence, His Theological Works and His Importance in the History of Humanism*. St. Petersburg, 1883. In Russian.

Saewulf. *Pilgrimage of Saewulf to Jerusalem and the Holy Land*. (Palestine Pilgrim's Text Society.) London, 1896.

Saidak, J. *Literatura Bizantyńska*. Warsaw, 1933. In Polish.

———. "Que Signifie Κυριώτης Γεωμέτρης?", *Byzantion*, VI (1931), 343–53.

Salaville, S. "L'Affaire de l'Hénotique ou le premier schisme byzantin au Ve siècle," *Échos d'Orient*, XVIII (1910), 225–65, 389–97; XIX (1920), 49–68, 415–33.

———. "Deux manuscrits du 'De vita Christi,' de Nicholas Cabasilas," *Bulletin de la section historique de l'Académie roumaine*, XIV (1928).

———. *Nicolas Cabasilas: Explication de la divine liturgie*. Intro. and trans. Paris and Lyons, 1944.

———. "Le second centenaire de Michel le Quien (1733–1933)," *Échos d'Orient*, XXXII (1933), 257–66.

Salomon, R. "Review: Silberschmidt, *Das orientalische Problem*," *Byzantinische Zeitschrift*, XXVIII (1928), 143–44.

Salutati, C. *Epistolario di Coluccio Salutati*. Ed. Novati, F. (*Fonti per la Storia d'Italia Epistolari*, XIV–XV.) Rome, 1891–1911.

Sanudo, Marino. *Istoria del regno di Roumaina*. Ed. Hopf, C. in *Chroniques gréco-romanes inédites ou peu connues*. Berlin, 1873.

Sathas, Constantin. *Bibliotheca graeca medii aevi*. 7 vols. Venice and Paris, 1872–94.

———. *Documents inédits relatifs à l'histoire de la Grèce au moyen âge*. 9 vols. Paris, 1880–90.

Savage, H. L. "Reguerrand de Coucy VII and the Campaign of Nicopolis," *Speculum*, XIV (1939), 423–42.

Scala, R. von. "Das Griechentum seit Alexander dem Grossen," in Helmolt, H. F. *Weltgeschichte*. Vol. V. Leipzig and Vienna, 1905.

Schaeder, H. *Moskau das Dritte Rom. Studien zur Geschichte der politischen Theorien in der slavischen Welt*. Hamburg, 1929. The author is very familiar with the Russian sources.

Schanz, Martin von. *Geschichte der römischen Literatur bis zum gesetzgebungswerk des Kaisers Justinian*. Vol. III. 2nd ed., Munich, 1905.

Schaube, A. *Handelsgeschichte der romanischen Völker des Mittelmeergebiets bis zum Ende der Kreuzzüge*. Munich and Berlin, 1906.

Schechter, S. "An Unknown Khazar Document," *Jewish Quarterly Review*, N.S. III (1912–13), 181–219.

Schenk, K. *Kaiser Leon III*. Vol. I. Halle, 1880.

———. "Kaiser Leons III Walten im Innern," *Byzantinische Zeitschrift*, V (1896), 257–301.

Schiller, H. *Geschichte der römischen Kaiserzeit*. Vol. II. Gotha, 1887. Very good for the political, superficial for the religious, side.

Schillmann, F. "Zur byzantinischen Politik Alexanders IV," *Römische Quartalschrift*, XXII (1908), 108–31.

Schiltberger, H. *Reisebuch*. Ed. Langmantel, V. (*Bibliothek des literarischen Vereins in Stuttgart*, CLXXII.) Tübingen, 1885.

Schlauch, M. "The Palace of Hugon de Constantinople," *Speculum*, VII (1932), 500–14.

Schlosser, F. C. *Geschichte der bilderstürmenden Kaiser des oströmischen Reiches*. Frankfurt, 1912. Out of date.

Schlumberger, G. *Byzance et croisades*. Paris, 1927.

——. *Un Empereur byzantin au dixième siècle. Nicéphore Phocas*. Paris, 1890. A reprint, without plates and illustrations, Paris, 1923.

——. "Un Empereur de Byzance à Paris et à Londres," *Revue des Deux Mondes*, XXX (1915), 786–817. Reprinted in his *Byzance et croisades*, Paris, 1927.

——. *L'Epopée byzantine à la fin du dixième siècle*. 3 vols. Paris, 1896–1905.

——. *Expédition des "Almugavares" ou routiers catalans en Orient*. Paris, 1902.

——. *Renaud de Chatillon*. Paris, 1898.

——. *Le Siège, la prise et le sac de Constantinople par les Turcs en 1453*. Paris, 1915. On the basis of E. Pear's book. Bibliography on pp. 365–69.

Schmidt, L. *Geschichte der deutschen Stämme bis zum Ausgange der Völkerwanderung*. Vol. I. Berlin, 1904.

Schmidt, T. "La 'Renaissance' de la peinture byzantine au XIVe siècle," *Revue archéologique*, Ser. 4, XX (1912), 127–42.

Schmitt, J. *Die Chronik von Morea. Eine Untersuchung über das Verhältnis ihrer Handschriften und Versionen*. Munich, 1889. English trans. London, 1904.

——. "La 'Théséide' de Boccace et la 'Théséide' grecque," *Études de philologie néo-grecque*. (*Bibliothèque de l'Ecole des hautes études. Sciences philologiques et historiques*, XCII.) Paris, 1892.

Schneider, G. A. *Der heilige Theodor von Studion, sein Leben und Werke*. Münster, 1900.

Schoenebeck, Hans von. *Beiträge zur Religionspolitik des Maxentius und Constantin*. Leipzig, 1939. Important.

Schramm, P. *Kaiser, Rom und Renovatio*. Leipzig and Berlin, 1929.

Schubart, W. *Einführung in die Papyruskunde*. Berlin, 1918.

——. *Justinian und Theodora*. Munich, 1943.

Schultze, F. *Geschichte der Philosophie der Renaissance. I. Georgios Gemistos Plethon und seine reformatorischen Bestrebungen*. Jena, 1874.

Schwartz, E. *Kaiser Constantin und die christliche Kirche*. Leipzig and Berlin, 1913.

——. *Kyrillos von Skythopolis*. Leipzig, 1939.

Schwarzlose, Karl. *Der Bilderstreit, ein Kampf der Griechischen Kirche um ihre Eigenart und ihre Freiheit*. Gotha, 1890. Important.

Scriptor incertus de Leone Bardae filio. Ed. Bekker, I. (*Corpus Scriptorum Historiae Byzantinae*; volume with Leo Grammaticus.) Bonn, 1842.

Scriptores originum Constantinopolitanarum. Ed. Preger, T. Leipzig, 1901.

Scylitzes, John. *Excerpta ex breviario historico*. Ed. Bekker, I. (*Corpus Scriptorum Historiae Byzantinae*.) Bonn, 1838–39.

Sebèos. *The History of the Emperor Heraclius*. Trans. from Armenian into Russian. Patkanov, K. St. Petersburg, 1862. Trans. into French. Macler, F. Paris, 1904.

Sedelnikov, A. "The Epic Tradition Concerning Manuel Comnenus," *Slavia*, III (1924–25), 608–18. In Russian.

Seeck, O. "Der Codex Justinianus," in his *Regesten der Kaiser und Päpste für die Jahre 311 bis 476 n. Chr.* Stuttgart, 1919.

———. "Collatio lustralis," *Real-Encyclopädie der Classischen Altertumswissenschaft.* Ed. Pauly, A. F., Wissowa, G. and others. 1 ser. IV (1901), cols. 370–76.

———. *Geschichte des Untergangs der antiken Welt.* 6 vols. Berlin and Stuttgart, 1895. Vol. I, 2nd ed., 1897; 3rd ed., 1910. Vols. II, III, 2nd ed., 1921.

———. "Die Quellen des Codex Theodosianus," in his *Regesten der Kaiser und Päpste für die Jahre 311 bis 476 n. Chr.* Stuttgart, 1919.

———. "Das sogenannte Edikt von Mailand," *Zeitschrift für Kirchengeschichte,* XII (1891), 381–86.

Sergius, Arch. *The Complete Liturgical Calendar. (Menelogion) of the Orient.* 2nd ed., Vladimir, 1901. In Russian.

Serruys, M. D. "Les Actes du Concile Iconoclaste de l'an 815," *Mélanges d'archéologie et d'histoire,* XXIII (1903), 345–51.

———. "Une source byzantine des *Libri Carolini,*" *Comptes rendus de l'Académie des inscriptions et belles-lettres,* I (1904), 360–63.

Setton, Kenneth M. "Athens in the Later Twelfth Century," *Speculum,* XIX (1944), 179–207. Very good.

———. *Catalan Domination of Athens 1311–1388.* Cambridge, Mass., 1948.

Sewell, R. "Roman Coins in India," *Journal of the Royal Asiatic Society,* XXXVI (1904), 620–21.

Shakhmatov, A. *The Story of the Current Times (Poviest vremennych liet).* Petrograd, 1916. In Russian.

Shanguin, M. A. "Byzantine Political Personalities of the First Half of the Tenth Century," *Vizantiysky Sbornik* (1945), 228–36. In Russian.

Shepard, A. M. *The Byzantine Reconquest of Crete (A.D. 960). (U.S. Naval Institute Proceedings,* LXVII, no. 462.) Annapolis, Md., 1941.

Shestakov, S. P. *Lectures on the History of Byzantium.* Vol. I, 2nd ed., Kasan, 1915. In Russian.

———. "Notes to the Poems of the Codex Marcianus gr. 524," *Vizantiysky Vremennik,* XXIV (1923–26), 46–47. In Russian.

———. "The Question of the Author of the Continuation of Theophanes," *Compterendu du deuxième congrès international des études byzantines, Belgrade, 1927.* Belgrade, 1929.

Siciliano, Villanueva L. "Diritto bizantino," *Enciclopedia Giuridica Italiana,* IV, 5 (1906), 72.

Sickel, W. "Die Kaiserwahl Karls des Grossen. Eine rechtsgeschichtliche Erörterung," *Mitteilungen des Instituts für österreichische Geschichtsforschung,* XX (1899), 1–38.

Siderides, X. "Μανουὴλ Ὁλοβώλου Ἐγκώμιον εἰς Μιχαὴλ Η' Παλαιόλογον," Ἐπετηρὶς Ἑταιρείας Βυζαντινῶν Σπουδῶν, III (1926), 168–91.

Silberschmidt, M. *Das orientalische Problem zur Zeit der Entstehung des Türkischen Reiches.* Leipzig and Berlin, 1923.

Simeon, Metropolitan of Varna and Preslava. *The Letters of Theophylact of Ochrida.* Trans. into Bulgarian. (*Sbornik of the Bulgarian Academy of Sciences,* XXVII.) Sofia, 1931.

Šišić, F. *Geschichte der Kroaten.* Zagreb, 1917.

Skabalanovich, N. *Byzantine State and Church in the Eleventh Century.* St. Peters-

788 *Bibliography*

burg, 1884. A history of the eleventh century from 1025; very important for the internal history of the Empire. In Russian.

Skok, P. "Les Origines de Raguse," *Slavia,* X (1931), 449–500.

Skrzinska, Elena. "Inscriptions latines des colonies génoises en Crimée," *Atti della Società Ligure di Storia Patria,* LVI (1928), 1–180.

Smirnov, V. D. *Turkish Legends on Saint Sophia.* St. Petersburg, 1898. In Russian.

Socrates Scholasticus. *Historia ecclesiastica.* English trans. Schaff, Philip, Ware, Henry, and others. *A Select Library of the Nicene and Post-Nicene Fathers of the Christian Church.* 2nd ser. Vol. II. New York, 1895.

Sölch, J. "Historisch-geographische Studien über bithynische Siedlungen. Nikomedia, Nikäa, Prusa," *Byzantinisch-neugriechische Jahrbücher,* I (1920), 263–86.

Sokolov, J. J. *The Eparchies of the Constantinopolitan Church of the Present Time.* St. Petersburg, 1914. In Russian.

———. "Large and Small Landlords in Thessaly in the Epoch of the Palaeologi," *Vizantiysky Vremennik,* XXIV (1923-26), 35–42. In Russian.

———. "Review: Works of G. Papamichael," *Journal of the Ministry of Public Instruction,* N.S. XLIV (1913), 378–93; XLV (1913), 159–85; XLVI (1913), 409–19; XLVII (1913), 114–39. In Russian.

Sokolsky, V. "Concerning the Nature and Meaning of the Epanagoge," *Vizantiysky Vremennik,* I (1894). In Russian.

Solovjev, A. V. "The Thessalian Archonts in the Fourteenth Century. Traces of Feudalism in the Byzantino-Serbian Order," *Byzantinoslavica,* IV, 1 (1932), 159–74. In Russian with a French summary.

Sommerard, L. du. *Deux princesses d'orient au XIIᵉ siècle. Anne Comnène témoin des croisades. Angès de France.* Paris, 1907.

Sorel, A. *Montesquieu.* 2nd ed., Paris, 1889.

Soteriou, G. "Die byzantinische Malerei des XIV. Jahrhunderts in Griechenland. Bemerkungen zum Stilproblem der Monumentalmalerei des XIV. Jahrhunderts," Ἑλληνικά, I (1928), 95–117.

Soyter, G. "Prokop als Geschichtschreiber der Vandalen- und Gotenkriege," *Neue Jahrbücher für Antike und Deutsche Bildung,* II (1939), 97–103.

Sozomenis, H. *Historia ecclesiastica.* Ed. Migne, J. (*Patrologia Graeca,* LXVII.) Paris, 1864.

Spassky, A. *The History of the Dogmatic Movements during the Period of the Ecumenical Councils.* Sergiev Posad, 1906. In Russian.

Speransky, M. N. "Digenis' Deeds," *Sbornik Otdeleniya Russkago Yazyka i Slovesnosti,* XCIX, 7 (1922). In Russian.

———. *From the Ancient Novgorod Literature of the Fourteenth Century.* Leningrad, 1934. In Russian.

———. "The South-Slavonic and Russian Texts of the Tale of the Construction of the Church of St. Sophia of Tzarigrad," *Memorial Volume in Honor of V. N. Zlatarsky.* Sofia, 1925. In Russian.

Spintler, R. *De Phoca imperatore Romanorum.* Jena, 1905.

Spulber, C. A. *L'Eclogue des Isauriens: texte, traduction, histoire.* Cernautzi, 1929. Greek text with French trans. and history of the Ecloga.

Stadelmann, H. *Theodora von Byzanz.* 2 vols. Dresden, 1926.

Stadtmüller, Georg. "Michael Choniates Metropolit von Athen (ca. 1138–ca. 1222)," *Orientalia Christiana,* XXXIII, 2 (Rome, 1934), 125–325. Best study on the subject.

Stanojevitch, S. *History of the Serbian People*. 3rd ed., Belgrade, 1926. In Serbian. Useful.

Stein, Ernst. *Geschichte des spätrömischen Reiches*. Vol. I. Vienna, 1928. Important.

――. *Histoire du Bas-Empire*. Vol. II. Paris, Brussels, and Amsterdam, 1949.

――. "Justinian, Johannes der Kappadozier und das Ende des Konsulats," *Byzantinische Zeitschrift*, XXX (1930), 376–81.

――. "Ein Kapitel vom persischen und vom byzantinischen Staate," *Byzantinisch-neugriechische Jahrbücher*, I (1920), 50–89. See especially pp. 70–82.

――. "Une Nouvelle Histoire de l'Église," *Revue belge de philologie et d'histoire*, XVII (1938), 1024–44.

――. "Review: Baynes, *The Byzantine Empire*," *Gnomon*, IV (1928), 410–14.

――. "Review: Vasiliev, *History of the Byzantine Empire*," *Byzantinische Zeitschrift*, XXIX (1930), 347–60.

――. *Studien zur Geschichte des byzantinischen Reiches vornehmlich unter den Kaisern Justinus II und Tiberius Constantinus*. Stuttgart, 1919. Very important.

――. *Untersuchungen über das Officium der Prätorianenpräfektur seit Diokletian*. Vienna, 1922.

――. "Untersuchungen zur spätbyzantinischen Verfassungs-und Wirtschaftsgeschichte," *Mitteilungen zur Osmanischen Geschichte*, II (1924).

――. "Untersuchungen zur spätrömischen Verwaltungsgeschichte," *Rheinisches Museum für Philologie*, N.S. LXXIV (1925), 347–54.

Stephen the Younger. *Vita*. Ed. Migne, J. P. (*Patrologia Graeca*, C, cols. 1070–1186.) Paris, 1860.

Stéphanou, P. E. "Études récentes sur Pléthon," *Échos d'Orient*, XXXI (1932), 207–17.

――. "Jean Italos, philosophe et humaniste," *Orientalia Christiana Analecta*, CXXXIV (1949), 121 ff.

――. "Spyridon Lambros (1851–1919); Xénophon Sidéridès (1851–1929)," *Échos d'Orient*, XXIX (1930), 73–79.

Stöckle, A. *Spätrömische und byzantinische Zünfte*. Leipzig, 1911. Interesting.

Streit, L. *Venedig und die Wendung des vierten Kreuzzugs gegen Konstantinopel*. Anklam, 1877.

Struck, A. "Die Eroberung Thessalonikes durch die Sarazenen im Jahre 904," *Byzantinische Zeitschrift*, XIV (1905), 535–62.

――. *Mistra, eine mittelalterliche Ruinenstadt*. Vienna and Leipzig, 1910.

Strzygowski, J. *Die Baukunst der Armenier und Europa*. Vienna, 1918.

――. *Ursprung der christlichen Kirchenkunst*. Leipzig, 1920. English trans. Dalton, O. and Braunholtz, H. Oxford, 1923.

Suetonius. "Caligula," *Vita 12 Caesarum*.

Suidas. *Lexicon*. Ed. Adler, Ada, I–V. Leipzig, 1928–38.

Sundwell, J. *Abhandlungen zur Geschichte des ausgehenden Römertums*. Helsingfors, 1919.

Suvorov, N. "Review: Grenier, *L'Empire Byzantin*," *Vizantiysky Vremennik*, XII (1906), 227–28. In Russian.

Suzumov, M. "On the Sources of Leo the Deacon and Scylitzes," *Vizantiyskoe Obozrenie*, II, 1 (1916), 106–66. In Russian.

Swift, E. H. *Hagia Sophia*. New York, 1940. Thirty-four figures and forty-six plates. Full bibliography.

——. "The Latins at Hagia Sophia," *American Journal of Archaeology*, XXXIX (1935), 458–59, 473–74.

Sybel, H. *Geschichte des ersten Kreuzzuges*. Leipzig, 1841. Two later editions came out (1881 and 1900) almost without change. Still the most important work on the subject today.

——. "Ueber den zweiten Kreuzzug," *Kleine Historische Schriften*. Vol. I. Munich, 1863.

Sykutres, I. "Περὶ τὸ σχίσμα τῶν Ἀρσενιτῶν," Ἑλληνικά II (1929), 267–332; III (1930), 15–44. The author said that the book of the Russian theologian, Ivan Troizsky, was absolutely inaccessible to him.

Symeon Magister (Logothete). *Chronicle*. Ed. Bekker, I. (*Corpus Scriptorum Historiae Byzantinae*). Bonn, 1838.

Synesius of Cyrene. *The Essays and Hymns of Synesius of Cyrene, including the Address to the Emperor Arcadius and the Political Speeches*. Trans. and ed. Fitzgerald, A. Oxford and London, 1930.

——. *The Letters of Synesius of Cyrene*. Ed. Fitzgerald, A. London, 1926.

——. *Opera*. Ed. Migne, J. P. (*Patrologia Graeca*, LXVII, cols. 1020–1615.) Paris, 1864.

Synodicon Orientale ou Recueil de Synodes Nestoriens. Trans. and ed. Chabot, J. B. in *Notices et extraits des manuscrits de la Bibiothèque Nationale*, XXXVII (1902).

Tabari. *Annales*. Ed. de Goeje, M. J. 15 vols. Leyden, 1879–1901.

Tacchi-Venturi, P. S. I. "Commentariolum de Joanne Geometra ejusque in S. Gregorium Nazianzenum inedita laudatione in cod. Vaticano-Palatino 402 adversata," *Studi e documenti di storia e diritto*, XIV (1893).

Tafel, G. L. F. *Komnenen und Normannen*. Stuttgart, 1870.

—— and Thomas, G. M. *Urkunden zur ältern Handels- und Staatsgeschichte der Republik Venedig*. (*Fontes rerum austriacarum. Diplomata et acta*, XII–XIV.) Vienna, 1856–57.

Tafrali, O. *Thessalonique au quatorzième siècle*. Paris, 1913.

——. *Thessalonique des origines au XIVᵉ siècle*. Paris, 1919.

Tafur, Pero. *Andanças e viajes de Pero Tafur por diversas partes del mundo avidos (1435-1439)*. (*Coleccion de libros españoles raros ó curiosos*, VIII–IX.) Madrid, 1874. Trans. and ed. Letts, Malcolm. New York and London, 1926.

Tales of the Russian People. Ed. Sakharov, T. St. Petersburg, 1849. In Russian.

Taylor, J. W. *Georgius Gemistus Pletho's Criticism of Plato and Aristotle*. Menasha, Wis., 1921.

Tchaadayev, P. Y.. *Works and Letters*. Ed. Herschensohn, M. Moscow, 1914. In Russian.

Tcherniavsky, N. *The Emperor Theodosius the Great and his Religious Policy*. Sergiev Posad, 1913. In Russian.

Tennent, J. E. *Ceylon*. 5th ed., London, 1860.

Ternovsky, F. A. *The Graeco-Eastern Church*. Kiev, 1879–82. In Russian.

Tessier, J. *Quatrième croisade. La diversion sur Zara et Constantinople*. Paris, 1884.

Testaud, G. *Des Rapports des puissants et petits propriétaires ruraux dans l'empire byzantin au Xᵉ siècle*. Bordeaux, 1898.

Thalloczy, L. von. *Illyrisch-albanische Forschungen*. Munich and Leipzig, 1916.

Thallon, Ida C. *A Medieval Humanist:Michael Akominatos*. (*Vassar Medieval Studies* by the members of the Faculty of Vassar College.) New Haven, 1923.

Theiner, A. *Vetera monumenta historica Hungariam sacram illustrantia.* Rome, 1859.

Theodore the Monk. Θεοδοσίου Μοναχοῦ τοῦ καὶ γραμματικοῦ ἐπιστολὴ πρὸς Λέοντα Διάκονον περὶ τῆς ʽαλώσεως Συρακούσης. Ed. Hase. Paris, 1819. New ed. Zuretti, C. *Centenario della nascita di Michele Amari,* I (Palermo, 1910), 165–68.

Theodore Scutariotae *Addimenta ad Georgii Acropolitae Historiam.* Ed. Heisenberg, A. Leipzig, 1903.

Theodoret, bishop of Cyrus. *Historia ecclesiastica.* Ed. Parmentier, Léon. Paris, 1911.

Theodosius II. *Theodosiani libri XVI.* Ed. Mommsen, T. and Meyer, P. 3 vols. Berlin, 1905. In English, *The Theodosian Code* by C. Pharr. Princeton, 1952.

Theophanes. *Chronographia.* Ed. de Boor, C. 2 vols. Leipzig, 1883–85.

Theophanes Continuatus. *Historia.* Ed. Bekker, I. (*Corpus Scriptorum Historiae Byzantinae.*) Bonn, 1838.

Theophylact, archbishop of Bulgaria. *Epistolae.* Ed. Migne, J. P. (*Patrologia Graeca,* CXXVI.) Paris, n. d.

Theophylact Simocatta. *Historiae.* Ed. de Boor, C. Leipzig, 1887.

Thomas, A. "La Légende de Saladin en Poitou," *Journal des Savants,* N. S. VI (1908), 467–71.

Thomas, C. *Theodor von Studion und sein Zeitalter.* Osnabrück, 1892.

Thompson, E. A. *A History of Attila and the Huns,* Oxford, 1948.

Thompson, James Westfall. "The Age of Mabillon and Montfaucon," *The American Historical Review,* XLVII (1942), 225–44.

———. *An Economic and Social History of the Middle Ages.* New York and London, 1928.

Thuasne, L. *Gentile Bellini et Sultan Mohammed II. Notes sur le séjour du peintre vénitien à Constantinople (1479–1480).* Paris, 1888.

Timario sive De passionibus ejus. Dialogus satyricus. See M. Hase, in *Notices et extraits des manuscrits de la Bibliothèque Nationale,* IX (1813). Ed. Ellissen, A. *Analecten der mittel- und neugriechischen Literatur.* Vol. IV, Leipzig, 1860.

Tomaschek, W. *Die Goten in Taurien.* Vienna, 1881.

Tozer, H. F. "A Byzantine Reformer (Gemistus Plethon)," *Journal of Hellenic Studies,* VII (1886), 353–80.

———. "Byzantine Satire," *Journal of Hellenic Studies,* II (1881), 233–70.

Traub, E. *Der Kreuzzugsplan Kaiser Heinrichs VI im Zusammenhang mit der Politik der Jahre 1195–97.* Jena, 1910.

Treu, M. *Dichtungen des Grosslogothet Theodoros Metochites.* Potsdam, 1895.

———. "Manuel Holobolos," *Byzantinische Zeitschrift,* V (1896), 538–59.

———. "Mazaris und Holobolos," *Byzantinische Zeitschrift,* I (1892), 86–97.

Troizky, J. *Arsenius, the Patriarch of Nicaea and Constantinople, and the Arsenites.* St. Petersburg, 1873. Originally published in the *Christianskoe Čtenie,* 1873. Very good description of the life of the Eastern Church in the second half of the thirteenth century, under Michael VIII and Andronicus II.

Trubezkoy, E. *Religious and Social Ideals of Western Christianity in the Fifth Century.* Moscow, 1892. In Russian.

Turaev, B. A. *History of the Ancient East.* 2nd ed. Petrograd, 1914. In Russian.

Turchi, N. *La civiltà bizantina.* Turin, 1915.

Twenty-five Years of Historical Study in the U.S.S.R. Ed. Levchenko, M. Moscow and Leningrad, 1942. In Russian.

Tzetzes, John. *Argumentum et allegoriae in Iliadem.* Ed. Metranga, P. *Anecdota Graeca.* Rome, 1850.

——. *Historiarum variarum Chiliades.* Ed. Kiesslingius, T. Leipzig, 1826.

Ubicini, J. H. "Chronique du règne de Mahomet II, par Critobule d'Imbros," *L'Annuaire de l'association pour l'encouragement des études grecques,* V (1871), 49–74.

Underhill, Clara. *Theodora. The Courtesan of Constantinople.* New York, 1932. Has a good bibliography.

Usener, H. "Vier Lateinische Grammatiker," *Rheinisches Museum für Philologie,* XXIII (1868), 490–507.

Uspensky, C. N. "Exkuseia-Immunity in the Byzantine Empire," *Vizantiysky Vremennik,* XXIII (1923), 99–117. In Russian.

——. *Outlines of the History of Byzantium.* Moscow, 1917. In Russian.

Uspensky, P. *The Christian Orient. Athos.* Vol. III. Kiev, 1877. 2nd ed., St. Petersburg, 1892. In Russian.

Uspensky, Th. I. "The Boundary Stone between Byzantium and Bulgaria under Simeon," *Transactions of the Russian Archaeological Institute at Constantinople,* III (1898), 184–94. In Russian.

——. "Byzantine Historians on the Mongols and Egyptian Mamluks," *Vizantiysky Vremennik,* XXIV (1923–26), 1–16. In Russian.

——. *A Byzantine Writer, Nicetas Acominatus, of Chonae.* St. Petersburg, 1874. In Russian.

——. "The Constantinopolitan Code of Seraglio," *Transactions of the Russian Archaeological Institute at Constantinople,* XII (1907), 30–31. In Russian.

——. "The Eastern Policy of Manuel Comnenus," *Accounts of the Russian Palestine Society,* XXIX (1926), 111–38. In Russian.

——. "The Emperors Alexius II and Andronicus Comnenus," *The Journal of the Ministry of Public Instruction,* CXII (1880), 95–130; CXIV (1881), 52–85. In Russian. Interesting but unfinished.

——. "The Eparch of Constantinople," *Transactions of the Russian Archaeological Institute at Constantinople,* IV, 2 (1890). In Russian.

——. *Essays on the History of Byzantine Civilization.* St. Petersburg, 1892. In Russian. Very important. Contains a great deal of new and fresh material on the Hesychast movement and the relation of Byzantium to the Renaissance. See also a very interesting review of this book by P. Bezobrazov in *Vizantiysky Vremennik,* III (1896), 125–50. In Russian.

——. *The Formation of the Second Kingdom of Bulgaria.* Odessa, 1879. In Russian.

——. *A History of the Byzantine Empire.* Vols. I, II, 1 (II, 2 never was published), III. St. Petersburg, Moscow, and Leningrad, 1914–48. In Russian.

——. *A History of the Crusades.* St. Petersburg, 1900. In Russian. Very important from the point of view of the history of Byzantium.

——. "The Last Comneni. The Beginning of a Reaction," *Vizantiysky Vremennik,* XXV (1927–28), 1–23. In Russian.

——. "Materials for Bulgarian Antiquities, Aboba-Plisca," *Transactions of the Russian Archaeological Institute at Constantinople,* X (1905). In Russian.

——. "The Military Organization of the Byzantine Empire," *Transactions of the*

Russian Archaeological Institute at Constantinople, VI, 1 (1900), 1–54. In Russian.

———. "The Official Report on the Accusation of John Italus of Heresy," *Transactions of the Russian Archaeological Institute at Constantinople,* II (1897), 1–66. In Russian.

———. "On the History of the Peasant Landownership in Byzantium," *Journal of the Ministry of Public Instruction,* CCXXV (1883). In Russian.

———. "On the Manuscripts of the History of Nicetas Acominatus in the National Library of Paris," *Journal of the Ministry of Public Instruction,* CXCIV (1877). In Russian.

———. "Opinions and Decrees of Constantinopolitan Local Councils of the Eleventh and Twelfth Centuries concerning the Distribution of Church Possessions," *Transactions of the Russian Archaeological Institute at Constantinople,* V (1900), 1–48. In Russian.

———. "Review of V. I. Barvinok's Work," *Sbornik otcětov o premiyach i nagradach Akademii Nauk za 1912 god,* (Petrograd, 1916), 101–24. In Russian.

———. "Significance of Byzantine and South-Slavonic Pronoia," *Collection of Articles on Slavonic Studies for the Twenty-fifth Anniversary of the Scholarly and Professorial Activities of V. J. Lamansky.* St. Petersburg, 1883.

———. "The Start and Development of the Eastern Problem," *Transactions of the Slavonic Charitable Society,* III (1886). In Russian.

———. *Synodikon for the First Sunday of Lent.* Odessa, 1893. In Russian.

———. "The Tendency of Conservative Byzantium to adopt Western Influences," *Vizantiysky Vremennik,* XXII (1916). In Russian.

Uspensky, Th. I. and Beneševič, V. *The Acts of Vazelon. Materials for the History of Peasant and Monastery Landownership in Byzantium from the Thirteenth Century to the Fifteenth.* Leningrad, 1927. Greek text and a commentary in Russian.

Vailhé, S. "Projet d'alliance turco-byzantine au VIe siècle," *Échos d'Orient,* XII (1909), 206–14.

Valdenberg, V. "An Oration of Justin II to Tiberius," *Bulletin of the Academy of Sciences of the Union of Soviet Socialist Republics,* no. 2 (1928). In Russian.

———. "The Philosophical Ideas of Michael Psellus," *Vizantiysky Sbornik* (1945), 249–55. In Russian.

Vance, J. M. *Beiträge zur byzantinische Kulturgeschichte am Ausgange des IV. Jahrhunderts aus den Schriften des Johannes Chrysostomos.* Jena, 1907.

Vandercook, John W. *Empress of the Dusk. A Life of Theodora of Byzantium.* New York, 1940.

Van Millingen, A. *Byzantine Constantinople, the Walls of the City and Adjoining Historical Sites.* London, 1899.

Vasiliev, Alexander A. *Byzantium and the Arabs.* Vols. I–II. St. Petersburg, 1900–2. In Russian. Trans. into French. Gregoire, Henri, Canard, M. and others. *Byzance et les Arabes.* Vols. I, II, 2 (II, 1 has not yet been published). Brussels, 1935–50. (*Corpus bruxellense historiae byzantinae,* I, II, 2.)

———. "Charlemagne and Harun ar-Rashid," *Vizantiysky Vremennik,* XX (1913), 63–116. In Russian.

———. "An Edict of the Emperor Justinian II, September, 688," *Speculum,* XVIII (1943), 1–13.

———. *The First Russian Attack on Constantinople in 860–61.* (*Medieval Academy of America Monographs,* no. 46.) Cambridge, Mass., 1946.

———. "Das genaue Datum der Schlacht von Myriokephalon," *Byzantinische Zeitschrift,* XXVII (1927), 288–90.

———. *The Goths in the Crimea.* (*Medieval Academy of America Monographs,* no. 11.) Cambridge, Mass., 1936.

———. (Ed.) "A Greek Text of the Life of 42 Martyrs of Amorion, after the MSS of the Bibliothèque Nationale de Paris, no. 1534," *Transactions of the Imperial Academy of Sciences,* St. Petersburg, III, 3 (1898).

———. "La Guerre de cent ans et Jeanne d'Arc dans la tradition byzantine," *Byzantion,* III (1926), 241–50.

———. "Harun-ibn-Yahya and His Description of Constantinople," *Annales de l'Institute Kondakov,* V (1932).

———. and I. Kratchkovsky. (Eds. and trans.) *Histoire de Yahya-ibn-Saïd d'Antioche. Continuateur de Saïd-ibn-Bitriq.* In *Patrologia Orientalis,* XVIII (1924), 699–834; XXIII (1932), 348–520.

———. *Justin the First: An Introduction to the Epoch of Justinian the Great.* Cambridge, Mass., 1950.

———. "Justin I (518–527) and Abyssinia," *Byzantinische Zeitschrift,* XXXIII (1933), 67–77. Bibliography is indicated.

———. "Justinian's Digest, in commemoration of the 1400th anniversary of the publication of the Digest (A.D. 533–1933)," *Studi Bizantini e neoellenici,* V (1939), 711–34.

———. *The Latin Sway in the Levant.* Petrograd, 1923.

———. *Lectures in Byzantine History.* I. *The Period Until the Beginning of the Crusades (1081).* Petrograd, 1917. II, part 1. *Byzantium and the Crusaders.* Petrograd, 1923. II, part 2. *Latin Domination in the East.* Petrograd, 1923. II, part 3. *The Fall of the Byzantine Empire.* Leningrad, 1925. In Russian. Trans. into English from the Russian. Ragozina, Sarra Mironovna. *History of the Byzantine Empire.* 2 vols. (*University of Wisconsin Studies in the Social Sciences and History,* nos. 13, 14.) Madison, Wis., 1928–29. Trans. into French from the English. Brodin, P. and Bourguina, A. Preface by Diehl, Charles. *Histoire de l'Empire Byzantine.* 2 vols. Paris, 1932. The first volume trans. into Turkish from French ed. by Professor Arif Müfid Manzel. Ankara, 1943. Ed. and trans. into Spanish from the French. Luaces, Juan G. de and Masoliver, Ramón. *Historia del Imperio Bizantino.* 2 vols. Barcelona, 1946.

———. "The Lifetime of Romanus the Melode," *Vizantiysky Vremennik,* VIII (1901), 435–78. In Russian.

———. "Medieval Ideas of the End of the World: West and East," *Byzantion,* XVI, 2 (1944), 462–502.

———. "The Origin of the Emperor Basil the Macedonian," *Vizantiysky Vremennik,* XII (1906), 148–65. In Russian.

———. "Pero Tafur, a Spanish Traveler of the Fifteenth Century and his visit to Constantinople, Trebizond and Italy," *Byzantion,* VII (1932), 75–122.

———. "The Problem of Justinian's Slavic Origin," *Vizantiysky Vremennik,* I (1894), 469–92. In Russian.

———. "Quelques remarques sur les voyageurs du moyen âge à Constantinople," *Mélanges Charles Diehl: Études sur l'histoire et sur l'art de Byzance.* Paris, 1930.

Bibliography

795

———. "Review: Diehl and Marçais, *Le Monde oriental*," *Byzantinisch-neugriechische Jahrbücher*, XIII, 1 (1937), 114–19.

———. "The Slavs in Greece," *Vizantiysky Vremennik*, V (1898), 404–38, 626–70. In Russian.

———. "The Transmission by Andreas Palaeologus of the Rights to Byzantium to the King of France, Charles VIII," *Papers Presented to N. I. Kareev*. St. Petersburg, 1914.

———. "Il Viaggio dell' Imperatore Bizantino Giovanni V Paleologo in Italia (1369–1371) e l'Unione di Roma del 1369," *Studi Bizantini e Neoellenici*, III (1931), 151–93.

Vasilievsky, V. G. "Byzantium and the Patzinaks," *Journal of the Ministry of Public Instruction*, CLXIV (1872). Reprinted in *Works*, I. (1908). A masterpiece. In Russian.

———. "The Alliance of the Two Empires," *Slavyansky Sbornik*, II (1877), 210–90. Reprinted in *Works*, IV (1930). Very important. In Russian.

———. "The Chronicle of Logothete in Slavonic and Greek," *Vizantiysky Vremennik*, II (1895), 78–151. In Russian.

———. "Epirotica saeculi xiii," *Vizantiysky Vremennik*, III (1896), 233–99.

———. "The Legislation of the Iconoclasts," *Journal of the Ministry of Public Instruction*, CXCIX, CC (1878). Reprinted in *Works*, IV (1930). In Russian.

———. "The Life of Stephen the Younger," *Works*, II (1909).

———. "Lives of Meletius the Younger by Nicolaus bishop of Methone and of Theodore Prodromus," *Pravoslavny Palestinsky Sbornik*, XVII (1886). In Russian.

———. "Materials for the Internal History of the Byzantine State. Measures in Favor of Peasant Landownership," *Journal of the Ministry of Public Instruction*, CCII (1879). Reprinted in *Works*, IV (1930), 250–331. Russian translation of the novels of the tenth century with a very important commentary.

———. "On the Life and Works of Simeon Metaphrastes," *Journal of the Ministry of Public Instruction*, CCXII (1880), 379–437. In Russian.

———. "The Regeneration of the Bulgarian Patriarchate under the Tsar John Asen II," *Journal of the Ministry of Public Instruction*, CCXXXVIII (1885). In Russian.

———. "Review: Th. I. Uspensky, *The Formation of the Second Bulgarian Kingdom*," *Journal of the Ministry of Public Instruction*, CCIV (1879), 144–217, 318–48. In Russian. Very important.

———. "Russian-Byzantine Fragments. II. On the History of the Years 976 to 986," *Journal of the Ministry of Public Instruction*, CLXXXIV (1876), 162–78. Reprinted in *Works*, II (1909), 107–24. In Russian.

———. "The South Italian War (1156–57)," *Slaviansky Sbornik*, III (1876). Reprinted in *Works*, IV (1930). In Russian.

———. *A Survey of Works on Byzantine History*. St. Petersburg, 1890. In Russian.

———. "An Unpublished Funeral Oration of Basil of Ochrida," *Vizantiysky Vremennik*, I (1894), 55–132. In Russian.

———. "The Varangian-Russian and Varangian-English Guard (druzhina) in Constantinople in the Eleventh and Twelfth Centuries," *Works*, I (1908), 265–66. In Russian.

———. *Works of V. G. Vasilievsky*. 4 vols. St. Petersburg and Leningrad, 1908–30. In Russian.

Vast, H. *Le cardinal Bessarion (1403–1472)*. *Étude sur la chrétienté et la renaissance vers le milieu du XVᵉ siècle*. Paris, 1878.

Veniero, A. "Paolo Silenziario," *Studio sulla letteratura bizantina del VI secolo*. Catania, 1916.

Vernadsky, G. "The Golden Horde, Egypt and Byzantium in their Mutual Relations in the Reign of Michael Palaeologus," *Annales de l'Institut Kondakov*, I (1927), 73–84. In Russian.

——. "Die kirchlich-politische Lehre der Epanagoge und ihr Einfluss auf das russische Leben im XVII. Jahrhundert," *Byzantinisch-neugriechische Jahrbücher*, VI (1928), 121–25.

——. "Notes on the Peasant Community in Byzantium," *Ucheniya Zapiski osnovanniya Russkoy Uchebnoy Kollegiey v Prage*, I, 2 (1924), 81–97. In Russian.

——. "Sur les Origines de la loi agraire byzantine," *Byzantion*, II (1926), 169–80.

——. "The Tactics of Leo the Wise and the Epanagoge," *Byzantion*, VI (1931), 333–35.

Vernet, F. "Nicolas Cabasilas," *Dictionnaire de théologie catholique*, II, 2 (1923), cols. 1292–95.

——. "Le second Concile oecuménique de Lyon, 7 mai—17 juillet 1274," *Dictionnaire de théologie catholique*, IX (1926), cols. 1374–91. Good bibliography.

"Versus Pauli Diaconi XII." *Poetae Latini Aevi Carolini*. (*Monumenta Germaniae Historica*.) Berlin, 1881.

Veselovsky, A. N. "Boccaccio, His Environment and Contemporaries," *Sbornik Otdeleniya Russkago Yazyka i Slovesnosti*, LIII (1893). Reprinted in *Works*, V (1915). In Russian.

——. "The Poem of Digenes," *Vestnik Evropy*, (1875). In Russian.

Vie de Saint Athanase l'Athonite. Ed. Petit, L. *Analecta Bollandiana*, XXV (1906), 5–89.

Villehardouin, G. de. *La Conquête de Constantinople*. Ed. Wailly, N. de. Paris, 1872. Ed. and trans. Faral, E. Paris, 1938–39.

Viller, M. "La Question de l'union des églises entre Grecs et Latins depuis le concile de Lyon jusqu'à celui de Florence (1274–1438)," *Revue d'histoire ecclésiastique*, XVI (1921), 260–305, 515–32.

Vincent, H. and Abel, F. N. *Bethléem: Le Sanctuaire de la Nativité*. Paris, 1914.

——. *Jérusalem. Recherches de topographie, d'archéologie et d'histoire*. Paris, 1914. 2nd ed., Paris, 1926. Bibliography.

Vinogradov, P. "The Origin of Feudal Relations in Lombard Italy," *Journal of the Ministry of Public Instruction*, CCVII (1880). In Russian.

Vita Agapeti papae. Ed. Duchesne, L. *Liber Pontificalis*. Paris, 1886.

Vita Euthymii: Ein Anecdoten zur Geschichte Leo's des Weisen A.D. 886–912. Ed. de Boor, C. Berlin, 1888. In addition to the Greek text, de Boor gives a very valuable study on the *Vita* from the historical point of view.

Vogt, A. *Basile Iᵉʳ empereur de Byzance (867–86) et la civilisation byzantine à la fin du IXᵉ siècle*. Paris, 1908.

——. "La Jeunesse de Leon VI le Sage," *Revue historique*, CLXXIV (1934), 389–428.

Vogt, J. *Constantin der Grosse und sein Jahrhundert*. Munich, 1949.

de Vogüé, M. *Les Églises de la Terre Sainte*. Paris, 1860.

Voigt, G. *Enea Silvio Piccolomini*. Vol. II. Berlin, 1862.

Wagner, W. *Trois Poèmes du moyen âge.* Berlin, 1881.

Warmington, E. *The Commerce Between the Roman Empire and India.* Cambridge, 1928.

Wartenberg, G. "Das Geschichtswerk des Leon Diakonos," *Byzantinische Zeitschrift,* VI (1897), 106–11, 285–317.

———. *Das mittelgriechische Heldenlied von Basileios Digenis Akritis.* Ostern, 1897.

Warton, T. *History of English Poetry.* Ed. Hazlitt, W. C. Vol. II. London, 1871.

Weil, G. *Geschichte der Chalifen.* 3 vols. Mannheim, 1846–51.

Wellhausen, J. *Das arabische Reich und sein Sturz.* Berlin, 1902.

———. *Die Kämpfe der Araber mit den Romäern in der Zeit der Umajaden.* (*Nachrichten von der Klassische Gesellschaft der Wissenschaften zu Göttingen. Philosophisch-historische Klasse.*) Göttingen, 1901.

Wellnhofer, M. *Johannes Apokaukos, Metropolit von Naupaktos in Aetolien (c. 1155–1233). Sein Leben und seine Stellung in Despotate von Epirus unter Michael Doukas und Theodoros Komnenos.* Freising, 1913.

Wendel, C. Planudes in *Paulys Real Encyclopädie.* Neue Bearbeitung. XX (1950), 2202–53.

Whittemore, Thomas. *The Mosaics of St. Sophia at Istambul.* Preliminary reports, I–IV. Oxford, 1933–52.

Wigram, W. A. *An Introduction to the History of the Assyrian Church.* London, 1910.

———. *The Separation of the Monophysites.* London, 1923.

Wilken, F. *Andronikus Comnenus. Historisches Taschenbuch von Raumer.* Vol. II. Leipzig, 1831. Out of date.

———. *Rerum ab Alexio I, Joanne et Manuele Comnenis Gestarum Libri IV.* Heidelberg, 1811. Brief and out of date.

Wilkenhauser, "Zur Frage der Existenz von Nizänischen Synodalprotocolen," *Gesammelte Studien.* Ed. Dölger, F. Freiburg, 1913.

William of Tyre. *Historia rerum in partibus transmarinis gestarum.* (*Recueil des historiens des croisades. Historiens occidentaux,* I, II.) Paris, 1869–81. Ed. and trans. Babcock, E. A. and Krey, A. C. *William Archbishop of Tyre. A History of Deeds Done Beyond the Sea.* New York, 1943. Ed. Paulin, M. *Guillaume de Tyr et ses continuateurs: texte français du XIIIe siècle.* 2 vols. Paris, 1879–80.

Willibaldi. *Vita.* Ed. Pertz, G. H. (*Monumenta Germaniae Historica. Scriptorum,* XV.) Hanover, 1887.

Winstedt, E. O. *The Christian Topography of Cosmas Indicopleustes.* Cambridge, 1909.

Wittek, P. "Deux Chapitres de l'histoire des Turcs de Roum," *Byzantion,* XI (1936), 285–302.

———. *Das Furstentum Mentesche. Studie zur Geschichte Westkleinasiens im 13.–15. Jahrhunderts.* Istambul, 1934.

———. *The Rise of the Ottoman Empire.* London, 1938. Interesting.

———. "Von der byzantinischen zur türkischen Toponymie," *Byzantion,* X (1935), 12–53.

Wolff, R. L. "The Second Bulgarian Empire; Its Origin and History to 1204," *Speculum,* XXIV (1949), 167–206.

Wolters, P. "De Constantini Cephalae Anthologia," *Rheinisches Museum für Philologie,* XXXVIII (1883), 97–119.

Wright, F. A. *A History of Later Greek Literature from the Death of Alexander in 323 B.C. to the Death of Justinian in 565 A.D.* New York, 1932.

Wright, W. C. *The Works of the Emperor Julian.* With English trans. Cambridge, 1913.

Wright, W. S. (Ed.) *The Chronicle of Joshua the Stylite, composed in Syriac A.D. 507.* Cambridge, 1882.

Wroth, W. *Catalogue of the Imperial Byzantine Coins in the British Museum.* London, 1908.

de Xivrey, B. *Mémoire sur la vie et les ouvrages de l'empereur Manuel Paléologue.* (*Mémoires de l'Institut de France. Académie des inscriptions et belles-lettres,* XIX, 2). Paris, 1853. Excellent work on the personality and literary activity of Manuel II together with a very good general description of his epoch.

Yaballah III. "Histoire de Mar Jabalaha III, patriarche des Nestoriens (1281–1317), et du moine Rabban Çauma, ambassadeur du roi Argoun en Occident (1287)," Ed. and trans. Chabot, J. B. *Revue de l'Orient Latin,* II (1894), 82–87.

———. *The History of Yaballaha III Nestorien Patriarch and of his vicar Bar Sauma.* Ed. and trans. Montgomery, J. A. New York, 1927.

Yacut (Yaqut). *Geographisches Wörterbuch.* Ed. Wüstenfeld, H. F. 6 vols. Leipzig, 1866–70.

Yahia Ibn Said Antiochensis. *Annales.* Ed. Cheikho. Beirut and Paris, 1909. Another ed. listed under Vasiliev.

Yakovenko, P. *On the History of Immunity in Byzantium.* Yuryev, 1908. In Russian.

———. "Review: Tafrali, *Thessalonique au quatorizième siècle,*" *Vizantiysky Vremennik,* XXI, 3–4 (1914). In Russian.

———. *Studies in the Domain of Byzantine Charters. The Charters of the New Monastery in the Island of Chios.* Yuryev, 1917. In Russian.

Yaqubi. *Historiae.* Ed. Houtsma, M. T. 2 vols. Leyden, 1883.

Yewdale, R. B. *Bohemond I, Prince of Antioch.* Princeton, 1924.

Yule, H. J. *Cathay and the Ways Thither.* (*Publications of the Hakluyt Society,* XXXVII.) London, 1914.

Zachariä von Lingenthal, K. E. *Collectio librorum juris graeco-romani ineditorum. Ecloga Leonis et Constantini.* Leipzig, 1852.

———. *Geschichte des griechisch-römischen Rechts.* 3rd ed., Berlin, 1892.

———. *Historiae juris graeco-romani delineatio.* Heidelberg, 1839.

———. "Wissenschaft und Recht fur das Heer vom 6. bis zum Anfang des 10. Jahrhunderts," *Byzantinische Zeitschrift,* III (1894), 437–57.

Zachariah of Mitylene. *The Syriac Chronicle.* Trans. Hamilton, F. J. and Brooks, E. W. London, 1899.

Zakythinos, D. A. *Le Chrysobulle d'Alexis III Comnène empereur de Trébizonde en faveur des Vénetiens.* Paris, 1932.

———. *Crise monetaire et crise économique à Byzance du XIIᵉ au XVᵉ siècle.* Athens, 1948.

———. *Le Despotat grec de Morée.* Paris, 1932. A very fine piece of work.

———. Οἱ Σλάβοι ἐν Ἑλλάδι. Συμβολαὶ εἰς τὴν ἱστορίαν τοῦ μεσαιωνικοῦ Ἑλληνισμοῦ. Athens, 1945. Important.

———. "Processus de féodalisation," *L'Hellénisme Contemporain* (1948), 499–534.

Zeller, C. F. *Andronikus der Komnene Römischer Kaiser. Ein historisches Gemälde aus dem ost-römischen Kaiserthume im zwölften Jahrhundert.* Vol. I. Stuttgart, 1804. Out of date.

Zenghelis, C. "Le Feu grégeois," *Byzantion,* VII (1932), 265–86.

Zepos, J. and P. (Eds.) *Jus graecoromanum.* Athens, 1930–31.

Zernin, A. *The Life and Literary Works of the Emperor Constantine Porphyrogenitus.* Kharkov, 1858. In Russian. Out of date.

Zervos, Chr. *Un Philosophe néoplatonicien du XIe siècle. Michael Psellus, sa vie, son oeuvre, ses luttes philosophiques, son influence.* Paris, 1920. Interesting.

Ziebarth, E. "Κυριακὸς ὁ ἐξ Ἀγκῶνος ἐν Ἠπείρῳ," Ἠπειρωτικὰ Χρονικά, II (1926), 110–19.

Zimmert, K. "Der deutsch-byzantinische Konflikt vom Juli 1189 bis Februar 1190," *Byzantinische Zeitschrift,* XII (1903), 42–77.

Zinsser, Hans. *Rats, Lice and History.* Boston, 1935.

Zlatarsky, V. N. "Accounts of the Bulgarians in the Chronicle of Simeon Metaphrastes and Logothete," *Sbornik za Narodni umotvoreniya, nauka i knizhnina,* XXIV (1908). In Bulgarian.

———. "Bulgarian Chronology," *Izvestia otdela russkago yazyka i slovesnosti Akademii Nauk,* XVII, 2 (1912), 28–59. In Russian.

———. *Geschichte der Bulgaren. I. Von der Grundung des bulgarischen Reiches bis zur Türkenzezit (679–1396). (Bulgarische Bibliothek.* Ed. Waigand, G. V.) Leipzig, 1918.

———. *The Greek-Bulgarian Alliance in the year 1204–5.* Sofia, 1914. In Bulgarian.

———. *A History of the State of Bulgaria in the Middle Ages.* Sofia, 1919–34. In Bulgarian. Excellent.

———. "John Asen II," *Historical Bulgarian Library,* III (1933), 1–55. In Bulgarian.

———. "The Letters of Nicholas Mysticus, Patriarch of Constantinople, to Simeon, Tsar of Bulgaria," *Sbornik za Ministerstvo Norodnago Prosvescheniya,* X (1894), 372–428; XI (1894), 3–54; XII (1895), 121–211. In Bulgarian.

———. *The Origin of Peter and Asen, Leaders of the Insurrection in 1185.* Sofia, 1933. In Bulgarian.

———. (Ed.) *The Works of Drinov.* Sofia, 1909.

Zoras, Giorgio. *Le corporazioni bizantine. Studio sull' Ἐπαρχικὸν Βιβλίον dell' imperatore Leone VI.* Rome, 1931.

Zosimus. *Historia nova.* Ed. Mendelssohn, L. Leipzig, 1887.

Zotos, A. Ἰωάννης ὁ Βέκκος πατριάρχης Κωνσταντινουπόλεως νέας Ῥώμης. Munich, 1920.

INDEX

of and Plethon, 699, 719; Chrysoloras at, 718

Florence, Council and Union of, 643, 647, 672–74

Florinsky, T. D.: 585, 613; on the Genoese of the Galata, 616; on Simeon, 618; on Stephen Dushan, 620, 621; on John Cantacuzene, 623–24; and the Athonian archives, 677

Follis, coinage: introduction of, 113

Foord, E.: survey of Byzantine history, 29

France: beginnings of Byzantine scholarship in, 3–6; Age of Reason and attitude toward Byzantine history, 6–8, 11–12; Era of the Revolution and Napoleon and attitude toward Byzantine history, 6–7, 12–13; and crusade studies, 389; and origin of crusades, 399; crusading enthusiasm in, 402; French chivalric romance and the problem of Byzantine romance, 556–59; and the crusade of Sigismund, 630; and the appeal of Manuel II, 631–32, 633–34, 635; Chrysoloras in, 719

Francis I, 3

Franciscan monks (Minorites): in Nicaea, 543

Franks: relations with Ostrogoths, 136; appealed to by Tiberius II against the Lombards, 172–73; relations with under Heraclius, 199; in the army of Romanus Diogenes, 356

Fravitta, Goth: defeats Gaïnas, 94

Frederick I Barbarossa: and Manuel I, 424, 425, 430; negotiations with Qilij Arslan, 425–26, 428; and the Congress of Vienna, 430; and the Third Crusade, 445, 446–47; matrimonial alliance with the Norman royal house and significance for Constantinople, 435–36, 446; relations with Constantinople after the death of Manuel I, 435–36, 445, 446–47; and Serbian-Bulgarian nationalist movement, 443, 445, 446, 612; negotiations with the King of Hungary, the Great Župan of Serbia, Isaac Angelus and the Sultan of Iconium, 445; and the Third Crusade, 445, 446–47; mentioned, 448, 476, 561

Frederick II Hohenstaufen: culture and ideology, 526–27, 529; papacy and the Latin Empire of Constantinople, 527–28; and Theodore Angelus, 528; and John Vatatzes, 528–30, 544; on the Orthodox Church, 529–30, mentioned, 561, 563, 591

Frederick III of Germany: on the fall of Constantinople, 655

Freeman, Edward A., on Gibbon, 10; on Finlay, 16; on Anglo-Saxon immigration to Byzantium, 484

Frohne, 568

Fustel de Coulanges, French historian, 82, 102

G̲ABALAS, Leon, governor of Rhodes: rebellion of, 548

Gabotto, F., Italian scholar: on Euphemius, 279

Gades, Straits of, 138

Gaïnas: Germanic party of, 92; and Tribigild, 93; and Eutropius, 93–94; and Arianism, 94; end of, 94

Gaius, jurist, 102

Galata: and the Fourth Crusade, 459; Genoese at, 588, 593, 616, 625, 684, 685; pillaged by the Venetians, 616

Galerius, Emperor: 44, Edict of Toleration, 50–51, 119; Caesar, 62; Augustus, 63

Galesinius, Petrus: on the Council of Lyons, 658

Galich: and the See of Constantinople, 665

Galich (Galicia), in Russia: Andronicus I at, 378

Galla Placidia, daughter of Theodosius I, 128, 190

Gallipoli, on the Hellespont: acquired by Venice, 463; occupied by the Catalans, 606; and the Ottomans, 622

Gallus: and Constantius, 65–66, 70

Gardner, A., 517

Gattilusio, dynasty of: Genoese rulers of the island of Lesbos, 589

Gaul: in the tetrarchy settlement, 63; prefecture of, 64; Julian in, 70; Roman population in, 111; barbarian kingdoms in, 115; under Justinian, 138

Gaza, in Palestine, 117, 120

Geffcken: on Julian, 77

Gelzer, H.: 23–24, 31; on the Arab conquest of Egypt, 210; on the effects of the Arab conquests on Byzantium, 213; on the themes, 249; on Isaac II, 439; on Athonian monasticism, 666, 670

Genesius, Joseph, Byzantine historian, 364

Gennadius Scholarius, Patriarch of Constantinople: 676, work and culture, 697

Genoa: and western Arabs, 399; trade privilege in Byzantium under John II, 413; relations with Manuel I, 425; position in Byzantium and Venice, 453; 458; privileges under the

Muralt, E., Swiss scholar in Russia: Byzantine chronology, 42

Mutasim, Caliph: campaign in Asia Minor, 276

Muzalon, George: regent of John IV, 536

Myriocephalon, battle of, 428–29

N

NAISSUS (Nish), 44, 58, 443

Naples: captured by Belisarius, 136; Constans II in, 221; Duchy of, 280, 327, 436; University of, 527; and Charles of Anjou, 590, 604; Serbian and Bulgarian envoys in, 595; Angevin archive in, 597; under Alfonso V, 643; John V in, 671

Napoleon I: on Byzantium, 6–7

Narses, Byzantine general: conquers Totila, 137; and the Lombard invasion, 172

Nasiri-Khusrau, Persian traveller: in Jerusalem, 312–13

Naupactus, 559

Navarrese: in the Catalan expedition, 604, 608

Nazareth: churches at, 127; recovered by John Tzimisces, 310

Nea, church: construction of, 372–73

Nea Moni, in Chios, 372

Nectarius, Patriarch of Constantinople, 81, 95

Nedjd, province of Arabia, 200

Nemanjas, dynasty: founders of the Serbian monarchy, 443, 609

Νέος Ἑλληνομνήμων, 41

Nestorianism, Nestorians: centers and opposition to, 99, 108; and Justinian, 149–50, 154; and the Fifth Ecumenical Council, 153; in Persia, 165, 196; in Ceylon, 165

Nestor Iskinder, 649

Nestorius, Antiochene presbyter: heresy of, 98–99, 108

New Church (Nea), 372–73

Nicaea, Empire of: and the Latin Empire, 50–59, 516–17, 536–38; and the Lascarids, 468–69; and the national cause, 507, 511; and the Sultanate of Iconium, 508, 514–15, 530–31; and the battle of Hadrianople, 510–11; and the city of Nicaea, 512–13; and the Despotat of Epirus, 518–22, 523; and John II Asen, 525–26; and the Mongols, 530–31; under John Vatatzes, 531–32; under Theodore II and Michael VIII, 534–38; relations with the papacy, 542–45; historian of, 553; letters in, 562–63

Nicaea, in Bithynia: First Council of, 55–56;

Seljuq Sultanate of, 385, 394, 402; and the First Crusade, 408; history of, 512–13; Council of 1234 in, 543; cultural center, 548–49; captured the Ottomans, 604, 608

Nicaea, Patriarchate of: religious leadership, 522, 541, 542, 545–46

Nika Riot, 135, 154–57

Nicephorus, Patriarch of Constantinople, historian and theologian: and the decree of the Council of 815, 251; opposition to, 283; and Leo V, 284, 285; work of, 292, 293

Nicephorus, Patriarch of Jerusalem, 312

Nicephorus I, Emperor: origin and succession to throne, 235, 271; and Charlemagne, 268; and Krum, 271, 281; uprising of the Slavs of the Peloponnesus under, 278; activity of the Arabs under, 278; religious policy of, 283; and the *allelengyon,* 348

Nicephorus II Phocas, Emperor: succession to throne, 302; Italian campaigns of, 306, 326; recovers Crete, 308; Syrian campaigns of, 308–9, 391; and Sviatoslav, 308; western policy of, 308–9; and Otto I, 308, 327–28; struggle with Bulgaria, 319; ecclesiastical policy of, 334–37; and the papacy, 336; and Athonian monasticism, 336–37; social legislation of, 347, 567; historian of, 364; "crusades" of, 403; mentioned, 313, 471, 481

Nicephorus III Botaniates: succession to throne, 353; mentioned, 357, 384, 489

Nicephorus Callistus, writer: on John Chrysostom, 118

Nicholaites, 333, 334

Nicholas I, Pope: sends *Breviarium* to Boris, 102; and the Bulgarian church, 282–83; and the Photian case, 290, 330–31

Nicholas V, Pope, 655

Nicholas Mysticus, Patriarch of Constantinople: and Photius, 297; relations with the Emir of Crete, 297, 306; and Simeon, 317; and the *Tome of Union,* 334; and Leo VI, 333–34; and the papacy, 334; his correspondence, 364

Nicholas of Otranto, Abbot of Casole, 541

Nicomedia, in Bithynia: Edict of, 51, 52; and Diocletian, 58, 62; Goths in, 84; mint at, 114; captured by the Ottomans, 609

Nicopolis, battle of, 630–31, 632

Nikon, Patriarch, 342

Nikov, P.: on Kalojan, 511

Nile River: under Justinian, 141

Nineveh, battle of, 197

Niphon: preacher of Bogomile doctrine, 473